MARK
1–8

VOLUME 27

THE ANCHOR BIBLE is a fresh approach to the world's greatest classic. Its object is to make the Bible accessible to the modern reader; its method is to arrive at the meaning of biblical literature through exact translation and extended exposition, and to reconstruct the ancient setting of the biblical story, as well as the circumstances of its transcription and the characteristics of its transcribers.

THE ANCHOR BIBLE is a project of international and interfaith scope: Protestant, Catholic, and Jewish scholars from many countries contribute individual volumes. The project is not sponsored by any ecclesiastical organization and is not intended to reflect any particular theological doctrine. Prepared under our joint supervision, THE ANCHOR BIBLE is an effort to make available all the significant historical and linguistic knowledge which bears on the interpretation of the biblical record.

THE ANCHOR BIBLE is aimed at the general reader with no special formal training in biblical studies; yet it is written with the most exacting standards of scholarship, reflecting the highest technical accomplishment.

This project marks the beginning of a new era of cooperation among scholars in biblical research, thus forming a common body of knowledge to be shared by all.

William Foxwell Albright
David Noel Freedman
GENERAL EDITORS

THE ANCHOR BIBLE

MARK
1–8

◆

A New Translation
with Introduction and Commentary

JOEL MARCUS

THE ANCHOR BIBLE
Doubleday
New York   London   Toronto   Sydney   Auckland

THE ANCHOR BIBLE
PUBLISHED BY DOUBLEDAY
a division of Random House, Inc.
1540 Broadway, New York, New York 10036

THE ANCHOR BIBLE, DOUBLEDAY, and the portrayal of an
anchor with the letters A and B are trademarks of
Doubleday, a division of Random House, Inc.

Library of Congress Cataloging-in-Publication Data
Bible. N.T. Mark I–VIII. English. Marcus. 1999.
    Mark 1–8: a new translation with introduction and commentary /
Joel Marcus. — 1st ed.
    p.   cm. — (The Anchor Bible ; v. 27)
Includes bibliographical references and indexes.
1. Bible. N.T. Mark—Commentaries. I. Marcus, Joel, 1951–   .
II. Title. III. Series: Bible. English. Anchor Bible.
1964; v. 27A.
BS192.2.A1   1964.G3 vol. 27
[BS2583]
220.7′7 s—dc21
[226.3′077]   98-8741
                                                                  CIP

ISBN 0-385-42349-7

10   9   8   7   6   5   4   3   2   1

CONTENTS

◆

APPENDICES

GLOSSARY

INDICES

PALESTINE IN NEW TESTAMENT TIMES

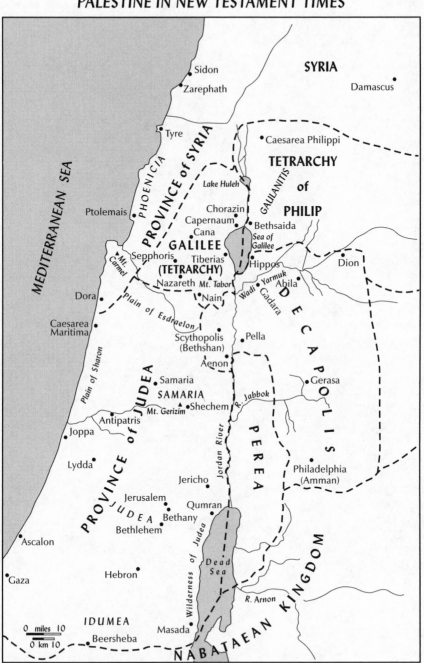

Palestine from 6 to 44 C.E.

PREFACE

◆

This is the first volume of a projected two-volume commentary on the Gospel of Mark, replacing C. S. Mann's 1986 volume in the Anchor Bible series. It includes the general INTRODUCTION to the commentary; the TRANSLATION, NOTES, and COMMENT on Mark 1:1–8:21; three appendices; a glossary; and a bibliography and indices for the first volume. The second volume will include the TRANSLATION, NOTES, and COMMENT on Mark 8:22–16:8; additional appendices; a supplementary glossary and bibliography; and indices covering both volumes.

Concerning translations, unless otherwise noted: translations of Markan texts are my own, while translations of other New Testament texts are from the New Revised Standard Version. Translations of the Pseudepigrapha are from Charlesworth, ed., *Old Testament Pseudepigrapha*. Translations of the Qumran literature are from García Martínez, *The Dead Sea Scrolls Translated*. Translations of the Mishnah are from Danby's edition, and translations from the Babylonian Talmud are from the Soncino edition. Translations of Philo, Josephus, and other classical writers are from the Loeb Classical Library. I have sometimes altered these translations slightly in the interests of accuracy, style, inclusive language, etc.

I have incurred a number of debts in the years I have been working on this commentary. The greatest of these is to the good friends — I hope they are still friends — who have read and commented on it, thereby saving me from a number of embarrassing errors, and often pushing my thought in unexpected and fruitful directions. The Anchor Bible editor, Noel Freedman, has devoted to the manuscript his tireless energy and exacting scrutiny, and has illuminated it with his massive knowledge of biblical texts and the ancient world. Dale Allison also read and commented on the whole manuscript, and I have garnered as much from his learned remarks as I have from the magisterial three-volume "Davies and Allison" ICC commentary on Matthew, of which he is the principal author (see the preface to volume 3 of that work). Bart Ehrman has given me the benefit of his detailed, penetrating, and often hilarious criticism of the commentary section, and Clifton Black has commented on the introduction, bringing to bear his unparalleled insight into the Markan text and Markan criticism. Michael Winger mobilized his sharp senses of logic and style in a critique of 2:1–3:6, and John Riches gave helpful feedback on the discussion of Synoptic relationships in the introduction. I would also like to thank the

Religion Editor at Doubleday, Mark Fretz, and his able assistant, Andrew Corbin, for their supervision of the project. I am especially grateful to Andrew and to Terry Karydes, the Senior Design Editor, for helping to rescue my charts. Thanks also to the creator of the Author and Ancient Literature Indexes, Shirley Warkentin, for her careful work.

I am also grateful for institutional support that has helped me to finish the manuscript, especially two sabbatical leaves from the University of Glasgow. The Interlibrary Loan Department at the university's library has swiftly provided necessary literature. And there are other, less formal kinds of support that have been given to me in Glasgow. My wife, Gloria, and daughter, Rachel (who was born just about the time I started work on the commentary), have endured with good grace my obsession with Mark. The Department of Theology and Religious Studies at the university has provided an atmosphere that is supportive of research, and I have tested out in seminars there a number of the ideas that have been developed in the commentary. I would like to single out for special thanks my New Testament colleagues, John Riches and John Barclay, from whom I have learned much in all sorts of ways. One could not have asked for better colleagues or for truer friends. I thank God for them, and it is to them that I dedicate this volume.

LIST OF FIGURES

◆

PRINCIPAL ABBREVIATIONS

◆

AB	Anchor Bible		*Greek Grammar of*
ABD	D. N. Freedman, ed.,		*the New Testament*
	The Anchor Bible	BETL	Bibliotheca ephemeri-
	Dictionary		dum theologicarum
ABRL	Anchor Bible Refer-		lovaniensium
	ence Library	*Bib*	*Biblica*
AGJU	Arbeiten zur Ge-	*BibLeb*	*Bibel und Leben*
	schichte des antiken	BibOr	Biblica et orientalia
	Judentums und des	*BibRev*	*Bible Review*
	Urchristentums	BJRL	*Bulletin of the John*
AnBib	Analecta biblica		*Rylands University Li-*
ANRW	*Aufstieg und Nieder-*		*brary of Manchester*
	gang der römischen	BJS	Brown Judaic Studies
	Welt	Black	M. Black, *An Aramaic*
Aram	Aramaic		*Approach to the Gos-*
ATANT	Abhandlungen zur		*pels and Acts*
	Theologie des Alten	BR	*Biblical Research*
	und Neuen Testa-	Bratcher	R. G. Bratcher, *A Trans-*
	ments		*lator's Guide to the*
b.	Babylonian Talmud		*Gospel of Mark*
BAGD	W. Bauer, W. F. Arndt,	Brown	R. E. Brown, *The Gos-*
	F. W. Gingrich, and		*pel according to John*
	F. W. Danker, *Greek-*	Bultmann	R. Bultmann, *History*
	English Lexicon of		*of the Synoptic*
	the New Testament		*Tradition*
BARev	*Biblical Archaeology*	Burton	E. D. Burton, *Syntax of*
	Review		*the Moods and*
BBB	Bonner biblische		*Tenses in New Testa-*
	Beiträge		*ment Greek*
BBET	Beiträge zur biblischen	BWANT	Beiträge zur Wissen-
	Exegese und Theo-		schaft vom Alten und
	logie		Neuen Testament
BDB	F. Brown, S. R. Driver,	BZ	*Biblische Zeitschrift*
	and C. A. Briggs,	BZNW	Beihefte zur ZNW
	Hebrew and English	CBQ	*Catholic Biblical*
	Lexicon of the Old		*Quarterly*
	Testament	CBQMS	Catholic Biblical Quar-
BDF	F. Blass, A. Debrunner,		terly—Monograph
	and R. W. Funk, A		Series

CGTC	Cambridge Greek Testament Commentaries	Freedman	Comments of D. N. Freedman, Anchor Bible editor, on manuscript of this commentary
ConB	Coniectanea biblica		
ConBNT	Coniectanea biblica, New Testament	FRLANT	Forschungen zur Religion und Literatur des Alten und Neuen Testaments
ConNT	Coniectanea neotestamentica		
CQR	*Church Quarterly Review*	Gesenius	E. Kautzsch and A. E. Cowley, *Gesenius' Hebrew Grammar*
Cranfield	C. E. B. Cranfield, *The Gospel according to Saint Mark*	Ginzberg	L. Ginzberg, *The Legends of the Jews*
Danby	H. Danby, *The Mishnah*	Gk	Greek
Davies and Allison	W. D. Davies and D. C. Allison, *A Critical and Exegetical Commentary on the Gospel according to Saint Matthew*	Gnilka	J. Gnilka, *Das Evangelium nach Markus*
		GTA	Göttingen theologische Arbeiten
		Guelich	R. A. Guelich, *Mark 1–8:26*
Dibelius	M. Dibelius, *From Tradition to Gospel*	Gundry	R. H. Gundry, *Mark: A Commentary on His Apology for the Cross*
Dupont-Sommer	A. Dupont-Sommer, *The Essene Writings from Qumran*	HBD	P. J. Achtemeier et al., eds., *Harper's Bible Dictionary*
Ebib	Études bibliques		
EDNT	H. Balz and G. Schneider, eds., *Exegetical Dictionary of the New Testament*	Heb	Hebrew
		HNT	Handbuch zum Neuen Testament
EEC	E. Ferguson, ed., *Encyclopedia of Early Christianity*	Hooker	M. D. Hooker, *A Commentary on the Gospel according to Saint Mark*
Eisenman and Wise	R. Eisenman and M. Wise, *The Dead Sea Scrolls Uncovered*	HTKNT	Herders theologischer Kommentar zum Neuen Testament
EKKNT	Evangelisch-katholischer Kommentar zum Neuen Testament	HTR	*Harvard Theological Review*
		HUCA	*Hebrew Union College Annual*
EncJud	*Encyclopaedia Judaica*	IBS	*Irish Biblical Studies*
ErFor	Erträge der Forschung	ICC	International Critical Commentary
ET	*Expository Times*		
ETL	*Ephemerides theologicae lovanienses*	IDB	G. A. Buttrick, ed., *The Interpreter's Dictionary of the Bible*
FB	Forschung zur Bibel		
FBBS	Facet Books, Biblical Series	IDBS	K. Crim, ed., *The Interpreter's Dictionary*

	of the Bible, Supple- mentary Volume		Logienquelle und des Markusevan-
Int	Interpretation		geliums
IRT	Issues in Religion and Theology	Lauterbach	J. Z. Lauterbach, Mekilta de-Rabbi Ishmael
JAAR	Journal of the American Academy of Religion	LB	Linguistica Biblica
JANES	Journal of the Ancient Near Eastern Society	LCL Lohmeyer	Loeb Classical Library E. Lohmeyer, Das
JAOS	Journal of the American Oriental Society		Evangelium des Markus
Jastrow	M. Jastrow, A Dictio- nary of the Targu- mim, the Talmud Babli and Yeru- shalmi, and the Mid- rashic Literature	Lohmeyer, Ergänzungsheft LQ LSJ	Ergänzungsheft (sup- plement) to above Lutheran Quarterly H. D. Liddell et al., A Greek-English Lexicon with a
JBL	Journal of Biblical Literature	Lührmann	Supplement D. Lührmann, Das
JBLMS	Journal of Biblical Lit- erature—Mono- graph Series	LXX m.	Markusevangelium Septuagint Mishnah
JE	The Jewish Encyclopedia	Mann	C. S. Mann, Mark
JJS	Journal of Jewish Studies	Metzger	B. M. Metzger, A
JR	Journal of Religion		Textual Commen-
JSJ	Journal for the Study of Judaism		tary on the Greek New Testament
JSJSup	Journal for the Study of Judaism—Supple- ment Series	MeyerK	H. A. W. Meyer, Kritisch-exege- tischer Kommentar
JSNT	Journal for the Study of the New Testament		über das Neue Testa- ment
JSNTSup	Journal for the Study of the New Testament— Supplement Series	MHT	J. H. Moulton, W. F. Howard, and N. Tur- ner, A Grammar of New Testament Greek
JSOTSup	Journal for the Study of the Old Testament— Supplement Series	M-M	J. H. Moulton and G. Milligan, The Vo-
JSS	Journal of Semitic Studies		cabulary of the Greek Testament
JTS	Journal of Theological Studies	Montefiore	C. G. Montefiore, The Synoptic Gospels
Juel	D. Juel, Mark	Moore	G. F. Moore, Judaism in
Lagrange	M. J. Lagrange, Évan- gile selon Saint Marc		the First Centuries of the Christian Era
Lane	W. Lane, The Gospel of Mark	Moule	C. F. D. Moule, An Idiom Book of New
Laufen	R. Laufen, Die Doppel- überlieferungen der	MT	Testament Greek Masoretic text

Neirynck and van Segbroeck	F. Neirynck and F. van Segbroeck, *New Testament Vocabulary*	Rawlinson	A. E. J. Rawlinson, *St Mark*
NICNT	New International Commentary on the New Testament	RB	*Revue biblique*
		RE	*Realencyklopädie für protestantische Theologie und Kirche*
NIGTC	The New International Greek Testament Commentary	RevQ	*Revue de Qumran*
		Rhoads and Michie	D. M. Rhoads and D. Michie, *Mark as Story*
Nineham	D. E. Nineham, *Saint Mark*	Robertson	A. T. Robertson, A *Grammar of the Greek New Testament in the Light of Historical Research*
NJBC	R. E. Brown et al., eds., *The New Jerome Biblical Commentary*		
NovT	*Novum Testamentum*		
NovTSup	Novum Testamentum, Supplements	SANT	Studien zum Alten und Neuen Testament
NT	New Testament	SBB	Stuttgarter biblische Beiträge
NTAbh	Neutestamentliche Abhandlungen		
NTOA	Novum Testamentum et Orbis Antiquus	SBLDS	Society of Biblical Literature — Dissertation Series
NTS	*New Testament Studies*	SBLMS	Society of Biblical Literature — Monograph Series
NTTS	New Testament Tools and Studies		
OBO	Orbis biblicus et orientalis	SBM	Stuttgarter biblische Monographien
OT	Old Testament	SBS	Stuttgarter Bibelstudien
OTL	Old Testament Library	SBT	Studies in Biblical Theology
OTP	J. H. Charlesworth, ed., *The Old Testament Pseudepigrapha*	ScEs	*Science et esprit*
		D. Schmidt	D. D. Schmidt, *The Gospel of Mark with Introduction, Notes, and Original Text*
Pesch	R. Pesch, *Das Markusevangelium*		
PG	J. Migne, *Patrologia graeca*	K. Schmidt	K. L. Schmidt, *Der Rahmen der Geschichte Jesu*
PGM	*Papyri graecae magicae*; English texts in H. D. Betz, *The Greek Magical Papyri in Translation*	Schmithals	W. Schmithals, *Das Evangelium nach Markus*
Pryke	E. J. Pryke, *Redactional Style in the Marcan Gospel*	Schürer	E. Schürer et al., *The History of the Jewish People in the Age of Jesus Christ*
QD	Quaestiones disputatae		
Räisänen	H. Räisänen, *The "Messianic Secret" in Mark's Gospel*	Schweizer	E. Schweizer, *The Good News according to Mark*

SJLA	Studies in Judaism in Late Antiquity			*Early Christian Tradition*
Smyth	H. W. Smyth, *Greek Grammar*		TLZ	*Theologische Literaturzeitung*
SNTSMS	Society for New Testament Studies Monograph Series		Tolbert	M. A. Tolbert, *Sowing the Gospel: Mark's World in Literary-Historical Perspective*
SNTW	Studies in the New Testament and Its World		TU	Texte und Untersuchungen
SPB	Studia postbiblica		*TynBul*	*Tyndale Bulletin*
SSEJC	Studies in Scripture in Early Judaism and Christianity		Vermes	G. Vermes, *The Dead Sea Scrolls in English*
ST	*Studia theologica*		*VT*	*Vetus Testamentum*
Strack-Billerbeck	H. L. Strack and P. Billerbeck, *Kommentar zum Neuen Testament aus Talmud und Midrasch*		WA	M. Luther, *Kritische Gesamtausgabe* (= "Weimar" edition)
			WBC	Word Biblical Commentary
SUNT	Studien zur Umwelt des Neuen Testaments		Wellhausen	J. Wellhausen, *Das Evangelium Marci übersetzt und erklärt*
SVTP	Studia in Veteris Testamenti pseudepigrapha		WMANT	Wissenschaftliche Monographien zum Alten und Neuen Testament
Swete	H. B. Swete, *The Gospel according to Saint Mark*		Wrede	W. Wrede, *The Messianic Secret*
t.	Tosephta		WUNT	Wissenschaftliche Untersuchungen zum Neuen Testament
Taylor	V. Taylor, *The Gospel according to Saint Mark*		y.	Yerushalmi = Jerusalem or Palestinian Talmud
TDNT	G. Kittel and G. Friedrich, eds., *Theological Dictionary of the New Testament*		ZDPV	*Zeitschrift des deutschen Palästina-Vereins*
TDOT	G. J. Botterweck and H. Ringgren, eds., *Theological Dictionary of the Old Testament*		Zerwick	M. Zerwick, *Biblical Greek Illustrated by Examples*
			ZKG	*Zeitschrift für Kirchengeschichte*
ThViat	*Theologia viatorum*		ZNW	*Zeitschrift für die neutestamentliche Wissenschaft*
Theissen	G. Theissen, *The Miracle Stories of the*			

MARK 1:1–8:21: A TRANSLATION

◆

Prologue (1:1–15)

1 ¹The beginning of the good news of Jesus Christ ²(as it has been written in Isaiah the prophet: "Look, I am sending my messenger before your face, who will set your way in order. ³The voice of someone shouting in the wilderness: 'Prepare the way of the Lord; make his paths straight!'"):

⁴John appeared, baptizing in the wilderness and proclaiming a baptism of repentance leading to the forgiveness of sins. ⁵All of the people from the region of Judaea, including all of the inhabitants of Jerusalem, were traveling out to him and being baptized by him in the Jordan River, confessing their sins. ⁶This John used to wear a garment made of camel's hair and a leather belt around his waist, and he would eat grasshoppers and wild honey. ⁷And he proclaimed this message: "There is coming after me the one stronger than me, of whom I am not worthy so much as to stoop down and loosen his sandals' thong. ⁸I myself have baptized you with water, but he will baptize you in the Holy Spirit."

⁹And it came to pass in those days that Jesus came from Nazareth in Galilee and was baptized in the Jordan by John. ¹⁰And as he was coming up out of the water, he immediately saw the heavens being ripped apart and the Spirit like a dove descending upon him; ¹¹and a voice came out of the heavens: "You are my beloved son; in you I have taken delight."

¹²And immediately the Spirit cast him out into the wilderness, ¹³and he was in the wilderness forty days, being tested by Satan; and he was with the wild animals; and the angels were serving him.

¹⁴But after John was handed over, Jesus came into Galilee proclaiming the good news of God ¹⁵and saying, "The time has been fulfilled, and the dominion of God has come near! Repent, and believe in the good news!"

First Major Section (1:16–3:6)

Honeymoon Period (1:16–45)

¹⁶And passing by along the Sea of Galilee, he caught sight of Simon and Andrew, Simon's brother, casting their nets in the sea—for they were fishers. ¹⁷And Jesus said to them: "Come on after me, and I'll make you become fishers of people!" ¹⁸And immediately they left their nets and followed him. ¹⁹And going on a little way, he caught sight of James the son of Zebedee and his brother John—they were in a boat preparing their nets—²⁰and immediately he called them. And they left their father Zebedee in the boat with the hired hands, and they went after him.

²¹And they entered Capernaum. And on the Sabbath he went into the synagogue and immediately began to teach. ²²And the people were amazed at his teaching; for he was teaching them as one who had authority, and not in the way the scribes did. ²³And immediately in their synagogue there was a man in

an unclean spirit, and he cried out, [24]saying, "What do we have to do with you, Jesus the Nazarene? Have you come to destroy us? I know who you are—the holy one of God!" [25]And Jesus rebuked him, saying, "Shut up and come out of him!" [26]And the unclean spirit came out of him after convulsing him and uttering a loud cry. [27]And they were all awestruck, so that they asked one another saying, "What is this? A new teaching with authority! He even gives orders to the unclean spirits, and they obey him!" [28]And immediately his fame spread everywhere, into all the region of Galilee.

[29]And leaving the synagogue, they immediately went into the house of Simon and Andrew with James and John. [30]Now Simon's mother-in-law was lying down because she had a fever, and immediately they told him about her. [31]And coming forward, he grasped her by the hand and raised her up; and the fever left her, and she began serving them.

[32]When evening had come, after the sun had gone down, the people began bringing to him all those who were sick and afflicted by demons; [33]and the whole city was gathered at the door. [34]And he healed many people who were sick with various diseases, and he cast out many demons; and he did not let the demons speak, because they knew him.

[35]And early in the morning, while it was still quite dark, he got up, went outside, and went away to a deserted place; and there he was praying. [36]And Peter and those who were with him hunted him down, [37]and they found him and said to him, "Everyone is looking for you." [38]And he said to them, "Let's go elsewhere, into the neighboring towns, so that I might preach there also. For this is why I have come forward." [39]And he came into their synagogues throughout the whole region of Galilee, preaching and casting out demons.

[40]And a man with scale-disease came up to him, pleading with him and saying, "If you want to, you are able to cleanse me." [41]And he, becoming incensed, stretched out his hand and touched him and said, "I *do* want to; be cleansed!" [42]And immediately the scale-disease left him, and he was cleansed. [43]And Jesus, growling at him, immediately cast him out [44]and said to him, "See that you don't say anything to anyone, but go and show yourself to the priest and offer for your cleansing what Moses commanded, as a witness to them." [45]But he went out and began to proclaim it all over and to spread the news abroad, so that Jesus was no longer able to go into a city openly, but had to remain out in deserted places. And the people came to him from everywhere.

The Opposition Asserts Itself (2:1–3:6)

2   [1]And he returned several days later to Capernaum, and it was rumored that he was at home. [2]And many people gathered together there, so that there was no room even in front of the door, and he was speaking the word to them. [3]And a paralytic was brought to him, carried by four of his friends; [4]and not being able to reach him because of the crowd, they unroofed the roof where he was, and digging through they lowered the pallet upon which the paralytic

was lying. [5]And Jesus, seeing their faith, said to the paralytic, "My child, your sins are forgiven."

[6]But some of the scribes were sitting there and pondering in their hearts: [7]"Why does this man speak in this way? He is blaspheming! Who can forgive sins except One, that is, God?" [8]And Jesus, immediately recognizing in his spirit that they were pondering within themselves in this way, said to them, "Why are you pondering in your hearts? [9]Which is easier, to say to the paralytic, 'Your sins are forgiven,' or to say, 'Get up, take up your pallet, and walk!'? [10]But so that you may know that upon the earth the Son of Man has authority to forgive sins"—he said to the paralytic: [11]"I say to you, get up, take up your pallet, and go to your house!" [12]And he got up, and immediately he took up his pallet and went out in front of them all, so that they all were amazed and glorified God, saying, "We have never seen anything like it!"

[13]And he went out beside the sea again. And the whole crowd came to him, and he was teaching them. [14]And moving along, he saw Levi, the son of Alphaeus, sitting at a tax booth; and he said to him, "Follow me!" And he got up and followed him. [15]And it came to pass that, as he was reclining at table in his house, many tax collectors and sinners were reclining with Jesus and his disciples—for they were many, and they followed him. [16]And the scribes of the Pharisees, seeing that he was eating with sinners and tax collectors, said to his disciples: "Why does he eat with tax collectors and sinners?" [17]And hearing it, Jesus said to them: "The strong don't need a doctor, but the sick. I did not come to call righteous people but sinners."

[18]And the disciples of John and the Pharisees were fasting. And they came and said to him: "Why do the disciples of John and the disciples of the Pharisees fast, but your disciples do not fast?" [19]And Jesus said to them, "Can the wedding guests fast while the bridegroom is with them? As long as they have the bridegroom with them, they cannot fast. [20]But the days will come when the bridegroom is taken away from them, and then they will fast on that day. [21]"No one sews a patch of unshrunk cloth on an old garment; for if he does, the fullness takes out from it, the new from the old, and a worse rip results. [22]And no one pours new wine into old wineskins; for if he does, the wine will burst the wineskins, and the wine will be lost—and the wineskins. But new wine into new wineskins!"

[23]And it came to pass that he was going through a grain field on the Sabbath, and his disciples began to make their way, plucking the ears of grain as they went along. [24]And the Pharisees said to him, "Look! Why are they doing what is not permissible on the Sabbath?" [25]And he said to them, "Haven't you ever read what David did when he was in need and hungry—he and those who were with him? [26]How he went into the house of God in the time of Abiathar the high priest and ate the loaves of presentation, which only the priests may eat—and gave them to those who were with him also?" [27]And he said to them, "The Sabbath was created for man, and not man for the Sabbath; [28]so the Son of Man is lord even of the Sabbath."

3 ¹And again he entered the synagogue; and there was a man there who had a withered hand. ²And they were watching him closely, to see whether he would heal him on the Sabbath, so that they might bring charges against him. ³And he said to the man with the withered hand, "Get up, and come to the middle of the room!" ⁴And he said to them, "Is it permissible to do good on the Sabbath or to do evil, to save life or to kill?" But they were silent. ⁵And he, glancing around with anger, and grieved at the hardness of their hearts, said to the man, "Stretch out your hand!" And he stretched it out, and his hand was restored. ⁶And the Pharisees immediately went out with the Herodians and took counsel against Jesus, in order that they might destroy him.

Second Major Section (3:7–6:6a):
The Struggle Intensifies

⁷And Jesus, together with his disciples, withdrew to the sea; and a great crowd from Galilee followed—and from Judaea ⁸and from Jerusalem and from Idumaea and from Transjordan and from the region around Tyre and Sidon, a great crowd that had heard the things he had done came to him. ⁹And he told his disciples to prepare a boat for him because of the crowd, so that they might not crush him; ¹⁰for he had healed many people, so that as many as had afflictions fell upon him in order to touch him. ¹¹And the unclean spirits, whenever they beheld him, fell down before him and yelled out, saying, "You are the Son of God!" ¹²And he sharply rebuked them, in order that they might not make him known.

¹³And he went up the mountain and called to himself those whom he himself wanted, and they came away to him. ¹⁴And he appointed twelve, in order that they might be with him and that he might send them out to preach ¹⁵and to have authority to cast out demons. ¹⁶And he appointed the Twelve, and he gave Simon the name Peter; ¹⁷and James the son of Zebedee and John, James' brother—and he gave them the name Boanerges, that is "sons of thunder"; ¹⁸and Andrew and Philip and Bartholomew and Matthew and Thomas and James the son of Alphaeus and Thaddaeus and Simon the Kananite—¹⁹and Judas Iscariot, who also betrayed him.

²⁰And he went into a house. And a crowd gathered again, so that they could not even eat their food. ²¹And his relatives, hearing about it, went out to seize him; for they said, "He has gone out of his mind."

²²And the scribes who had come down from Jerusalem said, "He has Beelzebul, and it's by the power of the ruler of the demons that he casts out demons." ²³And calling them to himself, he spoke to them in parables: "How can Satan cast out Satan? ²⁴If a dominion is divided against itself, nothing can make that dominion stand. ²⁵And if a household is divided against itself, nothing can make that household stand. ²⁶And if Satan has risen against himself and has become divided, he cannot stand, but is coming to an end. ²⁷But no one can enter into the strong man's house and plunder his things unless he first ties the strong man up—then he will plunder his house. ²⁸Amen, I say to

you: all things will be forgiven to people, both their sins and the blasphemies that they blaspheme. [29]But whoever blasphemes against the Holy Spirit never gains forgiveness, but is guilty of an eternal sin" [30](because they were saying, "He has an unclean spirit").

[31]And his mother and his brothers came, and standing outside they sent a message to him, calling him. [32]Now a crowd was sitting around him, and they said to him, "Look, your mother and your brothers and your sisters are outside looking for you." [33]And he answered and said, "Who are my mother and my brothers?" [34]And looking around at the group seated in a circle around him he said, "Look—my mother and my brothers! [35]For whoever does the will of God, that one is my brother and sister and mother."

4 [1]And again he began to teach beside the sea. And there gathered to him the biggest crowd yet, so that he got into a boat and sat on the sea; and the whole crowd was by the sea on the land. [2]And he was teaching them many things in parables, and he said to them in his teaching: [3]"Listen! Look! A sower went out to sow. [4]And it came to pass in the sowing that one part fell beside the way, and the birds came and ate it up. [5]And another part fell into the rocky ground where it did not have much earth, and immediately it sprang up because it did not have depth of earth; [6]and when the sun rose it was scorched, and because it did not have root it withered. [7]And another part fell into the thorns, and the thorns came up and choked it, and it did not yield fruit. [8]But other parts fell into the good earth, and they were yielding fruit, coming up and growing, and they were bearing thirtyfold and sixtyfold and a hundredfold." [9]And he said, "The one who has ears to hear, let him hear!"

[10]And when he was alone, those around him with the Twelve asked him about the parables. [11]And he said to them: "To you has been given the mystery of the dominion of God; but to those outside everything happens in parables [12]in order that 'in their looking they may look but not *see*, and in their hearing they may hear but not understand; lest they turn and it be forgiven them.'"

[13]And he said to them, "Don't you know this parable? How then will you know all the parables? [14]The sower is sowing the word. [15]And these are the seeds beside the path, where the word is sown; they who, when they hear, immediately Satan comes and takes away the word that has been sown in them. [16]And these are the seeds sown in the rocky ground: they who, when they hear the word, immediately receive it with joy, [17]and do not have root in themselves but are temporary and, when tribulation or persecution on account of the word arises, immediately fall away. [18]And others are the seeds sown among the thorns; these are they who hear the word, [19]but the cares of the age and the deceitfulness of wealth and desires for other things enter into them and strangle the word, and it becomes unfruitful. [20]And these are the seeds sown in the good earth: they who hear the word and accept it and bear fruit thirtyfold, sixtyfold, and a hundredfold.

[21]And he said to them, "Does the lamp come in order that it may be put under the bushel or under the bed? Doesn't it come in order that it may be put

on the lampstand? [22]For there is nothing hid, except in order that it may be made manifest; nor has anything become hidden, but in order that it might come to manifestation. [23]If anyone has ears to hear, let him hear!"

[24]And he said to them, "Pay attention to what you hear! With what measure you measure, it will be measured to you—and more will be added to you. [25]For, the one who has—more will be given to him; and the one who does not have—even what he has will be taken away from him.

[26]And he said, "The dominion of God is like this: as if a man should throw seed on the earth, [27]and should sleep and rise night and day, and the seed should sprout and grow up—how, even he does not know. [28]And by itself the earth yields fruit—first a shoot, then an ear, then full grain in the ear. [29]But when the condition of the fruit allows it, immediately he sends forth the sickle, for the harvest has come."

[30]And he said, "How shall we form a likeness for the dominion of God, or in what parable shall we put it? [31]It is as a mustard grain, which, when it is sown on the earth, is smaller than all the other seeds on earth, [32]but when it is sown, it grows up and becomes bigger than all other shrubs and puts out large branches, so that the birds of heaven can lodge under its shadow."

[33]And with many such parables he used to speak the word to them, as they were able to hear. [34]Indeed, without a parable he did not speak to them; but privately, to his own disciples, he explained everything.

[35]And that day, as evening was coming, he said to them: "Let's go to the other side." [36]And sending the crowd away, they took him off, when he had gotten back in the boat and other boats were with him. [37]And a great wind-storm arose, and the waves were breaking into the boat, so that the boat was beginning to fill with water. [38]And he was in the stern, sleeping on a cushion. And they woke him up and said to him, "Teacher, don't you care that we're about to die?" [39]And he roused himself and rebuked the wind, and said to the sea, "Silence! Shut up!" And the wind died down, and there was a great calm. [40]And he said to them, "Why are you cowardly? Don't you have faith yet?" [41]And they feared a great fear and said to each other: "Who then is this?—for even the wind and sea obey him!"

5   [1]And they came to the other side of the sea, to the region of the Gera-senes. [2]And he came out of the boat, and immediately there came out from the tombs to meet him a man in an unclean spirit [3]who had his dwelling among the tombs, and no one had ever yet been able to tie him up for long, not even with a chain—[4]for he had often been tied up with fetters and chains, but the chains had been torn apart by him and the fetters had been smashed, and no one had the power to subdue him. [5]And he was in the tombs and in the mountains continuously, night and day, shrieking and cutting himself with stones. [6]And seeing Jesus from far away, he ran up and threw himself down before him, [7]and shrieking with a loud voice he said, "What do I have to do with you, Jesus, Son of the Most High God? I adjure you by God: Don't torture me!" [8](For Jesus had said to him, "Let the unclean spirit come out of the man.") [9]And Jesus asked him, "What is your name?" And he said to him,

"My name is Legion, for we are many." [10]And they pleaded with him greatly not to send them out of the land.

[11]Now there was a large herd of pigs grazing on the mountain. [12]And the demons pleaded with him, saying, "Send us into the pigs, so that we may enter them." [13]And he permitted them; and the unclean spirits came out and entered the pigs—and the whole herd, about two thousand of them, rushed headlong over the cliff into the sea, and choked to death in the sea!

[14]And those who had been grazing the pigs ran away and spread the news into the city and the villages. And people came to see what had happened; [15]and they came to Jesus, and they beheld the one who had been demonized for so long, sitting, clothed, and sane, the man who had had the legion of demons. And they were afraid. [16]And the eyewitnesses described what had happened to the demoniac, and the story of the pigs. [17]And the townspeople began to plead with him to go away from their region.

[18]And as he was getting into the boat, the former demoniac began to plead with him that he might be with him. [19]And he didn't permit him, but said to him, "Go to your house, to your people, and announce to them what great things the Lord has done for you, how he has had mercy on you." [20]And he went out and began to proclaim in the Decapolis what great things Jesus had done for him; and everybody was amazed.

[21]And when Jesus had again crossed over to the other side, a great crowd gathered together around him, and he was beside the sea. [22]And there came one of the rulers of the synagogue, whose name was Jairus, and seeing him he fell at his feet [23]and pleaded with him urgently, saying, "My little daughter is about to die; come and lay your hands on her, so that she'll be cured and start to live again." [24]And he went off with him, and a great crowd followed him and was pressing against him.

[25]And a woman who had a flow of blood for twelve years, [26]and had suffered many treatments from many doctors, and had spent all her money on them and hadn't benefited a bit but had rather gotten worse, [27]heard about Jesus and came behind him in the crowd and touched his garment. [28]For she said, "Even if I just touch his clothes, I'll be cured." [29]And immediately the fountain of her blood dried up and she knew in her body that she had been healed of her scourge. [30]But immediately Jesus, knowing in himself that power had gone out of him, turned in the crowd and said, "Who touched my clothes?" [31]And his disciples said to him, "You see this crowd pressing against you and you say, 'Who touched me?'" [32]But he continued looking around to see the woman who had done this. [33]And the woman, fearing and trembling, knowing what had happened to her, came and fell down before him and told him the whole truth. [34]And he said to her, "Daughter, your faith has saved you. Go in peace and be well from your scourge."

[35]While he was still speaking some people came from the house of the synagogue ruler saying, "Your daughter has died. Why bother the teacher any more?" [36]But Jesus, ignoring what had been said, said to the synagogue ruler, "Don't be afraid, just keep on believing." [37]And he didn't let anyone follow

him except Peter and James and John, James' brother. [38]And they went into the house of the synagogue ruler, and he saw the commotion made by the people weeping and wailing loudly, [39]and as he entered he said to them, "Why are you making a commotion and weeping? The child hasn't died, but is sleeping." [40]And they laughed at him. But he, throwing them all out, took with him the father of the child and the mother and his companions and went in where the child was. [41]And taking the child's hand he said to her, "*Talitha koum*," which is translated, "Girl, I say to you: Rise!" [42]And immediately the girl arose and began walking around—for she was twelve years old. And immediately they were greatly amazed. [43]And he commanded them urgently that no one should know this, and said that she should be given something to eat.

6   [1]And he went out from there and came to his hometown, and his disciples followed him. [2]And when the Sabbath had come he began to teach in the synagogue. And many people, when they had heard him, were amazed, saying, "Where does this man get these things from? What wisdom has been given to him! And such works of power are performed by his hands! [3]Isn't this the carpenter, the son of Mary and the brother of James and Joses and Judas and Simon? And aren't his sisters here with us?" And they were scandalized by him. [4]And Jesus said to them, "A prophet is not dishonored, except in his hometown and among his relatives and in his own household." [5]And he could not do any work of power there, except that he laid hands on a few people and cured them. [6a]And he was dumbfounded at their lack of faith.

Third Major Section (6:6b–8:21): Feasts

[6b]And he made a circuit of the villages in that area, teaching. [7]And he summoned the Twelve and began to send them out two by two, and gave them authority over unclean spirits, [8]and instructed them that they not take anything for the way except a staff—no bread, no provision bag, no small change for the money belt—[9]"but have your sandals strapped up, and don't put on two tunics!" [10]And he said to them: "Into whatever house you go, there remain until you the leave that place. [11]And whatever place does not accept you or hear you, when you leave there shake off the dust from under your feet, as a witness against them." [12]And they went out and proclaimed that people should repent, [13]and they cast out many demons and anointed many sick people with oil and healed them.

[14]And King Herod heard about it, for Jesus' name had become well known, and people were saying that John the Baptist had been raised from among the dead, and on account of that the powers were at work in him. [15]But others said that he was Elijah. And still others said that he was a prophet, like a prophet in the Scriptures. [16]But Herod, when he heard these opinions, said, "The one I myself beheaded, John, has been raised."

[17]For Herod himself had sent out and arrested John and bound him in prison on account of Herodias, the wife of his brother Philip, because he had married her. [18]For John had said to Herod, "You're not allowed to marry your

brother's wife." [19]And after that Herodias had it in for him and wanted to kill him, but she wasn't able to. [20]For Herod was afraid of John, knowing that he was a righteous and holy man, and he protected him; and when he listened to him he was greatly perplexed, and yet he listened to him eagerly.

[21]But an opportune day arrived for Herodias when Herod, for his birthday, made a feast for his lords and military commanders and the magnates of Galilee; [22]and his daughter Herodias came in, danced, and pleased Herod and his guests. The king said to the girl, "Ask of me whatever you want, and I will give it to you." [23]And he swore to her, "Whatever you ask of me, I will give it to you, up to half my kingdom." [24]So she went out and said to her mother, "What shall I ask for?," and she said, "The head of John the Baptizer." [25]So she went in to the king with haste and immediately made her request, saying, "I want you to give me immediately, on a platter—the head of John the Baptist!" [26]And although he became very sad, still because of his oaths and his guests he didn't want to deny her. [27]So immediately the king sent one of his bodyguards and commanded him to bring him his head. And he went away and beheaded him in prison [28]and brought his head on a platter and gave it to the girl, and the girl gave it to her mother. [29]And his disciples heard about it and came and took up his corpse and buried it in a tomb.

[30]And the apostles congregated before Jesus and told him all that they had done and taught. [31]And he said to them, "Come by yourselves privately to a deserted place and rest up a little." For there were many people coming and going, and they didn't even have a chance to eat. [32]So they went away in a boat to a deserted place privately. [33]But they were seen going, and many people found out about it, and they ran together to the spot on foot and got there before them. [34]And when he got out of the boat Jesus saw a great crowd, and he took pity on them, for they were like sheep not having a shepherd, and he began to teach them many things.

[35]And since the hour was already late, the disciples came to him and said, "This place is deserted, and the hour is already late. [36]Send them away, so that they may go into the neighboring villages and towns and buy themselves something to eat." [37]But he answered and said to them, "Give them something to eat yourselves." And they said to him, "What do you want us to do? Shall we go out and buy two hundred denarii worth of bread and give it to them to eat?"

[38]And he said to them, "How many loaves do you have? Go and see." And they found out and said, "Five, and two fish." [39]And he commanded them to make them all recline eating-group by eating-group on the green grass. [40]So the people reclined cluster by cluster in groups of a hundred and in groups of fifty. [41]And taking the five loaves and the two fish, and looking up into heaven, he said the blessing and broke the loaves, and kept giving them to his disciples, in order that they might distribute them; and the two fish he divided among them all. [42]And they all ate and were satisfied; [43]and they took up twelve baskets full of bread fragments and fish. [44]And there were five thousand men who ate the loaves.

[45]And immediately he made his disciples get into the boat and go before him to the other side, toward Bethsaida, while he himself sent the crowd away. [46]And having dismissed them, he went away to the mountain to pray. [47]And when evening had come, the boat was in the middle of the sea, and he alone was on the land. [48]And seeing them making tortuous progress in their rowing—for the wind was against them—at around the fourth watch of the night he came toward them, walking on the sea, and intended to pass them. [49]But they, seeing him walking on the sea, thought that he was a ghost, and they cried out—[50]for they all saw him, and were disturbed. But he immediately spoke with them and said to them, "Be brave, I am here; don't be afraid!" [51]And he came up to them, into the boat, and the wind died down, and they were greatly amazed within themselves; [52]for they did not understand about the loaves, but their heart was hardened.

[53]And crossing over, they came to land at Gennesaret, and docked. [54]And when they got out of the boat he was immediately recognized, [55]and people ran through that whole region and began bringing the sick on pallets to wherever they heard that he was. [56]And wherever he went, into villages or cities or hamlets, they laid the sick down in the marketplaces and pleaded with him to let them touch just the fringe of his garment; and as many as touched him were cured.

7   [1]And the Pharisees, and some of the scribes who had come from Jerusalem, gathered together before him. [2]And when they saw that some of his disciples were eating loaves of bread with impure, that is unwashed, hands—[3]for the Pharisees, and all the Jews, unless they first wash their hands with the hand shaped into a fist refuse to eat, since they hold fast to the tradition of the elders; [4]nor, when they come from the marketplace, do they eat unless they immerse; and there are many other customs which they have received to preserve, immersions of cups and of pitchers and of copper utensils and of beds—[5]and the Pharisees and the scribes asked him, "Why don't your disciples walk according to the tradition of the elders?—but they eat bread with impure hands."

[6]And he said to them, "Isaiah did a good job of prophesying about you hypocrites; as it has been written: 'This people honors me with their lips, but their heart stands far off from me; [7]they worship me pointlessly, teaching as divine teachings the commandments of human beings.' [8]You forsake the commandment of God and hold fast to the tradition of human beings."

[9]And he said to them, "You do a good job of annulling the commandment of God, so that you may establish your tradition. [10]For Moses said, 'Honor your father and your mother,' and 'The person who curses father or mother, let him be executed.' [11]But you say, 'If a person says to his father or mother, "Whatever of mine you might have benefited from is korban, that is, a gift to God"'—[12]you no longer allow him to do anything for his father or mother, [13]thus voiding the word of God for the sake of your tradition which you have passed down. And you do many similar things of this sort."

[14]And summoning the crowd again he said to them, "Listen to me, all of you, and understand: [15]There is nothing from outside of a person which,

when it goes into the person, is able to defile him; but the things that come out of the person are the ones that defile the person."

[17]And when he went into a house, away from the crowd, his disciples asked him about this parable. [18]And he said to them, "Then are you also without understanding? Don't you know that anything from outside that goes into a person cannot defile him, [19]because it doesn't go into his heart but into his stomach, and goes out into the latrine?" (declaring all foods clean). [20]And he said, "What comes out a person—that is what defiles the person. [21]For from within, from the heart of human beings, the evil thoughts come out: sexual sins, robberies, murders, [22]adulteries, actions motivated by greed, wicked actions; deceit, indecency, an evil eye, abusive speech, arrogance, foolishness. [23]All of these evil things come out from within and defile the person.

[24]And he got up from there and went away to the region around Tyre. And he went into a house and didn't want anyone to know it, but he was unable to escape notice. [25]Rather, a woman whose daughter had an unclean spirit immediately heard about him and came and fell down at his feet. [26](This woman was a "Greek," a Syrophoenician by race.) And she asked him to cast the demon out of her daughter. [27]But he said to her, "Let the children first be satisfied; for it is not right to take the children's bread and throw it to the dogs." [28]But she answered and said to him, "Lord, even the dogs under the table eat from the children's leftovers." [29]And he said to her, "Because you have said this, go—the demon has gone out of your daughter." [30]And she went away to her house and found her child cast onto her bed, with the demon gone out of her.

[31]And he came out again from the region of Tyre and went through Sidon to the Sea of Galilee, going through the middle of the Decapolis region. [32]And they brought to him a man who was deaf and could scarcely speak, and they began to plead with him to put his hand on him. [33]So taking him away from the crowd privately, he thrust his fingers into his ears, spat, and touched his tongue, [34]and looking up to heaven he sighed and said to him, "*Ephphatha*," that is, "Be opened!" [35]And his ears were opened, and his tongue was unshackled, and he spoke normally. [36]And he commanded them not to tell anyone; but the more he commanded them, all the more greatly did they spread the news. [37]And they were exceedingly astonished, saying, "He has done all things well. He makes both the deaf to hear and the mute to speak."

8 [1]In those days, when there was again a big crowd and they did not have anything to eat, he summoned his disciples and said to them, [2]"I take pity on the crowd, for they have remained with me for three days, and they don't have anything to eat. [3]And if I send them home without eating, they will faint on the way; and some of them have come from a distance." [4]And his disciples answered him, "Where will anyone be able to get the loaves to satisfy these people here in the wilderness?"

[5]And he asked them, "How many loaves do you have?" And they answered, "Seven." [6]And he commanded the crowd to sit down on the ground. And taking the seven loaves, and giving thanks, he broke them and gave them to his disciples so that they might distribute them; and they distributed them to the

crowd. [7]And they had a few small fish. And he said the blessing over them and told the disciples to distribute them as well. [8]And they ate and were satisfied, and the disciples took up seven large baskets full of bread fragments. [9]And there were about four thousand people; and he sent them away.

[10]And immediately he entered the boat with his disciples and went to the region of Dalmanutha. [11]And the Pharisees came out and began to dispute with him, seeking from him a sign from heaven, testing him. [12]And he sighed in his spirit and said, "Why does this generation seek a sign? Amen, I say to you, God forbid that a sign should be given to this generation." [13]And he left them and again entered the boat and went away to the other side.

[14]And they had forgotten to take loaves of bread, and except for one loaf they did not have any with them in the boat. [15]And he commanded them, saying, "Look! Beware of the leaven of the Pharisees and the leaven of Herod!" [16]And they were reasoning among themselves that he had said it because they had no loaves. [17]And when he knew it he said to them, "Why are you reasoning that I said it because you had no loaves? Do you not yet perceive or understand? Has your heart been hardened? [18]Having eyes, do you not see, and having ears, do you not hear? And don't you remember? [19]When I broke the five loaves among the five thousand, how many baskets full of bread fragments did you take up?" They said to him, "Twelve." [20]"When I broke the seven loaves among the four thousand, how many big baskets full of bread fragments did you take up?" And they said, "Seven." [21]And he said to them, "Do you not yet understand?"

INTRODUCTION

◆

AUTHOR

◆

Who wrote the New Testament book referred to as the "Gospel according to Mark"? Most people will reflexively answer: Mark! But how do we *know* that "Mark" (Gk *Markos*, Latin *Marcus*) was the author's name? The evangelist does not identify himself within the body of his Gospel; for him his work is *not* "the gospel (= good news) of Mark" but "the good news of Jesus Christ" (1:1). This absence of self-identification is probably deliberate; unlike most Hellenistic biographers, but like most biblical authors, the evangelist does not consider his own authorial personality to be important (cf. Sternberg, *Poetics*, 33; Achtemeier, *Mark*, 125–26). The "one thing necessary" (cf. Luke 10:42) is rather to allow the good news to speak for itself—the good news that proclaims Jesus and that also is, in a sense, proclaimed *by* Jesus through the evangelist himself (see the COMMENT on 1:1). The absence of self-identification probably also reflects the fact that there was no need for it; the evangelist was well known to his original addressees, who were members of his own Christian community (see the discussion of the Markan community below).

If Mark does not identify himself, why is the name "Mark" commonly attached to his Gospel? It appears in most extant manuscripts as part of an appended title, either in the short form *Kata Markon* ("According to Mark") or in the long form *Euangelion kata Markon* ("Good News according to Mark"). This title, however, is sometimes located at the beginning of the manuscript, sometimes at its end, sometimes at both beginning and end, sometimes somewhere along the side. This variation suggests that the identification of Mark as the author is not original but was added independently by different later scribes. Harnack and Zahn influentially argued that the Gospel titles did not arise until the second century C.E., when the churches began to have collections of all four Gospels and needed to distinguish one from the other. Hengel (*Mark*, 64–84) has attempted to push this date back into the late first century, when churches began to have not four but only two Gospels, but he is not able to produce a convincing argument that the Gospel titles were an original part of the text. As late as the fourth century, moreover, some copies of Mark appear to have circulated anonymously (see C. Black, *Mark*, 151).

Despite the probability that our Gospel was originally anonymous, it is likely that it was actually written by someone named Mark, because it is hard to believe that anyone would adopt this name as a pseudonym. Mark was one of the commonest names in the Roman Empire, as well-known personages such as the emperor Marcus Aurelius or the general Marcus Antonius ("Mark Antony") attest. Despite this popularity of the name, there is only one Mark known to us from early church history, a rather minor associate of Paul who is mentioned in Acts and the Pauline correspondence. The relative insignificance of this person is one reason for thinking that the Gospel was actually written by a Mark; if, lacking a sure tradition of authorship, a scribe had wished to ascribe an anonymous Gospel fictionally to a church hero, he would have chosen a more illustrious name, probably that of one of Jesus' twelve disciples (see Streeter, Four Gospels, 560–62; Brown, "Rome," 195).

But if someone named Mark wrote our Gospel, which Mark was he? As just mentioned, a man by this name is spoken of glancingly as a coworker of Paul's in Col 4:10; Philemon 24, and 2 Tim 4:11. Luke's history of the early years of the Christian movement also refers to a Mark, a resident of Jerusalem who is associated with Paul (Acts 12:12, 25; 13:5, 13; 15:36–41) and whose other (Hebrew) name is given as "John" (Gk Iōannēs = Heb Yôḥanan) in Acts 12:12, 25; 15:37. Such double names were widespread among ancient Jews (see G. Horsley, "Names"), and John was a common Jewish name (cf. in the New Testament John the Baptist, John son of Zebedee, and the John mentioned in Acts 4:6 as a relative of Caiaphas). First Peter also supports a Pauline connection by mentioning a Mark along with Silvanus, which was the name of another coworker of Paul (1 Pet 5:12–13). First Peter, Acts, and the Pauline correspondence are probably all referring to the same person, since they agree in associating Mark with Paul or a Pauline circle, including Barnabas and Silvanus (against C. Black, Mark, 66–67, 72–73).

This being the case, we can sketch out a vague outline of Mark's career on the basis of these sources. According to Acts 12:12, the Jerusalem church met at John Mark's mother's house. Despite this claim to local fame, he does not cut a very creditable figure in Luke's narrative. Acts 13:13 relates that he abandoned Paul for some unknown reason in the middle of a missionary journey, and 15:36–41 describes this desertion as the cause of a subsequent quarrel between Paul and Barnabas, who may have been Mark's cousin (cf. Col 4:10). Barnabas wanted to take Mark along with them on a later mission, but Paul, because of the earlier experience, refused, and the two missionaries therefore parted acrimoniously. The reference in the Deutero-Pauline 2 Tim 4:11 to how "useful" Mark has been to Paul may either reflect a subsequent rehabilitation of Mark or represent a pious attempt to create one.

Could this "John Mark" be the author of our Gospel? It is probable that the scribe or scribes who first titled our Gospel "according to Mark" thought so, or wanted their readers to think so, since John Mark is the only Mark known from the New Testament; if another Mark had been intended, the scribes would have identified him more exactly. As we shall see below, moreover, the second-century church father Papias apparently identified the author of the Gospel with the John Mark of Acts. But these testimonies beg the question: were Papias and the early scribes right?

Hengel (*Mark*, 45–53) argues strongly for the identification, pointing to the unusual number of Aramaic words and phrases in the Gospel as evidence for authorship by a Jerusalemite. The author's Jewishness might also be inferred from his frequent utilization of biblical quotations and allusions (e.g. 1:2–3; 7:6–7; 12:10–11; 12:36), sometimes in subtle ways (e.g. the allusions to Psalm 22 in the account of Jesus' crucifixion, 15:24–34; cf. Marcus, *Way*, 16–17; C. Black, "Was Mark," 38). The Gospel's similarity to Pauline emphases (see the discussion of the history of interpretation of Mark below) might also be cited in defense of the John-Markan hypothesis, since John Mark is an associate of Paul both in Acts and in the Pauline correspondence. Nor is the fact that the Gospel is written in Greek necessarily an argument against its composition by the Jerusalemite John Mark. The quality of the Greek is not terribly high, and many Palestinian Jews seem to have possessed an elementary level of Greek competence (see Porter, "Use"). John Mark, moreover, could have been a "Hellenist," a Greek-speaking Jew originally from the Diaspora (on the Hellenists, see Acts 6:1 and cf. Hill, *Hellenists*, 19–24). The fact that he possessed a double name, one part of which was Greek, is compatible with this assumption.

Many critical scholars, however, have been skeptical about authorship by John Mark for three major reasons: the Gentile orientation of the Gospel, the supposed mistakes and/or unconcern about Jewish laws and customs, and the supposed errors about Palestinian geography. These arguments are of unequal weight. For example, the fact that the Markan Jesus relates frequently and positively with Gentiles, especially in 7:24–8:10, but often disputes with Jewish leaders, does not necessarily mean that Mark himself was a Gentile and thus could not have been the Jewish Christian John Mark. Paul, after all, was a Jewish Christian too, and perhaps one educated in Jerusalem (see Acts 22:3), and he related positively to Gentiles and sometimes had critical things to say concerning those of his fellow Jews who rejected Jesus (see e.g. 1 Thess 2:14–16 and Romans 9–11 passim). The Markan Jesus, moreover, is not one-sidedly anti-Jewish and pro-Gentile; he relates positively to Jews, especially to Jewish crowds, throughout the Gospel (e.g. 1:21–28, 32–39; 2:1–2, 12–13; 3:7–12; 10:17–22; 12:28–34), whereas one of his two experiences with a Gentile crowd is a negative one—he is summarily asked to leave the predominantly Gentile Decapolis region after healing the Gerasene demoniac (5:17). And even in Mark's special "Gentile" section we find his Jesus expressing a typically Jewish denigration of Gentiles, referring to them as "dogs" (7:27).

More weighty as evidence against John Markan composition is the argument that the author shows himself to be an outsider to Judaism when he misunderstands or is indifferent to Jewish customs and laws. In 7:3–4, for example, he says that "the Pharisees, and all the Jews" wash their hands before eating and observe other aspects of "the traditions of the elders." Handwashing and some of the other traditions described here, however, were not universal among Jews, being especially associated with the Pharisees, so that what Mark says is technically incorrect (see Niederwimmer, "Frage" 183–85). Similarly, some scholars think that Mark, as a Gentile, is ignorant of the Jewish method of counting days, which began at nightfall. S. Schulz, for example (*Stunde*, 126–27), points to 14:12, in which the Passover lamb's sacrifice is said to take place "on the first day of Unleavened Bread [= Passover]." By the usual method of Jewish reckoning, however, this day was Passover eve, not the first day of Passover, since the holiday did not begin until sundown. Sariola (*Gesetz*, 115–17) points to 15:42 as further evidence of Markan ignorance of Jewish customs; here Mark presents the day of preparation for the Sabbath as continuing into the night. In passages such as 1:40–45; 2:23–28, and 7:1–23, moreover, Sariola sees an affirmation of the principle of Law-observance combined with an indifference to the Law's details, including biblical food laws; this combination of an explicit yes and an implicit no to the Torah he declares to be un-Jewish (*Gesetz*, 56, 68, 102). And C. Black ("Was Mark," 38) adds that Mark's grasp of Jewish Scripture seems uncertain, citing the erroneous attribution to Isaiah in 1:2 and the mistaken reference to Abiathar in 2:26.

These texts, however, do not necessarily demand that Mark be a Gentile. With respect to "the Pharisees, and all the Jews" in 7:3, the phrase places the major emphasis on the Pharisees. Although the "all" is something of an exaggeration, it is the sort of exaggeration that ancient Jews themselves made; there is a close parallel in a Jewish document, *Epistle of Aristeas* (305; see the NOTE on "for the Pharisees, and all the Jews" in 7:3). Nor is the exaggeration totally unjustified; Deines (*Steingefässe*) has recently argued on the basis of archaeological evidence that Pharisaic purity rules were widely observed by first-century Palestinian Jews. With respect to 14:12 and 15:42, Mark may be adapting the Jewish time scheme to his predominantly Gentile readers (cf. Hengel, *Mark*, 147–48 n. 50), or he may simply be inexact. As Brown (*Death*, 2.1211 n. 13) points out in his comment on 15:42, "evening" seems to be an imprecise term for Mark, and in two other instances in which he uses it, 1:32 and 14:17, he finds it necessary to clarify it by a supplemental time indication. In the Old Testament and Jewish literature, moreover, the predominant evening–evening method of reckoning days sometimes coexists with a morning–morning pattern (see e.g. Lev 7:15–16; Judg 19:4–9; 1 Sam 19:11; 28:19; Bel and the Dragon 15–17; *Joseph and Aseneth* 20:5–21:1; Josephus *Ant.* 6.336 [cf. 1 Sam 28:8, 19]; cf. VanderKam, "Calendar," 814). Mark, therefore, is doing nothing extraordinary or un-Jewish by combining the two schemes.

Neither is the Markan combination of affirmation of the Law with looseness toward its details a decisive indication of Markan non-Jewishness. One finds this same combination in Paul, who both declares that he upholds the Law (Rom 3:31; cf. 1 Cor 7:19b) and pronounces null and void some specific Torah observances (e.g. 1 Cor 7:19a; Gal 5:6), including food laws (Rom 14:14). Indeed, this is exactly the sort of combination one would *expect* from a Jew who had had the necessity of Law-observance drummed into him from his youth up, but who had latterly become an apostle of the Law-free Christian mission to Gentiles. And as for the attributions in 1:2 and 2:26, these may not be mistakes but deliberate theological exegeses (see the COMMENT on 1:2–3 and the NOTE on "in the time of Abiathar the high priest" in 2:26), and even if they are mistakes, they are the sort of error that ancient Jews as well as non-Jews frequently committed.

The most difficult problem for the John-Markan hypothesis is the apparent geographical errors in the Gospel (see the NOTES on "Gerasenes" in 5:1, "toward Bethsaida" in 6:45, "crossing over" in 6:53, and "came out again" in 7:31; cf. also 10:1 and 11:1 and see Niederwimmer, "Frage," 178–82). These, however, are not decisive either. As Hengel points out (*Mark*, 148 n. 51), even today the geographical knowledge most people possess of their home country and its environs is pretty abysmal, and the situation was worse in antiquity, when maps were rare and accurate maps nonexistent. Some of Mark's errors, moreover, may have resulted from the fact that he was trying to fit localized pre-Markan traditions into his own geographical framework; this is obvious in the conflict between the intended goal of one journey, Bethsaida (6:45), and its actual terminus, Gennesaret (6:53). And the most problematic Markan case, the illogical journey described in 7:31, may reflect not geographical ignorance but a Markan desire to construct a tour of non-Jewish areas, in line with the Gentile theme of this section of the Gospel (see the NOTE on "came out again" in 7:31). This sort of theological geography was common in antiquity; it is well illustrated, for example, by the sixth-century mosaic Medeba Map (cf. Piccirillo, "Medeba").

THE PAPIAS TESTIMONY

The objections to the John-Markan hypothesis, then, are not compelling: neither the evangelist's attitude toward Jews and Gentiles nor the extent of his knowledge about Judaism and Palestinian geography is an unsuperable bar to the identification of him with John Mark of Jerusalem. On the other hand, the arguments so far adduced in favor of this identification (Aramaic, Pauline parallels) are not overwhelming either. There is, however, one other piece of evidence that needs to be considered, the testimony to Mark's authorship by the early-second-century Bishop of Hierapolis in Asia Minor, Papias. Papias' lost work "The Interpretation of the Oracles of the Lord," which was probably written near the beginning of the second century C.E. (see Gundry, 1026–29; Botha, "Setting," 36–37), is quoted by the fourth-century Christian historian Eusebius in his *Church History* (3.39.15). Papias in turn cites an elder named John for traditions on the origin of the Gospels, including the following information about Mark:

> And the Presbyter [= Elder] used to say this, "Mark became Peter's inter-
> preter and wrote accurately all that he remembered, not, indeed, in order,
> of the things said or done by the Lord. For he had not heard the Lord, nor

had he followed him, but later on, as I said, followed Peter, who used to give teaching as necessity demanded but not making, as it were, an arrangement of the Lord's oracles, so that Mark did nothing wrong in thus writing down single points as he remembered them. For to one thing he gave attention, to leave out nothing of what he had heard and to make no false statements in them."

If this tradition is reliable, we have probable confirmation that the author of our Gospel was John Mark, since Papias seems to have this man in mind when he speaks of Mark as the interpreter of Peter toward the end of the latter's life, presumably in Rome, where Peter died. On the one hand, Papias knew 1 Peter (Eusebius *Church History* 2.15.2 and 3.39.17), a letter that links the Mark known by Peter with Silvanus in Rome (1 Pet 5:12–13). On the other hand, in Acts 15:22–40 John Mark is described as a companion of Silvanus (Silas), Paul, and other Christians, and the same man (apparently) is pictured as being in Rome in Col 4:10 and 2 Tim 4:11. Papias' linkage of Mark both with Rome and with Silvanus, therefore, strongly suggests that he thought the evangelist was the John Mark of Acts and the Pauline correspondence (see Brown, "Rome," 191–94; Guelich, xxix; contrast the skepticism of Lührmann [5]).

But how reliable is the Papias testimony? Despite spirited defenses by Hengel (*Mark*, 47–53) and Gundry (1026–45), there remain several uncertainties and doubts about it. For one thing, it is impossible to know to what extent the information Eusebius transmits really comes from "the Elder," to what extent it comes from Papias, and to what extent it comes from Eusebius himself (see Botha, "Setting," 36). For another thing, the very tone of Papias' account renders it suspect. Although Papias has to admit that Mark himself was not an eyewitness to Jesus' ministry, he stoutly maintains that his Gospel is the next best thing, a faithful transcription of the memories of Peter, who was Jesus' most important disciple, and that it is accurate apart from its arrangement, which Papias seems to ascribe to Mark himself (thus anticipating the consensus of modern scholarship; cf. Glasson, "Place," 149–50). A strong claim is made here for the apostolic, and specifically Petrine, origin of Mark's Gospel.

The very vehemence of Papias' insistence upon the connection with Peter creates suspicion. The language is obviously what scholars call "apologetic"—not in the sense of being contrite, but in the sense of being defensive (in Greek an *apologia* is a defense speech, as in Plato's *Apology* of Socrates). Papias' language is apologetic in this sense, since it seems designed to ward off objections by vindicating Mark's trustworthiness: he "wrote accurately (*akribōs*)"; he "did nothing wrong"; his aim was "to leave out nothing of what he had heard and to make no false statements." Similar language is used in the preface to Luke's Gospel (Luke 1:1–4), even down to the word *akribōs*; both Papias and Luke are concerned to stress the accuracy of Gospels by emphasizing that they go back to apostolic eyewitnesses, and it is a good guess that Papias, like Luke, is defending a Gospel against other presentations of Jesus. In Papias' case, the other works against whose claims he (or the Elder) is defending Mark's accuracy could be the other canonical Gospels—that is, why does Mark tell the stories he shares with Matthew and Luke in a slightly different and often less polished way?—but it is also possible that the works he is opposing are Gnostic. Early-second-century "orthodox" Christians like him battled the members of the schismatic Gnostic movement by linking the canonical Gospels with Jesus' original followers and denying the apostolic origin of Gnostic works. The claim to Petrine inspiration, though perhaps partly inspired by the reference to a Mark in 1 Pet 5:13, could also have been part of this battle against the Gnostics. We know from Clement of Alexandria (*Stromateis* 7.106) that the Gnostic leader Basilides claimed to have been taught by Glaucias, the interpreter of Peter—a claim that is exactly comparable to that which Papias makes for Mark (see T. Smith, *Petrine*, 38). To be sure, Papias' claim to apostolicity for Mark is indirect, operating through Peter rather than directly through Mark himself. But it would *have* to be indirect if, as argued above, the name "Mark," which is not found in any of the lists of the Twelve, was already by his time securely attached to this Gospel.

Still, just because Papias' tone is defensive, that does not *necessarily* mean that he is lying; people *sometimes* tell the truth when they are defending themselves or something they hold dear. Papias' claim of a special Markan link with Peter must therefore be evaluated on its intrinsic probability: is this a particularly apostolic or Petrine Gospel? Unfortunately for Papias' credibility, the answer is: not really. Though Glasson ("Place") has done a good job of discrediting the old form-critical argument that the rounded, stereotyped form of the Markan stories means that they cannot be from eyewitnesses—even eyewitnesses sometimes tell stories in this way—it is at least fair to say that Mark does not give the impression of being any *closer* to the events he describes than are Matthew and Luke, the later evangelists who appropriated his work. And the supposition that between Jesus and Mark there was a lengthy course of development with many tradents helps to explain how, for example, two versions of the same narrative, the feeding of the multitude (6:30–44 and 8:1–9), had had time to crystallize before their incorporation into the Gospel.

Papias' postulated close connection of the Gospel with Peter, moreover, is at variance with many of the details of individual Markan stories. If, for example, the first Markan narrative that features Peter, the story of his call in 1:16–18, were a genuine personal reminiscence, we would expect more detail, such as an explanation of what it was about Jesus that made Peter and Andrew drop everything to follow him. (In this regard the rather different story in John 1:35–42 is more plausible psychologically.) And what about the many stories in the Gospel in which Peter and the other disciples are not present, such as those that occur before their call in 1:16–20 or most of those that occur after Jesus' arrest in 14:43–52? What about the other instances in which the disciples seem to have been superficially brushstroked into narratives that originally concerned Jesus alone (e.g. 1:21–28; 2:15–17; 3:1–6, 20–35; 5:1–20, 21–43; 6:1–6a; cf. the NOTES and COMMENT on these passages and the COMMENT on 3:13–15)? Even Rigaux and Hengel, who defend Papias' "interpreter of Peter" theory, have to admit that the Gospel contains sources other than eyewitness testimony (Rigaux, *Testimony*, 49–50) and that in Mark "Peter does not appear as a living individual, but as a type" (Hengel, *Mark*, 51).

Moreover, if Mark were the Petrine Gospel *par excellence*, we would expect that Peter would be more prominent here than he is in the other Gospels, but this is not the case. Peter plays a more important part, for example, in Matthew, where there are several significant traditions about him that are missing in Mark (see Matt 14:28–31; 16:17–19; 17:24–27; cf. Brown, "Rome," 195–96). And Luke gives a more humanly affecting account than Mark does of the most dramatic incident in Peter's life, his denial of Jesus (see Luke 22:61). The truth is that, were it not for Papias, one would never suspect that the Second Gospel was particularly Petrine (cf. Jülicher, "Marcus," 294). Indeed, Mark's picture of Peter is generally a rather negative one (see T. Smith, *Petrine*, 162–90, and cf. what Rofé, *Prophetical Stories*, 21–22, says about the unlikelihood that Gehazi is the main transmitter of the stories about Elisha, since the main narratives in which he appears paint a negative picture of him). Emden's assertion ("Debt," 67) that this modest, "warts-and-all" Markan portrait of Peter is a reflection of the latter's humility does not grapple with the circumstance that Peter was involved in some important and fiercely fought ideological battles within the early church (see e.g. Gal 2:11–14), so that his name even became a slogan among the combatants (1 Cor 1:12). He could ill have afforded, therefore, to weaken his position by passing on stories that put himself in a bad light or by withholding traditions that exalted him.

In conclusion, our Gospel probably was written by someone named Mark, but this Mark probably had no special connection with Peter, contrary to Papias' apologetic claim. The possibility cannot be excluded that this Mark was the John Mark of Acts and the Pauline correspondence. There is no definitive evidence in favor of this hypothesis either, to be sure, but one admittedly inconclusive consideration may be added to the Pauline parallels and usage of Aramaic that were mentioned in its favor above. Might not the searing Markan portrait of the (temporary) abandonment of Jesus by the disciples, particularly by Peter (14:27–31, 50, 66–71), partly reflect the traumatic experience of John Mark himself, who had similarly abandoned Paul at one point in his career (Acts 13:13; 15:38)? Both of the words used to describe Mark's defection in these Acts passages, *apochōrein* and *aphistanai*, can have the nuance of apostasy (see e.g. 3 Macc 2:33; Luke 8:13; 1 Tim 2:19; Heb 3:12), and as we shall see in the exegesis of the story of Peter's denial, that narrative also has been shaped by early Christian experiences of defection from the faith. Mark, therefore, may have highlighted the disciples' desertion of Jesus partly because it was so similar to his own desertion of Paul.

But speculation, however intriguing, is not demonstration, and the fairest judgment on John Markan authorship is the nonprejudicial Scottish legal verdict of "not proven."

SETTING: THE MARKAN COMMUNITY

◆

A TOPICAL GOSPEL

Whoever the author of the Gospel was, he seems to have written his work first and foremost for the Christian community of which he himself was a member. This sort of local destination for the Gospel is assumed by most recent studies of Mark, which have argued about the details of the geographical placement of the community for which the work was written, not about the contention that it was indeed written for a particular community. I will try to be more forthcoming here about the justification for this basic assumption.

One has already been alluded to in the previous section. The very anonymity of the Gospel may point in the direction of a local address; although not the only conceivable explanation, one possibility is that no byline was necessary because the author was personally known to his readers. Another reason to assume a local address has been pointed out by Best ("Readers," 857). Mark's notice in 15:21 that the man who carried Jesus' cross, Simon of Cyrene, was "the father of Alexander and Rufus" is most plausibly explained by the theory that Simon's sons were known to Mark's audience. Since, however, Alexander and Rufus are not mentioned elsewhere in early Christian literature, they were probably people who were familiar to the Markan community, perhaps even members of it, but little known elsewhere. Matthew and Luke, in retelling Mark's narrative about Simon of Cyrene, significantly omit his allusion to Alexander and Rufus. Some of the "prophecies" in Mark 13, moreover, are best interpreted as directions to people resident in a particular locality. In 13:14, for example, the Markan Jesus commands, "When you see the abomination of desolation, . . . then let those in Judaea flee to the mountains," stressing the relevance of this instruction to his addressees with the parenthetical, probably editorial remark "Let the reader understand!"

Bauckham, however, in a stimulating essay ("For Whom"), has challenged the consensus that Mark was directed to a particular community, suggesting instead that this and the other Gospels were intended for the instruction of the church at large. Bauckham believes that scholars have been misled by the analogy of the Pauline letters, which definitely *were* addressed to particular communities. Paul's letters, however, were a *substitute* for his personal presence; the author of Mark, by way of contrast, was, according to the consensus, a resident in the community for which he wrote—so there would have been no need for him to write to it. Oral instruction, rather, would have been a more effective mode: "It was distance that required writing, whereas orality sufficed for presence . . . Literature addressing a specific community in a specific locality is very rare . . . "

Bauckham's main positive evidence for encyclical Gospels is the cosmopolitanism of the ancient world and the ecumenical consciousness of the early church; roads were good, travel was relatively safe and cheap, and early Christian leaders such as Peter, Paul and his cohorts, Ignatius, and the teachers mentioned in the *Didache* traveled around a great deal. Through such missionaries and messengers, Christian writings, especially letters, were disseminated also. The Gospel authors, according to Bauckham, were not members of insular, sectarian communities but ecumenical evangelists who saw themselves as part of a worldwide movement; in Mark itself, to extrapolate Bauckham's argument, Jesus declares that before the end comes, "the good news must first be preached to all the nations" (13:10). Would not an author who believed so strongly in the necessity of worldwide proclamation have been interested in seeing his own encapsulation of the good news travel as far afield as possible?

Bauckham has made some worthy points, but he has not really mounted a convincing challenge to the common position that the Gospels were directed *in the first instance* to individual communities. Contrary to Bauckham, writing in antiquity was not always a substitute for presence; it could have other functions such as to preserve precious memories in the face of the potential decease of their bearers through old age (cf. Mark 9:1) or through violence (cf. Mark 13:9–13 etc.). Moreover, an author's commitment of a series of traditions to writing allowed him or her to shape an overall narrative whose parts mutually illuminated each other (cf. the discussion of the literary outline of Mark below in the section on Markan composition), secure in the knowledge that the work's preservation in a relatively fixed form would allow it to be heard over and over again until it began to reveal its deeper secrets of structure and meaning.

In addition, the very plurality of the Synoptics, and their combination of similarity to and divergence from each other, is in favor of the supposition that they were written, as Streeter puts it, "in and for different churches." If both Matthew and Luke hoped to provide an authoritative replacement for Mark (see the discussion of the Synoptic problem below), and if Mark nevertheless survived, these hopes and this survival are best explained by the hypothesis of local support for the individual Gospels and the distance of their target communities from each other—just as the existence of local manuscript types (Alexandrian, Western, Caesarean, Byzantine) is testimony to the strength and relative independence of the churches in which those manuscripts were preserved. Despite their obvious debt to a common body of tradition, Matthew and Luke are very different from each other, especially in their infancy and resurrection narratives, and "churches in which the traditions current were so completely independent in regard to points of such absorbing interest as these must, one would suppose, have been geographically remote from one another" (Streeter, *Four Gospels*, 11–12). Bauckham objects that Streeter here confuses the question of the local context *in which* a Gospel was written with the issue of the audience *for which* it was written, but his own position that these two issues are completely separable is not without its problems.

Contrary to Bauckham, moreover, we do know of several works in the ancient Jewish-Christian sphere, besides Pauline and other letters, that seem to have had local addressees. The *Epistle of Aristeas*, for example, appears to be largely designed to justify the adoption of the Septuagint by the Jewish community in Alexandria and to deal with problems of cultural convergence that had arisen there (see Shutt, "Letter," 10–11; Barclay, *Jews*, 138–50). A strong case has recently been made, similarly, that *Joseph and Aseneth* was originally directed to the Jewish residents of Heliopolis in order to bolster the legitimacy of the temple that Onias IV established in that Egyptian city in 145 B.C.E. (see Bohak, *Joseph and Aseneth*). The sectarian scrolls found at Qumran seem to have been written for the members of the particular community that had gone into the Judaean wilderness to prepare God's way there (cf. 1QS 8:13–14), even though that community may have been part of a larger Essene fellowship (see VanderKam, *Scrolls*, passim)—thus providing a close counterpart to the postulated address of Mark to a specific church that was part of a larger Christian movement. And, in the Christian sphere, *The Teaching of Addai* is an example of a work that was targeted to a particular Christian community, in this case the one in the Syrian city of Edessa, whose foundation legend it presents (see J. Segal, *Edessa*, 78–81). Contrary to Bauckham, then, writing does not necessarily imply absence.

Bauckham's theory of encyclical Gospels also conflicts with aspects of particular Markan texts. The Gospel, for example, contains a number of cryptic passages (e.g. 4:10–12; 8:14–21; 14:51–52; the possible ending at 16:8) that have had to be heavily edited and/or removed by Matthew and Luke and that would make it problematic as an encyclical. And Bauckham experiences real problems with the reference to Rufus and Alexander in Mark 15:21 (see his n. 27). He first suggests that Matthew and Luke may have omitted the reference simply because of their habit of abbreviating Mark (but why did they both abbreviate at precisely the same point?). In the next sentence, however, he admits that the omission of the names might indicate that Matthew and Luke "were less confident than Mark that readers of their Gospels would know of Alexander and Rufus," but this, he asserts, might merely mean that "Alexander and Rufus were well known in some, but only some of the churches to which Mark could expect his Gospel to circulate" (but apparently not in *any* of the churches to which Matthew and Luke expected *their* Gospels to circulate—and again one must ask why). Finally, he speculates that Alexander and Rufus might have been alive when Mark wrote but dead when Matthew and Luke wrote. But should not such figures, who according to Bauckham were so well known, have been mentioned even if—in fact, even more if—they had recently died?

Bauckham may well be correct in speculating that Mark hoped his Gospel would eventually reach a wider readership, and this desire may help explain its fairly quick appropriation by the Matthean and Lukan groups. But it was probably still intended in the first instance as a teaching tool for Mark's local church. One of the pieces of evidence that Bauckham cites actually supports this supposition: the Roman author of *The Shepherd of Hermas* did indeed make a copy of his book, so that it might be sent abroad (*Visions* 2.4.3). But the work was intended first and foremost for the instruction of the leaders and members of the local churches in and around Rome (*Visions* 2.2.6; 3.8.10; 3.9.7; cf. Quasten, *Patrology*, 1.96–97; Aune, "Hermas").

Some of the arguments against Bauckham's encyclical theory, such as the cryptic nature of the narrative and the specific reference to Rufus and Alexander, also apply to the suggestion that Mark is intended as an evangelistic tool (against e.g. Gundry, 1026, and Tolbert, 304). As Shiner points out (*Follow Me*, 185 n. 26), the Gospel's rhetoric presupposes Christian belief at a number of points, including its call narratives (1:16–20; 2:13–17). In contrast to similar tales in philosophical and wisdom literature, the Markan call stories neither suggest a motivation for the disciples to begin following Jesus nor argue for the benefit of such following, and are thus inappropriate for an evangelical discourse.

A PERSECUTED COMMUNITY

Besides all the evidence adduced above against Bauckham's encyclical theory, an address to a particular Christian community is also suggested by the addressees' apparent situation of persecution, since we know of no worldwide persecution of Christians in the first century, but only sporadic mistreatment in specific localities. There are several indications in the text that the addressees were indeed living in a situation of persecution. In 10:30, for example, Mark introduces the phrase "with persecutions" into a saying that appears to have previously lacked it (cf. Pesch, 2.145). A preoccupation with persecution, moreover, seems to be reflected in the very structure of the book; as van Iersel has pointed out ("Persecuted," 17–19), chapter 4 near the beginning and chapter 13 near the end correspond to each other in many ways (e.g. a concern with the fate of the word, exhortations to attention, harvest imagery), and both emphasize the suffering that true followers of Jesus will undergo (4:16–17; 13:9–13). The ostensible "prophecies" of chapter 13 are particularly graphic; here the Markan Jesus alerts his followers to the necessity of maintaining their Christian testimony before governors and kings (13:9) and warns them that they will be betrayed to death by members of their own families (13:12) and "hated by all for my name's sake"; only "the one who endures to the end will be saved" (13:13). Further, the middle section of the Gospel is dominated by three predictions of Jesus' suffering and death (8:31–33; 9:30–31; 10:32–34) that are closely linked with prophecies of the persecution of his followers (8:34–38; 9:42–48; 10:17–31, 38–39); Jesus, then, is presented as a paradigm of the way in which his disciples, including the Markan audience, should endure suffering. And the Gospel's ending, which portrays Jesus' courageous stand before the Jewish council and Pontius Pilate, and which contrasts it with the ignominious manner in which Peter and the other disciples give way under pressure, also seems deliberately designed to prepare readers for their own martyrdom (cf. Lampe, "Denial"; van Iersel, "Persecuted," 33–34).

It is theoretically possible, to be sure, that the persecution in view is potential rather than actual, as is pointed out by van Iersel ("Persecuted," 35), or that the persecution theme is meant to jolt a comfortable Christian group out of its complacency, as is hypothesized by Juel (20). But van Iersel also rightly asserts that "the significance of the book is most pregnant in an actual situation of persecution." For example, the two Markan narratives in which disciples in a boat are endangered by the raging sea are redolent of a situation of persecution (see the COMMENT on 4:37–39 and on 6:48–50), and the way in which Jesus in these passages rebukes the disciples for their fear and doubt (4:40) or tries to allay their terror (6:50) suggests that this persecution is actual rather than potential (cf. van Iersel, "Persecuted," 21–24, 35). And as for Juel's theory, would "Why are you cowardly?" (4:40) or "I am here; don't be afraid!" (6:50) make much sense if addressed to a complacent group (cf. Rhoads, review of Juel, *Master*, 162)?

Some additional observations strengthen the case for an address to a persecuted community. A secrecy motif, emphasis on predestination, and sharp, sectarian division between "insiders" and "outsiders" such as are found in Mark (see especially the "messianic secret" passages and 4:10–12) are typical of groups that view themselves as persecuted (see Watson, "Social Function"). The specific wording of two Markan "prophecies" of persecution, moreover, is more compatible with the hypothesis of an actual persecution than with the hypothesis of a potential one or of complacent addressees. Mark 10:30 associates the situation "*now, in this* time" with persecutions, and the emphasis created by the redundancy in this phrase makes it unlikely that Mark is merely employing a standard Jewish apocalyptic contrast with "the coming age" (against van Iersel, "Persecuted," 20). The intertextual echo of Dan 12:1 LXX in Mark 13:19 points in the same direction, for here Mark makes a significant change in his Danielic source. Daniel says, "That will be a day of tribulation such as has not been since they have been *until that day*." Mark, however, alters this to "For in those days there will be tribulation such as has not been from the beginning of the creation that God created *until now*." The change from "until that day" to "until now" is probably a reflection of the Markan situation: "that day" of eschatological tribulation, the like of which the world will never again see, has *now* become a terrifying reality.

A ROMAN GOSPEL?

Granted that Mark's Gospel was initially targeted at a particular Christian community, which saw itself as living through the time of eschatological tribulation, where was this community located in space and time? As we have seen above, the Papias testimony seems to assume that Mark's Gospel was written in Rome after Peter died there. Peter was probably martyred in Rome during the Neronian persecution around 64 C.E. (see *1 Clem.* 5:4–7; Ignatius *Romans* 4:2–3; Irenaeus *Against Heresies* 3.3.2; Eusebius *Church History* 2.25.7; cf. O'Connor, *Peter*, passim; C. Black, *Mark*, 229). Papias' words suggest that the Gospel's composition took place sometime shortly thereafter, perhaps in the late sixties or early seventies, and this may actually be right. Such a dating coheres with several references in Mark 13. There were at least two famous earthquakes in the sixties (in 60 and 63; see Tacitus *Annals* 14.27, and cf. Mark 13:8). There were documented persecutions of Christians in Jerusalem (the murder of James by a lynch mob in 62; see Josephus *Ant.* 20.200) and in Rome (the persecution under Nero in 64, in which Peter and Paul among others died; see *Annals* 15.44), and there may have been others (cf. Mark 13:9–13). And there were several "wars and rumors of war" (cf. Mark 13:7–8): the defeat of Rome by the Parthians in 62 (cf. *Annals* 15.13–17), the civil war after the death of Nero in 68, and above all the Jewish War of 66–73 C.E. Admittedly, earthquakes, persecutions, and wars were not unique to the seventh decade of the first century, and predictions of such catastrophes are standard apocalyptic fare; *2 Apoc. Bar.* 70:8, for example, mentions earthquakes and wars as part of the eschatological tribulation, as Davies and Allison note (3.340). But several of the events in the Jewish War correspond closely to details of Mark 13, as we shall see in a moment. A dating in the late sixties or early seventies is also in accord with the common view that Matthew and Luke incorporated Mark into their own narratives in the eighties or nineties (on the dating of Matthew and Luke, see Davies and Allison, 1.127–38, and Fitzmyer, *Luke*, 1.53–57); it allows time for Mark to be copied and distributed and to gain acceptance in two distant Christian communities. Even without Papias, then, a dating for Mark in the late sixties or early seventies makes sense (on all of the above, cf. Telford, *Mark*, 21–23).

As for the place of composition, although most modern scholars have questioned Papias' link between Mark and Peter, many have been sympathetic to the related theory of a Roman provenance (see recently Donahue, "Quest" and "Windows"). This sympathy partly reflects the concord between the events "prophesied" in Mark 13, on the one hand, and some known aspects of the history of first-century Roman Christianity, on the other. We have already seen that Mark 13 strongly emphasizes the tribulation that Christians will endure in the end-time; this warning comes in the context of a prophecy of the diffusion of the gospel from its home base in Palestine out into the whole world, presumably including the capital of the empire (13:10). Moreover, the exhortation to maintain Christian witness before governors and kings (13:9) and the warnings against betrayal by family members and universal hatred (13:12–13) make some sense in a Roman context. Tacitus (*Annals* 15.44), for example, describes the persecution experienced by the Roman Christians in 64 C.E., when the emperor Nero tried to deflect onto them the popular suspicion that he himself was responsible for the great Roman fire, in terms that can easily be related to Mark 13:9–13:

> To scotch the rumor, Nero substituted as culprits, and punished with the utmost exquisite cruelty, a class loathed for their abominations, whom the crowd styled Christians. Christus, from whom the name is derived, had undergone the death penalty in the reign of Tiberius, by sentence of the procurator Pontius Pilate. Checked for the moment, this pernicious superstition again broke out, not only in Judaea, the home of the disease, but in the capital itself [Rome]—that receptacle for everything hideous and degraded from every quarter of the globe, which there finds a vogue. Accordingly, arrest was first made of those who confessed [to being Christians]; next, on their disclosures, vast numbers were convicted, not so much on the charge of arson as for the hatred of the human race (*odio humani generis*). Every sort of derision was added to their deaths: they were wrapped in the skins of wild beasts and dismembered by dogs; others were nailed to crosses; others, when daylight failed, were set afire to serve as lamps by night. Nero had offered his gardens for the spectacle and gave an exhibition in the circus, mingling with the people in the costume of a charioteer or mounted on a car. Hence even for criminals who merited extreme and exemplary punishment, there arose a feeling of pity, due to the impression that they were being destroyed, not for the public good, but to gratify the cruelty of a single man. (Trans. alt. from C. Black, *Mark*, 228–29)

This description certainly corresponds to the Markan depiction of Jesus' followers being "hated by all for my name's sake" (13:13a); indeed, Tacitus' expression *odio humani generis* might be translated "because of the human race's hatred for them." His depiction of Christians turning in their fellow Christians may also be seen as corresponding to the Markan Jesus' prophecy that "brother will hand brother over to death" (13:12), since "brother" in early Christian writings often has the nuance of "fellow Christian" (see e.g. 1 Cor 1:1, 10–11, 26; cf. Mark 10:30 and C. Black, *Mark*, 235).

In addition to these correspondences with Tacitus' description of the Neronian persecution, linguistic arguments have been adduced in favor of a Roman provenance for Mark. Standaert (*Marc*, 470–73) and Hengel (*Mark*, 29), for example, have asserted that the Gospel's frequent Latinisms point toward such a provenance, since Latin was the first language of the Romans. These scholars focus especially on two passages (12:42 and 15:16) in which Mark uses Latin to clarify Greek terms for a coin and a palace respectively. For Standaert and Hengel these explanations are evidence that Mark's Roman readers were unfamiliar with realities in the eastern part of the empire, i.e. in

the vicinity of Palestine. Similarly, Standaert and Hengel assert that the ethnic designation Mark employs in 7:26, "Syrophoenician," would be unnecessary in the vicinity of Palestine but essential in Rome, where it would be used
to distinguish a Phoenician who hailed from Syria from another sort of Phoenician, a "Libyphoenician," i.e. one from the area of Carthage. And it is
sometimes asserted that the Rufus referred to as a member of the Roman
church in Rom 16:13 is the same person as the Rufus mentioned in Mark
15:21 and that this coincidence also points to a Roman provenance for Mark.

Other scholars, however, have not been impressed by these arguments for a
Roman provenance. The linguistic data, for example, have come under fire
from Theissen (*Gospels*, 245–49) and Marcus ("Jewish War," 443–46), who
have argued that in 12:42 and 15:16 Mark is not substituting western terms for
eastern equivalents but explaining imprecise Greek words by means of precise Latin ones. Similarly, the designation of the woman in 7:26 as a "Syrophoenician" may not be meant to specify that she is a particular kind of
Phoenician but that she is a particular kind of *Syrian*, one who either has married a Phoenician or is from the Phoenician part of the province of Syria.
(The province consisted of two main sections, the Phoenician portion, i.e. the
Palestinian coast, and Coele-Syria, which corresponded roughly to modern
Syria.) In either case the subtlety of the distinction would make more sense in
a Syrian context than elsewhere, including Rome. And Rufus was such a
common name (cf. J. Lightfoot, *Philippians*, 176) that nothing can be concluded from the fact that it appears both in Mark and in Romans. Since,
moreover, Paul does not call Rufus one of his "relatives" (contrast Androni-
cus, Iunias, and Herodion in the same list), it is probable that he is a Gentile
Christian, whereas the Rufus of the Markan account is the son of a Cyrenian
Jew; the two men, then, are probably not the same (cf. P. Lampe, *Christen*, 58;
idem, "Rufus").

More important, although the persecution of the Roman Christians under
Nero is the best-attested case of persecution of Christians in the first century, it
is not the *only* such instance (for surveys, see Beare, "Persecution," and Potter,
"Persecution"). Acts, the Pauline correspondence, and later church sources attest sporadic persecutions before Mark's time, in Judaea (Gal 1:13, 22), particularly in Jerusalem (e.g. Acts 5:40; 7:54–8:3; Acts 12:1–5; 21:27–36; 23:12–15;
Josephus *Ant.* 20.200); in Damascus in Syria (2 Cor 11:32–33; Acts 9:1–2, 23);
in several cities in Asia Minor (Acts 13:50; 14:19; 19:24–34); and in Greece
(Acts 16:19–24; 17:5–9, 13; 18:12–13). Some of these persecutions seem to have
been spontaneous acts of mob violence (cf. "hated by all" in Mark 13:13); Josephus, for example, mentions that James, the brother of Jesus and head of the
Jerusalem church, was killed by a Jewish mob in 62 C.E. (*Ant.* 20.200), and in
Acts the Christians' antagonists are often simply called "the Jews" (Acts 9:23;
12:3; 13:50; 14:19, etc.), though this term may sometimes denote Jewish authorities rather than the general populace (e.g. 13:50).

In any event, some of the actions against Christians involved rulers as well
(cf. the reference to trials before kings and rulers in Mark 13:9). In Acts 12:1–

5, for example, we hear of the involvement of Agrippa I of Palestine, sometime before his death in 44 C.E., in the execution of James the son of Zebedee and the incarceration of Peter in Jerusalem, and in 2 Cor 11:32–33 we are told of an attempted arrest of Paul by agents of the Nabataean King Aretas in Damascus. Official persecution of some sort is also implied, at least if the accounts in Acts are to be trusted, by Paul's arrests of Judaean Christians before his conversion (Acts 8:3), by the letters he obtained from the high priest in Jerusalem to authorize the arrest of Damascene Christians (Acts 9:1–2), and by the punishment meted out against him after his conversion by the magistrates of Derbe in Asia Minor (Acts 16:22–24). Examinations of Christians before rulers, moreover, are described as taking place in Corinth (Acts 18:12–17), Jerusalem (22:30–23:10), and Caesarea (23:33–26:32), and beatings in synagogues or other Jewish venues, similar to those mentioned in Mark 13:9, are referred to as occurring in Jerusalem (Acts 5:40) and unspecified locations (2 Cor 11:24). The persecutions described in Mark 13:9–13, therefore, do not necessarily point toward Rome or the events under Nero.

Indeed, it may even be questioned how well Mark 13 fits the circumstances of the Roman persecution described by Tacitus. If this chapter really reflected those events, in which Nero was such a dominating presence, would we not expect a Nero-like figure to be prominently featured in the Markan "prophecies"? Tacitus makes it clear that the persecution of 64 C.E. was instigated by Nero himself and that he played a central role in it, even using his private gardens for the slaughter of Christians. This information is intrinsically credible, since Nero would have had a plausible motive (scapegoating the Christians for a crime of which he himself was suspected) and since Tacitus himself had no love for the Christians and thus would probably not have invented the charge merely to slander Nero. But Mark 13 does not concentrate disproportionately on the wickedness of a Nero-like pagan king; there is only an incidental reference to hearings before rulers in 13:9, not the sort of preoccupation with regal wickedness that we see, for example, in the descriptions of the "beasts" in Daniel 7 and Revelation 13. And Nero is an unlikely candidate for the "abomination of desolation" in 13:14, since he never visited or even planned to visit Palestine, and the "abomination" is probably some sort of desecration of the Jerusalem Temple (see below). If Mark 13 really came out of the Neronian persecution, would we not expect it to focus more, as Daniel and Revelation do, on a bestial, anti-God figure?

A SYRIAN GOSPEL?

Rather than the Neronian persecution, Mark 13 and the Gospel in general seem to many scholars to mirror more closely the events of the revolt of Palestinian Jews against the Romans in 66–73 C.E. After all, the real bitterness in the Gospel is directed against Jews, not Romans, and the savage events of the Jewish War would provide a plausible setting for the development of such animosity.

And the course of events in chapter 13 matches the general course of events in the Jewish War. We hear, for example, of "wars and rumors of wars" (13:7) and of nation rising against nation (13:8). Admittedly, these are general predictions and by themselves would not prove much, but Mark brings them into connection with other, more specifically described experiences: the destruction of the Jerusalem Temple (13:1–2); betrayal to "councils," beatings in synagogues, and trials before rulers (13:9); the "abomination of desolation" (13:14); and the appearance of messianic pretenders and prophets (13:22; cf. 13:6). These Markan references permit a closer link with the events of the Jewish War against the Romans, since the Temple destruction described in 13:1–2, which took place in 70 C.E., was the effective end of that war. Most commentators, moreover, think that "abomination of desolation" also refers to some event related to the war and the Temple, partly because the expression is rooted in Daniel's prophecies of Temple defilement in association with war (see Dan 9:26–27; 11:31–33; 12:11; the original reference is probably to Antiochus Epiphanes' erection of a pagan altar in the Temple in 167 B.C.E., which precipitated the Maccabean Revolt). Further, Jewish "sign prophets" and messiahs seem to have catalyzed the war effort (on "sign prophets," see the end of the COMMENT on 8:10–13; on messianic pretenders, see Josephus J.W. 2.433–34, 444, 652; 6.313; 7.29–31), and so are good candidates for the Markan "false Christs and false prophets" (cf. Marcus, "Jewish War," 457–59). And Josephus describes the mock trials held by the revolutionary Zealots after they took over in Jerusalem, thus creating a possible link with the trials Mark depicts in 13:9 (see Josephus J.W. 4.335–44 and cf. Donahue, *Are You*, 217–24, though Donahue now favors a Roman setting, as noted above).

The weakest point in this argument for a setting in temporal and spatial proximity to the Jewish War in Palestine is the lack of direct evidence for persecution of Christians in the Jewish War. It does seem, however, that Christians were persecuted in the *second* revolt of Palestinian Jews against the Romans, in 132–35 C.E., for refusing to accept the messianic claims made on behalf of its leader, Bar Kokhba (Justin *First Apology* 31.6; *Apoc. Pet.* 2:8–13; cf. S. Wilson, *Strangers*, 5–7). It is therefore not implausible that they were similarly harassed in the first revolt, which also seems to have been catalyzed by messianic hope. Such persecution would have been especially likely if the church in Jerusalem included some Gentiles, a possibility that gains credence from the apparent reference to Christian evangelism of Judaean Gentiles in 1 Thess 2:14–16 (cf. J. Sanders, *Schismatics*, 8) and from the account of the Apostolic Conference in Acts 15, which suggests the openness of the Jerusalem church to Gentiles who observed certain conditions. Such a mixed group of Jewish and Gentile Christians would have come under the fire of the revolutionaries, since the revolt seems to have been inspired by a theology that was not only anti-Roman but also anti-Gentile (see Jewett, "Agitators," 204–6; Marcus, "Jewish War," 450 n. 47; Seland, *Violence*, 271–72).

Other elements of the Markan Gospel fall neatly into place under the assumption that the Gospel was composed in proximity to the Jewish War. In

Mark 11:17, for example, Jesus castigates those in charge of the Temple because this "house," which was meant to be a house of prayer for all nations (cf. Isa 56:7), has instead turned into "a den of brigands" (cf. Jer 7:11). "Brigands" is Josephus' term of opprobrium for the revolutionaries who in his view hijacked the Jewish people into the disastrous conflict with the Romans, and if Mark understands the term similarly, then the Markan Jesus' reproach exactly fits what happened early in the Jewish revolt: in the winter of 67–68 C.E. a group of revolutionary "brigands" or Zealots moved into Jerusalem under the leadership of Eleazar son of Simon and set up their headquarters in the inner Temple itself, remaining there until the fall of the city in 70 C.E. (Josephus *J.W.*, 4.151–57; 5.5). This action was probably related to the anti-Gentile attitude that prevailed among the revolutionary groups; the Zealots saw themselves as purifying the Temple from corrupting foreign influences. In Mark's view, however, this occupation transformed God's intended house of international prayer into a "den of brigands." The revolutionary leader responsible could thus easily be seen as "the abomination of desolation, standing where he should not" (Mark 13:14), who "desolated" the Temple by unlawfully entering the inner sanctuary, filling it with violence, and barring from the Temple the Gentiles whom God meant to find in it a house of prayer (cf. Josephus *J.W.* 4.182–83, 201, 388; 6.95).

Further, the fact that the revolution was apparently led by pretenders to Davidic messiahship probably goes a long way toward explaining Mark's ambivalence toward the Davidic image, which he sometimes seems to affirm as a model for Jesus (cf. 10:47–48; 11:9–10) and sometimes to deny (12:35–37). On the one hand, he wants to assert that Jesus *is* God's holy warrior, the Davidic messiah who battles the demonic powers arrayed against God's people, and thus is the fulfillment even of the distorted hopes of the revolutionaries. On the other hand, he wants to stipulate that Jesus fulfills these Davidic hopes in a different way from the conventional image and that the overarching truth about him is that he is not just the Son of David but the Son of God (see Marcus, "Jewish War," 456–60).

The sort of detailed knowledge of the course of the Jewish War that seems to be reflected in Mark 13 is most easily explained by the theory that the Gospel was composed in geographical and temporal proximity to it, i.e. somewhere in the vicinity of Palestine, either during the war or shortly thereafter. The setting was probably not Palestine itself, however; the older view of Lohmeyer (*Galiläa*), Marxsen (*Mark*), and Kelber (*Kingdom*), which placed the Markan community in Galilee, largely because that area plays such an important role in the Gospel, has not found many advocates recently. Galilee is probably prominent not because the Markan community is situated there but because that is where the main part of Jesus' ministry and some of the early resurrection appearances actually took place (cf. Mark 16:7; Matt 28:16–20; John 21); it is also the sort of place in which the Markan Jesus can plausibly interact with Gentiles (see Stemberger, "Galilee," 435–36 ; C. Black, *Mark*, 236–37 and 249 n. 60). As an actual setting for the Markan community, however, it is unlikely, partly because the community appears to be predominantly Gentile (cf. 7:3), whereas Galilee was overwhelmingly Jewish. (On the basis of the Gospel's presumption of its audience's scriptural knowledge and Jewish concerns, Juel [*Master*, 133–39] argues that they are Jewish Christians, but he does not really explain 7:3.) If the late sixties is the time of the Gospel's composition, moreover, a Galilean provenance is questionable because Galilee was then a war front, and a community living there would probably not have had the resources, time, or inclination to set about producing a Gospel.

Rather than arguing for Galilee, most of those who have advocated a location close to Palestine have pointed to the Roman province of Syria, which was contiguous to Palestine. Syria was close enough that contact with many traditions about Jesus was likely, but it was also a predominantly Gentile region and an area of Pauline influence, so that the Markan emphasis on Jesus' contact with non-Jews and on freedom from the Law, and the explanations of Jewish customs and Aramaic terms, might find a ready audience (see Koester, *Introduction*, 2.164–67). As was noted above in the discussion of the Roman hypothesis, moreover, the designation of the woman in 7:26 as a "Syrophoenician" may point toward Syrian composition, since it may be intended to distinguish her home from the Coele-Syrian part of the province. Further, if, as seems likely, the instruction to Judaean Christians to flee to the hills upon the appearance of the abomination of desolation (13:14–15) reflects the Markan community's history, the hills concerned are most likely those on the eastern edge of the Jordan Valley, in the Transjordanian Decapolis region in which Mark shows such interest (5:1–20; 7:31–37)—the nearest neutral territory to Judaea (cf. Wehnert, "Auswanderung," 251 and n. 41). Such a flight of Markan Christians from Jerusalem to the Decapolis would correspond to the report of Eusebius (*Church History* 3.5.3) and Epiphanius (*Panarion* 29.7.7–8; 30.2.7; *Weights and Measures* 15) that the Judaean church, warned by a divine oracle, fled to the Decapolis city of Pella before or in view of the war (*pro tou polemou*) or before the siege of Jerusalem (on the historicity of the Pella tradition, see C. Koester, "Origin," and Wehnert, "Auswanderung"). And a Syrian setting during or shortly after the war years would fit in with the Gospel's emphasis on persecution, since the war in Palestine spilled over into Syria, and there were frequent massacres there of Jews by Gentiles and vice versa (see Marcus, "Jewish War," 451–54). Christians, who were perceived to be a group standing somewhere between Jews and Gentiles, may have become targets to both sides (see Josephus *J.W.*, 2.463 and cf. Theissen, *Gospels*, 268–69).

In view of such evidence, the theory of a Syrian provenance seems to be the strongest one available, and it will be adopted in this commentary and used as the basis for inferences about how the Gospel's audience would have heard particular passages. To be sure, a Syrian provenance is not a mathematical certainty, and most of the exegesis would work just as well if the setting were Rome or some other place where Christians were under pressure. But historical reconstructions are important in trying to interpret a writing such as Mark, because he and other NT authors did not think they were writing timeless philosophical treatises or works of art but messages on target (cf. Beker, *Paul*, passim), as 13:14 so clearly demonstrates when it conjoins a reference to an event occurring in time and space with an urgent summons to the audience to grasp its significance: "Let the reader understand!" Mark's purpose in writing, then, is similar to that articulated by George Orwell:

> My starting point is always a feeling of partisanship, a sense of injustice. When I sit down to write a book, I do not say to myself, "I am going to produce a work of art." I write it because there is some lie that I want to expose, some fact to which I want to draw attention, and my initial concern is to get a hearing. ("Why I Write," 5)

Mark, too, begins with a feeling of partisanship, a concern to get a hearing, a desire to expose lies and to draw attention to "facts." And just as we would never understand Orwell's fable *Animal Farm* without some comprehension of early Soviet history, so we will never understand Mark if we do not try to enter imaginatively into his first-century world.

DATE

Aside from relating the composition of Mark's Gospel generally to the time of the Jewish War (66–73 C.E.), can we narrow down its date of composition any more exactly? Perhaps the most promising data for this quest are the references to the destruction of the Temple in 13:1–2, to the "abomination of desolation" in 13:14, and to flight to the mountains in the same verse. The first-mentioned event, the Temple's destruction, is datable almost to the day; it took place on the ninth or tenth of Ab (July-August) in 70 C.E. (on the sources' divergence about the exact date, see Schürer, 1.506 n. 115). The "abomination of desolation" is more difficult to date because of the controversy about the term's reference. This is a shame because it seems to be the occurrence most immediately related to the Gospel's composition, a dramatic event that the Markan audience has either recently seen or that Mark anticipates it will very shortly see; otherwise the exhortation to understand it would be hard to comprehend. Most scholars agree that it is some sort of event in the Temple because of the Danielic context of "abomination of desolation" (see the discussion of the Syrian hypothesis above); reasonable surmises of the Markan meaning range from the sanctuary's occupation by the Zealots in 67–68 (Marcus, "Jewish War") to its destruction in 70 by Titus (Pesch, *Naherwartungen*, 139–44) to the anticipated erection of a pagan sanctuary on its site at some point thereafter (Theissen, *Gospels*, 259–64). The flight to the mountains is the most difficult event to date. Even its possible identification with the Jerusalem church's removal to Pella does not help much, since that transfer itself is hard to pin down temporally; Eusebius dates it either before or during the war, depending on the translation of *pro*, Epiphanius dates it immediately before the siege of Jerusalem, and Luke 21:20–22, if it refers to the same event, dates it after the siege had begun.

The position adopted here is that for Mark and his community the abomination of desolation, which is the occupation of the Temple by the Zealots in 67–68, and the flight of the Christians from Jerusalem shortly thereafter, are events of the recent past. For these events appear to have inaugurated the time of great tribulation in which Mark and his addressees feel themselves to be now living (cf. 13:14–19). It is more difficult to pin down Mark's chronological relation to the Temple destruction in 70. Is this an event that he and his readers know has already happened, or is it merely one that they anticipate will occur very shortly?

On the one hand, in favor of a pre-70 dating is the probability that Jesus actually prophesied the Temple's destruction, as did other Jewish prophets down through the centuries (see e.g. Jer 7:1–15; Josephus J.W. 6.300–9; cf. Brown, *Death*, 1.450, and Evans, "Non-Christian Sources," 475–77); a prophecy of its end, therefore, would not require a post-70 date. And one would not even need prophetic powers to see that the Temple would probably end up being reduced to the rubble by the Romans once the Jewish rebels had occupied it in 67–68 and the Romans had begun preparations for besieging Jerusalem shortly thereafter. The case for a pre-70 dating might be strengthened by the observation that the prophecy in Mark 13:1–2 does not exactly correspond to what happened: even after the destruction in 70 C.E. there *were* still some stones left standing upon other stones in the Temple compound; indeed, they are still standing there today, nearly two thousand years later, as anyone who has visited the "Wailing Wall" in the Old City of Jerusalem knows. These standing stones, to be sure, are from the foundation and retaining wall of the edifice, not from the Temple proper, but the unnuanced nature of the Markan Jesus' language ("not one stone") might still be considered an argument against a postdestruction dating for the Gospel. Moreover, Mark makes no mention of the huge fire that actually precipitated the Temple's collapse, even though this fire features prominently in post-70 accounts of the war (Josephus J.W. 6.250–87; Dio Cassius 66.6; 'Abot R. Nat. [B] 7 [Saldarini 72–73]; cf. b. Ta'an. 29a).

Theissen (*Gospels*, 259) attempts to solve the problem of the unfulfilled "stone upon stone" prophecy by asserting that the word hōde ("here") in 13:2 is restrictive and thus "could be a hint that only the buildings on the temple platform, but not its foundation walls, would be destroyed." But there is no real reason to take the hōde restrictively; the most natural reading of the verse is that *all* of the stones belonging to the Temple compound will be cast down. On the other hand, the lack of precise consonance with the nature of the Temple's destruction is not a decisive argument that that event is still outstanding for Mark; Josephus, too, inaccurately asserts that the Temple was completely razed to the ground by Titus (J.W. 7.1–4), and he was an eyewitness to the occurrence (cf. Botha, "Setting," 34).

In view of these conflicting arguments, it does not seem to be possible to make a decision about whether Mark knows that the Temple has been demolished, or whether he merely is positive that it *will* be destroyed very soon. In either case, however, it seems safe to say that his Gospel was written in the shadow of its destruction. The Gospel might have been written as early as 69 C.E., allowing for a bit of time after the flight from Jerusalem in 67–68 for the re-formation of the Markan community (perhaps through incorporation into an already established, predominantly Gentile church in Syria) and for the actual composition of the Gospel. Or it might have been written as late as 74 or 75—still close enough to the Temple's destruction and the final end of the war for eschatological excitement to remain intense.

GOSPEL RELATIONSHIPS

◆

THE SYNOPTIC PROBLEM

Many of the conclusions in the foregoing section would have to be revised if Mark were not the first written Gospel. How secure is this postulate?

Almost all observers would agree that there is some literary relationship among the three Synoptic Gospels (Matthew, Mark, and Luke), that is, that one of the three was written first and was copied and adapted by the other two. This literary link is evident from the close verbal agreement among the Synoptics, not only in their description of characters' words (a congruence that might theoretically be attributable to the exact memories of retentive eyewitnesses) but also in their characterizations of characters' actions, which is very difficult to explain on the theory of literary independence (see e.g. Matt 7:28–29//Mark 1:22//Luke 4:32; Matt 15:35–38//Mark 8:6–9; Matt 21:1//Mark 11:1//Luke 19:28–29). Moreover, the Gospels usually show the same basic order of pericopes, even at places where this order is not strictly logical; as Tuckett notes, for example ("Synoptic Problem," 263), Matthew and Mark break their narrative of Jesus' ministry at precisely the same point in order to offer a flashback about the death of John the Baptist (Matt 14:3–12//Mark 6:17–29).

Since the work of Holtzmann in 1863 (*Evangelien*), most scholars have operated on the basis of the assumption that Mark was the first Gospel, that Matthew and Luke knew and adapted his work, and that they also had available to them another, hypothetical source dubbed "Q" (from the German *Quelle* = "source"). But this so-called Two-Source Hypothesis (the two sources being Mark and Q) has in the last generation or so been loudly challenged by Farmer (*Synoptic Problem*) and his students and followers. These scholars have advocated a return to the older theory, first advanced in 1789–90 by Griesbach ("Demonstration"), that Matthew was the first Gospel, that Luke used Matthew, and that Mark then conflated and abridged Matthew and Luke. (This "Griesbach Hypothesis" is sometimes referred to as the Two-Gospel Theory, the two Gospels being Matthew and Luke.)

Besides these two major contenders, other theories have also been advanced: that Matthew used Mark, and then Luke used both of them (Farrer, "Dispensing"); that Mark used Matthew, and then Luke used both of them (Butler, "Synoptic Problem"); and that all three Synoptics used not only the vanished Q but also a Proto-Gospel that has likewise disappeared (Lindsey,

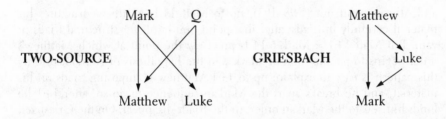

TWO-SOURCE   Mark   Q   Matthew
                  GRIESBACH   Luke
Matthew   Luke   Mark

"Modified"; Boismard, *Synopse*). Most scholars, however, have been reluctant to adopt the Proto-Gospel theory as a major part of the explanation for Synoptic peculiarities because of Occam's Razor, the principle that a theory should adopt no more hypothetical assumptions than necessary. And any theory of Lukan dependence on Matthew, including the Griesbach Hypothesis as formulated by Farmer, faces problems such as the differences in those two Gospels' birth and resurrection narratives, Luke's inexplicable scattering of the material found in Matthew's Sermon on the Mount and other Matthean sermons, and in general Luke's failure to insert the non-Markan material he shares with Matthew into the same context as Matthew does (see Fitzmyer, "Priority," 17–18). In a way it would be easier to argue for Matthean dependence on Luke, since Matthew is the more organized Gospel, though the two other problems would still remain; the fact that, with a few exceptions such as Lindsey's, this solution has not been tried may reflect the ancient church tradition—that Matthew was the first evangelist and a follower of the earthly Jesus, whereas Luke was not—rather than exegetical considerations.

It is obviously impossible to summarize here all the ins and outs of this complicated debate about Synoptic relationships, which has generated many conferences, articles, and monographs in recent years. The most important issue for our purposes is the question of whether or not Mark was the first written Gospel. Despite the challenge of Farmer and the others, Markan priority is still the consensus position, and it is the one that will be adopted in this commentary. The following are the principal reasons for preferring it over its most serious competitor, the Griesbach Hypothesis:

(1) It is easier to explain the general phenomenon of Matthew/Luke's expansion of Mark than it is to explain the general phenomenon of Mark's abbreviation of Matthew/Luke. Faced with a short Markan Gospel, Matthew and Luke might reasonably have wanted to supplement it with other material and to abbreviate the Markan passages they did include. But if Mark had Matthew and Luke before him, as the neo-Griesbachians posit, why would he on the one hand have left out useful material such as the Lord's Prayer, the Sermon on the Mount/Plain, and the preaching of John the Baptist, and on the other hand expand the stories he did include with so many inconsequential details (see Tuckett, "Synoptic Problem," 264)?

(2) It is easier to explain Matthew/Luke's rearrangement of Mark than it is to explain Mark's rearrangement of Matthew/Luke. For example, as Davies

and Allison point out (1.98–103), up to Matt 14:1, Matthew structures his material carefully in triads; after that point one hunts for structural triads in vain. But Matt 14:1 = Mark 6:14 is precisely the point at which Matthew's order begins to parallel that of Mark. On the hypothesis of Markan priority this pattern is easy to explain: up to 14:1 Matthew is imposing triads on his material, and he breaks apart the Markan sequence to do so; after 14:1 he binds himself to the Markan order, so the triads disappear. On the Griesbach hypothesis "Mark deviates significantly from Matthew only when the latter composes in triads; but as soon as Matthew quits presenting groups of three, Mark decides to get in line" (Davies and Allison, 1.103). Given that Mark does not seem to have an aversion to triads elsewhere, this procedure is difficult to explain on the theory of Matthean priority.

(3) One can understand why Matthew and Luke would have left out the few Markan passages they have both omitted. Most of these passages are either cryptic (4:26–29; 9:49–50; 11:16; 14:51–52), theologically or narratologically problematic (1:43, 2:27; 3:20–21; 7:32–37; 8:22–26; 9:39b; 15:44; 16:3), repetitious (15:25), or unnecessary (6:31; 7:2–4 for Matthew; see Kümmel, *Introduction*, 56–57; Davies and Allison, 1.108–9). On the other hand, on the Griesbach Hypothesis it is precisely such anomalous passages that have been added by Mark. But a consistent attempt to eliminate oddity seems more likely than a concerted effort to introduce it. As Davies and Allison put it, "Can one seriously envision someone rewriting Matthew and Luke so as to omit the miraculous birth of Jesus, the sermon on the mount, and the resurrection appearances, while, on the other hand, adding the tale of the naked young man [14:51–52], a healing miracle in which Jesus has trouble healing [8:22–26], and the remark that Jesus' family thought him mad [3:20–21]?" (109).

(4) In other cases, Matthew has, on the Two-Source Hypothesis, altered a feature of a Markan story for a rather obvious reason but thereby created a narrative problem for himself. In Mark 10:17–18, for example, the rich young man addresses Jesus as "good teacher" and asks him what he must do to inherit eternal life; Jesus responds, "Why do you call me good? No one is good except God." Matthew apparently found Jesus' denial of his own goodness offensive, as well a Christian might; he therefore changed Jesus' offensive question "Why do you call me good?" to the inoffensive "Why do you ask me concerning the good?" (Matt 19:17). But the continuation of Jesus' words, which essentially reproduces the continuation in Mark ("There is One who is good"), makes less sense than it did in the Markan context (see Beare, *Records*, 194–95). This redactional explanation of the Matthean incoherence works better than the assumption in the Griesbach Hypothesis that the incoherence was already part of the first Gospel's narrative. Similar remarks can be made about tensions that seem to result from Matthean editing of Mark in Matt 14:5, 9 and Matt 27:15–18 (see Davies and Allison, 1.107).

(5) The doublet sayings in Matthew and Luke also favor the Two-Source Hypothesis (see figure 1 and cf. Neirynck, "Synoptic Problem," 591–92). These

Figure 1: Doublet Sayings in the Synoptics

Tradition	Mark	Matthew	Luke
In Mark and Luke			
If want to be first, become last	9:35		9:38b
	10:43–44	20:26–27	18:26
In Matthew and Luke			
To him who has	4:25	13:12	8:18
Q:		25:29	19:26
Taking up cross	8:34	16:24	9:23
Q:		10:38	14:27
Losing one's life	8:35	16:25	9:24
Q:		10:39	17:33
Receiving Jesus as a child	9:37	18:5	9:48
Q:		10:40	10:16
In Matthew			
Beelzebul accusation	3:22	9:34	
Q:		12:24	11:15
Sign of Jonah	8:11–12	16:1–2a	
Q:		12:38–42	11:29–32
Divorce	10:11–12	19:9	
Q:		5:32	16:18
First shall be last	10:31	19:30	
Q:		20:16	13:30
Faith moves mountains	11:22–23	21:21	
Q:		17:19–20	17:5–6
In Luke			
The lamp	4:21		8:16
Q:		5:15	11:33
Hidden and revealed	4:22		8:17
Q:		10:26	12:2
Ashamed of Jesus	8:38		9:26
Q:		10:32–33	12:9
Spirit's help	13:9–11		21:12–15
Q:		10:19	12:11–12

are instances in which either Matthew or Luke, or both, have two forms of a saying. In all of these cases but one (the first in the figure), one of the sayings is similar in form to a saying that occurs in Mark, while the other is similar to the form that occurs in the other large Synoptic Gospel but not in Mark. For example, Jesus' saying forbidding divorce ("Whoever divorces his wife . . .") occurs in both Mark and Matthew in the context of a controversy with the Pharisees (Mark 10:11–12//Matt 19:9). But it also occurs as part of Matthew's Sermon on the Mount (Matt 5:32), and this form of the saying ("*Everyone* who divorces his wife . . . ") is paralleled in Luke 16:18.

According to the Two-Source Hypothesis, on the one hand, these doublets are easy to understand: they result from Matthew/Luke's interweaving of their two written sources, Mark and Q, each of which contained a version of the saying. About half of the time one or the other of the later evangelists eliminated the resultant repetition, in accordance with his policy of abbreviating the Markan traditions he transmitted; about half of the time he did not bother and let the doublet stand. (*Both* Matthew and Luke may have eliminated the repetition in other instances, but in such cases we would never know that a doublet had existed.)

According to the Griesbach Hypothesis, on the other hand, the picture looks more complicated: Matthew's Gospel contains nine doublets, presumably resulting from different oral sources he used and/or from written sources that are lost to us. (Nine, however, is a lot of doublets to be created in these ways. Mark, the first Gospel in the Two-Source Hypothesis, has only one.) Luke retained four of these Matthean doublets and eliminated five by dropping one of the doubled sayings in each case; he then created five more by supplementing pericopes he had inherited from Matthew with other traditions that were available to him. Mark then came along and eliminated all of the doublets except one. The weak points in this reconstruction are the unexplained presence of so many doublets in Matthew and the weird Lukan combination of elimination and creation of doublets.

(6) The Greek style of the respective Synoptics is also in favor of Markan priority. As Allen points out (*Matthew*, xxvi–xxvii), there are several verses in which Mark's vocabulary is rare or unusual, Matthew's more common (e.g. Mark 1:10, 12, 16; 2:11, 21; 3:28; 9:3; 10:25; 11:8; 14:68, 72; 15:11). It is easier to explain why Matthew would try to make Mark more understandable than it is to explain why Mark would want to replace a common Matthean word with a rare Markan one. Moreover, despite Davies and Allison's disclaimer (1.103), the generally better Greek style of Matthew and Luke is also an argument for Markan priority and against the Griesbach Hypothesis. It is true that, were Mark retelling Matthew/Luke freely, he would probably use his own characteristic, inferior Greek style. But in the Griesbach Hypothesis he is *not* retelling his source stories freely but copying them, sometimes word for word. In these circumstances why would he constantly choose a less felicitous way of expressing himself than that present in his sources?

(7) The Christological tendencies of the respective Gospels also provide a powerful argument in favor of Markan priority and against the Griesbach Hypothesis. In a well-reasoned monograph, Head (*Christology*) has shown that, in the Two-Source Hypothesis, one can come up with plausible reasons for Matthean editing of Markan passages that deal with Jesus' identity, reasons that are consistent with other Matthean passages on the same subjects. The reverse, however, is not true: Markan Christological editing of Matthew in the Griesbach Hypothesis turns out to be implausible, since in this theory Mark omits themes that elsewhere are important to him (e.g. Jesus as "Lord" or the future Son of Man); nor does he replace them with consistent alternatives.

THE MINOR AGREEMENTS

The cumulative evidence for the Two-Source Hypothesis, therefore, seems very strong. The biggest problem for this hypothesis is the "minor agreements"—that is, passages in the Triple Tradition in which the versions of Matthew and Luke depart in similar ways from that of Mark (for a cumultative display of them, see Neirynck, *Minor Agreements*). These Matthean/Lukan agreements, which are few in comparison with the "major," Q agreements, are still a problem for the Two-Source Hypothesis and *prima facie* evidence for the neo-Griesbach Hypothesis, because the former posits no direct literary relationship between Matthew and Luke, whereas the latter does. A few examples will illustrate the nature of the phenomena involved: (1) In the account of Jesus' baptism (Matt 3:13–17//Mark 1:9–11//Luke 3:21–22) Mark says that Jesus saw the heavens *ripped apart* (*schizomenous*) and the Spirit descending *eis auton* ("upon him", but lit. "into him"). In both Matthew and Luke, however, the heavens are *opened* (*ēneōchthēsan/aneǫchthēnai*) rather than ripped, and this breach is described as an objective event rather than a visionary experience of Jesus; in both, moreover, the Spirit descends *ep' auton*, the more usual term for "upon him." (2) In Mark 4:11 Jesus says to his disciples, "To you has been given the *mystery* [singular] of the dominion of God." Matt 13:11 and Luke 8:10, however, render this "To you has been given *to know* the *mysteries* [plural] of the dominion of heaven/of God." (3) In the story of Jesus' encounter with his family in Matt 12:46–50//Mark 3:20–21, 31–35//Luke 8:19–21, neither Matthew nor Luke frames this story around the Beelzebul controversy, as Mark does, and both lack the Markan notes about Jesus' going into a house with his disciples, being surrounded by a crowd, being unable to eat because of the press, and being pronounced mad by his relatives. In Matthew and Luke, moreover, the people describe the position outside the house of Jesus' mother and brothers with the phrase "they are standing outside" (*exō hestēkasin/hestēkasin exō*), whereas in Mark they describe it with the phrase "outside, they are seeking you" (*exō zētousin se*). (4) In Mark 14:65 the mocking soldiers strike Jesus and say, "Prophesy!" In both Matt 26:68 and Luke 22:64 they add, "Who is it who struck you?" (*tis estin ho paisas se*).

The first thing to be said about these agreements is that they are indeed minor, not only in relation to Q but also in relation to the total number of departures of Matthew and Luke from Mark. Stoldt (*Marcan Hypothesis*), for example, cites 272 minor agreements. As Davies and Allison point out, however (1.112–13), there are literally thousands of Matthean and Lukan departures from Mark, since the two later evangelists are constantly revising their source and going their own ways. It would not be surprising, then, if Matthew and Luke, purely by chance, should occasionally have made the same alteration to Mark.

The minor agreements become even less impressive when individual cases are considered. Then it becomes clear that Matthew and Luke often deal with a problematic Markan text in the same predictable way. In example number 1 above, for example, the violence of the Markan picture of the ripped heavens is potentially embarrassing, whereas the "open heaven" is a common motif in ancient Jewish and Christian texts (see the index to Rowland, *Open Heaven*, under "Open Heaven"); Mark's *eis auton*, moreover, is potentially misleading (did the Spirit actually enter Jesus?). The change from ripped to open heavens and from *ep' auton* to *eis auton*, then, is unsurprising. Also unremarkable is the shift from visionary experience to public event; Mark's restriction of perception of the visionary events to Jesus is part of his messianic secret motif (see the APPENDIX "The Messianic Secret Motif"), and Matthew and Luke feel no need to retain it, especially since in their narratives Jesus has been proclaimed "king of the Jews" (Matt 2:2) and "Son of God" (Luke 1:32, 35) from his birth. In example number 3, similarly, one should not be astounded that Matthew and Luke have scrapped the hard-to-follow Markan intercalation technique, have omitted the verses in which Jesus' relatives allege that he is insane, and have changed the awkward *exō zētousin* to the unexceptional *exō hestēkasin*.

It is more difficult to explain instances such as numbers 2 and 4 (though it should immediately be added that the bulk of the minor agreements are more like 1 and 3). The *combination* in example 2 of the change to the plural "mysteries" and the addition of "to know," or the fact that in example 4 Matthew and Luke have added the exact same five words in the exact same sequence, makes ascription to independent editing harder though by no means impossible ("to be given" a mystery is enigmatic without "to know"; "mysteries of the dominion of God" is a less puzzling locution than the Markan singular; and "Who is it who struck you?" brings out the meaning of the unclear "Prophesy!"). In any event, although such agreements are a problem for the Two-Source Hypothesis, it is unclear that the other major source theory fares better with them. Tuckett, for example ("Synoptic Problem," 267), cogently asks why Mark would have omitted "Who is it that struck you?" if it stood in both of his sources, as the Griesbach Hypothesis would have it.

Proponents of the Two-Source Hypothesis who feel that independent editing is an inadequate explanation for the Matthean/Lukan agreements have had recourse to a number of expedients. Some have pointed to the influence of oral tradition, which is especially likely in the case of important material such as the passion narrative (this might help explain "Who is it who struck you?" in example 4). Others have argued for the possible influence of Q; we do not know exactly what was in that source, and it may have included some of the agreement passages. Textual assimilation of Matthew and Luke to each other is often invoked as well; one or the other of the larger Synoptics, in other words, may originally have had a reading that followed Mark, but a scribe adapted it to the form found in the other major Synoptic, which was better known.

Finally, some have argued for Matthew/Luke's usage of a version of Mark different from that which has come down to us. This other version could either be "Proto-Mark," the lost original recension (see e.g. Wendling, *Entstehung*) or "Deutero-Mark," a forgotten revision of the present Gospel (see recently Fuchs, "Seesturmperikope," and Ennulat, *Minor Agreements*). The Deutero-Mark theory seems slightly more likely than the Proto-Mark theory, since the Matthew/Luke agreements are often easier to understand or less theologically problematic than the Markan version; but this consideration also increases the chance that they result from independent editing.

Moreover, both the Proto- and Deutero-Mark theories confront two difficulties: Why would anyone bother to reissue Mark in a new version that was minimally different from the old one—in other words, that varied only in the "minor agreement" passages? And why has Proto- or Deutero-Mark vanished completely, although it was such a well-known text that it was used by Matthew and Luke, who presumably wrote in localities distant from each other? It is not wholly satisfactory to counter, as H. Koester does (*Ancient Christian*, 275), that the other major source for Matthew and Luke, namely Q, has also vanished. The two cases are dissimilar: an independent version of Mark *has* survived, whereas an independent version of Q has not; texts of Mark apparently had more "sticking power" than texts of Q did. (This makes sense, since Mark was a freestanding Gospel, while Q may not have been.) And it is odd that, according to both the Proto- and Deutero-Mark theories, the surviving text is less felicitous than the vanished one. If textual history teaches us anything, it is that smooth, unproblematic texts survive and eventually predominate, whereas difficult texts fall by the wayside (see e.g. the dominance of the Byzantine family in the NT textual tradition).

SECRET GOSPEL?

Despite these reservations, an elaborate "Proto-Mark" theory proposed by Koester ("History"; *Ancient Christian*, 273–303), involving what is known as "the Secret Gospel of Mark," is worthy of more extended consideration. According to Koester, the Gospel developed in several stages:

(1) "Original Mark" was formed from oral traditions (a passion narrative, miracle stories, a parable collection, etc.). It was even shorter than the present Gospel, lacking 6:45–8:26 (the section omitted by Luke), and it contained some of the passages that turn up in the Matthew/Luke agreements. It is this abbreviated form that was used by Luke.

(2) Original Mark was augmented by the addition of 6:45–8:26 and was then used by Matthew.

(3) This augmented form later became the basis for "the Secret Gospel of Mark," an esoteric, "more spiritual" version of Mark produced in early-second-century Alexandria, which is mentioned in a letter by Clement of Alexandria discovered and published by M. Smith (*Clement*). (Some commentators, however, have expressed doubts about the genuineness of this letter. The only scholar who claims to have seen it is Smith, and some maintain that it is an ancient or modern forgery; for discussion, see Crossan, *Four Other*, 100–3, and the literature cited in H. Koester, *Ancient Christian*, 293 n. 8.) The Secret Gospel, according to Koester, made numerous editorial changes in the text of "Augmented Mark," pushing it in the direction of esotericism; many of Mark's references to "teaching," for example, come from this level of redaction, as can be seen by the frequency with which Matthew and Luke omit such references. Some Markan disagreements with Matthew/Luke are places where the author of the Secret Gospel altered the text after Matthew and Luke had copied Original Mark. For example, the singular "mystery" in Mark 4:11, which refers to baptism, and the magical practices described in 7:32–36 and 8:22–26, comport with the Secret Gospel's mystical atmosphere and are additions from this stage.

The Secret Gospel redactor also added two passages quoted in Clement's letter and one associated with them that remained in Canonical Mark: (a) a long text following 10:34 in which a young man is raised from death by Jesus, comes to him by night dressed in a linen cloth, and is taught the mystery of the dominion of God; (b) a description of the flight of the same young man at Jesus' arrest; this text is retained in Canonical Mark 14:51–52; (c) a short text following 10:46a in which Jesus, in Jericho, refuses to receive the young man's sister and mother and Salome.

(4) The Secret Gospel in turn became the basis for a risqué edition of Mark that is denounced by Clement in his letter. This version included the phrase "naked man with naked man," and it was produced by the Gnostic sect of the Carpocratians, whom orthodox churchmen accused of libertinism.

(5) To counter the Carpocratians, an orthodox redactor expurgated Secret Mark of the two passages Clement quotes and thereby produced the Canonical Mark that we find in our Bibles. This did not happen before the middle of the second century or so, since Carpocrates was active during the emperor Hadrian's reign (117–38 C.E.).

Koester's proposal, then, can be summed up in the following diagram from Sellew's excellent review article ("Secret Mark," 245):

[Pre-Markan Traditions]
:
:

Original Mark (without 6:45–8:26)

Augmented Mark (Original Mark + Mark 6:45–8:26)

Matthew

Luke

Secret Mark

Carpocratian Mark

Canonical Mark

This is a bold theory that places the development of Mark interestingly into a school context similar to that of the development of John, which many scholars think went through several recensions over a number of years. And it does offer an explanation for the different versions of Mark mentioned by Clement, for some of the minor agreements, and for certain other odd features in the present Markan text. The strange story of the anonymous, scantily clad young man who comes out of nowhere and then runs away naked in 14:51–52, for example, is now seen to be part of a series of narratives about this youth. The awkward verse 10:46, in which Jesus enters Jericho and immediately exits it without doing anything, is also explained: originally he *did* do something in Jericho, namely reject the young man's sister and mother and Salome, and this rejection helps to explain his hasty departure.

Nevertheless, Koester's arguments are ultimately unconvincing. Narrative fissures in the Markan text, for example, could have been filled in by subsequent redactors rather than being created by awkward editing. A later editor, for example, might have realized the strangeness of the young man's appearing out of nowhere in the Markan passion narrative, and he might have attempted to give this character some background by shaping a story about his first encounters with Jesus. Similarly, he might have realized that there was an awkward lacuna in the account of Jesus' trip to Jericho, and so he might have sketched in the little vignette of rejection there; troublesome gaps of this sort are often the basis for subsequent expansions of biblical texts (cf. Kugel, *Potiphar's House*, 247–51). The presence of such gaps, indeed, is no great surprise to readers of Mark; as Gundry (606) points out, for example, 10:46 is not the only place in Mark in which Jesus goes somewhere and then does nothing there (cf. 7:31; 11:11).

There are, moreover, logical problems with Koester's theory about the origin of the youth clad only with a linen cloth. Sellew ("Secret Mark," 251–52)

notes that if this character had already been presented in chapter 10, it is surprising that Mark should describe him in 14:51 as "*a certain* young man"
(*neaniskos tis*); in the Gospels, rather, this would normally be the way to introduce a previously unmentioned character (cf. Luke 10:30; 15:11; 16:1, 20;
19:12). And Gundry (612) cogently asks why, if this youth was interpolated
into both chapters 10 and 14 by the Secret Gospel author, he was purged from
the former but not from the latter by the author of Canonical Mark.

Even more important than these questions about individual passages are
reservations about the plausibility of the overall theory. Sellew, for example,
disputes that the original version of Mark lacked 6:45–8:26, pointing out that
Luke's omission of this section comports with his tendency to avoid repetition
(if the section remained, Luke would have two boat trips, two feeding miracles, and two healings of blind men, as Mark does). The section's presence in
Original Mark, moreover, is confirmed by its cruciality for developing a central aspect of the Markan plot, the theme of the increasing incomprehension
of the disciples (6:52; 7:18; 8:14–21), which also appears elsewhere in the
Gospel (e.g. 4:13; 14:68). The presence of this major plot theme in the Gospel from the beginning of its development is much more plausible than its
introduction at a later stage.

Sellew also undermines Koester's conclusion that many of the Markan references to "teaching" were absent in Original Mark; usually such references
are in fact retained in Matthew and/or Luke (cf. Neirynck and Van Segbroeck, 233), and in many of the cases in which they have been eliminated
they are not in fact appropriate to the miracle context and so would have been
prime candidates for independent abbreviation (cf. Räisänen, 110 n. 116). As
Räisänen notes, moreover, Koester's theory is self-contradictory in that "the
author of the Secret Gospel inserted several remarks on 'teaching' in order to
underline the idea of *esoteric* instruction, and yet he made Jesus give this instruction to the *crowd* (e.g. 1:27; 2:13; 4:1–2; 10:1; 11:17; 12:35, 37–38)." The
combined attacks of Räisänen and Sellew on this point weaken a major plank
in Koester's program, since a supposed tendency to introduce references to
pedagogy would obviously go along with the esoteric concern for deep understanding in Secret Mark.

Like Koester, Crossan (*Four Other*, 91–121) has tried to fit Secret Mark into
a genealogy of Markan versions, but his attempt is even less convincing than
Koester's. Like the latter, Crossan argues that Canonical Mark is a redaction
of Secret Mark. He has a simpler picture of the overall development of the
versions, however, because he rejects the Proto-Mark theory. (See diagram,
next page.)

Gundry (613–23) has written a thoughtful, detailed refutation of Crossan's
treatment of individual passages. But it also weakens Crossan's case fatally that,
because he rejects the Proto-Mark theory that Koester embraces, he must place
Matthew and Luke's appropriation of Markan tradition, and hence their composition, after the time of the Carpocratians—that is, in the middle of the second
century. But this is an absurdly late date for the two larger Synoptics. Probably

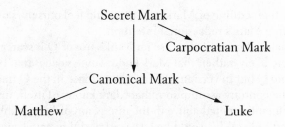

for this reason, in his later book *Historical Jesus* (329–30, 429–30), Crossan does not describe Canonical Mark's predecessor as Carpocratian Mark but as a version of Mark concocted by "libertine Gnostics, proleptic Carpocratians as it were, similar to those Paul encountered at Corinth"—that is, first-century Gnostics, not second-century ones. But this new reconstruction forfeits the connection with Clement's letter and its mention of the Carpocratians, which is the only secure foundation for the thesis of an antilibertine redaction of Mark. It is better to go along with Koester and treat Secret Mark—if it ever existed— as a late edition of Mark that reveals the concern for esotericism typical of second-century Alexandrian Christianity. Contrary to Koester, however, Secret Mark is more likely a redaction of Canonical Mark than the other way around.

DID MARK USE Q?

In the sketch of the Synoptic problem given above, Q was defined as the body of material not present in Mark but evidently used by both Matthew and Luke. There are, however, several overlaps between Markan and Q material—places where the same tradition is transmitted but in a different way. I have already given some examples in my discussion of doublets in the section on Synoptic relationships above. To cite a few other instances, both Mark and Matthew/ Luke have narratives about Jesus' temptation by Satan, but Mark's is only two verses long and relates no dialogue between Jesus and Satan (Mark 1:12–13), whereas Matthew's and Luke's (Matt 4:1–11//Luke 4:1–13) are eleven and thirteen verses respectively and describe in detail Satan's attempts to make Jesus turn a stone into bread, worship him, and cast himself from the Temple pinnacle. Similarly, both Mark (4:30–32) and Matthew/Luke (Matt 13:31–32// Luke 13:18–19) have a version of the Parable of the Mustard Seed, but the Matthew/Luke forms are so different from the Markan one and so close to each other that they obviously come from a different source other than Mark.

These Mark/Q overlaps suggest to some exegetes (e.g. Lambrecht, "John"; Catchpole, "Beginning"; Fleddermann, *Mark and Q*) that Mark actually knew and used Q. Such a result would be of great significance for exegesis of Mark, since it would mean that we have what we otherwise sadly lack, fairly direct access to one of Mark's sources. We could then observe Mark's editing of this source in a way similar to that in which commentators on Matthew and Luke can observe their editing of Mark, and we would feel ourselves on surer ground in interpreting Mark's redactional intention.

Unfortunately, however, the case for Mark's use of Q is scarcely overwhelming. It is more likely, rather, that Mark knows some sayings that have also found their way into Q but in versions different from those in the Q tradition (see e.g. Laufen). The contrary assumption, that Mark knows Q itself, involves some of the same difficulties noted above in the discussion of his possible awareness of Matthew and Luke: Why would he leave out useful material such as the Lord's Prayer, the Sermon on the Mount, and John the Baptist's preaching? Why would he so drastically reduce the temptation narrative and render it so cryptic? Why would he, in his version of the Beelzebul controversy (3:22–30), expunge the saying about casting out demons by the finger of God (Matt 12:28// Luke 11:20), when its assertion that Jesus' exorcisms demonstrate the arrival of God's dominion seems to be exactly the point of the Markan Parable of the Strong Man? Why, in his narration of Jesus' refusal to give a sign (8:10–13), would he omit the sayings about the sign of Jonah and the repentance of the men of Nineveh (Matt 12:39–41//Luke 11:29–32), when they would fit so well with the theme of Gentile inclusion in this section of the Gospel?

Moreover, if Mark used Q, then his versions of Q sayings should always be more developed than those in Q, and he should show awareness of Q redaction, not just of Q's raw material. This, however, does not seem to be the case; contrary to the claim of Fleddermann (*Mark and Q*), Mark never gives unambiguous proof of knowledge of Q redaction (see Tuckett, "Mark and Q," and Neirynck, "Mark and Q"). In some instances, as a matter of fact, the Q form of a saying seems to be secondary to that of Mark. This happens several times, for example, in material found in Mark 4. The beginning of the Q form of the saying about hiddenness and revelation (Matt 10:26//Luke 12:2), "nothing is hidden," seems to smooth out a roughness found in the Markan form, "there is nothing hid" (Mark 4:22). Similarly, Q's version of Mark 4:25 (Matt 25:29// Luke 19:26) is smoother than the Markan version, and one of the awkward features of the latter is a redundant pronoun ("given *to him*"), which is a feature of Semitic syntax and likely to be primitive.

The Parable of the Mustard Seed in the same chapter (Mark 4:30–32//Matt 13:31–32//Luke 13:18–19) is another good argument for Mark's independence from Q. Mark's omission of the Parable of the Leaven (Matt 13:33//Luke 13:20–21), with which the Mustard Seed parable is coupled in Q, is difficult to explain on the theory that Mark knew Q, since this parable would fit in superbly with the theme in Mark 4 of the hidden spread of the dominion of God. Considering the parable itself, moreover, Mark 4:30–32 and Luke 13:18–19 = Q "have virtually nothing in common beyond the barest essentials necessary for telling a parable comparing the Kingdom of God to a mustard seed" (Tuckett, *Revival*, 81), so the thesis of Markan dependence on Q faces an uphill battle.

Further, while certain Markan differences from the Q form might represent Markan redaction (see the introduction to the COMMENT on 4:26–34), others are difficult to explain in this way. In the introduction to the parable, for example, why does Mark not follow Q in providing 4:31 with a main verb instead of beginning the sentence awkwardly with "as"—a form that corresponds to rabbinic parables but not to Greek syntax (cf. Jeremias, *Parables*, 101–2; Tuckett, *Revival*, 79)? In the body of the parable, why would he have eliminated the figure of the sower who appears in Q, when this figure would fit in well with the sower in 4:3–8 and 4:26–29 (cf. Marcus, *Mystery*, 207–8; Friedrichsen, "Matthew-Luke Agreements," 659)? And at the parable's end, why would he have changed the primary OT allusion from Dan 4:21 to Ezek 17:23, when the former could make his point as well as the latter (cf. Tuckett, *Revival*, 83)? Partisans of Markan use of Q can come up with answers to such questions (see e.g. Lambrecht, "Redaction," 291–97; Fleddermann, *Mark and Q*, 90–99), but these solutions often give the impression of trying to make water flow uphill (see the detailed refutations in Tuckett, "Mark and Q," 172–74, Friedrichsen, "Matthew-Luke Agreements"; and Neirynck, "Mark and Q," 277–78). Mark, then, probably did not know Q as a literary document.

MARK AND JOHN

In some ways the issue of the relationship between Mark and the Johannine tradition is similar to the issue of the relationship between Mark and Q: is this a case of direct literary influence of Mark and/or the other Synoptics on John? (With the notable exception of J. A. T. Robinson [*Priority*], scholars almost universally agree that John is the later Gospel.) Or is it a case of the independent use of a common stream of tradition by the Synoptics and John? John is so different from the Synoptics that, if he did use them, he has transformed them radically in pursuance of his own theological and narrative interests. But there are also instances in which striking similarities exist between John and the Synoptics (see the survey by Kysar, "John," 920). The question is whether this combination of similarities and differences points toward John's dependence on the Synoptics or his independence from them. Although this question may seem at first to be more relevant for a commentary on John than it is for one on Mark, it is also important for the latter. Even though John is later than Mark, if he is independent he may in some cases preserve traditions that are earlier, and similar to pre-Markan ones, and thus may occasionally provide a clue as to how Mark has edited his material.

Not only this question but also some of the arguments that are used to investigate it are similar to those we have reviewed in the previous section (see the excellent survey of the contemporary discussion in D. M. Smith, *John Among*). Like proponents of Markan use of Q, advocates of Johannine use of the Synoptics explain differences between parallel traditions as redaction of the earlier Gospels by the later one, and they point out cases in which they think that John has used redactional material from the Synoptics (see e.g. Neirynck, "John and the Synoptics"). On the other hand, advocates of Johannine independence from the Synoptics deny such use of redactional material and point to instances in which the putative Johannine redaction seems to lack an obvious motive or in which the Johannine tradition seems to be more primitive than the Synoptic one.

The advocates of independence seem to have the edge here again, though it must be admitted that the number and influence of the advocates of dependence of John on one or more of the Synoptics have been growing in recent years. But the latter group of scholars has still not been able to present convincing evidence for Johannine usage of Synoptic redaction. For example, the contacts that Neirynck points out between John 20:1–10 and Luke 24:12, on the one hand, and between John 20:11–18 and Matt 28:9–10, on the other, are too slight a base to support the thesis of dependence on Lukan and Matthean redaction and might be due to contact with common tradition (see Davies and Allison, 3.668–69; Fitzmyer, *Luke*, 2.1547–48). The textual uncertainty of Luke 24:12, moreover, renders the argument for dependence even more uncertain; Ehrman (*Orthodox Corruption*, 212–17) has recently contended at length that this verse was not an original part of Luke's text but a later "orthodox corruption of scripture" that fuses features of John 20:1–10 together. Moreover, the Johannine narratives shared with the Synoptics are sometimes less theologically developed than the Synoptic versions, a circumstance that goes against the general thrust of Johannine theology (see e.g. the discussion of the Johannine version of the story of the walking on the water in the introduction to the COMMENT on 6:45–52). And there are cases in which John relates inconsequential details that are not matched in any of the Synoptics and that do not seem to have theological significance; in the story of the miraculous feeding, for example, he is unique in specifying that the fish distributed were *dried* fish (*opsaria*, John 6:8, 11; see Brown, 1.246, and generally 1.236–50). Dodd (*Historical Tradition*) has used such cases to mount an impressive argument that there is actually historical tradition in John, tradition that is not simply an elaboration of the Synoptics, even when it occurs in passages that parallel them. But this demonstration poses a significant challenge to the theory of Johannine dependence on the Synoptics.

THE *GOSPEL OF THOMAS*

Similar arguments and conflicting conclusions about dependence on or independence from the Synoptics arise with respect to the *Gospel of Thomas*, a collection of aphorisms that purport to be sayings delivered by the risen Jesus to Thomas and the other disciples. The extant manuscripts of *Thomas* are in Coptic, but Greek versions of eighteen individual *Thomas* sayings have been found in the papyrus fragments from Oxyrhynchus, Egypt, and most scholars believe Greek to be the original language of the writing (see Fitzmyer, "Oxyrhynchus," and Tuckett, "Thomas," 134). *Thomas* seems to have been influenced by second-century Gnostic beliefs such as a radically negative attitude toward the world (see e.g. *Gos. Thom.* logion 56 and cf. Marjanen, "Gnostic") and a soteriology that emphasizes self-realization and the heavenward ascent of the soul (see e.g. logion 9 and cf. Klauck, *Allegorie*, 199–200; on other Gnostic elements in *Thomas*, see Meier, *Marginal Jew*, 1.125–27). Partly because of such Gnostic features, most scholars date *Thomas* to the second century C.E. Such a late date, however, does not necessarily rule *Thomas* out *a priori* as a source for early Jesus tradition, since the date of documents is not necessarily identical with the date of the traditions they transmit; the Gospel of John is also relatively late, and as we have just seen, this has not ruled *it* out as a source for Jesus tradition. The question has been raised, therefore, whether *Thomas* preserves independent and perhaps historical forms of Gospel sayings, as claimed, for example, by Crossan (*Four Other*, 35–37), H. Koester (*Ancient Christian*, 84–86), and the members of the Jesus Seminar, or whether it is dependent on the canonical Gospels and thus useless as a source for the historical Jesus and the pre-Synoptic tradition, as argued by Schrage (*Verhältnis*), Tuckett ("Thomas"), and Meier (*Marginal Jew*, 1.124–39).

A large part of this debate has revolved around the forms of the individual sayings. About half of them have twins in the Synoptic Gospels (see Patterson, *Thomas*, 95–97), though the *Thomas* forms are usually shorter, formally simpler, and sometimes more paradoxical; Jesus' parables in *Thomas*, for example, lack explanatory allegories and, for the most part, applications (see Scott, *Hear Then*, 30). These characteristics have been used by some scholars as justification for their contention that the *Thomas* tradition is earlier than that found in the canonical Gospels (see e.g. H. Koester, "Thomas Parables"), though others interpret the same characteristics as signs of a later, Gnostic reworking (see e.g. Meier, *Marginal Jew*, 1.133). It is difficult to avoid the suspicion that in part this debate reflects extrascientific factors; on the one hand, a prejudice against *Thomas* because of its noncanonical status; on the other hand, a predilection for it for the very same reason.

In view of the equivocal nature of the other evidence and the prevalence of subjective factors in the debate, it is doubly important to mobilize an argument that we have used above with respect to Mark's use of Q and John's use of the Synoptics—namely, whether or not *Thomas* uses redactional material from the earlier sources. In this case the evidence seems to point toward *Thomas*'s dependence on the Synoptics. Tuckett ("Thomas") adduces passages such as *Gos. Thom.* logion 5//Luke 8:17; *Gos. Thom.* logion 16//Luke 12:51–53; and *Gos. Thom.* logion 20//Mark 4:30–32 (the Parable of the Mustard Seed again) as instances in which *Thomas* seems to reflect Synoptic editing, and Uro ("Thomas") builds a strong case for the secondary nature of *Gos. Thom.* logion 14//Matt 15:11 (see also the discussion in Meier, *Marginal Jew*, 1.134–37).

This evidence, however, does not completely close the question of whether or not *Thomas* preserves early tradition. That some of the *Thomas* sayings reflect Synoptic editing or second-century Gnosticism does not necessarily mean that all of them do, for as R. Wilson ("Thomas," 232) says, "The vital question is not so much the date of our present Gospel of Thomas, or of its immediate Greek original, but that of the nucleus from which the whole collection grew." And certain evidence seems to point away from *direct* use of the canonical Gospels by *Thomas*: why, for example, does *Thomas* not seem to follow the order of any of the canonical Gospels in his use of Synoptic-like material (see de Solages, "Thomas")? Tuckett ("Thomas," 139–40) tries to meet this objection by demonstrating that the lack of order may be more apparent than real, but this rebuttal, while possible, is speculative. It may be better to go with Uro, who deals with the problem of order by suggesting that *Thomas* is an example of "secondary orality"; the *Gospel of Thomas* is using the Synoptics not directly but as mediated by oral performance. The author, in other words, may once have heard the Synoptics, but he does not have them in front of him while he writes (cf. Meier, *Marginal Jew*, 1.131–32). But nothing in his analysis precludes the possibility that other *Thomas* sayings, also mediated orally, may reflect early, pre-Synoptic tradition. While, therefore, a healthy dose of skepticism is warranted in using the *Thomas* tradition, its relevance for reconstructing pre-Synoptic tradition cannot be dismissed altogether.

MARKAN COMPOSITION

◆

RAW MATERIALS

Mark, then, probably did not draw on other Gospels in composing his narrative. He wrote before Matthew, Luke, John, and Thomas did; and even if it were correct (as it probably is not) to call Q a Gospel, Mark seems not to have used that document. What, then, *were* the raw materials out of which he composed his story of Jesus' life?

The longest and most elaborate of them was probably a pre-Markan passion narrative: an account of Jesus' last days in Jerusalem, leading up to his suffering and death. A detailed argument for the existence of this source will be presented in volume 2 of this commentary, as will a discussion of the possibility that the eschatological discourse in chapter 13 has crystallized around a pre-Markan core.

The other major discourse section in Mark, the "parable chapter" in 4:1–34, probably also expands a pre-Markan nucleus, the three seed parables in 4:3–8, 26–29, and 30–32. Collections of parables using a common image were widespread in antiquity; in *Lam. Rab.* 1.1, 2.2, and 3.7, for example, there are batches of rabbinic "king" parables, and in *Gen. Rab.* 3.1 there is a series of palm-tree parables. Such written records are probably just the tip of an oral iceberg; in a famous Talmudic passage R. Yoḥanan refers to the three hundred fox parables of R. Meir, of which all but three have been lost (*b. Sanh.* 38b)! The fact that exactly three survived is probably not an accident, since groupings of three parables are common in ancient sources (though not as common as double parables such as Mark 4:21–25); there are parabolic threesomes, for example, in *Gos. Thom.* logia 63–65 and 96–98, as well as frequently in the Synoptic tradition (Mark 2:18–22; Matt 13:24–33; 13:44–48; 21:28–22:14; Luke 15), with all or most of these threesomes probably harking back to oral collections (cf. Jeremias, *Parables*, 90–96). A pre-Markan collection of three seed parables, therefore, is *prima facie* likely, and this supposition is enhanced by the fact that the material that interrupts the three seed parables is often identifiable as redactional on other grounds (see the introduction to 4:1–34).

It is also possible that the cores of the controversy sections in 2:1–3:6 and 11:27–12:37 are pre-Markan. Here again, the plausibility of a source is supported both by redactional analysis (see the introduction to the COMMENT on 2:1–3:6) and by parallels in ancient literature. In extra–New Testament literature one sometimes finds collections of stories that go back to oral sources and that portray a leader or leaders of one's own group refuting the group's opponents. The Talmud, for example, transmits clusters of disputes between rabbis and their adversaries, who are usually either hostile pagans or Jewish sectarians, including Jewish Christians (see e.g. the series of disputes in b. Sanh. 90b–91b and b. ʿAbod. Zar. 54b–55a and cf. Ben-Sasson, "Disputations"). The obvious intention of such collections is to provide fellow religionists with both the sort of example that will encourage them to confront their own adversaries and the intellectual ammunition that will help them to emerge victorious from such encounters (see Bultmann, 39–54).

Ancient sources, however, do not just present folk heroes *talking*; they also present them *doing* things, including miracles. Descriptions of a hero's or god's miracles had great propaganda value, both as a testimony to outsiders and as an encouragement to insiders, since they demonstrated that God was with the hero (cf. Acts 10:38) or that the god really was a god. In the non-Jewish world, for example, the fame of the healing god Asclepius was spread by inscriptions at his temples about the wonders he had accomplished there; some of these inscriptions seem to go back to oral sources that have been grouped together by content (see LiDonnici, *Epidaurian*, 50–60). Philostratus' second-century *Life* of the first-century Pythagorean philosopher Apollonius of Tyana, similarly, is full of accounts that describe Apollonius' supernatural feats of miracle working, healing, and prophecy, and that undergird Philostratus' claim that a divine power operated through him. Some of these miracle narratives probably reflect local traditions about Apollonius' wonder-working that originally circulated orally (see Flinterman, *Power*, 68). Even closer parallels are found in the Jewish sphere. Already the biblical tales about the miracle working of the prophets Elijah and Elisha are probably derived from oral cycles of stories (see Gunkel, *Elias*, and Rofé, *Prophetical Stories*, 13–18). Similarly, in rabbinic literature there are many narratives of wonder-workers, which are sometimes arranged in catenae or chains of miracles that go back to oral sources (see e.g. the stories about Ḥoni the Circle-Drawer and his descendants in b. Taʿan. 23a–b and the stories about R. Ḥanina b. Dosa in b. Ber. 34b and b. Taʿan. 24b–25a; cf. Achtemeier, "Origin," 204–5). Aside from their entertainment value, which is considerable, these rabbinic miracle catenae also magnify the human miracle worker and the God of Israel who was active in him (cf. Green, "Holy Men," 639–47).

Miracle cycles, then, were known in the New Testament environment, and it is unsurprising that the early Christians developed them too; indeed, the reputation of Jesus and his followers for performing miracles was probably a major reason for the success of the Christian movement, and Jesus the miracle worker is one of the most frequently portrayed subjects in early Christian art (see Mac-Mullen, *Christianizing*, index s.v. "Miracles," and Mathews, *Clash*, 54–91). This emphasis on miracles was presumably present from Christianity's inception. Scholars, for example, have detected a collection of Jesus' miracles, which they have dubbed the "Signs Source," at the base of the Gospel of John (see D. M. Smith, *Johannine Christianity*, 39–93, for a history of the discussion), and it is probable that Mark has made use of pre-Gospel miracle catenae as well (see Achtemeier, "Origin"). The most easily identifiable of these are the one that describes Jesus' wonder-working in the Galilean city of Capernaum, which has been taken up more or less whole into the Gospel (see the introduction to 1:16–45), and the one that links a miraculous feeding of thousands with a miracle at sea (see the introduction to the COMMENT on 6:30–44). Other pre-Markan catenae are possible, but more difficult to identify (see e.g. the attractive but uncertain theory about a pre-Markan boat cycle, which is discussed in the introduction to 3:7–6:6a; cf. also H. Koester, *Ancient Christian*, 202–3).

Besides the passion narrative, the eschatological discourse, a parable collection, one or two controversy story collections, and some miracle cycles, other types of joined sources may also have been incorporated into Mark's Gospel. The miscellaneous nature of 9:33–50, for example, may reflect its appropriation from a preexistent oral source, perhaps a primitive catechism, in which tales about and sayings of Jesus were strung together loosely on the basis of catchwords ("in my name," "lose his reward," "fire," "salt") and so were made easier to remember (cf. Bultmann, 149–50; Best, "Preservation," 124).

Aside from such collections, Mark apparently knew many traditions about Jesus that were free-floating. We can see Mark introducing such independent traditions into preexistent sources at various places (e.g. 1:40–45; 2:1–12; 3:1–6, and 4:10–12; cf. the introductions to 1:16–45, 2:1–3:6, and 4:1–34). More often, however, he seems not to have expanded existing sources but to have created whole sections by combining originally independent traditions. It is Mark himself, then, who appears to be responsible for the basic "framework of the history of Jesus," to quote the title of K. L. Schmidt's famous book from the beginning of this century (*Der Rahmen der Geschichte Jesu*).

CONSERVATIVE REDACTOR OR CREATIVE THEOLOGIAN?

In accepting Schmidt's claim, I side with those scholars who see Mark as a creative shaper of inherited traditions. This view has two aspects. On the one hand, it recognizes Mark's *continuity* with tradition. He has not created his picture of Jesus totally out of his own head, but has been inspired and, to a certain extent, constrained by the memories of Jesus' words and deeds that have been passed down to him in the church. On the other hand, it recognizes that there is also a degree of *discontinuity* between Mark and the tradition; he has not reproduced these memories mechanically, but has elaborated them creatively to address the situation of his own time and place.

Thus, on the one hand, Mark did have a substantial amount of raw material to work with when he sat down to write his Gospel. As we have seen in the previous section, this literary ore included both individual traditions and pre-formed collections; the rough edges of this preexistent matter, which Mark has only imperfectly pounded into its present, more or less unified shape, are still visible beneath the surface. Examples of this imperfect fit include 2:1–12, in which Mark's introduction of a controversy element (2:5b–10a) into an original miracle story has led to the anomaly that the hostile scribes praise Jesus; 4:1–34, in which his insertion of the motif of secret instruction (4:10–12) has resulted in confusion about whether the audience for the subsequent parables is the "in group" of disciples or the crowd in general; and 6:45–53, where the juxtaposition of two originally independent traditions has produced the strange situation that Jesus and the disciples set out for Bethsaida but land in Gennesaret (see the introduction to the COMMENT on 2:1–12 and on 6:53–56 and the introduction to 4:1–34). Another trace of pre-Markan traditions, as Best ("Preservation") has argued, is superfluous identifications of disciples, such as "the sons of Zebedee" in 10:35 (cf. 1:19; 3:17) and "one of the Twelve" in 14:43 (cf. 3:19; 14:10).

Mark, then, does not always seem to be entirely in control of his material; he is occasionally guilty of what Meagher (Clumsy) terms "clumsy construction," which partly results from his attempt to preserve the traditions passed down to him. His Greek style, moreover, is frequently awkward and has had to be corrected by his later adapters, Matthew and Luke. As opposed to scholars who regard him and other New Testament writers as sophisticated practitioners of the Hellenistic rhetorical arts (e.g. Standaert, Marc; Robbins, Teacher; Mack and Robbins, Patterns), we should never forget the dismay felt by the rhetorically trained Augustine when he first turned to the biblical writings after years of studying the classics: "To me they seemed quite unworthy of comparison with the stately prose of Cicero" (Confessions).

Not only are Mark's writing style and arrangement of material frequently awkward, but Best ("Preservation") has also shown that his adoption of pre-existent tradition has meant that he passes on narratives that are in tension with his own theology in minor ways. Thus, for example, the obscure title shouted out by the demon in 1:24, "holy one of God," is never repeated in the Gospel; if Mark had been composing freely, he would probably have had the demon use the Gospel's most important Christological title, "Son of God," as the unclean spirits do in the redactional 3:11. In 8:38 and 14:61–62, similarly, the implied distinction between Jesus and the Son of Man is at odds with Markan theology, in which Jesus is the Son of Man. Mark is similarly inconsistent about the disciples; according to 1:16–20 and 10:28, they have left house, family, livelihood, and "everything," but according to 1:29, Peter still has a house to go back to, and according to 3:9; 4:1, 36, the disciples still have a boat at their disposal.

Mark, then, is not a totally unfettered author who is subject only to his own imagination and theological convictions, as he has been presented in the work of some recent critics such as Kermode (Genesis), Kelber (Oral, 1–139), Tolbert (306–7), and Mack (Myth). He is neither an "ancient Henry James" (Kermode,

Genesis, 68), manipulating his characters subtly with sovereign authorial freedom, nor the revolutionary creator of "a myth of innocence" (Mack), the previously unheard-of fantasy of an apocalyptic, transcendental Jesus. His Gospel, as Hurtado ("Evolutionary") puts it, is an evolutionary rather than a revolutionary document; he is not an autonomous author but a link in a chain of tradition. Best, therefore, provides a helpful image when he suggests that we should think of Mark not as a painter who confronts a blank canvas but as an artist who creates a collage out of preexistent material ("Preservation," 128).

Still, no one would deny that makers of collages are creative artists, and Best himself later changed his comparison to reflect Mark's vital role in shaping his material: he is perhaps more like a composer who transforms traditional folk songs to accommodate them to the new composition in which he incorporates them (see *Gospel*, 121–22). For as Best and other redaction critics recognize, the evangelists are not simply collectors (as the old form-critics styled them) but writers who have shaped and arranged the traditions that have come down to them in order to express overarching themes that address their own situation. In the case of Mark, this is most obvious from his pervasive use of the "messianic secret motif," the way in which the Markan Jesus throughout the Gospel tries to hide his identity as Messiah and Son of God (see the APPENDIX, "The Messianic Secret Motif"). It is scarcely accidental, moreover, that Jesus is proclaimed "Son of God," the most important Christological title in the Gospel, in "pillar" passages strategically located at the beginning, middle, and end of the work (1:11; 9:7; 15:39; see Ambrozic, *Hidden Kingdom*, 23). Even Mark's style is not as inept as has sometimes been claimed; while it may at times be ungrammatical, it has the rough-and-ready forcefulness of good popular writing or speech and is admirably suited to the Markan portrait of a dynamic, abrasive, intensely emotional Jesus who is the passionate instrument for the advent of the dominion of God.

This insight into Mark's deliberate, pervasive editorial activity is somewhat obscured in the otherwise impressive two-volume commentary of Pesch (*Das Markusevangelium*). Pesch minimizes the evangelist's own contribution to the Gospel; Mark, for him, is not a true author but a conservative redactor (= editor), with the emphasis on the adjective "conservative." His work is not so much a reinterpretation of the traditions about Jesus as a faithful reproduction of extensive, often historically accurate sources. According to Pesch, it is these sources that really determine the shape and character of the Gospel; the pre-Markan passion narrative, for example, began all the way back at 8:27! As Luz points out in a penetrating review ("Markusforschung"), however, Pesch's commitment to Markan historicity sometimes leads him to adopt implausible explanations of features of the text, rather in the manner of eighteenth-century rationalists (for a critique of similar expedients in Gundry's commentary, see Marcus, "Review of Gundry"). Luz, moreover, convincingly challenges Pesch's contention that Mark used a distinct, unitary, historically accurate source in the second half of his Gospel. The vocabulary in the second half is not radically different from that in the first half, and there is plenty of evidence

that this supposedly unitary "source" incorporates different preexistent traditions and has been shaped by Markan redaction (for other criticisms of Pesch,
see Neirynck, "L'Évangile").

It would be a mistake, then, to tip the balance too far either toward the
"creative theologian" or toward the "conservative redactor" side of the evaluation of Markan literary activity. Mark's work has been strongly influenced *both*
by the traditions he has inherited and by his own theological convictions,
which flow out of the situation he and his community confront. For Mark,
then, as for the Old Testament authors studied by Fishbane (*Biblical Interpretation*), "tradition" is a matter both of a *traditum*, a thing passed down from
the past that influences the present, and of a *traditio*, a traditioning process
that inevitably involves adaptation to a new situation.

LITERARY OUTLINE

This combination of conservatism and creativity is illustrated by the literary
outline of the Gospel. On the one hand, there is some truth in Kähler's characterization of Mark and all the Gospels as "passion narratives with extended
introductions" (Kähler, *So-Called*, 80 n. 11), and thus the influence on the
Gospel's structure of preformed sources, especially the pre-Markan passion
narrative, has been great. On the other hand, Mark himself has been responsible for putting these pieces of tradition together, and he has shaped the Gospel
into a comprehensive, structured whole. Like other Hellenistic biographers,
he has created an overall chronological framework, but within this framework
he arranges his material topically, in a historically artificial way (see Burridge,
What, 139–41, 169–71, 200–2). It is inherently unlikely, for example, that the
historical Jesus spent two days doing nothing but performing miracles (1:21–
45), then spent several days doing nothing but arguing with his opponents
(2:1–3:6). The Markan suggestion that Jesus did not begin his ministry until
John's arrest (1:14), moreover, may owe more to the theological conviction
that John was Jesus' Elijah-like forerunner (cf. 1:2–3; 9:11–13) than to historical reality (cf. John 3:22–24, where their ministries overlap); and the Markan
implication that he did not have a ministry in Jerusalem until the last few days
of his life is called into question by various evidence in and outside of Mark
(see e.g. Mark 14:3; Matt 23:37//Luke 13:34, and in general the Gospel of
John; cf. Baarlink, *Anfängliches*, 81).

But what is the overall structural plan of Mark's Gospel? Of the making of
many Markan outlines there is, seemingly, no end (for surveys, see Baarlink,
Anfängliches, 73–88; Matera, *What*, 77–83; and Telford, *Mark*, 101–4). Baarlink, in his 1977 monograph, divided these outlines into geographical types
(e.g. Galilee/Jerusalem) and theological types (e.g. those that see Peter's confession and Jesus' response to it in 8:27–33 as a turning point); to this we may now
add literary types, such as those of Standaert (*Marc*) and van Iersel ("Locality"),

which make extensive use of concentric structures, and that of Beavis (*Audience*, 163–65), which separates the Gospel into action and teaching sections. It is perhaps a mistake to be too dogmatic about which sorts of criteria should be used or about where Markan sections begin and end; as Dewey ("Tapestry") has reminded us, oral narrators as well as writers strongly influenced by oral techniques can use a variety of overlapping methods for relating sections to each other, and they often do not draw hard-and-fast lines between sections but let them melt imperceptively into each other, as happens in modern-day films.

Nevertheless, there does seem to be an overarching geographical framework to the Gospel, within which literary and theological structures play their roles: the first ten chapters take place outside of Jerusalem, whereas chapters 11–16 are set in the holy city. As for further subdivisions, these are easier to discern if we take Kähler's hint and start at the end. The story of the empty tomb in 16:1–8 seems to form an epilogue to the main body of the Gospel and to correspond to the prologue in 1:1–15; both emphasize the theme of "going before" and speak of a movement of Jesus into Galilee. Moving backward, the passion narrative (14:1–15:47) is a discrete section; its beginning is signaled in 14:1–2 by the attention-grabbing hypotactic construction (see GLOSSARY), by one of the Gospel's rare time notices, which sets the subsequent events within a Passover context, and by a reference to the plot by the scribes and Pharisees, which will quickly result in Jesus' death. The previous subdivision of the Gospel concerns Jesus' Jerusalem ministry before the passion; Jerusalem and the Temple are a pervasive theme in this section, and it starts with a clairvoyant dispatching of disciples that parallels that of a passage near the beginning of the passion narrative (14:12–16).

Moving still further backward into the pre-Jerusalem section, the middle portion of the Gospel, 8:22–10:52, also seems to be a distinct section. This segment is structured around three passion predictions (8:31; 9:30–32; 10:32–34) and frequent references to "the way" and "the dominion of God." Its most striking structural feature, however, is the fact that it is framed by two stories of healings of blind men (8:22–26 and 10:46–52). This framing device fits the content of the section, which is overwhelmingly concerned with the "illumination" of the disciples as to the meaning of the Christian life—Jesus' teaching about what it means to suffer with him, to follow him "in the way," and so to enter into the dominion of God. Thus it implicitly begins to answer the question that had concluded the previous section, "Do you not yet understand?" (8:21).

As for the chapters that precede this central segment, it is obvious that the Gospel's prologue (1:1–15, in my judgment) is a distinct section. But how is 1:16–8:21 structured? As will be noted in the introduction to 1:16–45, the first passage in this large section is a narrative of the commissioning of disciples (1:16–20), and later there are two similar narratives (3:13–19; 6:7–13). All three of these commissioning stories use a form of the verb *kalein* ("to call"), and each follows a transitional summary of Jesus' activity (1:14–15; 3:7–12; 6:6b). Despite these similarities, there is a progression among these three commissioning narratives: the first is a call, the second is an appointment, and the third is a sending out on mission. It makes sense, then, to regard the commissioning narratives as the initiation of literary units within the Gospel (see Schweizer, "Mark's," 57–58; Perrin and Duling, *Introduction*, 239–40). Each of these units, moreover, ends with a passage in which Jesus confronts misunderstanding and/or opposition, though the people involved change in a significant and worrying way: from the Pharisees (3:1–6) to Jesus' townspeople (6:1–6a) to his own disciples (8:14–21).

The proposed structure for the Gospel, therefore (which is close to that of Schweizer), looks like this (I have included a count of verses and words so that the reader can see the approximate size of the sections):

    I. 1:1–15—PROLOGUE (15 verses, 248 words)
    II. 1:16–8:21—ACT I: Jesus' Early Ministry (290 verses, 4,813 words)
        A. 1:16–3:6: FIRST MAJOR SECTION—Honeymoon and Beginning of Opposition (64 verses, 1,095 words)
        B. 3:7–6:6a: SECOND MAJOR SECTION—The Struggle Intensifies (118.5 verses, 1,958 words)
        C. 6:6b–8:21: THIRD MAJOR SECTION—Feasts (107.5 verses, 1,760 words)
    III. 8:22–10:52—ACT II: FOURTH MAJOR SECTION—"On the Way" (117 verses, 2,076 words)
    IV. 11:1–15:47—ACT III: Jerusalem Ministry (231 verses, 3,828 words)
        A. 11:1–13:37: FIFTH MAJOR SECTION—Teaching (113 verses, 1,963 words)
        B. 14:1–15:47: SIXTH MAJOR SECTION—Dying (118 verses, 1,865 words)
    V. 16:1–8: EPILOGUE (The Empty Tomb; 8 verses, 136 words)

It will be noticed that the major sections are all of approximately equal length (about 1,800–2,000 words) apart from the first one (1:16–3:6), which is about half the length of the others. The general consistency of the sections in terms of size, while far from probative, would suggest that the analysis may be on the right track.

GENRE

The observations in the previous sections about Mark's structure, literary level, and indebtedness to tradition may help to explore another controversy, that concerning its literary genre. This is a potentially important issue, since readers' conceptions about what sort of book they are reading can shape their experience of the book; we pick up a historical novel, for example, with different sorts of expectations from those with which we pick up a biography or a history. This analogy is not chosen at random, since in recent scholarship Mark has been treated as a biography (e.g. Burridge, *What*), as a work of apocalyptic history (A. Collins, "Is Mark's"), and even as a novel (Tolbert). This last, "novel" suggestion is the most difficult to agree with; although Mark has certain novelistic features, it differs from ancient novels in having as its central character a real person of the recent past rather than fictional, star-crossed lovers. The Gospel, moreover, presupposes a communal readership, which is reflected, for example, in the many scenes in which Jesus addresses crowds or a group of disciples. Ancient novels, on the other hand, were addressed to individuals (cf. Dowd, "Gospel," 55–56).

If Mark is not a novel, what is it? Much of the twentieth-century discussion has revolved around the question of whether or not it and the other Gospels are biographies of Jesus. Early in the century Votaw (*Gospels*) asserted that they were, but he was swiftly opposed by Bultmann (369–74) and K. Schmidt ("Stellung"). For these influential scholars the Hellenistic *bios* (lit. "life," as in Plutarch's *Parallel Lives*) was a sophisticated type of literature that reflected a self-conscious authorial personality, whereas the anonymous Gospels were unsophisticated folk literature that arose out of the communal experience and cultic needs of early Christian communities. This position was theologically attractive to Bultmann, since it enabled him to maintain that the Gospels were preaching rather than history or biography and thus to refute fundamentalists who regarded them as historically accurate accounts (cf. Gamble, *Books*, 36). Bultmann, indeed, thought that the Gospel genre was a Christian invention and absolutely unprecedented, and this position also had a theological payoff: it was compatible with his emphasis on the uniqueness of the Christian message.

Partly because of the enormous stature of Bultmann, the Bultmann/Schmidt position on the nonbiographical nature of the Gospels held the field until well into the post–World War II period. But it has gradually been eroded in recent years, on the one hand, by the demonstration that some Hellenistic biographies are more popular than Bultmann and Schmidt gave them credit for being, and, on the other hand, by the argument of redaction and literary critics that the Gospels are more sophisticated than had previously been thought (see e.g. Talbert, *What*; Aune, *New Testament*, 17–76; and Burridge, *What*). The Gospels and Hellenistic biographies, then, have seemed to meet somewhere in the middle.

Still, there remain problems with calling Mark a biography of Jesus. The first is that in some ways the work is more like an ancient history, especially a biblical history, than it is like an ancient biography. As Hartman points out ("Markusevangelium," 157), Mark's style consciously imitates the OT historical narratives by its use of expressions such as "and it came to pass in those days" (1:9), "answered and said" (3:33; 6:37, etc.), and even the ubiquitous Markan phrase "and immediately" (cf. the NOTE on "and as he was coming up out of the water, he immediately" in 1:10). The title of Mark's composition, moreover, does not designate it as a *bios* but as *archē tou euangeliou* ("beginning of the good news"; 1:1), and A. Collins ("Is Mark's," 18) points out that the word *archē* is more often used to begin a historical narrative than a biography.

Furthermore, Mark's narrative does not start, as most biographies do, with the birth of the hero (in this way Matthew and Luke are more typical of biographies) but with an Old Testament citation (1:2–3) and the description of a prophetic forerunner (1:4–8), features that point toward Jesus' advent as the climax of redemptive history. The narrative, then, is not only about Jesus as a teacher, miracle worker, and martyr worthy of emulation but also about what God was doing through his ministry (cf. Guelich, "Gospel Genre," 191; Boring, "Beginning," 70 n. 9). Mark is more the biography of a movement, or at least that movement's beginnings (archē), than it is the biography of an individual, and the narrative points toward the continuation of that movement after Jesus' death, both through explicit prophecies (e.g. chapter 13) and through the way in which Jesus and his followers and opponents constantly become symbols for groups in the Markan present.

In this orientation toward a movement's history, Mark resembles two books that appeared in the 1980s, David Garrow's Bearing the Cross: Martin Luther King, Jr., and the Southern Christian Leadership Conference and Taylor Branch's Troubling the Waters: America in the King Years 1954–63. Although Mark is not trying to be a historian/biographer in the modern, "critical" sense, as Garrow and Branch are, there are some striking similarities between Mark's account of the inception of Christianity and their accounts of the inception of the Civil Rights Movement in the United States. Both Garrow's and Branch's books revolve around the figure of Martin Luther King, as Mark's revolves around the figure of Jesus, but each is less a biography of King than a description of the movement he led. Neither, significantly enough, begins with its main character's birth, as a real biography would do, but with the start of his public ministry, as in Mark's story of Jesus; and Branch's book even prefaces this description, as Mark's does, with a chapter about a "forerunner" (Vernon Johns)!

Besides Mark's orientation toward redemptive history, a second way in which his Gospel differs from a typical ancient biography is in the assumed nature of its subject. To be sure, as Robbins (Teacher, 10) and Dowd (Prayer, 24–26) point out, there is a certain analogy to Mark in ancient biographies of disciple-gathering teachers who started philosophical or religious movements and whose influence was palpable through those movements. This is not the same thing, however, as the Markan account of a figure who is believed still to be present in the most realistic way possible with the community he founded—empowering it day by day, performing miracles on its behalf, and guiding it through the stormy waters of the present evil age toward the imminent parousia (see Boring, Sayings, 202). Indeed, Mark may understand the genitive "of Jesus Christ" in 1:1 in a subjective as well as an objective way: his story is not only the good news about Jesus but also the good news that Jesus himself preaches through the evangelist (see the COMMENT on 1:1). But this "present" quality of the Markan Jesus raises a question about the propriety of calling the Gospel simply a bios, a biography, the story of the completed life of a revered (or reviled) figure of the past. For Mark and his readers, Jesus' *bios* is not completed, indeed can never be completed, which is perhaps part of the reason that the Gospel ends as abruptly as it does (if the original ending is 16:8): Mark's writing describes only the *beginning* of the good news of Jesus (1:1), because in Mark's day Jesus' good news *continues* through his presence with the church and in the world. As Boring ("Review of Lührmann," 345) puts it, then, it may be asked whether Christology and biography are really compatible categories.

Still, there are similarities between Mark and Hellenistic *bioi* that are striking enough that some ancient readers would have been tempted to place them on the same bookshelf. And if Mark and the other Gospels differ from most "lives" in the assumed nature of their subject, they are not absolutely unique in this. As K. Schmidt already noted ("Stellung," 91–118), there are close parallels between the Gospels and saints' lives, including Hasidic biographies of wonderfully wise, miracle working rabbis who mediate between God and humans, whose presence frequently extends beyond the grave, and who are sometimes even worshiped (see Landau, *Piety*, 28, and Rapoport-Albert, "God and Zaddik").

But if Mark himself were asked to define what sort of work he had written, what would he say? One important clue is provided by the word he uses to refer to his work, *euangelion* or "good news" (usually translated with the Middle English word "gospel"). Elsewhere in the NT this term is always used for the oral proclamation of the message about Jesus, either in a missionary setting (so usually) or within the church (see e.g. Rom 1:15; 16:25; 1 Cor 15:1–2; 1 Thess 3:2; 2 Tim 1:10–11; 2:8). Despite Mark's structural similarity to Peter's missionary speech in Acts 10:34–43 (cf. Dodd, *Apostolic Preaching*, 46–52), it does not seem likely that the Gospel is "good news" in the sense of preaching to outsiders (see the discussion of this issue in the section on the Markan community above). It is more likely that it is *euangelion* in the sense that it embodies the sort of message that was proclaimed *within* the church at worship services (cf. Bultmann, 371, who calls Mark an "expanded cult legend," and more recently Best, *Gospel*, 38; Hengel, *Mark*, 52; and especially the illuminating essay of Hartman, "Markusevangelium"). As Hengel points out, the division of the text into short, often rhythmic cola (see GLOSSARY) suggests composition for oral recitation in a community. Moreover, some of the traditions that later became part of Mark were passed down in the context of Christian worship (see e.g. the account of the Lord's Supper in 1 Cor 11:23–26), and Mark and the other Gospels eventually found a place in the lectionary of the church. The likelihood is that the same was true in Mark's day as was true before and afterward: the text formed part of the liturgy. Indeed, scholars such as Carrington (*Primitive*) and Goulder (*Calendar*) have argued that Mark actually began as an early Christian lectionary, a collection of texts that were recited at successive Christian worship services and that followed Jewish Sabbath or festal readings. This theory, however, has not met with general approval, partly because of the paucity of evidence for early Jewish lectionary practices or for serial lectionary readings in churches before the fourth century (see Aune, *New Testament*, 26–27) and partly because the Gospel is more cohesive than a loosely linked series of lectionary readings (see Best, *Gospel*, 145).

Standaert, noting the Gospel's overall literary unity, more plausibly suggests that the work *as a whole* was meant to be read in a single service. This would take somewhere around two hours, without intermission. It is not implausible that early Christians would have been willing to attend such a long recitation, especially if the reading were done in a dramatic manner; Justin Martyr reports that at Sunday services "the memoirs of the apostles [= Gospels] or the writings of the prophets are read *for as long as time permits*" (*Apology* 1.67; cited by Gamble, *Books*, 205), and even today Russian Orthodox churchgoers stand for hours in their services.

Can we be any more exact about what sort of liturgy might have accommodated a reading of Mark's Gospel? Standaert points to the Easter vigil service, which culminated with the baptism of new Christians at daybreak on Easter morning, and he links this service with baptismal and paschal themes he finds throughout Mark: its beginning with John the Baptist and with Jesus' baptism, its intense concentration on Jesus' passion, the two young men clad with linen cloths, which Standaert (following Scroggs and Groff, "Baptism") thinks may be baptismal garb (14:51–52; 16:5), and the work's conclusion at Easter sunrise (cf. also the Gospel's strong emphasis on exorcism and on "illumination" of the blind, both of which are associated with baptism in the early church). This is an intriguing hypothesis, but up to the present it has not won widespread support (cf. the sharp critique of Best, *Gospel*, 95–98), partly because some of Standaert's exegesis seems strained (see e.g. Neirynck's attack ["Fuite"] on the link between baptism and the two "young men") and partly because hard-and-fast evidence for an Easter baptismal vigil is not attested before the late second century (cf. Talley, *Origins*, 33–37).

In any event, whether or not our Gospel originally belonged in a baptismal setting, the idea that it played a central role in the liturgy of Mark's Christian community is a compelling one. One of the points in its favor is that in such a setting the cryptic nature of Mark's narrative, far from giving offense, would be very much at home. For it is characteristic of liturgy, and indeed an aspect of its numinous power, that it contains elements that are disjunctive and mysterious, "half-revealed, half-concealed" in order to elicit worshipers' awe. Rudolf Otto's protest against the efforts of latter-day liturgical reformers to eliminate such elements could almost be read as a reminder of what the later church lost when Mark slipped into obscurity, pushed out by the more rational narratives of Matthew and Luke:

> In these [new liturgies] we find carefully arranged schemes worked out with the balance and coherence of an essay, but nothing unaccountable, and for that very reason suggestive; nothing accidental, and for that very reason

pregnant in meaning; nothing that rises from the deeps below consciousness to break the rounded unity of the wonted disposition, and thereby
point to a unity of a higher order—in a word, little that is really spiritual.
(*Idea*, 64–65)

Like the older liturgies whose disappearance Otto laments, Mark lacks "the
balance and coherence of an essay" but is full of disruptive, mysterious, allusive elements that hint at spiritual depths. As Käsemann ("Problem," 22) puts
it, in Mark "the life history of Jesus becomes almost the subject of a mystery
play." And in this way the Gospel may reflect its origin within the liturgy of
the early church.

In conclusion, Mark may very well be a dramatization of the good news
that was originally staged in the context of a Christian worship service (on the
similarity of the Gospel's structure to that of a drama, see Bilezikian, *Liberated Gospel*, and Beavis, *Audience*, 31–35, 128–29; a demonstration of Mark's
dramatic potential can be seen in the recent one-man staging of it by Alec
McCowen). Perhaps the different roles in this liturgical drama were read by
different readers in this service, as happens today in extended lectionary readings at special times such as Christmas and Easter; the preponderance of direct discourse over the indirect mode favored by Hellenistic biography perhaps
points in this direction. While this dramatization may borrow generic features
from known forms such as dramas, biographies, and biblical histories, it is
also a new creation because of its close link with the Christian liturgical setting. It is *euangelion*, a proclamation of good news: a redemptive story re-
enacted and reexperienced in the church's celebration of the compassionate,
suffering, risen Lord who not only has gone before it in the way of suffering
and death but is also present in its midst, traveling with it "on the way."

THE PLACE OF MARK IN CHRISTIAN LIFE AND THOUGHT

◆

MARK IN THE HISTORY OF RELIGIONS

We have seen that Mark may have originally been written to play a role within a particular setting in the life of the church. But where more generally does it fit within the history of Christian life and thought? And where does it fit, even more generally, within the history of religions?

The first thing to be said about Mark's Gospel is that it is an eclectic writing. As we have already seen, some of its descriptions of Jesus as a miracle worker correspond to tales that were told not only about Old Testament prophets and Palestinian rabbis but also about wonder-workers in the larger Hellenistic world. Other motifs, such as several involved in the story of John the Baptist's execution, seem to be borrowed from the folklore of Greco-Roman paganism, and some of the Markan Jesus' proverbial wisdom and instructions to his disciples are akin to snippets of popular Hellenistic philosophy (see the NOTES on "The strong don't need a doctor, but the sick" in 2:17, on "staff" and "provision bag" in 6:8, and on "two tunics" in 6:9, and the COMMENT on 6:14–16 and on 6:21–28). Even if, as has been argued above, Mark was a native of Palestine, that does not mean that he (and Jesus before him) were untouched by Hellenistic influences, since first-century Palestine was Hellenized to a significant extent (see Hengel, *Judaism*); and if Mark subsequently became a member of a Syrian Christian community, he would have been exposed to such influences even more. And even if, as I shall argue below, he was an apocalyptic thinker, that still does not remove him from the Hellenistic realm, since apocalypticism itself was a general phenomenon in the Greco-Roman world (see Hellholm, *Apocalypticism*).

But this important observation about Mark's cosmopolitanism, and that of the New Testament in general, has its limits. One of them is pointed out at the beginning of Stauffer's *New Testament Theology* (17–18): the only writing that is extensively quoted in the New Testament is the Old Testament. The Old Testament—not Homer, Plato, or Cicero. It is only the Old Testament books that are called "the writings" (*hai graphai*; Mark 12:10, 24; 14:49); it is only to them that the significant perfect passive verb *gegraptai* ("it has been written") is made to refer (Mark 1:2; 7:6; 9:12–13; 11:17; 14:21, 27; cf. 12:19).

Mark's particular way of interpreting these writings, moreover, follows in the footsteps of the Old Testament exegesis of Jewish writers (see Marcus, *Way*, 199–202). The God whose advent the Markan Jesus announces, to whom he calls his hearers to turn in penitence and faith, the God whom he trusts to raise him from the dead (an un-Hellenistic concept), is the God of Abraham, Isaac, and Jacob (cf. 12:26), and not of the philosophers (cf. Pascal, "Memorial," *Pensées*). The basic Jewishness of the outlook in Mark's Gospel, then, is apparent from its opening verses, whatever we may think of Mark's own ethno-religious background and the ethnic makeup of his community.

MARK'S APOCALYPTIC ESCHATOLOGY

Mark's mode of OT interpretation is particularly close to that found in Jewish apocalyptic writings, since he like the Jewish apocalypticists sees the OT prophecies being fulfilled in the events of his own day (see Marcus, *Way*, index s.v. "apocalyptic eschatology" and "eschatological interpretation of OT"). Nor is this the only way in which Mark is an apocalyptic thinker. His outlook can be termed "apocalyptic" because his narrative is from start to finish set within the context of the approaching end of the world (on the definition of "apocalyptic eschatology" and "apocalypticism," see Hanson, "Apocalypse, Genre" and "Apocalypticism"; J. J. Collins, *Apocalyptic Imagination*, 2; de Boer, "Paul"). The Markan Jesus' inaugural sermon announces that the time has been fulfilled and that the dominion of God is at hand (1:14–15). Later he tells his hearers that some of them will not taste death before they see that dominion come in power (9:1); for Mark's audience, hearing these words forty years after Jesus' death, the impression that the time was growing short would be unavoidable. Nor would they *want* to escape it, since the cutting short of the present time of tribulation is the basis of their hope (13:19–20): the horror they are experiencing cannot last long; soon the Son of Man will return on the clouds of heaven and send his angels to gather the elect (13:24–27).

At the same time, however, Mark holds this note of imminent expectation in tension with a sense of present fulfillment. This he does both by including individual sayings and stories that imply the presence of salvation already in Jesus' ministry (2:19–22, 27–28; 3:27; 4:35–41, etc.) and by juxtaposing stories about Jesus' earthly life with eschatological predictions. Thus the Markan Jesus' powerful revelation of his divine glory to three disciples on the Mount of Transfiguration (9:2–8) immediately follows his prophecy about some not tasting death before they see the arrival of God's dominion with power (9:1), and the correlation between the two suggests that the Transfiguration is some sort of foretaste of the dominion of God. Similarly, the juxtaposition of the eschatological prophecies in chapter 13 with the passion narrative that immediately follows suggests that Mark wants his readers to see the latter as in some sense a fulfillment of the former (see R. Lightfoot, *Gospel Message*, 48–59). As Jesus has prophesied will happen at "the end," some disciples cannot stay awake and are unready when "the hour" of eschatological crisis comes (14:32–42; cf. 13:35–37); even the elect are led astray and desert (14:50–52; cf. 13:22); the climactic events unfold in three-hour intervals (15:25, 33–34; cf. 13:35); and the good news makes its way to the Gentiles (15:39; cf. 13:10).

The Markan correspondences between prophecies and narrative fulfillments, however, do not eliminate the note of future expectation. In fact, for Mark the belief that the eschatological fulfillment began in Jesus' ministry probably feeds the sense of imminent expectation, as it already did for Jesus himself (cf. Kümmel, *Promise*, on the combination of present and futuristic elements in Jesus' eschatology). The redemptive events of a generation ago were the start of the final age; if that generation is now seen to be drawing to a close, the end must surely be in sight (cf. Ravitzky, *Messianism*, 140, for a parallel from modern-day Jewish apocalypticism).

THE COSMIC BATTLE

But Mark's expectation of a near end is not the only way in which he is an apocalyptic thinker. A certain type of apocalypticism, which de Boer ("Paul") terms "cosmic apocalyptic eschatology," is characterized by the notion that the earth is in subjection to cosmic forces of evil, which human beings are helpless to combat through their own efforts, and that the only hope for them is an eschatological act of God that will utterly transform the conditions of human existence and defeat the oppressive powers. This description fits Mark's narrative perfectly. The situation before the advent of Jesus is one in which the realm of the human is sharply opposed to the realm of the divine (cf. 8:33). The human condition is one of bondage to a "strong man," a demonic power that humans are incapable of countering until Jesus, the "Stronger One," arrives on the scene to free them (3:27). As in this passage, Mark often uses the verb *dynasthai*, "to be able," or the cognate adjective *dynatos*, "possible," to emphasize what God and/or Jesus alone can do (1:40; 2:7; 5:3; 8:4; 9:3, 22, 28; 10:26–27; 14:35–36) or what human beings can do only through the power of God (9:23, 29). The whole issue is summed up in the terse pronouncement in 10:26–27: salvation is impossible for human beings, but not with God.

For Mark as for other Jewish apocalypticists, this salvation is above all a liberation of humanity from the cosmic powers that oppress it; Jesus' main mission is to clear the earth of demons (Käsemann, *Jesus*, 55), and even his teaching is a weapon in this struggle (cf. 1:27). It is not accidental, therefore, that the Markan Jesus' first action after his baptism is a life-or-death struggle with Satan (1:12–13), that the first extended passage in the Gospel is a description of a dramatic exorcism (1:21–28), that subsequent exorcisms are also dramatically highlighted (see 5:1–20 and 9:14–29 and the summaries in 1:32–34, 39; 3:11–13), that exorcistic ability is recognized as a sign of apostolic authority (3:15; 6:13), and that even some healings take on exorcistic features (1:31, 41–43; 7:33–35). Moreover, as Robinson has shown in an important monograph (*Problem*, 91–94), for the evangelist the human opposition to Jesus, which is visible, for example, in the controversy stories, is an extension of the cosmic opposition, which is visible especially in the exorcisms (cf. the COMMENT on 5:14–17 and 6:1–3).

This intertwined demonic/human opposition culminates in Jesus' crucifixion. Mark probably means his readers to understand that the Jewish leaders' conspiracy to liquidate Jesus (3:6; 11:18) reflects the demons' fear that he will liquidate *them* (1:24); the verb *apolesai* is used in both cases and resurfaces in the description of a demon's intention to destroy a human being in 9:22. This demonic interpretation of Jesus' death is supported by the way in which Mark portrays it as a scene of cosmic darkness (15:33); darkness suggests demonic powers elsewhere in the NT (e.g. Eph 6:12) and in Jewish sources (e.g. 1QS 3:15–4:26), and Mark himself links an apocalyptic darkening of the sun with the disturbance of cosmic (demonic?) powers (13:24–25). In his passion narrative, moreover, Mark uses exactly the same words to describe Jesus' death-cry (*phōnē megalē*, "a loud cry"; 15:34, 37) as he has employed previously to describe the screams of demoniacs (1:26; 5:7). This apparent defeat of Jesus by Satan, however, actually turns out to be Jesus' victory over him (15:38–39; cf. 1 Cor 2:8).

How does Mark come by this cosmic apocalyptic eschatology, which is simultaneously so pessimistic (about human capabilities) and so hopeful (about divine possibilities)? We cannot ignore the possible influence of Mark's religious background (did he perhaps grow up in a Jewish apocalyptic milieu, such as the Qumran sect?) and personal temperament. Apocalyptic modes of thinking, moreover, are often accentuated in situations of war, persecution, and other forms of stress, such as the Markan community apparently experienced in the wake of the Jewish War. But it is hard to agree with Mack (*Myth*) that Mark simply *invented* Christian apocalypticism out of his own psychological needs and the stress his community was undergoing. A line of Christian apocalyptic thinking, rather, can be traced back to Jesus himself, through the earliest Christians, and on to Paul and other first-generation Christians (cf. Allison, "Plea"; Hurtado, "Evolutionary," 19–25; Wedderburn, "Paul and Jesus"). And Mark could theoretically have been influenced by all of these sources, since he followed them in time.

MARK AND PAUL

The really controversial issue here is whether or not Mark was influenced by Paul. We could be confident that Mark had been exposed to Paul's influence if we knew that he really was the John Mark of Acts, but unfortunately we cannot be sure of that (see the discussion of Markan authorship above). Certainly, however, there are a number of similarities between Mark's theology and Paul's (see Fenton, "Paul and Mark," for an extensive comparison; cf. also C. Black, "Christ Crucified"). Both, for example, term the message about Jesus "good news" (*euangelion*) and make this word a central aspect of their theology (e.g. Mark 1:1; Gal 1:6–9; Rom 1:16–17; cf. Marxsen, *Mark*, 117–50). Both stress the significance of Jesus' crucifixion as the apocalyptic turning point of the ages (cf. Martyn, "Epistemology"; Marcus, "Mark 4:10–12"), although neither ignores the resurrection either. Both highlight Jesus' victory over demonic powers (the Markan exorcisms; Rom 8:38–39; 1 Cor 15:24, etc.) and see his advent as the dawn of the age of divine blessing prophesied in the Scriptures (e.g. Mark 1:1–15; Rom 3:21–22). Both emphasize the importance of faith in Jesus and in God, sometimes picturing this faith in a dualistic way as a new mode of seeing that God grants to his elect people while condemning outsiders to blindness (Mark 4:10–12; Rom 11:7–10; 1 Cor 2:6–16; cf. Romaniuk, "Problème," 273–74). In both cases, however, such dualism sometimes yields to a universalistic perspective (e.g. Mark 10:45; Rom 11:25–32). Both Mark and Paul have negative things to say about Peter and about members of Jesus' family (e.g. Mark 3:20–21, 31–35; 8:31–33; Galatians 2). Both assert that Jesus came not for the righteous but for ungodly sinners (e.g. Mark 2:17; Rom 4:15; 5:18–19), on whose behalf he died an atoning death (Mark 10:45; Rom 3:25; 5:8), and that he came for the Jews first (*prōton*) but also for the Gentiles (Mark 7:27–29; Rom 1:16; cf. Romans 11). And both think that the widening of God's purposes to incorporate the Gentiles was accomplished by an apocalyptic change in the Law that had previously separated Jews from Gentiles, a change that included an abrogation of the OT food laws; in the new situation that pertains since Jesus' advent, all foods are pure (*katharizōn panta ta brōmata*, Mark 7:19; *panta men kathara*, Rom 14:20).

Such similarities, however, have not convinced everyone about Pauline influence on Mark. Werner, in a monograph that is often cited as definitive (*Einfluss*), concludes that the themes shared by the two authors are not distinctively Pauline but universally Christian; specifically Pauline ideas are either absent or explicitly contradicted in Mark, and Paul obviously does not share Mark's concern with the earthly career of Jesus. Taylor (12), similarly, asserts that Mark lacks "the great Pauline ideas of justification by faith, faith union with Christ, and life in the Spirit." Mark, I would add, does not mention the particular issue upon which the question of Law-observance is usually focused in Paul, namely circumcision; nor does he link his polemic against Peter and Jesus' family directly with the Law-observance issue, as Paul does in Galatians 2.

But the similarities between Paul and Mark cannot simply be brushed aside; nor are all the differences spotlighted by people such as Werner and Taylor as significant as they might at first appear. Although they may not always have been confined to Pauline circles, such emphases as the abrogation of the Law, a critical attitude toward Peter, and even to a certain extent the theology of the cross were matters of controversy and precisely the sorts of issues that landed Paul in hot water (on the controversiality of Paul's theology of the cross, see Käsemann, "Saving Significance"). The combination of the same polemical emphases in Mark suggests some sort of relation to the Pauline mission. Some of the terminological similarities noted above, moreover, are really quite striking, especially that between Mark 7:19 and Rom 14:20. Furthermore, the absence from Mark of themes such as "being in Christ" and circumcision may have other explanations than alienation from Pauline concerns. It would be difficult, for example, to picture "being in Christ" in a literal way within the Markan story. And the lack of reference to the circumcision issue in Mark could very well be because Jesus had not said anything on the subject, and Mark is not in the habit of inventing (as opposed to expanding) passages that have no grounding in the life of Jesus.

Werner, moreover, sometimes overlooks ways in which Mark subtly makes theological points that are similar to Paul's more explicit statements. For example, in discussing the theology of the cross (*Einfluss*, 60–72), he contends that a crucial difference between Mark and Paul is that Mark ascribes responsibility for Jesus' death to human beings, namely the Jewish leaders and Judas, whereas Paul characteristically ascribes it to demonic powers. But 1 Cor 2:8 is the only passage Werner cites for the "characteristic" Pauline view, and he acknowledges that elsewhere Paul does attribute Jesus' death to the enmity of human beings (1 Thess 2:15). It may be true, as Werner claims, that Paul would have seen "the Jews" in this passage (as well as the Roman authorities) as the tools of the demons, but this is probably Mark's view as well (see the discussion above of the cosmic battle motif).

The theology of the cross, then, including the role of evil cosmic powers in Jesus' death, *is* a similarity between Mark and Paul, and there are many others. At the same time, the legitimate differences between the two authors noted above must also be given their due weight. The most reasonable conclusion would seem to be that Mark writes in the Pauline sphere of activity and shows some sort of Pauline influence on his thought, although he is not a member of a Pauline "school" in the same sense that the authors of Colossians-Ephesians and the Pastorals are; unlike them, he has not studied, internalized, and imitated Paul's letters. But neither is he hermetically sealed off from the influence of Paul, and as a matter of fact in some ways is quite close to him (cf. Bacon, *Gospel*, 271).

CORRECTIVE CHRISTOLOGY

One of the differences between Mark and Paul that *does* seem to be significant is that Paul appears to be relatively uninterested in the earthly career of Jesus, whereas Mark is obviously very interested in it. Indeed, scholars such as Schweizer ("Mark's," 42–43) and Martin (*Mark*, 156–62) think that the purpose of Mark's Gospel is to prevent the Pauline kerygma from floating off into space by grounding it in the story of Jesus of Nazareth. For them, Mark is a

Pauline disciple who is concerned with the threat posed by Christians in his community who emphasize their union with the heavenly Christ, as Paul's gnosticizing antagonists in Corinth did. Mark mobilizes the Jesus tradition as well as the theology of the cross to fight against the incipient docetism (see GLOSSARY) of these opponents. A similar theory is propounded by Weeden ("Heresy"; *Traditions*), though without making the Pauline connection explicit; he links Mark's enemies with Paul's "divine man" opponents in Corinth but does not relate Mark to Paul.

These are only two of a number of theories that classify Mark as a polemical document. Other scholars think that Mark is battling not against Christian gnosticism but against an opposite type of heresy, a Law-observant Jewish Christianity similar to what Paul confronted in Antioch (Galatians 2), Galatia (the rest of Galatians), Jerusalem (Rom 15:31; cf. Acts 15), and some sections of the Roman church (Rom 14:1–15:13). Markan evidence for this sort of internal battle is seen in the Gospel's denigration of Peter, the Twelve, and Jesus' family, all of whom were active in the Law-observant Jerusalem Christian community, and in its emphasis on the Gentile mission and abrogation of the Jewish food laws. Proponents of this view are split between those such as Loisy (*L'Évangile*, 37–44) and Goulder ("Those Outside") who think that Mark is a Paulinist continuing Paul's battles in narrative form and those such as Trocmé (*Formation*, 130–37, 145–46) who think that it is merely a case of two different exponents of Gentile Christianity running into similar problems with the Law-observant Jerusalem church. Still another "corrective" approach sees the Gospel as an attempt to cool down the overheated eschatology of some Markan Christians, as Paul or a Pauline disciple does in 2 Thessalonians 2 (see e.g. Best, *Gospel*, 42–43; Hooker, "Trial").

But is the "corrective" approach to Markan theology itself correct? Was Mark really trying to face down strong internal opposition within his own Christian community? We may evaluate some of the strengths and weaknesses of this approach by examining the interrelated views of Weeden ("Heresy"; *Traditions*) and Perrin (*Redaction Criticism*, 51–57; "Christology"). According to these scholars, Mark's opponents are "divine man" theologians who believe that, through union with the risen Lord (cf. "I am he" in 13:6), they are able to participate in the resurrection life already in their earthly existence and thereby possess miracle working power. Mark opposes this glorious, divine man theology, which is represented in the narrative by the disciples and linked with the Christological title "Son of God," by means of his portrait of the suffering Jesus, which is linked with the title "Son of Man." In 14:61–62, for example, he has Jesus reformulate the high priest's question about "the Christ" and "the Son of the Blessed" (= Son of God) in terms of the Son of Man. Similarly, in the first half of his Gospel, Mark incorporates the miracle traditions that are so emphasized by his enemies, but he does so only to qualify them in the second half through the theology of the cross. And he discredits the whole divine man approach by showing its proponents, the disciples, abandoning Jesus and fleeing when persecution comes; he implies that this apostasy was definitive when he concludes the Gospel with the failure of the women to deliver the message about meeting Jesus in Galilee (16:8).

This particular form of the "corrective Christology" approach to Mark has come in for serious attack (see especially Kingsbury, *Christology*) for a number of reasons:

(1) "Divine man" does not seem to have been a fixed term in first-century Hellenism, and when the term is used, it does not seem to be particularly connected with miracles or with the title "Son of God" (cf. Kingsbury, "Divine Man").

(2) It is far from clear that Mark is as negative about miracles as Weeden and Perrin think he is. Although they gradually dwindle in the second half of the Gospel, at the point of emphasis at the very end comes the biggest miracle of all, the resurrection. An interesting parallel is suggested by the observation of Rofé, (*Prophetical Stories*, 42, 55) that in OT prophetic narratives such as 2 Kgs 2:1–18 and 13:14–17, as well as in Hasidic tales about wonder-working rabbis, the end of the seer's life is often marked by a struggle with the forces of Sheol that issues in even greater miracles than at any previous time in his career. In the case of the Elisha cycle, the concluding story in 2 Kgs 13:14–17 "contains allusions to many of his earlier miracles, juxtaposed by one which equals them all"—remarks that could equally be applied to the resurrection of Jesus. The presence of miracles in the first half of Mark's narrative is so massive, moreover, and they are so positively evaluated by onlookers, that it is difficult to believe that Mark dislikes them—although he recognizes their ambivalence, since false Christs and false prophets can do them also (13:22). But the only people in the Gospel who evaluate *Jesus'* miracles negatively are his enemies, the scribes—and Jesus accuses them of blasphemy against the Holy Spirit for doing so (3:28–30)!

(3) The Markan disciples are confused bumblers, not traitors; whatever their failings, they do for most of the story follow Jesus, even in spite of their fear (10:32–34), and their desertion of him at the end seems to be overruled by his promise of renewed fellowship after the resurrection (14:28; 16:7). That in Mark's view this promise was eventually fulfilled is confirmed by the prophecies that members of the Twelve will face martyrdom for Jesus' sake and the gospel's (10:29; 13:9–13). As is the case with some great Old Testament heroes (e.g. Abraham, Moses, David, and Jonah), the Markan disciples' failings and sins do not prevent them from becoming the earthen vessels for God's transcendent power (cf. 2 Cor 4:7).

(4) In 14:61–62 "Son of Man" does not qualify the glorious connotation of "Son of God" but reinforces it, since here the Son of Man is not a suffering figure but a triumphant one who comes on the clouds of heaven to judge his enemies, in accordance with the picture in the primary biblical background, Daniel 7.

Pointing out the glaring weaknesses in the views of Weeden and Perrin, however, does not completely discredit the idea that there is a corrective element in Mark's Christology (against Kingsbury, *Christology*, 33–45). The Markan Jesus explicitly warns his disciples about "false Christs and false prophets," deceivers who will come and lead astray, "if it were possible," the very elect (13:5–6, 21–22). The disciples, moreover, persistently misunderstand Jesus, and Jesus often rebukes them for this misunderstanding (see the rebukes in 4:13; 7:18; 8:14–21, 33, and the other instances of misunderstanding or incomplete perception in 4:41; 8:4; 9:6, 10, 32; 14:40). It seems inherently likely that their confusion reflects some perceptual problem in the Markan community (cf. Reploh, *Lehrer*, 81), especially when two of the rebukes (4:13; 7:18) occur after Jesus has taken the disciples aside for private instruction, a Markan device to allow the risen Lord to address the concerns of Mark's own day (see e.g. 10:10–12; 13:3–37). Some of the misunderstandings, moreover, concern Christology. This is most obvious in Peter's inability to accept the notion of a suffering Messiah (8:11–13; cf. 14:40) and in his failure to grasp the meaning of Jesus' transfigured glory (9:6). But it is probably also implicit in the disciples' misunderstanding "about the loaves" (6:52; 8:14–21), which seems to mean their inability to intuit Jesus' presence in the eucharistic meal of the community (see the COMMENT on 6:51–52 and on 8:17–21).

A part of what these rebukes and corrections appear to be getting at is that the absence of Jesus from the Markan community (cf. 2:20) is only apparent; he is actually present with it, massively present, in the meal that they communally share (cf. the eucharistic "loaves"), in the eschatological fullness that meal symbolizes (cf. the numbers emphasized in 8:19–20), and in the eschatological power demonstrated by their own exorcisms and healings (cf. 6:7, 12–13). The failure of some of Mark's congregants to grasp the radical consequences of this presence, and of the eschatological change that it represents, leads them to cling to old, outmoded ways of being in the world such as Mosaic food laws (7:17–18). The vivifying, explosive power of the God who is present in Jesus negates such attempts (cf. 2:21–22), but it is visible only to the eye of faith, since it is not manifested in a way that eliminates weaknesses, suffering, and death from the lives of community members, any more than it shielded the life of Jesus himself (cf. 8:31–33). It is revealed, rather, in the very midst of those contrary realities (cf. 4:13–20). This message, again, is remarkably similar to that of Paul, who boasts about the power of Christ that rests on him in his weaknesses: "When I am weak, then I am strong" (1 Cor 12:10).

Mark's Christology, then, and his theology in general are not corrective in the radical sense envisaged by Weeden. Mark is not anxious to anathematize a heretical group within his community. The "deceivers" of 13:6–7, 22–23 are not within the community but outside of it; the concern is that they may "deceive the elect" as they have deceived others. But Mark's theology does seek to correct a tendency of some members of his church to forget the massive change that Jesus' death and resurrection have brought about. This "Christological amnesia" (cf. Martyn, "Galatians 3:28") may have led some Markan community members to take refuge in the certainties of the Mosaic Law (cf. 7:17–18). But a far more pervasive concern of the Gospel is that the Markan Christians may simply be overwhelmed by their present situation of "tribulation such as has not been from the beginning of creation" (13:19), and that they may be tempted, like the disciples in the storm-tossed boat, to cry out, "Teacher, don't you care that we're about to die?" (4:38). Mark responds to their fear and despair by retelling the story of Jesus, who conquers wind and waves and comes to his disciples over the stormy sea of death (cf. 6:45–52); he thereby recalls his audience to Christological memory—in other words, to faith (cf. 4:41).

THE APPROACH OF
THIS COMMENTARY

◆

In accordance with the traditional Anchor Bible format, the commentary is divided into sections for TRANSLATION, NOTES, and COMMENT.

In the TRANSLATION I have aimed at a fairly literal rendering—literal enough to convey some of the awkwardness of Mark's grammar, as well as some of its rough-hewn power. For example, I have retained Mark's sturdy, forceful method of connecting clauses by means of the simple word "and," heeding Sternberg's sensible complaint: "How can one prevail on translators to leave the Bible's art of parataxis alone?" (*Poetics*, 525 n. 8). But there are occasions upon which a completely literal rendering leaves the text impossible to understand or conveys a misleading impression. For example, in the first draft I began by translating historical presents as English presents, thinking that this translation conveyed the vividness of the Greek idiom. But in reading my own translations I found the constant shuttling between present and past tenses distracting, and so was happy when I became convinced that in Koine Greek the historical present is usually a means not of conveying vividness but of indicating some sort of transition in the narrative (see Osburn, "Historical Present"; Fanning, *Verbal Aspect*, 226–39). This sort of transition is often impossible to reproduce in translation; an oral performer might leave a brief pause, but starting a new paragraph may be too much of a break. So I have usually just translated historical presents with English past tenses, and left it at that. I have tried to use the same English word throughout to translate the same Greek word so that even readers with no Greek can see connections within the Markan text, but I have sometimes sacrificed this principle for the sake of clarity.

The NOTES explain choices made in the TRANSLATION, highlight exegetical problems with respect to specific words and phrases, including text-critical questions, and convey other technical information. Readers who are impatient, not technically minded, and/or mainly concerned with the central significance of the passage may safely skip the NOTES and go directly to the COMMENT, though they will often find that the COMMENT sends them back to individual NOTES.

I view the COMMENT section as the heart of the commentary. It is the section I would like every reader to read, from the pastor trying to get a "fix" on a particular passage for a Sunday sermon to the professional scholar attempting to situate it within the development of early Christian life and thought. Here I present my vision of what each pericope is centrally about. The COMMENT sections begin with an "introduction" that describes the passage's relation to what precedes it, makes an attempt to reconstruct its redactional history (i.e. to separate Mark's own contribution from the tradition he has inherited), and outlines its structure. They then move on to an exposition of the passage, usually broken up into the smaller subsections discerned in the analysis of structure. In these expositions I have tried to keep two things constantly in mind: that Mark has produced a narrative text and that he intended it for specific first-century readers, or, better, for specific first-century hearers. So my attempt has been to read myself and my own readers back into the first hearers' sequential experience of the unfolding passage, asking how its development would have impressed *them* in their own particular historical situation; how they would have answered such questions as "why the text says this and not that" (Keck and Tucker, "Exegesis," 298) and why it says it here and not there.

I have tried to show that sometimes the first readers' rootedness in a situation different from ours would have meant that passages that are puzzling to us would not have been enigmatic to them. Sometimes, however, they would probably have been just as baffled as we are and would have heard as addressed to themselves the words with which the Gospel's first act closes: "Do you not *yet* understand?" (8:21). Our Gospel is written by someone who thinks that the path of interpretation is arduous and beset with pitfalls, and who does not set out to make things too easy for his readers, partly because he believes that human puzzlement is a necessary part of the revelation of divine mysteries (cf. the reference to Otto in the discussion of Markan composition above). No commentator on Mark, then, can hope to solve all its perplexing problems; the best an exegete can hope to do is to help his readers (and himself) reproduce the situation of the disciples and place themselves on the road that leads to understanding. Further steps are up to the reader and, Mark would say, to God, for Mark presents the healing of blindness as a divine miracle that takes place in the context of the miracle of discipleship: "And his sight was restored, and he followed him in the way" (10:52).

BIBLIOGRAPHY

◆

BIBLIOGRAPHY

◆

Works are cited in the text according to the word or words printed below in **boldface**.

Åalen, S.
  1961–62   "'**Reign**' and 'House' in the Kingdom of God in the Gospels." *NTS* 8: 215–40.
Aberbach, M.
  1972   "**Pharaoh**." In *EncJud*, 13.359–63.
Achtemeier, P. J.
  1986   **Mark**. 2nd ed. Proclamation Commentaries. Philadelphia: Fortress.
  1972   "The **Origin** and Function of the Pre-Marcan Miracle Catenae." *JBL* 91: 198–221.
Achtemeier, P. J., et al., eds.
  1985   *Harper's Bible Dictionary*. San Francisco: Harper & Row. [Cited as **HBD**]
Adler, C., et al., eds.
  1881   *The Jewish Encyclopedia: A Descriptive Record of the History, Religion, Literature, and Customs of the Jewish People from the Earliest Times to the Present Day*. 12 vols. New York and London: Funk & Wagnalls. Reprint, New York: KTAV Publishing House, 1964. [Cited as **JE**]
Albertz, M.
  1921   *Die synoptischen **Streitgespräche***. Berlin: Trositzsch & Sohn.
Allen, W. C.
  1912   *A Critical and Exegetical Commentary on the Gospel according to St. **Matthew***. 3rd ed. ICC. Edinburgh: T. & T. Clark.
Allison, D. C.
  1992   "The **Baptism** of Jesus and a New Dead Sea Scroll." *BARev* 18: 58–60.
  1985   *The **End** of the Ages Has Come: An Early Interpretation of the Passion and Resurrection of Jesus*. Philadelphia: Fortress.
  1986   "The **Living Water** (John 4:10–14; 6:35c; 7:37–39)." *St Vladimir's Theological Quarterly* 30: 143–57.
  1993   *The **New Moses**: A Matthean Typology*. Edinburgh: T. & T. Clark.
  1993   "A **Plea** for Thoroughgoing Eschatology." *JBL* 113: 651–68.
  1983   "**Psalm 23** (22) in Early Christianity: A Suggestion." *IBS* 5: 132–37.
  1989   "**Who Will Come** from East and West?" *IBS* 11: 158–70.
Alon, G.
  1977   "The **Levitical Uncleanness** of Gentiles." In *Jews, Judaism and the Classical World: Studies in Jewish History in the Times of the Second Temple and Talmud*, 146–89. Jerusalem: Magnes.

Ambrozic, A. M.
1972   *The Hidden Kingdom: A Redaction-Critical Study of the References to
             the Kingdom of God in Mark's Gospel*. CBQMS 2. Washington, D.C.:
             Catholic Biblical Association.
1975   "**New Teaching** with Power (Mk 1:27)." In *Word and Spirit: Essays in
             Honor of David Michael Stanley, S.J. on His 60th Birthday*, ed. J. Plevnik,
             113–49. Willowdale, Ont.: Regis College.
Anderson, B. W.
1962   "**Exodus Typology** in Second Isaiah." In *Israel's Prophetic Heritage: Essays
             in Honor of James Muilenburg*, ed. B. W. Anderson and W. Harrelson,
             177–95. New York: Harper & Row.
Anderson, B. W., ed.
1985   *Creation in the Old Testament*. IRT 6. Philadelphia: Fortress; London:
             SPCK.
Anderson, G. A.
1997   "The **Exaltation** of Adam and the Fall of Satan." *Journal of Jewish
             Thought and Philosophy* 6: 105–34.
1999   "The **Garments** of Skin in Apocryphal Narrative and Biblical Commen-
             tary." In *Studies in Ancient Midrash*, ed. J. Kugel. Harvard: Harvard Uni-
             versity Press.
Anderson, J. C.
1992   "Feminist Criticism: The **Dancing Daughter**." In *Mark and Method:
             New Approaches in Biblical Studies*, ed. J. C. Anderson and S. D. Moore,
             103–34. Minneapolis: Augsburg Fortress.
Anderson, S. M.
1994   *An Exegetical Study of Mark 9:14–29*. B.D. Honours diss., University of
             Glasgow.
Arens, E.
1976   *The ĒLTHON-Sayings in the Synoptic Tradition: A Historico-Critical
             Investigation*. OBO 10. Göttingen: Vandenhoeck & Ruprecht.
Ashton, J.
1991   *Understanding the Fourth Gospel*. Oxford: Clarendon.
Augustine, Saint
1961   *Confessions*. Penguin Classics. Middlesex: Penguin.
Aune, D. E.
1990   "**Hermas**." In *EEC*, 421. New York and London: Garland.
1989   *The New Testament in Its Literary Environment*. Library of Early Chris-
             tianity. Philadelphia: Westminster.
Aus, R.
1988   *Water into Wine and the Beheading of John the Baptist*. BJS 150. Atlanta:
             Scholars Press.
Baarlink, H.
1977   *Anfängliches Evangelium: ein Beitrag zur näheren Bestimmung der theo-
             logischen Motive im Markusevangelium*. Kampen: Kok.
Bacon, B. W.
1925   *The Gospel of Mark: Its Composition and Date*. New Haven: Yale Uni-
             versity Press; London: Oxford University Press.
Bailey, R. C.
1992   "**Jerubbesheth**." In *ABD*, 3.747.

Baird, J. A.
1987   "The Holy **Word**: The History and Function of the Teachings of Jesus in the Theology and Praxis of the Early Church." *NTS* 33: 585–99.
1957   "A Pragmatic **Approach** to Parable Exegesis: Some New Evidence on Mark 4:11, 33–34." *JBL* 76: 201–7.

Balch, D. L.
1990–93 "**Household Codes**." In *ABD*, 3.318–20.

Balz, H., and G. Schneider, eds.
1990–93 *Exegetical Dictionary of the New Testament*. 3 vols. Grand Rapids: Eerdmans. [Cited as **EDNT**]

Barclay, J. M. G.
1996   *Jews in the Mediterranean Diaspora from Alexander to Trajan (323 BCE– 117 CE)*. Edinburgh: T. & T. Clark.
1988   *Obeying the Truth: A Study of Paul's Ethics in Galatians*. SNTW. Edinburgh: T. & T. Clark.

Barnett, P. W.
1980–81 "The Jewish **Sign Prophets**—A.D. 40–70: Their Intentions and Origin." *NTS* 27: 679–97.

Barrett, C. K.
1947   *The Holy Spirit and the Gospel Tradition*. London: SCM; New York: Macmillan.
1947   "The **Old Testament** in the Fourth Gospel." *JTS* 48: 155–69.

Batto, B. F.
1987   "The **Sleeping** God: An Ancient Near Eastern Motif of Divine Sovereignty." *Bib* 68: 153–77.

Bauckham, R.
1994   "The **Brothers** and Sisters of Jesus: An Epiphanian Response to John P. Meier." *CBQ* 56: 686–700.
1997   "**For Whom** Were Gospels Written?" In *The Gospels for All Christians: Rethinking the Gospel Audiences*, ed. R. Bauckham. Grand Rapids: Eerdmans.
1994   "**Jesus** and the Wild Animals (Mark 1:13): A Christological Image for an Ecological Age." In *Jesus of Nazareth: Lord and Christ: Essays on the Historical Jesus and New Testament Christology*, ed. J. B. Green and M. Turner, 3–21. Grand Rapids: Eerdmans; Carlisle: Paternoster.
1990   *Jude and the Relatives of Jesus in the Early Church*. Edinburgh: T. & T. Clark.

Baudoz, J.-F.
1995   "**Mc** 7, 31–37 et Mc 8,22–26. Géographie et théologie." *RB* 102: 560–69.
1995   *Les **Miettes** de la Table. Étude synoptique et socio-religieuse de Mt 15,21– 28 et de Mc 7,24–30*. Ebib n.s. 27. Paris: Gabalda.

Bauer, J. B.
1958   "**Drei Tage**." *Bib* 39: 354–58.

Bauer, W., et al.
1979   *A Greek-English Lexicon of the New Testament and Other Early Christian Literature*. 2nd ed. Chicago and London: University of Chicago Press. [Cited as **BAGD**]

Bauernfeind, O.
1927   *Die Worte der Dämonen im Markusevangelium.* BWANT 44. Stuttgart: Kohlhammer.

Baumgärtel, F.
1968   "Spirit in the OT." In *TDNT*, 6.359–67.

Baumgarten, A. I.
1998   "Greco-Roman Voluntary Associations and Jewish Sects." In *Jews in the Greco-Roman World*, ed. M. Goodman. Oxford: Oxford University Press.
1984   "*Korban* and the Pharisaic *Paradosis.*" *JANES* 16: 5–17.
1983   "The Name of the Pharisees." *JBL* 102: 411–28.
1987   "The Pharisaic *Paradosis.*" *HTR* 80: 63–77.
1991   "Rivkin and Neusner on the Pharisees." In *Law in Religious Communities in the Roman Period: The Debate over Torah and Nomos in Postbiblical Judaism and Early Christianity*, ed. P. Richardson and S. Westerholm, 109–26. Waterloo, Ont.: Wilfred Laurier University Press.
1996   "The Temple Scroll, Toilet Practices, and the Essenes." *Jewish History* 10: 9–20.

Baumgarten, J. M.
1976   "The Duodecimal Courts of Qumran, Revelation, and the Sanhedrin." *JBL* 95: 59–78.
1990   "The 4Q Zadokite Fragments on Skin Disease." *JJS* 41: 153–65.

Beardslee, W. A.
1992   "James." In *ABD*, 1.790–94.

Beare, F. W.
1962   *The Earliest Records of Jesus: A Companion to the Synopsis of the First Three Gospels by Albert Huck.* New York and Nashville: Abingdon.
1962   "Persecution." In *IDB*, 3.735–37.

Beasley-Murray, G. R.
1962   *Baptism in the New Testament.* London: Macmillan.

Beavis, M. A.
1989   *Mark's Audience: The Literary and Social Setting of Mark 4.11–12.* JSNTSup 33. Sheffield: Sheffield Academic Press.

Beckett, S.
1929   "Dante. Bruno. Vico. Joyce." In *Our Examination round His Factification for Incamination of Work in Progress*, ed. S. Beckett et al. London: Faber & Faber.

Behm, J.
1965   "*Kardia, ktl.*" In *TDNT*, 3.603–14.

Behm, J., et al.
1967   "*Metanoeō, metanoia.*" In *TDNT*, 4.975–1008.

Beker, J. C.
1980   *Paul the Apostle: The Triumph of God in Life and Thought.* Philadelphia: Fortress.

Ben-Sasson, H. H.
1881   "Disputations and Polemics." In *JE*, 6.82–103.

Bengel, J. A.
1866   *Gnomon Novi Testamenti.* Stuttgart: J. F. Steinkopf; London: Dulau (orig. 1773).

Berger, K.
1976   Die **Auferstehung** des Propheten und die Erhöhung des Menschensohnes: Traditionsgeschichtliche Untersuchungen zur Deutung des Geschickes Jesu in frühchristlichen Texten. SUNT 13. Göttingen: Vandenhoeck & Ruprecht.
1972   Die **Gesetzauslegung** Jesu. Ihr historischer Hintergrund im Judentum und im Alten Testament. Teil 1, Markus und Parallelen. WMANT 40. Neukirchen: Neukirchener Verlag.

Bergren, T. A.
1989   "The '**People** Coming from the East' in 5 Ezra 1:38." *JBL* 108: 675–83.

Berkey, R. F.
1963   "**ENGIZEIN, PHTHANEIN**, and Realized Eschatology." *JBL* 82: 177–87.

Bertram, G.
1972   "**Hypsos, ktl.**" In *TDNT*, 8.602–20.

Best, E.
1981   *Following Jesus: Discipleship in the Gospel of Mark*. JSNTSup 4. Sheffield: JSOT.
1983   *Mark: The Gospel as Story*. Edinburgh: T. & T. Clark.
1975–76 "**Mark III**.20,21,31–35." NTS 22: 309–19.
1985   "Mark's **Preservation** of the Tradition." In *The Interpretation of Mark*, ed. W. Telford. IRT 7, 119–33. Philadelphia: Fortress; London: SPCK (orig. 1974).
1992   "Mark's **Readers**: A Profile." In *The Four Gospels 1992: Festschrift Frans Neirynck*, eds. F. Van Segbroeck et al. BETL 100, 2.839–58. Leuven: Leuven University Press.
1977   "Mark's **Use** of the Twelve." ZNW 69: 11–35.
1977   "The **Role** of the Disciples in Mark." NTS 23: 377–401.
1990   *The **Temptation** and the Passion: The Markan Soteriology*. 2nd ed. SNTSMS 2. Cambridge: Cambridge University Press (orig. 1965).

Betz, H. D.
1992   "**Apostle**." In *ABD*, 1.309–11.
1992   *The Greek **Magical Papyri** in Translation Including the Demotic Spells*. 2nd ed. Chicago and London: University of Chicago Press.

Beyer, H. W.
1964   "**Diakoneō, ktl.**" In *TDNT*, 2.81–93.

Bilezikian, G. G.
1977   *The **Liberated Gospel**: A Comparison of the Gospel of Mark and Greek Tragedy*. Grand Rapids: Baker.

Black, C. C.
1996   "**Christ Crucified** in Paul and in Mark: Reflections on an Intracanonical Conversation." In *Theology and Ethics in Paul and His Interpreters: Essays in Honor of Victor Paul Furnish*, ed. E. H. Lovering and J. L. Sumney, 80–104. Nashville: Abingdon.
1994   *Mark: Images of an Apostolic Interpreter*. Studies on Personalities of the New Testament. Columbia, S.C.: University of South Carolina Press.
1993   "**Was Mark** a Roman Gospel?" ET 105: 36–40.

Black, M.
1967   *An Aramaic Approach to the Gospels and Acts*. 3rd ed. Oxford: Clarendon. [Cited as **Black**]

1961   *The Scrolls and Christian Origins: Studies in the Jewish Background of the New Testament.* London: Thomas Nelson & Sons.

Blackburn, B.
1991   *Theios Anēr and the Markan Miracle Traditions.* WUNT, 2.40. Tübingen: J. C. B. Mohr (Paul Siebeck).

Blass, F., et al.
1961   *A Greek Grammar of the New Testament and Other Early Christian Literature.* Chicago and London: University of Chicago Press. [Cited as **BDF**]

Blau, L.
1914   *Das altjüdische Zauberwesen.* 2nd ed. Berlin: Louis Lamm.

Blenkinsopp, J.
1992   *The Pentateuch: An Introduction to the First Five Books of the Bible.* London: SCM.

Blevins, J. L.
1981   *The Messianic Secret in Markan Research, 1901–1976.* Washington, D.C.: University Press of America.

Böcher, O.
1972   *Christus Exorcista. Dämonismus und Taufe im Neuen Testament.* BWANT 96. Stuttgart: W. Kohlhammer.

Bockmuehl, M.
1995   "The **Noachide** Commandments and New Testament Ethics," *RB* 102: 72–101.

Bohak, G.
1996   *Joseph and Aseneth and the Jewish Temple in Heliopolis.* Early Judaism and Its Literature 10. Atlanta: Scholars Press.

Boismard, M.-É.
1972   *Synopse des quatre évangiles en français.* Vol. 2, *Commentaire.* Paris: Édition du Cerf.

Bokser, B.
1984   *The Origins of the Seder: The Passover Rite and Early Rabbinic Judaism.* Berkeley: University of California Press.

Bolyki, J.
1992   "**Menge**—Tischgemeinschaft—Gruppe." *Communio Viatorum* 24: 20–26.

Bonner, C.
1927   "Traces of **Thaumaturgic Technique** in the Miracles." *HTR* 20: 171–81.

Boobyer, G. H.
1952   "The **Eucharistic** Interpretation of the Miracles of the Loaves in St. Mark's Gospel." *JTS* n.s. 3: 161–71.
1954   "**Mark II,10a** and the Interpretation of the Healing of the Paralytic." *HTR* 48: 115–20.

Booth, R. P.
1986   *Jesus and the Laws of Purity: Tradition History and Legal History in Mark 7.* JSNTSup 13. Sheffield: JSOT.

Borg, M.
1984   *Conflict, Holiness and Politics in the Teaching of Jesus.* New York: Edwin Mellen Press.

Borgen, P.
1965   *Bread from Heaven: An Exegetical Study of the Concept of Manna in the Gospel of John and the Writings of Philo.* NovTSup 10. Leiden: Brill.

Boring, M. E.
1990   "Mark 1:1–15 and the **Beginning** of the Gospel." *Semeia* 52: 43–81.
1989   "**Review of** D. **Lührmann**, *Das Markusevangelium.*" *JBL* 108: 343–45.
1982   *Sayings of the Risen Jesus: Christian Prophecy in the Synoptic Tradition.* SNTSMS 46. Cambridge: Cambridge University Press.

Bornkamm, G.
1968   "*Presbys, ktl.*" In *TDNT,* 6.651–83.

Boswell, J.
n.d.   *Boswell's Life of Johnson.* London: Oxford University Press.

Botha, P. J. J.
1993   "The Historical **Setting** of Mark's Gospel: Problems and Possibilities." *JSNT* 51: 27–55.

Botterweck, G. J., and H. Ringgren
1977–94   *Theological Dictionary of the Old Testament.* 8 vols. Grand Rapids: Eerdmans. [Cited as **TDOT**]

Bovon, F.
1989   *Das Evangelium nach **Lukas** (Lk 1,1–9,50).* EKKNT 3.1. Zürich: Benziger; Neukirchen-Vluyn: Neukirchener.

Boyarin, D.
1994   *A **Radical Jew**: Paul and the Politics of Identity.* Contraversions 1. Berkeley, Los Angeles, and London: University of California Press.

Branch, T.
1988   *Parting the Waters: America in the King Years 1954–63.* Touchstone Books. New York: Simon & Schuster.

Bratcher, R. G.
1981   *A Translator's Guide to the Gospel of Mark.* Helps for Translators. London, New York and Stuttgart: United Bible Societies. [Cited as **Bratcher**]

Braude, W. G.
1968   *Pesikta Rabbati: Discourses for Feasts, Fasts, and Special Sabbaths.* Yale Judaica Series 18. 2 vols. New Haven and London: Yale University Press.

Braumann, G.
1963–64   "Die **Schuldner** und die Sünderin. Luk. VII.36–50." *NTS* 10: 487–93.

Braund, D. C.
1992   "**Herodian Dynasty.**" In *ABD,* 3.173–74.

Breuer, J., and S. Freud
1974   *Studies on Hysteria.* Penguin Freud Library. London: Penguin (orig. 1895).

Broadhead, E. K.
1992   *Teaching with Authority: Miracles and Christology in the Gospel of Mark.* JSNTSup 74. Sheffield: JSOT.

Brown, F., et al.
1907   *A Hebrew and English Lexicon of the Old Testament* (Oxford: Clarendon). [Cited as **BDB**]

Brown, R. E.
1993   *The **Birth** of the Messiah: A Commentary on the Infancy Narratives in Matthew and Luke.* ABRL. New York: Doubleday (orig. 1979).
1979   *The **Community** of the Beloved Disciple.* New York: Paulist.
1994   *The **Death** of the Messiah: From Gethsemane to the Grave. A Commentary on the Passion Narratives in the Four Gospels.* ABRL. New York: Doubleday.

1966–70   *The Gospel according to John.* AB 29 and 29A. Garden City, N.Y.: Doubleday. [Cited as **Brown**]

1971   "**Jesus and Elisha.**" *Perspective* 12: 85–104.

1968   "**Parable** and Allegory Reconsidered." In *New Testament Essays.* Garden City, N.Y.: Doubleday (orig. 1962).

1968   *The Semitic **Background** of the Term "Mystery" in the New Testament.* FBBS 21. Philadelphia: Fortress (orig. 1958–59).

Brown, R. E., and J. P. Meier

1983   "**Rome.**" In *Antioch and Rome: New Testament Cradles of Catholic Christianity,* 87–210. New York: Paulist.

Brown, R. E., et al.

1978   *Mary in the New Testament: A Collaborative Assessment by Protestant and Roman Catholic Scholars.* Philadelphia: Fortress; New York: Paulist.

1973   *Peter in the New Testament: A Collaborative Assessment by Protestant and Roman Catholic Scholars.* Minneapolis: Augsburg; New York: Paulist.

Brown, R. E., et al., eds.

1990   *The New Jerome Biblical Commentary.* Englewood Cliffs, N.J.: Prentice-Hall. [Cited as **NJBC**]

Brownmiller, S.

1976   *Against Our Will: Men, Women, and Rape.* London: Penguin.

Bruce, F. F.

1982   *The Epistle to the **Galatians**: A Commentary on the Greek Text.* NIGTC. Exeter: Paternoster; Grand Rapids: Eerdmans.

Buber, M.

1948   "And **If Not Now**, When?" In *Israel and the World: Essays in a Time of Crisis,* 234–39. New York: Schocken (orig. 1932).

1991   *Tales of the Hasidim.* New York: Schocken (orig. 1947).

Büchler, A.

1909–10   "The **Law** of Purification in Mark VII.1–23." *ET* 21: 34–40.

Bultmann, R.

1964   "*Aphiēmi, ktl.*" In *TDNT,* 1.509–12.

1971   *The Gospel of **John**: A Commentary.* Philadelphia: Westminster (orig. 1964).

1963   *History of the Synoptic Tradition.* New York: Harper & Row (orig. 1921). [Cited as **Bultmann**]

1951–55   *Theology of the New Testament.* New York: Scribner's.

Bultmann, R., et al.

1964   "*Alētheia, ktl.*" In *TDNT,* 1.232–51.

Bunyan, John.

1907   *Grace Abounding and the Pilgrim's Progress.* Cambridge: Cambridge University Press.

Burkill, T. A.

1967   "The Historical **Development** of the Story of the Syrophoenician Woman (Mark Vii:24–31)." *NovT* 9: 161–78.

1968   "**Mark 3:7–12** and the Alleged Dualism in the Evangelist's Miracle Material." *JBL* 87: 409–17.

1966   "The Syrophoenician Woman: The **Congruence** of Mark 7,24–31." *ZNW* 57: 23–37.

Burrelli, R. J.
1993   *A Study of Psalm 91 with Special Reference to the Theory That It Was In-tended as a Protection against Demons and Magic.* Ph.D. diss., Cambridge University.

Burridge, R. A.
1992   *What Are the Gospels? A Comparison with Graeco-Roman Biography.* SNTSMS 70. Cambridge: Cambridge University Press.

Burton, E. D. W.
1976   *Syntax of the Moods and Tenses in New Testament Greek.* Grand Rapids: Kregel (orig. 1900). [Cited as **Burton**]

Buse, I.
1956   "The **Markan Account** of the Baptism of Jesus and Isaiah LXIII." *JTS* n.s. 7: 74–75.

Butler, B. C.
1985   "The **Synoptic Problem.** " In *The Two-Source Hypothesis: A Critical Appraisal,* ed. A. J. Bellinzoni, 97–118. Macon, Ga.: Mercer University Press (orig. 1969).

Buttrick, G. A., ed.
1962   *The Interpreter's Dictionary of the Bible: An Illustrated Encyclopedia.* 4 vols. Nashville: Abingdon. [Cited as **IDB**]

Cadbury, H. J.
1933   "Note XXIV. **Dust and Garments.**" In *The Beginnings of Christianity.* Part 1, *The Acts of the Apostles,* ed. F. J. F. Jackson and K. Lake, 269–77. London: Macmillan.

Caird, G. B.
1978   "**Review of** M. **Pesce,** *Paolo e Gli Arconti a Corinto.*" *JTS* 29:543–44.

Campbell, R. A.
1994   *The **Elders:** Seniority within Earliest Christianity.* SNTW. Edinburgh: T. &. T. Clark.

Capps, D.
1990   *Reframing: A New Method in Pastoral Care.* Minneapolis: Fortress.

Carlston, C. E.
1975   *The **Parables** of the Triple Tradition.* Philadelphia: Fortress.

Carrington, P.
1952   *The **Primitive** Christian Calendar: A Study in the Making of the Markan Gospel.* Cambridge: Cambridge University Press.

Casey, M.
1988   "Culture and Historicity: The **Plucking** of the Grain (Mark 2.23–28)." *NTS* 34: 1–23.

1987   "**General, Generic and Indefinite:** The Use of the Term 'Son of Man' in Aramaic Sources and in the Teaching of Jesus." *JSNT* 29: 21–56.

1995   "**Idiom** and Translation: Some Aspects of the Son of Man Problem." *NTS* 41: 164–82.

1980   *Son of Man: The Interpretation of and Influence of Daniel 7.* London: SPCK.

Catchpole, D. R.
1992   "The **Beginning** of Q: A Proposal." *NTS* 38: 205–21.

Charlesworth, J. H.
1992   "The **Lost Tribes**" In *ABD,* 4.372.

Charlesworth, J. H., ed.
1983   *The Old Testament Pseudepigrapha*. 2 vols. Garden City, N.Y.: Double-
        day. [Cited as **OTP**]

Childs, B. S.
1974   *The Book of Exodus: A Critical, Theological Commentary*. OTL. Phila-
        delphia: Westminster.
1962   "**Orientation**." In *IDB*, 3.608–9.

Chilton, B. D.
1992   "**Amen**." In *ABD*, 1.184–86.
1984   A *Galilean Rabbi* and *His Bible: Jesus' Own Interpretation of Isaiah*.
        London: SPCK.
1970   *God in Strength: Jesus' Announcement of the Kingdom*. Studien Zum
        Neuen Testament und Seiner Umwelt. Serie B, Teil 1. Freistadt: Plöch.
1987   *The Isaiah Targum: Introduction, Translation, Apparatus and Notes*. Ara-
        maic Bible 11. Wilmington: Glazier.

Clark, S.
1997   *Thinking with Demons: The Idea of Witchcraft in Early Modern Europe*.
        Oxford: Clarendon.

Cohen, A.
1975   *Everyman's Talmud*. New York: Schocken (orig. 1931).

Cohen, S. J. D.
1989   "**Crossing** the Boundary and Becoming a Jew." *HTR* 82: 13–33.
1991   "**Menstruants** and the Sacred in Judaism and Christianity." In *Women's
        History and Ancient History*, ed. S. B. Pomeroy, 273–99. Chapel Hill and
        London: University of North Carolina Press.
1984   "The Significance of **Yavneh**: Pharisees, Rabbis, and the End of Jewish
        Sectarianism." *HUCA* 55: 27–53.
1993   "'**Those Who Say** They Are Jews and Are Not': How Do You Know a Jew
        in Antiquity When You See One?" In *Diasporas in Antiquity*, ed. S. J. D.
        Cohen and E. S. Frerichs. BJS 288, 1–45. Atlanta: Scholars Press.

Collins, A. Y.
1996   *Cosmology and Eschatology in Jewish and Christian Apocalypticism*.
        JSJSup 50. Leiden, New York, and Köln: Brill.
1992   "**Is Mark's** Gospel a Life of Jesus? The Question of Genre." In *The Be-
        ginning of the Gospel: Probings of Mark in Context*, 1–38. Minneapolis:
        Augsburg Fortress.

Collins, J. J.
1984   *The Apocalyptic Imagination: An Introduction to the Jewish Matrix of
        Christianity*. New York: Crossroad.
1996   "Jesus and the **Messiahs** of Israel." In *Geschichte-Tradition-Reflexion*.
        Festschrift für Martin Hengel zum 70. Geburtstag. Band 3, *Frühes Chris-
        tentum*, ed. H. Cancik et al., 287–302. Tübingen: J. C. B. Mohr (Paul
        Siebeck).
1995   *The Scepter and the Star: The Messiahs of the Dead Sea Scrolls and
        Other Ancient Literature*. ABRL. New York: Doubleday.

Collins, J. N.
1990   *Diakonia: Re-interpreting the Ancient Sources*. New York and Oxford:
        Oxford University Press.

Conybeare, F. C., and St. George Stock
1980   A *Grammar of Septuagint Greek*. Grand Rapids: Zondervan (orig. 1905).
Cope, O. L.
1976   *Matthew: A Scribe Trained for the Kingdom of Heaven*. CBQMS 5. Washington, D.C.: Catholic Biblical Association.
Cover, R. C.
1992   "Sin, Sinners (OT)." In *ABD*, 6.30–40.
Cranfield, C. E. B.
1975–79   *A Critical and Exegetical Commentary on the Epistle to the Romans*. ICC. Edinburgh: T. & T. Clark.
1974   *The Gospel according to Saint Mark*. CGTC. Cambridge: Cambridge University Press (orig. 1959). [Cited as **Cranfield**]
Crim, K., ed.
1976   *The Interpreter's Dictionary of the Bible, Supplementary Volume*. Nashville: Abingdon. [Cited as **IDBS**]
Cronin, A.
1997   *Samuel Beckett: The Last Modernist*. London: Flamingo.
Crossan, J. D.
1976   "**Empty Tomb** and Absent Lord (Mark 16:1–8)." In *The Passion in Mark: Studies on Mark 14–16*, ed. W. H. Kelber, 135–52. Philadelphia: Fortress.
1985   *Four Other Gospels: Shadows on the Contours of the Canon*. Minneapolis, Chicago, and New York: Winston.
1991   *The Historical Jesus: The Life of a Mediterranean Jewish Peasant*. San Francisco: Harper.
1973   "Mark and the **Relatives** of Jesus." *NovT* 15: 81–113.
1973   *In Parables: The Challenge of the Historical Jesus*. New York: Harper & Row.
1973   "The *Seed Parables* of Jesus." *JBL* 92: 244–66.
Cullmann, O.
1962   *Peter: Disciple, Apostle, Martyr: A Historical and Theological Study*. 2nd ed. London: SCM.
Cuvillier, E.
1993   *Le Concept de PARABOLĒ dans le second évangeile. Son arrière-plan littéraire, sa signification dans le cadre de la rédaction marcienne, son utilisation dans la tradition de Jésus*. Ebib n.s. 19. Paris: Gabalda.
Dahl, N. A.
1976   "The **Parables** of Growth." In *Jesus in the Memory of the Early Church*, 141–66. Minneapolis: Augsburg (orig. 1951).
Dahl, N. A., and A. F. Segal
1978   "**Philo** and the Rabbis on the Names of God." *JSJ* 9: 1–28.
Dalman, G.
1902   *The Words of Jesus Considered in the Light of Post-biblical Jewish Writings and the Aramaic Language*. Edinburgh: T. & T. Clark.
Danby, H.
1933   *The Mishnah: Translated from the Hebrew with Introduction and Brief Explanatory Notes*. Oxford University Press. [Cited as **Danby**]
Danker, F. W.
1963   "**Mark 8:3**." *JBL* 82: 215–16.

Daube, D.
   1972–73   "**Responsibilities** of Master and Disciples in the Gospels." *NTS* 19: 1–15.
   1964   *The Sudden in the Scriptures*. Leiden: Brill.
Davies, S. L.
   1995   *Jesus the Healer: Possession, Trance, and the Origins of Christianity*. London: SCM.
Davies, W. D., and D. C. Allison
   1988–97   *A Critical and Exegetical Commentary on the Gospel according to Saint Matthew*. 3 vols. Edinburgh: T. & T. Clark. [Cited as **Davies and Allison**]
de Boer, M. C.
   1995   "**God-Fearers** in Luke-Acts." In *Luke's Literary Achievement: Collected Essays*, ed. C. M. Tuckett. JSNTSup 116, 50–71. Sheffield: Sheffield Academic Press.
   1996   *Johannine Perspectives on the Death of Jesus*. Contributions to Biblical Exegesis and Theology 17. Kampen: Kok Pharos.
   1989   "**Paul** and Jewish Apocalyptic Eschatology." In *Apocalyptic in the New Testament: Essays in Honor of J. Louis Martyn*, ed. J. Marcus and M. L. Soards. JSNTSup 24, 169–90. Sheffield: Sheffield Academic Press.
de Lacey, D. R.
   1992   "In **Search** of a Pharisee." *TynBul* 43: 353–72.
de Solages, B.
   1979   "L'évangile de **Thomas** et les évangiles canoniques: l'ordre des péricopes." *BLE* 80: 102–8.
de Vaux, R.
   1965   *Ancient Israel*. New York: McGraw-Hill.
Dean-Jones, L.
   1994   *Women's Bodies in Classical Greek Science*. Oxford: Clarendon.
Deines, R.
   1993   *Jüdisches Steingefässe und pharisäische Frömmigkeit*. WUNT, 2.52. Tübingen: J. C. B. Mohr (Paul Siebeck).
Deissmann, A.
   1978   *Light from the Ancient East: The New Testament Illustrated by Recently Discovered Texts of the Graeco-Roman World*. Grand Rapids: Baker (orig. 1922).
Denaux, A.
   1992   *John and the Synoptics*. BETL 101. Leuven: Leuven University Press.
Derrett, J. D. M.
   1979   "**Contributions** to the Study of the Gerasene Demoniac." *JSNT* 3: 2–17.
   1977   "**Judaica** in St. Mark." In *Studies in the New Testament*, 1.85–100. Leiden: Brill.
   1979   "**Spirit-Possession** and the Gerasene Demoniac." *Man* n.s. 14: 286–93.
DeVries, S. J.
   1985   *1 Kings*. WBC 12. Waco: Word.
Dewey, J.
   1991   "Mark as Interwoven **Tapestry**: Forecasts and Echoes for a Listening Audience." *CBQ* 53: 221–36.
   1980   *Markan Public Debate: Literary Technique, Concentric Structure, and Theology in Mark 2:1–3:6*. SBLDS 48. Chico, Calif.: Scholars Press.

Dibelius, M.
1971   *From Tradition to Gospel*. Cambridge: James Clarke (orig. 1933). [Cited as **Dibelius**]
1911   *Die urchristliche Überlieferung von Johannes der Täufer*. FRLANT. Göttingen: Vandenhoeck & Ruprecht.

Dickinson, E.
1970   *The Complete Poems of Emily Dickinson*, ed. T. H. Johnson. Boston and Toronto: Little, Brown.

Dillon, R. J.
1995   "'As One Having **Authority**' (Mark 1:22): The Controversial Distinction of Jesus' Teaching." *CBQ* 57: 92–113.

Dimant, D.
1995   "**Review of** P. A. **Tiller**, *A Commentary on the Animal Apocalypse of 1 Enoch*." *JBL* 114: 726–29.

Dodd, C. H.
1952   *According to the Scriptures: The Sub-structure of New Testament Theology*. London: Nisbet.
1980   *The Apostolic Preaching and Its Developments: With an Appendix on Eschatology and History*. Grand Rapids: Baker (orig. 1936).
1963   *Historical Tradition in the Fourth Gospel*. Cambridge: Cambridge University Press.
1961   *The Parables of the Kingdom*. Glasgow: Collins (orig. 1935).

Dölger, F. J.
1909   *Der Exorzismus im altchristlichen Taufritual. Eine religionsgeschichtliche Studie*. Studien zur Geschichte und Kultur des Altertums 3. Paderborn: Ferdinand Schöningh.

Donahue, J. R.
1973   *Are You the Christ?* SBLDS 10. Missoula: Society of Biblical Literature.
1996   "**Mark** 7:1–23: A Key to the Setting of Mark?" Conference paper for Mark seminar, Studiorum Novi Testamenti Societas. Strasbourg.
1992   "The **Quest** for the Community of Mark's Gospel." In *The Four Gospels 1992: Festschrift Frans Neirynck*, ed. F. Van Segbroeck et al. BETL 100, 2.817–38. Leuven: Leuven University Press.
1986   "**Recent Studies** on the Origin of 'Son of Man' in the Gospels." *CBQ* 48: 484–98.
1992   "**Tax Collector**." In *ABD*, 6.337–38.
1995   "**Windows** and Mirrors: The Setting of Mark's Gospel." *CBQ* 57: 1–26.

Donfried, K. P.
1980   "The **Feeding Narratives** and the Marcan Community: Mark 6,30–45 and 8,1–10." In *Kirche. Festschrift für Günther Bornkamm zum 75. Geburtstag*, ed. D. Lührmann and G. Strecker, 95–103. Tübingen: J. C. B. Mohr (Paul Siebeck).

Doty, M.
1990   "**Amazed** in Mark." *Notes on Translation* 4: 49–58.

Doudna, J. C.
1961   *The Greek of the Gospel of Mark*. JBLMS 12. Philadelphia: Society of Biblical Literature and Exegesis.

Douglas, M.
1984　　　*Purity and Danger: An Analysis of the Concepts of Pollution and Taboo.*
　　　　　London: Ark (orig. 1966).
Dowd, S. E.
1991　　　"The Gospel of Mark as Ancient Novel." *Lexington Theological Quarterly* 26: 53–59.
1988　　　*Prayer, Power, and the Problem of Suffering.* SBLDS 105. Atlanta: Scholars Press.
Downing, F. G.
1988　　　*Christ and the Cynics: Jesus and Other Radical Preachers in First-Century Tradition.* JSOT Manuals 4. Sheffield: Sheffield Academic Press.
Drinkard, J. F.
1992　　　"Direction and Orientation." In *ABD*, 2.204.
Drury, J.
1987　　　"Mark." In *The Literary Guide to the Bible*, ed. R. Alter and F. Kermode, 402–17. Cambridge, Mass.: Belknap Press of Harvard University Press.
1985　　　"Mark 1.1–15: An Interpretation." In *Alternative Approaches to New Testament Study*, ed. A. E. Harvey, 25–36. London: SPCK.
1985　　　*The Parables in the Gospels: History and Allegory.* London: SPCK.
Dschulnigg, P.
1984　　　*Sprache, Redaktion und Intention des Markus-Evangeliums. Eigentümlichkeiten der Sprache des Markus-Evangeliums und ihre Bedeutung für die Redaktionskritik.* SBB 11. Stuttgart: Katholisches Bibelwerk.
Dunderberg, I.
1998　　　"'Thomas' I-Sayings and the Gospel of John." In *Thomas at the Crossroads: Essays on the Gospel of Thomas*, ed. R. Uro. SNTW. Edinburgh: T. & T. Clark.
Dunn, J. D. G.
1970　　　*Baptism in the Holy Spirit.* London: SCM.
1990　　　*Jesus, Paul and the Law: Studies in Mark and Galatians.* Louisville: Westminster/John Knox.
1983　　　"The Messianic Secret in Mark." In *The Messianic Secret*, ed. C. Tuckett. IRT 1, 116–31. Philadelphia: Fortress; London: SPCK (orig. 1974).
Dupont, J.
1975　　　"Encore la parabole de la semence, qui pousse toute seule (Mk. 4,26–29)." In *Jesus und Paulus. Festschrift für Werner Georg Kümmel zum 70. Geburtstag*, ed. E. E. Ellis and E. Grässer, 96–101. Göttingen: Vandenhoeck & Ruprecht.
1967　　　"Le Parabole du semeur." *Foi et Vie* 66: 3–25.
1982　　　"La Transmission des parables de Jésus sur la lampe et la mesure dans Marc 4,21–25 et dans la tradition Q." In *Logia. Les Paroles de Jésus—the Sayings of Jesus. Memorial Joseph Coppens*, ed. J. Delobel. BETL 59, 201–36. Leuven: Leuven University Press/Peeters.
Dupont-Sommer, A.
1973　　　*The Essene Writings from Qumran.* Gloucester, Mass.: Peter Smith.
　　　　　[Cited as Dupont-Sommer]
Eckert, J.
1991　　　"*Kaleō, ktl.*" In *EDNT*, 2.240–44.

Edersheim, A.
1971   *The Life and Times of Jesus the Messiah.* Grand Rapids: Eerdmans (orig.
          1883).
Edwards, D.
1992   "Gennesaret." In *ABD*, 2.963.
Egger, W.
1976   *Frohbotschaft und Lehre. Die Sammelberichte des Wirkens Jesu im
          Markusevangelium.* Frankfurter Theologische Studien 19. Frankfurt:
          Knecht.
Ehrman, B. D.
1993   *The Orthodox Corruption of Scripture: The Effect of Early Christological
          Controversies on the Text of the New Testament.* New York and Oxford:
          Oxford University Press.
1991   "The Text of Mark in the Hands of the Orthodox." *LQ* 5: 143–56.
Eichrodt, W.
1961–67   *Theology of the Old Testament.* OTL. Philadelphia: Westminster.
Eisenman, R., and M. Wise
1992   *The Dead Sea Scrolls Uncovered: The First Complete Translation and In-
          terpretation of 50 Key Documents Withheld for Over 35 Years.* Shaftesbury,
          Dorset, and Rockport, Mass.: Element. [Cited as **Eisenman and Wise**]
Eisenstein, J. D.
1881   "The Sun, Rising and Setting of." In *JE*, 11.591–97.
Eitrem, S.
1966   *Some Notes on the Demonology in the New Testament.* 2nd ed. Symbolae
          Osloenses Fasc. Supplet. 20. Oslo: Universitetsforlaget.
Elbogen, I.
1913   *Der jüdische Gottesdienst in seiner geschichtlichen Entwicklung.* Leipzig:
          Fock.
Elliott, J. K.
1971   "The Conclusion of the Pericope of the Healing of the Leper and Mark
          i.45." *JTS* n.s. 22: 153–57.
Emden, C.
1953   "St. Mark's Debt to St. Peter." *CQR* 154: 61–71.
Encyclopaedia Judaica
1971–72   16 vols. Jerusalem: Keter. [Cited as ***EncJud***]
Ennulat, A.
1994   *Die "Minor Agreements." Untersuchungen zu einer offener Frage des
          synoptischen Problems.* WUNT, 2.62. Tübingen: J. C. B. Mohr (Paul
          Siebeck).
Ernst, J.
1989   *Johannes der Täufer. Interpretation—Geschichte—Wirkungsgeschichte.*
          BZNW 53. Berlin and New York: De Gruyter.
Evans, C. A.
1994   "Jesus in Non-Christian Sources." In *Studying the Historical Jesus: Eval-
          uations of the State of Current Research,* ed. B. Chilton and C. A. Evans.
          NTTS 19, 443–78. Leiden, New York, and Köln: Brill.
1989   *To See and Not Perceive: Isaiah 6.9–10 in Early Jewish and Christian In-
          terpretation.* JSOTSup 64. Sheffield: JSOT.

Evans, C. F.
1990   *Saint Luke*. New Testament Commentaries. London: SCM; Philadelphia: Trinity Press International.
Fanning, B. M.
1990   *Verbal Aspect in New Testament Greek*. Oxford: Clarendon.
Farmer, W. R.
1964   *The Synoptic Problem: A Critical Analysis*. New York: Macmillan.
Farrer, A. M.
1985   "On Dispensing with Q." In *The Two-Source Hypothesis: A Critical Appraisal*, ed. A. J. Bellinzoni, 321–56. Macon, Ga.: Mercer University Press (orig. 1955).
Faulkner, W.
1965   *The Mansion*. New York: Vintage Books (orig. 1955).
Fay, G.
1989   "Introduction to Incomprehension: The Literary Structure of Mark 4:1–34." *CBQ* 51: 65–81.
Fee, G. D.
1991   *The First Epistle to the Corinthians*. NICNT. Grand Rapids: Eerdmans.
Feldmeier, R.
1994   "Die Syrophönizierin (Mk 7,24–30)—Jesus 'verlorenes' Streitgespräch?" In *Die Heiden. Juden, Christen und das Problem des Fremden*, ed. R. Feldmeier and U. Heckel. WUNT 70, 211–27. Tübingen: J. C. B. Mohr (Paul Siebeck).
Fenton, J. C.
1957   "Paul and Mark." In *Studies in the Gospels: Essays in Memory of R. H. Lightfoot*, ed. D. E. Nineham, 89–112. Oxford: Basil Blackwell.
Ferguson, E., ed.
1990   *Encyclopaedia of Early Christianity*. New York and London: Garland. [Cited as *EEC*]
Field, F.
1899   *Notes on the Translation of the New Testament*. Cambridge: At the University Press.
Filson, F. V.
1960   *A Commentary on the Gospel according to St. Matthew*. Black's New Testament Commentaries. London: A. & C. Black.
Finley, M. I.
1980   *Ancient Slavery and Modern Ideology*. London: Penguin.
Finn, T. M.
1990   "Anointing." In *EEC*, 42–44. New York and London: Garland.
Finney, P. C.
1994   *The Invisible God: The Earliest Christians on Art*. New York and Oxford: Oxford University Press.
Fishbane, M.
1985   *Biblical Interpretation in Ancient Israel*. Oxford: Clarendon.
Fitzmyer, J. A.
1974   "The Aramaic Qorbān Inscription from Jebel Hallet et-Turi and Mk 7:11/Mt 15:5." In *Essays on the Semitic Background of the New Testament*. SBS 5, 93–100. Missoula: Scholars Press (orig. 1959).

1971   "'4Q Testimonia' and the New Testament." In *Essays on the Semitic Background of the New Testament*. SBS 5, 59–89. Missoula: Scholars Press.

1971   *The Genesis Apocryphon of Qumran Cave 1: A Commentary*. 2nd ed. BibOr 18A. Rome: Biblical Institute Press.

1981–85 *The Gospel according to Luke*. AB 28 and 28A. New York: Doubleday.

1971   "The Oxyrhynchus *Logoi* of Jesus and the Coptic Gospel according to Thomas." In *Essays on the Semitic Background of the New Testament*. SBS 5, 355–433. Missoula: Scholars Press (orig. 1959).

1981   "The Priority of Mark and the 'Q' Source in Luke." In *To Advance the Gospel: New Testament Studies*, 3–40. New York: Crossroad (orig. 1970).

1979   "The Semitic Background of the New Testament Kyrios-Title." In *A Wandering Aramean: Collected Aramaic Essays*. SBLMS 25, 115–42. Missoula: Scholars Press (orig. 1975).

Fleddermann, H. T.

1995   *Mark and Q: A Study of the Overlap Texts: With an Assessment by F. Neirynck*. BETL 122. Leuven: Leuven University Press.

Flinterman, J.

1995   *Power, Paideia and Pythagoreanism: Greek Identity, Conceptions of the Relationship between Philosophers and Monarchs, and Political Ideas in Philostratus' Life of Apollonius*. Dutch Monographs on Ancient History and Archaeology 13. Amsterdam: J. C. Gieben.

Flusser, D.

1988   "Qumran und die Zwölf." In *Judaism and the Origins of Christianity*, 134–46. Jerusalem: Magnes (orig. 1965).

1981   *Die rabbinischen Gleichnisse und der Gleichniserzähler Jesus. Teil 1, Das Wesen der Gleichnisse*. Judaica et Christiana 4. Bern, Frankfurt am Main, and Las Vegas: Peter Lang.

Focant, C.

1993   "Mc 7,24–31 par. Mt 15,21–29. Critique des sources et/ou étude narrative." In *The Synoptic Gospels: Source Criticism and the New Literary Criticism*, ed. C. Focant. BETL 110, 39–75. Leuven: Leuven University Press.

Foerster, W.

1964   "Eirēnē, *ktl.*" In *TDNT*, 2.400–420.

1964   "Exestin, *ktl.*" In *TDNT*, 2.560–75.

Foerster, W., and G. Fohrer.

1971   "Sǭzō, *ktl.*" In *TDNT*, 7.965–1024.

Forsyth, N.

1987   *The Old Enemy: Satan and the Combat Myth*. Princeton: Princeton University Press.

Fowler, R. M.

1981   *Loaves and Fishes: The Function of the Feeding Stories in the Gospel of Mark*. SBLDS 54. Chico: Scholars Press.

Francis, D.

1994   *Evil in the Gospel of Mark: An Exploration*. B.D. honours diss., University of Glasgow.

N.d.   *Jesus and the Self in the Gospel of Mark*. Ph.D. diss., University of Glasgow. Forthcoming.

Fredriksen, P.
1995   "**Did Jesus** Oppose Purity Laws?" *BibRev* 11: 18–25, 42–47.

Freedman, D. N., ed.
1992   *The Anchor Bible Dictionary*. 6 vols. New York: Doubleday. [Cited as **ABD**]

Freedman, H., and M. Simon, eds.
1977   *The Midrash Rabbah*. 5 vols. London, Jerusalem, and New York: Soncino (orig. 1938).

Friedman, M.
1982   *Martin Buber's Life and Work: The Early Years 1878–1923*. London and Tunbridge Wells: Search.

Friedrich, G.
1964   "*Euangelizomai, ktl.*" In *TDNT*, 2.707–37.
1965   "*Kēryx, ktl.*" In *TDNT*, 3.683–718.

Friedrichsen, T. A.
1992   "'Minor' and 'Major' **Matthew-Luke Agreements** against Mk 4,30–32." In *The Four Gospels 1992: Festchrift Frans Neirynck*. BETL 100, 1.649–76. Leuven: Leuven University Press.

Fuchs, A.
1993   "Die 'Seesturmperikope' Mk 4,35–41 parr. im Wandel der urkirklichen Verkündigung." In *Minor Agreements: Symposium Göttingen 1991*, ed. G. Strecker. GTA 50, 65–92. Göttingen: Vandenhoeck & Ruprecht.

Funk, R. W.
1973   "The **Looking-Glass** Tree Is for the Birds: Ezekiel 17:22–24; Mark 4:30–32." *Int* 27: 3–9.

Fusco, V.
1982   "L'Accord mineur Mt 13,11a/Lk 8,10a contre Mc 4,11a." In *Logia. Les Paroles de Jesus. Memorial Joseph Coppens*, ed. J. Delobel. BETL 59, 355–61. Leuven: Peeters.
1980   *Parola e regno. La sezione delle parabole (Mc. 4,1–34) nella prospettiva marciana*. Alosiana 13. Brescia: Morcelliana.

Gamble, H. Y.
1995   *Books and Readers in the Early Church: A History of Early Christian Texts*. New Haven and London: Yale University Press.

García Martínez, F.
1994   *The Dead Sea Scrolls Translated: The Qumran Texts in English*. Leiden: Brill.

García Martínez, F., and J. Trebolle Barrera
1995   *The People of the Dead Sea Scrolls: Their Writings, Beliefs and Practices*. Leiden, New York, and Köln: Brill.

Garrett, S. R.
1989   *The Demise of the Devil: Magic and the Demonic in Luke's Writings*. Minneapolis: Fortress.

Garrow, D. J.
1986   *Bearing the Cross: Martin Luther King, Jr., and the Southern Christian Leadership Conference*. New York: William Morrow.

Gärtner, B.
1959   *John 6 and the Jewish Passover*. ConNT 17. Lund: Gleerup.

Geddert, T. J.
1989   *Watchwords: Mark 13 in Markan Eschatology.* JSNTSup 26. Sheffield: JSOT.

Geller, M. J.
1977   "Jesus' **Theurgic** Powers: Parallels in the Talmud and Incantation Bowls." *JJS* 28: 141–55.

Gibson, J. B.
1990   "Jesus' **Refusal** to Produce a 'Sign' (Mk 8.11–13)." *JSNT* 38: 37–66.
1995   *The Temptations of Jesus in Early Christianity.* JSNTSup 112. Sheffield: Sheffield Academic Press.

Ginzberg, L.
1909–38   *The Legends of the Jews.* 7 vols. Philadelphia: Jewish Publication Society. [Cited as **Ginzberg**]

Glasson, T. F.
1981   "The **Place** of the Anecdote: A Note on Form Criticism." *JTS* 32: 142–50.

Gnilka, J.
1978–79   *Das Evangelium nach Markus.* 2 vols. EKKNT 2. Zürich: Benziger; Neukirchen: Neukirchener Verlag. [Cited as **Gnilka**]
1973   "Das **Martyrium** Johannes' des Täufers (Mk 6,17–29)." In *Orientierung an Jesus. Zur Theologie der Synoptiker. Für Josef Schmid,* ed. P. Hoffmann, 78–92. Freiburg, Basel, and Wien: Herder.
1961   *Die Verstockung Israels. Isaias 6,9–10 in der Theologie der Synoptiker.* SANT 3. München: Kösel.

Goodenough, E. R.
1954   *Jewish Symbols in the Greco-Roman Period.* Vol. 4, *The Problem of Method: Symbols from the Jewish Cult.* Bollingen Series 37. New York: Pantheon.

Goulder, M. D.
1978   *The Evangelists' Calendar: A Lectionary Explanation of the Development of Scripture.* London: SPCK.
1991   "**Those Outside** (Mk. 4:10–12)." *NovT* 33: 289–302.

Grabbe, L. L.
1992   *Judaism from Cyrus to Hadrian.* 2 vols. Minneapolis: Fortress.

Grässer, E.
1975   "Beobachtungen zum **Menschensohn** in Hebr 2,6." In *Jesus und der Menschensohn. Für Anton Vögtle,* ed. R. Pesch and R. Schnackenburg, 404–14. Freiburg, Basel, and Wien: Herder.
1969–70   "Jesus in Nazareth (**Mark VI.1–6a**): Notes on the Redaction and Theology of St Mark." *NTS* 16: 1–23.

Gray, R.
1993   *Prophetic Figures in Late Second Temple Jewish Palestine: The Evidence from Josephus.* New York and Oxford: Oxford University Press.

Green, W. C.
1979   "Palestinian **Holy Men**: Charismatic Leadership and Rabbinic Tradition." In ANRW II.19.2, 619–47.

Greeven, H.
1968   "*Peristera.*" In *TDNT,* 6.63–72.

Griesbach, J. J.
1977   "A Demonstration That Mark Was Written after Matthew and Luke." In
           J. J. Griesbach: Synoptic and Text-Critical Studies 1776–1976, ed. B. Or-
           chard and T. R. W. Longstaff, 103–35. Cambridge: Cambridge University
           Press (orig. 1789–90).
Griffin, M. T.
1992   "Nero." In ABD, 4.1076–81.
Gruenwald, I.
1980   Apocalyptic and Merkavah Mysticism. AGJU 14. Leiden and Köln: Brill.
Guelich, R.
1982   " 'The Beginning of the Gospel': Mark 1:1–15." BR 27: 5–15.
1983   "The Gospel Genre." In Das Evangelium und die Evangelien, ed. P. Stuhl-
           macher. WUNT 28, 183–219. Tübingen: J. C. B. Mohr (Paul Siebeck).
1989   Mark 1–8:26. WBC 34. Dallas: Word. [Cited as Guelich]
Guillemette, P.
1978   "Mc 1,24 est-il une formule de défense magique?" ScEs 30: 81–96.
Gundry, R. H.
1993   Mark: A Commentary on His Apology for the Cross. Grand Rapids: Eerd-
           mans. [Cited as Gundry]
1967   The Use of the Old Testament in St. Matthew's Gospel. NovTSup 18.
           Leiden: Brill.
Gunkel, H.
1906   Elias, Jahve und Baal. Leipzig.
Hahn, F.
1963   Christologische Hoheitstitel. Ihre Geschichte im frühen Christentum.
           FRLANT 83. Göttingen: Vandenhoeck & Ruprecht.
Hamilton, G. H.
1996   "A New Hebrew-Aramaic Incantation Text from Galilee: 'Rebuking the
           Sea.' " JSS 41: 215–49.
Hanson, P. D.
1976   "Apocalypse, Genre." In IDBS, 27–28.
1976   "Apocalypticism." In IDBS, 28–34.
Harder, G.
1948–49   "Das Gleichnis von der selbstwachsenden Saat Mk 4,26–29." ThViat 1:
           51–70.
Harrington, D. J.
1991   "Sabbath Tensions: Matthew 12:1–14 and Other New Testament Texts."
           In The Sabbath in Jewish and Christian Traditions, ed. T. Eskenazi et al.,
           45–56. New York: Crossroad.
Harrington, H. H.
1995   "Did the Pharisees Eat Ordinary Food in a State of Ritual Purity?" JSJ
           26: 42–54.
Harris, R.
1916–20   Testimonies. 2 vols. Cambridge: Cambridge University Press.
Hartman, L.
1996   "Das Markusevangelium, 'für die lectio sollemnis im Gottesdienst abge-
           fasst'?" In Geschichte-Tradition-Reflexion. Festschrift für Martin Hengel
           zum 70. Geburtstag. Band 3, Frühes Christentum, ed. H. Cancik et al.,
           147–71. Tübingen: J. C. B. Mohr (Paul Siebeck).

Hassler, I.
1934 "The **Incident** of the Syrophoenician Woman (Matt XV,21–28; Mark VII,24–30." *ET* 45: 459–61.

Hastings, J., et al.
1909 *Dictionary of the Bible*. Edinburgh: T. & T. Clark.

Hauck, F.
1965 "*Koinos, ktl*." In *TDNT*, 3.789–809.

Hauptman, J.
1974 "**Images** of Women in the Talmud." In *Religion and Sexism*, ed. R. E. Ruether, 184–212. New York: Simon & Schuster.

"**Havdalah**."
1972 In *EncJud*, 7.1481–89.

Head, P. M.
1997 *Christology and the Synoptic Problem: An Argument for Markan Priority*. SNTSMS 94. Cambridge: Cambridge University Press.

Hedrick, C. W.
1984 "The Role of '**Summary Statements**' in the Composition of the Gospel of Mark: A Dialog with Karl Schmidt and Norman Perrin." *NovT* 26: 289–311.

Heil, J. P.
1981 *Jesus Walking on the Sea: Meaning and Gospel Functions of Matt 14:22–33, Mark 6:45–52 and John 6:15b–21*. AnBib 87. Rome: Biblical Institute Press.

Heilman, S.
1992 *Defenders of the Faith: Inside Ultra-Orthodox Jewry*. New York: Schocken.

Held, M.
1968 "The **Root** ZBL/SBL in Akkadian, Ugaritic and Biblical Hebrew." *JAOS* 88: 90–96.

Hellholm, D., ed.
1983 *Apocalypticism in the Mediterranean World and the Near East: Proceedings of the International Colloquium on Apocalypticism, Uppsala, August 12–17, 1979*. Tübingen: J. C. B. Mohr (Paul Siebeck).

Hengel, M.
1981 *The Charismatic Leader and His Followers*. SNTW. New York: Crossroad (orig. 1968).
1974 *Judaism and Hellenism: Studies in Their Encounter in Palestine during the Early Hellenistic Period*. 2 vols. in 1. Philadelphia: Fortress.
1969 "**Mc 7.3** PUGMĘ. Die Geschichte einer exegetischen Aporie und der Versuch ihrer Lösung." ZNW 60: 182–98.
1985 *Studies in the Gospel of Mark*. Philadelphia: Fortress.
1989 *The Zealots: Investigations into the Jewish Freedom Movement in the Period from Herod I until 70 A.D.* Edinburgh: T. & T. Clark (orig. 1961).

Herr, M.
1979 "**Continuum** in the Chain of Torah Transmission" (in Hebrew). *Zion* 44: 43–56.

Herzog, J. J.
1896– *Realencyklopädie für protestantische Theologie und Kirche*. 24 vols. Ed.
1913 A. Hauck. Leipzig: J. H. Hinrichs. [Cited as *RE*]

Hiers, R. H.
1985   "'Binding' and 'Loosing': The Matthean Authorizations." *JBL* 104: 233–50.
Hill, C. C.
1992   *Hellenists and Hebrews: Reappraising Division within the Earliest Church.* Minneapolis: Fortress.
Hock, R. F.
1992   "Cynics." In *ABD*, 1.1221–26.
Hoehner, H. W.
1972   *Herod Antipas.* SNTSMS 17. Cambridge: Cambridge University Press.
Hofius, O.
1994   "Jesu Zuspruch der Sündenvergebung. Exegetische Erwägungen zu Mk 2,5b." *Jahrbuch für Biblische Theologie* 9: 125–45.
Hogan, L. P.
1992   *Healing in the Second Temple Period.* NTOA 21. Freiburg: Universitätsverlag Freiburg; Göttingen: Vandenhoeck & Ruprecht.
Holtzmann, H. J.
1863   *Die synoptischen Evangelien. Ihr Ursprung und geschichtlicher Charakter.* Leipzig: Wilhelm Engelmann.
Hooker, M. D.
1991   A *Commentary on the Gospel according to St Mark.* Black's New Testament Commentaries. London: A&C Black. [Cited as **Hooker**]
1967   *The Son of Man in Mark: A Study of the Background of the Term "Son of Man" and Its Use in St. Mark's Gospel.* London: SPCK.
1982   "Trial and Tribulation in Mark XIII." *BJRL* 65: 78–99.
Horbury, W.
1986   "The Twelve and the Phylarchs." *NTS* 32: 503–27.
Horman, J.
1979   "The Source of the Version of the Parable of the Sower in the Gospel of Thomas." *NovT* 21 (1979): 326–43.
Horsley, G. H. R.
1992   "Names, Double." In *ABD*, 4.1011–17.
Horsley, R. A.
1993   *Jesus and the Spiral of Violence: Popular Jewish Resistance in Roman Palestine.* Minneapolis: Fortress.
Horsley, R. A., and J. S. Hanson
1985   *Bandits, Prophets, and Messiahs: Popular Movements at the Time of Jesus.* New Voices in Biblical Studies. San Francisco: Harper & Row.
Howard, G.
1977   "The Tetragram and the New Testament." *JBL* 96: 63–83.
Hübner, H.
1973   *Das Gesetz in der synoptischen Tradition.* Witten: Luther-Verlag.
Hull, J. M.
1974   *Hellenistic Magic and the Synoptic Tradition.* SBT Second Series 28. London: SCM.
Hultgren, A. J.
1979   *Jesus and His Adversaries: The Form and Function of the Conflict Stories in the Synoptic Tradition.* Minneapolis: Augsburg.
Hunkin, J. W.
1924   "'Pleonastic' ARCHOMAI in the New Testament." *JTS* 25: 390–402.

Hurtado, L. W.
1990   "The Gospel of Mark: **Evolutionary** or Revolutionary Document?"
        JSNT 40: 15–32.
1988   *One God, One Lord: Early Christian Devotion and Ancient Jewish Mono-theism.* London: SCM.

Ilan, T.
1992   "'**Man** Born of Woman . . .' (Job 14:1): The Phenomenon of Men Bear-ing Metronymes at the Time of Jesus." *NovT* 34: 23–45.

Jacobson, H.
1983   *The **Exagoge** of Ezekiel.* Cambridge: Cambridge University Press.

Jastrow, M.
1982   *A Dictionary of the Targumim, the Talmud Babli and Yerushalmi, and the Midrashic Literature.* New York: Judaica (orig. 1886–1903). [Cited as **Jastrow**]

Jeremias, J.
1966   *The **Eucharistic** Words of Jesus.* Philadelphia: Fortress.
1969   *Jerusalem in the Time of Jesus: An Investigation into Economic and So-cial Conditions during the Time of Jesus.* Philadelphia: Fortress.
1971   *New Testament Theology.* Part 1, *The Proclamation of Jesus.* London: SCM.
1959   "**Paarweise** Sendung im Neuen Testament." In *New Testament Essays: Studies in Memory of Thomas Walter Manson 1893–1958,* ed. A. J. B. Higgins, 136–43. Manchester: Manchester University Press.
1972   *The **Parables** of Jesus.* 2nd rev. ed. New York: Scribner's (orig. 1954).

Jervell, J.
1960   *Imago Dei. Gen. 1,26f. im Spätjudentum, in der Gnosis und in den pauli-nischen Briefen.* FRLANT 76. Göttingen: Vandenhoeck & Ruprecht.

Jewett, R.
1970–71 "The **Agitators** and the Galatians Congregation." *NTS* 17: 198–212.
The Jewish Encyclopedia. See under Adler 1881.

Juel, D. H.
1990   *Mark.* Augsburg Commentary on the New Testament. Minneapolis: Augsburg. [Cited as **Juel**]
1994   *A Master of Surprise: Mark Interpreted.* Minneapolis: Fortress.
1973   *Messiah and Temple: The Trial of Jesus in the Gospel of Mark.* SBLDS 31. Missoula: Scholars Press.

Jülicher, A.
1910   *Die **Gleichnisreden** Jesu.* 2nd ed. Tübingen: Mohr (orig. 1888).
1903   "**Marcus** im NT." In *RE,* 12.288–97.

Kahle, P.
1957   "**Problems** of the Septuagint." In *Studia Patristica.* TU 63, 1.329–32. Berlin: Akademie.

Kähler, M.
1964   *The **So-Called** Historical Jesus and the Historic Biblical Christ.* Philadel-phia: Fortress (orig. 1892).

Kalmin, R.
1994   "**Christians** and Heretics in Rabbinic Literature of Late Antiquity." *HTR* 87: 155–69.

Käsemann, E.
1969   "The **Beginnings** of Christian Theology." In *New Testament Questions of Today*, 82–107. Philadelphia: Fortress (orig. 1960).
1969   *Jesus Means Freedom*. Philadelphia: Fortress.
1964   "The **Problem** of the Historical Jesus." In *Essays on New Testament Themes*, 15–47. Philadelphia: Fortress (orig. 1954).
1971   "The **Saving Significance** of the Death of Jesus in Paul." In *Perspectives on Paul*, 32–59. Philadelphia: Fortress.

Kautzsch, E., and A. E. Cowley
1910   *Gesenius' Hebrew Grammar*. 2nd ed. Oxford: At the Clarendon. [Cited as **Gesenius**]

Kazmierski, C. R.
1979   *Jesus, the Son of God: A Study of the Markan Tradition and Its Redaction by the Evangelist*. FB 33. Würzburg: Echter.

Keck, L. E.
1965–66   "The **Introduction** to Mark's Gospel." *NTS* 12: 352–70.
1965   "**Mark 3:7–12** and Mark's Christology." *JBL* 84: 341–58.
1970   "The **Spirit** and the Dove." *NTS* 17: 41–67.

Keck, L. E., and G. M. Tucker
1976   "**Exegesis**." In *IDBS*, 296–303.

Kee, H. C.
1975   "The **Function** of Scriptural Quotations and Allusions in Mark 11–16." In *Jesus und Paulus. Festschrift für Werner Georg Kümmel zum 70. Geburtstag*, ed. E. E. Ellis and E. Grässer, 165–88. Göttingen: Vandenhoeck & Ruprecht.
1967–68   "The **Terminology** of Mark's Exorcism Stories." *NTS* 14: 232–46.

Kelber, W.
1974   *The **Kingdom** in Mark: A New Place and a New Time*. Philadelphia: Fortress.
1979   *Mark's Story of Jesus*. Philadelphia: Fortress.
1983   *The Oral and the Written Gospel: The Hermeneutics of Speaking and Writing in the Synoptic Tradition, Mark, Paul, and Q*. Philadelphia: Fortress.

Kelly, H. A.
1985   *The **Devil** at Baptism: Ritual, Theology, and Drama*. Ithaca and London: Cornell University Press.

Kennedy, D.
1992   "**Roman Army**." In *ABD*, 5.789–98.

Kermode, F.
1979   *The **Genesis** of Secrecy: On the Interpretation of Narrative*. Cambridge, Mass., and London: Harvard University Press.

Kertelge, K.
1970   *Die Wunder Jesu im Markusevangelium. Eine redaktionsgeschichtliche Untersuchung*. SANT 23. München: Kösel.

Kiilunen, J.
1985   *Die **Vollmacht** im Widerstreit. Untersuchungen zum Werdegang von Mk 2,1–3,6*. Annales Academiae Scientiarum Fennicae Dissertationes Humanarum Litterarum 40. Helsinki: Suomalainen Tiedeakatemia.

Kilpatrick, G. D.
1946   *The **Origins** of the Gospel according to St. Matthew*. Oxford: Clarendon.

Kimelman, R.
1997 "The **Messiah** of the Amidah: A Study in Comparative Messianism."
JBL 116: 313–20.

Kingsbury, J. D.
1983 *The Christology of Mark's Gospel.* Philadelphia: Fortress.
1981 "The 'Divine Man' as the Key to Mark's Christology—the End of an
Era?" *Int* 35: 243–57.

Kittel, G.
1964 "*Akoloutheō, ktl.*" In *TDNT*, 1.210–16.
1967 "*Legō, ktl.*" In *TDNT*, 4.69–192.

Kittel, G., and G. Friedrich, eds.
1964–76 *Theological Dictionary of the New Testament.* 10 vols. Grand Rapids:
Eerdmans. [Cited as **TDNT**]

Klauck, H. J.
1978 *Allegorie und Allegorese in synoptischen Gleichnistexten.* NTAbh 13.
Münster: Aschendorff.
1981 "Die **Frage** der Sündenvergebung in der Perikope von der Heilung des
Gelähmten (Mk 2,1–12 parr.)." *BZ* n.f. 25: 223–48.

Klausner, J.
1929 *Jesus of Nazareth: His Life, Times, and Teaching.* New York: Macmillan
(orig. 1925).
1955 *The Messianic Idea in Israel: From Its Beginning to the Completion of the
Mishnah.* New York: Macmillan.

Kloppenborg, J. S.
1988 *Q Parallels: Synopsis, Critical Notes and Concordance.* Foundations &
Facets Reference Series. Sonoma, Calif.: Polebridge.

Koch, D.-A.
1975 *Die Bedeutung der Wundererzählungen für die Christologie des Markus-
evangeliums.* Berlin: De Gruyter.

Koester, C.
1989 "The **Origin** and Significance of the Flight to Pella Tradition." *CBQ* 51:
90–106.

Koester, H.
1990 *Ancient Christian Gospels: Their History and Development.* London:
SCM; Philadelphia: Trinity Press International.
1983 "**History** and Development of Mark's Gospel (from Mark to Secret Mark
and 'Canonical' Mark)." In *Colloquy on New Testament Studies: A Time
for Reappraisal and Fresh Approaches,* ed. B. Corley, 35–57. Macon, Ga.:
Mercer University Press.
1982 *Introduction to the New Testament.* 2 vols. Philadelphia: Fortress.
1971 "A **Test Case** of Synoptic Source Theory (Mark 4:1–34 and Parallels)."
SBL Gospels Seminar. Atlanta.
1983 "Three **Thomas Parables.**" In *The New Testament and Gnosis: Essays in
Honour of Robert McL. Wilson,* ed. A. H. B. Logan and A. J. M. Wedderburn, 195–203. Edinburgh: T. & T. Clark.

Kohler, K.
1991 "**Habdalah.**" In *JE,* 6.118–21.

Kollmann, B.
1991 "Jesu **Schweigegebote** an die Dämonen." *ZNW* 82: 267–73.

1996 *Jesus und die Christen als Wundertäter. Studien zu Magie, Medizin und Schamanismus in Antike und Christentum.* FRLANT 170. Göttingen: Vandenhoeck & Ruprecht.

Kraft, R. A.
1994 "Re: Which James?" IOUDAIOS-L Electronic Bulletin Board, November 11, 1994.

Kramer, W.
1966 *Christ, Lord, Son of God.* SBT 50. London: SCM.

Kruse, H.
1954 "Die 'dialektische Negation' als semitisches Idiom." *VT* 4: 385–400.
1977 "Das Reich Satans." *Bib* 58: 29–71.

Kugel, J. L.
1981 *The Idea of Biblical Poetry: Parallelism and Its History.* New Haven: Yale University Press.
1990 *In Potiphar's House: The Interpretive Life of Biblical Texts.* Cambridge, Mass., and London: Harvard University Press.

Kuhn, H.-W.
1971 *Ältere Sammlungen im Markusevangelium.* SUNT 8. Göttingen: Vandenhoeck & Ruprecht.

Kümmel, W. G.
1975 *Introduction to the New Testament.* Nashville: Abingdon.
1957 *Promise and Fulfillment: The Eschatological Message of Jesus.* London: SCM.

Kuthirakkattel, S.
1990 *The Beginning of Jesus' Ministry according to Mark's Gospel (1,14–3,6): A Redaction Critical Study.* AnBib 123. Rome: Pontifical Biblical Institute.

Kysar, R.
1992 "John, the Gospel of." In *ABD*, 3.912–31.

Lagrange, M. J.
1920 *Évangile selon Saint Marc.* 2nd ed. Ebib. Paris: Lecoffre (orig. 1910). [Cited as **Lagrange**]

Lambrecht, J.
1992 "John the Baptist and Jesus in Mark 1.1–15: Markan Redaction of Q?" *NTS* 38: 357–84.
1974 "Redaction and Theology in Mk. IV." In *L'Évangile selon Marc. Tradition et rédaction*, ed. M. Sabbe. BETL 34, 269–307. Leuven: Leuven University Press.

Lampe, G. W. H.
1951 *The Seal of the Spirit: A Study in the Doctrine of Baptism and Confirmation in the New Testament and the Fathers.* London, New York, and Toronto: Longmans, Green.
1972–73 "St. Peter's Denial." *BJRL* 55: 346–68.

Lampe, P.
1992 "Rufus." In *ABD*, 5.839.
1989 *Die stadtrömischen Christen in den ersten beiden Jahrhunderten. Untersuchungen zur Sozialgeschichte.* WUNT, 2.18. Tübingen: J. C. B. Mohr (Paul Siebeck).

Landau, D.
1993   *Piety and Power: The World of Jewish Fundamentalism*. London: Secker & Warburg.

Lane, W. L.
1974   *The Gospel of Mark*. NICNT. Grand Rapids: Eerdmans. [Cited as **Lane**]
1991   *Hebrews*. WBC 47AB. Dallas: Word.

Lang, F. G.
1978   "'Über Sidon Mitten ins Gebiet der Dekapolis.' Geographie und Theologie in Markus 7,31." *ZDPV* 94: 145–60.

LaSor, W. S.
1972   *The Dead Sea Scrolls and the New Testament*. Grand Rapids: Eerdmans.

Laufen, R.
1980   *Die Doppelüberlieferungen der Logienquelle und des Markusevangeliums*. BBB 54. Bonn: Peter Hanstein. [Cited as **Laufen**]

Lauterbach, J.
1961   *Mekilta de-Rabbi Ishmael*. 3 vols. Philadelphia: Jewish Publication Society (orig. 1933–35). [Cited as **Lauterbach**]

Lehmann, K.
1968   *Auferweckt am dritten Tag nach der Schrift. Früheste Christologie, Bekenntnisbildung und Schriftauslegung im Lichte von 1 Kor. 15,3–5*. QD 38. Freiburg, Basel, and Wien: Herder.

Lemcio, E. E.
1978   "External **Evidence** for the Structure and Function of Mark IV.1–20, VII.14–23 and VIII.14–21." *JTS* 29: 323–38.

Lentzen-Deis, F.
1970   *Die Taufe Jesu nach den Synoptikern*. Frankfurter Theologische Studien 4. Frankfurt: Knecht.

Levenson, J. D.
1993   *The Death and Resurrection of the Beloved Son: The Transformation of Child Sacrifice in Judaism and Christianity*. New Haven and London: Yale University Press.

Lewis, T. J.
1992   "**Beelzebul**." In *ABD*, 1.638–40.

Liddell, H. G., R. Scott, and S. Jones
1968   *A Greek-English Lexicon with a Supplement*. Oxford: Clarendon. [Cited as **LSJ**]

LiDonnici, L. R.
1995   *The Epidaurian Miracle Inscriptions: Text, Translation and Commentary*. Texts and Translations 36; Graeco-Roman Religion Series 11. Atlanta: Scholars Press.

Lieberman, S.
1955   *Tosefta Ki-Fshuṭah: A Comprehensive Commentary on the Tosefta*. 9 vols. New York: Jewish Theological Seminary.

Lightfoot, J. B.
1980   *Saint Paul's Epistle to the Philippians: A Revised Text with Introduction, Notes, and Dissertations*. London: Macmillan.

Lightfoot, R. H.
1950   *The Gospel Message of St. Mark*. Oxford: Clarendon.
1935   *History and Interpretation in the Gospels*. London: Hodder & Stoughton.

Lincoln, A. T.
1990   *Ephesians*. WBC 42. Dallas: Word.
Lindars, B.
1983   *Jesus Son of Man: A Fresh Examination of the Son of Man Sayings in the Gospels in the Light of Recent Research*. Grand Rapids: Eerdmans.
Lindeskog, G.
1950   "Logia-Studien." *ST* 4: 129–84.
Lindsey, R. L.
1953   "A Modified Two-Document Theory of Synoptic Dependence and Interdependence." *NovT* 6: 239–63.
Linton, O.
1965   "The Demand for a Sign from Heaven. Mk 8,11–12 and Parallels." *ST* 19: 112–29.
Lohmeyer, E.
1951   *Das Evangelium des Markus*. 11th ed. MeyerK. Göttingen: Vandenhoeck & Ruprecht (orig. 1937). [Cited as Lohmeyer]
1936   *Galiläa und Jerusalem*. FRLANT. Göttingen: Vandenhoeck & Ruprecht.
Loisy, A.
1912   *L'Évangile selon Marc*. Paris: Émile Nourry.
Lövestam, E.
1995   *Jesus and "This Generation": A New Testament Study*. ConBNT 25. Stockholm: Almqvist & Wiksell.
Lührmann, D.
1992   "Faith" and "Faith, New Testament." In *ABD*, 2.744–60.
1987   *Das Markusevangelium*. HNT 3. Tübingen: J. C. B. Mohr (Paul Siebeck). [Cited as Lührmann]
1987   "Die Pharisäer und die Schriftgelehrten im Markusevangelium." *ZNW* 78: 169–85.
Luz, U.
1980   "Markusforschung in der Sackgasse?" *TLZ* 9: 641–55.
1983   "The Secrecy Motif and the Marcan Christology." In *The Messianic Secret*, ed. C. Tuckett. IRT 1, 75–96. Philadelphia: Fortress; London: SPCK (orig. 1965).
Mack, B.
1988   *A Myth of Innocence: Mark and Christian Origins*. Philadelphia: Fortress.
Mack, B., and V. K. Robbins
1989   *Patterns of Persuasion in the Gospels*. Foundations and Facets. Sonoma, Calif.: Polebridge.
MacMullen, R.
1984   *Christianizing the Roman Empire* (A.D. 100–400). New Haven and London: Yale University Press.
1981   *Paganism in the Roman Empire*. New Haven and London: Yale University Press.
Madden, P. J.
1997   *Jesus' Walking on the Sea: An Investigation of the Origin of the Narrative Account*. BZNW 81. Berlin and New York: De Gruyter.
Magill, T. F.
1996   *Markan Controversy Dialogues and the Chreia Tradition: An Investigation of the Rhetorical Dimensions of Selected Markan Pericopes (2.15–17,*

18–22, 23–28, 3.22–30; 7.1–23; 11.27–33) in Light of Their Redaction, Form, and Transmission Histories. Ph.D. diss., University of Glasgow.

Mahnke, H.
1978   *Die Versuchungsgeschichte im Rahmen der synoptischen Evangelien. Ein Beitrag zur frühen Christologie.* BBET 9. Frankfurt am Main, Bern, and Las Vegas: Peter Lang.

Maier, J.
1978   *Jesus von Nazareth in der talmudischen Überlieferung.* ErFor 82. Darmstadt: Wissenschaftliche Buchgesellschaft.

Malbon, E. S.
1983   "**Fallible Followers**: Women and Men in the Gospel of Mark." *Semeia* 28: 29–48.
1985   "*TĒ OIKIA AUTOU*: **Mark 2.15** in Context." *NTS* 31, 282–92.

Malherbe, A. J.
1980   "**Medical Imagery** in the Pastoral Epistles." In *Texts and Testaments: Critical Essays on the Bible and Early Church Fathers,* ed. W. E. March, 19–35. San Antonio: Trinity University Press.

Maloney, E. C.
1981   *Semitic Interference in Marcan Syntax.* SBLDS 51. Chico, Calif.: Scholars Press.

Mánek, J.
1958   "**Fishers** of Men." *NovT* 2: 138–41.

Mann, C. S.
1986   *Mark: A New Translation with Introduction and Commentary.* AB 27. Garden City, N.Y.: Doubleday. [Cited as **Mann**]

Manson, T. W.
1949   *The Sayings of Jesus as Recorded in the Gospels according to St. Matthew and St. Luke.* London: SCM (orig. 1937).
1935   *The Teaching of Jesus.* 2nd ed. Cambridge: Cambridge University Press (orig. 1931).

Marcus, J.
1994   "**Authority** to Forgive Sins upon the Earth: The Shema in the Gospel of Mark." In *The Gospels and the Scriptures of Israel,* ed. C. A. Evans and W. Stegner. JSNTSup 104/SSEJC 3, 196–211. Sheffield: Sheffield Academic Press.
1999   "The **Beelzebul** Controversy and the Eschatologies of Jesus." In *Authenticating the Activities of Jesus,* ed. B. Chilton and C. A. Evans, 247–77. NTTS 28.2. Leiden: Brill.
1997   "**Blanks** and Gaps in the Parable of the Sower." *Biblical Interpretation* 5: 1–16.
1986   "**Entering** into the Kingly Power of God." *JBL* 107: 663–75.
1982   "The **Evil Inclination** in the Epistle of **James**." *CBQ* 44: 606–21.
1986   "The **Evil Inclination** in the Letters of **Paul**." *IBS*: 8–21.
1995   "**Jesus' Baptismal** Vision." *NTS* 41: 512–21.
1992   "The **Jewish War** and the Sitz im Leben of Mark." *JBL* 111: 441–62.
1988   "**Mark 14:61**: Are You the Messiah-Son-of-God?" *NovT* 31: 125–41.
1984   "**Mark 4:10–12** and Marcan Epistemology." *JBL* 103: 557–74.
1989   "**Mark 9,11–13**: As It Has Been Written." *ZNW* 80: 42–63.

1995   "**Mark and Isaiah.**" In *Fortunate the Eyes That See (David Noel Freedman Festschrift)*, ed. A. H. Bartelt et al., 449–66. Grand Rapids: Eerdmans.

1996   "Modern and Ancient **Jewish Apocalypticism.**" *JR* 76: 1–27.

1986   *The Mystery of the Kingdom of God.* SBLDS 90. Atlanta: Scholars Press.

1994   "**Review of** R. H. **Gundry,** *Mark: A Commentary on His Apology for the Cross.*" *JTS* 45: 648–54.

1997   "**Scripture** and Tradition in Mark 7." In *The Scriptures in the Gospels*, ed. C. M. Tuckett. BETL 131, 145–63. Leuven: Leuven University Press.

1989   "'The **Time** Has Been Fulfilled!' (Mark 1:15)." In *Apocalyptic in the New Testament: Essays in Honor of J. Louis Martyn*, ed. J. Marcus and M. L. Soards. JSNTSup 24, 49–68. Sheffield: Sheffield Academic Press.

1992   *The Way of the Lord: Christological Exegesis of the Old Testament in the Gospel of Mark.* Louisville: Westminster/John Knox; Edinburgh: T. & T. Clark.

Marjanen, A.
1998   "Is Thomas a **Gnostic** Gospel?" In *Thomas at the Crossroads: Essays on the Gospel of Thomas*, ed. R. Uro, 107–39. SNTW. Edinburgh: T. & T. Clark.

Marshall, C. D.
1989   *Faith as a Theme in Mark's Narrative.* SNTSMS 64. Cambridge: Cambridge University Press.

Martin, R.
1979   *Mark: Evangelist and Theologian.* Grand Rapids: Zondervan (orig. 1972).

Martyn, J. L.
1997   "**Epistemology** at the Turn of the Ages." In *Theological Issues in the Letters of Paul.* SNTW, 89–110. Edinburgh: T. & T. Clark; Nashville: Abingdon.

1982   "**Galatians 3:28,** Faculty Appointments and the Overcoming of Christological Amnesia." *Katallagete* 8: 39–44.

1979   *History and Theology* in the Fourth Gospel. 2nd ed. Nashville: Abingdon (orig. 1968).

1997   *Theological Issues in the Letters of Paul.* SNTW. Edinburgh: T. & T. Clark; Nashville: Abingdon.

Marxsen, W.
1969   *Mark the Evangelist.* Nashville: Abingdon.

Matera, F. J.
1982   *The Kingship of Jesus: Composition and Theology in Mark 15.* SBLDS 66. Chico, Calif.: Scholars Press.

1988   "The **Prologue** as the Interpretative Key to Mark's Gospel." *JSNT* 34: 3–20.

1987   *What Are They Saying about Mark?* New York: Paulist.

Mathews, T. F.
1993   *Clash of the Gods.* Princeton: Princeton University Press.

Mauser, U.
1963   *Christ in the Wilderness: The Wilderness Theme in the Second Gospel and Its Basis in the Biblical Tradition.* SBT 39. Naperville, Ill.: Allenson.

Maynard, A. H.
1985   "**TI EMOI KAI SOI.**" *NTS* 31: 582–86.

McArthur, H. K.
1971   "**Parable** of the Mustard Seed." *CBQ* 33: 198–210.

1973   "'**Son of Mary.**'" *NovT* 15: 38–58.

McCullough, W. S.
1962   "**Bed**." In *IDB*, 1.372–73.

McIver, R.
1994   "One **Hundred-fold** Yield—Miraculous or Mundane? Matthew 13.8,23; Mark 4.8,20; Luke 8.8." *NTS* 40: 606–8.

McKay, H. A.
1994   *Sabbath and Synagogue: The Question of Sabbath Worship in Ancient Judaism*. Leiden: Brill.

McKnight, Scot.
1991   *A **Light** among the Gentiles: Jewish Missionary Activity in the Second Temple Period*. Minneapolis: Fortress.

Meagher, J. C.
1979   *Clumsy Construction in Mark's Gospel: A Critique of Form- and Redaktionsgeschichte*. Toronto Studies in Theology 3. New York and Toronto: Mellen.

Meeks, W. A.
1973   "The **Image** of the Androgyne: Some Uses of a Symbol in Earliest Christianity." *Journal of the History of Religions* 13: 165–208.

1968   "**Moses** as God and King." In *Religions in Antiquity: Essays in Memory of Erwin Ramsdell Goodenough*, ed. J. Neusner. Studies in the History of Religions 14, 354–71. Leiden: Brill.

1972   *The **Writings** of St. Paul*. Norton Critical Editions. New York: Norton.

Meier, J. P.
1991   *A **Marginal** Jew: Rethinking the Historical Jesus*. 3 vols. ABRL. New York: Doubleday [1994 and forthcoming].

Mell, U.
1996   "**Jesu Taufe** durch Johannes (Markus 1:9–15)—zur narrativen Christologie vom neuen Adam." *BZ* n.f. 40: 161–78.

Mendels, D.
1992   *The **Rise** and Fall of Jewish Nationalism: Jewish and Christian Ethnicity in Ancient Palestine*. ABRL. New York: Doubleday.

Metzger, B. M.
1971   *A Textual Commentary on the Greek New Testament*. London and New York: United Bible Societies. [Cited as **Metzger**]

Meyers, E. M.
1992   "**Synagogue**." In *ABD*, 6.251–60.

Michaelis, W.
1951   "Zum jüdischen **Hintergrund** der Johannestaufe." *Judaica* 7: 81–120.

Milgrom, J.
1991   *Leviticus 1–16: A New Translation with Introduction and Commentary*. AB 3A. New York: Doubleday.

Milik, J. T.
1976   *The **Books** of Enoch*. Oxford: Clarendon.

Miller, S.
N.d.   *Mark's Apocalyptic Gospel*. Ph.D. diss., University of Glasgow. Forthcoming.

Millgram, A. E.
1971   *Jewish Worship*. Philadelphia: Jewish Publication Society.

Mitton, C. L.
1972–73   "New Wine in Old Wine Skins: IV. **Leaven**." *ET* 84.
Montefiore, C. G.
1927   *The Synoptic Gospels*. 2nd ed. 2 vols. London: Macmillan. [Cited as **Montefiore**]
Moore, C. A.
1974   "**Mk 4,12**: More Like the Irony of Micaiah Than Isaiah." In *Light unto My Paths: Old Testament Studies in Honor of Jacob M. Meyers*. Gettysburg Theological Studies 4, 335–44. Philadelphia: Temple University Press.
Moore, G. F.
1971   *Judaism in the First Centuries of the Christian Era*. 2 vols. New York: Schocken (orig. 1927–30). [Cited as **Moore**]
Morrison, T.
1987   *Beloved*. London: Picador.
Moule, C. F. D.
1967   "**Fulfillment Words** in the New Testament: Use and Abuse." *NTS* 14: 293–320.
1959   *An Idiom Book of New Testament Greek*. 2nd ed. Cambridge: Cambridge University Press. [Cited as **Moule**]
Moulton, J. H., and G. Milligan
1930   *The Vocabulary of the Greek Testament*. Grand Rapids: Eerdmans. [Cited as **M-M**]
Moulton, J. H., et al.
1908–65   *A Grammar of New Testament Greek*. 4 vols. Edinburgh: T. & T. Clark. [Cited as **MHT**]
Muddiman, J.
1992   "**Fast**, Fasting." In *ABD*, 2.773–76.
Müller, M.
1996   *The First **Bible** of the Church: A Plea for the Septuagint*. JSOTSup 206. Sheffield: Sheffield Academic Press.
Murphy-O'Connor, J.
1986   *The **Holy Land**: An Archaeological Guide from Earliest Times to 1700*. 2nd ed. Oxford and New York: Oxford University Press.
1990   "**John** the Baptist and Jesus: History and Hypotheses." *NTS* 36: 359–74.
Mussies, G.
1984   "The **Use** of Hebrew and Aramaic in the Greek New Testament." *NTS* 30: 416–32.
Mussner, F.
1960   "Ein **Wortspiel** in Mk 1,24?" *BZ* 4: 285–86.
Myers, C.
1988   *Binding the Strong Man: A Political Reading of Mark's Story of Jesus*. Maryknoll, N.Y.: Orbis.
Naveh, J., and S. Shaked
1985   *Amulets and Magic Bowls: Aramaic Incantations of Late Antiquity*. Jerusalem: Magnes; Leiden: Brill.
1993   *Magic Spells and Formulae: Aramaic Incantations of Late Antiquity*. Jerusalem: Magnes.

Neirynck, F.
1972   *Duality in Mark: Contributions to the Study of the Markan Redaction*. BETL 31. Leuven: Leuven University Press.
1977   "L'Évangile de Marc. À propos d'un nouveau commentaire." *ETL* 53: 153–81.
1979   "La Fuite du jeune homme en Mc 14,51–52." *ETL* 55: 43–66.
1975   "Jesus and the Sabbath. Some Observations on Mark II,27." In *Jésus aux origines de la christologie*, ed. J. Dupont. BETL 40, 227–70. Leuven: Leuven University Press.
1984   "John and the Synoptics: The Empty Tomb Stories." *NTS* 30: 161–87.
1995   "Mark and Q." In H. T. Fleddermann, *Mark and Q: A Study of the Overlap Texts*. BETL 122, 263–397. Leuven: Leuven University Press.
1974   *The Minor Agreements of Matthew and Luke against Mark with a Cumulative List*. Leuven: Leuven University Press.
1981   "The Redactional Text of Mark." *ETL* 57: 144–62.
1990   "Synoptic Problem." In *NJBC*, 587–95.
Nierynck, F., and F. van Segbroeck
1984   *New Testament Vocabulary: A Companion Volume to the Concordance*. BETL 65. Leuven: Leuven University Press. [Cited as **Neirynck and van Segbroeck**]
Nestle, E.
1906   "Dalmanutha." In *Dictionary of Christ and the Gospels*, ed. J. Hastings, 1.406–7. Edinburgh: T. & T. Clark; New York: Scribner's.
Neusner, J.
1973   *From Politics to Piety: The Emergence of Pharisaic Judaism*. Englewood Cliffs, N.J.: Prentice-Hall.
1973   *The Idea of Purity in Ancient Judaism*. SJLA 1. Leiden: Brill.
Nickelsburg, G. W. E.
1992   "Son of Man." In *ABD*, 6.137–50.
Nicolson, F. W.
1897   "The Saliva Superstition in Classical Literature." *Harvard Studies in Classical Philology* 8: 23–40.
Niederwimmer, K.
1967   "Johannes Markus und die Frage nach dem Verfasser des zweiten Evangeliums." *ZNW* 58: 172–88.
Nineham, D. E.
1963   *Saint Mark*. Pelican New Testament Commentaries. Middlesex: Penguin. [Cited as **Nineham**]
Nolland, J.
1989   *Luke*. WBC 35AB. Dallas: Word.
O'Callaghan, J.
1972   "New Testament Papyri in Qumrân Cave 7?" Supplement to *JBL* 91/2: 1–14.
O'Connor, D. W.
1969   *Peter in Rome: The Literary, Liturgical and Archeological Evidence*. New York: Columbia University Press.
O'Connor, F.
1979   "Parker's Back." In *The Complete Stories*, 510–30. New York: Farrar, Straus & Giroux.

O'Neill, J. C.
1993   "The **Kingdom** of God." *NovT* 35: 130–41.
O'Rourke, J. J.
1966   "A **Note** Concerning the Use of EIS and EN in Mark." *JBL* 85: 348–51.
Oepke, A.
1964   "*Baptō, ktl.*" In *TDNT*, 1.529–46.
1965   "*Iaomai, ktl.*" In *TDNT*, 3.194–215.
1967   "*Pais, ktl.*" In *TDNT*, 5.636–54.
Opie, I., and M. Tatem
1996   A *Dictionary of Superstitions*. Oxford Paperback Reference. Oxford and New York: Oxford University Press.
Orwell, G.
1984   "**Why I Write.**" In *The Penguin Essays of George Orwell*, 1–7. London: Penguin (orig. 1946).
Osburn, C. D.
1983   "The **Historical Present** in Mark as a Text-Critical Criterion." *Bib* 64: 486–500.
Otto, R.
1929   *The **Idea** of the Holy: An Inquiry into the Non-rational Factor in the Idea of the Divine and Its Relation to the Rational*. London: Oxford University Press.
Overman, J. A.
1990   *Matthew's **Gospel** and Formative Judaism: The Social World of the Matthean Community*. Minneapolis: Fortress.
Pascal, B.
1995   *Pensées and Other Writings*. The World's Classics. Oxford and New York: Oxford University Press.
Patrick, D.
1992   "**Election**, Old Testament." In *ABD*, 2.434–41.
Patterson, S. J.
1993   *The Gospel of **Thomas** and Jesus*. Foundations and Facets: Reference Series. Sonoma, Calif.: Polebridge.
Payne, P. B.
1978   "The **Order** of Sowing and Ploughing in the Parable of the Sower." *NTS* 25: 123–29.
Peisker, C. H.
1968   "**Konsekutives** HINA in Markus 4:12." *ZNW* 59: 126–27.
Perrin, N.
1985   "The **Christology** of Mark: A Study in Methodology." In *The Interpretation of Mark*, ed. W. Telford. IRT 7, 95–108. Philadelphia: Fortress (orig. 1971, 1974).
1969   *What Is **Redaction Criticism**?* Guides to Biblical Scholarship, New Testament Series. Philadelphia: Fortress.
Perrin, N, and D. C. Duling
1982   *The New Testament: An **Introduction**: Proclamation and Parenesis, Myth and History*. 2nd ed. New York: Harcourt Brace Jovanovich.
Pesce, M.
1977   *Paolo e gli arconti a Corinto. Storia della ricerca (1888–1975) ed esegi di I Cor 2,6–8*. Brescia: Paideia.

Pesch, R.
1968   "Levi-Matthäus (Mc 2,14/Mt 9,9; 10,3). Ein Beitrag zur Lösung eines alten Problems." *ZNW* 59: 40–56.
1971   "The Markan Version of the Healing of the Gerasene Demoniac." *Ecumenical Review* 21: 349–76.
1976   *Das Markusevangelium.* 2 vols. HTKNT 2. Freiburg: Herder. [Cited as Pesch]
1968   *Naherwartungen. Tradition und Redaktion in Mk 13.* Kommentare und Beiträge zum Alten und Neuen Testament. Düsseldorf: Patmos.
1968   "Ein Tag vollmächtige Wirkens Jesu in Kapharnaum (Mk 1,21–34.35–39)." *BibLeb* 9: 114–95.

Petzke, G.
1990   "*Dialogizomai, ktl.*" In *EDNT*, 1.308.

Pfammatter, J.
1991   "*Oikodespotēs.*" In *EDNT*, 2.495.

Phillips, J. B.
1961   *Your God Is Too Small.* New York: Macmillan.

Piccirillo, M.
1992   "Medeba." In *ABD*, 4.656–58.

Pietersma, A.
1987   "Kyrios or Tetragram: A Renewed Quest for the Original LXX." In *De Septuaginta: Studies in Honour of John William Wevers on His 65th Birthday*, ed. A. Etal and C. Cox, 85–101. Mississauga, Ont.: Benben.

Poirier, J. C.
1996   "Why Did the Pharisees Wash Their Hands?" *JJS* 47: 217–33.

Pokorny, P.
1995   "From a Puppy to a Child: Some Problems of Contemporary Biblical Exegesis Demonstrated from Mark 7.24–30/Matt 15.21–8." *NTS* 41: 321–37.

Popkes, W.
1993   "Paradidōmi." In *EDNT*, 3.18–20.

Porter, J. R.
1985   "Levites." In *HBD*, 557–58.

Porter, S. E.
1992   *Idioms of the Greek New Testament.* Biblical Languages: Greek 2. Sheffield: JSOT.
1994   "Jesus and the Use of Greek in Palestine." In *Studying the Historical Jesus: Evaluations of the State of Current Research*, ed. B. Chilton and C. A. Evans. NTTS 19, 123–54. Leiden, New York, and Köln: Brill.

Potter, D. S.
1992   "Persecution of the Early Church." In *ABD*, 5.231–35.

Preuss, J.
1923   *Biblisch-talmudische Medizin. Beiträge zur Geschichte der Heilkunde und der Kultur überhaupt.* Berlin: S. Karger.

Price, J.
1992   *Jerusalem under Siege: The Collapse of the Jewish State 66–70 C.E.* Brill's Series in Jewish Studies 4. Leiden, New York, and Köln: Brill.

Procksch, O.
1964   "Hagios, *ktl.*" In *TDNT* 1.88–115.

Pryke, E. J.
1978   *Redactional Style in the Marcan Gospel: A Study of Syntax and Vocabulary as Guides to Redaction in Mark.* Cambridge: Cambridge University Press. [Cited as **Pryke**]
Puech, É.
1992   "Une **Apocalypse** Messianique (4Q521)." *RevQ* 15: 475–522.
1992   "**Fragment** d'une Apocalypse en Araméen (4Q246 = Pseudo-Dand^d) et le 'Royaume de Dieu.'" *RB* 99: 93–131.
Quasten, J.
1983   *Patrology.* 3 vols. Westminster, Md.: Christian Classics (orig. 1950–60).
Quesnell, Q.
1969   *The **Mind** of Mark: Interpretation and Method through the Exegesis of Mark 6:52.* AnBib 38. Rome: Pontifical Biblical Institute.
Rabinowitz, I.
1962   "'**Be Opened**' = EPHPHATHA (Mark 7.34): Did Jesus Speak Hebrew?" ZNW 53: 229–38.
Rabinowitz, L. I.
1972   "Ḥameẓ." In *EncJud*, 7.1235–37.
Räisänen, H.
1976   *The Idea of Divine **Hardening**: A Comparative Study of the Notion of Divine Hardening, Leading Astray and Inviting to Evil in the Bible and the Qur'an.* Publications of the Finnish Exegetical Society 25. Helsinki: Finnish Exegetical Society.
1992   "Jesus and the Food Laws: Reflections on **Mark 7.15**." In *Jesus, Paul and Torah: Collected Essays.* JSNTSup 43, 127–48. Sheffield: Sheffield Academic Press (orig. 1982).
1990   *The "Messianic Secret" in Mark's Gospel.* SNTW. Edinburgh: T. & T. Clark. [Cited as **Räisänen**]
Rapoport-Albert, A.
1991   "**God and** the **Zaddik** as the Two Focal Points of Hasidic Worship." In *Essential Papers on Hasidism: Origins to Present,* ed. G. D. Hundert. Essential Papers on Jewish Studies, 299–329. New York and London: New York University Press (orig. 1977).
Rau, G.
1985   "Das **Markusevangelium**. Komposition und Intention der ersten Darstellung christlicher Mission." In *ANRW* II.3.15.2036–2257.
Ravitzky, A.
1996   *Messianism, Zionism, and Jewish Religious Radicalism.* Chicago Studies in the History of Judaism. Chicago and London: University of Chicago Press.
Rawlinson, A. E. J.
1925   *St Mark: With Introduction, Commentary and Additional Notes.* London: Methuen. [Cited as **Rawlinson**]
Realencyklopädie für protestantische Theologie und Kirche. See under Herzog 1896–1913.
Rebell, W.
1993   "*Chitōn.*" In *EDNT,* 3.468.

Reiser, M.
1984   *Syntax und Stil des Markusevangeliums im Licht der hellenistischen Volks-literatur.* WUNT, 2.11. Tübingen: J. C. B. Mohr (Paul Siebeck).

Rengstorf, K. H.
1964   *"Apostellō, ktl."* In *TDNT*, 1.398–447.

Reploh, K. G.
1969   *Markus, Lehrer der Gemeinde.* SBM 9. Stuttgart: Katholisches Bibelwerk.

Rey-Coquais, J.-P.
1992   "Decapolis." In *ABD*, 2.116–21.

Reynolds, J., and R. Tannenbaum
1987   *Jews and God-Fearers at Aphrodisias: Greek Inscriptions with Commentary.* Cambridge Philological Society Supplementary Volume 12. Cambridge: Cambridge Philological Society.

Reynolds, S. M.
1966   *"PYGMI* (Mark 7:3) as 'Cupped Hand.'" *JBL* 85: 87–88.

Rhoads, D. M.
1976   *Israel in Revolution 6–74 C.E.: A Political History Based on the Writings of Josephus.* Philadelphia: Fortress.

1994   "Jesus and the Syrophoenician Woman in Mark: A Narrative-Critical Study." *JAAR* 62: 343–75.

1997   "Review of D. H. Juel, *A Master of Surprise: Mark Interpreted. CBQ* 59: 144.

1992   "Zealots." In *ABD*, 6.1043–54.

Rhoads, D. M., and D. Michie
1982   *Mark as Story: An Introduction to the Narrative of a Gospel.* Philadelphia: Fortress. [Cited as **Rhoads and Michie**]

Riches, J. K.
1980   *Jesus and the Transformation of Judaism.* London: Darton, Longman & Todd.

Riches, J. K., and A. Millar
1985   "Conceptual Change in the Synoptic Tradition." In *Alternative Approaches to New Testament Study*, ed. A. E. Harvey, 37–60. London: SPCK.

Rigaux, B.
1966   *The Testimony of St. Mark.* Chicago: Franciscan Herald Press.

Ritner, R. K.
1993   *The Mechanics of Ancient Egyptian Magical Practice.* Studies in Ancient Oriental Civilization 54. Chicago: Oriental Institute.

Robbins, V. K.
1992   *Jesus the Teacher: A Socio-Rhetorical Interpretation of Mark.* Minneapolis: Fortress (orig. 1984).

1976   "Last Meal: Preparation, Betrayal, and Absence (Mark 14:12–25)." In *The Passion in Mark: Studies on Mark 14–16*, ed. W. H. Kelber, 21–40. Philadelphia: Fortress.

1994   "The Woman Who Touched Jesus' Garment: Socio-Rhetorical Analysis of the Synoptic Accounts." In *New Boundaries in Old Territory: Form and Social Rhetoric in Mark*, ed. D. B. Gowler. Emory Studies in Early Christianity 3, 155–84. New York: Peter Lang (orig. 1987).

Robertson, A. T.
1934   *A Grammar of the Greek New Testament in the Light of Historical Re-search*. Nashville: Broadman (orig. 1914). [Cited as **Robertson**]
Robinson, J. A. T.
1985   *The Priority of John*, ed. J. F. Coakley. London: SCM.
Robinson, J. M.
1982   *The Problem of History in Mark and Other Marcan Studies*. Philadelphia: Fortress (orig. 1957).
Rochais, G.
1981   *Les Récits de résurrection des morts dans le Nouveau Testament*. SNTSMS 40. Cambridge: Cambridge University Press.
Rofé, A.
1988   *The Prophetical Stories: The Narratives about the Prophets in the Hebrew Bible, Their Literary Types and History*. Perry Foundation for Biblical Research. Jerusalem: Magnes.
Romaniuk, K.
1976–77   "Le **Problème** des Paulinismes dans l'Évangile de Marc." NTS 23: 266–74.
Rook, J. T.
1981   "'**Boanerges**, Sons of Thunder' (Mark 3:17)." *JBL* 100: 94–95.
Roubos, K.
1986   "**Biblical Institutions**." In *The World of the Bible*, ed. A. S. van der Woude. Bible Handbook, 1.350–92. Grand Rapids: Eerdmans.
Rowland, C.
1982   *The Open Heaven: A Study of Apocalyptic in Judaism and Early Christianity*. New York: Crossroad.
Russell, D. S.
1964   *The Method and Message of Jewish Apocalyptic*. Philadelphia: Westminster.
Saldarini, A. J.
1975   *The Fathers according to Rabbi Nathan (Abot de Rabbi Nathan) Version B*. SJLA 11. Leiden: Brill.
1994   *Matthew's Christian-Jewish Community*. Chicago and London: University of Chicago Press.
1988   *Pharisees, Scribes and Sadducees in Palestinian Society*. Wilmington: Glazier.
Sanders, E. P.
1985   *Jesus and Judaism*. Philadelphia: Fortress.
1990   *Jewish Law from Jesus to the Mishnah: Five Studies*. London: SCM; Philadelphia: Trinity Press International.
1992   *Judaism: Practice and Belief 63 BCE–66 CE*. London: SCM; Philadelphia: Trinity Press International.
1977   *Paul and Palestinian Judaism: A Comparison of Patterns of Religion*. Philadelphia: Fortress.
1992   "**Sin**, Sinners (NT)." In *ABD*, 6.40–47.
1983   "**Testament** of Abraham." In *OTP*, 1.871–902.
Sanders, J. T.
1993   *Schismatics, Sectarians, Dissidents, Deviants: The First One Hundred Years of Jewish-Christian Relations*. London: SCM.

Sariola, H.
1990   *Markus und das Gesetz. Eine redaktionskritische Untersuchung.* Annales
         Academiae Scientiarum Fennicae Dissertationes Humanarum Littera-
         rum 56. Helsinki: Suomalainen Tiedeakatemia.
Saunders, S. P.
1990   *"No One Dared Ask Him Anything More": Contextual Readings of the Con-
         troversy Stories in Matthew.* Ph.D. diss., Princeton Theological Seminary.
Saxer, V.
1988   *Les Rites de l'initiation chrétienne du IIe au VIe siècle. Equisse historique
         de signification d'après leurs principaux témoins.* Spoleto: Centro Italiano
         di Studi Sull'Alto Medioevo.
Schaberg, J.
1985   *"Daniel 7–12 and the New Testament Passion-Resurrection Predic-
         tions." NTS:* 208–22.
Schäfer, P.
1972   *Die Vorstellung vom heiligen Geist in der rabbinischen Literatur.* SANT
         28. München: Kösel.
Schechter, S.
1961   *Aspects of Rabbinic Theology.* New York: Schocken (orig. 1909).
Schenke, L.
1974   *Die Wundererzählungen des Markusevangeliums.* SBB 5. Stuttgart:
         Katholisches Bibelwerk.
Schlatter, A.
1963   *Der Glaube im Neuen Testament.* Darmstadt: Wissenschaftliche Buch-
         gesellschaft (orig. 1927).
1956   *Johannes der Täufer.* Basel: Reinhardt (orig. 1880).
Schlier, H.
1964   *"Amēn."* In *TDNT,* 1.335–38.
1964   *"Eleutheros, ktl."* In *TDNT,* 2.487–502.
1967   *"Parrēsia, ktl."* In *TDNT,* 5. 871–86.
Schlosser, J.
1980   *Le Règne de Dieu dans les dits de Jesus.* 2 vols. Ebib. Paris: Gabalda.
Schmahl, G.
1974   *Die Zwölf im Markusevangelium. Eine redaktionsgeschichtliche Untersu-
         chung.* Trier Theologische Studien 30. Trier: Paulinus-Verlag.
Schmidt, D. D.
1990   *The Gospel of Mark with Introduction, Notes, and Original Text.* Scholars
         Bible. Sonoma, Calif.: Polebridge. [Cited as **D. Schmidt**]
Schmidt, K. L.
1965   *"Kaleō, ktl."* In *TDNT,* 3.487–536.
1918   "Die literarische **Eigenart** der Leidengeschichte Jesus." *Die christliche Welt.*
1919   *Der Rahmen der Geschichte Jesu. Literarkritische Untersuchungen zur ältes-
         ten Jesusüberlieferung.* Berlin: Trowitzsch & Sohn. [Cited as **K. Schmidt**]
1981   "Die **Stellung** der Evangelien in der allgemeinen Literaturgeschichte."
         In *Neues Testament. Judentum. Kirche: kleine Schriften herausgegeben zu
         seinem 90. Geburtstag am 5. Februar 1981,* ed. G. Sauter. Theologische
         Bücherei, 37–130. München: Chr. Kaiser (orig. 1923).
Schmidt, K. L., and M. A. Schmidt
1967   *"Pachynō, ktl."* In *TDNT,* 5.1022–31.

Schmidt, W. H., et al.
1978   "Dābar." In TDOT, 3.84–125.
Schmithals, W.
1979   Das Evangelium nach Markus. 2 vols. Ökumenischer Taschenbuchkom-
            mentar zum Neuen Testament. Gütersloh: Mohn; Würzburg: Echter.
            [Cited as Schmithals]
Schnackenburg, R.
1968–82   The Gospel according to St. John. 3 vols. New York: Crossroad.
Schneck, R.
1994   Isaiah in the Gospel of Mark, I–VIII. Bibal Dissertation Series 1. Vallejo,
            Calif.: Bibal.
Scholem, G. G.
1965   Jewish Gnosticism, Merkabah Mysticism, and Talmudic Tradition. New
            York: Jewish Theological Seminary.
1980–81   "Havdala De-Rabbi 'Aqiva: A Source for the Tradition of Jewish Magic
            during the Geonic Period" (in Hebrew). Tarbiz 50: 243–81.
1971   "Toward an Understanding of the Messianic Idea in Judaism." In The
            Messianic Idea in Judaism and Other Essays on Jewish Spirituality, 1–36.
            London: George Allen & Unwin (orig. 1959).
Scholtissek, K.
1992   Die Vollmacht Jesu. Traditions- und redaktionsgeschichtliche Analysen zu
            einem Leitmotif markinischer Christologie. NTAbh n.f. 25. Münster:
            Aschendorff.
Schrage, W.
1964   Das Verhältnis des Thomas-Evangeliums zur synoptischen Tradition und zu
            den koptischen Evangelienübersetzungen. TU 125. Berlin: Töpelmann.
Schrenk, G.
1964   "Dialegomai, ktl." In TDNT, 2.93–98.
Schulz, A.
1962   Nachfolgen und Nachahmen. Studien über das Verhältnis der neu-
            testamentlichen Jüngerschaft zur urchristlichen Vorbildethik. SANT 6.
            München: Kösel-Verlag.
Schulz, S.
1970   Die Stunde der Botschaft. Einführung in die Theologie der vier Evangel-
            isten. 2nd ed. Hamburg: Furche.
Schürer, E.
1973–87   The History of the Jewish People in the Age of Jesus Christ (175 B.C.–A.D. 135),
            ed. G. Vermes et al. 3 vols. Edinburgh: T. & T. Clark. [Cited as Schürer]
Schürmann, H.
1969   Das Lukasevangelium. HTKNT 3/1. Freiburg: Herder.
Schütz, R.
1967   Johannes der Täufer. ATANT 50. Zürich: Zwingli.
Schwartz, D. R.
1992   "'Kingdom of Priests'—a Pharisaic Slogan?" In Studies in the Jewish Back-
            ground of Christianity. WUNT 60, 57–80. Tübingen: J. C. B. Mohr (Paul
            Siebeck) (orig. 1979–80).
1992   "'Scribes and Pharisees, Hypocrites': Who Are the 'Scribes' in the New
            Testament." In Studies in the Jewish Background of Christianity. WUNT
            60, 89–101. Tübingen: J. C. B. Mohr (Paul Siebeck).

1992 "Temple and Desert: On Religion and State in Second Temple Period Judaea." In *Studies in the Jewish Background of Christianity.* WUNT 60, 29–43. Tübingen: J. C. B. Mohr (Paul Siebeck) (orig. 1987).

Schwartz, S.
1990 *Josephus and Judaean Politics.* Columbia Studies in the Classical Tradition 18. Leiden: Brill.

Schweitzer, A.
1968 *The Quest of the Historical Jesus: A Critical Study of Its Progress from Reimarus to Wrede.* New York: Macmillan (orig. 1906).

Schweizer, E.
1970 *The Good News according to Mark.* Atlanta: John Knox. [Cited as **Schweizer**]
1985 "**Mark's** Theological Achievement." In *The Interpretation of Mark,* ed. W. Telford. IRT 7, 42–63. Philadelphia: Fortress; London: SPCK (orig. 1964).
1978 "The **Portrayal** of the Life of Faith in the Gospel of Mark." *Int* 32: 387–99.
1983 "The Question of the **Messianic Secret** in Mark." In *The Messianic Secret,* ed. C. Tuckett. IRT 1, 65–74. Philadelphia: Fortress; London: SPCK (orig. 1965).
1990 "**What Do We** Really **Mean** When We Say 'God Sent His Son . . .'?" In *Faith and History: Essays in Honor of Paul W. Meyer,* ed. J. T. Carroll et al., 298–312. Atlanta: Scholars Press.

Schweizer, E., et al.
1972 "*Huios, huiothesia.*" In *TDNT,* 8.363–92.

Schweizer, E., et al.
1968 "*Pneuma, pneumatikos.*" In *TDNT,* 6.332–454.

Schwier, H.
1989 *Tempel und Tempelzerstörung. Untersuchungen zu den theologischen und ideologischen Faktoren im ersten jüdisch-römischen Krieg (66–74 n. Chr.).* NTOA 11. Göttingen: Vandenhoeck & Ruprecht.

Scott, B. B.
1989 *Hear Then the Parable: A Commentary on the Parables of Jesus.* Minneapolis: Fortress.
1981 *Jesus, Symbol-Maker for the Kingdom.* Philadelphia: Fortress.

Scroggs, R., and K. I. Groff
1973 "**Baptism** in Mark: Dying and Rising with Christ." *JBL* 92: 531–48.

Segal, A. F.
1977 *Two Powers in Heaven: Early Rabbinic Reports about Christianity and Gnosticism.* SJLA 25. Leiden: Brill.

Segal, J. B.
1970 *Edessa 'the Blessed City.'* Oxford: Clarendon.

Seland, T.
1995 *Establishment Violence in Philo and Luke: A Study of Non-conformity to the Torah and Jewish Vigilante Reactions.* Biblical Interpretation Series. Leiden: Brill.

Sellew, P.
1991 "**Secret Mark** and the History of Canonical Mark." In *The Future of Early Christianity: Essays in Honor of Helmut Koester,* ed. B. A. Pearson, 242–57. Minneapolis: Fortress.

Selvidge, M. J.
    1984   "**Mark 5:25–34** and Leviticus 15:19–20: A Reaction to Restrictive Purity
                 Regulations." *JBL* 103: 619–23.
Shepherd, M. H.
    1960   *The **Paschal Liturgy** and the Apocalypse*. Ecumenical Studies in Wor-
                 ship. London: Lutterworth.
Shiner, W. T.
    1995   *Follow Me! Disciples in Markan Rhetoric*. SBLDS 145. Atlanta: Scholars
                 Press.
Shutt, R. J. H.
    1983   "The **Letter** of Aristeas." In *OTP*, 2.7–34.
Smith, D. E.
    1992   "**Greco-Roman** Meal Customs." In *ABD*, 4.650–53.
    1989   "The **Historical Jesus** at Table." In *SBL 1989 Seminar Papers*, ed. D. Lull,
                 466–86. Atlanta: Scholars Press.
    1992   "**Messianic Banquet.**" In *ABD*, 4.788–91.
Smith, D. M.
    1984   *Johannine Christianity: Essays on Its Setting, Sources, and Theology*.
                 Columbia, S.C.: University of South Carolina Press.
    1992   *John among the Gospels: The Relationship in Twentieth-Century Re-
                 search*. Minneapolis: Fortress.
Smith, J. Z.
    1978   "Towards **Interpreting** Demonic Powers in Hellenistic and Roman An-
                 tiquity." In ANRW II.17.1, 425–39.
Smith, M.
    1973   *Clement of Alexandria and a Secret Gospel of Mark*. Cambridge, Mass.:
                 Harvard University Press.
    1978   *Jesus the Magician*. New York: Harper & Row.
    1982   *The Secret Gospel: The Discovery and Interpretation of the Secret Gospel
                 according to Mark*. Laughing Man Series. Clearlake, Calif.: Dawn Horse
                 (orig. 1973).
Smith, T. V.
    1985   *Petrine Controversies in Early Christianity*. WUNT, 2.15. Tübingen:
                 J. C. B. Mohr (Paul Siebeck).
Smyth, H. W.
    1956   *Greek Grammar*. Cambridge, Mass.: Harvard University Press (orig. 1920).
                 [Cited as **Smyth**]
Snodgrass, K. R.
    1980   "**Streams** of Tradition Emerging from Isaiah 40:1–5 and Their Adapta-
                 tion in the New Testament." *JSNT* 8: 24–45.
Snoy, T.
    1974   "**Marc 6,48**: '. . . et il voulait les dépasser.' Proposition pour la solution
                 d'une énigme." In *L'Évangile selon Marc. Tradition et rédaction*, ed.
                 M. Sabbe. BETL 34, 347–63. Leuven: Leuven University Press.
Sommer, B. D.
    1996   "**Did Prophecy** Cease? Evaluating a Reevaluation." *JBL* 115: 31–47.
Spencer, A. B.
    1981   "**Šᵉryrwt** as Self-Reliance." *JBL* 100: 247–48.

Spiegel, S.
1993   *The* **Last Trial**: *On the Legends and Lore of the Command to Abraham to Offer Isaac as a Sacrifice: The Akedah*. Woodstock, Vt.: Jewish Lights (orig. 1950).

Stählin, G.
1967   "**Orgē**, *ktl.*" In *TDNT*, 5.382–447.
1971   "**Skandalon**, *skandalizō*." In *TDNT*, 7.339–58.

Standaert, B. H. M. G. M.
1978   *L'Évangile selon* **Marc**. *Composition et genre littéraire*. Nijmegen: Stichting Studentenpers.

Stanton, G.
1995   *Gospel* **Truth?** *New Light on Jesus and the Gospels*. Valley Forge, Pa.: Trinity Press International.

Stauffer, E.
1969   "**Jeschu** ben Mirjam. Kontroversgeschichtliche Anmerkungen zu Mk 6:3." In *Neotestamentica et Semitica: Studies in Honour of Matthew Black*, ed. E. E. Ellis and M. Wilcox, 119–28. Edinburgh: T. & T. Clark.
1955   *New Testament Theology*. London: SCM (orig. 1941).

Steichele, H.-J.
1980   *Der* **leidende** *Sohn Gottes: Eine Untersuchung einiger alttestamentlicher Motive in der Christologie des Markusevangeliums*. Biblische Untersuchungen 14. Regensburg: Pustet.

Stein, S.
1957   "The **Influence** of Symposia Literature on the Literary Form of the Pesah Haggadah." *JJS* 7: 13–44.

Stemberger, G.
1974   "**Galilee**—Land of Salvation?" Appendix 4 in W. D. Davies, *The Gospel and the Land: Early Christianity and Jewish Territorial Doctrine*, 409–38. Berkeley: University of California Press.

Stendahl, K.
1968   *The* **School** *of St. Matthew and Its Use of the Old Testament*. Philadelphia: Fortress.

Stern, D.
1991   **Parables** *in Midrash: Narrative and Exegesis in Rabbinic Literature*. Cambridge, Mass., and London: Harvard University Press.
1981   "**Rhetoric** and Midrash: The Case of the Mashal." *Prooftexts* 1: 261–91.

Stern, M.
1991   "**Herod and Rome**" (in Hebrew). In *Studies in Jewish History: The Second Temple Period*, 165–79. Jerusalem: Yad Izhak Ben-Zvi.
1991   "The **House of Herod** and the Roman Empire after the Death of Herod" (in Hebrew). In *Studies in Jewish History: The Second Temple Period*, 232–45. Jerusalem: Yad Izhak Ben-Zvi.

Sternberg, M.
1985   *The* **Poetics** *of Biblical Narrative*. Bloomington: Indiana University Press.

Stock, K.
1975   **Boten** *aus dem Mit-Ihm-Sein. Das Verhältnis zwischen Jesus und den Zwölf nach Markus*. AnBib 70. Rome: Pontifical Biblical Institute.

Stoldt, H.-H.
1980   *History and Criticism of the **Marcan Hypothesis**.* SNTW. Edinburgh: T. & T. Clark.

Stone, M. E.
1990   ***Fourth Ezra**: A Commentary on the Book of Fourth Ezra.* Hermeneia. Minneapolis: Fortress.

Strack, H. L., and P. Billerbeck
1924–61 *Kommentar zum Neuen Testament aus Talmud und Midrasch.* 6 vols. München: Beck. [Cited as **Strack-Billerbeck**]

Strack, H. L., and G. Stemberger
1991   *Introduction to the Talmud and Midrash.* Edinburgh: T. & T. Clark.

Strange, J. F.
1992   "**Bethsaida**." In *ABD*, 1.692–93.
1992   "**Dalmanutha**." In *ABD*, 2.4.

Strauss, D. F.
1972   *The **Life** of Jesus Critically Examined.* Philadelphia: Fortress (orig. 1840).

Streeter, B. H.
1924   *The **Four Gospels**: A Study of Origins.* London: Macmillan.

Stuebe, I. C.
1968–69 "The **Johannisschüssel**: From Narrative to Reliquary to *Andachtsbild*." *Marsyas* 14: 1–16.

Stuhlmacher, P.
1968   *Das paulinische **Evangelium**. Vorgeschichte.* FRLANT 95. Göttingen: Vandenhoeck & Ruprecht.
1981   *Versöhnung, Gesetz und Gerechtigkeit. Aufsätze zur biblischen Theologie.* Göttingen: Vandenhoeck & Ruprecht.

Stuhlmann, R.
1973   "**Beobachtungen** und Überlegungen zu Markus 4.26–29." *NTS* 19: 153–62.
1983   *Das eschatologische **Mass** im Neuen Testament.* FRLANT 132. Göttingen: Vandenhoeck & Ruprecht.

Styler, G. M.
1985   "The **Priority** of Mark." In *The Two-Source Hypothesis: A Critical Appraisal*, ed. A. J. Bellinzoni, 63–75. Macon, Ga.: Mercer University Press (orig. 1962).

Swanson, D. D.
1995   *The **Temple Scroll** and the Bible: The Methodology of 11QT.* Studies on the Texts of the Desert of Judah 14. Leiden, New York, and Köln: Brill.

Swete, H. B.
1906   *The **Apocalypse** of St. John: The Greek Text with Introduction Notes and Indices.* London: Macmillan.
1898   *The Gospel according to St Mark.* London and New York: Macmillan. [Cited as **Swete**]

Swetnam, J.
1987   "Some **Remarks** on the Meaning of HO DE EXELTHŌN in Mark 1,45." *Bib* 68: 245–49.

Tabory, J.
1995   ***Jewish Festivals** in the Time of the Mishnah and Talmud* (in Hebrew). Jerusalem: Magnes.

Tagawa, K.
1966   *Miracles et évangile. Le Pensée personelle de l'évangéliste Marc*. Études
         d'Histoire et de Philosophie Religieuses 62. Paris: Presses Universitaires
         de France.
Talbert, C. H.
1977   *What Is a Gospel? The Genre of the Canonical Gospels*. Philadelphia:
         Fortress.
Talley, T. J.
1986   *The Origins of the Liturgical Year*. New York: Pueblo.
Tannehill, R. E.
1985   "The Disciples in Mark: The Function of a Narrative Role." In *The
         Interpretation of Mark*, ed. W. Telford. IRT 7, 134–57. Philadelphia: For-
         tress (orig. 1977).
Taylor, V.
1949   *The Formation of the Gospel Tradition*. London: Macmillan.
1981   *The Gospel according to Saint Mark*. 2nd ed. Grand Rapids: Baker (orig.
         1950). [Cited as **Taylor**]
Telford, W. R.
1997   *Mark*. New Testament Guides. Sheffield: Sheffield Academic Press.
Theissen, G.
1991   *The Gospels in Context: Social and Political History in the Synoptic Tra-
         dition*. Minneapolis: Fortress.
1983   *The Miracle Stories of the Early Christian Tradition*. SNTW. Edinburgh:
         T. & T. Clark, 1983. [Cited as **Theissen**]
Thomas Aquinas
1842   *Catena Aurea: Commentary on the Four Gospels Collected out of the
         Works of the Fathers*. 4 vols. Oxford: Parker.
Thyen, H.
1964   "*Baptisma Metanoias Eis Aphesin Hamartiōn*." In *Zeit und Geschichte.
         Dankesgabe an Rudolph Bultmann zum 80. Geburtstag*, ed. E. Dinkler,
         97–125. Tübingen: J. C. B. Mohr (Paul Siebeck).
Tolbert, M. A.
1989   *Sowing the Gospel: Mark's World in Literary-Historical Perspective*. Phila-
         delphia: Fortress. [Cited as **Tolbert**]
Toombs, L. E.
1962   "Rod." In *IDB*, 4.103–4.
Trever, J. C.
1962   "Mustard." In *IDB*, 3.476–77.
Trocmé, E.
1975   *The Formation of the Gospel according to Mark*. Philadelphia: Westmin-
         ster (orig. 1963).
Tuckett, C. M.
1993   "Mark and Q." In *The Synoptic Gospels: Source Criticism and the New
         Literary Criticism*. BETL 110, 149–75. Leuven: Leuven University Press.
1982   "The Present Son of Man." *JSNT* 14: 58–81.
1983   *The Revival of the Griesbach Hypothesis: An Analysis and Appraisal*.
         SNTSMS 44. Cambridge: Cambridge University Press.
1992   "Synoptic Problem." In *ABD*, 6.263–70.
1988   "Thomas and the Synoptics." *NovT* 30: 132–57.

Tuckett, C. M., ed.
  1983   *The Messianic Secret*. IRT 1. Philadelphia: Fortress.
Turner, N.
  1962   "Dog." In *IDB*, 1.862.
Twelftree, G. H.
  1993   *Jesus the Exorcist: A Contribution to the Study of the Historical Jesus*.
            Peabody, Mass.: Hendrickson; Tübingen: J. C. B. Mohr.
Urbach, E. E.
  1979   *The Sages: Their Concepts and Beliefs*. 2 vols. Publications of the Perry
            Foundation. Jerusalem: Magnes, Hebrew University.
Urman, D.
  1995   "The House of Assembly and the House of Study: Are They One and
            the Same?" In *Ancient Synagogues: Historical Analysis and Archaeologi-
            cal Discovery*, ed. D. Urman and P. V. M. Flesher. SPB 47, 1.232–55.
            Leiden, New York, and Köln: Brill (orig. 1988).
Uro, R.
  1998   "Thomas and Oral Gospel Tradition." In *Thomas at the Crossroads: Es-
            says on the Gospel of Thomas*, ed. R. Uro. SNTW. Edinburgh: T. & T.
            Clark.
van der Horst, P. W.
  1978   *The Sentences of Pseudo-Phocylides: With Introduction and Commen-
            tary*. SVTP 4. Leiden: Brill.
van der Loos, H.
  1965   *The Miracles of Jesus*. NovTSup 9. Leiden: Brill.
van Iersel, B. M. F.
  1983   "Locality, Structure and Meaning in Mark." *LB* 53: 45–54.
  1980   "The Gospel according to St. Mark—Written for a Persecuted Commu-
            nity?" *Nederlands Theologisch Tijdschrift* 34: 15–36.
Vancil, J. M.
  1992   "Sheep, Shepherd." In *ABD*, 5.1187–90.
VanderKam, J. C.
  1992   "Calendar, Ancient Israelite and Jewish." In *ABD*, 1.814–20.
  1994   *The Dead Sea Scrolls Today*. Grand Rapids: Eerdmans; London: SPCK.
Vawter, B.
  1977   *On Genesis: A New Reading*. Garden City, N.Y.: Doubleday.
Vermes, G.
  1995   *The Dead Sea Scrolls in English*. 4th ed. London: Penguin. [Cited as
            Vermes]
  1981   *Jesus the Jew: A Historian's Reading of the Gospels*. Philadelphia: Fortress.
  1993   *The Religion of Jesus the Jew*. London: SCM.
  1971   *Scripture and Tradition in Judaism: Haggadic Studies*. SPB 4. Leiden:
            Brill.
  1967   "The Use of BR NŠ/BR 'NŠ in Jewish Aramaic." In M. Black, *An
            Aramaic Approach to the Gospels and Acts*, 310–28. 3rd ed. Oxford:
            Clarendon.
Vielhauer, P.
  1965   "Apocalypses and Related Subjects—Introduction." In *New Testament
            Apocrypha*, ed. E. Hennecke and W. Schneemelcher, 2.579–607. Phila-
            delphia: Westminster.

1964 **"Erwägungen** zur Christologie des Markusevangeliums." In *Zeit und Geshichte. Dankesgabe an Rudolf Bultmann zum 80. Geburtstag,* ed. E. Dinkler, 155–69. Tübingen: J. C. B. Mohr (Paul Siebeck).

Voelz, J. W.
1984 "The **Language** of the New Testament." In *ANRW* II.25.2, 893–977. Berlin and New York: De Gruyter.

Vögtle, A.
1972 "Die sogennante **Taufperikope** Mk 1,9–11. Zur Probelmatik der Herkunft und des ursprünglichen Sinns." In *EKKNT: Vorarbeiten,* 4.105–39. Zürich: Benziger; Neukirchen: Neukirchener Verlag.

von Dobbeler, S.
1988 *Das **Gericht** und das Erbarmen Gottes. Die Botschaft Johannes des Täufers und ihre Rezeption bei den Johannesjüngern im Rahmen der Theologiegeschichte des Frühjudentums.* BBB 70. Frankfurt: Athenäum.

Votaw, C. W.
1970 *The **Gospels** and Contemporary Biographies in the Graeco-Roman World.* Facet Books. Philadelphia: Fortress (orig. 1915).

Wachsmann, S.
1988 "The Galilee **Boat**: 2,000-Year-Old Hull Recovered." *BARev* 14: 18–33.

Walker, W. O.
1983 "The **Son of Man**: Some Recent Developments." *CBQ* 45: 584–607.

Walsh, J. T., and C. T. Begg.
1990 "**1–2 Kings**." In *NJBC*, 160–85.

Watson, F.
1985 "The **Social Function** of Mark's Secrecy Theme." *JSNT* 24: 49–69.

Webb, R. L.
1991 *John the **Baptizer** and Prophet: A Socio-Historical Study.* JSNTSup 62. Sheffield: JSOT.

Wedderburn, A. J. M.
1985 "**Paul and Jesus**: The Problem of Continuity." *SJT* 38: 189–203.

Weeden, T. J.
1985 "The **Heresy** That Necessitated Mark's Gospel." In *The Interpretation of Mark,* ed. W. Telford. IRT 7, 64–77. Philadelphia: Fortress (orig. 1968).
1971 *Mark: **Traditions** in Conflict.* Philadelphia: Fortress.

Wegner, J. R.
1988 ***Chattel** or Person? The Status of Women in the Mishnah.* New York and Oxford: Oxford University Press.

Wehnert, J.
1991 "Die **Auswanderung** der Jerusalemer Christen nach Pella—historisches Faktum oder theologische Konstruktion?" *ZKG* 102: 231–55.

Weiss, W.
1989 *Eine neue **Lehre** in Vollmacht. Die Streit- und Schulgespräche des Markus-Evangeliums.* BZNW 52. Berlin: De Gruyter.

Wellhausen, J.
1909 *Das Evangelium Marci übersetzt und erklärt.* 2nd ed. Berlin: Georg Reimer. [Cited as **Wellhausen**]

Wendling, E.
1908 *Die **Entstehung** des Marcus-Evangeliums.* Tübingen: J. C. B. Mohr (Paul Siebeck).

Wenham, J. W.
1950   "Mark 2,26." *JTS* n.s. 1: 156.
Werner, M.
1923   Der *Einfluss* paulinischer Theologie im Markusevangelium. *Eine Studie zur neutestamentlichen Theologie.* BZNW 1. Giessen: Töpelmann.
Westerholm, S.
1978   *Jesus and Scribal Authority.* ConB 10. Lund: Gleerup.
Westermann, C.
1969   *Isaiah 40–66.* OTL. London: SCM.
Whitelam, K.
1992   "Abiathar." In *ABD*, 1.13–14.
Whittaker, M.
1984   *Jews and Christians: Graeco-Roman Views.* Cambridge Commentaries on Writings of the Jewish and Christian World 200 BC to AD 200. Cambridge: Cambridge University Press.
Wibbing, S.
1959   Die *Tugend- und Lasterkataloge im Neuen Testament.* BZNW 25. Berlin: Alfred Töpelmann.
Wilckens, U.
1972   "*Hypokrinomai, ktl.*" In *TDNT*, 8.559–71.
1973   "Vergebung für die Sünderin (Lk 7,36–50)." In *Orientiergun an Jesus. Zur Theologie der Synoptiker. Für Josef Schmid,* ed. P. Hoffmann, 394–424. Freiburg, Basel, and Wien: Herder.
Wilcox, M.
1984   "Semitisms in the New Testament." In ANRW, II.25/2.978–1029.
Wilkins, M. J.
1992   "Brother, Brotherhood." In *ABD*, 1.782–83.
Wilson, R. McL.
1960   "'Thomas' and the Growth of the Gospels." *HTR* 53: 231–50.
Wilson, S. G.
1995   *Related Strangers: Jews and Christians 70–170* c.e. Minneapolis: Fortress.
Windisch, H.
1964   "*Hellēn, ktl.*" In *TDNT*, 2.504–16.
Wink, W.
1968   *John the Baptist in the Gospel Tradition.* SNTSMS 7. Cambridge: Cambridge University Press.
Wise, M. O., and J. D. Tabor
1992   "The Messiah at Qumran." *BARev* 18: 60–65.
Wrede, W.
1971   *The Messianic Secret.* Cambridge: James Clarke (orig. 1901). [Cited as Wrede]
Wright, D. P., and R. N. Jones
1992   "Leprosy." In *ABD*, 4.277–82.
Wuellner, W.
1967   The *Meaning of "Fishers of Men."* Philadelphia: Westminster.
Wynne, G. R.
1909   "'Mending Their Nets' (Note on the Call of the Apostles James and John)." *Expositor* 7th ser. 8: 282–85.

Yadin, Y.
    1962   "The **Scroll** of the War of the Sons of Light against the Sons of Darkness." Oxford: Oxford University Press.

    1971   "The **Temple Scroll**." In *New Directions in Biblical Archaeology*, ed. D. N. Freedman and J. C. Greenfield, 156–66. Garden City, N.Y.: Doubleday (orig. 1969).

Yarnold, E.
    1972   *The **Awe-Inspiring** Rites of Initiation: Baptismal Homilies of the Fourth Century*. Middlegreen, Slough: St. Paul Publications.

Zahn, T.
    1900   *Einleitung in das Neue Testament*. 2nd ed. Leipzig: Deichert.

Zerwick, M.
    1963   *Biblical Greek Illustrated by Examples*. Rome: Pontifical Biblical Institute, 1963. [Cited as **Zerwick**]

Zimmerli, W.
    1983   *Ezekiel 2*. Hermeneia. Philadelphia: Fortress.

TRANSLATION, NOTES, AND COMMENTS

◆

THE MARKAN PROLOGUE
(MARK 1:1–15)

◆

INTRODUCTION

The first few verses of Mark's Gospel are set off from the bulk of the work in several ways. Whereas John the Baptist plays a major role in them, he does not appear after 1:10 except in brief reminiscences (e.g. 1:14; 9:13; 11:30) and in one extended flashback (6:14–29). Similarly, only in 1:12–13 is Satan a true character in the narrative. On the other hand, the three collective figures who play such an important role in the continuation of the story—the disciples, the crowd, and the opponents—do not put in appearances until 1:16–20; 1:29–34; and 2:1–12. The common designation of the first few verses of the Gospel as a "prologue," then, seems justified. But just how far does this prologue extend?

As Boring ("Beginning," 54) points out, the answer to this question depends in part upon the way in which one construes the literary genre of the Gospel. If the Gospel were simply a biography of Jesus, it would make sense to assert that 1:2–8 was its prologue, since these verses speak of Jesus' forerunner John; the body of the Gospel would begin in 1:9, where the subject of the biography was introduced. In the discussion of genre in the INTRODUCTION, however, it is argued that Mark is doing more than simply writing a biography of Jesus; he is situating him, rather, at the end of a line of salvation-historical fulfillment that begins with Isaiah's prophecy and continues through the Baptist. A "biographical" division between 1:8 and 1:9, therefore, would be inappropriate.

Neither does a division after the baptismal pericope in 1:9–11 make sense, since this passage is tightly bound with the one that follows it by Mark's favorite adverb, "immediately," and by the shared motif of the Spirit. The basic choice, therefore, is to locate the conclusion of the prologue at the end of the narrative of Jesus' testing by Satan in 1:12–13 or to locate it at the end of the account of his inaugural preaching in 1:14–15. In favor of a division at the end of 1:13 are the absence of the motif of the Spirit in 1:14–15, the change in grammar represented by the first two words in 1:14 (see the NOTE), and the change of locale from the wilderness to Galilee, where most of the first half of the Gospel takes place (cf. Matera, "Prologue," 5). In favor of a division between 1:15 and 1:16 is the inclusion between *euangelion* ("good news") in 1:1 and its double occurrence in 1:14–15; the latter verses, moreover, are bound to 1:12–13 by the linkage between Satan's implied defeat in 1:12–13 and God's implied victory in 1:14–15 (see Keck, "Introduction," 359–62). Moreover, two significant verbs, *kēryssein* ("to proclaim") and *erchesthai* ("to come"), tie 1:14–15 to the previous passages (cf. 1:4, 7, 9), and Jesus' call to repentance in 1:15 recalls John's preaching in 1:4. Perhaps the wisest course is not to be overly dogmatic but to recognize that 1:14–15 functions transitionally both as the end of 1:1–15 and as the beginning of 1:14–45 (cf. Dewey, "Tapestry," 225–26).

Within the prologue, two subsections are discernible: that dealing primarily with John the Baptist (1:1–8) and that dealing primarily with Jesus (1:9–15). As Boring points out, each subsection identifies a character (John or Jesus), places him in the wilderness, and describes his preaching ("Beginning," 59). This parallelism between John and Jesus is reinforced by the fact that the verbs *kēryssein* ("to proclaim," 1:4, 7, 14) and *egeneto* ("appeared," "came to pass," 1:4, 9) are used of both. On the other hand, the superiority of Jesus to John is suggested by the greater fullness and biblical resonance of the phrase in which *egeneto* is employed in 1:9: whereas John "appeared" (1:4), Jesus' advent "came to pass in those days." Only Jesus' advent, moreover, is described with the significant verb *erchesthai* ("to come," 1:7, 9, 14). The relationship of John to Jesus in the flow of 1:1–15 can be summed up as follows:

1:2–3   Old Testament prophecy of John as Jesus' forerunner
1:4–8   John appears and points the way toward Jesus
1:9–11   John and Jesus come together at Jesus' baptism, but Jesus is the center of attention
1:12–15 John drops out of the picture but is recalled in 1:14a

John, then, is announced, moves to center stage, points toward his successor, recedes from view in favor of him, and vanishes, leaving only an echo behind. Mark 1:1–15 thereby expresses obliquely, by dramatic inference, what the Fourth Evangelist has the Baptist declare openly: "He must increase, but I must decrease" (John 3:30).

Who is responsible for this artfully constructed narrative? Pesch (1.71–73) thinks that 1:2–15 already existed as a pre-Markan unit and is essentially historical. But it is hard to imagine this section existing by itself as a separate collection; it makes sense only as the introduction to a larger work such as Mark or Q (cf. Gnilka, 1.39–40). There are indeed those, such as Catchpole ("Beginning") and Lambrecht ("John"), who think that Mark 1:1–15 reflects knowledge of Q, but if so, it is difficult to explain Mark's omission of Matt 3:7–10//Luke 3:7–9 (cf. Davies and Allison, 1.286) and his disfigurement of the Q temptation narrative (on the general question of Mark's relation to Q, see the INTRODUCTION). On the other hand, 1:1–15 is probably not a free Markan composition, since there are tensions within it; the description in 1:9 of Jesus' baptism "in the Jordan by John" needlessly repeats information previously transmitted in 1:4–5, and the notice in 1:12 about the Spirit driving Jesus out into the wilderness creates a certain tension with 1:4, 9, which suggests that Jesus is already in the wilderness. The alternative is to regard the section as a Markan conglomeration of originally disparate material, and in favor of this suggestion, two of the linking phrases, "and it came to pass" in 1:9 and "and immediately" in 1:12, are especially characteristic of Mark.

One of the organizing principles of this Markan composition seems to be the demonstration that the beginning of the good news happened "as it has been written in Isaiah the prophet" (1:2). This is not just a reference to the citation of Isa 40:3 in Mark 1:3; rather, echoes of Isaiah, particularly of the second part of the book, which is commonly ascribed to an anonymous postexilic author ("Deutero-Isaiah"), permeate the entire Markan prologue. Forgiveness of sins, for example (1:4), is a major theme in Deutero-Isaiah (e.g. Isa 43:25 and 44:22), as is the wilderness (Mark 1:4, 12; cf. Isa 40:3; 43:19; 48:20–21, etc.), and the phrase "proclaiming . . . forgiveness" (*kēryssōn . . . aphesin*) recalls "to proclaim release" (*kēryxai aphesin*) in Isa 61:1. The tearing of the heavens, the descent of the Spirit, and the content of the heavenly voice (Mark 1:10–11) recall Isa 63:11–64:1; 11:1–2, and 42:1. The picture of Jesus living at peace with the animals (Mark 1:13) is reminiscent of Isa 11:6–8 and 65:25, and Jesus' initial announcement of the good news of the nearness of the dominion of God (Mark 1:14–15) echoes Deutero-Isaiah's proclamation of the good news of the advent of Yahweh's royal rule in Isa 40:9–10; 52:7; 61:1–15. Thus each of the initial five pericopes in Mark's Gospel has strong connections with the second half of the book of Isaiah.

Deutero-Isaiah has been called "the father of apocalyptic" (Stuhlmacher, *Evangelium*, 116, 122), and so the setting of Mark's prologue in a context stamped by Deutero-Isaiah may suggest that Mark, too, has significant connections with apocalyptic ways of thought. This suggestion is borne out by the details of the passage. Mark 1:1, for example, uses the word "beginning" to launch the Gospel's account of the marvelous things accomplished by God, and this commencement inevitably awakens echoes of the first phrase of Genesis, "in the beginning" (cf. the similar allusion in John 1:1). This allusion has affinities with apocalypticism, since in apocalyptic literature the "beginning-time" of Genesis becomes the prototype for the "end-time"; the world that will come into being at the eschaton will be as new and as dependent on the power of God as was the cosmos created by God "in the beginning" (see Russell, *Method and Message*, 280–84). This typology of "beginning-time/end-time," indeed, is a central element in Deutero-Isaiah itself, where God's act of eschatological redemption recapitulates but surpasses his action "in the beginning" (see Isa 40:21; 51:9, etc., and cf. B. Anderson, "Exodus Typology"). Since Mark follows the word "beginning" with the Deutero-Isian concept of "good news" (1:1) and with an explicit quotation of Isa 40:3 (1:3), this proto-apocalyptic, Deutero-Isian typology of "beginning-time/end-time" seems to be explicitly in his mind as he pens the Gospel's first few verses. As the treatment of the following pericopes will make clear, moreover, the forgiveness of sins (1:4), the advent of the Spirit and the splitting of the heavens (1:8–11), the assault by demonic powers and the implicit Adam typology (1:12–13), are all apocalyptic features. And Jesus' inaugural preaching (1:15) is thoroughly apocalyptic, since it speaks of the death of the old age, the birth of the new, and the human reorientation necessitated and elicited by this cosmic change. From start to finish, then, Mark's prologue is shot through with apocalyptic features, and the apocalyptic character of the prologue has a decisive effect upon the way in which the remainder of the narrative is to be read.

This apocalypticism probably reflects Mark's setting in the Jewish War against the Romans of 66–73 C.E. For that war, as is argued in the INTRO-DUCTION, was probably catalyzed by apocalyptic hopes. It had been pre-ceded by several incidents in which prophets appeared and led people out to the wilderness, promising to show them there "the signs of deliverance" from the Romans, in fulfillment of biblical oracles such as Isaiah 40 (see the con-clusion to the COMMENT on 8:10–13 and D. Schwartz, "Temple"). The way in which Mark begins his Gospel with a section that is set in the wilder-ness and that quotes Isaiah 40, therefore, may well reflect the revolutionary situation. The leaders of the war, moreover, probably saw themselves in royal terms, as messianic kings empowered by God for an eschatological task. For this reason the thrust of the story of Jesus' messianic anointing in 1:9–11, which employs the Davidic imagery of Psalm 2, would not be totally foreign to anyone familiar with the ideological underpinnings of the anti-Roman movement. Nor would the accounts of Jesus' battle with Satan in 1:12–13 and his proclamation of the victory of God's royal power in 1:14–15 strike a false chord in an environment in which the Romans could be dubbed "the army of Belial [= Satan]" (1QM 1:1, 13) and the revolutionaries saw their work—or rather, God's work through them—as the overthrow of this Satanic imperium and the establishment of the royal dominion of God: "For long ago we determined . . . neither to be slaves to the Romans nor to anyone else except God, for he alone is the true and righteous ruler of human beings" (Josephus J.W. 7.323). Indeed, Jesus' inaugural preaching in Mark 1:15, which sums up the eschatological thrust of everything that has gone before, expresses themes that were undoubtedly dear to the revolutionaries' hearts: the fulfillment of the term set for the evil world-kingdom, the imminent arrival of the dominion of God, and the call for human beings to turn from allegiance to the old-age powers and instead put all their trust in the good news of God's victory on the battlefield.

But who is the king who leads God's people to victory against the foe? This is the question to which the prologue addresses itself, and the presentation ends up implying a stinging critique of the messianic figures who inspired the rebellion. Jesus, and not the "false Christs" of the revolt (cf. 13:6, 22), is the fulfillment of Israel's messianic hopes; in this context the divine voice that sounds forth at the climax of the prologue emphatically addresses him to the exclusion of all other aspirants: "*You* are my beloved son; in *you* I have taken delight" (1:11).

THE BEGINNING OF THE GOOD NEWS (1:1–3)

1 ¹The beginning of the good news of Jesus Christ ²(as it has been written in Isaiah the prophet: "Look, I am sending my messenger before your face, who will set your way in order. ³The voice of someone shouting in the wilderness: 'Prepare the way of the Lord; make his paths straight!'"):

NOTES

1 1. *The beginning.* Gk *archē*. The Greek lacks the definite article "the," but the article is frequently absent in the first word of a title (see e.g. the beginnings of Hosea, Proverbs, and Song of Solomon in the LXX and of Matthew and Revelation in the NT). Pesch (1.74–76) interprets *archē* as "the rudiments" of the message about Jesus Christ, but Mark elsewhere uses *archē* only with a temporal nuance (cf. 10:6; 13:8, 19), and that nuance is most appropriate at the beginning of a narrative.

of Jesus Christ. Gk *Iēsou Christou.* Mark knows that the Greek word "Christ" refers to the Jewish concept of an anointed one from the line of David (Heb *māšîaḥ,* Aram *mĕšîḥā',* and Gk *Christos* all mean "anointed one"), as is shown by Mark 12:35 as well as by the fact that most of the Markan usages employ the definite article (*"the* Christ"; for a good survey of the Jewish Messiah concept, see J. J. Collins, *Scepter*). Only here in 1:1 and in 9:41 does Mark use "Christ" without the definite article, probably because it is in the genitive case. The situation in Mark, then, is different from that in Paul's writings, where the term is normally used without the article and seems to be on its way to becoming something like a second name for Jesus (cf. Kramer, *Christ*, 203–14).

Most manuscripts, including some quite good and early ones, add "the Son of God" to "of Jesus Christ," but it is absent in Sinaiticus and several other important textual witnesses. It is more likely that an early scribe added the title "Son of God" than that one omitted it; an intentional omission of such a ubiquitous and important epithet is improbable, and it is also unlikely that a scribe freshly started on the transcription of a manuscript would be careless or tired enough to skip over these important words on the very first line of his text (see Ehrman, "Text," 149–52)! It is true that ancient Jewish writings (e.g. Tobit, Baruch, Matthew) often begin with a superscription identifying the author or subject as the son of someone else (see Davies and Allison, 1.152), but this custom could explain a scribe's addition of "Son of God" as well as Mark's original inclusion of it.

2. *as it has been written.* Gk *kathōs gegraptai.* This is a typical Jewish formula for the citation of scripture (see 4 Kgdms 14:6 and cf. Marcus, *Way*, 18 n. 22, for parallels from Qumran and rabbinic traditions).

Taylor (153) and others have argued that "as it has been written" is the beginning of a second sentence independent of 1:1, citing Luke 11:30; 17:26; John 3:14, and 1 Cor 2:9 as parallels. As Guelich ("Beginning," 6) shows, however, in its Jewish occurrences as well as in its numerous NT usages, the formula is transitional in function, acting as a bridge between a previously mentioned fact or event and the OT citation that follows and confirms it. Of the passages cited by Taylor, only 1 Cor 2:9 contains the full formula "as *it has been written*," and there the formula is preceded by the strongly disjunctive word "but," which creates a separation from the preceding sentence that is not present in Mark 1:2.

in Isaiah the prophet. Gk *en tǭ Ēsaiǭ tǭ prophētǭ.* Many manuscripts, including Alexandrinus, change this to "in the prophets," but this is obviously an attempt to evade the difficulty that the passages cited in 1:2 are not from Isaiah. On the reason for this Markan attribution to Isaiah, see the COMMENT on 1:2–3.

Only here and in Rom 9:25 does a NT author cite an OT passage with the word "in" plus the name of the author, and Billerbeck can find no example from rabbinic literature that is exactly comparable (Strack-Billerbeck, 2.1). Since *en* can mean not only "in" but also "by means of" (cf. BAGD, 261), the phrase may have a double meaning: both "as it has been written in the book of Isaiah" and "as it has been written through the instrumentality of Isaiah," with God being presumed to be the real author (cf. the use of *dia* = "through" in Matt 1:22; 2:15, 17, etc.). The latter nuance would go well with the beginning of the scriptural citation, in which God speaks in the first person through the prophet.

Look, I am sending my messenger before your face. Gk *idou apostellō ton angelon mou pro prosōpou sou.* These words are from the LXX of Exod 23:20, though Mark has omitted the superfluous and perhaps emphatic *egō* = "I myself." In Exodus the words refer to the angel whom God promises to send before the Israelites in the desert. (The Gk *angelos*, like the Heb *mal'āk*, can mean either an earthly messenger or a heavenly one, i.e. an angel; contrary to the sense of the original, Mark understands it as a reference to a human envoy, John the Baptist.)

Most exegetes think that Mark understands the messenger as John; Tolbert, however (239–48), suggests that he is Jesus, who prepares the way for God. But there are too many links between 1:2–3 and 1:4–8 for this interpretation to be plausible; just as the messenger of 1:2–3 proclaims a message in the wilderness and prepares the way for the person designated "you," so John in 1:4–8 proclaims a message in the wilderness and lays the groundwork for the ministry of Jesus. The words "who will prepare your way" in 1:2, moreover, are from Mal 3:1, and later in this chapter of Malachi the preparer of the way is explicitly identified as Elijah (Mal 3:23; ET 4:5). Since John the Baptist is, for Mark, the returning Elijah (cf. the COMMENT on 1:4–8 and 9:11–13), as Tolbert herself acknowledges, the preparer of the way in Mark 1:2 is probably also the Elijah-like figure, John.

who will set your way in order. Gk *hos kataskeuasei tēn hodon sou.* This part of the citation is from Mal 3:1, a passage that is probably dependent on Exod 23:20 and that is conflated with it in various Jewish traditions (e.g. *Exod. Rab.* 32.9; *Deut. Rab.* 11.9) and in Q (Matt 11:10//Luke 7:27; see figure 2). Mark's version of Mal 3:1 is exactly like that of Q except that Mark lacks the words "before you," which are not in the Malachi text anyway. It is uncertain whether or not Mark knew the same version as Q did (on Mark/Q overlaps, see the discussion of Gospel relationships in the INTRODUCTION); if he did, he may have eliminated "before you" in order to increase the parallelism between "your way" and "the way of the Lord" in 1:3 (see the COMMENT on 1:2–3 on Mark's desire to link Jesus with God).

3. *The voice of someone shouting in the wilderness: 'Prepare the way of the Lord; make his paths straight!'* Gk *phōnē boōntos en tȩ̄ erēmȩ̄, Hetoimasate tēn hodon kyriou, eutheias poieite tas tribous autou.* Here Mark cites Isa 40:3 according to the LXX. Like the LXX, Mark connects the phrase "in the wilderness" with the shouting voice, whereas the MT connects it with the imperative "Prepare!" (see figure 2). D. Schwartz ("Temple," 37–38) claims that 1QS 8:13–16; 9:19–20 also connect "in the wilderness" with the voice, but these texts do not mention the "voice calling" part of Isa 40:3. Gundry's assertion (*Use*, 9–10) that the Targum, Peshitta, and Vulgate connect the voice with the wilderness also seems to be a mistake; see Marcus, *Way*, 13–15 n. 9.

of the Lord. Gk *tou kyriou.* In most manuscripts of the Greek translation of the OT, the Septuagint, God's personal name YHWH is rendered as *kyrios* or *ho kyrios*, "the Lord." Some scholars, however (e.g. Kahle, "Problems"; Howard, "Tetragram"), have argued that this usage of *kyrios* is a Christian invention and that the original LXX manuscripts had the Hebrew tetragrammaton (see the GLOSSARY). This theory, however, is unable to explain certain data, such as two passages in which Philo comments on the meaning of *kyrios* as a divine appellation and in one of which he cites the LXX of Gen 21:33; 28:21 (*On Noah's Work as a Planter* 85–90; cf. *On Abraham* 121 and see Dahl and Segal, "Philo," and Pietersma, "Kyrios"). Thus, no matter how the divine name was *written* in the LXX, it was probably *pronounced* as *kyrios.* The issue is important, since with the LXX usage as background the NT application of *kyrios* to Jesus implies some sort of divinity. Mark, however, never unambiguously calls Jesus *kyrios* in this sense (see the COMMENT on 1:2–3).

COMMENT

Introduction. Mark begins his work with a title (1:1) that introduces both the prologue (1:1–13 or 1:1–15) and the Gospel as a whole; this title then flows seamlessly into a conflation of three OT citations (Mark 1:2–3; cf. Exod 23:20; Mal 3:1; Isa 40:3) that present John the Baptist and Jesus as the eschatological fulfillment of biblical hope (1:2–3).

Mark has undoubtedly penned the first verse of the Gospel. The tradition history of the three OT citations, however, is complicated (see figure 2). Mark 1:3 (= Isa 40:3), which follows the LXX almost exactly, is unparalleled in Q, but Mark 1:2 (= Exod 23:20 + Mal 3:1), which differs from the LXX, has a Q parallel. The Hebrew originals behind the OT passages cited in 1:2 and 1:3 are linked by the phrase *pnh drk*, but this linkage is not present either in the LXX

Figure 2: OT Passages in Mark 1:2–3

Exodus 23:20 LXX	Malachi 3:1 MT	Malachi 3:1 LXX	Matthew 11:10 = Luke 7:27 (Q)	Mark 1:2
Look, I myself am sending (egō apostellō) my messenger before your face	Look, I am sending my messenger	Look, I am sending (exapostellō) my messenger	Look, I [Matt: + egō = "myself"] am sending (apostellō) my messenger before your face	Look, I am sending (apostellō) my messenger before your face
to guard you on the way	and he will examine/clear a way (pnh drk) before my face	and he will examine (epiblepsetai) a way before my face	who will set in order (kataskeuasei) your way before you	who will set your way in order (kataskeuasei)

Isaiah 40:3 MT	Isaiah 40:3 LXX	Mark 1:3 = Matthew 3:3 = Luke 3:4	John 1:23
The voice of one crying	The voice of one crying in the wilderness	The voice of one crying in the wilderness	I am the voice of one crying in the wilderness
In the wilderness examine/clear the way (pnh drk) of the Lord	Prepare (hetoimasate) the way of the Lord	Prepare (hetoimasate) the way of the Lord	Straighten (euthynate) the way of the Lord
Straighten in the desert a highway for our God	Straight make (eutheias poieite) the paths of our God	Straight make (eutheias poieite) his paths	

or in Mark's Greek, though it is in the Targum. This suggests that 1:2 and 1:3 were already connected in an early Semitic milieu. Some scholars (e.g. Fitzmyer, "4Q Testimonia," 62–63) have suggested that Mark took these linked texts from a book of "testimonies," a collection of OT texts that early Christians applied to the events concerning Jesus. Such a theory might also explain the attribution of the whole catena to Isaiah; all the texts on "preparing the way" would have appeared under the label "Isaiah," since there are several Isaian passages with that theme (40:3; 57:14; 62:10). This theory, however, would be more convincing if the citation from Isaiah *preceded* the conflation from Exodus/Malachi rather than following it. It is more likely, as Stendahl (*School*, 51–52) has suggested, that Exod 23:20; Mal 3:1, and Isa 40:3 were linked orally using the principle of *gĕzērāh shāwāh* (analogy)—perhaps even in circles associated with John the Baptist. The linked texts were eventually translated into Greek, drawing on both LXX and non-LXX textual traditions, and in one form of the tradition (Q) Exod 23:20/Mal 3:1 became detached from Isa 40:3. (Contrary to Catchpole ["Beginning," 214], it is unlikely that Mark 1:2 reflects Markan knowledge of Q; see Tuckett, "Mark and Q," 162–68.)

In any case, these texts were very important to Mark, since he has chosen to cite them at the very opening of his Gospel, right after the title in 1:1. Grammatically, 1:2–3 is in the nature of a parenthesis, since the real "beginning of the good news" comes in 1:4, with the appearance of John to pave the way for Jesus; 1:2–3 parenthetically establishes that this appearance is the fulfillment of scriptural prophecy. The scriptural citations themselves progress from God's promise to Jesus to send a messenger before him (1:2b), to a description of the messenger as a voice crying in the wilderness (1:3a), to a summary of his message, which consists of two parallel imperatival clauses (1:3b). The scriptural citations are tied together phonetically in the Greek by *ou* sounds and thematically by the motif of the way, and they are all included by Mark under the rubric "As it has been written in Isaiah the prophet."

1:1: title. The first words of Mark's work are "the beginning of the good news of Jesus Christ" ("the Son of God" is probably not part of the original text; see the NOTE on "of Jesus Christ" in 1:1). Each word here is momentous.

"The beginning" probably has a double reference, encompassing both the first thirteen or fifteen verses of the Gospel, its prologue (see the introduction to 1:1–15), and Mark's work as a whole. (Mark's composition, therefore, is technically speaking not a "gospel," but the *beginning* of a gospel.) There is ample precedent for this sort of double referent. Several biblical and early Jewish works start with a sentence that, like Mark 1:1, lacks a predicate and that functions most immediately as the beginning of the work's opening section, but that also serves as a summary of the whole work (see e.g. Prov 1:1–6; Eccl 1:1–2; Cant 1:1–2; *1 Enoch* 1:1; Rev 1:1–3). The title of the first book of the LXX, Genesis, is the prototype for such double referents, since it relates both to the first words of the book, "in the beginning," which state the theme of the first chapter, and to the whole book, which is a book of beginnings.

With respect to the Gospels themselves, Davies and Allison argue forcefully that Matthew intends his opening words, "the book of the origin of Jesus Christ," to be read "telescopically"—that is, as referring at one and the same time to the genealogy that immediately follows, to the birth narrative as a whole, and to the entire work (1.149–55). "The beginning of the good news of Jesus Christ" is an appropriate title for Mark's work, since Mark intends to relate to his audience only the initial portion of the good news about Jesus, the portion that tells the story of his earthly life, which ends with his resurrection (cf. Acts 1:1–2, "all that Jesus *began to* do and teach until the day when he was taken up"). Interpreting 1:1 as the title of the book, therefore, helps make sense of the abrupt ending at 16:8—the *beginning* of the good news is over on Easter morning; after that "the good news of Jesus" will continue through the life of the church.

The genitive "of the good news" reproduces the Greek *tou euangeliou*. The Greek *euangelion*, which is usually rendered in English as "gospel" (from the Old English *gōdspell* = "good tale"), literally means an announcement of something good. The parallels in Deutero-Isaiah are especially important for the NT concept (see Stuhlmacher, *Evangelium*, 109–79, 218–25) and for Mark in particular, since Isa 40:3 LXX, the passage that is cited in Mark 1:3, is shortly followed by two references to "the announcer of good news" (*euangelizomenos*) to Zion and Jerusalem (Isa 40:9). Both in Deutero-Isaiah and elsewhere the term and its cognates are associated with military victory (see e.g. Philostratus *Life of Apollonius of Tyana* 5.8; Isa 40:9–10; 41:25–27), a nuance that Boring ("Beginning," 56) captures nicely when he translates *euangelion* as "good news of victory from the battlefield." As we shall see throughout this commentary, this nuance of military victory is extremely important for Mark, who interprets Jesus' ministry as a triumph over demonic forces and their human agents.

Partly because of the natural association between battles and kings, *euangelion* and its cognates are frequently linked with royalty. In Deutero-Isaiah, for example, the "announcer of good news" proclaims the victory of Yahweh, Israel's true king, over hostile forces (Isa 40:9–10; 41:25–27) and the reclamation of royal power that follows upon that victory (Isa 52:7; cf. *Tg. Isa* 40:9). Similarly, in non-Jewish sources *euangelion* is used of announcements about the birth, coming of age, and accession of the emperor, as in the famous Priene inscription concerning Augustus: "The birthday of the god began for the world the announcements of good news (*euangeliōn*) that have gone forth because of him" (cf. Friedrich, "*Euangelizomai*," 722, 724–25). This inscription is especially close to Mark 1:1 because it speaks of the *beginning* of the announcements of good news. The usage of *euangelion* at the start of the prologue, therefore, forms an inclusion (see GLOSSARY) not only with the two uses of *euangelion* in 1:14–15 but also with the theme of the dominion of God there.

The good news that Mark proclaims is specifically "the good news of Jesus Christ." "Of Jesus Christ" could be taken either as an objective genitive (the good news about Jesus Christ), as a subjective genitive (the good news that Jesus Christ himself announces), or as a combination of the two. The objective nuance is certainly present, as is shown by comparison with 1:14, where "the good news of God" is the good news *about* God. But the subjective nuance cannot be excluded, since passages such as 1:8 and 13:11 imply the presence of Jesus and the Spirit with the Markan community (cf. Boring, "Beginning," 71 n. 16). As in Rev 1:1, then, "of Jesus Christ" may be understood as having both objective and subjective nuances; Mark's composition is not only the good news *about* Jesus but also the good news that Jesus himself proclaims through Mark.

1:2–3: *the Old Testament prophesies John the Baptist's ministry.* "Good news" implies newness, an announcement that has not been heard before; but it is also important to Mark to affirm that what happened in Jesus followed the plan of salvation laid out by God in the prophecies of the Scriptures. Therefore he, like the authors of Matthew, John, Romans, and Hebrews, relates the story of Jesus to the Old Testament at the beginning of his work through the common NT citation formula "as it has been written" (*kathōs gegraptai*). The Greek perfect tense ("has been written"), which implies a past action with permanent results (cf. Smyth, §1945), is particularly appropriate for such a formula, since it suggests that the ancient writing is not just a dead letter but a living force in the present.

The formula links the good news specifically to the writings of "Isaiah the prophet." This ascription is technically incorrect, since only 1:3 (the description of the voice crying in the wilderness) is actually from Isaiah, while 1:2b (the description of the messenger) is a mélange of Exod 23:20 and Mal 3:1. Such conflation of OT texts is familiar from postbiblical Judaism, especially from the Dead Sea Scrolls, and is common in Mark (see 1:11; 12:36; 14:24; 14:27, 62; cf. Kee, "Function," 181) and elsewhere in the New Testament (e.g. Matt 27:9–10; Rom 3:11–18; 9:25–26; 1 Pet 2:6–8). Mark's ascription of the whole catena to Isaiah could simply be a mistake, but it is more likely that Mark is deliberately setting his story in an Isaian context. Mark seems to have a special attachment to Isaiah; he is the only OT author mentioned by name in the Gospel (here and in 7:6), and the prologue is full of allusions to Deutero-Isaiah (see the introduction to 1:1–15).

Speaking through "Isaiah," God announces to Jesus that he will send a messenger before him (1:2b–3). Right from the beginning of the Gospel, then, an extraordinary intimacy between Jesus and God is portrayed; the direct address to Jesus foreshadows the heavenly voice that only he hears in 1:11. An unprecedentedly close relationship between Jesus and God is also implied by the way in which the OT citations parallel Jesus' "way" to "the way of the Lord" (*tou kyriou*). The latter is the circumlocution used by the LXX writers or their readers to render YHWH, the unutterable name of God, and hence becomes a common name for God in the NT (see the NOTE on "of the Lord" in 1:3). The close connection made by Mark between Jesus and "the Lord" is borne out by other passages in the Gospel (2:28; 11:3; 12:36–37) in which the term "lord" is used for Jesus. In all of these passages, to be sure, "lord" *could* be understood in its secular sense of "master," and the last of them *distinguishes*

David's lord (= Christ) from *the* Lord, God. Such a distinction coheres with several Markan passages that emphasize Jesus' subordination to God (10:18, 40; 13:32; 14:36; 15:34) and with the fact that, in 1:2-3, Mark has not effaced the difference between "your way" and "the way of the Lord." Mark, then, does not want simply to *identify* Jesus with "the Lord," even though he seems to think that the way of Jesus is the way of the Lord. Perhaps the best way of putting all these observations together is to say that, for him, where Jesus is acting, there God is acting (see the COMMENT on 5:18-20 and cf. Matt 1:23).

It is not an accident, then, but an intimation of the divine initiative in the drama of salvation that the very first "lines" spoken in the Gospel belong to God: "Look, I am sending . . . " (cf. Kingsbury, *Christology*, 56-57). Specifically, God speaks of "sending" (*apostellō*) a messenger, whom the reader soon discovers to be John the Baptist (1:4-8; for Tolbert's theory that the messenger is Jesus, see the NOTE on "Look, I am sending my messenger before your face" in 1:2). John is thus the culmination of the series of prophets whom God has sent out into the world (cf. 12:2-6, and on the linkage of *apostellein* with the prophets in the OT, cf. Rengstorf, "*Apostellō*," 400-1), and he foreshadows the disciples whom Jesus and God will send out in the course of the narrative (cf. 3:14; 6:7; 11:1; 14:13; cf. 9:37).

John's mission is described as preparation of the way of Jesus. As the Gospel progresses, we will learn that John has prepared the way for Jesus both by his preaching and by his martyrdom; as Perrin and Duling have observed (*Introduction*, 110, 239), first John preaches and is delivered up (1:7, 14), then Jesus preaches and is delivered up (1:14; 9:31; 10:33), and finally the Christians preach and are delivered up (3:14; 13:9-13). John's going before Jesus in the way of suffering and death also seems to be implied in 9:11-13 (see COMMENT).

But it is the first of John's "preparations" for Jesus, his preaching, that is emphasized in our passage. Indeed, Mark 1:3 presents John not so much as a person but as a voice, shouting in the wilderness and calling on human beings to prepare the way of the Lord. If, as Stendahl thinks (*School*, 215), this application of Isa 40:3 to John goes back to Baptist circles, these were probably building on a known exegetical tradition; the Qumran group, too, saw its existence in the same area of the Judaean desert as fulfilling the prophecy of Isa 40:3 by "separat[ing] from the habitation of unjust men and . . . go[ing] into the wilderness to prepare there the way of Him" (1QS 8:13, Vermes trans.).

In Isa 40:3 itself, "the way of the Lord" is not so much the way in which the Lord intends people to walk as it is the Lord's *own* way, his triumphant march through the wilderness and into the holy city as he leads his people back from exile in a magnificent demonstration of saving power. Since, as we have seen, Mark seems to be aware of the larger Isaian context, and since *euangelion* itself implies military victory, this meaning of the phrase in Isaiah may be relevant for the Gospel as well; Mark may understand "the good news about Jesus" to be a fulfillment of Isaiah's vision of saving holy war. This is especially likely if it is correct that the background to Mark is the Jewish revolt against the Romans (see the INTRODUCTION); Isaiah 40 is a passage that would have been very useful to the Jewish revolutionaries, as it could easily be interpreted as calling for holy war against the Romans. In Mark, however, the fulfillment of this well-known Isaian expectation of holy war victory will take place in a paradoxical way. "The way of the Lord," as we have already seen, is Jesus' "way" (1:2–3), and the latter will become the leitmotiv of the Gospel's central section, where it will refer to his path up to suffering and death in Jerusalem (see 8:27; 9:33–34; 10:17, 32, 46, 52). Mark may thus wish to imply, for frequent hearers of his message, that it is not the revolutionary struggle against the Romans but Jesus' way up to suffering and death in Jerusalem that truly represents the triumphant return of Yahweh to Zion prophesied by Isaiah.

Despite his opposition to revolutionary activism, Mark himself is not quietistic. John the Baptist's proclamation is summed up, in the concluding words of our passage, as a call to prepare the Lord's way and to make his paths straight, and the next verse will relate his baptism to repentance, which is a human action. Correspondingly, as Snodgrass ("Streams") points out, Isa 40:3 is interpreted in the Qumran literature as a reference to the human actions of studying, teaching, and carrying out the Law to prepare for the advent of God (1QS 8:12–16; 9:17–20). Although Mark does not put the same sort of emphasis on the Law that the Qumran literature does, there is a certain parallel in his emphasis on the necessity of proclaiming the gospel worldwide, an event that seems in some way to pave the way for Jesus' return and the end of the world (cf. 13:10).

Already in the first few verses of Mark, then, a characteristic, apocalyptic tension that will pervade the entire Gospel is foreshadowed. The decisive "fact" that characterizes the world now is the good news of what God has done, and is doing, in Jesus Christ, creating through him a "way" of redemption, a way of escape from the captive universe. Yet human beings have a role to play within this divine drama. In the Gospel's next passage this paradox will be explored further, as John proclaims both a baptism of repentance and a baptism in the Holy Spirit (1:4–8).

THE MINISTRY OF JOHN THE BAPTIST (1:4–8)

1 [4]John appeared, baptizing in the wilderness and proclaiming a baptism of repentance leading to the forgiveness of sins. [5]All of the people from the region of Judaea, including all of the inhabitants of Jerusalem, were traveling out to him and being baptized by him in the Jordan River, confessing their sins. [6]This John used to wear a garment made of camel's hair and a leather belt around his waist, and he would eat grasshoppers and wild honey. [7]And he proclaimed this message: "There is coming after me the one stronger than me, of whom I am not worthy so much as to stoop down and loosen his sandals' thong. [8]I myself have baptized you with water, but he will baptize you in the Holy Spirit."

NOTES

1 4. *John appeared, baptizing.* Gk *egeneto Iōannēs baptizōn.* Some manuscripts (e.g. Sinaiticus), for which "John the Baptist" has become a fixed expression, insert the definite article before *Iōannēs*, so that the reading becomes "John the-Baptizing-One appeared"; others (e.g. Vaticanus), after making this insertion, eliminate the "and" after "in the wilderness" to smooth out the grammar.

baptizing. Greek *baptizōn.* In pre-NT Greek, including the LXX, this verb means "to dip, plunge, or immerse" and can be used, for example, of dipping a cup in a wine bowl, sinking a ship, or plunging a sword into someone's body (LSJ, 305–6). It can also have a figurative sense, being used, for example, for the immersion of people in various sorts of evils (cf. 10:38–39 and see Oepke, "*Baptō*," 530, 545). Before the NT, the word does not have the technical sense of an act of water initiation.

proclaiming. Gk *kēryssōn.* This verb is derived from the Greek noun *kēryx*, "proclaimer" or "herald"; in later times the verb came into Hebrew and Aramaic as a loanword (see Jastrow, 665). The herald's office was an important one throughout the ancient world, but the verb *kēryssein* has particularly important background in the OT (see the COMMENT on 1:4). The NT usage of *kēryssein*, however, transcends its dual parentage in the Gentile and Jewish worlds; here the verb becomes, with very few exceptions (Luke 12:3; Acts 15:21; Rom 2:21), a technical term for the proclamation of God's redemptive eschatological action in Christ (see Friedrich, "*Kēryx*," 683–718).

repentance. Gk *metanoias*, lit. "change of mind." The Greek word, which is used outside of the biblical sphere only for regret for individual acts, has been immeasurably deepened by the influence of the Jewish concept of *tĕšûbāh* (lit. "turning" or "return"), which has its root in the call of the OT prophets for the nation to return to its God and implies a total change in spiritual orientation (see Behm, "*Metanoeō*," 976–89). Repentance was a prominent theme in first-century Judaism; in the fifth of the Eighteen Benedictions of daily prayer, for example, Israel prays that God would cause her to return to him in complete repentance and blesses him as a God "who delights in repentance." In some forms of Judaism the concept takes on an eschatological coloring; the Qumran covenanters, for example, call themselves "the penitents of the desert" (*šby hmdbr*, 4QpPs37 3:1) and see themselves as people who have returned to God on the eve of his eschatological advent (see LaSor, *Dead Sea Scrolls*, 156; cf. *T. Jud.* 23:5 and *b. Sanh.* 97b).

leading to the forgiveness of sins. Gk *eis aphesin hamartiōn. Aphesis* literally means a sending away or release; the NT sense of release from guilt before God is derived from the LXX (see Bultmann, "*Aphiēmi*").

5. *All of the people from the region of Judaea.* Gk *pasa hē Ioudais chōra*, lit. "all of the Judaean region." The name of the region is transferred to its inhabitants, just as one might say, "All of America loves baseball."

including all of the inhabitants of Jerusalem. Gk *kai hoi Ierosolymitai pantes.* Since Jerusalem itself lay in the province of Judaea, the *kai*, which normally means "and," is best taken in an inclusive sense, as in 16:7 (cf. BAGD, 392 [I1c]).

were traveling out to him. Gk *ekporeuesthai*. This word is applied in the OT to the exodus of the Israelites from Egypt under Moses (see e.g. Exod 13:4, 8; Deut 23:4[5]; Josh 2:10), and Mark may be deliberately invoking the exodus/ Moses typology here, as Lohmeyer (15) suggests. This typology is especially likely, since Mark sets his whole story, and in particular the prologue, in the context of the new exodus prophesied in Deutero-Isaiah (see the COMMENT on 1:2–3), and since Elijah, who is the model for the Baptist, is in many ways a Mosaic figure (see Allison, *New Moses*, 39–45).

6. *used to wear a garment made of camel's hair and a leather belt around his waist.* Gk *kai ēn . . . endedymenos trichas kamēlou kai zōnēn dermatinēn peri tēn osphyn autou*. Down through the ages, ascetics have worn rough and uncomfortable clothing as a sign of penitence; see, for example, the "clothing from trees" (= leaves or bark) worn by the hermit Bannus in Josephus' *Life* (2.11) and the hair shirt of the Middle Ages. For other implications of John's clothing, see the COMMENT on 1:5–6.

grasshoppers. Gk *akridas*. Grasshoppers or locusts are a permissible food according to Lev 11:22, and in *m. Ḥul.* 8:1 they are distinguished from "flesh." This makes our verse compatible with Matt 11:18//Luke 7:33, in which John is described as one who does not eat meat.

7. *stronger.* Gk *ischyroteros*, the comparative of *ischyros*. It is questionable that this saying of John originally had reference to Jesus. It only gains such a reference by the Markan juxtaposition with 1:9–11, and Matt 11:2–6//Luke 7:18–23 depicts John pondering the possibility of Jesus' messiahship but by no means convinced of it. Josephus, moreover, draws no line from John to Jesus, even though he mentions both men (on the substantial authenticity of Josephus' testimony to Jesus, see Meier, *Marginal Jew*, 1.56–88). In texts from the early Christian era we hear of people who had undergone John's baptism but were not Christians (Acts 19:3; cf. 18:25) and of a non-Christian Baptist sect that continued to exist for several centuries after its founder's death (Pseudo-Clementine *Recognitions* 1.54, 60; cf. Wink, *John the Baptist*, 98–105).

Some scholars, such as Lohmeyer (18 n. 1), think that the "stronger one" whose coming John awaited was God. In Isa 40:10 LXX the Lord comes with might (*ischys*), and in Rev 18:8 he is described as strong (*ischyros*; cf. Eccl 6:10 and see Schneck, *Isaiah*, 38). Such an interpretation, however, would have John putting himself almost on a par with God ("the one stronger *than me*") and speaking about loosening God's sandal thong; both seem implausible. Rather, for John the "stronger one" was probably the Messiah. As Davies and Allison point out, *Pss. Sol.* 17:37, drawing on the language of Isa 11:2, speaks of the Messiah as "powerful (*dynatos*) in the Holy Spirit" and ascribes strength (*ischys*) to him (cf. *1 Enoch* 49:3); the combination of the motifs of strength and the Holy Spirit is very similar to Mark 1:7–8 (1.314–15). Moreover, if "stronger one" was in circulation as an epithet for the Messiah, it is easy to see how the church could have come to think that John was referring to Jesus when he spoke of that figure.

loosen his sandals' thong. Gk *lysai ton himanta tōn hypodēmatōn autou.* The thong (*himanta*) was the leather strap that held the sandal on the foot (see BAGD, 376). In rabbinic sources the untying of the master's shoe is the task of a slave and unworthy of a disciple; in *b. Ketub.* 96a R. Joshua b. Levi says that "a pupil does for his teacher all the tasks that a slave does for his master, *except* untying his shoe." John, however, says that he is unworthy even of this humble, slavelike service. Mark's version of his words, by adding the reference to stooping down, emphasizes this inferiority even more strongly.

8. *I myself have baptized.* Gk *egō ebaptisa.* The *egō* (= "I") is superfluous, and probably emphatic, so that I have added "myself" in the translation; cf. the NOTE on "Give . . . yourselves" in 6:37.

he will baptize you in the Holy Spirit. Gk *autos de baptisei hymas en pneumati hagiǭ.* Rabbinic traditions (e.g. *Qoh. Rab.* 7.4) speak of the Holy Spirit resting (*šrh/šr'*) on people; the same root can mean "dissolve, soak, or steep" (Jastrow, 1629–30), and this variation in meaning may help account for the NT concept of baptism in the Holy Spirit. The *en* ("in") in our passage could be instrumental (cf. BDF, §195), making the meaning of *en pneumati* parallel to that of *hydati* ("with water"), but *en* could also be taken literally to suggest immersion in the Spirit, conceived as a liquidlike, supernatural substance.

As E. Sjöberg points out (in Schweizer, "*Pneuma*," 384), the Spirit is possessed by an anointed one or the Messiah in the OT (2 Sam 23:1–2; Isa 11:1–2; 61:1), the Pseudepigrapha (*Pss. Sol.* 17:37; *1 Enoch* 49:3; 62:2), and the Targum (*Tg. Isa* 42:1–4); the idea is also present in rabbinic literature (e.g. *y. Šabb.* 78a and the frequent references to Lam 4:20). It would be a short step from a Spirit-endowed Messiah to a Spirit-endowing one. Also having OT and Jewish roots is the linkage of the Spirit with water (e.g. Isa 32:15; Ezek 36:25–27; 1QS 4:21), which appears elsewhere in the NT (e.g. 1 Cor 12:13; Titus 3:5–6; see Allison, "Living Water," 151–52). As Guelich (25) points out, Ezek 36:25–27 provides an especially striking parallel: "I will sprinkle clean water upon you, and you shall be clean from all your uncleanness . . . I will put my spirit within you, and cause you to walk in my statutes." Here sprinkling with water parallels endowment with the Spirit, and the passage is immediately followed by a classic expression of the wilderness theme (Ezek 36:33–36), a theme that is prominent in the Markan context (1:3–4, 12–13).

In the COMMENT on 1:7–8, Jesus' baptism of his disciples in the Spirit is linked both with his endowment of them with exorcistic power and with his inspiration of their speech (cf. the combination of exorcism and powerful speech in 1:21–28 and 3:15). This speech component of "baptism in the Holy Spirit" may include the restoration of prophecy, since rabbinic traditions link the Holy Spirit so strongly with prophecy that the two become virtually synonymous (cf. Sommer, "Did Prophecy," 33, 37), and Acts 2:17–18 interprets Joel 2:28–29, which speaks of an eschatological gift of prophecy, as a reference to baptism

Figure 3: Mark 1:7–8 and Parallels

Mark 1:7–8	*Matthew 3:11–12 = Q*	*Luke 3:16 = Q*	*John 1:26–27, 33*
there is coming after me the one stronger than me	I myself baptize you with water — into repentance	I myself baptize you with water —	I myself baptize in water
of whom I am not worthy (*hikanos*) so much as to stoop down and loosen his sandals' thong	but the one coming after me is stronger than me	but there is coming the one stronger than me	but among you stands . . . the one coming after me
I myself have baptized you with water	of whom I am not worthy (*hikanos*) to —— carry his sandals	of whom I am not worthy (*hikanos*) to —— loosen the thong of his sandals	of whom I am not worthy (*axios*) that I might loosen the thong of his sandal . . .
but he will baptize you in the Holy Spirit ——	he will baptize you in the Holy Spirit and fire ——	he will baptize you in the Holy Spirit and fire ——	this is the one baptizing in the Holy Spirit

in the Spirit (cf. *Num. Rab.* 15.25, which looks forward to an eschatological extension of the gift of prophecy to all of Israel).

The Q form of the saying speaks not only of a baptism in the Holy Spirit but also of a baptism in fire (see figure 3). Some scholars (e.g. Guelich, 26) think Mark knew this version but edited out the reference to baptism in fire because he was uncomfortable with the idea of Jesus judging "by fire." Mark, however, retains several references to judgment by Jesus and God (see e.g. 8:35–38; 9:42–50; 12:9), and the primitiveness of the Markan form of the saying is supported by the independent witness of John 1:33 (see figure 3 again).

COMMENT

Introduction. After laying out the scriptural basis for John the Baptist's ministry in 1:2–3, Mark immediately brings John onto the scene in 1:4–8. In the course of the passage, however, the focus shifts from John to Jesus, the "coming one" whose way John prepares.

The passage seems to have been composed by Mark from individual traditions about the Baptist that he had at his disposal: a baptismal formula (1:4b), a tradition about John's clothing and food (1:6), and a comparison of him with the "stronger one" (1:7–8), which is also present in Q (Matt 3:11//Luke 3:16), and fragments of which appear in the fourth Gospel (John 1:26–27, 33). The parallels to Mark 1:7–8 have a chiastic structure, in which the references to baptism frame the references to John's inferiority to Jesus; in Mark, however, the themes of inferiority and baptism are sequential (see figure 3). Mark's own editing can be glimpsed in 1:4a, which is part of the framework of the Gospel and contains the redactional vocabulary "in the wilderness" and "proclaiming"; in the geographical description in 1:5, which is similar to 3:7–8 and contains two instances of "all," which is one of Mark's favorite words; and perhaps in certain aspects of 1:7–8. It is unlikely that these latter verses represent a reworking of Q (cf. the discussion of the Mark/Q overlaps in the INTRODUCTION and the NOTE on "he will baptize you in the Holy Spirit" in 1:8), but certain non-Q features are probably Markan; these include the usage of the finite verb *erchetai* ("there is coming"), the aorist *ebaptisa* ("I have baptized"), and perhaps the sequence of themes (cf. Laufen, 120–22, and von Dobbeler, *Gericht*, 53; note that these Markan features are unparalleled in John). *Erchetai* prepares for the usages of the same verb for Jesus in 1:9 and 1:14 and throughout the Gospel, the aorist *ebaptisa* corresponds to Mark's strong emphasis on John's status as a forerunner (cf. 1:2–3, 14; 9:11–13), and the concentration of the baptismal references at the end prepares for Jesus' baptism, which immediately follows in Mark.

The passage as a whole has a sandwichlike structure; two summaries of John's proclamation (*kēryssein*) in 1:4 and 1:7–8 surround an account of his baptismal activity and ascetic way of life in 1:5–6. Verse 7 is a turning point in the pericope and indeed in the prologue as a whole, for here the focus shifts from John's own ministry to his prophecy of the advent of the "stronger one" who will baptize with the Holy Spirit.

1:4: John's proclamation of baptism. The passage begins by clarifying the mysterious scriptural citation in 1:2–3, which spoke of a "voice shouting in the wilderness." Mark now identifies this "voice" as John the Baptist, who proclaimed and practiced in the wilderness a baptism of repentance leading to the forgiveness of sins. The verb "to proclaim" (*kēryssein*), which appears both here and in 1:7, has its most important background in the prophets, where it is sometimes linked with repentance (e.g. Jonah 1:2; 3:2, 4), which can be eschatological (Zeph 3:11–15). The verb is also sometimes linked with the arrival of an anointed one or Messiah (Isa 61:1; Zech 9:9–10); one of these messianic passages, Isa 61:1, even uses the phrase *kēryxai aphesin* ("to proclaim release/forgiveness"), which appears in Mark 1:4 (on the importance of Isa 61:1–3 in early Christianity, see Davies and Allison, 1.436–39).

The object of John's initial proclamation is his baptism. Various kinds of ritual washings were practiced in the ancient world, but the most direct connection of John's rite was with the Old Testament via later Judaism. In the Old Testament period, priests washed themselves before taking part in sacrifices, and ordinary people did likewise if they had contracted some sorts of ritual impurity (cf. de Vaux, *Ancient Israel*, 2.460–61); the latter practice continues today in the use of the *mikveh*, or ritual bath, by religious Jews. This ritual washing was eventually extended to Gentile proselytes to Judaism, who thereby purged themselves of the uncleanness of their pagan life; immersion in a ritual bath therefore became a requirement for conversion (see e.g. *m. Pesah.* 8:8; *b. Yebam.* 46a), though it is a matter of controversy whether or not proselyte baptism was a fixed requirement in the New Testament period (cf. McKnight, *Light*, 82–85). The Dead Sea sect at Qumran laid great stress on ritual bathing, and here, as in John's baptism, the bath was linked with the end-time cleansing and renewal to be accomplished by God's Spirit (1QS 3:1–12). This similarity is not surprising, since John operated in the same area of the Judaean wilderness as the Qumran group did; he may, indeed, have been a member of the Qumran community at one time. His baptism, however, departed from the Qumran pattern by being a onetime rite performed by a second party, not a continually repeated self-immersion.

Mark 1:4b speaks specifically of John proclaiming a "baptism of repentance leading to the forgiveness of sins." Thyen (*Baptisma*, 97–98) argues that this phrase is a baptismal formula that goes back to Baptist circles, noting the compressed, technical vocabulary, which lacks definite articles, and the tension with early Christian theology, in that the formula seems to ascribe the power of absolution to John's baptism rather than to Jesus' death. In this formula, however, it is unclear whether it is baptism or repentance that leads to forgiveness. Interestingly, the Jewish historian Josephus comments on this very issue when he says that in John's view a reformed life "was a necessary preliminary if baptism was to be acceptable to God" and that its recipients "must not employ it to gain pardon for whatever sins they had committed, but as a consecration of the body implying that the soul was *already* thoroughly cleansed by righteousness" (*Ant.* 18.117, LCL trans., alt.). For Josephus, then, it is repentance rather than baptism that leads to forgiveness, but his statement has an apologetic ring to it (cf. Schlatter, *Johannes*, 60–63), and it is probable that things were not so clear-cut either for John and his followers or for Mark. In our passage what John proclaims is not in the first instance repentance but baptism; the people are baptized by John *as* (not *after*) they confess their sins, and the verb "were baptized" precedes the participle "confessing." All of this suggests that, for Mark at least, baptism has some sort of logical priority over repentance, though the two are interrelated.

But how exactly? Perhaps a hint is provided by Zech 12:10–13:1, an OT passage that is extensively used in the NT (see Dodd, *According*, 65) and that shares several motifs with our text: water imagery, repentance, confession, forgiveness of sins, and even a reference to the inhabitants of Jerusalem. In this passage God *pours out* a spirit of *remorse and supplication* on the inhabitants of Jerusalem. The mass repentance prophesied in Zechariah, then, is an activity

that must ultimately be traced back to God himself; we could even say that
God here *baptizes* (i.e. envelops and immerses) the people in a wave of eschatological repentance and spiritual cleansing. Correspondingly, the Markan
context (1:6) suggests that both the baptism of the people and their confession
of sin result from the same eschatological initiative of God that has brought
"all Judaea and all the Jerusalemites" out to the wilderness (see the COM-
MENT on 1:5–6). The reader is left with the impression that a powerful action
of God is taking place, one that expresses itself both in the baptism of myriads of
people and in their being moved to confess their sins, which epitomizes their repentance. Repentance, then, is strongly associated with forgiveness of sins, but
the relationship is not a simple causal one.

When was the forgiveness of sins that was associated with John's baptism supposed to take place? The rite of baptism itself suggests cleansing and therefore
forgiveness, but the rite might merely be intended to foreshadow a remission of
sins that will take place at the eschaton; certainly the *eis* ("leading to") in 1:4
could be interpreted in this way. Moreover, since John thought of the eschatological condemnation of the wicked as a future event (see Matt 3:7–10//Luke
3:7–9 and Matt 3:11–12//Luke 3:16–17), he probably thought of the forgiveness
of the sins of the righteous as a future event also (see Ernst, *Johannes*, 334–36).
This is especially likely because John associated the future coming of the
"stronger one" with the advent of the Spirit (Mark 1:7–8), and the Spirit is often
linked with forgiveness in OT prophetic and Jewish apocalyptic texts (Ezek
36:25–26; Zech 12:10–13:1; 1QS 4:20–21), where forgiveness is not so much a
possibility for everyday life as it is a hope for the eschatological future (cf.
Eichrodt, *Theology*, 2.457–60). In any case, in *Mark's* understanding, John's
baptism was only a proleptic cleansing from sinfulness, since the true remission
resulted from Jesus' death as a "ransom for many" (10:45).

1:5–6: John's baptismal activity and asceticism. After sketching one aspect
of John's proclamation, his announcement of a baptism of repentance, Mark
portrays the effect of this proclamation and then pauses to describe John's
clothing and food, before returning to the other aspect of his proclamation.
Mark's claim that *all* of the Judaeans, including the Jerusalemites, flocked to
John—not just *many*, as in Josephus *Ant.* 18.116–19—is clearly hyperbolic
and may convey an eschatological nuance: the end-time has arrived, in which
all of Israel will repent (cf. Zech 12:10–13:1; Acts 3:19–21; *b. Sanh.* 98a).

This eschatological nuance would fit well with the Elijah-like features of the
Baptist, since by the late OT period Elijah had become an eschatological figure
(see Mal 3:23–24; cf. Mark 6:15; 8:28). The word "all" itself recalls Elijah, since
in 1 Kgs 18:21 Elijah calls *all* the people of Israel to choose between Yahweh and
Baal. John's clothing, moreover, is similar to that of Elijah, since the latter is described in 2 Kgs 1:8 as a hairy man with a leather belt around his waist; by the first
century this description may have been combined with that of the prophet with
a hairy mantle in Zech 13:4 (see Hengel, *Charismatic Leader*, 36 n. 71). Furthermore, Elijah preaches a message of repentance (e.g. 1 Kgs 18:21), and he is

associated with both the wilderness (1 Kgs 17:3; 19:3–18) and the Jordan (2 Kgs 2:4–11); the latter linkage, moreover, occurs in the important passage in which Elijah is taken up into heaven and a "double portion" of his spirit falls on his disciple Elisha (2 Kgs 2:6–14). Although originally this may merely have meant that Elisha inherited Elijah's birthright (Freedman), later Jewish tradition apparently interpreted it as Elisha's reception of double Elijah's power (Ginzberg, 4.239; 6.343–44). Jesus, similarly, comes to the Jordan to be baptized by John, and there he receives an endowment of the divine spirit that makes him the "stronger one" who supersedes John (cf. Brown, "Jesus and Elisha," 87–88 and nn. 12–13).

Even apart from these Elijan connections, the description of John the Baptist has a strongly eschatological flavor. His garment of camel hair, his leather belt, and his food of wild honey lend him a certain primal, back-to-the-earth quality, reminiscent of the Garden of Eden narrative and Jewish elaborations thereof. The hair garment and leather belt, for example, recall Gen 3:21 LXX, in which God clothes Adam and Eve with leather tunics (*chitōnas dermatinous*), and the honey is reminiscent of *Joseph and Aseneth* 16:14(8), where Aseneth eats a honeycomb made by the bees of the Garden of Eden; several later Jewish legends, moreover, describe a river of honey in Eden (see Ginzberg, 5.29 n. 79). These Edenic features anticipate Mark 1:13, where Jesus is with the wild animals in the wilderness, a scene that also recalls Eden (cf. Drury, "Mark 1.1–15," 31). In both passages the reminiscence of Eden looks forward to the eschaton, since the end-time will be, in a sense, a return to paradise, when the "natural" world was all that existed. Even some non-Jewish readers might have picked up this hint; Virgil's *Fourth Eclogue* 30, for example, mentions miraculous provision of honey as a feature of the coming Golden Age.

1:7–8: the prophecy of the "stronger one." The Elijan and eschatological features of the Markan portrait of the Baptist lead logically into the Markan description of John's prophecy of the coming of the "stronger one," since Elijah was expected to be the forerunner of the end-time Messiah (see the COMMENT on 9:11–13). Mark leaves his readers in no doubt as to the identity of this "stronger one" who baptizes in the Holy Spirit; he follows John's prophecy immediately with the narrative of Jesus' own baptism and reception of the Spirit, using the verb *erchesthai* ("to come") in both places. Although it is unlikely that the historical Baptist was actually speaking of Jesus in the prophecy (see the NOTE on "stronger" in 1:7), this is certainly the impression intended by Mark.

But in what way is Jesus "stronger" than John the Baptist for Mark? Jesus' strength is connected with his baptism in the Spirit, and in the context of Mark 1:12–13, 21–28 the Spirit is above all the divine power that enables Jesus and his followers to do battle with the *evil* spirits. The only other Markan use of the adjective *ischyros* ("strong"), moreover, is in 3:22–27, where Jesus shows himself to be stronger than Satan by casting out demons. And in 9:14–29 he proves himself superior to his disciples by his exorcistic capability; their question "Why did we *not have the strength to cast it out?*" (9:28) uses a verb cognate to "strong" (*ischyein* = "to have strength"). All of this suggests that for Mark Jesus' strength and his baptism in the Spirit manifest themselves first and foremost in his ability to rout the forces of Satan, and that Jesus is stronger than John because of his ability to perform exorcisms and other miracles (cf. John 10:41: "John performed no sign").

In Mark's conception Jesus is apparently imbued with his exorcistic "strength" at his baptism, when he receives the Holy Spirit (1:9–11). This would suggest that Christians, too, are "baptized in the Holy Spirit" at their own water baptisms (cf. Acts 2:38; 1 Cor 6:11; 12:13; Titus 3:5; see Beasley-Murray, *Baptism*, 275–79). Although during Jesus' earthly ministry, his disciples receive authority to cast out demons (3:15) and actually go out and do so on one occasion (6:7, 13), they later are unable to perform an exorcism (9:14–29), and the overall Markan picture of the bumbling followers of Jesus does not exactly leave an impression of them as powerful, Spirit-filled individuals. In order to become consistently effective exorcists, they will need the later, postresurrectional baptism in water and the Spirit, which will also enable them to bear witness to Jesus fearlessly and eloquently (see 13:11 and cf. the NOTE on "he will baptize you in the Holy Spirit" in 1:8). Mark, then, like Paul (Rom 8:15–17), Luke (Acts 2), and John (20:22), thinks of the reception of the Spirit, and therefore of baptism in it, as a postresurrectional event, albeit one that was foreshadowed in the earthly ministry of Jesus and his disciples. The agent of this postresurrectional baptism in the Spirit, according to 1:8, will be Jesus, and this means that Mark conceives of Jesus as present and active in the post-Easter period (cf. the COMMENT on 2:20 and 6:45–50).

In our passage, then, John's proclamation of baptism gives way to his proclamation of the coming of the crucial end-time figure, the "stronger one" or Messiah, and his final words testify to his inferiority to this figure. Our passage thus elaborates on the emphasis of 1:2–3 that the divinely ordained role of John the Baptist was to prepare the way for Jesus. It also leads into the next passage (1:9–11), in which Jesus will make his Markan debut.

THE BAPTISM OF JESUS (1:9–11)

1   [9]And it came to pass in those days that Jesus came from Nazareth in Galilee and was baptized in the Jordan by John. [10]And as he was coming up out of the water, he immediately saw the heavens being ripped apart and the Spirit like a dove descending upon him; [11]and a voice came out of the heavens: "You are my beloved son; in you I have taken delight."

NOTES

1   9. *And it came to pass.* Gk *kai egeneto*. These words, in conjunction with a finite verb (cf. 4:4), are an OT idiom that is not found in nonbiblical Greek (see Maloney, *Semitic Interference*, 81–86).

in the Jordan. Gk *eis ton Iordanēn.* The word for "in," *eis*, means "into" in classical Greek, but in Koine Greek the line between it and *en* ("in") becomes blurry (cf. 6:8; 10:10; 13:3, etc.; see O'Rourke, "Note," 349–51).

10. *And as he was coming up out of the water, he immediately.* Gk *kai euthys anabainōn ek tou hydatos.* This is the first instance of *euthys* ("immediately"), a favorite term in Mark, which has forty-one of the fifty-one NT usages. Matthew and Luke usually omit it, but sometimes they substitute the synonym *eutheōs*, which is the more normal Greek form (although Philo and Josephus, like Mark, prefer *euthys*; see BAGD, 320). The adverb imparts vividness to the narrative and leaves readers with the impression that the divinely willed series of events is unfolding at great speed (cf. Dschulnigg, *Sprache*, 84–86). It also has a biblicizing effect, since *kai euthys* is used in the LXX to translate the common OT formula *wĕhinnēh* ("and behold": Gen 15:4; 38:29; see Pesch, 1.90). Indeed, Mark seems to be so fond of this biblical phrase that he sometimes violates grammatical sense to retain it, as in our passage where *euthys* modifies a later verb ("he saw"), not the participial phrase that immediately ensues ("as he was coming up out of the water"; cf. 1:21, 29; 6:25; 9:15; 11:2; 14:43; see Davies and Allison, 1.328).

being ripped apart. Gk *schizomenous.* This harsh word is not the usual one for the opening of the heavens in visionary contexts. But its Hebrew counterpart, *qrʿ*, appears in the MT of Isa 63:19 (Eng. 64:1): "O, that you would rip the heavens apart and come down!" (cf. the COMMENT on 1:10–11). The Matthean/Lukan parallels to our passage use the more common verb *anoigein*, "to open," which also appears in the striking parallel in *T. Levi* 18:6–12. In the latter the heavens are opened, the glory of God bursts forth on the eschatological high priest "with a fatherly voice, as from Abraham to Isaac," the Spirit rests upon him in the water, and Beliar (= Satan) is bound (cf. Mark 1:12–13; 3:27).

the Spirit. Gk *to pneuma.* Bultmann (251) asserts that one finds this absolute use of "the Spirit," rather than qualified expressions such as "the Spirit of holiness" or "the Spirit of truth," only in non-Jewish texts. While this assertion is generally true, Num 11:26 does speak of "the Spirit" resting on Eldad and Medad, and 1QS 4:6 describes "the counsels of the Spirit for the sons of truth" (cf. Gnilka, 1.50).

like a dove. Gk *hōs peristeran.* Is it the *Spirit* that is like a dove, or only its descent? Scholars often opt for the latter interpretation (see e.g. Keck, "Spirit"), but the former at least explains how Jesus could have *seen* the Spirit. In any case, as Davies and Allison point out (1.331), the word "like" (*hōs*) points toward the world of apocalyptic symbolism, where earthly comparisons are used to approximate heavenly realities; it is no accident that *hōs* occurs more often in Revelation than in any other NT book.

What is the significance of the dove symbolism? Pesch (1.91) points out that a bird makes an appropriate symbol for the Spirit because it can cross the barrier between heaven and earth, but this does not explain why a dove rather than some other bird is used. Davies and Allison (1.331–34) list sixteen(!) different possibilities, of which the most plausible is the theory that dove is meant to echo Gen 1:2, where the Spirit soars, birdlike, over the waters. This theory is supported by *b. Ḥag.* 15a, in which the Spirit's hovering over the primeval waters is compared with a dove's brooding over its young, and by 4Q521 1:6, which reapplies the vocabulary of Gen 1:2 to an eschatological empowerment of human beings ("over the poor his Spirit will hover"; see Allison, "Baptism"); *Gen. Rab.* 2.4, moreover, interprets Gen 1:2 as an allusion to "the spirit of the Messiah" and adds a reference to Isa 11:2, on which see the next NOTE.

   descending. Gk *katabainon.* Codex א adds *kai menon* = "and remaining," but this is probably an assimilation to John 1:33 (cf. figure 4). The reconstruction of fragment 10 of 4Q287 by Wise and Tabor ("Messiah," 62) is close to these two verses: "The Holy Spirit rested on his Messiah." But this reconstruction is very speculative in view of the fragmentary state of the manuscript; for example, only the last letter of the word translated "rested," a *he*, is visible (IOUDAIOS-L posting from Tabor, 4.29.96). See, however, Isa 11:1-2, in which the Spirit of the Lord rests on a Davidic figure.

   The descent of the Spirit at Jesus' baptism might be taken to imply that it was at this point that he became the Messiah and Son of God. Messiah/ Christ, after all, means "anointed one," and Isa 61:1, which is cited elsewhere in the NT (Luke 4:16-22; Acts 10:38), speaks of a figure who is anointed with the Spirit and who proclaims good news, which is what Jesus does shortly af- ter his baptism, in Mark 1:14-15. The descent of the Spirit upon Jesus, there- fore, could be understood as his induction into messianic office; such a view would cohere with an interpretation of the divine pronouncement in 1:11, "You are my son," that sees it as performative, i.e. accomplishing what it pro- claims. On the other hand, the aorist *eudokēsa* ("have taken delight") in 1:11 implies God's delight with Jesus prior to the baptism (see the NOTE on "I have taken delight" in 1:11). These two views are not wholly incompatible with each other; God could have planned a long time before to make Jesus Messiah at his baptism. Or Mark may not be sure in his own mind when Jesus became Messiah.

   upon him. Gk *eis auton.* In classical Greek *eis* means "into." This has led Hahn (*Hoheitstitel,* 342-43) to claim that Mark pictures the Spirit as uniting itself with Jesus in a way that reflects Hellenistic conceptions. But in Koine Greek, including Mark, *eis* + accusative can be equivalent to *epi* + accusative, which means "upon" (see 4:5, 8; 11:8; 12:14; 13:3), and is the construction in the Matthean, Lukan, and Johannine parallels to 1:10 (see figure 4; cf. Kings- bury, *Christology,* 62-63). The vast majority of Markan manuscripts also change *eis* to *epi,* probably in order to defuse "the Gnostic claim that at Jesus' baptism a divine being entered into him" (Ehrman, *Orthodox Corruption,* 141).

   11. *voice.* Gk *phōnē.* The voice here and in 9:7 is similar to the rabbinic *bat qôl,* or "daughter of a voice," a voice that sounds forth from heaven to express God's will and may quote scripture and/or declare a favorable evaluation of a person. As the term itself suggests, however, the *bat qôl* is not the unmediated voice of God but its echo, and traditions such as *t. Soṭa* 13:2 explicitly contrast

Figure 4: Mark 1:10–11 and Parallels

Mark 1:10	*Matthew 3:16*	*Luke 3:21–22a*	*John 1:32–34*
(and was baptized . . .)	and when Jesus was baptized	and Jesus having been baptized, and while he was praying	
and as he was coming up out of the water	immediately he came up from the water		
he immediately saw the heavens being ripped apart	and look, the heavens were opened	the heaven was opened	I have seen
and the Spirit like a dove descending upon (*eis*) him	and he saw the Spirit of God descending like a dove upon (*epi*) him	and the Holy Spirit descended in bodily form like a dove upon (*epi*) him	the Spirit descending like a dove from heaven and it remained upon (*epi*) him

Mark 1:11	*Matthew 3:17*	*Luke 3:22b*	*John 1:34*
and a voice from the heavens:	and look, a voice from the heavens, saying:	and there was a voice from heaven:	and I have seen and borne witness that
"You are my beloved son, in you I have taken delight"	"This is my beloved son, in whom I have taken delight"	"You are my son, in you I have taken delight"	this is the chosen one of God

it with the Holy Spirit. Some of this devaluation of the *bat qôl* may be polemic against Christian claims of extraordinary revelation such as are made in our passage (cf. Davies and Allison, 1.335–36).

came. The verb *egeneto* is missing in the original text of Sinaiticus and in Bezae. It is possible that it was not present in the Markan original, but also possible that it has been omitted unintentionally by homoeoarcton (see GLOSSARY). In any case, even if it was not present originally, some such verb must be understood by the reader.

You are my . . . son. Gk *sy ei ho huios mou.* This is a near-exact quotation of Ps 2:7 LXX, the only difference being that the psalm verse puts the predicate nominative first ("my son you are"). Gundry (*Use*, 30 n. 2), among others, asserts that the change from the LXX reflects a desire to emphasize that *Jesus*, rather than some other figure such as John the Baptist, is the Son of God ("*You* are my son"). This interpretation, however, is questionable, since Mark 8:29 has an exactly similar structure, and in the latter verse the "you" is not emphatic (see Steichele, *Leidende*, 136–37 n. 104). As Freedman points out, the MT and LXX of Ps 2:7 are chiastic:

> my son
>
>   you are
>   I today
> have begotten you

Since Mark, however, has omitted the second colon ("I today have begotten you"), he switches the order back to a more natural sequence.

In the OT, Israel (Exod 4:22; Hos 11:1, etc.), angels (Gen 6:2, 4; Job 1:6, etc.), or the king (2 Sam 7:14; Ps 2:7) may be referred to as Yahweh's son (see Fohrer in Schweizer, "*Huios*," 347–53). The royal usage is the one that is most important for Mark, especially for our passage, where a royal psalm is being cited. In postbiblical Judaism such royal texts are sometimes interpreted messianically; in the Dead Sea Scrolls, for example, 4QFlor 1:10–13 applies 2 Sam 7:14 ("I will be his father, and he will be my son") to the Davidic Messiah, and rabbinic traditions such as *b. Sukk.* 52a quote Ps 2:7 with reference to the Messiah. The Qumran text 4Q246, moreover, probably speaks of the Messiah as the Son of God (see J. J. Collins, *Scepter*, 154–69).

beloved. Gk *agapētos.* This word is not present in Ps 2:7, the source of "You are my son"; Mark has moved on to a different biblical background. In the LXX *agapētos* can mean "only," but the present context, in which God goes on to declare his delight with Jesus, argues for "beloved" (cf. Davies and Allison, 1.340). It is possible to construe *agapētos* as a substantive adjective and hence as a separate title, as in Eph 1:6, so that the divine voice acclaims Jesus as "my son, the beloved one." But "beloved son/daughter" is biblical language, which is used in the LXX (e.g. Jdt 9:4; Tob 3:10S) and in postbiblical traditions (e.g. *T. Isaac* 2:7; *T. Jacob* 1:13; *4 Baruch* 7:24), most importantly in the story of Abraham's binding of his son Isaac for sacrifice (Gen 22:2, 12, 16). Isaac's binding (*'ăqēdāh*) becomes an important focus of attention in rabbinic traditions, where his obedience to God's will, even unto death, is elaborated upon; in some forms of the story Isaac actually dies, thereby making atonement (see Spiegel, *Last Trial*). Such conceptions may already have been extant in NT times, and if so, they could have influenced passages such as ours and Rom 8:32 (see e.g. Vermes, *Scripture*, 222–23, and Kazmierski, *Jesus*, 53–56).

I have taken delight. Gk *eudokēsa*. This is an allusion to Isa 42:1, a verse that Matt 12:18 renders as *ho agapētos mou eis hon eudokēsen hē psychē mou*, "my beloved one, in whom my soul has taken delight." The Isaian verse, moreover, continues, "I have put my Spirit upon him," and there is thus a connection with the descent of the Spirit in Mark 1:10. The aorist *eudokēsa* is usually translated as a present ("I take delight, I am well pleased"). This is grammatically possible (see Robertson, 837) but unusual; aorists are usually translated as pasts, and that is the sense of the corresponding term in Isaiah, where God's past choice of Israel is made the surety for the new thing he is about to do for it. Similarly, in Mark, the reference is probably to a past divine choice of Jesus that is now being ratified at the baptism. In support of such an interpretation, some Jewish traditions imply God's choice of the Messiah before the creation (see e.g. *1 Enoch* 48:3, 6; *b. Pesaḥ*. 54a), and Eph 1:4–6 uses the *eudok-* root in a reference to God's delight with his elect from the foundation of the world (on the other links between this passage and ours, see Marcus, *Way*, 124).

COMMENT

Introduction. Mark's readers have just heard John prophesying the arrival of his superior, the "stronger one," an eschatological figure who will baptize in the Holy Spirit. With this prophecy still ringing in their ears, they are now presented with a tableau in which Jesus appears on the scene and is baptized by John, endowed with the Spirit of the all-powerful God, and acknowledged by a heavenly voice to be God's son. Jesus' superiority to John is emphasized by the very grammar of 1:9–10, where he becomes the subject of all of the main verbs, even of the one dealing with John's act of baptizing him (1:9–10). Mark, moreover, had in 1:4 introduced John with the single verb *egeneto* ("appeared"); he now introduces Jesus with a much more impressive biblical formula incorporating the same verb, *kai egeneto en ekeinais tais hēmerais* ("and it came to pass in those days"; cf. Exod 2:11; Judg 18:31; 1 Kgdms 28:1). This formula is not only biblical but also eschatological, since "in those days" alludes to the end-time in the OT prophetic books (e.g. Jer 31:33; Joel 3:1; Zech 8:23) and the first two Gospels (e.g. Matt 7:22; 9:15; Mark 13:17, 19, 24; cf. Davies and Allison, 1.288). The cumulative effect is to suggest unmistakably that Jesus is the coming eschatological figure to whom John pointed.

The passage shows clear signs of Markan editing, especially in its first verse, which is transitional and has several features that are typical of Markan redaction ("in those days" [cf. 8:1; 13:24], "came" [*erchesthai*], and "Galilee"). It is also possible that Mark is behind the usage in 1:10 of the violent verb "to rip apart" (*schizein*; contrast Matthew and Luke's "to open"), a verb that appears again in conjunction with the "Son of God" title in the climactic scene at the end of the Gospel (15:38). It is more debatable whether or not Mark is responsible for the fact that in his Gospel the baptismal narrative takes the form of a private vision to Jesus. In Mark, Jesus alone sees the heavens split and the

Spirit descending upon him like a dove, and he alone hears the voice from heaven: "*You are* my beloved son; *in you* I have taken delight." In all of the other Gospels these supernatural events take on a more public character, in that John the Baptist and/or the crowd also perceives them (see figure 4). It is possible that this more public form of the baptismal tradition reflects an apologetic desire of the later Gospels to emphasize the objective truth of the baptismal events. On the other hand, the private nature of the vision in Mark's Gospel coheres with Mark's messianic secret motif, in which no human being besides Jesus himself knows of his divine sonship until his death on the cross; the private vision, then, could reflect Markan redaction (see Greeven, "*Peristera*," 68 n. 57). The choice between these two alternatives would be easier if it were certain that Q had a baptismal narrative, because this would increase the likelihood that the public form was older and the Markan private vision a later redaction; unfortunately, however, the question of whether or not Q included the baptism is quite controversial (see Kloppenborg, *Q Parallels*, for a summary of the arguments).

Mark 1:9–11 is structured in two parts: the baptism itself (1:9) and Jesus' vision (1:10–11), with the emphasis falling on the latter. The vision consists of two things seen by Jesus (torn heavens, Spirit descending) and one thing heard by him (heavenly voice). Of these components, the final one, the voice, is climactic because of its position at the end, the change from sight to sound, the greater number of words devoted to it, and its role in interpreting the visual elements (cf. Marcus, *Way*, 81). In the overall structure of Mark the baptismal events anticipate those that occur at the end of the Gospel: Jesus breathes out his *spirit*, the curtain of the Temple is *ripped apart*, and the centurion acclaims Jesus as *the Son of God* (15:37–39; see Juel, 34–35).

1:9: the baptism itself. The baptism itself is described laconically; we hear nothing of Jesus' personal relationship with John, of his motivation for joining in John's baptism, or of his feelings during the experience. Early Christians, indeed, were rather embarrassed by John's baptism of Jesus, both because of the possible implication of Jesus' sinfulness (cf. 1:4) and because of his apparent subordination to John the Baptist (Matt 3:14–15 and Luke 3:21 are early attempts to deal with these problems; see Marcus, "Jesus' Baptismal," 512 n. 1). Historically, it is probable that Jesus began his career as a disciple of John (see Meier, *Marginal Jew*, 2.116–30), but if Mark knows of this relationship, he has suppressed any overt reference to it.

1:10–11: Jesus' vision. Instead, Mark concentrates on a description of the things Jesus sees (1:10) and hears (1:11) immediately after his baptism. It may well be that Jesus did experience a vision at his baptism (see Marcus, "Jesus' Baptismal"), but our account has been strongly shaped by the OT and by Christian convictions about Jesus' identity. It may also have been influenced by the institution of Christian baptism, since early Christians believed that *they* had become children of God in *their* baptisms by receiving the Spirit, which showed God's delight in them (cf. Gal 4:5–6; Rom 8:15; Eph 1:5–14).

As far as the OT echoes are concerned, Buse ("Markan Account") has pointed out that the description in 1:10 echoes Isa 63:11–64:1:

> Where is he that brought up from the sea the shepherd of his flock?
> Where is he who put within him his Holy Spirit? . . .
> O that you would rip the heavens apart and descend! (LXX: a spirit from
> the Lord descended) (Buse trans., alt.)

This passage has in common with Mark 1:10 that it describes a coming up from the water, an endowment with the Holy Spirit, a ripping of the heavens, and a divine descent (in the LXX, a descent of the Spirit). Significantly, the Isaian passage is part of a proto-apocalyptic section; the prophet prays for God to rend the barrier between heaven and earth and to pour forth his Spirit into the lower realm as part of his act of creating a new heaven and a new earth (Isa 65:17). As Juel (33) notes, Mark also implies an irreversible cosmic change with his picture of the torn heavens, which contrasts with the tamer Matthean/ Lukan scenario, in which they are merely "opened": "What is opened may be closed; what is torn apart cannot easily return to its former state."

In Mark, then, God has ripped the heavens irrevocably apart at Jesus' baptism, never to shut them again. Through this gracious gash in the universe, he has poured forth his Spirit into the earthly realm. Like the tearing of the heavens, this advent of the Spirit is an eschatological event. Although in early OT narratives the Holy Spirit frequently "comes upon" people and enables them to prophesy or perform superhuman feats of strength (see Baumgärtel in Schweizer, *"Pneuma,"* 362–67), the prophets sometimes depict it as an eschatological gift (see e.g. Isa 32:15; Ezek 36:26–27; Joel 2:28–29), and rabbinic traditions portray it as having ceased with the death of the canonical prophets (see e.g. *b. Sanh.* 11a), only to be renewed at the dawn of the age to come (see e.g. *Tanhuma* on Num 8:2 [*Běhaʿălōtka* 6, end], and cf. Schäfer, *Vorstellung,* 112–15). Even the Qumran texts that claim the presence of the Spirit (e.g. 1QH 4:31; 7:6–7; 12:11–12) do not refute this point, since the Qumran community was gratefully aware of living at the dawn of the eschaton (see Sommer, "Did Prophecy," 33–34, 36–37).

Not only the fact of the Spirit's advent but also the manner of its descent fits into an apocalyptic framework; the symbolic language (*"like* a dove") is typical of apocalypses, and the dove itself is probably meant to evoke Genesis 1, where the Spirit broods, birdlike, over the primeval chaos (see the NOTE on "like a dove" in 1:10). An apocalyptic parallelism of beginning-time with end-time, then, is implicit in the portrayal of the Spirit as a dove: with its descent the new creation begins.

That new creation is focused in Jesus, who is now singled out as God's son by a heavenly voice employing biblical expressions. The first part of the voice, "You are my . . . son," is a near-exact citation of Ps 2:7 LXX; the second part, "in you I have taken delight," is a reference to Isa 42:1; and "beloved" may echo Genesis 22 (see the NOTES on 1:11). It should come as no surprise that on this and the other occasion on which God speaks directly in Mark's story (9:7), he uses scriptural language to do so; that is, so to speak, his native tongue, and Mark has already indicated in the first three verses of the Gospel that his story will unfold in accordance with scriptural "prophecy."

The OT allusions, however, do not just function as scriptural proof texts but contribute importantly to the message of the passage. Psalm 2 was interpreted messianically in early Judaism, so that its citation here gives a divine imprimatur to Mark's assertion in 1:1 that Jesus is the Christ (see e.g. 4QFlor 1:18–2:2 and *Tg. Isa* 42:1). In the psalm, moreover, the kingship of the "anointed one" is congruent with that of God, and it is against *both* of their kingships that the evil rulers array themselves, only to be swiftly destroyed. In later Jewish exegesis this opposition to the Messiah and his God sometimes assumes cosmic dimensions (see Marcus, *Way*, 102–5). The similarity to the basic "plot" of Mark 1:9–15 is striking: Jesus, God's anointed one, is acclaimed as his son (1:9–11) and challenged by the personification of an opposing kingship (1:12–13; cf. 3:23–27). The anointed king then proclaims the victory of God's royal rule and, by implication, the eschatological shattering of the hostile kingship (1:14–15)—a claim that is shortly thereafter demonstrated by the exorcisms and healings in 1:21–34.

The second half of the divine voice, the allusion to Isa 42:1 ("in you I have taken delight"), points in a similar eschatological direction, since in that passage the Lord's righteous servant has been chosen for an eschatological task (cf. the messianic interpretation in *Tg. Isa* 42:1). There may also be here an echo of Genesis 1, which would reinforce the eschatological point by using the apocalyptic typology between beginning-time and end-time: "The good-pleasure of God, his delight in his creation, his life-giving conviction that 'it is very good' (cf. Gen 1:31), is reborn in the baptismal waters, rises from them in the person of Jesus, and goes out with him to . . . do battle against the forces of negation that crush the hopes of humanity" (Marcus, *Way*, 75).

Mark 1:9–11 constitutes the most dramatic moment in the entire prologue, giving the reader access to a series of apocalyptic events of transcendent importance, a veritable theophany (see Vögtle, "Taufperikope," 135–36). After ages of alienation, heaven itself has drawn near; the barrier between it and earth has been ripped apart, the power of the new age has begun to flood the earth, and "the Father's voice spreads everywhere" (Pseudo-Hippolytus *Theophany* 6). Yet if Mark's baptismal scene is a theophany, it is a strange one, since there is only one ear attuned to hear God's voice, that of Jesus himself. Mark's readers, to be sure, are invited to identify with Jesus, in that they, too, see the secret vision and hear the secret voice; and by the end of the Gospel the mystery of Jesus' identity will begin to dawn even on the characters in the story (see 15:39).

Before the truth about Jesus can begin to be seen, however, the enemy who blocks its perception must first be confronted, and this confrontation will pervade the subsequent narrative and will ultimately lead to Jesus' death on the cross. The first engagement in that battle is the subject of the next passage.

JESUS IN THE WILDERNESS (1:12–13)

1   ¹²And immediately the Spirit cast him out into the wilderness, ¹³and he was in the wilderness forty days, being tested by Satan; and he was with the wild animals; and the angels were serving him.

NOTES

1   12. *cast . . . out*. Gk *ekballei*. The verb is in the present tense, but the sense is past; this is the first Markan instance of the historical present, which the evangelist uses frequently to signal transitions in the story—here, as often, the beginning of a new passage (see Fanning, *Verbal Aspect*, 232). *Ekballein* does not always carry a connotation of force and can merely mean "send out" (see e.g. Matt 9:38//Luke 10:2; John 10:4; cf. BAGD, 237). But most of the Markan usages are in exorcisms (1:34, 39, etc.), and nothing in nonexorcistic instances (1:43; 5:40; 9:47; 11:15; 12:8) suggests anything other than forceful ejection. In biblical contexts, moreover, the Spirit often acts in a violent, coercive manner, inducing ecstasy (e.g. 1 Sam 10:10), snatching people up and throwing them down (e.g. 1 Kgs 18:12; 2 Kgs 2:16), and miraculously transporting them to a different place (e.g. Ezek 8:3; Acts 8:39).

13. *being tested*. Gk *peirazomenos*. This word can be used in a neutral sense to mean "attempt" (e.g. Acts 9:26), in a positive sense, for trying to determine a person's mettle (e.g. 1 Cor 10:13), or in a negative sense, for trying to find a person's weaknesses or to entice him to sin. The negative sense predominates in the NT. Unlike Matthew and Luke, who record three specific temptations, Mark does not portray Satan as enticing Jesus to commit any particular sins; the emphasis instead is on the implacable hostility between the two combatants.

by Satan. Gk *hypo tou Satana*, a transliteration of Aram *Śātānā'*. The OT knows very little of Satan or the devil; *haśśātān* = "the adversary" is a sort of angelic prosecuting attorney to whom God has delegated the task of accusing human beings (Job 1–2 and Zech 3:1–2). Only in 1 Chr 21:1 is the noun used without the definite article to denote an evil figure who entices Israel to sin. The prominence of Satan in the NT reflects the development of demonology in intertestamental Judaism, particularly in the apocalyptic writings (see Russell, *Method and Message*, 235–62).

he was with the wild animals. Gk *ēn meta tōn thēriōn*. The important parallel in *T. Naph.* 8:4 (see the COMMENT on 1:12–13) might suggest that the animals are hostile to Jesus, but as Bauckham points out ("Jesus"), elsewhere in Mark *einai meta tinos* generally has the sense of close, friendly association (3:14; 5:18; 14:67; cf. 4:36), and in the OT and later Jewish writings the enmity between human beings and wild animals is regarded as a distortion of the original harmony that existed between them in Eden. In the eschaton, that enmity will be reversed (see Isa 11:6–9), and God will make for humanity a new covenant with the wild animals, so that people may live in peace with them once more (see Hos 2:18). Mark apparently believes that this restoration has now happened in Jesus, the new Adam (see again the COMMENT on 1:12–13). Many monastic texts, similarly, link living in peace with the animals with the recovery of paradise (see e.g. Athanasius *Life of Anthony* 14; Sulpicius Severus *Dialogue* 1.13; cf. the legends about St. Francis).

angels. Gk *angeloi*. On this word, see the NOTE on "Look, I am sending my messenger before your face" in 1:2.

were serving. Gk *diēkonoun*. On its most concrete level, *diakonein* describes the waiter's task of supplying someone with food and drink, though the word then comes to mean "to serve" generally and becomes particularly important in this transferred sense in early Christianity (cf. Beyer, "*Diakoneō*"). In our passage, however, the concrete meaning is to be preferred; it makes sense in the context, corresponds to 1:31, and coheres with the Adamic typology that can be observed throughout the narrative, since a Jewish legend depicts "ministering angels" (*ml'ky hšrt*) preparing food and drink for Adam in Eden (*b. Sanh.* 59b). *Diakonein* can also, like Heb *'bd*, mean "worship" (see e.g. Josephus *Ant.* 7.365), and this may be a secondary nuance in our passage, in view of the legend in which Adam is worshiped by angels (see the COMMENT on 1:12–13).

COMMENT

Introduction. The Spirit, which Jesus has just received, now challenges Satan by hurling Jesus out into the wilderness, where the two will inevitably clash; for the wilderness, in addition to being the site of God's past and future redemption, is also the abode of evil spirits in the OT and later Jewish and Christian traditions (see e.g. Lev 16:10; *1 Enoch* 10:4–5; Matt 12:43//Luke 11:24). It is as though the Spirit, having finally found the human instrument through whom it can accomplish its ends, is now spoiling for a fight with the Adversary (see the NOTE on "by Satan" in 1:13 and cf. Matt 12:28 on the Spirit as the conqueror of demons).

Mark is probably drawing on pre-Markan tradition in his account of Jesus' testing, since 1:12 is jarring in its context: how can Jesus be driven out to the wilderness when according to 1:4–11 he is already there? It is unlikely that the source from which he derives the narrative is the extended account in Q

(Matt 4:1–11//Luke 4:1–13; against Lambrecht, "John"). Not only is a drastic Markan abbreviation of Q difficult to explain, but the two accounts are rather different in substance: Q does not mention the animals, whereas Mark does not mention fasting. Mark's own contributions to the passage are probably minimal; he may be responsible for the usage of "immediately" in 1:12 and for the reference to the wilderness in 1:13, since it is superfluous and the wilderness theme is important to him (cf. 1:3, 4, 35, 45, etc.).

Structurally, the passage consists of four clauses beginning with "and." The last three of these clauses have a balanced structure:

A   and he was in the wilderness forty days
B   being tested by Satan
A'   and he was with the wild animals
B'   and the angels were serving him

Parts A and A' situate Jesus, using clauses that begin with the words "and he was." Parts B and B' describe what happens to him, contrasting the assault of Satan with the ministrations of the angels.

1:12–13: Jesus' sojourn in the wilderness. After being driven by the Spirit into the wilderness, Jesus spends forty days there—like Elijah, who was also sustained by an angel's provision of food (1 Kgs 19:5–8; cf. 1 Kgs 17:5–6). But the primary biblical model for our passage's portrait of Jesus is not Elijah but Adam (cf. Mahnke, *Versuchungsgeschichte,* 28–38, and Mell, "Jesu Taufe"). Adam was tested by God's adversary, the snake, who in later Jewish interpretation became Satan (see e.g. *Apoc. Mos.* 17:4). Adam, moreover, lived at peace with the wild animals before the Fall (Gen 2:19–20), and according to a Jewish legend, his meals were catered by angels—catering being one of the nuances of *diēkonoun* ("were serving") in 1:13 (see the NOTE on "were serving" in 1:13). The motif of forty days also appears in an influential pseudepigraphal account of the Fall (*Adam and Eve* 6). In this same account, which probably reflects a widespread tradition (see G. Anderson, "Exaltation"), Adam is raised by God to a preeminent position, opposed out of jealousy by Satan, and worshiped by the other angels (*Adam and Eve* 12–15). Similarly, in Mark 1:9–13 Jesus is proclaimed or even installed as God's son, combated by Satan, and worshiped by angels, if *diēkonoun* is given one of its alternate meanings (see the NOTE on "were serving" in 1:13). This interpretation has the advantages of linking our passage with the previous one and of providing a motivation for Satan's hostility to Jesus, namely jealousy. And it fits in with the Markan prologue's general emphasis on new creation (see the introduction to 1:1–15).

Other OT passages may also have influenced Mark 1:9–13. For example, Isa 11:1–9 speaks of the endowment of a Davidic figure with the Spirit, as does Mark 1:9–11, and it goes on to describe an idyllic future in which the enmity between wild animals and human beings will be miraculously overcome, as in

Mark 1:13 (see Bauckham, "Jesus," 14–16). Jesus' testing by Satan, moreover, is reminiscent of Jewish traditions in which Abraham is tested by Satan in the *ʿăqēdāh*, the sacrifice of Isaac (see e.g. *Jub.* 17:15–16; *b. Sanh.* 89b)—a story that may have influenced the description of Jesus as God's beloved son in the previous passage (see the NOTE on "beloved" in 1:11).

Mark does not specifically describe the outcome of the struggle between Jesus and Satan, but the context suggests that Jesus comes out on top, succeeding where Adam failed, in resisting Satan. The narrative is immediately followed by Jesus' triumphant proclamation of the advent of God's dominion (1:14–15); for the apocalyptic mind-set presupposed throughout Mark, that announcement would imply that the opposing dominion of Satan had been undermined (cf. Keck, "Introduction," 361–62). Shortly afterward, moreover, a powerful exorcism takes place (1:21–28), suggesting that the Satanic side in the cosmic warfare has been substantially weakened (cf. Luke 10:17–18). This understanding is reinforced by *T. Naph.* 8:3–4, a passage that combines several of the motifs found in 1:12–13 and 1:14–15:

> Through his *kingly power* (*skēptros*) God will appear to save the race of
>   Israel . . .
> If you achieve the good, my children,
> human beings and *angels* will bless you . . .
> The *devil* will flee from you;
> *wild animals* will be afraid of you,
> and the *angels* will stand by you.

Here we find the same three actors associated with Jesus in Mark 1:13 (Satan, wild animals, and angels) in a passage that deals with the revelation of God's kingly power (cf. 1:15) and the consequent dethronement of the devil.

This reading would have important corollaries for Mark's readers, for they would probably read Jesus' struggle as prototypical of their own. Whatever demonic powers they might confront, they would know that they, like Jesus before them, had been impelled into the fray by the Spirit and were armed with its power, so that they need not be afraid. Moreover, the narrative linkage between Jesus' baptism (1:9–11) and his Spirit-filled contention with Satan (1:12–13) might well remind them of their own baptism, in which they were equipped with the Spirit to fight demonic powers (see Standaert, *Marc*, 506–8, and cf. Kelly, *Devil*, on the exorcistic dimension of baptism throughout church history). An echo of baptismal theology is especially likely here because in early Christianity the newly baptized person is often associated with Adam (see Jervell, *Imago Dei*, 197–213, and Meeks, "Image," 185), and as we have seen, our passage is strongly stamped with an Adamic typology.

For Mark as for Paul, then, Jesus is the firstborn of a new humanity (cf. Rom 5:12–21; 1 Cor 15:21–22). Like Adam, moreover, he has been granted worldwide dominion, thereby becoming the instrument through whom God's own dominion over the earth may be realized (cf. Gen 1:26–28). In the next passage Jesus will leave his Eden in the wilderness, not, like Adam, because he has been exiled from it but in order to proclaim to God's people the coming of God's royal rule.

JESUS' INAUGURAL PREACHING (1:14–15)

1 ¹⁴But after John was handed over, Jesus came into Galilee proclaiming the good news of God ¹⁵and saying, "The time has been fulfilled, and the dominion of God has come near! Repent, and believe in the good news!"

NOTES

1 14. *But after.* Gk *meta de*, the reading of ℵ, A, and the majority of witnesses. A few, however, join B and D in reading *kai meta*, "and after." This would correspond to Mark's usual paratactic style (see GLOSSARY) but may for that very reason be a scribal harmonization; the superiority of the textual testimony to *meta de* is forceful. Mark's *meta de* construction suggests a certain discontinuity with what has gone before (see Taylor, 165, and cf. the introduction to 1:1–15).

handed over. Gk *paradothēnai.* Mark does not specify an agent of this "handing over." The Greek term can refer to human activity and can simply mean "to turn over to the custody of" (see BAGD, "*Paradidōmi,*" 614–15), but in the famous "suffering servant" passage (Isa 53:6, 12) and in the psalms of the righteous sufferer (Pss. 27:12; 41:2, etc.) it refers to God's action of delivering his chosen servants up to suffering and death. Perhaps both nuances are intended here, since Mark knows of the arrest of John by Herod's agents (cf. 6:17), yet the immediate context speaks of the fulfillment of the divine plan (cf. "the time has been fulfilled" in 1:15).

Galilee. Gk *Galilaia[n].* For a good survey of the theme of Galilee in Mark, see Stemberger, "Galilee." Influential scholars such as Lohmeyer, Lightfoot, and Marxsen have seen Galilee as the land of salvation, in contrast to Jerusalem, the locus of rejection. Stemberger objects that Jesus often encounters opposition and hostility in Galilee (see 3:20–35; 6:1–6; 7:1–23), but none of these passages employs the *word* "Galilee." The word itself has overwhelmingly positive connotations (1:14, 28, 39; 3:7; 14:28; 15:41; 16:7); there are only a few cases in which it may be a neutral datum (1:9, 16) or negative in its import (6:21). It is also significant that almost half of Mark's usages of the word (five of twelve) occur in his first chapter; the word is thus especially associated with the beginning of Jesus' ministry, and this helps to illuminate its usage in 14:28 and 16:7, where it occurs in a promise of a new beginning for Jesus' ministry after the resurrection.

the good news of God. Gk *to euangelion tou theou,* the reading of ℵ, B, L, etc. Many texts, however, insert *tēs basileias* ("of the dominion") after *euangelion,* thus making Jesus into a preacher of the good news *of the dominion of God.* But as Metzger (74) points out, "the good news of God" is the harder reading, and it was probably expanded by later scribes "in order to bring the unusual Markan phrase into conformity with the much more frequently used expression," i.e. "the dominion of God."

The primary nuance of the genitive *tou theou* ("of God") is objective ("the good news about God"), as is demonstrated in the next verse, where Jesus proclaims the good news of the advent of God's dominion. But a subjective nuance ("God's good news") may also be present; cf. the COMMENT on 1:1. The similarity and contrast between our phrase and "the good news of Jesus Christ" in 1:1 is significant: Jesus proclaims "the good news about God" (1:15), but after Easter the burden of the message becomes "the good news about *Jesus Christ*" (1:1). Mark shows an awareness here of the difference between the pre-Easter and post-Easter periods; in the interim "the proclaimer has become the proclaimed," in Bultmann's classic formulation (*Theology,* 1.33; see Rau, *Markusevangelium,* 2047–72).

15. *and saying.* Gk *kai legōn hoti.* Lit. "and saying that," but in Koine Gk *hoti* before quoted speech often loses its proper sense and becomes equivalent to a colon plus quotation marks (see BDF, §470[1]).

The time has been fulfilled. Gk *peplērōtai ho kairos. Kairos* can mean either "decisive moment" (cf. 12:2; 13:33) or "span of time" (cf. 10:30; 11:13). Because of the combination with *plēroun,* "to fulfill," which implies linearity, the meaning "span of time" is to be preferred in the present instance (see Marcus, "Time," 50–53).

the dominion of God. This is the first Markan reference to *hē basileia tou theou,* a phrase that the King James translators rendered as "the kingdom of God" but that most modern scholars have recognized is not so much the *place* where God rules as the *fact* that he rules or the *power* by which he manifests his sovereignty; hence the translation "dominion of God." This is the basic nuance of the Hebrew and Aramaic expression "dominion of heaven" (*malkût šāmayim/malkûtā᾿ dĕ šĕmayyā᾿*), which is reflected by the NT phrase; Åalen ("Reign") can argue against this interpretation of *basileia tou theou* in the NT only by taking the unlikely position that Jesus deliberately rejected the nuance given to the phrase in Judaism. The present instance is a strong argument for a dynamic, apocalyptic interpretation of the phrase in Mark, since here the *basileia* is said to have come near (cf. Marcus, "Entering").

has come near. Gk *ēngiken.* Dodd (*Parables,* 36–37) influentially argued that the original meaning of this clause was that the dominion of God had *arrived,* citing LXX passages in which *engizein* is used to translate the Heb *ngᶜ* or the Aram *mṭ᾿*. In the LXX, however, *engizein* almost always translates two other verbs, *ngš* and *qrb,* which mean "to come near," and this is the most obvious meaning of the Greek verb in the other NT passages as well as in its rare occurrences in nonbiblical Greek (see Kümmel, *Promise*, 19–25; Schlosser, *Règne*, 1.106–8). There are, admittedly, NT examples in which *engizein could* connote arrival; Berkey ("*ENGIZEIN*," 183), for example, points to Luke 24:15 and Acts 21:33. But both of these instances of *engizein* are aorist participles, probably of antecedent action (cf. Burton, §§134–38), and they probably imply only that a drawing-near *preceded* the actual arrival.

Ambrozic (*Hidden Kingdom*, 21) tries to buttress Dodd's case by pointing to the parallelism between the first two clauses of Jesus' announcement in 1:15. This argument, however, misunderstands biblical parallelism, which can imply anything from identity to contradiction, and which in this case probably indicates a sharpening of the first clause by the second (cf. Kugel, *Idea*, 51): "The time has been fulfilled, and *what is more*, the dominion of God has drawn near."

Repent. Gk *metanoeite*. See the NOTE on "repentance" in 1:4.

believe in the good news. Gk *pisteuete en tǭ euangeliǭ*. Here and in 8:35; 10:29; 13:10, and 14:9 Mark uses *to euangelion*, "the good news," in the absolute, i.e. without a qualifying phrase such as "of Jesus Christ" (as in 1:1) or "of God" (as in 1:14). This absolute usage is never found outside of the early church, and it reflects a distinctively Christian "absolutizing" of the *euangelion* concept (cf. Koester, *Ancient Christian*, 5). Surprisingly, it is never picked up by Matthew, who prefers the qualified phrase "the good news of the dominion [of God]" (Matt 4:23; 9:35; 24:14), or by Luke, who in his Gospel eschews the substantive entirely in favor of the cognate verb *euangelizesthai* (though see Acts 15:7). John also lacks *euangelion* entirely. The absolute usage of the term, however, is ubiquitous in Paul's writings (see Marxsen, *Mark*, 147). On other Pauline features in Mark, see the INTRODUCTION.

COMMENT

Introduction. Having, through God's power, stood his ground against Satan in personal combat and thus exposed the hollowness of the latter's pretension to universal sovereignty (cf. Matt 4:9//Luke 4:6), Jesus now comes into Galilee, the homeland of salvation (see the NOTE on "Galilee" in 1:14), proclaiming the good news that God himself is about to reassert his claim over the world: "the dominion of God has come near!" A similar connection between the end of Satan's rule and the beginning of God's is evident in the eschatological prophecy in *T. Mos.* 10:1: "Then his [God's] dominion (*regnum*) will appear throughout his whole creation. Then the devil will have an end." The transition to the theme of the dominion of God is also helped by the typology between Adam and Christ, which pervaded 1:12–13, since the pre-Fall Adam is the earthly representative of God's universal reign (Gen 1:26–28) and is often portrayed as a king (see e.g. 2 *Enoch* 30:12 and the iconographic representations described in G. Anderson, "Garments," section I). Moreover, in one ancient version of the Adam story (*Apoc. Mos.* 39:1–3), God prophesies to Adam that at the eschaton Adam's dominion will replace that of Satan, that he will sit on Satan's throne, and that this transfer of power will be a cause for rejoicing— a parallel not only with the Markan theme of the replacement of Satan's dominion by God's but also with the theme of good news.

Of the two verses in 1:14–15, the first seems to be Markan in origin; it is transitional and full of characteristically Markan vocabulary ("hand over," "Jesus came," "Galilee," "proclaiming," "good news"), and it corresponds to Mark's idea of John as Jesus' forerunner (cf. 1:2–3; 9:11–13). The précis of Jesus' message in 1:15, however, probably incorporates pre-Markan tradition, since it is similar to other NT passages that have been identified as baptismal formulae (see figure 5). The parallelism is most striking in the case of Rom 13:12, where we find exactly the same four elements as in Mark 1:15 in exactly the same order: (1) announcement of the termination of the old age, (2) announcement of the beginning of the new age, (3) call to turn away from the old age, and (4) call to turn toward the new age (see Marcus, "Time"). The motifs of repentance, faith, and the dominion of God, moreover, are often associated with baptism in NT texts (see e.g. Acts 2:38; John 3:5; 1 Cor 6:9–11; Col 1:13; Heb 6:1–2). This identification of 1:15 as a baptismal formula, however, does not mean that its gist cannot go back to the historical Jesus; later baptismal formulae may have incorporated some of his characteristic themes.

Figure 5: Mark 1:15 and Other Baptismal Formulae

Mark 1:15	*Romans 3:12*	*1 Thessalonians 5:5–6*	*Colossians 1:13*	*Acts 26:18*
time has been fulfilled	night is far gone	you are children of light and of day	rescued us from power of darkness	
dominion of God has come near	day has drawn near	we are not of night or of darkness	transferred us into dominion of beloved son	
repent	let us put off works of darkness	let us not sleep like others		to turn from darkness to light
believe in the good news	let us put on weapons of light	let us wake up and be sober		from power of Satan to God

Despite their diverse origin, the two verses hang together as a cohesive Markan unit. The final words of 1:14, "the good news of God," are taken up in reverse order in 1:15 ("dominion of God," "believe in *the good news*"). More-over, the contrast between the old and new eons, which pervades 1:15 in an alternating pattern, is also implicit in 1:14. The arrest of John the Baptist (1:14a) shows the way in which the old-age powers react to those who an-nounce God's eschatological action. But Jesus' return to his homeland to pro-claim the good news (1:14b) demonstrates that the opposition of those powers cannot silence the voice of God.

1:14–15: Jesus' inaugural proclamation. Mark introduces the passage with a subordinate clause that implies that Jesus' public ministry did not begin until after Herod had incarcerated John (see 6:14–29). Actually, Jesus' ministry seems to have overlapped with John's for some time (see John 3:22–30 and cf. Dodd, *Historical Tradition*, 279–87). If Mark knows of this overlap, he has obscured it, probably because of his idea that John's role was to be Jesus' forerunner (cf. 1:2–3) both in proclaiming the eschaton (cf. 1:4–8) and in enduring arrest, suffering, and unjust death (cf. 6:14–29; 9:11–13).

The first action that Mark records in Jesus' public ministry is his proclama-tion of "the good news of God," just as he begins his entire Gospel with a ref-erence to "the good news of Jesus Christ." This correspondence is scarcely accidental; it shows, rather, that Jesus' preaching foreshadowed that of the church, while it also acknowledges the distance between them (see the NOTE on "the good news of God" in 1:14). The content of the good news is specified in a pair of sentences that are carefully balanced in structure (1:15). The first consists of two main clauses connected by "and," each of which contains a per-fect tense indicative verb ("has been fulfilled," "has drawn near"). The second consists of two imperatives ("repent," "believe"), again connected by "and." The two sentences are structurally parallel both horizontally and vertically:

time has been fulfilled	AND	dominion of God has come near
repent	AND	believe in the good news

This parallelism is to be understood in the context of apocalyptic eschatology. The *kairos*, the old evil age of Satan's dominion, is now fulfilled, i.e. at an end (1:15a; see the NOTE on "The time has been fulfilled" in 1:15 and cf. Gal 4:4; Eph 1:10); the new age of God's rule is about to begin (1:15b). The first imper-ative, "repent" (1:15c), corresponds to the first indicative: the hearers are called to turn away from the old age that is now on its deathbed. The second imperative, "believe" (1:15d), corresponds to the second indicative: the hear-ers are called to turn in faith toward the new age that is dawning, in which God will reign as king.

As argued above, this announcement probably incorporates an early Chris-tian baptismal formula. If so, Mark's readers may well have been reminded by it of the moment when they themselves approached the baptismal waters.

"The time has been fulfilled, and the dominion of God has come near!"—at their baptism they would have heard this announcement of cosmic juncture as a promise that they might now enter the dominion of God. "Repent, and believe in the good news!"—at their baptism they would have heard this exhortation as a call to bury the moribund world in the water and to rise from it to view, through the eyes of faith, God's new creation. They would, in short, have been reminded by Mark 1:15 of the moment when they became disciples of Jesus.

It is only logical, then, that the next passage in the Gospel relates the call of Jesus' first four followers.

FIRST MAJOR SECTION
(MARK 1:16–3:6)

THE HONEYMOON PERIOD
(MARK 1:16–45)

◆

INTRODUCTION

After the prologue (1:1–15), the first major section of Mark begins with the call of four men from their fishing nets to a life of following Jesus (1:16–20). In the first six chapters of the Gospel, there are three such extended narratives of the commissioning of disciples (1:16–20; 3:13–19; 6:7–13; cf. 2:14), all of which use a form of the verb *kalein* ("to call"; see Schweizer, "Portrayal," 388–89). In all three cases the commissioning follows a transitional summary of Jesus' activity (1:14–15; 3:7–12; 6:6b; see Perrin and Duling, *Introduction*, 239–40). It seems reasonable to suppose that Mark has deliberately placed the three commissioning narratives at the beginning of literary units, the first of which is 1:16–3:6.

Within this larger unit, 1:16–45 forms the first subsection. It is strikingly different in tone from what follows in 2:1–3:6, where Jesus is constantly in conflict with the scribes and Pharisees. Here in 1:16–45 Jesus' human audience consists wholly of friends and neighbors, who receive him with open arms and thank God for his presence among them. Notices of the profound and favorable impression he makes on his Galilean compatriots punctuate this section: his fame spreads everywhere throughout Galilee (1:28), the whole city of Capernaum gathers at his doorstep (1:33), and the people stream to him from everywhere (1:45). It is really a "honeymoon" period.

Of the five passages in this section, the first four are set either in the village of Capernaum (1:21–28; 1:29–34) or on its outskirts (1:16–20; 1:35–39). These Capernaum passages are distinctive because most of them mention Peter by the name "Simon" (1:16 [2x], 29, 30, 36) and because, contrary to the general Markan pattern outside of the passion narrative, most of them contain an indication of time (1:21, 32, 35; see Jeremias, *Eucharistic Words*, 92 n. 1). These distinctive features suggest that in 1:16–39 Mark is drawing on a pre-Gospel source that described a day in Capernaum filled with miracles and suffused with the disciples' dawning sense of Jesus' mission, as is suggested by Pesch, who refers to the section as "Jesus' Day of Powerful Work in Capernaum" and describes it as a "community-founding tradition" ("Tag," 272–74). It arose, in other words, to serve the needs of the Christian community in Capernaum, specifically to explain the origin of the house-church there (on the archaeological evidence for this house-church, see the NOTE on 1:29).

Mark seems to have adapted the source in a couple of ways. He may, for example, be responsible for moving the story of the call of the first four disciples (1:16–20) forward to the beginning of this section; originally, perhaps, it followed the healings and exorcisms in 1:21–34 (cf. Luke 5:1–11, where Peter begins to follow Jesus only after witnessing a miracle). The source, then, may have looked something like this:

(1) 1:21–28: exorcism in Capernaum synagogue on Sabbath day (minus disciples)
(2) 1:29–31: healing of Peter's mother-in-law
(3) 1:32–34: healing of many people in the early evening, at the end of the Sabbath
(4) 1:16–20: call of Peter, Andrew, James, and John away from their fishing, implicitly at night (see the NOTE on "preparing" in 1:19)
(5) 1:35–39: Jesus' withdrawal from his new disciples in the early morning, their pursuit of him, and his announcement of his mission to neighboring towns

Not only would such an order be chronologically and psychologically plausible, but it would alleviate the difficulty that in the present narrative Peter and Andrew seem to abandon everything to follow Jesus in 1:18, yet are back in their own house in Capernaum in 1:29. Besides moving 1:16–20, Mark may also be responsible for appending the story of the healing of the man with the skin disease (1:40–45) to the end of the source. This story, in which the man is told to offer for his healing "what Moses commanded," is only loosely connected with what precedes it; Mark may have added it in order to provide a transition to the stories of conflict over the Law in 2:1–3:6.

Whatever its genesis, 1:16–45 contains an important message for Mark's community, whose members perceive themselves to be undergoing a tribulation unparalleled since the world began, hated by all for the sake of Jesus' name, and pushed to the very brink of extinction (13:13, 19–20; cf. the discussion of the Markan community in the INTRODUCTION). The section gives them an image to counterpose to this picture of horror—a preview of what the world will look like when it has been transformed by the healing touch of Jesus. Jesus is portrayed here as the one who gives purpose to human existence, who integrates lives that have been physically and psychologically shattered, and who enables the living dead to reenter the world from which they have been banished; in short as the one who restores to life its God-given wholeness and peace—its *šālôm*. Now the Markan community is harried and hated by all, but it will not always be so. Soon Jesus will return and turn this hell on earth into a realm of life, integrity, and joyful lucidity. The tableau of healing miracles in chapter 1 thus provides Mark's readers with a vision to hold on to throughout all the terror of the present—an anticipation of the redeemed world that will materialize through Jesus' power when God cuts the terror short and reclaims the universe for himself (cf. 13:20).

THE CALL OF THE FIRST DISCIPLES (1:16–20)

1   [16]And passing by along the Sea of Galilee, he caught sight of Simon and Andrew, Simon's brother, casting their nets in the sea—for they were fishers. [17]And Jesus said to them: "Come on after me, and I'll make you become fishers of people!" [18]And immediately they left their nets and followed him. [19]And going on a little way, he caught sight of James the son of Zebedee and his brother John—they were in a boat preparing their nets—[20]and immediately he called them. And they left their father Zebedee in the boat with the hired hands, and they went after him.

NOTES

1 16. *passing by*. Gk *paragōn*. In 1 Kgs 19:19 Elijah passes by Elisha before commissioning him, which recalls the previous passage, in which God passes by Elijah (19:11); the latter in turn recalls the theophany to Moses in Exod 33:18–23 (see Walsh and Begg, "1–2 Kings," 172). Since the Exodus passage is alluded to later in Mark (see the COMMENT on 6:48–50), it is possible that Jesus is being portrayed not only as Elijah-like but also as godlike; cf. the NOTE on "called" in 1:20.

the Sea of Galilee. Gk *tēn thalassan tēs Galilaias*. This "sea" (actually an inland lake) is not known by this name outside of the New Testament; in Jewish sources it is usually called the Sea of Kinneret (already Num 34:11; Josh 13:27), the Sea of Gennesaret (cf. Luke 5:1), or the Sea of Tiberias (cf. John 21:1). In the New Testament, however, it is usually simply "the sea"; the full phrase is found only in the present passage and in 7:31, in the Matthean parallels, and in John 6:1, where it is glossed with the phrase "of Tiberias." Mark's usage of the full phrase probably reflects his interest in the Galilee theme (cf. Gnilka, 1.72).

Simon . . . Andrew. Gk *Simōna . . . Andrean*. Simon is Simon Peter, the most famous disciple of the earthly Jesus. Jesus gives Simon the nickname "Peter" in 3:16, and from that point on in the narrative this nickname displaces his birth name, with the exception of 14:37. His name is given pride of place not only in 1:16 but also in the list of the Twelve in 3:16–19 and in the passages in the Gospel in which Jesus segregates three (5:37; 9:2; 14:33) or four (13:3) disciples. Throughout the Gospel, moreover, he is by far the commanding presence among the Twelve, though he distinguishes himself by folly as well as by insight (see 8:32–33; 9:5–6; 14:29–31, 66–72). Peter's precedence probably reflects both his position among the followers of the historical Jesus and his stature as the first of the Twelve to experience a resurrection appearance (1 Cor 15:5; cf. Mark 16:7). Some in Mark's Syrian Christian community (see the discussion of the Markan community in the INTRODUCTION) may have had personal memories of Peter, since he traveled to Syrian Antioch (Gal 2:11) and perhaps to other Syrian cities as well. His brother Andrew did not rise to a position of prominence in the early church, and this relative obscurity is reflected in the need to identify him by his relation to Simon (cf. Reploh, *Lehrer*, 33); his listing after Simon may also reflect the fact that he was the younger brother (cf. the NOTE on "James the son of Zebedee and his brother John" in 1:19).

casting their nets. Gk *amphiballontas*, lit. "throwing around." The reference is to a circular casting net which could be tossed into the water by fishers either wading near the shore or standing in boats (see BAGD, 47; Wuellner, *Meaning*, 9). Best (*Following*, 168) suggests that the term may have been an unfamiliar one, and this is why Mark glosses it with the clause "for they were fishers."

17. *Come on after me.* Gk *deute opisō mou.* In rabbinic literature a pupil sometimes "goes after" his teacher, i.e. joins him on his journey and maintains a respectful distance behind him (see e.g. *b. ʿErub.* 30a; *b. Ketub.* 66b); the following thus displays the pupil's deference for his teacher, his personal commitment to him, and his desire to learn from the way in which the teacher handles the concrete problems of his journey through life. As Hengel points out, however (*Charismatic Leader*, 52), in rabbinic literature teachers do not command prospective disciples to follow them. For other dimensions of "coming after" and the synonymous "following," see the COMMENT on 1:16–18.

19. *James the son of Zebedee and his brother John.* Gk *Iakōbon ton tou Zebedaiou kai Iōannēn ton adelphon autou.* Zebedee is mentioned in order to distinguish James and John from two other famous people with the same names, James the Lord's brother and John the Baptist. The sons of Zebedee are always mentioned together in the Synoptic tradition, often along with Peter in a special inner circle of three disciples (Mark 5:37; 9:2; 14:33; cf. 1:29), once with Peter and Andrew (13:3), but sometimes by themselves (Mark 10:35–45; Luke 9:51–56). James is usually mentioned first, presumably because he was older. His brother John became, along with Peter and James the brother of the Lord, one of the three "pillars" of the Jerusalem church (Gal 2:9); though Paul does not specify that this John is the son of Zebedee, scholars assume that it is he because John is associated with Peter on a couple of important occasions in Acts (3:1–4:22; 8:14–25; see Bruce, *Galatians*, 122). James was killed by Herod Agrippa I in 43 C.E., and Mark 10:39 seems to imply that John, too, was martyred.

"James" is an odd English rendering for a name whose Hebrew original is *Yaʿăqôb* = "Jacob" and whose Greek transliteration is *Iakōbos.* The etymological process of transformation is roughly: Gk *Iakōbos* to Latin *Jacobus* to Late Latin *Jacomus* (nasalization; cf. Italian *Giacomo*) to *Jāmus* (loss with compensatory lengthening) to James (Kraft, "Which James?"). Freedman notes that the name "Iago," the villain of Shakespeare's *Othello*, is also a contraction of "Jacob" and that "San Diego" is a misdivision of "Saint Iago" (Santiago).

preparing. Gk *katartizontas.* This word is often translated "mending" (e.g. NRSV, JB), creating an apparent conflict with 1:16, since mending of nets was a daytime occupation, whereas fishing itself was a nighttime occupation (see Gnilka, 1.72). *Katartizein,* however, basically means "to put in order" (see BAGD, 417) and can cover a variety of activities besides mending, such as preparing or folding the nets before casting them (see Wynne, "Mending"). The present scene, then, probably takes place at night (see the introduction to 1:16–45).

20. *called.* Gk *ekalesen.* This word is not found in Elijah's commissioning of Elisha in 1 Kgs 19:19–21, which otherwise has served as Mark's model (see the COMMENT on 1:19–20), but it is found in several passages in Deutero-Isaiah that speak of God's commissioning of Israel (Isa 41:9; 42:6, etc.) or (perhaps) of an individual prophet (Isa 49:1; see K. Schmidt, "*Kaleō*," 490). Taking up these Deutero-Isaian passages and other OT texts that speak of prophetic commissioning, Paul uses *kalein* and cognate words for his own divine commissioning to apostleship (e.g. Gal 1:1, 15–16; Rom 1:1; 1 Cor 1:1) or for God's induction of his addressees into the church (e.g. Rom 1:6; 9:24; 1 Cor 7:17–24; see Eckert, "*Kaleō*"). Our passage may reflect this background, and if so, the thought may be that the call of God undergirds the call of Jesus.

they left their father Zebedee . . . with the hired hands. Gk *aphentes ton patera autōn Zebedaion en tǭ ploiǭ meta tōn misthōtōn.* According to most translations of 1 Kgs 19:20, Elijah permits Elisha to say farewell to his parents and to make provision for them; if so, our passage and Matt 8:21–22//Luke 9:59–60 would be a radicalization of the OT pattern. But it is also possible that Elijah's response ("Go back again then; for what have I done to you?") is ironical, and that he is actually challenging Elisha to choose between his parents and Elijah (see already the medieval Jewish commentator Rashi and cf. the survey of scholarly opinion in A. Schulz, *Nachfolgen,* 101–2 n. 92). Josephus, however, explicitly says that Elijah permitted Elisha to bid his parents farewell (see *Ant.* 8.354), and this may have been the prevalent interpretation of the passage in the first century (cf. Hengel, *Charismatic Leader,* 16). The Markan phrase "with the hired hands," which is missing in the Matthean parallel, may be intended to reassure the reader that James and John did not leave their father totally helpless (cf. Gnilka, 1.74). As Freedman points out, however, it is a realistic detail that suggests the middle-class status of these apostles.

COMMENT

Introduction. In 1:14–15 Jesus has begun his public ministry as a lone preacher in Galilee; but he does not stay solitary for long. Immediately afterward, in

1:16–20, he calls two pairs of brothers to be his disciples: Simon and Andrew (1:16–18) and James and John, the sons of Zebedee (1:19–20). Almost from the beginning of his ministry, then, Jesus lives in community with a group of followers, and this community will last until almost the ministry's end (see 14:50). Although no simple causality is implied, the placement of the double call narrative after Jesus' inaugural proclamation also suggests that the preaching of the gospel is somehow linked to the appearance of disciples (cf. the similar pattern in 2:13–14; see Best, *Following*, 169).

Mark seems to be relying on pre-Markan tradition for this double call narrative; one indication of this dependence is the explanatory *gar* ("for") clause in the first story (1:16), since Mark normally uses this sort of clause to comment on received tradition (see Best, *Following*, 166). This pre-Markan tradition probably included the second story as well, since the two stories fit together hand in glove; not only are they very similarly structured, but Jesus' direct address in 1:17 alternates with his reported speech in 1:20a, and the notice that "they followed him" in 1:18 alternates with the synonymous "they went after him" in 1:20b (see Gnilka, 1.72). Mark himself may be responsible for the specification of the sea as "the sea *of Galilee*" (see the NOTE on "the Sea of Galilee" in 1:16), for the *gar* clause in 1:16, and for his favorite phrase, "and immediately," in 1:18 and 1:20. He may also be behind the references to Jesus *seeing* the prospective disciples, since elsewhere in his Gospel he frequently draws attention to the way in which Jesus looks at people (cf. 2:14; 3:34; 6:34; 8:33; 9:25; 10:21, 23, 27; 12:34; see Best, *Following*, 168). And it is likely that he has moved our passage to its present position after 1:14–15 (see the introduction to 1:16–45).

The similar structure of 1:16–18 and 1:19–20 is also paralleled in the short narrative of Levi's call in 2:14 (cf. Best, *Following*, 166). The three passages share the following sequence:

(1) a participle describing Jesus' movement followed by the finite verb *eiden*, "he saw" (1:16ab; 1:19a; 2:14a)
(2) a brief participial phrase describing the persons whom Jesus sees, engaged in their occupation (1:16c; 1:19b; 2:14b)
(3) Jesus' summons of them (1:17; 1:20a; 2:14c)
(4) their abandonment of their occupation to follow him (1:18; 1:20b; 2:14d)

In each case, the central figure is Jesus himself; the prospective followers are introduced in a rather incidental way, by means of a participial phrase, and they become grammatical subjects only at the conclusion of the passage, when they abandon their occupation to follow Jesus (cf. Gnilka, 1.73). These are stripped-down, stereotypical narratives that make no effort to fill in the features of the characters or to explain what happens to them in psychological terms; the stories, rather, have something of the simplicity and power of a medieval woodcut (cf. Kuthirakkattel, *Beginning*, 114).

1:16–18: the call of Peter and Andrew. The passage begins with a portrayal of Jesus in motion: he passes along the shore of the Sea of Galilee (1:16a). From the very start, then, the initiative of Jesus, his forward movement into the lives of human beings, is emphasized (see Best, *Following*, 171). This theme is driven home by Jesus' next action: he *sees* Peter and Andrew (1:16b). This seeing is not to be interpreted as passive observation but as an active, "possessive gaze" by means of which Jesus lays claim to something through a thorough inspection of it (cf. 11:11)—though this claim can sometimes be refused (see 10:21; cf. Ambrozic, "New Teaching," 143 n. 53). It is thus not principally the brothers' detection of some special quality in Jesus that leads to their becoming his followers, as in the typical disciple-teacher relationship (cf. Hengel, *Charismatic Leader*, 50–51; Robbins, *Teacher*, 87–108), but *his* perception of *them*, his prophetic vision of what they will become under the impact of his presence (cf. 1:17, "I will make you . . . ").

After passing by and seeing Peter and Andrew, Jesus orders them to come after him (1:17a). The entire course of events here and in 1:19–20 is modeled on the calling of Elisha by Elijah in 1 Kgs 19:19–21:

1 Kgs 19:19–21	*Mark 1:16–18*
Elijah found Elisha and passed by him	Passing by . . . , Jesus caught sight of Simon and Andrew; cf. 1:19: he caught sight of James and John
Elijah cast his cloak over Elisha [signifying that Elisha should accompany him and become his successor]	Jesus: "Come on after me" (*deute opisō mou*); cf. 1:20: he called them
Elisha: "I will follow after you" (*akolouthēsō opisō sou*); he went after Elijah (*eporeuthē opisō Ēliou*)	They followed him (*ēkolouthēsan autǭ*); cf. 1:20: they went after him (*apēlthen opisō autou*)

The point of this parallel is not that Jesus is Elijah (cf. 6:15; 8:28); that role is assumed in Mark's Gospel by John the Baptist (see 1:2–8; 9:11–13). But the general theme of prophetic authority is important to Mark (cf. the stress on Jesus' authority in the next passage: 1:22, 27), as is the notion that Jesus shares this authority with his followers and successors (cf. 3:14–15; 6:17; 13:34).

This Elijah/Elisha typology is combined with another influential OT tradition that is especially prominent in Judges and 1 Samuel and works based on these books: a charismatic military leader calls for the Israelites to follow him into holy war, and they go after him (see e.g. Judg 3:28; 6:34; 1 Sam 11:6–7) or follow him (Josephus *Ant.* 6.77). In Judg 6:34 and 1 Sam 11:6–7, moreover, the call of the leader for followers is preceded by the coming of the Spirit upon him, just as Jesus' call of the first four disciples is preceded by his reception of the Spirit in 1:9–11. This tradition of summons to holy war continued in the intertestamental period; in 1 Macc 2:27–28, for example, the priest Mattathias exhorts those zealous for the Law to "come out after me " (*exelthetō opisō mou*); he and his sons then flee to the hills, leaving all their possessions in the city. Here the wording of the call to follow, as well as the theme of abandonment of possessions, is similar to Mark 1:18, 20. This sort of holy war tradition was still very much alive among the Jewish revolutionaries who rose up against Roman rule closer to Mark's time; Acts 5:37 says that Judas the Galilean "stirred up the people *after him* (*opisō autou*)," and Josephus thrice applies the verb *hepesthai*, a synonym for *akolouthein*, to the enthusiastic crowds who followed various revolutionary leaders into the wilderness (*Ant.* 20.97, 167, and 188). It seems likely, then, that Jesus is being portrayed in our passage not only as a prophet but also as a leader who demands from his followers the same sort of total dedication that the Jewish revolutionaries in the Markan environment demanded from their followers (cf. Hengel, *Charismatic Leader*, 18–21).

The Markan Jesus, however, does not issue orders only; he also issues a promise: "Come on after me, and I'll make you become fishers of people!" (1:17b). There are several shades of meaning in this promise:

(1) In the Greco-Roman environment a fisher of people is often a teacher (see e.g. Plato *Sophist* 218d–222d), and similar images can be found in Jewish circles; in 'Abot R. Nat. (A) 40, for example, different kinds of pupils are compared to different kinds of fish (cf. Wuellner, *Meaning*, 12–15, 111–12). In support of this interpretation, the very next Markan passage describes Jesus, accompanied by his new disciples, teaching in the synagogue in Capernaum (1:21–22, 27).

(2) In the Qumran literature the members of the elect community are warned about the "three nets of Belial [= Satan]" (CD 4:15–16; cf. 1QH 3:26), and with this background in mind a people-fisher would be someone who plucks human beings out of the net of Satan and transfers them securely into the net of God (see Mánek, "Fishers of Men"). In support of this interpretation, the following Markan passage describes a powerful exorcism (1:23–27).

(3) In the OT prophets the fishing metaphor usually occurs in contexts having to do with warfare (Jer 16:16; Ezek 29:4–5; Amos 4:2; Hab 1:14–17), and with this background in mind Jesus might be commissioning the disciples to participate in God's eschatological holy war. The military nuances of "going after" and "following" would support this interpretation.

(4) In Jer 16:16, an OT passage that is rather close to Mark 1:17 in wording ("I am sending for many fishers"), part of the fishers' task seems to be the eschatological regathering of the people of Israel in a new exodus (see Jeremias, *New Testament Theology*, 132–33). This sort of nuance would be supported by the exodus typology found elsewhere in Mark 1 (see the NOTE on "were traveling out to him" in 1:5) and in the Gospel as a whole (e.g. 6:30–52; 8:1–13).

(5) Jesus' own action of calling disciples in our passage may easily be construed as "fishing for people" and may be intended as a paradigm of what the disciples will later do (see Shiner, *Follow Me*, 175–76).

There may not be any need to choose among these different interpretations; the disciples' fishing for people is probably a multivalent image that includes their future missionary preaching, their future teaching, and their future exorcisms (cf. 3:14–15; 6:7, 12–13, 30; 13:9–10), all of which are understood as a participation in God's eschatological war against demonic forces; this war, moreover, recapitulates God's redemption of Israel from Egyptian bondage.

Hearing Jesus' word of command and promise, Peter and Andrew instantly drop their nets and follow him (1:18). While, in the pre-Markan Capernaum source, this reaction may have been rendered more plausible by the brothers' having previously witnessed miracles of Jesus (see the introduction to 1:16–45), Mark's movement of the call narrative to the head of the section has made the obedience itself into a miracle. The very absence of psychological motivation here and in 2:14, which as Shiner has shown (*Follow Me*, 183–86) is unusual for an ancient call narrative, serves to emphasize the overwhelming power of Jesus' word; all human reticence has been instantaneously washed away because *God* has arrived on the scene in the person of Jesus, and it is *his* compelling voice that speaks through Jesus' summons (cf. the NOTES on "passing by" in 1:16 and "called" in 1:20). Mark's Christian readers would no doubt identify with Peter and Andrew in their response; Rev 14:4 demonstrates that "following" can be a term for discipleship to the risen Lord after the resurrection (cf. Hengel, *Charismatic Leader*, 62).

1:19–20: the call of James and John. The second call narrative repeats the basic pattern of 1:16–18 but adds a few significant details. Again, the tale begins with Jesus' forward movement ("going on a little way") and his seizure of the brothers with his gaze (1:19). This time, however, instead of relating the words of Jesus' summons, Mark simply encapsulates it with a short, significant phrase: "he called them" (1:20a; cf. the NOTE on "called" in 1:20). Again, the brothers' reaction is one of instantaneous obedience (1:20b). But there is an escalation from the previous occasion, since James and John not only abandon their property, as Peter and Andrew do, but also abandon their father (the same participle, *aphentes*, is used on both occasions). Mark's readers may again have been reminded of the revolutionary situation, since Josephus says that, in their pursuit of freedom, the exponents of the "Fourth Philosophy" disregarded family ties (*Ant.* 18.23; cf. Hengel, *Charismatic Leader*, 23). Jesus is as radical as the rebels against Rome, and their uncompromising dedication to their eschatological cause can be a model even to Mark's community (cf. 8:34–37; 10:28–31; 13:12–13), who have felt the sting of their fanaticism.

As was pointed out in the introduction to this passage, the disciples become grammatical subjects only at the end of each call narrative, when they begin following Jesus. This grammatical circumstance probably has a theological point: for Mark, authentic human identity is found only in discipleship to Jesus. In the next passage this principle will be upheld through the presentation of a horrifying counterexample, in which a demonic power that opposes

Jesus will swallow up the identity of its human host. But such a monstrous distortion of God's will, Mark will make clear, cannot last long when confronted by Jesus' eschatological power.

THE OPENING BATTLE (1:21–28)

1   [21]And they entered Capernaum. And on the Sabbath he went into the synagogue and immediately began to teach. [22]And the people were amazed at his teaching; for he was teaching them as one who had authority, and not in the way the scribes did. [23]And immediately in their synagogue there was a man in an unclean spirit, and he cried out, [24]saying, "What do we have to do with you, Jesus the Nazarene? Have you come to destroy us? I know who you are—the holy one of God!" [25]And Jesus rebuked him, saying, "Shut up and come out of him!" [26]And the unclean spirit came out of him after convulsing him and uttering a loud cry. [27]And they were all awestruck, so that they asked one another saying, "What is this? A new teaching with authority! He even gives orders to the unclean spirits, and they obey him!" [28]And immediately his fame spread everywhere, into all the region of Galilee.

NOTES

1 21. *Capernaum.* Gk *Kapharnaoum.* A fishing village at the north end of the Sea of Galilee, in the northwest quadrant. The magnificent restored synagogue now on the site is from the fourth or fifth century C.E., but it is built on the remains of a first-century synagogue, presumably the one in this story (see Murphy-O'Connor, *Holy Land*, 188–93).

on the Sabbath. Gk *tois sabbasin*, which is a plural form. This plural does not necessarily refer to teaching on several Sabbaths, as Lohmeyer (35 n. 4) suggests; in classical Greek, the papyri, and the NT, plurals are commonly used for festivals (see e.g. Mark 6:21 and 14:1 and cf. MHT, 3.26–37).

synagogue. Gk *synagōgē*, from the verb *synagein*, "to gather together"; a meeting-place of Jews for worship, scriptural study, and other religious and social functions. Recently, Urman ("House of Assembly") and McKay (*Sabbath*) have argued that synagogues in first-century Palestine were used for scriptural study and social activities rather than for prayer. This would appear to be a false dichotomy (see e.g. the references to prayer in synagogues in Matt 6:5; Josephus *Life* 290–95; and Philo *Flaccus* 121–24; cf. Barclay, *Jews*, 416–17 n. 29). It is interesting, however, that most of the New Testament allusions to the synagogue link it with scriptural reading and exposition rather than specifically with public prayer.

immediately. Gk *euthys.* As elsewhere in Mark, the word is misplaced in the Greek; it should go right before the word it modifies, *edidasken* ("began to teach"), instead of going before *tois sabbasin* ("on the Sabbath"; see the NOTE on "And as he was coming up out of the water, he immediately" in 1:10).

began to teach. Gk *edidasken*. Ambrozic ("New Teaching," 143–49) asserts that, for Mark, teaching, which is directed at insiders, is sharply distinguished from proclamation, which is directed at outsiders. This seems unlikely; in 6:12, 30 the two terms seem to be nearly synonymous, and 1:38 ("so that I might preach there *also*") suggests that the teaching in Capernaum was simultaneously preaching (see Broadhead, *Teaching*, 69). In the present instance, moreover, it is the synagogue crowd that is taught, not just the disciples.

22. *the people were amazed*. Gk *exeplēssonto*, lit. "they were amazed." Here, as often in Mark, the third person plural is used impersonally, to denote an amorphous crowd or unidentified people (cf. 1:27, 32, 45; 2:3; 3:32, etc. and see Pryke, 107). Black (126–28) identifies the construction as an Aramaism.

23. *immediately*. Gk *euthys*. This probably means "immediately after Jesus had finished teaching"; it cannot mean "immediately after he had started teaching," since he teaches enough to elicit the reaction described in 1:22.

their synagogue. Gk *tē̦ synagōgē̦ autōn*. Hooker (Hooker, 22) suggests that this phrase points to a division of Mark's community from Judaism, but here and in 1:39 "their synagogue(s)" may mean nothing more than "the synagogue(s) of the people just mentioned."

in. Gk *en*. This renders the Heb and Aram *bĕ*, which can also mean "with" or "having" (see e.g. Num 20:20; Josh 22:8; Judg 11:34), and many therefore translate *en pneumati akathartō̦* as "with an unclean spirit" (see e.g. NRSV; Taylor, 173). But perhaps the *en* should be taken literally; see the COMMENT on 1:23–26.

unclean spirit. Gk *pneumati akathartō̦*. This is Jewish terminology for a demon; see, for example, *T. Benj.* 5:2 and the rabbinic phrase "spirit of uncleanness" (*rûaḥ ṭûmʾāh*; see e.g. *b. Ḥag.* 3b; *b. Soṭa* 3a); 1QM 13:5, similarly, speaks of the uncleanness of the spirits of Belial's lot.

24. *What do we have to do with you*. Gk *ti hēmin kai soi*, lit. "what [is there] to us and to you?" This is an OT idiom with two shades of meaning: (1) "What cause of enmity is there between us?" (e.g. Judg 11:12; 2 Chr 35:21; 1 Kgs 17:18) and (2) "What do we have in common?" (e.g. 2 Kgs 3:13; Hos 14:8; see Brown, 1.99). Both nuances may be implied here; the demons want to know why Jesus is taking such a hostile attitude toward them (cf. the next clause, "Have you come to destroy us?"), but they are also expressing their consciousness of their difference in nature from Jesus (cf. 3:22–27, in which Jesus denies that he casts out demons by means of the ruler of the demons). Maynard ("TI EMOI KAI SOI," 584) notes that every Synoptic usage of the idiom involves demons' recognition of Jesus' identity.

As Lohmeyer (36) suggests, the demon's use of biblical language may represent an attempt to employ "holy words" and thus may be part of its effort to control Jesus, almost to exorcise *him* (see the COMMENT on 1:23–26); for an example of the use of a biblical phrase in an amulet, see Deissmann, *Light*, 405–6.

Jesus the Nazarene. Gk *Iēsou Nazarēnē*. In ancient magical texts the magician often invokes the name of a god or demon and uses "I know you" or a similar formula in order to gain control over it (Bauernfeind, *Worte*, 3–10).

Although the situation is reversed in our passage—here it is the demon that is trying to gain control over the exorcist—the principle is the same, contrary to Koch (*Bedeutung*, 55–61) and Guillemette ("Mc 1,24"), who think the difference makes the parallel irrelevant. Cf. 5:7, in which the demon adjures Jesus by God not to torment it; this is exactly the sort of reversal that Koch terms "nonsensical" (cf. the NOTE on "I adjure you by God" in 5:7).

Mussner ("Wortspiel") connects the demon's identification of Jesus as "the Nazarene" (*Nazarēne*) and "holy one of God" with the version of the Samson story in Judg 13:7 LXX, which translates "Nazirite of God" as "holy one of God"; the demon, then, is punning on the similarity between "Nazarene" and "Nazirite." Pesch (1.122 n. 20) adds that Mark's readers would not even have had to know Hebrew or Aramaic to recognize the pun, since Judg 13:5 LXX retains the term "Nazirite" (*Nazir*).

Have you come to destroy us? Gk *ēlthes apolesai hymas*. Since the earliest manuscripts lacked punctuation, this might be interpreted as an alarmed statement: "You have come to destroy us!" (see Hooker, 64). But the clause is immediately preceded by another question, and the reader would probably assume that the questions continued until there was a syntactical marker of a change to statement, which comes only with "I know" (cf. Swete, 18). "Come" could simply mean "come to Capernaum," but it probably also designates the overall purpose of Jesus' mission (cf. 1:38; 2:17; 4:21–22; 10:45; see Arens, *ĒLTHON-Sayings*, 219–21).

I know who you are. Gk *oida se tis ei*. The demons recognize Jesus, because they, like him, are spiritual beings (see Wrede, 25). Cf. 11Q11 2:8–9, in which the demons know God's wonderful acts.

the holy one of God. Gk *ho hagios tou theou.* "Holy," *hagios*, a term of cultic origin, is roughly synonymous with "clean" (*katharos*) and the antonym of "unclean" (*akathartos*; cf. Procksch, "*Hagios*," 88). As used in the Bible, its basic meaning is "separated from the profane realm" and hence from sin; the intrinsic relation between holiness, separation, and cleanness can be seen in Lev 20:24–26; 1QS 9:5–9, and throughout the Temple Scroll (cf. Douglas, *Purity*, 41–57). Reflecting this idea of holiness as separation from impurity, the unclean spirit in Mark acknowledges its estrangement from Jesus, "the holy one of God," by saying, "What do we have to do with you?"

In the OT itself the Messiah is never called a "holy one," but Aaron, the prototypical priest, is termed "the holy one of the Lord" (Ps 106:16). One fragmentary Qumran text, 1Q30, appears to speak of "the holy Messiah"; this may be a reference to the sect's expected priestly Messiah, who for them is more important than the Davidic Messiah; cf. *T. Levi* 18:6–12, in which the eschatological high priest is a holy being who, in the end-time, and through the Holy Spirit, will have authority over Beliar (= Satan), the king of the evil spirits, and will grant the same authority to his "children" (cf. Mark 3:15). Perhaps, therefore, some of the priestly associations of "holy one" carry over to Mark; on other priestly aspects of the Markan Jesus, see the NOTES on "being ripped apart" in 1:10 and "your sins are forgiven" in 2:5. "Holy one of God" may also echo 2 Kgs 4:9, in which Elisha is referred to as a "holy man of God" (see Kollmann, "Schweigegebote," 273); for later Jewish reflection on the holiness of Elisha, see *Pirqe R. El.* 33 and *b. Ber.* 10b, and for Elisha as the prototype of Jesus, see the COMMENT on 1:5–6.

25. *rebuked.* Gk *epetimēsen.* On the significance of this word, see the COMMENT on 1:23–26.

Shut up. Gk *phimōthēti,* the aorist passive imperative of *phimoun,* "to muzzle"; literally, then, Jesus says, "Be muzzled!" The effect is slangy and rude, like our "Shut up!" or "Shut your trap!," and this rudeness probably explains the rarity of the verb in literary Greek (see M-M, 672).

26. *after convulsing him.* Gk *sparaxan auton.* The verb literally means to tear or to rend and is used especially of the action of dogs, carnivorous animals, etc. (see LSJ).

uttering a loud cry. Gk *phōnēsan phōnę̄ megalę̄,* lit. "after crying a great cry." Is this merely the unclean spirit's attempt to terrify its human host and the bystanders as it flees, or is it its death cry? The parallel in 15:37, where Jesus utters a loud cry before expiring, might suggest the latter, as does the juxtaposition with "Have you come to destroy us?" in 1:24 (cf. Gnilka, 1.82). On the question of whether exorcised demons perish or simply move elsewhere, see Marcus, "Beelzebul."

27. *were . . . awestruck.* Gk *ethambēthēsan.* In the Greco-Roman world in general, stories about miracle workers occasionally conclude with a notice about the crowd's amazement (see Theissen, 70). More important, perhaps, is the Jewish background to the motif; in the OT and apocalyptic literature one sometimes finds a description of God's action, which can be eschatological, followed by a description of human astonishment, which is sometimes expressed by a question (e.g. Gen 42:28; Dan 3:24–25 [a miracle story]; Wis 5:1–8; cf. Ambrozic, "New Teaching," 127–28).

What is this? Gk *Ti estin touto.* Mark often uses rhetorical questions to highlight matters of importance (see e.g. 4:13, 41; 6:2; 16:3). There is perhaps an ironic contrast between the crowd's uncertainty about what is going on and the demon's assurance ("I *know* who you are," 1:24)

A new teaching with authority! He even gives orders to the unclean spirits. Gk *didachē kainē kat' exousian kai tois pneumasi tois akathartois epitassei.* It is unclear whether *kat' exousian* ("with authority") modifies Jesus' teaching or his exorcism. On the one hand, Mark's readers have just heard the phrase linked with Jesus' teaching in 1:22, and this is the stronger connection, especially since there is no syntactical indication of a stop after "new teaching." On the other hand, later in the Gospel (3:15; 6:7) a linkage is made between Jesus' authority and his exorcisms; cf. 2 Macc 3:24, which speaks of God as "the Sovereign of spirits and of all authority." Contrary to Pesch ("Tag," 127), Mark does not *identify* the exorcism as a teaching so as to deemphasize miracle in favor of teaching. Mark's summary passages, as a matter of fact, put great emphasis on exorcism (1:34; 3:11; cf. also 3:15; 6:7), and he has deliberately placed a dramatic exorcism near the start of the first major section of his Gospel; see the introduction to the COMMENT.

28. *immediately ... everywhere.* Gk *euthys pantachou.* Daube (*Sudden,* 46) denies that *euthys* ever means "suddenly"; its function, rather, is merely "to express the inevitable, one-after-the-other succession of events" (ibid., 60). But here at least, because of the extraordinary pileup of words implying the rapid extension of Jesus' fame (*"immediately, everywhere,* into *all* the region"), suddenness is implied. Mark 1:28, therefore, fits into a strand of Jewish and early Christian expectation concerning the suddenness of God's eschatological action (see Isa 48:3; Mal 3:1; Matt 24:37–39; Mark 13:36; Luke 21:34; 1 Thess 5:3).

all the region of Galilee. Gk *holēn tēn perichōron tēs Galilaias,* lit. "all the surrounding region of Galilee." This could also be understood as "all the portion of Galilee in the neighborhood of Capernaum" or as "all the region surrounding Galilee," which would include predominantly Gentile regions (see Swete, 21). But if the former were Mark's meaning, he probably would have written "all the surrounding region of *Capernaum,*" and if the latter were his meaning, he probably would have said so explicitly, as Matt 4:24 does (cf. Mark 3:7–8).

COMMENT

Introduction. In Mark 1:16–20 Jesus has called four men to abandon their day-to-day pursuits and follow him into battle in the eschatological war that was inaugurated in 1:13 by his one-on-one combat with Satan. These same four disciples now become witnesses to the first extensively reported encounter in that war, a powerful exorcism. As Meier (*Marginal Jew,* 1.409) points out, Mark consciously places this striking set piece near the outset of Jesus' public ministry, just as Matthew leads his Gospel off with the Sermon on the Mount, Luke with the inaugural sermon in the Nazareth synagogue, and John with the wedding feast at Cana (Matthew 5–7; Luke 4:16–30; John 2:1–11). Each evangelist thereby tips his hand as to what, in his mind, Jesus was, and is, all about. In Mark's case, it is "clearing the earth of demons" (Käsemann, *Jesus,* 58); the whole mission of the Markan Jesus is encapsulated in the implicit affirmative response to the demon's question, "Have you come to destroy us?" (1:24). It is not surprising, therefore, that later in the Gospel the unpardonable sin will be identified as misinterpretation of Jesus' exorcisms (3:28–30).

The disciples, whose presence links this passage with the previous one, vanish after the first four words, popping back into view only at the beginning of the next pericope (1:29). This disappearing-and-reappearing act, together with the awkward shift in the referent of "they" from the disciples in 1:21 to the crowd in 1:22 (see the NOTE on "the people were amazed" in 1:22), probably reflects Mark's rather maladroit introduction of the disciples into a story that did not originally include them. Verse 1:22 is probably also redactional; it is extravagant to have two reactions of astonishment in one passage (cf. 1:27), and both Jesus' teaching (2:13; 4:1–2; 6:2, 6, etc.) and the opposition between him and the scribes (2:6, 16; 3:22, etc.) are frequent Markan themes. Much of the vocabulary of 1:22, moreover, is distinctively Markan; besides words about teaching and scribes, we also find here "were astonished," the *gar* ("for") clause, and "authority." Similarly redactional is the reference to "new teaching with authority" in 1:27, which repeats the vocabulary of 1:22 and is out of place after an exorcism. It is also likely that 1:28 is redactional, since 1:27 ends the exorcism story, whereas 1:28 expresses the typically redactional theme of the spreading of Jesus' fame (e.g. 1:45; 3:7–8; 5:20; 6:14). As in many Markan passages, then, Mark's hand is most evident at the beginning and the end (cf. Koch, *Bedeutung*, 45–46).

The passage falls into three sections: the setting (1:21–22), the confrontation between Jesus and the demon (1:23–26), and the crowd's praise of Jesus (1:27–28). The first and third sections focus on the crowd's reaction to Jesus, whereas the second highlights the struggle between the two supernatural antagonists. In the first section the theme is Jesus' teaching, and in the second it is his exorcistic power; the third section brings these two themes together by having the crowd praise Jesus for both.

1:21–22: setting the stage. The passage begins with "them," i.e. Jesus and his four new disciples, going into Capernaum, the hometown of the four (1:21a). As argued above, Mark himself has probably introduced the plural; he has done so in order to link the passage with the previous one, in which the four disciples were chosen, and thus to convey the impression that from the outset of his ministry Jesus always lived in community with a band of followers (see Reploh, *Lehrer*, 31, and cf. the COMMENT on 3:13–15).

When Sabbath comes, Jesus goes into the synagogue and immediately begins to teach. We know scarcely anything about the customs in synagogues at the time, but presumably visitors taught or preached only at the invitation of the leaders of the synagogue (cf. Acts 13:14–16). That Jesus does not wait for such an invitation, or at least that the invitation is not recorded, implies his amazing charismatic power. This point is immediately made explicit by the editorial comment about the authority of his teaching. The word for "authority," here, *exousia*, denotes " 'ability to perform an action' to the extent that there are no hindrances in the way" (Foerster, "*Exestin*," 560–62); it is therefore often applied to kings (e.g. Dan 4:31, 37; 1 Macc 6:11; Rev 17:12–13), including the divine king (e.g. Dan 4:27, 31; Philo *Cherubim* 27; cf. Matt 28:18). The crowd's recognition of Jesus' authority thus indirectly testifies that the dominion of God, which was declared to be near in 1:15, is beginning to make itself felt ("authority" is parallel to "dominion" in Dan 7:14, 27; Rev 12:10; 17:12). *Exousia*, moreover, is particularly associated with God's reassertion of his royal authority in the end-time; it is therefore no accident that it appears most frequently in the eschatologically oriented books of Daniel in the Old Testament and Revelation in the New (cf. Ambrozic, "New Teaching," 123–24).

Jesus' eschatological divine power, his "authority," is immediately contrasted with the impression made by the teaching of the scribes, who will turn out to be

Jesus' constant opponents throughout the Gospel (see 2:6, 16; 3:22, etc.; cf. the APPENDIX "The Scribes and the Pharisees"). Lührmann ("Pharisäer," 182) notes that the scribes are terminologically linked with the theme of authority throughout Mark's narrative (see 1:22; 2:6, 10; 3:15, 22; 11:27, 28, 29, 33). This is partly because of their role as the custodians of traditional interpretation; the eschatological newness of Jesus' teaching is bound to clash with a way of teaching that takes its point of departure from precedent and tradition (see 7:1–13). In Mark's view the scribes' teaching is a merely human one that nullifies the commandment of God (see 7:8–9), and such a preference for the human will over the divine will places them, in Mark's dualistic universe, on the side of Satan (cf. 8:33; see Ambrozic, "New Teaching," 115–21). It is no accident, then, that the contrast between Jesus and the scribes is immediately followed by an exorcism, which demonstrates Jesus' authority in an even more astonishing fashion.

1:23–26: *the confrontation.* The exorcism is touched off by the frighteningly sudden appearance in the synagogue of a man possessed by an unclean spirit. The suddenness of the manifestation underlines the impression that supernatural forces are at work; as Francis (*Evil*, 15) puts it, "He appears *euthys* ["immediately"], as if from nowhere . . . The Gerasene demoniac makes a similar sudden appearance in 5:2, and Satan swoops down immediately when people hear the word in 4:15." The terror of the scene is increased by the description of the demoniac as "a man in an unclean spirit." This phrase is usually interpreted as a Semitic idiom meaning "a man *with* an unclean spirit" (see the NOTE on "in" in 1:23). But a literal interpretation has a great deal to commend it: the man's personality has been so usurped by the demon that the demon has, as it were, swallowed him up. The fusion of the man's identity with that of the demon is underlined by the grammar of the passage; in 1:23–24 it is the man who cries out, but in the next verse Jesus rebukes "him," which now means the unclean spirit. Since normal human beings keep their distance from uncleanness or dirt, this picture of "a man in an unclean spirit," enclosed by that which contaminates him, is horrifying.

Like most of the figures in Mark's drama, the unclean spirit confirms its character by an utterance, in this case a loud cry. It would probably have been smarter for the demon to keep a low profile than to call attention to itself in this manner, but Markan demons seem to experience a fatal attraction to Jesus (cf. 5:6). The spirit's words to Jesus progress logically from (feigned?) surprise at Jesus' hostility ("What do we have to do with you?") to alarm at his power ("Have you come to destroy us?") in an attempt to gain magical control over him through disclosure of his identity ("I know who you are—the holy one of God!"). The key here is the middle clause, in which the demon, speaking in the first person plural on behalf of all demons, expresses their terror at Jesus' advent. For Jesus is no ordinary exorcist, who has learned techniques for channeling and manipulating spirits; he comes, rather, as the sign and agent of God's eschatological reign, in which there will be no room for demonic opposition to God (cf. 3:27 and see Kee, "Terminology," 243). As Zech 13:2 puts it, in an eschatological passage that is associated with exorcisms in rabbinic traditions: "On that day, says the Lord of hosts . . . I will remove from the land . . . the unclean spirit" (cf. e.g. *Num. Rab.* 19.8; *Pesiq. Rab Kah.* 4:7). In later Jewish traditions, the agent for this eschatological removal could be the Messiah, as in *Pesiq. R.* 36:1: "And when he saw him, Satan was shaken, and he fell upon his face and said: Surely, this is the Messiah who will cause me and all the counterparts in heaven of the princes of the earth's nations to be swallowed up in Gehenna . . . " (Braude trans.).

The demon's identification of Jesus as "the holy one of God" is compatible with this eschatological interpretation, since "holy" and related words are often used in eschatological contexts in apocalyptic texts. The root meaning of holiness is separation from the profane realm (see the NOTE on "the holy one of God" in 1:24); apocalypticists believed that this separation could be accomplished only on the far side of this present profane and evil age. A fragmentary text from Qumran, therefore, speaks of the redemptive role to be played by "the holy Messiah" (1Q30), and the War Scroll uses "holy" numerous times in contexts that speak of the coming eschatological battle (1QM 1:16; 3:5; 6:6, etc.). Moreover, one eschatological War Scroll passage, in a striking parallel to our story, blesses God "because of all his plan of holiness" (Dupont-Sommer trans.), which includes a curse on Belial (Satan) and all his spirits, to whom are attributed uncleanness and hostility to God (1QM 13:2–6). Given such parallels, it is perhaps permissible to apply to Mark the Qumran concept that the instrument for the final purification of the world from unclean spirits will be God's holy Spirit (see e.g. 1QS 4:18–23; cf. *T. Levi* 18:6–12 and the antithesis in rabbinic texts between "the spirit of holiness" and "a spirit of uncleanness" — e.g. *Sipre*, Šopetîm 30, etc.). For Mark, similarly, Jesus is God's holy one, and therefore able to conquer the unclean spirits, because he himself possesses God's Spirit, the power of the new age (cf. 1:8, 9–11; see Procksch, 101–2).

Confronted by this eschatological power of God's "holy one," the demon fights back; its invocation of Jesus' name and disclosure of his status ("Jesus of Nazareth . . . the holy one of God"), and as its use of biblical language, are probably attempts at magical counterattack (see the NOTES on "What do we have to do with you" and "Jesus the Nazarene" in 1:24). Seen in this light, the narrator's repetition of Jesus' name in 1:25 may represent his symbolic reclamation of it after the demon's attempted manipulation.

Jesus responds to the demon's counterattack by peremptorily ordering it to be silent and to come out of the man. Mark characterizes this response as a "rebuke," and this word reinforces the atmosphere of apocalyptic battle suggested by the demon's utterance. Kee ("Terminology"), on the basis of a survey of Josephus, Philo, the Qumran literature, the Greek magical papyri, and rabbinic traditions, argues that "to rebuke" is unusual terminology for an exorcism narrative, but this assertion now needs to be qualified in view of the frequent use of $g^{c}r$ = "to rebuke" in recently published Aramaic and Hebrew incantation texts, where it almost becomes a synonym for "to exorcise" (see

Hamilton, "Rebuking," 230). Kee is right, however, to emphasize the mythic background of the term; it invokes the primordial battle in which God "rebuked" and subdued the demonic power of the sea and thereby created the world (see Job 26:10–12; Naveh and Shaked, *Amulets*, Geniza 4:3–8; idem, *Magic Spells*, Amulet 27:16–19)—a myth to which Mark will refer in a later usage of "rebuke" (4:39). Since, in the apocalyptic worldview, the end-time will correspond to the beginning-time, it is not surprising to find elsewhere in OT and Jewish texts the idea that at the end God will rebuke the chaotic evil powers ranged against him and his people in order to usher in the new age (e.g. Isa 17:13; Nahum 1:4; the latter OT text is cited in the Hebrew-Aramaic exorcistic spell in Hamilton, "Rebuking," 223, lines 1–3). These rebuked evil powers are personified as Satan, "the Adversary," in Zech 3:2, a passage that forms the background for 1QM 14:10, where God rebukes the spirits of Belial's lot, and 1QH fragment 4, 1:6, where he rebukes "every destroying adversary" (*śṭn*) as part of the cosmic struggle that will soon end in the establishment of his undisputed dominion over the earth. Although "to rebuke" as an exorcistic term can also be used in noneschatological contexts (cf. above on its employment in magical spells), the apocalyptic context of its use in our passage ("Have you come to destroy us?" 1:24) and of the Gospel in general (cf. the discussion of Mark's apocalyptic eschatology in the INTRODUCTION) support Kee's conclusion that in Mark it becomes "a technical term for the commanding word, uttered by God or by his spokesman, by which evil powers are brought into submission, and the way is thereby prepared for the establishment of God's righteous rule in the world" (Kee, "Terminology," 235).

The submission of the demon, however, is not accomplished quietly. Although it obeys Jesus' order to "shut up and come out of him," it does so under violent protest, tearing at its human host in a last expression of malice even as it evacuates him. But depart it does, thus demonstrating that Jesus truly is "the holy one of God," since he manages by God's eschatological power to accomplish the miracle of separating the sacred from the profane and sinful, the man made in the image of God from the unclean old-age spirit that has devoured him. This separation is signaled by a grammatical shift: the agent of the demon's departing scream is no longer the man, as in 1:24 (*legōn*, "saying," a masculine participle), but only the spirit (*phōnēsan*, "crying," a neuter participle).

1:27–28: *the reaction.* The conclusion of the story with the awed reaction of the crowd ties together the pericope's themes. Their wonder underlines the impression that God's end-time power has just been manifested, since wonder is the response to some eschatological displays in the OT (see the NOTE on "were . . . awestruck" in 1:27). The rhetorical question "What is this?" reinforces the point, since it focuses on the nature of the event that has just taken place (compare and contrast "Who is this?" in 4:41). The response to this question drives the eschatological point home, since it characterizes Jesus' teaching as "new" (*kainē*) and employs the military imagery of commanding and obeying to recap his exorcism (see LSJ, 664, 1851). And the conclusion of the passage, with the instantaneous spreading of Jesus' fame everywhere throughout Galilee, can also be seen in an eschatological light. It is compatible with this interpretation, since suddenness is a characteristic of God's anticipated action at the end of the age (see the NOTE on "immediately . . . everywhere" in 1:28).

Mark's portrayal of the inauguration of eschatological holy war against demonic foes would be topical for his community. On the one hand, it is likely that the Jewish revolutionaries against the Romans interpreted their struggle in similar terms (see Hengel, *Zealots*, 271–90); indeed, those of them who knew of its existence would probably have regarded the ethnically mixed Markan community as part of the Satanic side in that war. On the other hand, for Mark and his community such hostility toward Jesus, the holy one of God, is itself Satanic and recapitulates the enmity that the demons displayed to Jesus. In this regard it is particularly significant that the terrifying epiphany of the demon (1:23–24) is immediately preceded by Jesus' teaching (1:21–22), as though this display of eschatological power had provoked a demonic counterattack. In a sense, then, Jesus' advent is responsible for the demonic attack, just as the Spirit is the real instigator of the struggle between Jesus and Satan in 1:12–13. For Mark's community, which feels itself to be the focus of the hatred of the whole world because of its preaching of the good news about Jesus (13:9–13), this feature of the initial exorcism would function as a reassurance that the world's reaction of convulsive hatred does not invalidate the community's claim that its preaching imparts God's eschatological message. On the contrary, it substantiates it; the violence of the response testifies to the force of the shock wave that has rocked the cosmos in the word of Jesus, just as the persecution and hatred prophesied in chapter 13 will prove that "it is not you who speak but the Holy Spirit" (13:11).

In the next passage the eschatological redemption that Jesus has brought to a single man by the defeat of an individual demon will be generalized as he heals many people and casts out many demons.

HEALINGS IN PETER'S HOUSE (1:29–34)

1   ^{29}And leaving the synagogue, they immediately went into the house of Simon and Andrew with James and John. ^{30}Now Simon's mother-in-law was lying down because she had a fever, and immediately they told him about her. ^{31}And coming forward, he grasped her by the hand and raised her up; and the fever left her, and she began serving them.

^{32}When evening had come, after the sun had gone down, the people began bringing to him all those who were sick and afflicted by demons; ^{33}and the whole city was gathered at the door. ^{34}And he healed many people who were sick with various diseases, and he cast out many demons; and he did not let the demons speak, because they knew him.

NOTES

1 29. *And leaving the synagogue, they immediately went.* Gk *kai euthys ek tēs synagōgēs exelthontes ēlthon.* As is common in Mark, *euthys* ("immediately") is misplaced; see the NOTE on "And as he was coming up out of the water, he immediately" in 1:10. Some manuscripts (Vaticanus, Bezae, Θ, etc.) have a singular participle and finite verb ("And leaving the synagogue, *he* immediately went into the house"), but the plural is better attested and more difficult, since from 1:16–21 readers would assume that James and John were among the group designated "they." Matthew (8:14) and Luke (4:38) both have editorial reasons for altering the plural to a singular (see Koch, *Bedeutung*, 135 n. 5), and later scribes may have assimilated Mark's reading to theirs.

the house of Simon and Andrew. Gk *tēn oikian Simōnos kai Andreou.* A few yards away from the site of the Capernaum synagogue (see the NOTE on "Capernaum" in 1:21) are the remains of a group of small one-room houses; over one of them an octagonal church was built in the fifth century, presumably on the assumption that it was the home of Peter. This assumption may be right, considering the early Christian graffiti scratched on the walls (see Murphy-O'Connor, *Holy Land*, 189–91). If so, the word "immediately" in 1:29 may be literally correct; people exiting from the synagogue might find themselves at the door of Peter's house almost at once!

30. *Simon's mother-in-law.* Gk *hē . . . penthera Simōnos.* As Lohmeyer (40) notes, Peter's mother-in-law is depicted here as the lady of the house, and there is no mention of his wife; we might think that he was a widower, were it not for 1 Cor 9:5.

31. *and the fever left her, and she began serving them.* Gk *kai aphēken autēn ho pyretos, kai diēkonei autois.* Hooker (70) wryly observes that Mark's narrative implies that she regained her strength immediately, "but for once he omits to say so!" It is interesting that the Gospel's final usage of *diakonein* ("to serve"), in 15:41, is also a reference to women who ministered to Jesus "when he was in Galilee"; thus, in a way, the vast bulk of the Gospel is framed by the service that women render to Jesus (cf. Malbon, "Fallible Followers," 41). The translation takes the imperfect of *diakonein* as indicating the beginning of an action; Fanning (*Verbal Aspect*, §4.2.4) points out that this inceptive usage occurs in contexts that involve "the close collocation of two verbs . . . such that the first [here "to leave"] indicates the beginning-point of the second [here "to wait on"]." These conditions are also met by the imperfect *epheron* ("began bringing") in 1:32.

32. *When evening had come, after the sun had gone down.* Gk *opsias de genomenēs hote edy ho hēlios.* This is the first of many dual time expressions in Mark (see 1:35; 2:20; 4:35; 10:30; 13:24; 14:12, 43; 15:42; 16:2; on Markan duality generally, see Neirynck, *Duality*). Often the second expression specifies the first, which is somewhat vague; here, for example, "when evening had come" could indicate the time before sunset as well as the time after it (see BAGD, 601). "When the sun had gone down," then, adds an important detail in view of Jewish law, according to which the Sabbath and other festivals be-

gin and end at or around sundown (see e.g. Lev 23:32; Neh 13:19; Luke 23:54; John 19:31–42; Josephus *J.W.* 4.582; *b. Šabb.* 34b, and cf. Eisenstein, "Sun"; VanderKam, "Calendar," 814); Mark himself shows awareness of this timing elsewhere in 15:42. Since the Sabbath is over, the people can bring their sick to Jesus for healing; the objection of Sariola (*Gesetz*, 114) that Mark ignores the problematic of the Sabbath in the previous two healing stories (1:21–28, 29–31) glosses over the different contexts: the exorcism in 1:21–28 is self-defense against the assault of the demon (see the COMMENT on 1:23–26; on self-defense on the Sabbath, see the NOTE on "to save life or to kill" in 3:4), and the healing of Peter's mother-in-law in 1:29–31 is performed in private, not in public like the healings in 1:32–34, so no Pharisaic objection such as that in 3:1–6 arises.

the people began bringing. Gk *epheron,* lit. "they were bringing." Another impersonal plural (see the NOTE on "the people were amazed" in 1:22); on the inceptive translation, see the NOTE on "and the fever left her, and she began serving them" in 1:31.

34. *many . . . many.* Gk *pollous . . . polla.* As Jeremias has argued (*Eucharistic Words,* 180–81), these two instances of *polys* probably reflect the Semitic term *rabbîm,* which in the OT and later Jewish literature can be an inclusive term for the whole community; *pollous* in 1:34 is scarcely a smaller group than *pantas* ("all") in 1:32, and the inclusive sense is confirmed by the parallels in Matt 8:16 and Luke 4:40.

and he did not let the demons speak, because they knew him. Gk *kai ouk ēphien lalain ta daimonia, hoti ēdeisan auton.* Certain manuscripts (e.g. ℵ^c, B, C, f^{13}) have different versions of a longer reading, "because they knew that he was the Christ," but this reading is easily explainable as a scribe's way of highlighting Jesus' identity and of elucidating Mark's cryptic "because they knew him" by conforming it to Luke 4:41. It is difficult, on the other hand, to explain how the short reading could have arisen if the long reading had been original (see Metzger, 75).

COMMENT

Introduction. Jesus' battle with an unclean spirit in 1:21–28 is now complemented by his healing of Peter's mother-in-law in 1:29–31, and then the exorcism and healing are generalized in 1:32–34.

Most commentators would agree that the bulk of the healing story, 1:29–31, is a pre-Markan tradition because of its specificity, though it seems safe to ascribe at least "and . . . immediately" and the awkward "with James and John" to Mark (on the latter, see the COMMENT on 1:29–31). Many, however, share Bultmann's suspicion (341) that the summary in 1:32–34 represents Markan redaction because of its transitional function and similarity to other Markan summaries of healings (cf. 3:9–12; 6:54–56); it contains, moreover, typical elements of Markan style (the double time notice, "when evening had come," "all," "many," "demon") and the Markan theme of the attempt to prevent the disclosure of

Jesus' identity (see 1:34; 3:12; 5:43; 7:24, 36; 8:30; 9:9; cf. Gnilka, 1.86). Nevertheless, the way in which the time notice of 1:32 fits into the chronology of the pre-Markan "Capernaum Day" source (see the introduction to 1:16–45), the usage of *episynagesthai* for "to be gathered" in 1:33, instead of the usual Markan *synagesthai* (2:2; 4:1; 5:21; 6:30; 7:1), and the strikingly positive attitude toward Jewish Sabbath observance (see below on 1:32–34) all make it likely that the passage represents a Markan reworking of a pre-Markan tradition in 1:32–34 (cf. K. Schmidt, 67; Kertelge, *Wunder*, 31–32; Räisänen, 168–69).

Structurally, our passage forms a pendant to the exorcism in 1:21–28, which is the most striking episode in this section of the Gospel. The themes treated in 1:21–34 appear in a chiastic (ABBA) pattern:

A   1:21–28: exorcism

B   1:29–31: healing

B′   1:34a: healings

A′   1:34b: exorcisms

Although the two subsections, 1:29–31 and 1:32–34, have different forms— 1:29–31 is a healing story and 1:32–34 is a summary statement—the whole passage does have a certain unity in that it all takes place in the same location, namely Peter's house.

1:29–31: the healing of Peter's mother-in-law. The beginning of our passage is tightly linked with the previous one by the notice that, immediately after the striking exorcism in the Capernaum synagogue, Jesus leaves the synagogue and goes into Peter's nearby house. By this immediate exit Jesus gives an additional proof of his "authority" (cf. 1:22, 27): he does not remain at the synagogue to savor the applause of the crowd, but straightaway moves on to the next place to which God has called him (cf. 1:38).

The syntax of the sentence that describes this movement is very awkward, since it speaks of "them" going into the house of Simon and Andrew—the "them," one would assume, includes James and John—but then adds, "with James and John." Zahn (*Einleitung*, 2.246) ingeniously suggests that this awkwardness reflects the conversion of Peter's first-person reminiscence of Jesus into Mark's third-person narrative; originally, Peter would have said something like, "And leaving the synagogue, we went into my house with James and John." This explanation, however, presupposes a redactor who is implausibly wooden, retaining the plural merely because it was there in his source (see Nineham, 81); it is more likely that the reference to James and John was added by Mark in order to link our passage with 1:16–20 (see Guelich, 61). This hypothesis comports with the theory advanced in the introduction to 1:16–45 that in the pre-Markan tradition the call of James and John followed our passage rather than preceding it; James and John, then, would not have been present in the original of 1:29–31.

The story that unfolds after this entrance is a classic healing narrative (cf. Bultmann, 221–26):

Description of illness: "She had a fever."
Request for healing: "They told him about her."
Healing touch: "Coming forward, he grasped her hand and raised her up."
Accomplishment of cure: "The fever left her."
Demonstration of cure: "She began serving them."

Even this bare-bones narrative, however, would have symbolic significance for Mark's readers. In the Greek, for example, the phrase about Jesus grasping the woman's hand is belated, coming *after* "he raised her" (Luke eliminates it, and Matthew moves it to the beginning of the sentence). This unusual position may be designed to concentrate attention on the charismatic power of Jesus' touch, which Mark elsewhere emphasizes (see 1:41; 3:10; 5:27–30, 41, etc.); it is perhaps relevant in this regard that the Septuagint uses the same vocabulary for God grasping the hand of his chosen ones (Isa 42:6; Ps 72[73]:23). Even more significant is the verb used to describe Jesus' lifting of the woman from her sickbed, *ēgeiren* ("he raised"; the same verb is used in the story of the resuscitation of the dead girl in 5:41–42). While certainly appropriate to the context, this verb would probably also have reminded Mark's readers of the general resurrection of the dead (see 12:26) and of Jesus' resurrection in particular (see 6:14, 16; 14:28; 16:7). A similar connection between Jesus' "raising" of people from sickness and death, on the one hand, and his own resurrection and/or the general resurrection, on the other, is found elsewhere in the NT (cf. the usage of *egeirein* in Luke 7:14, 22 and John 11:23–26, 44). This connection between healing and resurrection probably has roots in pre-Christian Judaism; the Qumran fragment 4Q521, for example, links the healing of the sick by an eschatological figure, who may be the Messiah, with his resurrection of the dead. Mark probably wishes to imply, therefore, that the "raising" power that was manifested in Jesus' healing miracles was the same eschatological power by which God later resurrected him from death.

The reactions to Jesus' healing touch also have symbolic dimensions that relate to the larger Markan story. Mark says that "the fever left" the woman, and this wording parallels the description of the unclean spirit departing from the demoniac a few verses earlier in the chapter (1:26). Although Mark does not go so far as to identify healings with exorcisms (see Hooker, 71), he does link them closely together: both shrieking demons and bodily afflictions are distortions of the divine will that flee at the advent of Jesus (cf. J. M. Robinson, *Problem*, 88–89). On the other side of the spiritual divide, the healed woman's "serving" (*diēkonei*) of Jesus and his disciples is reminiscent of 1:13, where the same tense of the same verb was used to describe the angels' support of Jesus during his testing by Satan. The ministry of Peter's mother-in-law, therefore, literarily mirrors that of the angels and anticipates that of Jesus himself (10:45). The conceptual world presupposed in our passage is thus that of certain apocalyptic texts: on one side are Satan, the demons, and certain human beings; on the other are God and Jesus, the angels, and other human beings, though until the eschaton the demons can harass even those in God's "lot" (see e.g. 1QS 3:15–4:26).

1:32–34: *many healings and exorcisms*. The woman's service to Jesus and his companions now gives way to Jesus' service to the people of Capernaum (*etherapeusen* ["healed, served"] in 1:34 is a synonym of *diēkonei* ["began serving"] in 1:32). Peter's house now becomes a scene not of private but of public healing, as the inhabitants of Capernaum bring their afflicted friends and relatives to Jesus to experience his therapeutic touch.

The setting of these healings at the conclusion of the Sabbath is significant for a couple of reasons. First, it shows that reverence for Jesus is not necessarily incompatible with Jewish piety (cf. the COMMENT on 1:43–45). The passage, indeed, has something of the positive, nostalgic attitude toward Jewish Law-observance that is found in Luke 1–2: the godly folk of Capernaum wait patiently for the sun to go down and the Sabbath to end before bringing their ill and afflicted ones to the new healer who has arisen in their midst.

The end-of-Sabbath context is also important because this period was marked in Jewish homes by the *Havdālāh* service, in which God's creation of the world was celebrated; this custom seems to go back to Second Temple times (the Houses of Hillel and Shammai already debate some of its details; see *m. Ber.* 8:5 and cf. "Havdalah," 1481). In some rabbinic and Jewish magical texts and formulae, the *Havdālāh* period is associated with the fight against demonic powers and other magical procedures (see *b. Pesaḥ.* 53b–54a; *Gen. Rab.* 11.2; Geniza 16:5:1; cf. Kohler, "Habdalah"; Scholem, "*Havdala*"; Naveh and Shaked, *Magic Spells*, 220–21). These associations of the *Havdālāh* period perhaps provide part of the background for Mark's picture of the divine act of eschatological re-creation whereby Jesus heals and casts out demons in Peter's house at the conclusion of the Sabbath. The eschatological dimension of Jesus' actions is underscored by the repeated emphasis on completeness: *all* the sick and demon-possessed are brought to the house where Jesus is, and *the whole* city gathers at its door (cf. the COMMENT on 1:4).

Not only the setting of our passage in time but also its setting in space is significant. Peter's house may well have become a house-church at which the Christians of Capernaum gathered (see the NOTE on "the house of Simon and Andrew" in 1:29). For Mark's readers, who themselves worship in house-churches, our passage and later descriptions of Jesus active in houses (2:1–2, 15; 3:20, etc.) would probably have a contemporary ring: as Jesus manifested his power in houses during his earthly ministry, so he is *now* manifesting it in houses through his continued presence with tiny Christian communities (cf. Gnilka, 1.84). Mark's readers may even have seen contemporary significance in the scene shift from a synagogue in 1:21–28 to a house(-church) in 1:29–34: it is to the latter, not to the former, that the populace throngs.

The Markan description skillfully builds up the tension toward the manifestation of Jesus' eschatological healing power in this house, delaying it by the repetition of the thought of 1:32 in 1:33. The reader, therefore, like the inhabitants of Capernaum, must wait until Jesus is ready to manifest his power. When Mark finally does describe Jesus' healings and exorcisms, he adds that Jesus did not allow the demons to speak, "because they knew him." This injunction to silence is reminiscent of the one in 1:25, though the motivations are slightly different: in the pre-Markan tradition taken up in 1:25, Jesus prevents the demon from manipulating his name to launch a demonic counterattack, whereas in 1:34 he suppresses disclosure of his identity, because the time is not yet right for it (cf. Räisänen, 168–74). Both gagging orders, however, fit into the Gospel's apocalyptic framework: that in 1:25 is part of God's eschatological "rebuke" of the power of chaos, while that in 1:34 has to do with eschatological timing, since a premature revelation of divine secrets would risk disaster on the eschatological battlefield (cf. *1 Enoch* 9:6; 65:10–11; 1QS 9:17, 21–22; 1 Cor 2:7–8). In this particular case, the squelched secret is probably Jesus' divine sonship (cf. 3:11–12), and at least part of the reason for its suppression may be that its open proclamation by demons would expose Jesus to charges of Satanic collusion and blasphemy (cf. 3:22–30 and 14:61–64 and see the APPENDIX "The Messianic Secret Motif").

Despite the conclusion of our passage on a note of secrecy, which is linked to a sectarian element in Markan theology (see Watson, "Social Function"), overall it presents a beautiful, nonsectarian picture of Jesus fulfilling the universal human longing for wholeness: not just an elect few but *the whole city* congregates at the house where he is staying, and he heals *all* of them (see the NOTE on "many . . . many" in 1:34 and cf. 1:37: "Everyone is looking for you"). The same world-embracing aspect of the Markan Jesus will come to the fore in the following passage when Jesus tells his disciples that he must move on to the neighboring villages and proclaim the good news there also: "For this is why I have come forward" (1:38).

DEPARTURE ON MISSION (1:35–39)

1 ³⁵And early in the morning, while it was still quite dark, he got up, went outside, and went away to a deserted place; and there he was praying. ³⁶And Peter and those who were with him hunted him down, ³⁷and they found him and said to him, "Everyone is looking for you." ³⁸And he said to them, "Let's go elsewhere, into the neighboring towns, so that I might preach there also. For this is why I have come forward." ³⁹And he came into their synagogues throughout the whole region of Galilee, preaching and casting out demons.

NOTES

1 35. *early in the morning, while it was still quite dark.* Gk *prōi ennycha lian.* Another of Mark's double time expressions in which, as in 1:32, the second part makes the first more precise: *prōi* indicates the period from 3:00 to 6:00 A.M.,

while *ennycha lian* specifies the portion of this period when it is still quite dark (see Neirynck, *Duality*, 47).

went outside. Gk *exēlthen.* It is not clear whether *exēlthen* here means "left Capernaum" or "went outside," i.e. left the house that has been the scene of the action since 1:29.

36. *hunted . . . down.* Gk *katediōxen.* This is rather a strange verb to use, since it is a compounded form of *diōkō* ("to pursue or persecute") and is almost always used in a hostile sense, for hunting down one's enemies (see e.g. Ps 17:38 [MT 18:37], *Pss. Sol.* 15:8; cf. LSJ, 889; BAGD, 410). It does, ironically, fit in with the military atmosphere of 1:16–20; 21–28: Jesus has called the disciples to become fishers (a kind of hunter) of human beings, but instead they immediately hunt *him* down.

37. *is looking.* Gk *zētousin.* Lohmeyer (43) notes that this word, in combination with "I have come forth" in 1:38, gives this passage an almost Johannine air (see e.g. John 7:10–36; 16:27–30).

38. *elsewhere, into the neighboring towns.* Gk *allachou eis tas echomenas kōmopoleis.* As in the duplicate time expression in 1:35, here the second term makes the first one more precise. A *kōmopolis* ("town") is a municipality that is too big to be called simply a village (*kōmē*), but not important enough to be a true city (*polis*); BAGD (461) suggests the translation "market-town."

39. *came into their synagogues throughout the whole region of Galilee, preaching and.* Gk *ēlthen kēryssōn eis tas synagōgas autōn eis holēn tēn Galilaian kai,* lit. "came preaching into their synagogues into all Galilee and." On "their synagogues," see the NOTE on 1:23. Many manuscripts read *ēn kēryssōn,* "he was preaching," instead of *ēlthen kēryssōn,* "came preaching," but *ēlthen kēryssōn* could easily have become *ēn kēryssōn* either deliberately (the combination is awkward; I have had to move the participle to a later point in the sentence in the translation) or accidentally, through haplography (see GLOSSARY). Mark also combines the verbs "come/go" and "preach" in 1:14, 38, 45; 5:20; 6:12 (cf. 1:4). The repetition of *eis* is awkward but corresponds to Markan style (cf. 11:11); some manuscripts smooth the grammar out by changing the *eis* to an *en* (on the interchange between these two words in Hellenistic Greek, see MHT, 3.254–57).

COMMENT

Introduction. The secrecy implied by the injunction against demonic proclamation in 1:34 is reinforced at the beginning of our passage, where Jesus hides himself even from his own disciples. Yet by the end of the passage the Markan dialectic between hiding and disclosure has again asserted itself, as Jesus announces and carries out his intention of proclaiming the good news of God's advent throughout Galilee.

In line with the theory outlined in the introduction to 1:16–45, our story probably rounded off the pre-Markan "Day at Capernaum" source, which enshrined the Capernaum church's foundation story. Verses 1:35–39 would make a fitting conclusion to this source: after demonstrating his credentials through the dramatic exorcism in the Capernaum synagogue (1:21–28) and the healings and exorcisms in Peter's house (1:29–34), Jesus has called the first four disciples from their nighttime fishing, and they have responded immediately (1:16–20). Early in the morning, however, he slips away from them (1:35); alarmed, they hunt him down and imply that he should stay with them in Capernaum (1:36–37). Mark himself has probably added 1:39, which is a "framework" passage containing typical Markan vocabulary ("preach/proclaim," "whole," "Galilee," "cast out," "demon").

In form the passage is a pronouncement story; everything in it leads up to Jesus' saying in 1:38, where he reveals the reason for his "having come forward" and thus explains the elusive behavior that has dismayed his disciples.

1:35–39: pursuit of Jesus, and Jesus' pursuit. One might expect that, after his day and night of strenuous activity in Capernaum (see 1:21–34), Jesus would want to sleep late, but instead he gets up early the next morning and goes off to pray in the wilderness without awakening his disciples (1:35). This behavior is typical of biblical charismatics, who go where the Spirit leads them without so much as a fare-thee-well (see 1 Kgs 18:12; 2 Kgs 2:16; Acts 8:39–40; cf. John 3:8); it is therefore another sign of the fact that Jesus acts according to the guidance of a superhuman will and is not answerable to human beings (cf. 1:22, 27; 11:27–33).

His disciples, however, are alarmed upon discovering his absence; there is something touching about the desperation of their pursuit of him, as this is expressed in 1:36 in the verb *katediōxen* ("they hunted him down"; see the NOTE on "hunted . . . down" in 1:36). A similar feature appears in the resurrection story in Luke 24:28–31, in which two disciples implore the risen Jesus to remain with them; as in our story, however, he vanishes from their sight. For Mark, then, Jesus is by nature elusive; yet, as the continuation of our story shows, he can be found by people who pursue him single-mindedly. At the same time, however, the negative nuance of *katediōxen* perhaps hints at the friction to come between the disciples and Jesus (cf. Kelber, *Mark's Story*, 22).

When the disciples finally catch up to Jesus, they report to him that it is not only they but everyone who is looking for him (1:37)—another sign of the deep and pervasive longings that he has aroused in the populace of Capernaum (cf. 1:32–33). Jesus, however, again shows his authority, his independence of human expectations, by refusing to return to the scene of his former triumph. Instead he insists on going to preach in the neighboring towns as well: "For this is why I have come forward" (1:38).

This statement, which is the climax of the passage, can be understood on different levels, which are not necessarily contradictory to each other. At its most prosaic, "came forward" (*exēlthon*) means simply "went out from Capernaum" (cf. the NOTE on "went outside" in 1:35) and thus corresponds to

Jesus' intention of preaching in the neighboring towns. But it is also part of an important group of Markan sayings about the purpose of Jesus' "coming" (1:24; 1:38; 2:17, and 10:45), all of which have in view the reasons for his entire ministry, not just the motivation for a particular change of location (cf. Lohmeyer, 43). It is especially significant that the Markan Jesus links his "coming forward" with his intention of preaching; this makes him similar to the prophet Amos, who emerges from obscurity into the public limelight to proclaim God's message (Amos 7:14–15), and to some later Jewish figures such as Josephus, who portrays himself as a messenger who has come (hēkō) from God (Ant. 3.400). It also calls to mind some more-than-human figures in ancient literature; the Stoic philosopher Cornutus, for example, speaks of Hermes as a herald (kēryx) sent from the gods to humanity (Summary of the Traditions Concerning Greek Mythology 16), and in Dan 9:21–23 the archangel Gabriel uses exēlthon for his coming forth from the heavenly world with a message of divine grace for Daniel (cf. Dan 10:14; 11:2; see Schweizer, "What Do We Mean," 303, and Arens, ELTHON-Sayings, 272). In 1:38, then, Mark is applying to Jesus the sort of language that was used of divine envoys in the ancient world, and Luke is only bringing out Mark's implication when he changes "this is why I came forward" to "this is why I was sent out" (Luke 4:43). It is possible that exēlthon, which literally means "came out," implies Jesus' preexistence with God (cf. the NOTE on "I have taken delight" in 1:11), but if so, the idea remains largely undeveloped elsewhere in Mark.

But there is one other nuance of exēlthon that is strongly supported by the Markan context, and that is a military one: in the redactional conclusion of the passage Jesus comes into Galilee, not only preaching but also prosecuting his war against demonic powers. Indeed, the previous "I have come" saying, in 1:24, identified the purpose of Jesus' coming as the destruction of the demons, and Mark portrays a very close connection between exorcism and the preaching of the good news: the latter is about the eschatological advent of God upon the scene, and God's arrival means the destruction of the evil powers that have usurped his rightful rule over the world (cf. 1:12–15). So it is doubly significant that one of the nuances of exerchesthai from classical times is "to come forward for battle" (cf. LSJ, 591 [1c]); as Francis puts it (Evil, 13–14), the verb's usage here and in 14:48 "suggests that Jesus and his opponents are indeed engaged in battle over disputed territory, are warriors coming out from their respective positions."

Jesus not only announces his intention of carrying this war to the neighboring towns; he also includes the disciples in his plan. Thus the suspenseful question of whether or not Jesus intends to get rid of the disciples, which has lain beneath the surface since the beginning of the passage, is now resolved by his usage of the first person plural agōmen, "Let's go." Mark's Christian readers would probably hear this exhortation as addressed to themselves (cf. Gnilka, 1.89), and if so, the alternation between the first person plural agōmen and the first person singular kēryxō ("I might preach") may carry a contemporary significance: the Markan Christians are included in Jesus' triumphal progress through the world, and it is he who proclaims the good news through them (cf. 13:11).

At the conclusion of the passage, Jesus fulfills and even surpasses the plan he has enunciated in 1:38 by extending his ministry not only to the surrounding towns but to "the whole region of Galilee" (1:39). Thus there is an escalation beyond the previous passages: not merely a whole Galilean city (cf. 1:33) but the whole region now experiences Jesus' power in word and deed, and Galileans who had previously heard about him secondhand (cf. 1:28) now experience the miracle of his personal presence. The geographical extent of Jesus' influence, moreover, is already beginning to match that of John the Baptist (cf. 1:5: "all of . . . the region of Judaea").

In the next passage that influence will spread still more widely after a notable healing transforms a sufferer not only into a servant of Jesus (cf. 1:31) but into a proclaimer of him.

JESUS HEALS A MAN WITH A SKIN DISEASE (1:40–45)

1   [40]And a man with scale-disease came up to him, pleading with him and saying, "If you want to, you are able to cleanse me." [41]And he, becoming incensed, stretched out his hand and touched him and said, "I *do* want to; be cleansed!" [42]And immediately the scale-disease left him, and he was cleansed. [43]And Jesus, growling at him, immediately cast him out [44]and said to him, "See that you don't say anything to anyone, but go and show yourself to the priest and offer for your cleansing what Moses commanded, as a witness to them." [45]But he went out and began to proclaim it all over and to spread the news abroad, so that Jesus was no longer able to go into a city openly, but had to remain out in deserted places. And the people came to him from everywhere.

NOTES

1   40. *a man with scale-disease.* Gk *lepros.* "Scale disease" is Milgrom's translation (*Leviticus,* 1.768 passim) for the Hebrew term *ṣāra'at,* which the Septuagint renders as *lepra.* "Leper," the usual translation, is misleading; *ṣāra'at/lepra* designates a variety of conditions in which the skin becomes scaly, but not what today is called leprosy (Hansen's disease). As described in Leviticus 13–14, the ailment is one that develops quickly, and people sometimes recover from it; leprosy, on the other hand, develops over a number of years and is incurable apart from modern drug therapy (see Wright and Jones, "Leprosy," 278).

pleading with him. Gk *parakalōn auton.* Some manuscripts (ℵ, A, C, L, etc.) follow these words with "and kneeling" (*kai gonypetōn*), and the idea of kneeling, though not the exact phrase, is supported by the Matthean and Lukan parallels. *Kai gonypetōn,* however, is omitted in B, D, W, and other texts. The phrase could have been added by scribes to assimilate our verse to 10:17 and to highlight Jesus' divinity. Metzger (76) thinks the words were original and were inadvertently dropped by homoeoteleuton (see GLOSSARY), but the preceding word, *auton*, has only its last letter in common with *gonypetōn*.

41. *becoming incensed.* Gk *orgistheis*, a text read by Western witnesses (D, Old Latin, Ephraem), though a much more widely attested reading is *splanchnistheis* ("moved with compassion"; ℵ, A, B, C, etc.). The latter, however, is probably a scribal amelioration, though it may also reflect the interchange of the gutturals *ḥeth* and *ʿayin* in the Aramaic words *ethraʿem* (= "he was enraged") and *ethraḥam* (= "he had pity on"; see Stählin, "*Orgē*," 5.427 n. 326). It is irrelevant for Metzger (76–77) to object against the amelioration theory that copyists have let Jesus' anger stand in Mark 3:5 and 10:14; in these passages the anger is easily comprehensible, whereas in 1:41 it is not. If *splanchnistheis* was the original reading, moreover, Matthew and Luke would probably have included it in their parallels, since they use the term elsewhere of Jesus (Matt 9:36; Luke 7:13), whereas if *orgistheis* was original, it is easy to understand why scribes and the later Gospels changed it (see Guelich, 72, and Hooker, 79–80). The Scholars Bible accepts *orgistheis* but translates it concessively ("*although* Jesus was indignant"), but the related participle *embrimēsamenos* ("growling") in 1:43 is causal, and in John 11:33, 38, which also use *embrimēsamenos*, Jesus' indignation at the power of death is the motivation for a miraculous healing (see Brown, 1.425–26).

stretched out his hand and touched him. Gk *ekteinas tēn cheira autou hēpsato*, lit. "having stretched out his hand, he touched." Chrysostom (*Homily on Matthew* 23.2) asserts that this description is deliberately provocative, since it overlooks OT/Jewish scruples about touching ritually impure people, and he contrasts it with 2 Kgs 5:1–14, where Elisha avoids contact with the man whom he cures of scale-disease (similarly Num 12:9–15; see Davies and Allison, 2.13). Sariola (*Gesetz*, 66–67) thinks that Mark is unconscious of this problem of contact with a scale-diseased person, but the repetition in "stretched out and touched" and the omission in the Greek of the pronoun "him" make Jesus' act of touching the sufferer emphatic, and this emphasis is most easily explained by the man's impurity.

be cleansed! Gk *katharisthēti*. This is probably a "divine passive," a reverent Jewish circumlocution used to suggest God's action without mentioning him directly, and it thus implies that God is the active agent in the cure (on the divine passive, see Jeremias, *New Testament Theology*, 1.9–14).

43. *growling.* Gk *embrimēsamenos*. As Guelich (72) points out, in classical Greek this verb refers to the snorting of a horse; as applied to human beings, it means to express indignation by an explosive expulsion of breath. The nuance of anger continues in the LXX (see Lam 2:6; Dan 11:30) and is obvious in the other Markan usage (14:5); there is no reason to deny it in our passage, especially when it follows the reference to Jesus' anger in 1:41 (cf. the NOTE on "becoming incensed" in 1:41). The word is also used in healing contexts in Matt 9:30 and John 11:33, 38.

cast . . . out. Gk *exebalen.* This is the same term that is used for the exorcism of demons in 1:34, 39; 3:15, etc.

44. *as a witness to them.* Gk *eis martyrion autois.* This phrase could modify either "what Moses commanded," in which case "them" refers to Israel, or "show yourself and offer," in which case "them" refers to the priests (see Cranfield, 95). A reference to the priests is more probable because of the parallelism between the datives *tǭ hierei* ("to the priest") and *autois* ("to them"). The dative could be translated either as "to them" or as "against them"; the latter is supported by the parallel in 6:11, but is unlikely at this point in the story, before the outbreak of hostilities between Jesus and the Jewish leaders. The man's appearance before the priest will testify both to Jesus' miracle working power and to his obedience to the Mosaic Law (cf. ibid.).

45. *But he . . . Jesus.* Gk *ho de . . . auton,* lit. "But he . . . he." Elliott ("Conclusion") argues that the first "he" is not the healed man but Jesus, who goes out and proclaims the good news, since the contrary position, which is adopted here, involves an abrupt change of subject at the beginning of 1:45 and a change back to Jesus in the middle of the verse. Elsewhere in Mark, Elliott adds, *logos* ("news") always means the message of salvation, not a report about a particular incident. But Swetnam ("Remarks") defends the more usual translation by noting that elsewhere in Mark *ho de* always indicates a change of subject, that *auton* is grammatically superfluous if Jesus has been the subject up to this point, and that in Matt 28:15, the only other NT passage linking *diaphēmizein* ("to spread . . . abroad") with *logos,* the latter means an account of a particular incident, not the message of salvation. For other examples of people proclaiming (*kēryssein*) a cure, see 5:20 and 7:36.

went out. Gk *exelthōn,* lit. "going out." It is clear that the man disobeys Jesus' injunction to be silent; what is unclear is whether or not he also disobeys his command to show himself to the priest and offer the required sacrifice (see Hooker, 79).

all over. Gk *polla,* lit. "greatly."

And the people came to him. Gk *kai ērchonto,* lit. "and they were coming to him," with the exact subject unspecified (see the NOTE on "the people were amazed" in 1:22).

COMMENT

Introduction. As an appendix to the "Capernaum Day" section (see the introduction to 1:16–45), Mark adds a healing story, bringing to three the number of therapeutic miracles that Jesus performs on behalf of individuals in 1:16–45 (cf. 1:21–28 and 1:29–31). Like the other two healings, this one has pronounced exorcistic features, but it also hints at the sort of issue of Jewish Law-observance that will come to prominence in the next section of the Gospel (2:1–3:6). It is thus ideally suited for its role as a transition between the two sections, a role that is signaled literarily by the usage of the historical present at its beginning (*erchetai,* "came," lit. "comes").

This is an originally independent story that did not form part of the "Capernaum Day" source, as can be seen from the abrupt way in which the man with scale-disease is introduced (see Kertelge, *Wunder*, 70–71); in contrast to the previous four pericopes, the beginning of this one neither describes the setting nor has Jesus as its subject. The most obvious redactional feature is the final verse, 1:45, which is replete with Markan vocabulary ("went out," "began to," "proclaim," adverbial *polla* ["greatly"], "was able," "go into," "openly," "deserted places," "came," "every[where]"). The command in 1:44, "See that you don't say anything to anyone," fits smoothly and without strain into its context and is a provisional, temporary injunction, in contrast to the other commands to be silent in Mark; it is therefore likely to be an original part of the tradition rather than an instance of the Markan messianic secret motif (see Räisänen, 146–47). On the other hand, the exorcistic features of the story (the anger of Jesus in 1:41 and 1:43, the departure of the disease from the man in 1:42, and the expulsion of the man in 1:43) may well be Markan, since they are rather strange in the context of a healing story but fit into the exorcistic theme of this section of the Gospel. The phrase "as a witness to them," which recurs in 6:11 and 13:9, may also reflect Mark's editing.

The structure of the passage is dominated by repetition and contrast. At the beginning the sufferer "comes" (*erchetai*) to Jesus and expresses confidence in his *ability* (*dynasai*) to heal him; at the end he "goes out" (*exelthōn*) from Jesus, and Jesus' *inability* (*mēketi . . . dynasthai*) to appear in public is noted. The story is dominated by the motif of cleansing ("you are able to cleanse me," "be cleansed!," "he was cleansed," "offer for your cleansing"), and it follows the typical outline of a healing story: (1) request for healing, with gravity of illness implied (1:40), (2) healing gesture and word (1:41), (3) accomplishment of cure (1:42), and (4) demonstration of cure (1:43–45). But the amount of attention devoted to the last element—half of the story—is unusual.

1:40–42: the healing itself. The problematic of the story is immediately introduced along with its main character: at some point in the missionary journey described in 1:39, a man with scale-disease approaches Jesus (1:40; on the nature of this disease, see the NOTE on scale-disease in 1:40). This skin disorder was treated as a grave anger to the cultic purity of the community in ancient Israelite religion (see Leviticus 13–14) and in later Judaism. Sufferers were regarded as, in effect, corpses, and physical contact with them produced the same sort of defilement as touching dead bodies (see Num 12:12; Job 18:13; 11QTemple 45:17–18; *b. Nid.* 64b; cf. Milgrom, *Leviticus*, 1.819). The resultant ostracism is pathetically described in Lev 13:45–46:

> The person with scale-disease shall wear torn clothes and let the hair of his head be disheveled; and he shall cover his upper lip and cry out, "Unclean, unclean." He shall remain unclean as long as he has the disease; he is unclean. He shall live alone; his dwelling shall be outside the camp. (NRSV alt.; cf. Josephus *Ag. Ap.* 1.281)

In the present instance, the desperation of the outcast's plight is underlined by the repetition in the opening verse: he pleads with Jesus and urges him to use his power to "cleanse" him (1:40a).

At the same time, the man expresses faith in Jesus' healing power: "If you want to, you are able to cleanse me" (1:40b). His usage of *dynasai* ("you are able") is significant, since in Mark this verb often implies the ability of Jesus to do what is impossible for mere human power (see 3:27; 5:3; 8:4, 22–23, 28–29). But it is important to remember that, in the overall Markan context, this ability of Jesus is derived from that of God (cf. *dynasthai* in 9:3; 10:26); 9:28–29 uses *dynasthai* to emphasize that the divine power to work miracles comes about only through prayer, and it is probably not just a coincidence that the passage previous to ours shows Jesus praying (1:35). Jesus' power, therefore, is derivative of that of God, a point also made by the shift from the active voice of *katharizein* ("you are able to cleanse me") to the divine passives "be cleansed!" and "he was cleansed" (on the divine passive, see the NOTE on "be cleansed!" in 1:41).

Jesus responds to the man's entreaty with a puzzling mixture of emotions: he becomes incensed, yet stretches out his hand and touches the supplicant, accompanying this action with words that highlight his desire to help: "I *do* want to" (1:41). Scholars have been puzzled by Jesus' anger and have suggested some unlikely explanations of it: the petitioner is ritually unclean, for example (but why would this make Jesus angry?), or he has doubts about Jesus' willingness to heal, or he has interrupted Jesus' preaching mission. All of these explanations read too much into the narrative and fail to account for the duality of Jesus' response; rather, as Hooker (80) argues, Jesus' rage is directed not at the man but at the demonic forces responsible for his affliction (cf. *b. Ketub.* 61b, where scale-disease is ascribed to an evil spirit, and perhaps already 4Q272; see J. Baumgarten, "4Q Zadokite," 162). This explanation is supported by the usage in 1:43 of *exebalen* ("threw . . . out"), the term used elsewhere for Jesus' ejection of demons (1:34, 39, etc.). There are, moreover, especially close parallels between our passage and the exorcism a few verses earlier in 1:21–28: Jesus encounters uncleanness and engages in an angry rebuke, the impurity "comes out" of the man, and the result is the spreading of Jesus' fame (see Kertelge, *Wunder*, 72).

Thus Jesus' rage at the disease or at the demon that has caused it is mixed with his compassion for the man whom it has attacked, and by his gesture of touching the man he even risks contracting ritual impurity himself. But instead of impurity passing from the man to Jesus, the purity of Jesus' holiness (cf. 1:24) passes from him to the man, and the latter is cured (1:42; cf. Chrysostom *Homily on Matthew* 25.2).

1:43–45: the response to the healing. Illogically, however, Jesus now treats the man as if he were the disease, ejecting him from his presence as he would a demon (1:43; see the NOTE on "cast . . . out" in 1:43). Mark's desire to emphasize the exorcistic aspect of the cure has apparently gotten the better of his quest for narrative coherence. In any case, the more important point is Jesus' parting instruction to the cured man (1:44): he is not to speak to anyone, but to go to the priest and offer the sacrifice commanded by Moses in Leviticus 14 for those healed of scale-disease (either three lambs or one lamb and four birds, depending on the person's wealth). By this instruction Jesus seems to acknowledge the authority of the priestly establishment, and at least part of Mark's reason for placing our passage here, ahead of the controversy stories in 2:1–3:6, is to show that Jesus respects the Law, in spite of the clashes with its scribal interpreters that will immediately ensue (see Hooker, 82).

The man, however, disobeys Jesus and begins to spread the news about the miracle, as described in the final verse of the pericope (1:45). This conclusion is full of ironies. On the one hand, the man who previously would not have been allowed to appear in public now goes about everywhere proclaiming Jesus' deeds, but Jesus himself cannot appear openly because of the fame this publicity brings. Moreover, an ability of Jesus, namely his power to heal (*dynasai*, 1:40), has now become the cause of his inability to move about (*mēketi auton dynasthai*, 1:45).

It is hard to see this result as a bad one, even though it contradicts Jesus' intention: the man's disobedience causes Jesus' fame to spread further abroad—not only to all of Galilee (cf. 1:39) but "everywhere." This result would no doubt remind Mark's readers of the situation in their own day, when the gospel was being disseminated to all the nations (cf. 13:10). Indeed, the man healed of scale-disease seems in some ways to be a prototypical missionary: he broadcasts the good news everywhere, and this proclamation causes others to repeat his experience of coming to Jesus (cf. the parallel between "and he came to him" in 1:40 and "and they came to him" in 1:45). In this context the note that the man *began to* proclaim the news all over the place could point to the way in which his preaching foreshadows that of the post-Easter church (cf. the NOTE on "began to send them out" in 6:7).

For Mark such universal promulgation of the good news is itself an eschatological sign (see again 13:10), and the conclusion of the passage with people coming to Jesus from everywhere reinforces this eschatological nuance. The healing itself fits into such a context, since the cure of one afflicted with scale-disease was sometimes seen as equivalent to a resurrection from the dead (cf. *b. Sanh.* 47a) and is thus a sign of the dawning of the new age and of Jesus' centrality in it (cf. Matt 11:5//Luke 7:22 and see Kertelge, *Wunder*, 65).

But this entrance of the eschaton into history threatens to efface the Law's sharp structuring distinction between the realm of the pure and that of the impure (see Marcus, "Jewish Apocalypticism," 24). Although Jesus does nothing strictly illegal in our passage (see Fredriksen, "Did Jesus"), and although he signals his respect for the Law by sending the healed man to the priest, he is still treading on dangerous ground by venturing into the realm of impurity through deliberate contact with an unclean person, when he is not a trained expert in such matters (see the NOTE on "stretched out his hand and touched him" in 1:41). This is the sort of theological bravado that will, in the next section of the Gospel, get him into hot water with the religious professionals (see especially 2:13–17).

Our passage, then, foreshadows both Jesus' eschatological freedom vis-à-vis the Law and his insistence that he upholds it. Both will become major themes in the following section of the Gospel.

THE OPPOSITION ASSERTS ITSELF
(MARK 2:1–3:6)

◆

INTRODUCTION

In 1:16–45 Jesus has battled with demons and disease, but his relations with human beings have been remarkably harmonious, even idyllic. All this changes in 2:1–3:6, where he finds himself constantly in conflict with the Jewish religious leaders, the scribes, and members of the sect of the Pharisees. In a way this tension was foreshadowed at the beginning of the exorcism in 1:21–28, where the evangelist contrasted Jesus' authoritative teaching with the instruction of the scribes; that may have already been a hint to perceptive hearers that, for Mark, the scribes were on the side of Satan. The juxtaposition between 1:16–45 and 2:1–3:6 drives this point home: though routed for the moment by Jesus' exorcisms and healings, the demons now counterattack through human instruments, perhaps with special fierceness because they know that Jesus has been sent to destroy them and their time is short (see 1:24; cf. Rev 12:12).

This counterattack takes the form of arguments with the scribes and Pharisees about the way in which Jesus is carrying out his ministry. Typically, the argument is initiated by the opponents questioning Jesus' reason for doing something, as can be seen through the repetition of the word "why" in the following verses:

2:7   Why *(ti)* does this man speak in this way?

2:16   Why *(hoti)* does he eat with tax collectors and other sinners?

2:18   Why *(dia ti)* do the disciples of John and the disciples of the Pharisees fast, but your disciples do not?

2:24   Why *(ti)* are they doing what is not permissible on the Sabbath?

The "why" is missing only in the final passage, 3:1–6, where the opponents' objection is implied but not described.

In each of the stories Jesus responds to the objection in a forceful manner, either by an answer that silences his opponents (2:17, 19–22, 25–27) or by an answer in combination with a miracle that drives the point home (2:9–11; 3:4–5). In each case the answer expresses the central point of the passage:

2:10   But so that you may know that upon the earth the Son of Man has authority to forgive sins

2:17   The strong don't need a doctor, but the sick. I did not come to call righteous people but sinners.

2:19–20   Can the wedding guests fast while the bridegroom is with them? As long as they have the bridegroom with them, they cannot fast. But the days will come when the bridegroom is taken away from them, and then they will fast on that day.

2:27–28   The Sabbath was created for man, and not man for the Sabbath; so the Son of Man is lord even of the Sabbath.

3:4   Is it permissible to do good on the Sabbath or to do evil, to save life or to kill?

Scholars call such narratives controversy stories, because of their argumentative nature, or pronouncement stories, because they climax in an authoritative declaration by Jesus (see Bultmann, 12–27, and Taylor, *Formation*, 63–87).

There is something artificial about the way in which Mark and the other Gospels group such stories together. It strains credulity, for example, to imagine that Jesus spent several days doing nothing but performing exorcisms and other healings (1:21–45), then spent several more days doing nothing but arguing with his opponents (2:1–3:6). Rather, the concatenation of material in 2:1–3:6 probably reflects later collectors' organization of originally disparate narratives. It is most likely, as Guelich (82–83) argues, that there first arose a pre-Markan core collection (2:13–28), which was then expanded by Mark's imposition of a "frame" around it (2:1–12; 3:1–6). The three central controversies (2:13–17; 2:18–22; 2:23–28) all concern the theme of eating, are pure examples of the controversy form, and have a consistent cast of characters: Jesus, his opponents, and the disciples; three, moreover, is a good number of units to have in such a collection (cf. the introduction to Mark 4:1–34 on the three seed parables in the pre-Markan parable collection). The two "frame" passages, on the other hand, lack the eating theme, mix the controversy form with a healing miracle, and do not mention the disciples.

The framing stories, 2:1–12 and 3:1–6, have a number of striking parallels, which probably reflect Markan redactional activity, though the core stories themselves are pre-Markan. Both mix controversy elements with miracle elements, both begin with a nearly identical phrase (*kai eiselthōn/eiselthen palin eis*), and in both Jesus perceives his opponents' unspoken objection supernaturally, interrupts his miracle to address the objection, and answers in two addresses to the sufferer that are expressed in almost identical terms ("he said to the paralytic"/"he said to the man"; cf. Dewey, *Debate*, 100–101). In both stories, moreover, Jesus says *egeire* ("Get up!") to the sufferer. And if the man's "withered hand" is a form of paralysis (see the NOTE on 3:1), then both passages deal with the healing of paralytics.

In spite of Mark 2:1–3:6 being a mixture of a pre-Markan collection with Markan expansions, the section as a whole has a tight structure that gives it a powerful overall effect, which has been perceptively analyzed by Joanna Dewey. As she points out (*Debate*, 115–16), the complex is preceded (1:45) and followed (3:7–8) by summary passages stressing Jesus' popularity. The first two stories, 2:1–12 and 2:13–17, have to do with sin, whereas the last two, 2:23–28 and 3:1–6, have to do with the Sabbath law. The middle three, as already noted, share the motif of eating, whereas the first and the last (2:1–12 and 3:1–6) are mixed controversy and healing stories with a number of striking literary parallels (see the introduction to the COMMENT on 3:1–6). We thus obtain the following overall picture:

SIN $\begin{cases} \text{2:1–12:} & \text{the healing of the paralytic} \\ \text{2:13–17:} & \text{the call of Levi/eating with sinners} \end{cases}$

$\left.\begin{matrix} \text{2:18–22:} & \text{the sayings on fasting and on the} \\ & \text{old and the new} \end{matrix}\right\}$ EATING

SABBATH $\begin{cases} \text{2:23–28:} & \text{plucking grain on the Sabbath} \\ \text{3:1–6:} & \text{the healing on the Sabbath} \end{cases}$

Dewey goes too far, however, in asserting that the whole section is concentrically arranged (*Debate*, 110); 2:13–17 and 2:23–28 do not correspond to each other either structurally or thematically, as such an arrangement would require. More important than any such circular pattern is the linear progression within the section toward greater and greater tension between Jesus and his opponents. The opponents move from questioning Jesus silently (2:7) to interrogating the disciples about him (2:16) to interrogating him about them (2:18, 24) to seeking legal grounds for condemning him (3:2) to plotting his murder (3:6; see Dewey, *Debate*, 116).

Although the section is not concentrically structured, it is still true, as Dewey claims, that its central passage, 2:18–22, makes explicit the unifying theme of the entire section, the incompatibility between the old and the new. In 2:1–12 Jesus claims to possess the eschatological authority to forgive sins; then in 2:13–17 he demonstrates an unprecedented openness in his table fellowship; next in 2:18–22 he separates himself from his contemporaries' penitential practices in view of the advent of the era of God's grace; and finally in 2:23–28 and 3:1–6 he bends the letter of the Sabbath law because he is an eschatological figure, the Son of Man, and therefore the lord of the Sabbath. Upon each of these occasions, those who question Jesus' authority for making such departures from precedent are scandalized, and in the course of the section their upset increases until it ripens into a murderous intent.

JESUS HEALS A PARALYTIC (2:1–12)

2 ¹And he returned several days later to Capernaum, and it was rumored that he was at home. ²And many people gathered together there, so that there was no room even in front of the door, and he was speaking the word to them. ³And a paralytic was brought to him, carried by four of his friends; ⁴and not being able to reach him because of the crowd, they unroofed the roof where he was, and digging through they lowered the pallet upon which the paralytic was lying. ⁵And Jesus, seeing their faith, said to the paralytic, "My child, your sins are forgiven."

⁶But some of the scribes were sitting there and pondering in their hearts: ⁷"Why does this man speak in this way? He is blaspheming! Who can forgive sins except One, that is, God?" ⁸And Jesus, immediately recognizing in his spirit that they were pondering within themselves in this way, said to them, "Why are you pondering in your hearts? ⁹Which is easier, to say to the paralytic, 'Your sins are forgiven,' or to say, 'Get up, take up your pallet, and walk!'? ¹⁰But so that you may know that upon the earth the Son of Man has authority to forgive sins"—he said to the paralytic: ¹¹"I say to you, get up, take up your pallet, and go to your house!" ¹²And he got up, and immediately he took up his pallet and went out in front of them all, so that they all were amazed and glorified God, saying, "We have never seen anything like it!"

NOTES

2 1. *at home.* Gk *en oikǭ*. This could simply mean "in a house," but *en oikǭ* is a fixed idiom for "at home" from classical times onward (see BAGD, 560 [1aα]; cf. 1 Cor 11:34; 14:35). We are, therefore, probably meant to understand that Jesus is at Peter's house, his base of operations at the beginning of his ministry (cf. 1:29; see Pesch, 153 n. 5).

2. *even in front of the door.* Gk *mēde pros tēn thyran.* The unexpressed implication is: much less inside the house.

the word. Gk *ton logon.* On the absolute use of "the word," see the NOTE on "the word" in 4:14.

3. *And a paralytic was brought to him, carried by four of his friends.* Gk *kai erchontai pherontes pros auton paralytikon airomenon hypo tessarōn*, lit. "And they came bringing to him a paralytic, carried by four"—an awkward sentence because the subject is the same as the the object of the preposition "by," namely the four friends of the paralytic. But "they came bringing" is another

example of the third person plural used impersonally, and here it is the equivalent of a passive (see the NOTE on "the people were amazed" in 1:22).

4. *they unroofed the roof.* Gk *apestegasan tēn stegēn.* Access to the roof,
which would have been necessary for repair and for enjoying cool nighttime
breezes during the summer, would have been by means of an outside wood
ladder (see Roubos, "Biblical Institutions," 350). The roofs of the dwellings of
common people in Israel were "made of wooden beams placed across stone or
mudbrick walls; the beams were covered with reeds, matted layers of thorns,
and several inches of clay" (Fitzmyer, *Luke,* 1.582).

pallet. Gk *krabatton.* The *krabattos* was the poor person's bed (BAGD, 447), a
wooden frame which could double as a litter or stretcher (McCullough, "Bed").
The more usual term for bed, *klinē,* is used in 4:21; 7:30, and perhaps 7:4.

5. *seeing their faith.* Gk *idōn . . . tēn pistin autōn.* On "seeing" used for spiritual insight, cf. 4:12. It is unclear whether the reference is to the faith of the
bearers alone or whether it also includes the faith of the paralytic; the paralytic
is, in any case, not singled out.

your sins are forgiven. Gk *aphientai sou hai hamartiai.* Many manuscripts
have the perfect *apheōntai* = "have been forgiven" both here and in the
Matthean parallel (Matt 9:2), but in both instances this is probably a harmonization with Luke 5:20 (see Klauck, "Frage," 241). "Are forgiven" can be interpreted as a divine passive (see Jeremias, *New Testament Theology,* 11, and cf.
4:12, in which a divine passive is used in a statement about God *not* forgiving
sins). If this were the case, the declaration would be very much like that of a
priest, who according to Lev 4:26, 31, etc. "shall make atonement on his behalf
for his sin, and he shall be forgiven" (NRSV)—the implied forgiver being God.
Although there is no explicit statement that such atonement rituals were
accompanied by the priest's declaration of divine forgiveness, it can be assumed that they were (see Klauck, "Frage," 237). Part of Jesus' offense, then,
may be his usurpation of priestly prerogatives, and this makes particularly good
sense if scribes were priests (see the APPENDIX "The Scribes and the Pharisees"). But "are forgiven" is probably not just a divine passive in the Markan
context; see the COMMENT on 2:6–10.

6. *pondering.* Gk *dialogizomenoi;* cf. the two usages of this verb in 2:8. The
repetition emphasizes the verb, which has a connotation of calculation and is
almost always used in a negative sense in the NT (see Petzke, "*Dialogizomai*"). Later in Mark the term will again be used for the hostile deliberations
of the Jewish leaders (11:31) and also for the misguided ones of the disciples
(8:16–17; 9:33).

hearts. In the OT the "heart" is used in a way very similar to the modern (and
ancient Greek) use of "mind," for the center of individual human cognitive existence, the seat of volition and of emotional, intellectual, and spiritual life.
The NT follows this holistic OT usage (see Behm, "*Kardia,*" 605–13); in our
passage, for example, "in their/your hearts" alternates with "in themselves." Because of the concealment of the heart within the body, the image readily lends
itself to the nuance of secret thoughts and plans (see e.g. 1 Sam 16:7). For some

biblical authors, moreover, the heart is easily corruptible (see e.g. Gen 6:5; 8:22; Jer 17:9), and this may help explain the contrast in 2:8 between the scribes' pondering in their *hearts* and Jesus' perception in his *spirit* (cf. 8:12).

7. *Who can forgive sins except One, that is, God?* Gk *tis dynatai aphienai hamartias ei mē heis ho theos.* On the OT idea that forgiveness is a prerogative of God, see the COMMENT on 2:6–10. Hofius ("Jesu Zuspruch," 127 n. 11) cites a close parallel from a late midrash: "No one (*'êyn eḥād*) can forgive transgressions except you [God]" (*Midrash Psalms* 17:3). Koch (*Bedeutung*, 117–48) claims that the Messiah is a forgiver of sins in *Tg. Isa* 53:4 and that the eschatological high priest is one in *T. Levi* 18:9, but these figures only make intercession for sinners or announce God's forgiveness to them; God himself remains the actual agent of forgiveness (see Guelich, 87). Similarly, when *Pesiq. R.* 37:2 says that "the utterance of [the Messiah's] tongue is pardon and forgiveness for Israel" (Braude trans.), the meaning is that he will beseech God to forgive Israel, as the context makes clear. But in a fragmentary Qumran text, the *Prayer of Nabonidus* (4Q242), a Jewish exorcist or diviner (*gzr*) forgives Nabonidus' sins (see Dupont-Sommer, 322 n. 3, and cf. the translations of Vermes and García Martínez). Klauck ("Frage," 239–40), Tuckett ("Present Son," 74–75 n. 29), and Hogan (*Healing*, 149–57) question this reading and argue that God rather than the exorcist/diviner is the forgiver in the passage, but the proposed reconstructions involve either textual emendation or tortuous Aramaic grammar; it is better to go with Fitzmyer (*Luke*, 1.585) and recognize the text as "an important piece of evidence showing that some Palestinian Jews thought that a human being on earth could remit sins for God" (interpreting *lh* as "for him" = God).

8. *in his spirit.* Gk *tǭ pneumati autou,* lit. "by means of his spirit." In the OT "spirit" can be used as an anthropological term for the seat of the emotions, the will, or the intellect (see Baumgärtel, "Spirit," 360–62). This approximates the meaning of "heart," and indeed the two words can appear in synonymous parallelism (see Ps 77:6), but because of its association with the breath of God, "spirit" as an anthropological term usually has a more positive nuance than "heart" (see the NOTE on "hearts" in 2:6). As Gundry (113) points out, moreover, "spirit" is associated with power, and here Mark is emphasizing the clairvoyant power of Jesus.

9. *Which is easier, to say to the paralytic, 'Your sins are forgiven,' or to say, 'Get up, take up your pallet, and walk!'?* Gk *ti estin eukopōteron, eipein tǭ paralytikǭ, Aphientai sou hai hamartiai, ē eipein, Egeire kai aron ton krabatton sou kai peripatei.* But which *is* easier? From the standpoint of systematic theology, it may be simpler to perform a miraculous cure than to forgive a person's sins, but in terms of external proof, which is what is at stake in our passage, it is easier to declare sins forgiven than to declare a person cured. One may *say*, "Your sins are forgiven," but are they? Outside observers have no immediate way of knowing, whereas they can at once verify a miraculous cure (see Taylor, 197). Thus Jesus' ability to heal is an argument "from the greater to the lesser": if he can do a hard thing such as healing a paralytic, he

can certainly do the "easier" thing of forgiving his sins (cf. Lagrange, 37). The miracle thus confirms the claim to forgive sins, although the logic is, from the systematic point of view, flawed.

10. *so that you may know*. Gk *hina . . . eidēte*. Boobyer ("Mark II, 10a," 115–20) suggests that 2:10 is, like 13:14, an aside to the reader from Mark himself, but in the absence of a clear literary signal such as "let the reader understand" it is better to take the verse as the continuation of Jesus' words to the scribes (cf. Tolbert, 136 n. 18). The phrasing here may be modeled on the repeated instances of "so that you may know" (LXX *hina eidēs*) in the Exodus narratives about Moses' confrontation with Pharaoh (Exod 7:17; 8:10, 22; 9:14; 10:2; cf. C. F. Evans, *Luke*, 301). The context is particularly close to that of Exod 9:14, which deals with God's incommensurability on earth ("so that you may know that there is none like me in all the earth"), and to that of Exod 8:22, which deals with his sovereignty over the earth ("so that you may know that I am the Lord in the midst of the earth"; RSV alt.). If Mark is aware of these echoes of Exodus, it is significant that he has transformed divine oracles against the ancient, archetypical Gentile enemy of Israel into a prophetic judgment against Israel's own religious leaders.

upon the earth. Gk *epi tēs gēs*. The position of this phrase varies greatly in the manuscripts; it follows either "sins," "to forgive," or "the Son of Man," and some manuscripts omit it altogether. The most difficult text, and therefore probably the original one, is that of **א**, C, D, L, etc., *exousian echei ho huios tou anthrōpou epi tēs gēs aphienai hamartias*, lit. "authority has the Son of Man upon the earth to forgive sins." The position of "upon the earth" before "to forgive sins" makes it more emphatic than it would be if it came after "to forgive sins"; on the reason for this emphasis, see the COMMENT on 2:6–10a.

the Son of Man. Gk *ho huios tou anthrōpou*. On the meaning of this self-reference, and its connection with Daniel 7, see the APPENDIX "The Son of Man."

11. *get up*. Gk *egeire*. The usage of the active for the intransitive meaning of this verb is restricted to the imperative, which is formulaic (see BAGD, 214 [1b]); usually, the aorist passive is used for the intransitive meaning (see the next NOTE).

12. *he got up*. Gk *ēgerthe*, lit. "was raised," the aorist passive of the same verb that is used in the active imperative in 2:11 ("Get up!"). The aorist passive of this verb is usually translated as an intransitive active, but this form can also, depending on the context, have a true passive sense (see MHT, 1.163).

COMMENT

Introduction. Like the previous passage, 2:1–12 describes a notable healing. Now, however, the Jewish leaders, the scribes, enter the picture, and along with them comes controversy and polemic, which will dominate all of 2:1–3:6 and dog the Markan Jesus until the end of the Gospel.

This tension, however, is found only in the middle of the story, in 2:6–10a; in 2:6 the scribes, whose presence has not been mentioned before, suddenly and unexpectedly pop up, object to something Jesus has said, and are roundly answered by him. The presence of these hostile scribes, moreover, makes the ending of the story problematic: are they among the "all" who praise Jesus in 2:12, as Gundry (121–22) thinks? If so, they have had a notable conversion, and one that is immediately reversed in 2:13–17! It is more likely that the controversy in 2:6–10a has been introduced into a healing story that originally lacked controversy, and this hypothesis is supported by the awkward repetition of "he said to the paralytic" from 2:5 in 2:10. This sort of narrative resumption often frames Markan redactional insertions (see e.g. 3:7–8; 3:14–16; 4:31–32) and is a commonly recognized editorial technique both in the OT (cf. Rofé, *Prophetical Stories*, 63 n. 13) and in later Jewish literature (cf. Kugel, *Potiphar's House*, 34). Here it creates a typically Markan sandwich structure (cf. 3:20–35; 6:7–32; 11:12–26; 14:1–11; 14:54–72). Mark himself, then, may have expanded the story, a hypothesis supported by the presence in 2:6–10a of Markan vocabulary such as "authority," "scribes," "consider," and "speak" (cf. Scholtissek, *Vollmacht*, 150–63), and of the phrase "except one, that is, God," which is repeated word for word in 10:18 (cf. 12:29, 32). Verses 2:6–8, moreover, foreshadow the pattern of 8:16–17:

(1) People consider (*dialoginzontai*) among themselves something that Jesus has said;
(2) Jesus perceives it;
(3) Jesus asks, "Why do you consider . . . ?" (*ti dialogizesthe*).

Since 8:16–17 are themselves probably redactional verses (see the introduction to the COMMENT on 8:14–21), the redactional nature of 2:6–8 is confirmed. Besides inserting 2:6–10a, Mark is probably also responsible for several elements in 2:1–2 that make the transition from the previous passage or reflect redactional themes (most of 2:1 and "speaking the word to them" in 2:2; cf. Bultmann, 14; Guelich, 83).

In its present form our story has a roughly chiastic structure (cf. Marshall, *Faith*, 83–84):

A   Introduction (2:1–2)
B   Spiritual healing (2:3–5)
C   Controversy (2:6–10a)
B'   Physical healing (2:10b–12a)
A'   Conclusion (2:12b)

In such a structure the middle element usually represents the point of greatest emphasis, and this is underlined in the present case by the hypotaxis of 2:6–10a, which makes it stand out from the usual Markan parataxis (see the GLOS-SARY for these terms). These structural and stylistic observations correspond to the thematic centrality of 2:6–10a: according to 2:10, the whole purpose of the healing of the paralytic is to demonstrate Jesus' power to forgive, which is what is stressed in these verses.

2:1–5: the setting for the healing. The story begins with a description of the physical setting: Jesus returns to Capernaum, his base of operations for the early portion of his ministry, and is "at home" there, preaching "the word," presumably the good news about the arrival of the dominion of God (cf. 1:14–15). His presence draws to him not only a crowd of people who are eager to hear this news but also a man in search of healing, a paralytic, whose helpless condition is underlined by the fact that he has to be carried on a stretcher by four of his friends.

Nor is his condition the man's only problem. As happens elsewhere in healing stories, there is an obstacle that hinders the suppliant from approaching Jesus (cf. e.g. 5:27–28; 10:46; see Theissen, 52–53). In the present case Jesus' fame and the power of his preaching have attracted such a huge throng of listeners that it is impossible for the paralytic to gain access to him in the ordinary way, even with the assistance of his friends. Thus, as in 5:24–34, a manifestation of Jesus' grace to one person or group creates a problem for someone else. This sort of barrier to healing functions literarily to heighten the tension and thus to sustain narrative interest. It also gives the suppliants the chance to display an extraordinary initiative, which our passage terms "faith," in order to overcome the obstacle (cf. 5:34; 10:52; Matt 15:28). Faith is thus, as Theissen (129) puts it, "a boundary-crossing motif." In the present case the boundary is crossed through a bold move by the paralytic's friends, one that probably causes discomfort to and demands physical courage of the man himself: they carry him up to the roof of the house, presumably by the outside ladder typical of such dwellings, dig through the reeds and clay that compose the roof (see the NOTE on "they un-roofed the roof" in 2:4), and then lower him precipitously on his stretcher, either by means of ropes or by handing the stretcher to the crowd below.

Jesus perceives this improvisation as an expression of faith. Although the motif of trust in the healer's power is a standard part of ancient stories of miraculous healing, outside of the NT people usually "hope" in the healer's power rather than believing in it (see Theissen, 129–33). The Gospel stories' preference for "faith" (*pistis*) and "to believe in" (*pisteuein*) probably reflects the fact that in the church these words had become technical terms for believing in Jesus and in the God who had raised him from the dead (see Lührmann, "Faith," 752–56). Moreover, the progression within our story from "the word" of Jesus (2:2) to "faith" in him (2:5) is reminiscent of Rom 10:17 and may reflect the tendency of early Christians to retell stories about Jesus in the light of post-Easter experiences. And the fact that his friends' faith triggers the paralytic's healing, and that they physically carry him into Jesus' presence, may relate to the Christian practice of intercessory prayer and to the imperative of "bearing one another's burdens" (Gal 6:2; cf. Klauck, "Frage," 244).

The possible reverberations of early Christian life continue in Jesus' response to the faith of his suppliants. He turns to the paralytic and says, "My child, your sins are forgiven." These words are easy to imagine in church contexts such as the Lord's Supper (cf. Matt 26:28) and Christian baptism (cf. Acts 2:38 etc.; see Klauck, "Frage," 243–44). They also, however, fit well into the healing miracle, since sin was associated with sickness and thus could be viewed as another obstacle to healing. In the OT, for example, transgression can lead to illness (see e.g. Deut 28:27 and Ps 107:17–18), and therefore healing and forgiveness are often closely related to each other (e.g. Ps 103:3; Isa 38:17); in places the terms become almost interchangeable (see the use of "to heal" for "to forgive sin" in Ps 41:3–4; Hos 14:4; Isa 57:18–19, etc.; cf. Marshall, *Faith*, 88 n. 2). As Freedman points out, moreover, Isa 1:4–6 and 33:24 combine the ideas of sin and sickness and form an inclusion around First Isaiah. Closer to the time of Mark, the Qumran text *Prayer of Nabonidus* (lines 3–4) links an exorcism with forgiveness of the possessed man's sins. And a rabbinic tradition, *b. Ned.* 41a, offers a striking parallel to our passage when it says that "a sick person does not arise from his sickness until all his sins are forgiven him." Here, as in Mark, we find a linkage between sin and sickness, the phrase "sins are forgiven," and a reference to the healed person "rising" from his bed. New Testament passages such as the present one and John 5:14, then, move along a well-trodden Jewish path when they link disease with sin and healing with forgiveness.

This linkage is problematic to many modern people, who are wary of connecting illness with transgression too directly, as if diseases were always the fault of their sufferers. In the present case the exact nature of the connection between the patient's spiritual and physical conditions is left obscure; to ask what has caused his paralysis is to pose a question unsuited to the genre of the narrative, which after all is a healing story, not a narrative in which someone is stricken with illness. Moreover, the fact that the healing is triggered not by the man's repentance but by his friends' faith warns against making a simpleminded causal connection between "getting oneself right with God" and being cured. Perhaps the best commentary on the issue is provided by John 9:2–3, where Jesus shifts his disciples' attention away from their cruel preoccupation with the blind man's presumed responsibility for his affliction and redirects it to the witness that his cure will bear to the advent of God's eschatological grace: "It was not that this man sinned, or his parents, but that the works of God might be made manifest in him" (RSV).

Nevertheless, given the strong traditional association between sin and sickness, Jesus' declaration of forgiveness to the paralytic fulfills the function of reassuring him, as is made explicit in the Matthean parallel (Matt 9:2). Such reassurance is a frequent feature in other NT healing stories (see e.g. Matt 9:22; Mark 5:36; 10:49) as well as in nonbiblical examples of the genre (cf. Theissen, 58–59). In the pre-Markan story, therefore, Jesus' statement may have meant nothing more than that he trusted in God's power to forgive the man's sins and to heal him (see the NOTE on "your sins are forgiven" in 2:5).

2:6–10a: the controversy with the scribes. But in the context of the intercalated controversy story, Jesus' assurance to the paralytic takes on a deeper meaning, probably reflecting the developing Christology of the church, especially baptismal theology. Immersion in water was already associated with remission of sins in Judaism (see the COMMENT on 1:4), but when the Christians took over such practices, they added the idea that Jesus was present and active in baptism (see e.g. Rom 6:3 and the terminology of baptism "into the name of" Jesus). It was a short step to thinking of him as the active agent of baptismal forgiveness.

This step, however, was bound to cause offense to Jews concerned to guard the uniqueness of God, and this is what happens in our passage, where the scribes interpret "your sins are forgiven" as a claim that Jesus himself has the power of absolution, and angrily reject this claim. Although it is not totally unprecedented for a Jewish healer to forgive sins (see the NOTE on "Who can forgive sins except One, that is, God?" in 2:7), such forgiveness might seem to the scrupulous to encroach on a prerogative of God, who according to several OT texts is the one who has the power to forgive sins (see e.g. Exod 34:6–7; Isa 43:25; 44:22). The scribes underline their objection by alluding to the *Shema,* the famous passage in Deut 6:4 which from ancient times has formed the center of the synagogue liturgy: "Hear O Israel, the Lord our God is one" *(heis ho theos).* Against the background of this confession, the scribes reason within themselves that no one can forgive sins "except One, that is, God" *(ei mē heis ho theos),* a phrase that deliberately and somewhat awkwardly recalls the *Shema.* The *Shema,* significantly, was a touchstone of the debates about "two powers in heaven" between Jews and Christians in the first Christian centuries, with the Jews claiming that the Christians violated the *Shema*'s assertion of divine unity through their high claims for Jesus (see *Deut. Rab.* 2.32–33 and cf. Segal, *Two Powers,* passim). Something like these debates seem already to be reflected in the Gospel of John (cf. e.g. John 10:30–33 and see Barrett, "Old Testament," 161–62, and Ashton, *Understanding,* 141–47), and it is possible that the scribes' objection in our story reflects a similar Jewish discomfort with the perceived violation of the *Shema* in the Christology of the Markan community (see Marcus, "Authority").

The Markan Jesus does not draw back from the implication of near-divinity that gives rise to this objection. The fact that he can discern and expose the scribes' innermost thoughts already supports his more-than-human status, especially since God is described in the OT as the one who knows people's hearts (see e.g. 1 Sam 17:28; Ps 139:23; Prov 24:12; cf. Pesch, 1.159). Jesus goes on to imply that the healing itself will demonstrate his credentials (see the NOTE on "Which is easier" in 2:9). But the scribes' objection must also be engaged at a deeper scriptural level, and Jesus does so with his assertion that "upon the earth the Son of Man has authority to forgive sins." The juxtaposition of the phrases "upon the earth," "Son of Man," and "authority" calls to mind

Daniel 7, in which God transfers royal power to "one like a son of man," i.e. a humanlike figure, who is given the authority to rule earthly nations at the eschaton (see the APPENDIX "The Son of Man"). Thus, for Mark, the heavenly God remains the ultimate forgiver, but at the climax of history he has delegated his power of absolution to a "Son of Man" who carries out his gracious will in the earthly sphere; therefore "*upon the earth* the Son of Man has the authority to forgive sins" (see Pesch, 1.160–61; Klauck, "Frage," 243).

Mark, then, has drawn on Daniel 7 and perhaps other OT traditions (see the NOTE on "so that you may know" in 2:10) to answer objections that his readers may have heard from some of their Jewish neighbors. His interpretation of these traditions, however, is not always straightforward or in line with the way in which other Jews would have interpreted them. In this first of his Markan appearances, for example, the Son of Man is not pictured as a judge of sinners, as he is in Daniel 7 and *The Similitudes of Enoch* (*1 Enoch* 45:3; 46:4–6; 50:1–5, etc.), but as a forgiver of sins. It may be that this novel twist on the Son of Man image is directed against a competing interpretation of the Danielic Son of Man prevalent among the Jewish revolutionaries of the Great Revolt. For the latter, the coming of the Son of Man probably meant not forgiveness for sinners but the establishment of God's kingship on earth through a cleansing act of divine judgment on them, especially on Israel's Gentile oppressors—an interpretation that is very much in agreement with Daniel 7 in its original context (cf. Marcus, *Way*, 167–68). The Markan Jesus, in contrast, extends God's dominion from heaven to earth through forgiveness (cf. Matt 18:18; John 20:23).

2:10b–12: the healing. But anyone can *claim* to forgive sins; it is more difficult to demonstrate that one has the right to make such a claim. Jesus now does so by healing the paralytic; assuming the traditional connection between sin and sickness, the healing establishes the reality of the forgiveness. As was already the case in 1:31, the use of the language of "raising" may imply for informed readers that the power by which Jesus heals the man is the same power by which God will raise Jesus himself from the dead (see the COMMENT on 1:29–31), and the close correspondence between Jesus' order to the paralytic in 2:11 and its fulfillment in 2:12a emphasizes once again his messianic authority:

I say to you, get up (*egeire*)	And he got up (*ēgerthē*, lit. "was raised")
take up your pallet	and immediately he took up his pallet
and go to your house	and went out in front of them all

Despite this pronounced parallelism, the small differences are also interesting, particularly in the first line: whereas Jesus stresses his own agency in the cure ("*I* say to you"), the usage of the passive in the description of the man's rise allows the inference that God's power is responsible for it (see the NOTE on "he got up" in 2:12), and this inference is supported when the crowd glorifies not Jesus but God for what has happened. Our passage thus evidences a characteristic Markan ambiguity about whether Jesus himself is acting or whether God is acting through him; in Mark's view both perspectives contain aspects of the truth (cf. the COMMENT on 1:1–3 and on 5:18–20). The conclusion thus drives home the point of 2:10, with its background in Daniel 7: Jesus acts on behalf of the heavenly king, fulfilling his will eschatologically on the earth; his mighty actions, therefore, do not compromise the uniqueness of God. The eschatological nuance is reinforced by the conclusion of the narrative, which emphasizes the universality of the response ("they were all amazed") and the radical newness of the deed ("We have never seen anything like it!"). As Schmithals (1.163) puts it, the crowd's words imply that "the new aeon, which no eye has previously seen (Isa 64:4; 1 Cor 2:9), is here breaking in."

It is significant that this first Markan controversy story, which has been placed deliberately at the beginning of 2:1–3:6 by Mark, is overtly Christological; it concerns not simply the question of Jesus' behavior but also and more particularly the issue of his identity (see especially 2:7, "Who can forgive sins . . . ?"). Christological questions are primary for Mark, as the first verse of the Gospel already shows, and they may have primacy in the Markan community's disputes with outsiders as well (cf. 13:5–6a). On the other hand, the issue of who Jesus is cannot be separated for long from the question of what he does. Having enunciated the principle that the Son of Man has the authority to forgive sins on earth, the Markan Jesus will, in the next passage, demonstrate it in a very "earthly" way—by eating with sinners.

JESUS EATS WITH TAX COLLECTORS AND OTHER SINNERS (2:13–17)

2 ¹³And he went out beside the sea again. And the whole crowd came to him, and he was teaching them. ¹⁴And moving along, he saw Levi, the son of Alphaeus, sitting at a tax booth; and he said to him, "Follow me!" And he got up and followed him. ¹⁵And it came to pass that, as he was reclining at table in his house, many tax collectors and sinners were reclining with Jesus and his disciples—for they were many, and they followed him. ¹⁶And the scribes of the Pharisees, seeing that he was eating with sinners and tax collectors, said to his disciples: "Why does he eat with tax collectors and sinners?" ¹⁷And hearing it, Jesus said to them: "The strong don't need a doctor, but the sick. I did not come to call righteous people but sinners."

NOTES

2 13. *And the whole crowd came to him.* Gk *kai pas ho ochlos ērcheto pros auton.* It is unclear whether this is the same crowd as was present in 2:1–12, or whether that crowd has dispersed and another crowd has gathered. If it is the

same crowd, their pursuit of Jesus testifies to his charismatic power and fore-shadows Levi's following of him.

14. *Levi, the son of Alphaeus.* Gk *Leuin ton tou Alphaiou.* This is a cameo appearance, since Levi never reappears in Mark or, apart from the Lukan parallel (Luke 5:27–29), in the rest of the New Testament. But James son of Alphaeus, who was perhaps his brother, is included in the list of the Twelve in Mark 3:16–19. The Matthean parallel to our passage changes Levi's name to Matthew and thus identifies him with one of the Twelve (Matt 9:9; cf. Matt 10:3); the same desire to make him a member of the Twelve is probably behind the alteration of his name to James in certain manuscripts.

In the first century most people named Levi were Levites, i.e. people who were presumed to be descended from the biblical Levi, the third son of Jacob, and whose hereditary job was service in the Temple (see Jeremias, *Jerusalem*, 213 n. 209). Since the NT scribes were probably Levites as well (see the APPENDIX "The Scribes and the Pharisees"), the scribal objection in 2:16 may be a reflection of a "family quarrel" among Levites.

15. *reclining at table.* Gk *katakeisthai*, lit. "to lie." This was the usual posture for dining at feasts in the Greco-Roman world, including among the Jews; guests reclined on banqueting-couches arranged around low tables (see D. E. Smith, "Greco-Roman"). At regular meals, however, poor Jews generally sat at table rather than reclining on luxurious dining couches (see Jeremias, *Eucharistic Words*, 48–49; Bokser, *Origins*, 130 n. 48).

in his house. Gk *en tē oikiā autou.* Malbon ("Mark 2.15") argues that this is a reference to Jesus' house, pointing out that Jesus has just commanded Levi to follow him; Levi, therefore, probably follows him to his (Jesus') house, and the "calling" imagery of 2:17 confirms the impression that Jesus is the host. But there is no other evidence, Markan or otherwise, for Jesus' possessing a house in Capernaum; the house he stays in is Peter's, not his own (cf. 1:32–34). In favor of the house being Levi's is the literary parallel with chapter 1, where Jesus calls Simon (1:16–18) and later eats a meal in his house (1:29–31; cf. Dewey, *Debate*, 81). Luke's specification of the house as Levi's, then (Luke 5:29), is probably a clarification of the Markan sense rather than an alteration of it.

tax collectors. Gk *telōnai.* This term denotes collectors of indirect taxes, especially on the transport of goods; hence it is sometimes translated "toll collectors" (see Donahue, "Tax Collector," 337). Indirect taxes were farmed out to the highest bidder, who was then at liberty to charge as much as he wished; the system bred abuse, and Luke 3:13 implies that overcharging was usual (cf. Luke 19:8). The dishonesty and general unsavoriness of tax collectors became proverbial; in *m. Ned.* 3:4, for example, they appear in parallel with murderers and robbers, and in *t. B. Meṣ* 8:26 they are described as people for whom repentance is difficult (see Davies and Allison, 1.558). This dishonesty is probably one of the reasons they were considered to be ritually impure by the Pharisees and their successors, the rabbis; in *m. Ṭohar.* 7:6, for example, a tax collector's entry into a house renders it unclean. Other reasons might include their association with Gentiles, who were deemed to be impure (cf. Matt 5:46–47 and 18:17 and see the end of the COMMENT), and their direct contact with Roman coins, some of which carried the idolatrous image of the emperor (Freedman; cf. Finney, *Invisible God*, 70–72).

and sinners. Gk *kai hamartōloi*. It is possible that this is simply a hendiadys (see the GLOSSARY) and that the two terms designate the same group (Freedman), but the parallel in Matt 11:19//Luke 7:34 suggests that "tax collectors and sinners" was a fixed phrase and that the groups were distinct (cf. the pairing in the Q passage with "a glutton and a drunkard," which are distinct but related categories). In addition to its simple copulative function, the Greek *kai* ("and") can either generalize or particularize; in classical Greek literature, for example, we find both "Zeus and the gods" (= "Zeus and the other gods") and "the gods and Zeus" (= "the gods and above all Zeus"; see Smyth, §2869). Correspondingly, *telōnai kai hamartōloi* in the present verse seems to denote tax collectors *and other* sinners, since tax collectors are a subset of sinners according to 2:17 (generalizing *kai*; cf. Schmithals, 168); in 2:16, where the phrase is reversed, it denotes sinners *such as* tax collectors (particularizing *kai*; cf. 16:7).

Who are these "sinners"? According to Jeremias (*New Testament Theology*, 108–13) and many other exegetes, they are the "people of the land" (*'ammê hā'āreṣ*), the ritually impure common people with whom the members of Pharisaic eating fellowships would not eat meals (cf. e.g. *t. Dem.* 2:2). E. Sanders (*Jesus*, 174–211), however, has argued strongly against this identification, asserting that sin has little to do with impurity and that the Pharisees would not have considered the "people of the land" to be sinners; for him, rather, the "sinners" are flagrant violators of the Mosaic covenant. This conclusion about the identity of the sinners seems to be correct; in our passage, for example, it is not only the Pharisees but also the narrator and Jesus himself who refer to "sinners," and it is incredible that Mark or the Markan Jesus would consider ritual impurity in and of itself to constitute a sin (cf. 7:17–23). Verses 7:21–22 probably give the best insight into the identity of the Markan "sinners": people who engage in sexual immorality, robbery, murder, and other actions of an equally heinous nature. Sanders, however, goes too far when he asserts that for the Pharisees themselves sin had little to do with impurity (cf. *Jewish Law*, 131–254); the references to *eating* in 2:16 and Matt 11:19//Luke 7:34 suggest purity concerns, and it is difficult to believe that the ritual impurity of tax collectors in the Mishnah is unconnected with their reputation for moral laxity (see the NOTE on "tax collectors" in 2:15 and cf. Dunn, *Jesus*, 71–77, and the APPENDIX "The Scribes and the Pharisees").

for they were many, and they followed him. Gk *ēsan gar polloi, kai ēkolouthēsan autǭ*. It is unclear whether the "many" who follow Jesus are the tax collectors and sinners mentioned at the start of the verse or the disciples mentioned near the end. Malbon ("Mark 2.15," 284) thinks they must be the tax collectors and sinners, since these groups have just been described as "many," but Best (*Following*, 178 n. 2) thinks that they cannot be the tax collectors and sinners, since then "many" would be superfluous—a good example of the reversibility of scholarly arguments. On balance Malbon is probably right; in Mark "following" is not restricted to disciples (cf. 3:7; 5:24; 11:9; cf. 14:13), and interpreting the "followers" as the tax collectors and other sinners allows a nice transition to 2:16, where part of the scribes' disturbance could result from the large numbers of sinners involved. Delayed parentheses, such as this interpretation requires, are common in Mark; see, for example, the delayed *gar* clauses in 5:8; 6:18; 10:22; 12:12; 16:4, and cf. 3:29–30 (cf. MHT, 4.26).

16. *the scribes of the Pharisees.* Gk *hoi grammateis tōn Pharisaiōn.* This implies that while some scribes were Pharisees, others were not. On the identities of these two groups, see the APPENDIX "The Scribes and the Pharisees." Given their subsequent objection to Jesus' eating with the tax collectors and sinners, the scribes' own presence at the meal is difficult to explain; are they, as R. Horsley (*Spiral*, 215–16) ironically asks, spying through the window? Gundry (128–29) tries to save the realism of the story by asserting that "it is normal near eastern custom for people to stand around observing a banquet." But the passages he cites, Luke 7:37 and *b. Ta'an.* 23ab, describe extraordinary intrusions into banquets, not "normal near eastern custom." The implausible stage management testifies to the artificiality of the scene (see Bultmann, 18 n. 3).

Why does he eat with tax collectors and sinners? Gk *Hoti meta tōn hamartōlōn kai telōnōn esthiei.* In classical usage *hoti* introduces an indirect question rather than a direct one, but Mark is particularly fond of using it for direct questions; cf. 9:11, 28 and possibly 2:7; 8:12; cf. Taylor, 61; BDF, §300 (2).

Most scholars accept that Jesus was known as one who associated with tax collectors and other sinners and that this reputation got him into trouble with the Pharisees. Horsley (*Spiral*, 212–23), to be sure, argues that this association is a fabrication of the early church, but this hypothesis seems to be motivated partly by a concern to show that Jesus was a social revolutionary who would not do anything as counterrevolutionary as fraternizing with lackeys of imperial Rome (for another dissent from the consensus, see D. E. Smith, "Historical Jesus"). But the contemptuous tone of the phrase "tax collectors and sinners" suggests its origination as an accusation by Jesus' opponents (cf. Matt 11:18–19//Luke 7:33–34), and such accusations usually contain at least an element of truth; Jesus' fellowship with such people, moreover, is attested in a variety of streams of Synoptic tradition and in a variety of forms. And the early church was not known for its high tolerance of "sinners," so Jesus' association with them is not likely to be a retrojection of the church's own practice (Jeremias, *New Testament Theology*, 109; E. Sanders, *Jesus*, 174–75).

Part of the problem with Jesus' table fellowship with sinners would have been that his ritual purity might be compromised. He might be offered non-kosher food or food that had not been properly tithed, or he might be defiled by contact with the clothes of ritually unclean people in the close quarters of a meal situation (see *m. Ḥag.* 2:7) or by contact with their dishes or furniture (see Nineham, 95; Booth, *Jesus*, 110). Table fellowship with such people may also have been avoided because of fear of their negative influence; *b. Ber.* 43b, for example, says that a scholar should not recline in the company of ritually impure common people (*'ammê hā'āreṣ*), "lest he be drawn into their ways" (see

Carlston, *Parables*, 111 n. 4). Cf. the warning in *1 Enoch* 97:4 about "becoming bedfellows with sinners."

17. *The strong don't need a doctor, but the sick.* Gk *Ou chreian echousin hoi ischyontes iatrou alla hoi kakōs echontes.* It was probably already traditional in Jesus' time to relate this adage to the spiritually sick (cf. Malherbe, "Medical Imagery"); according to Plutarch, for example, Pausanias applied to philosophers the observation that "doctors . . . are not to be found among the well but customarily spend their time among the sick" (*Apophthegmata Laconica* 230–31; trans. alt. from Lane, 104 n. 43). In a context informed by the OT and Judaism, however, the saying would take on additional ramifications because of the idea that *God* is the only true healer (see e.g. Exod 15:26, "I am Yahweh your healer") and especially that, in a figurative sense, he is the sole "healer" of people's sins (see the COMMENT on 2:6–10a). Reflecting this OT conception, Philo describes God as "the only doctor for the sicknesses of the soul" (*Sacrifices of Abel and Cain* 70; see Oepke, "*Iaomai*," 203).

I did not come to call righteous people but sinners. Gk *ouk ēlthon kalesai dikaious alla hamartōlous.* If this statement goes back to the historical Jesus, it may have originally acknowledged differing missions within God's plan: the Pharisees were righteous and did not need Jesus, but the "sinners" did, and he must go to them (see Lane, 105; Hooker, 97). In the overall context of Mark's narrative, however, "righteous people" takes on an ironic nuance; see the COMMENT. Luke 5:32 lessens the radicality of the saying by adding "to repentance."

COMMENT

Introduction. Having shown by healing the paralytic that he has the authority to forgive sins, Jesus now further demonstrates this authority by calling to discipleship a man whose profession puts him automatically in the "sinner" category (see the NOTE on "tax collectors" in 2:15) and by eating with this man and his fellow sinners (cf. Dewey, *Debate*, 85).

Mark 2:13–17 is a composite unit consisting of a call story (2:13–14) and a controversy story (2:15–17). These two stories probably did not originally belong together, as is shown not only by their different forms but also by the fact that Levi disappears from view in the controversy section (see Guelich, 98). The call story is sketchy and follows the pattern of those in 1:16–20 closely (see the introduction to the COMMENT on 1:16–20), and some (e.g. Pesch, "Levi-Matthäus," 43–45) have thought it to be a Markan invention modeled on 1:16–20. But the inconspicuousness of Levi in subsequent Christian history is against this theory (see the NOTE on "Levi, the son of Alphaeus" in 2:14), since a call narrative is not likely to have been fabricated for such a relative nonentity (cf. Gundry, 127). As Best suggests, Mark may have pared down a preexistent tradition to its bare essentials and retold it in his own words (*Following*, 176). The opening verse is editorial; it is transitional in function, and the sea setting, which is typical of Mark, plays no role in the subsequent action; the vocabulary and themes, moreover, are characteristically Markan ("again," "beside the sea," "whole," "crowd," "teaching"; see K. Schmidt, 82; Best, *Following*, 175). As for the controversy section, 2:15b is a *gar* ("for") clause, a typical Markan intervention in a pre-Markan story. It is also probable that Mark has added the references to the disciples in 2:15–16, since they are entirely superfluous to the story but fit into the overall Markan framework; the phrase in which they appear in 2:15, moreover, is grammatically awkward, and in 2:16 the scribes take offense only at *Jesus'* eating with sinners, not with that of the disciples (see Kiilunen, *Vollmacht*, 137–39).

As it stands, 2:13–17 is a little drama in four scenes: (1) Jesus teaches the crowd by the seashore, (2) he calls the tax collector Levi to discipleship, (3) he eats in Levi's house with a group of tax collectors and other sinners, and (4) he responds to the scribes' objection about this table fellowship. The scenes are bound together by the words "tax collector" ("tax booth") and "sinners," which form a daisy chain pattern (see Dewey, *Debate*, 84):

2:14	sitting at a *tax booth*	A
2:15	*tax collectors* and *sinners* were reclining with him	AB
2:16a	seeing that he was eating with *sinners* and *tax collectors*	BA
2:16b	"Why does he eat with *tax collectors* and *sinners* ?"	AB
2:17	"I did not come to call righteous people but *sinners*"	B

The pattern is a nice combination of repetition and movement, and the vista widens from the situation of a single individual (Levi at his tax booth) to that of a larger group (the tax collectors and sinners who join him at dinner) to a universal perspective (Jesus' outreach to sinners in general).

2:13–14: the teaching of the crowd and the call of Levi. The passage begins with a return to the seashore, perhaps partly to remind readers of the callings in 1:16–20; the edge of the vast sea is also a good setting for a passage that will end on a universalistic note, speaking of the salvific purpose of Jesus' mission. Here, as later in Mark (4:1–2), the seashore becomes a classroom, as Jesus resumes the instruction of the people begun in 2:2; the pattern of teaching followed by commission recalls 1:14–20 (cf. 6:6–7) and underlines the point that when the gospel is preached, people are won to the Christian community (cf. Best, *Following*, 177).

Passing by him, Jesus fastens his eyes on Levi the tax collector and calls him to follow in his footsteps. Jesus' choice of human material would be amazing to first-century readers, especially in remote parts of the empire where the tax collector was often perceived as a corrupt toady of a hated imperial presence. In the NT and rabbinic sources tax collectors are presented as being inherently dishonest, and their presence renders a room unclean (see the NOTE on "tax collectors" in 2:15); yet it is just such a disreputable person whom Jesus calls, and who immediately obeys, as Peter and Andrew and the sons of Zebedee did before him. One aspect of the call narratives in 1:16–20, however, is missing here: there is no commissioning of Levi to become a "fisher of people," perhaps reflecting the fact that he did *not* become one, or at least not a notable one. Our story, then, is not intended to trace a great missionary career back to its inception; its interest, rather, lies in the questionable nature of the person called, the surprising fact of his choice, and what this choice reveals about the caller (see Kiilunen, *Vollmacht*, 135–36).

2:15–17: the controversy with the scribes. These implications are brought out in the follow-up story, in which Jesus debates with the scribes his choice of people like Levi as meal companions. The stage is set by a description of these companions: not only Levi but also a great many other tax collectors and "sinners" (see the NOTE on "and sinners" in 2:15), as well as Jesus' disciples, who have not been mentioned since 1:35–39. There are also some unwelcome guests, the Pharisaic scribes, whose presence inside Levi's house is rather dubious historically (see the NOTE on "the scribes of the Pharisees" in 2:16), but who voice what was undoubtedly an objection to Jesus from rigorist circles during his lifetime: "Why does he eat with tax collectors and sinners?" (see the NOTE on these words in 2:16). This hostile question, Mark implies, arises out of spiritual shortsightedness; whereas Jesus "saw" (*eiden*) Levi as a potential disciple (2:14), the scribes "see" (*idontes*) him and his companions only as sinners. The question that this distorted perception elicits is not addressed directly to Jesus but to his disciples; while this makes sense in an ancient context, where a master and his disciples were answerable for each other's behavior (see Daube, "Responsibilities," 11–12), it probably also reflects the way in which Jesus' association with sinners continued to be an issue for the later church (see Bultmann, 49).

This was an issue partly because tax collectors were ritually unclean, and those who ate with them risked defiling themselves (see the NOTES on "tax collectors" in 2:15 and "Why does he eat with tax collectors and sinners?" in 2:16). The Pharisees, who formed themselves into pure-eating fellowships in order to avoid such ritual contagion, and whose very name may mean "those who have separated from sin," would have seen Jesus' courting of impurity as a reckless act. But the Pharisaic objection probably went beyond purity issues, for "sinners" were not only people who were careless about ritual matters but also people who were actively involved in breaking the laws of God and human beings by fraud, treachery, prostitution, etc. (see E. Sanders, *Jesus*, 174–211). Some of these traitors to the covenant, such as the tax collectors, were also traitors in a literal sense, since they collaborated with the Romans in fleecing their own people, and in general the "sinners'" style of life reflected in destructive ways the societal breakdown caused by the impact of foreign ways on Jews in the Greco-Roman period. Jesus' public association with "sinners" would therefore have been anathema to the Pharisees, for it would have seemed to encourage a cavalier attitude toward the Law and thus to hasten the process of societal distintegration, whereas the Pharisees saw their mission as sanctifying God's name and redeeming society by observance of God's Law.

The issue of separation from impurity and sin may still be a live one for Mark and his community, as is suggested by Mark's introduction of the disciples into the pericope. The relevance may have partly to do with the fact that Mark's community is a predominantly Gentile one in proximity to revolutionary Palestine; the Jewish revolutionaries battling the Romans would probably identify such Gentiles as sinners (see e.g. Ps 9:17; *Pss. Sol.* 2:1–2) and would have considered them to be unclean (see *m. Tohar.* 7:6 and cf. Alon, "Levitical Uncleanness"). In the eyes of the revolutionaries, therefore, Jewish Christians such as Mark, who shared table fellowship with Gentile sinners, were traitors giving aid and comfort to the enemy. It is also possible that some Jewish Christians in the Markan community had scruples about sharing meals with Gentiles (cf. Kuhn, *Sammlungen*, 91–94, and cf. the COMMENT on 7:17–23).

In our passage Jesus responds to the Pharisees' censure of his table fellowship with tax collectors and sinners by means of a double-barreled proverb: "The strong don't need a doctor, but the sick. I did not come to call righteous people but sinners." This response shifts the frame of reference from the Pharisees' anxiety about the contagion of impurity and sin to the human need of the sinners and the new situation created by Jesus' advent ("I have come"). In that new situation holiness rather than sin turns out to be contagious; as in 1:40–45 and 5:25–34, Jesus is not defiled by his contact with impurity but instead vanquishes it through the eschatological power active in him (see Borg, *Conflict*, 134). Our passage, then, ascribes to Jesus the same sort of divine authority that was evident in 2:1–12, for it implies that he is not one who is susceptible to sin's infection but the doctor who heals it, and in so doing it transfers to him an image customarily used for God in the Old Testament and later Judaism (see the NOTE on "The strong don't need a doctor but the sick" in 2:17).

Once the problem has been "reframed" with this doctor image (see Capps, *Reframing*), the concluding statement can respond more directly to the Pharisees' challenge—though no doubt in an unsatisfactory manner, as far as a Pharisee would be concerned. For whatever it may have meant to the historical Jesus (see the final NOTE on 2:17), in the Markan context "I did not come to call righteous people but sinners" satirizes the Pharisees' claim to have achieved righteousness by separation from sin; they, who are consistently hostile to Jesus in this section of the Gospel and will soon initiate a plot against his life (3:6), are certainly not in Mark's opinion righteous (see Arens, *ĒLTHON-Sayings*, 53–54). Indeed, despite 6:20, in which John the Baptist is described as "a righteous and holy man," and which perhaps should not be pressed too hard, it is questionable whether from Mark's perspective any human being is really "righteous." Are there for Mark such things as "righteous persons who need no repentance" (Luke 15:7; cf. the discussions in Genesis 18 and Ezek 14:20 about the saving effect of a few righteous people in a city or land)? Or would Mark agree with Paul that "there is . . . not even one" who has attained to this state (Rom 3:10; cf. Mark 10:18)? In any case, Jesus' ministry is not to those who consider themselves to be righteous, not to the "healthy," but to the "sick," to those who know their unrighteousness and their need for God's help.

In extending his grace to sinners Jesus not only acts on behalf of God but also follows his example; a Jewish pseudepigraphon, for example, praises God in terms remarkably similar to Jesus' self-description: "You . . . did not appoint grace for the righteous ones . . . but you appointed grace for me, who am a sinner" (*Prayer of Manasseh* 8; cf. Matt 5:45). But the fact that it is Jesus, a human being, who takes on this godlike role is bound to raise the hackles of those who insist on a strict interpretation of divine uniqueness (see the COMMENT on 2:6–10a). This blurring of the distinction between God and humanity is of a piece with the blurring of the fundamental structuring distinction between the realm of the pure and that of the impure; and both are related to the conviction that now, at the world's end, the grace of the heavenly world is beginning to break through into the earthly sphere (cf. Marcus, "Jewish Apocalypticism," 23–25). This conviction will dominate the passage that follows.

THE NEW AND THE OLD (2:18–22)

2   [18]And the disciples of John and the Pharisees were fasting. And they came and said to him: "Why do the disciples of John and the disciples of the Pharisees fast, but your disciples do not fast?" [19]And Jesus said to them, "Can the wedding guests fast while the bridegroom is with them? As long as they have the bridegroom with them, they cannot fast. [20]But the days will come when the bridegroom is taken away from them, and then they will fast on that day.
    [21]"No one sews a patch of unshrunk cloth on an old garment; for if he does, the fullness takes out from it, the new from the old, and a worse rip results. [22]And no one pours new wine into old wineskins; for if he does, the wine will burst the wineskins, and the wine will be lost—and the wineskins. But new wine into new wineskins!"

NOTES

2   18. *the disciples of John and the Pharisees were fasting.* Gk *ēsan hoi mathētai Iōannou kai hoi Pharisaioi nēsteuontes.* On John's own fasts, which were related to his pervasively eschatological orientation, see Mat 11:19//Luke 7:34. This fasting may have been influenced by a similar practice at Qumran, although the evidence for the latter is indirect; Philo *On the Contemplative Life* 34 speaks of the fasting of the Therapeutae, who were probably related to the Essenes and the Qumran community (cf. Muddiman, "Fast," 774). The Pharisaic practice of fasting twice a week is attested in Luke 18:12 and *Did.* 8:1 (cf. *b. Ta'an.* 12a). For

some Pharisees this practice may have been connected with eschatological hopes and even a desire to hasten the end (cf. *b. Sanh.* 97b–98a; on the apocalyptic orientation of some pre-70 Pharisees, see Hengel, *Judaism*, 1.253).

they came and said to him. Gk *erchontai kai legousin autǭ.* From the flow of the narrative, the questioners would seem to be the disciples of John and the Pharisees, but since they go on to speak of these groups in the third person, this seems unlikely; they may be either an undefined group (cf. Cranfield, 108) or the scribes who have opposed Jesus in the two previous pericopes (2:6–7, 16; cf. Kiilunen, *Vollmacht*, 167–68). The latter seems slightly more likely in the overall Markan context, since all of the other challenges to Jesus in 2:1–3:6 come from scribes and/or Pharisees.

the disciples of the Pharisees. Gk *hoi mathētai tōn Pharisaiōn.* This is an odd locution, because "disciple" implies adhesion to a particular master such as John the Baptist, Jesus, or Hillel, not membership in a group such as the Pharisaic party. It is not surprising that Matt 9:14 omits "the disciples of."

your disciples. Gk *hoi . . . soi mathētai.* According to many scholars (e.g. Hooker, 99), the charge is brought against Jesus' disciples rather than against Jesus himself because the story reflects a dispute between the early church and its Jewish opponents. Since, however, the early church did fast and was conscious of a difference from Jesus in this regard (see the NOTE on "on that day" in 2:20), and since another Synoptic tradition defends Jesus against the charge that he was a glutton and a drunkard (Matt 11:19//Luke 7:34), it is better to see our passage as rooted in Jesus' ministry. As Daube points out ("Responsibilities"), the rabbinic assumption that masters were responsible for their disciples' behavior presumably applied to Jesus and his disciples as well.

19. *Can . . . ?* Gk *Mē dynantai.* As Bultmann (41) notes, an answer in the form of a counterquestion is frequent in Synoptic controversy stories (e.g. 2:25–26; 3:4; 11:29). This method probably reflects Jesus' Jewish environment; cf. the rabbinic examples in Strack-Billerbeck, 1.861–62.

wedding guests. Gk *hoi huioi tou nymphōnos,* lit. "the children of the bridal chamber." This corresponds exactly to the Talmudic expression *běnê haḥuppâ,* which can indicate either the bridegroom's attendants or the wedding guests in general (see e.g. *b. Sukk.* 25b–26a; *t. Ber.* 2:10). In Jewish law wedding guests were freed from certain religious obligations that were deemed to be incompatible with the joy of the occasion; in a tradition attributed to R. Abba b. Zabda in *b. Sukk.* 25b, for example, we read that when a wedding occurs during the holiday of Sukkot, all the wedding guests (*běnê haḥuppâ*) are freed from the obligation of living in booths for the seven days of wedding celebration. "What is the reason? Because they have to rejoice."

bridegroom. Gk *nymphios.* The bridegroom motif recurs in John 3:25–30, where it is also used in a parable that responds to a question raised by the disciples of John the Baptist, has joy as a central motif, and speaks of the bridegroom's attendants (see Dodd, *Historical Tradition*, 282–85). It is interesting, in view of the fact that the next two Markan passages concern the Sabbath, that Jewish sources also use bridal imagery for the Sabbath (see e.g. *b. Šabb.* 119a) and forbid fasting on the Sabbath (see *y. Ta'an.* 3:11).

20. *the days will come.* Gk *eleusontai . . . hēmerai.* As Gnilka (1.115) notes, this formula often refers to eschatological events; see Luke 17:22; 21:6 and cf. many OT passages, such as Amos 8:11; Jer 16:14; 19:6, where the formula is only slightly different ("days are coming").

on that day. Gk *en ekeinę tę hēmerą.* Although "on that day" could simply mean "then," its significance is probably deeper here. The phrase is used in apocalyptic contexts in the OT (e.g. Mal 3:19; Zeph 1:15; Amos 8:9) and the NT, including Mark (see Mark 13:32; 14:25; Matt 7:22; 2 Thess 1:10, etc.). In both bodies of literature it indicates the Last Day, the day of judgment and/or salvation (see Carlston, *Parables*, 120; Klauck, *Allegorie*, 161). One of the OT passages, Amos 8:9–14, has several other connections with Mark 2:20 besides "on that day": "days are coming" and the themes of fasting ("I will turn your feasts into mourning") and of grief for a loved one ("like the mourning for an only son"; NRSV). This passage from Amos also forms the background for a later Markan allusion to Jesus' death as an apocalyptic event, Mark 15:33. Besides these apocalyptic nuances, the phrase may also allude to the later church's practice of fasting on Fridays, the day of Jesus' death (cf. *Did.* 8:1), or on Good Friday, a fast that was linked with the expectation of the parousia (cf. *Apostolic Constitutions* 5.3.19; see Kuhn, *Sammlungen*, 68–71, and Gnilka, 1.117).

21. *old garment.* Gk *himation palaion.* Jeremias (*Parables*, 117–18) points out that the cosmos is compared to a garment in numerous religious traditions and that in Heb 1:10–12, following Ps 106:26–28, Christ rolls up this old world-garment and unfurls the new cosmos. The imagery of a garment, then, is a natural one to use for an eschatological change.

rip. Gk *schisma*, from which our word "schism" comes. All other NT usages of this term refer to sociological ruptures (John 7:43; 9:16; 10:19; 1 Cor 1:10; 11:18; 12:25); on the relevance of this nuance to our passage, see the COMMENT on 2:21–22.

22. *pours.* Gk *ballei*, lit. "throws," but used here in the softened sense of "pours"—a common enough usage (see BAGD, 131[2b]). The forceful nuance of *ballei*, however, is important not only because it comports with the sense of radical newness in our passage but also because of the echo of 1:12, where a compounded form of the verb is used for the violent action of the Spirit.

new wine. Gk *oinon neon.* Jeremias (*Parables*, 118) makes a good case for this being a symbol of the new age, citing John 2:11, which links the wine miracle at Cana with Jesus' eschatological "glory"; see also Mark 14:23–25 and 1QSa 2:17–20, in which the Messiah of Israel leads the congregation in blessing the new wine at the eschaton. The Qumran sect's Festival of New Wine (11QTemple 19:11–21:10) perhaps looks forward to this eschatological event (cf. Yadin, *Temple Scroll*, 93).

wineskins. Gk *askous.* Wine was kept in leather skins; old skins were less flexible, and fermenting wine kept inside of them would expand and sometimes burst the skins.

But new wine into new wineskins! Gk *alla oinon neon eis askous kainous.* These words are omitted in D and many Old Latin manuscripts, perhaps accidentally, because of the repetition of the words "wine" and "wineskins" (Metzger, 79), perhaps deliberately, for example in order to combat Marcion, the Christian heretic who insisted that Jesus had nothing to do with the Old Testament or with Judaism. Many manuscripts add *blēteon*, "let . . . be poured," after *askous kainous*. This makes the sense clearer but obscures the fact that the words are a slogan.

COMMENT

Introduction. Having defended his table fellowship with tax collectors and sinners, Jesus is now called upon to defend another eating practice. This time, however, he is asked to explain not why he *does* something but why his disciples do *not* do something, namely fast. Located strategically at the center of the five controversy stories in Mark 2:1–3:6, this defense reveals the underlying cause of the growing tension between Jesus, on the one hand, and the scribes and Pharisees, on the other: the incompatibility between the eschatological newness of Jesus' ministry and a way of doing things that, in Mark's view, takes its cues from the old age.

The passage seems to have grown over time, since it careens from a defense of nonfasting (2:19) to a prophecy that at some future point Jesus' disciples will fast (2:20) to a pair of parables that returns to the point about not fasting (2:21–22). In view of his reputation for avoiding fasting (cf. Matt 11:19//Luke 7:34), it is plausible that Jesus did, in his ministry, say something in his defense like 2:19 (+ 2:21–22?). Verse 2:20, however, reflects the early church's practice of fasting (cf. Matt 6:16–18; Acts 13:2–3; 14:23; *Did.* 1:3; 8:1) and was inserted either by a pre-Markan tradent (so most source critics) or by Mark himself (so Bultmann, 19). We can be more sure about ascribing to Mark himself the transitional "framework" sentence 2:18a, which creates some confusion as to the subject by its juxtaposition with 2:18b (see the NOTE on "they came and said to him" in 2:18). Originally, perhaps the questioners mentioned only the fasting of John the Baptist's disciples, not that of "the disciples of the Pharisees" (see the NOTE on this phrase in 2:18); the Pharisees may have been introduced into the picture at the pre-Markan stage in order to adapt the passage to the rest of 2:13–28. Mark himself, however, may be responsible for the gloss in 2:21 ("the new from the old"), since he seems to be very fond of explanatory additions (cf. the ubiquitous *gar* ["for"] clauses), and this gloss coheres with the "new teaching" theme of 1:27 (cf. Kiilunen, *Vollmacht*, 173).

After the introductory question in 2:18, the passage divides into two sections: the parable on fasting at weddings in 2:19–20 and the two parables on the theme of the old and the new in 2:21–22 (on the definition of a parable, see the NOTE on "in parables" in 4:2). Each of these sections consists of two sentences that are closely related to each other, followed by a third that is contrastive:

A   Can the wedding guests fast while the bridegroom is with them?

B   As long as they have the bridegroom with them, they cannot fast.

C   But the days will come when the bridegroom is taken away . . .

A'   No one sews a patch of unshrunk cloth . . . , for if he does . . .

B'   And no one pours new wine into old wineskins; for if he does . . .

C'   But new wine into new wineskins!

The bulk of the passage (ABA'B') is focused on things that are impossible to do: to fast while the bridegroom is present, to sew unshrunk cloth on a new garment, or to pour new wine into old wineskins. This concentration on what cannot be done corresponds to the negative phrasing of the opening question, "Why do . . . your disciples . . . not fast?" The ending of the passage, however, resolves things on a positive note that sums up the theme of 2:1–3:6: new wine in new wineskins.

2:18–20: *fasting and the bridegroom*. The passage begins with a question to Jesus from some disciples of John the Baptist and some Pharisees, who want to know why Jesus' disciples do not fast, whereas the groups posing the question do. In the OT and early Judaism, the mortification involved in voluntary abstinence from food was a sign of repentance before God and an act of self-purification that was believed to give power to prayer (see e.g. Dan 9:3; 10:3; Tob 12:8; cf. Muddiman, "Fast," 773–74). All Jews physically capable of doing so fasted on the Day of Atonement (cf. Lev 16:29–31; 23:26–29). Our passage does not concern Jesus' avoidance of this prescribed yearly fast, which would have caused a greater outcry than the present passage evinces, but his failure to engage in the additional voluntary fasts practiced by spiritual virtuosi such as the Pharisees and the disciples of John Baptist. These groups, however, did not engage in fasting solely out of individualistic motives, despite the impression conveyed by the parody of Pharisaic fasting in Luke 18:12; both, rather, probably fasted in order to prepare for and even to hasten the redemption of Israel and of the world (see the NOTE on "the disciples of John and the Pharisees were fasting" in 2:18). Such a motivation, as Lane (109) points out, makes sense of the transition from 2:18 to 2:19: Jesus' interlocutors are trying to trigger the messianic redemption by their asceticism, but he hints that it has already arrived, so that their fasting is no longer necessary. Contrary to Davies and Allison (2.109 n. 118), this connection could have been understood by Mark and at least some of his readers, since fasting in anticipation of eschatological redemption is attested in connection with the Jewish Revolt that forms the background to his Gospel (Josephus *Life* 290), and this practice continued a venerable Jewish tradition of abstaining from food in preparation for holy war victory (1 Sam 7:6; 1 Macc 3:47; see Hengel, *Zealots*, 272, 286).

Jesus expresses his conviction that the messianic age has arrived, and that therefore penitential practices are no longer necessary or appropriate, through wedding imagery. Already in Isa 62:5 the future redemption is compared to a wedding feast in which God will marry Israel. This image is rooted in earlier prophets, who use the metaphor of a marriage (often a strained one) for Yahweh's relationship with Israel (see e.g. Hosea 2; Ezekiel 16; Jer 2:2; Isa 54:5; cf. Klauck, *Allegorie*, 162). Several NT passages reapply the marriage or wedding metaphor to the relation between Christ and the church (Matt 25:1–3; Eph 5:23–33; Rev 19:7–9; 21:2, 9; cf. Hultgren, *Adversaries*, 79). In Jewish sources, however, "bridegroom" as a metaphor for the Messiah is not attested until the sixth-to-seventh-century work *Pesiqta Rabbati* (37:2), so that Jesus' use of the metaphor in Mark 2:19a may have originally been simply a way of evoking the joy of the dominion of God (see Jeremias, *Parables*, 52 n. 13).

For Mark, however, Jesus certainly is a bridegroom, albeit a tragic one. For the reference to the wedding guests' joy in the bridegroom's presence suddenly and surprisingly gives way to a reference to the coming days when he will be taken away from them, "and then they will fast on that day." As Drury points out (*Parables*, 10, 44), there is a certain analogy in Ezek 18:2, where a parable is quoted only to be ruled out of order; the difference is that in our passage the same person, Jesus, utters the parable and then overrules it. This anomaly is best explained by the hypothesis that the perspective of later Christians has qualified a saying of the historical Jesus; Jesus' death (the taking away of the bridegroom in 2:20) has created a new situation in which the original tradition can be preserved only by altering it radically. Both "on that day" and "the days will come" place Jesus' death in an eschatological context (see the NOTES on these expressions in 2:20); thus, in a startling reversal of the usual Jewish eschatological pattern, the period of messianic redemption (2:19) is *followed* rather than preceded by the period of messianic woes (2:20; on the usual pattern, see Allison, *End*, 5–25).

For some exegetes, such as Kelber (*Kingdom*, 20, 123), this reversal indicates that the present is a time of Jesus' absence from the Markan community, and this viewpoint might garner support from the structural centrality of 2:20 within 2:18–22 and indeed within 2:1–3:6. This interpretation, however, is unbalanced in that it removes the verse from its Markan context. For this section of the Gospel is studded with ringing affirmations of Jesus' eschatological authority and saving mission: "the Son of Man has authority [on earth] to forgive sins" (2:10); "I did not come to call righteous people but sinners" (2:17); "the Son of Man is lord even of the Sabbath" (2:28). It is hard to imagine that such statements would not have been heard by Mark's audience as references to their present situation and therefore Jesus is, in some sense, present for them. Within 2:18–22 itself, moreover, the verse about the bridegroom's absence is surrounded by parables implying that Jesus brings a joyful new reality into the world. Thus both elements, absence/death and presence/life, are given their due weight within Markan Christology: Jesus has been physically absent since his death, but that absence is, paradoxically, the means by which his presence is achieved. For it is through the eschatological events of his death and exaltation to God's right hand that he has gained the power to be dynamically present with his church everywhere (see 12:35–37 and 14:62 and cf. John 16:16–24, which also uses the expression "on that day").

2:21–22: *parables of new and old.* After the digression prophesying the disciples' future fasting, the Markan Jesus returns to his main theme, the reason that they cannot fast in the present. Now his defense switches from the psychological to the metaphysical sphere: not only would no one want to fast during a time of messianic fulfillment, but to do so would contradict the very nature of that fulfillment. Here Jesus twice uses a characteristic type of Wisdom saying (cf. Luke 5:39; 8:16; 16:1) that implies that the behavior he opposes contradicts the innermost structure of the (redeemed) universe, since "no one" would do the analogous thing in daily life.

Both of these parables speak of the destructive consequences of trying to mix old with new—a patch made of new cloth will rip out the old, and new wine will burst old wineskins. Similarly, the eschatological newness of Jesus' mission cannot be contained within the old structures of Judaism; if one tries to do so, the consequences will be disastrous for both. The language of these parables invokes previous Markan references to the violent, apocalyptic change that Jesus' advent involves. The word "rip" (*schisma*), for example, recalls the baptism, where the heavens were ripped (*schizomenous*) as the Spirit of the new age descended on Jesus (1:10), and the verb used for "pours," *ballei*, is the same one that is used for the Spirit's subsequent action of casting Jesus out into the wilderness (1:12), as well as for his own exorcisms (1:34, 39, etc.). This divine violence inevitably produces counterviolence from the human side, as is suggested by the literary linkage between *airei* ("takes"), which is used in 2:21 for the destructive effect of the new patch on the old garment, and the compounded form of the same verb, *aparthḗ* ("is taken away"), which is used in 2:20 for the removal of the bridegroom. The old order, then, must sooner or later take away Jesus' life, because he has violently disturbed it with his new teaching, which tears at its very fabric. Some of the language here sounds as if it may be directed not only against external opponents but also against followers of Jesus who are trying to mediate between him and Judaism. In particular, the warning that a worse rip (*schisma*) may develop from the attempt to patch things up may be read as a reference to the futility of trying to mend the schism between Jewish Christians and other Jews (see the NOTE on "rip" in 2:21 and cf. the introduction to the COMMENT on 7:17–23).

This basic point about the incompatibility between the new and the old orders and the necessity of preserving, undiluted by compromise with the structures of the old age, the eschatological power that has broken into the world in Jesus' advent, is summed up by the battle cry that ends the passage: "New wine into new wineskins!" This slogan was probably especially important to the Markan community, which was conscious of the singularity of its claim that, despite consisting largely of Gentiles, it was the true Israel (cf. 12:1–9). In a context decisively influenced by the Old Testament and Judaism, however, the slogan necessarily raises the question of whether or not the old-age structures swept away by the eschaton include not only Pharisaic purity rules and various fasting practices but also the Law of Moses itself. In the next pericope the Markan Jesus will confront this pressing question.

THE LORD OF THE SABBATH (2:23–28)

2 ²³And it came to pass that he was going through a grain field on the Sabbath, and his disciples began to make their way, plucking the ears of grain as they went along. ²⁴And the Pharisees said to him, "Look! Why are they doing what is not permissible on the Sabbath?" ²⁵And he said to them, "Haven't you ever read what David did when he was in need and hungry—he and those who were with him? ²⁶How he went into the house of God in the time of Abiathar the high priest and ate the loaves of presentation, which only the priests may eat—and he gave them to those who were with him also?" ²⁷And he said to them, "The Sabbath was created for man, and not man for the Sabbath; ²⁸so the Son of Man is lord even of the Sabbath."

NOTES

2 23. *began to make their way, plucking the ears of grain as they went along.* Gk *ērxanto hodon poiein tillontes tous stachyas,* lit. "began to make a way, plucking the ears of grain." The grammar seems to put the emphasis on the disciples' movement, not on the plucking of the grain, but it is the latter that is chiefly at issue in the subsequent controversy; in 2:25–26 Jesus invokes the example of David and his followers, stressing their hunger. It therefore seems an exaggeration for Derrett ("Judaica," 90) and Dewey (*Debate,* 97) to deny that hunger is a motive for the disciples' action.

On the other hand, there must be some reason for Mark to express himself as he does, and it does not solve the problem totally to suggest that the participle can occasionally convey the leading idea in NT Greek (see e.g. Rom 4:19 and Heb 2:10; cf. Taylor, 215). There are certainly more straightforward ways of expressing such a meaning. Mark's choice of grammar may rather reflect a desire to suggest (without pressing) the notion of the disciples clearing a path for Jesus. Although *hodon poiein* can mean "to make one's way, to journey" (cf. Judg 17:8 LXX), it usually signifies "to create a road." Mark may wish to play on this meaning, as the twelfth-century commentator Euthymius already suggested (see Field, *Notes,* 25). If so, the disciples' action would become a partial fulfillment of the prophecy of Isaiah that is cited in 1:3: they are preparing the way of the Lord. This picture presents a contrast to the usual one of Jesus leading the disciples (e.g. 10:32), but it is appropriate in a pericope that hints at Jesus' royal authority, since royal visits were often prepared for by roadworks (see Westermann, *Isaiah 40–66,* 38, on Isa 40:3 and Babylonian texts; and cf. M-M, 438, on the use of a related substantive in a papyrus). Gundry (140) objects that plucking ears of grain would not really create a road, but Mark's imagery may function on a more allusive level than he allows.

24. *the Pharisees.* Gk *hoi Pharisaioi*. What are the Pharisees doing in or near a grain field on the Sabbath? For E. Sanders (*Jesus,* 265), this is an example of "the extraordinarily unrealistic settings of many of the conflict stories . . . Pharisees did not organize themselves into groups to spend their Sabbaths in Galilean cornfields in the hope of catching someone transgressing." Casey, however, points out that rabbis or groups of rabbis are reported to be in fields on Sabbaths for a variety of reasons, so the Pharisees' presence is not impossible ("Plucking," 1, citing *b. Šabb.* 127a as an example). Still, Sanders' point is well taken; it is suspicious that, throughout this section of the Gospel, whenever Jesus is doing something a bit questionable, the Pharisees and/or their allies the scribes always seem to conveniently turn up, even in very unlikely places (see 2:6, 16).

Why are they doing. Gk *ti poiousin*. Bultmann (16) remarks: "Jesus is questioned about the disciples' behaviour; why not about his own?" He concludes that our story is an attempt by the church to ascribe to Jesus its own attitude toward the Sabbath (cf. the NOTE on "your disciples" in 2:18). Daube, however, points out that in the ancient world the master was responsible for the behavior of his disciples; he appositely cites Seneca *Troades* 290: "He who forbids not sin when in control commands it" ("Responsibilities," 5).

what is not permissible on the Sabbath. Gk *tois sabbasin ho ouk exestin*. Plucking grain was viewed as "work" and hence was forbidden on the Sabbath, when no labor was allowed (Exod 20:10); Philo, for example, asserts that on the Sabbath Jews are not allowed to pluck fruit or cut any kind of tree or plant (*Life of Moses* 2.22; cf. Casey, "Plucking," 6). Although it is not specifically mentioned in the Mishnah's list of activities prohibited on the Sabbath (*m. Šabb.* 7:2), plucking is viewed as a subset of reaping, which *is* prohibited, in *y. Šabb.* 7:9b and *t. Šabb.* 9:17. It is also possible, in view of the grammar of 2:23, that the removal of the ears of grain is regarded as creating a road (see the NOTE on "began to make their way, plucking the ears of grain as they went along" in 2:23). There is a discussion in *b. Šabb.* 127a of the legality of making a path through a field with one's feet on the Sabbath; the question is answered in the affirmative, but other rabbis might not have been so lenient.

25. *And he said to them.* Gk *kai legei autois*. This is the historical present usage of the verb; contrast 2:27, where Mark uses the imperfect form.

Haven't you ever read . . . ? Gk *Oudepote anegnōte*. On responding to a question with a counterquestion, see the NOTE on "Can . . . ?" in 2:19.

those who were with him. Gk *hoi met' autou*. As Daube ("Responsibilities," 5–6) points out, David's followers are *not* with him in 1 Samuel 21, and there is no suggestion that he shares the loaves with them, either in the text or in Jewish interpretations of it. David does, to be sure, mention "the young men," presumably his companions, in 21:2–6, but this is a trick to get the priest to give him all five loaves. The New Testament retelling thus rehabilitates David by effacing his lie; this sort of "improvement" of fallible OT heroes is common in Jewish and Christian exegesis (see e.g. Sternberg, *Poetics*, 188–89). More important, however, the Markan Jesus brings in David's companions because the Pharisees' challenge concerns the actions of Jesus' disciples; this sort of reshaping of a biblical story in order to make one's point stronger is also a common feature in ancient biblical interpretation.

26. *in the time of Abiathar the high priest.* Gk *epi Abiathar archiereōs.* Actually, the high priest with whom David dealt in 1 Samuel 21 was Abiathar's father, Ahimelech (cf. 1 Sam 30:7). Some manuscripts of our passage, as well as the Matthean and Lukan parallels, deal with the problem simply by omitting *epi Abiathar archiereōs.* Modern scholars have also tried to save Mark's accuracy in various ways. Wenham, for example ("Mark 2,26"), noting the way in which *epi* + the genitive is used in 12:26, suggests that the meaning is "in the section of scripture having to do with Abiathar." As Lane points out (116 n. 86), however, the phrase in question is far away from "have you not read," Abiathar is not the central character in this portion of 1 Samuel, and rabbinic documents tend to designate a section by a term that occurs earlier rather than later in it (Abiathar does not appear until 1 Samuel 22). Similarly questionable is Derrett's suggestion ("Judaica," 91–92) that *epi Abiathar archiereōs* means "in the presence of Abiathar the high priest" and anticipates Abiathar's future office. As Gundry (146) notes, there is no indication in 1 Samuel 21 either that Abiathar is present along with Abiathar or that "high priest" is meant prospectively.

These explanations failing, the reference to Abiathar may simply be a mistake. Abiathar and Ahimelech are sometimes confused with each other in textual transmission, and Abiathar is certainly the better known of the two (see Whitelam, "Abiathar"). As Freedman notes, a better-known name often supplants a lesser-known one in the development of traditions: the famous Nebuchadnezzar replaces the historical Nabonidus as the father of Belshazzar (Dan 5:2, 11, 18), and Noah may have replaced his son Ham in the cursing of his grandson Canaan (Gen 9:20–27; cf. Vawter, *Genesis*, 138–39). The reverse can also happen: a famous son (such as Abiathar) can supplant his lesser-known father (such as Ahimelech). Abraham, for example, may have replaced his father, Terah, as the recipient of the divine command to move to Canaan (compare Gen 11:31 with Gen 12:1–4).

Whether or not Mark was aware of this technical error, the substitution of Abiathar for Ahimelech certainly suits his purposes in this passage. Gundry (141) points out Abiathar's linkage with the "house of God," i.e. the Temple, in Jerusalem (2 Sam 15:24, 35, etc.). The reference to Abiathar may also be meant to invoke the larger biblical context in 2 Samuel 15, which would have numerous points of contact with the Markan situation in the Jewish War. In 2 Samuel King David and his companions are forced by the persecution of the authorities in Israel to go into exile among Gentiles. The rule of these wicked authorities falls under a divine curse, and judgment is soon meted out to them. This story line might well remind Mark and his readers of the way in which some of the disciples of the true king of Israel, Jesus, have been forced to leave

Jerusalem and settle among Gentiles by the persecution of the Jewish authorities during the Great Revolt of 66–73 C.E. In this context the reference to Abiathar would be especially significant, since he is strongly linked with David in the OT and is especially remembered for transferring the ephod, the symbol of spiritual legitimacy and Yahweh's favor, from Saul to David after the slaughter of the priests of Nob (1 Sam 22:18–23; 23:6; cf. Weiss, *Lehre*, 53 n. 55). This story would reverberate strongly in the Markan situation, in which the authorities' persecution of Jesus and the Christians has, in Mark's view, de-legitimized them and caused the vineyard of Israel to be transferred to others (12:9).

the loaves of presentation. Gk *tous artous tēs protheseōs.* On these loaves, called "the bread of the presence" in Exod 25:30 and Num 4:7, see especially Lev 24:5–9. Twelve loaves were placed on a table in the sanctuary of the Tabernacle and Temple every Sabbath as an offering to God (hence the NT term "loaves of presentation"); the old loaves were then removed and given to the priests to eat.

27. *And he said to them.* Gk *kai elegen autois.* Here Mark uses the imperfect form of the verb; contrast 2:25. This verse is missing in the parallels in Matthew and Luke and in Western texts of Mark, which has led some to suggest that it was not part of the original text of Mark or of its first edition (see e.g. Koester, "History," 39–40). The textual evidence, however, is unimpressive, and plausible reasons can be adduced for the omission of 2:27 by Matthew and Luke—namely, the verse's denigration of the Sabbath and the desire of Matthew and Luke to heighten the Christological element in the passage by eliminating an anthropologically based argument (see Neirynck, "Sabbath," 230; Hultgren, *Adversaries*, 112 and 138 n. 50). In favor of the verse being an original part of the Markan text is also its closeness in thought to 3:4–5.

The Sabbath was created. Gk *to sabbaton . . . egeneto.* On the translation of *egeneto* as "was created," see BAGD, 158 (2). Mark 2:27 is probably an allusion to Gen 2:1–3, although *egeneto* does not occur there; the verb, however, is prominent throughout the LXX of Genesis 1. The Sabbath was so closely connected with the creation of the world that it could be called "the Sabbath of creation" to distinguish it from the sabbatical year (see e.g. *Mekilta* on Exod 23:12 and cf. Casey, "Plucking," 13–14). It is doubtful, however, that Jesus is arguing that humanity overrides the Sabbath because it was created first (Pesch, 1.184); not only is this not stated, but in Gen 1:26–29 it is what is created *later* that takes precedence over what is created earlier.

man. Gk *anthrōpon.* This term is not gender-specific, and in 1:17 its plural is translated "people."

and not man for the Sabbath. Gk *kai ouch ho anthrōpos dia to sabbaton.* A roughly contemporary parallel can be found in 2 *Apoc. Bar.* 14:18 (man was not created for the world, but the world for man), and the opposite thought is expressed by Pausanias, the King of Sparta from 408 to 394 B.C.E.: "For the laws should be lords (*kyrious*) of men, not men of laws" (Plutarch, *Moralia* 2.230F; cf. Weiss, *Lehre*, 49). More striking is the rabbinic parallel cited in the COMMENT on 2:27–28.

COMMENT

Introduction. Having just enunciated the principle "new wine in new wine-skins" to conclude the dispute about fasting, Jesus now makes this theme even more concrete by expressing approval of his disciples' choice to meet their need for food in a way that, in the Pharisaic view at least, violates the Sabbath code. Mark 2:23–28 thus continues the eating motif of the last two passages, but an escalation of tension is evident: Jesus' disciples are implicitly accused not just of a break with Pharisaic traditions of table fellowship and fasting but of a violation of the written Law's injunction against working on the Sabbath (Exod 20:10; cf. Dewey, *Debate*, 96–97).

Many scholars think that either the discussion of David in 2:25–26 or one or both of the concluding assertions in 2:27–28 must be secondary (see the survey in Sariola, *Gesetz*, 77–87). The Pharisees' challenge in 2:24 receives two answers (2:25–26 and 2:27–28), each in a different form (scriptural proof in 2:25–26, pronouncement in 2:27–28) and each with its own introductory formula (two different versions of "and he said to them" in 2:25 and 2:27). The two answers, moreover, deal with two different issues: eating forbidden food (2:25–26) and the relation of humanity to the Sabbath (2:27–28; see Dewey, *Debate*, 94). But if one of these responses is secondary, which is it? On the one hand, the second response (2:27–28) might be deemed original, since it forms a logical answer to the question of Sabbath observance posed in 2:23–24, whereas the first response (2:25–26) does not. On the other hand, the second response might have been devised because a later tradent perceived that the first response did not really address the Sabbath issue raised by the question; moreover, the formula that introduces it, *kai elegen autois* ("and he said to them"), is usually redactional in Mark (4:2, 11; 6:10; 7:14; 8:21; 9:1; 11:17).

When the evidence is so equivocal, it is best to be cautious. Moreover, it may be asked whether it is really so extraordinary for a question to receive two answers, or for those answers to be in different forms, or to be introduced by slightly different formulae, or even for one of them to be slightly illogical. All of these features can be paralleled, for example in the Talmud. Similarly, while it is possible that the phrase "those who were with him" in 2:25–26 is a Markan addition, as Weiss claims (*Lehre*, 44), the phrase does seem to be integral to the story, since it links David's action with that of his followers and thus is of a piece with the way in which Jesus answers a charge brought against his disciples. While it is likely that Mark intervened in this passage as he seems to do nearly everywhere else, his penmanship cannot be identified with any degree of certainty.

The passage divides itself naturally into three parts: the stage-setting description of the disciples' action and the Pharisees' objection to it (2:23–24), Jesus' first answer, based on 1 Samuel 21 (2:25–26), and his second answer, based on the original purpose of the Sabbath (2:27–28; cf. Dewey, *Debate*, 95). Throughout the passage the focus keeps shifting from leader to followers in a symmetrical pattern:

2:23	A	Jesus		
	B			disciples
2:24	B			disciples
2:25	A	David		
	B			followers
2:26	A	David		
	B			followers
2:27	B			humanity
2:28	A		Son of Man	

This arrangement is significant. Although more space is devoted to the followers than to the leader, the passage begins and ends with the leader.

2:23–26: the Pharisees' challenge and Jesus' appeal to David. It is probably deliberately ironic that a passage in which Jesus' disciples are to be accused of violating a biblical law begins with the Old Testament formula "and it came to pass" (see the NOTE on this phrase in 1:9). The continuation of the passage will extend this irony, as Jesus will appeal to biblical precedent in 2:25–26.

What comes to pass is that Jesus and his disciples make their way through a grain field on the Sabbath. Under the watchful eyes of the Pharisees, the disciples begin to pluck ears of grain, presumably to still their hunger (see the NOTE on "began to make their way, plucking the ears of grain as they went along" in 2:23). The Pharisees object that this action is illegal, though not because the disciples are appropriating another's property; a compassionate biblical law allowed the poor to cull the standing grain left in fields (Lev 19:9; 23:22; cf. Deut 23:25; see Casey, "Plucking," 2–3). Rather, the implicit objection is that the disciples are performing work, here apparently that of reaping (see the NOTE on "what is not permissible on the Sabbath" in 2:24).

Jesus' first response to this Pharisaic objection is to appeal to a biblical precedent, that of David in 1 Sam 21:1–6, for an example of a blameless violation of a rule having to do with eating. David, Jesus asserts, ate the "bread of the presence," which is allowed only to priests (Lev 24:9), and he gave it to his followers too. Unfortunately, the example is not entirely appropriate, since the transgression of Jesus' disciples has to do not with *what* they eat but with the work involved in procuring it. Even Casey's observation ("Plucking," 9–10) that rabbinic sources such as *b. Menaḥ.* 95b assume that the OT incident took place on the Sabbath does not really meet the problem, since the Markan Jesus does not mention any violation of Sabbath laws in referring to David, just that David and his followers ate that "which only the priests may eat."

It may be that Mark has other reasons for citing the example of David. As Dewey (*Debate,* 98) points out, Jesus' allusion to 1 Samuel 21 links the authority of a leader with that of his followers ("those who were with him"; see the NOTE on this phrase in 2:25). When Jesus proclaims himself "lord of the Sabbath" at the end of the passage, therefore, the implication is that his disciples may share in his sovereignty over the law of the Sabbath. Moreover, it is important to Mark to show Jesus playing a Davidic role. While the evangelist has some reservations about the title "Son of David" (12:35–37), he can still use it for Jesus (10:48) or otherwise link him positively with David's dominion (11:9–10). The Messiah expected by most people, after all, was to be Davidic not only in lineage but also in likeness, and Mark can affirm a properly nuanced understanding of this royal expectation (see Marcus, *Way*, chapter 7). Mark, indeed, accentuates Jesus' kingly role in our passage by the way in which he describes the disciples' plucking of grain, since it creates the impression that a path is being cleared for Jesus, as would be done in preparation for a royal visit (see the NOTE on "began to make their way, plucking the ears of grain as they went along" in 2:23).

Still, the story itself seems implicitly to recognize that 2:25–26 is in the end inadequate as an answer to the objection in 2:24, for Jesus immediately proceeds to another, more pertinent reply.

2:27–28: humanity, the Sabbath, and the Son of Man. This reply consists of two pronouncements, the first having to do with human beings in general, the second with the Son of Man in particular.

The first response, "The Sabbath was created for man, and not man for the Sabbath," is related to ideas found both in the Old Testament and in postbiblical Judaism. Some OT passages imply that the Sabbath has a humanistic purpose, namely the refreshment of people after the strenuous labor of the week (see Exod 23:12; Deut 5:14). In rabbinic traditions this idea is generalized into a saying that is strikingly similar in form to the one enunciated by Jesus: "The Sabbath is handed over to you, not you to it" (*Mekilta* on Exod 31:14; *b. Yoma* 85b). To be sure, nothing is said here about the *creation* of the Sabbath, but it is a natural inference that a divine institution functioning for humanity's welfare was designed for that purpose. This implication becomes explicit in *t. Ber.* 3:7: "From your love, O Lord our God, with which you loved your people Israel, and from your compassion, our king, which you bestowed on the son of your covenant, you have given us, O Lord our God, this great and hallowed seventh day in love." As in 10:2–9, then, Jesus appeals to God's intention in creation in order to qualify a Mosaic ordinance (see Dewey, *Debate*, 98).

While 2:27 has important Jewish analogies, the conclusion of the passage in the following verse does not. Here the argument suddenly modulates from the human level to the Christological one: "So the Son of Man is lord even of the Sabbath." The "so" at first seems puzzling: why does a declaration that the Sabbath was meant for humans justify the assertion that the Son of Man is its sovereign?

One influential response has been to assert that "son of man" here does not refer to Jesus or to a particular figure at all. The passage, rather, uses an OT idiom in which "son of man" simply means "human being" (see the APPENDIX "The Son of Man")—an idiom of which Mark is aware, as 3:28 demonstrates. The saying, therefore, may just mean "so humanity is lord over the Sabbath," which would make a good continuation from 2:27 (see Neirynck, "Sabbath," 237–38).

But whatever the *original* meaning of 2:28 was, it is unlikely that *Mark* understands it merely as a statement about a prerogative of humanity in general. For him, rather, the Son of Man is an individual figure based on Daniel 7. Mark uses the definite form ("*the* Son of Man"), whereas the indefinite form ("a son of man") would be expected if a general anthropological statement were being made; the line between these two forms may be blurred in Aramaic, but it is not in Greek. Further, in the Markan context the reference to the Son of Man in 2:28 follows closely the reference in 2:10, and the latter definitely alludes to Jesus himself; both Markan passages, moreover, refer to the authority of the Son of Man and thus echo Daniel 7 (see the COMMENT on 2:6–10a and cf. Dewey, *Debate*, 99; Sariola, *Gesetz*, 102–3). In our passage, moreover, the immediately preceding 2:25–26 directs the reader's attention not to humanity in general but to a particular person from whom other human beings derive authority, namely David, the prototype of the Messiah. And for Mark the Davidic Messiah and the Danielic Son of Man are one and the same, and their name is Jesus (see 14:61–62 and cf. 8:29, 31, 38).

Two other considerations may be more helpful for thinking about the transition from 2:27 to 2:28 than the assertion that "son of man" refers to humanity in general. First, even though the "Son of Man" figure is not *identical* to the elect people in Daniel 7 and writings dependent on it, he is still strongly linked with them, and this linkage carries over to the New Testament usages of the term (see Marcus, *Way*, 167–71, and the APPENDIX "The the Son of Man"). The transition from 2:27 to 2:28, therefore, may not be a matter of identity but of very close connection. This is especially likely because, as we have just seen, our passage strongly associates Jesus with a group of human beings, his own disciples.

Second, one of the important backgrounds for Daniel's figure of the "one like a son of man" is the portrait of Adam in Genesis 1–3 (see Grässer, "Menschensohn," 412–14). Since Mark 2:27 already recalls the Adam story, the transition to 2:28 is a natural one: the Sabbath was a divine gift for the benefit of the first Adam, and so his eschatological counterpart has sovereignty over it as well (see D. Schmidt, 34–35). It may be that Mark thinks that Jesus restores the compassionate aspect of the original Sabbath, which in the interim has been effaced by a human hard-heartedness that has transformed the good Sabbath into a source of destruction (see 3:4 and cf. again 10:1–9).

In our passage, then, the Markan Jesus appeals to God's original will in creation, and its eschatological renewal in his own ministry, in order to defend his disciples' infraction of Sabbath regulations. There may have been echoes of this approach even among non-Christian Jews in Mark's environment, since some of the revolutionaries seem to have believed that the waging of holy war was not only allowed on the Sabbath (cf. the NOTE on "to save life or to kill" in 3:4) but actually *mandated* on it (see Hengel, *Zealots*, 287–90, citing Josephus *J.W.* 2.456). Josephus' sarcastic remark that "in their case, the Sabbath was kept holy in a special way" (*J.W.* 2.517, Hengel trans.) may reflect the revolutionaries' own self-understanding: they were sanctifying the Sabbath by fighting the battles that would bring in the new age, of which the Sabbath was a customary symbol (cf. e.g. Heb 4:4; *Adam and Eve* 51:2–3; *m. Tamid* 7:4). Similarly, the frequency with which the Sabbath became a flash point between Jesus and his opponents is easily explicable on the theory that he, and the church after him, regarded it as a day upon which his work of national and cosmic restoration was particularly appropriate, since it transformed the celestial Sabbath rest into a terrestrial reality by extending God's dominion from heaven to earth (cf. John 5:1–18 and see Hooker, *Son of Man*, 102, and Stuhlmacher, *Versöhnung*, 148).

The Christian reinterpretation of the concept of Sabbath rest, however, was bound to leave unimpressed those who did not believe that Jesus was the commander in chief whom God had appointed to lead his eschatological host into battle. The continuation in 3:1–6 will once more remind Mark's readers that the Pharisees belong among these skeptics.

JESUS HEALS ON THE SABBATH (3:1–6)

3 ¹And again he entered the synagogue; and there was a man there who had a withered hand. ²And they were watching him closely, to see whether he would heal him on the Sabbath, so that they might bring charges against him. ³And he said to the man with the withered hand, "Get up, and come to the middle of the room!" ⁴And he said to them, "Is it permissible to do good on the Sabbath or to do evil, to save life or to kill?" But they were silent. ⁵And he, glancing around with anger, and grieved at the hardness of their hearts, said to the man, "Stretch out your hand!" And he stretched it out, and his hand was restored. ⁶And the Pharisees immediately went out with the Herodians and took counsel against Jesus, in order that they might destroy him.

NOTES

3 1. *the synagogue.* Gk *tēn synagogue.* Codices ℵ and B omit the definite article and thus read "a synagogue," but this is probably either a case of homoeoteleuton (see GLOSSARY) or an attempt to deal with the question of which synagogue is being referred to, none having been mentioned since 2:1–12. Both Matthew (12:9) and Luke (6:6) appear to have read the definite article in their Markan text.

withered. Gk *exērammenēn,* the perfect passive participle of *exērainein,* "to dry up." The word may be meant figuratively as an image of paralysis (cf. 3 Kgdms 13:4).

2. *were watching . . . closely.* Gk *paretēroun*. In Gal 4:10 this same verb is used for fulfillment of the cultic commandments of the Law, and Josephus links it particularly with observance of the Sabbath (*Ag. Ap.* 2.282; *Ant.* 3.91; 14.262). Mark thus may be playing on the verb's ambiguity: the Pharisees are watching Jesus closely because they are concerned about Sabbath observance.

so that they might bring charges against him. Gk *hina katēgorēsōsin autou*. Theoretically, deliberate transgression of the Sabbath law carried the death penalty (Exod 31:14–15; Num 15:32–36); the Mishnah specifies that the transgressor must be warned by two witnesses, and only executed if he persists (*m. Sanh.* 7:8). But both CD 12:3–6 and *m. Šabb.* 7:1 suggest that capital punishment was usually avoided in favor of lesser penalties (see E. Sanders, *Jewish Law*, 16–19).

3. *Get up, and come to the middle of the room!* Gk *egeire eis to meson*, lit. "get up to the middle," an abbreviated way of expressing two thoughts at once.

4. *And he said to them* etc. Gk *kai legei autois* etc. Mark implies that Jesus is clairvoyant, as in 2:8. The question about what is permissible on the Sabbath suggests that he divines the Pharisees' unspoken intention of accusing him of doing what is not allowed on that day (cf. 3:2), and the question as to whether or not one may kill on the Sabbath anticipates their action in 3:6 of conspiring with the Herodians to murder him. Matt 12:10 and Luke 6:8 merely make Mark's implication explicit (cf. Kiilunen, *Vollmacht*, 223).

to save life or to kill. Gk *psychēn sōsai ē apokteinai*. It is a good rabbinic principle that "saving life overrules the Sabbath" (*b. Yoma* 85b); if someone's life is in danger, the Sabbath laws may and indeed must be broken to rescue him or her. This principle grew out of experiences during the Maccabean Revolt, when pious Jews who refused to defend themselves on the Sabbath were slaughtered by the Syrians (see 1 Macc 2:29–41 and cf. E. Sanders, *Jewish Law*, 13). By rabbinic times it applied to all illnesses in which there was even a slight chance that death might be the result—the case discussed in *m. Yoma* 8:6 is that of a sore throat (see Vermes, *Religion*, 22–23)! In the present instance, however, the man's life is not threatened, and according to both the Dead Sea Scrolls and the Mishnah, diseases that are not life-threatening should not be treated on the Sabbath (see CD 11:9–10 and *m. Šabb.* 14:3–4 and cf. the synagogue ruler's question in Luke 13:14).

they were silent. Gk *esiōpōn*. By silencing his opponents, Jesus has publicly humiliated them, as he will do later in 11:33 (cf. 12:34). It is interesting that *m. 'Abot* 3:12 lists "putting one's fellow to shame publicly" as an offense that removes one from the world to come, along with other offenses that might with ill will be ascribed to the Markan Jesus: defiling holy things, despising appointed times, and interpreting the Torah contrary to the traditional norm (*hălākāh*).

5. *grieved.* Gk *syllypomenos*. As Taylor points out (223), elsewhere this verb in the passive means "to share in grief, sympathize, condole," never "to be grieved with," which seems to be the meaning required by the context here; cf., however, the COMMENT on 3:5–6.

at the hardness of their hearts. Gk *epi tēs pōrōsei tēs kardias autōn.* "Hardness of heart" corresponds to the Hebrew phrase *šĕrirût lēb* (lit. "sinewiness of heart"), which is particularly common in Jeremiah (3:17; 7:24; 9:13, etc.) and in the Community Rule of the Dead Sea Scrolls (1QS 1:6; 2:14; 3:3, etc.; see K. Schmidt and M. Schmidt, "*Pachynō*," 1026 n. 3, and Spencer, "*Šryrwt*"). Since the heart is a soft muscle and was thought of as the seat of the feelings as well as of the intellect (see the NOTE on "hearts" in 2:6), its petrification can signify an inability to respond in an emotionally appropriate manner.

And he stretched it out, and his hand was restored. Gk *kai exeteinen kai apekatestathē hē cheir autou,* lit. "and he stretched out and was restored his hand." The awkward grammar probably reflects an Aramaic original (cf. Peshitta).

6. *the Herodians.* Gk *tōn Hērǭdianōn.* No one really knows what this term means, since it occurs only here and in 12:13//Matt 22:16, neither of which provides a clear contextual clue. It is usually interpreted as a reference to supporters of the dynasty founded by Herod the Great, who ruled Jewish Palestine from 37 to 4 B.C.E.; this is the meaning of the related term *tōn Hērōdeiōn,* which occurs in Josephus *J.W.* 1.319. Particularly important scions of the family for the early Christians were Herod's son Herod Antipas, tetrarch in Galilee and Perea from 4 B.C.E. to 39 C.E.; his grandson Agrippa I, ruler of a kingdom restored to the size of that of Herod from 41 to 44 C.E.; and his great-grandson Agrippa II, tetrarch of certain areas in the north from 53 C.E. until the end of the first century. For a family tree of the descendants of Herod, see figure 14 in the NOTES to 6:14–29.

The Herodian dynasty's legitimacy was questionable in the eyes of some, since Herod was not from a family of Jewish ancestry; his mother was a Nabataean and his father an Idumaean, a member of a people who had been forcibly converted to Judaism by John Hyrcanus in 129 B.C.E. and were regarded as half-breeds by other Jews (see Josephus *Ant.* 14.403). Herod worked hard to establish his Jewish credentials, for example by his energetic work in expanding the Temple and by his marriage with the Jewish Hasmonaean princess Mariamne I, but his subsequent execution of her did not help the cause, nor was it forgotten that he had usurped the dynasty that had ruled Judaea for nearly one hundred years and that his position as king was wholly dependent on the backing of Rome (see M. Stern, "Herod and Rome," 165–79). He himself clashed with the Pharisees (Josephus *J.W.* 1.571; *Ant.* 17.41–47; see Grabbe, *Judaism,* 2.471), and there is no evidence that his son Herod Antipas, the ruler of Galilee at the time of Jesus, had particularly close relations with them, so that the alliance alluded to in 3:6 is puzzling on a historical level.

It may, however, reflect later realities. Herod's grandson and great-grandson Agrippa I and II had more impressive Jewish credentials than he and Antipas had; they were descendants of Herod's union with the Jewish Hasmonaean princess Mariamne, and this branch of the family identified with the Israelite side of its ancestry and was zealous for Jewish concerns—including persecution of at least one prominent Christian (see Acts 12:2–3 and cf. 26:3 and Josephus

Ant. 19.331; 20.139; see M. Stern, "House of Herod," 236–41). The two Agrippas were popular with the Pharisees' successors, the rabbis (see e.g. *m. Soṭa* 7:8), who were not always successful in distinguishing between them, and this popularity may go back to the pre-70 Pharisees (cf. S. Schwartz, *Josephus*, 158–69). Mark's report about an alliance between the Pharisees and the Herodians, therefore, may reflect the situation in his own time rather than in the time of Jesus (cf. Lohmeyer, 67 n. 2).

against Jesus. Gk *kat' autou,* lit. "against him." The translation introduces Jesus' name to make it clear that the murder plot is not directed at the healed man (contrast John 12:10).

COMMENT

Introduction. The series of five controversy stories that began in 2:1 is rounded off with a second argument taking place on and concerning the Sabbath (cf. 2:23–28). This time, however, it is not an action of Jesus' disciples that is called into question but one of Jesus himself.

Mark's own discernible contributions to the passage come at the beginning and end of the pericope and include the introductory clause "and again he entered the synagogue" in 3:1 and the conclusion in 3:6, both of which link our passage with the section and with the Gospel as a whole; the cast of characters and the grammar in 3:6, moreover, are similar to those in 8:15; 11:18; and 12:13, all of which are either totally or partly redactional (cf. Kiilunen, *Vollmacht*, 225–33). Also possibly redactional are two features of 3:5, the participle "looking around" (cf. 3:34; 5:32; 9:8; 10:23; 11:11) and the reference to the Pharisees' hardness of heart (cf. 6:52; 8:17–18; see Hultgren, *Adversaries*, 82, and Kiilunen, *Vollmacht*, 235).

Despite its wide-ranging structural parallels with the first story in the section, 2:1–12 (see the introduction to 2:1–3:6), our concluding narrative is more thoroughly saturated with the element of conflict, as befits its position at the end of the controversy section. In the course of the pericope one sees from the side of Jesus provocative behavior (3:3), anger, and sorrow (3:5); from the side of the Pharisees, a desire to condemn Jesus (3:2), hostile silence (3:4), hardness of heart (3:5), and the instigation of a murder plot (3:6; see Kiilunen, *Vollmacht*, 222, 239–44). It is symptomatic of the difference between 3:1–6 and 2:1–12 that the latter begins and ends with references to a friendly crowd, whereas our pericope begins and ends with references to hostile opponents (see Dewey, *Debate*, 104). Atypically for a miracle story, there is no acclamation of the miracle from the audience; instead its Pharisaic observers go out and begin to plot Jesus' murder (cf. John 11:45–54). Corresponding to this stress on conflict, the man who is healed plays a relatively minor role in the story, serving primarily as a lightning rod to focus the tension between Jesus and the Pharisees (see Guelich, 133).

The passage falls naturally into three parts, the first two of which will be treated together below. In the first part (3:1–2) Mark sets the stage by describing Jesus' entry into the synagogue, the presence of the man with the "withered" arm, and the hostile, watchful Pharisees. In the second part (3:3–4) Jesus challenges the Pharisees by moving the man to center stage and asking them whether it is lawful to do good on the Sabbath. In the third part (3:5–6) he defies them by healing the man, and they consequently go out to plot his murder. There is a series of correspondences between these sections:

```
1a Jesus entered synagogue
1b         man with withered hand
2a                  Pharisees watched Jesus closely
2b                           to see if he would heal on Sabbath


3a                                    And he said to the man
3b "Come to the middle [of the synagogue]!"
4a                                             "Is it permissible on the Sabbath to save life or to kill?"


5a                           Jesus looked angrily at Pharisees
5b                                    And he said to the man
5c         "Stretch out your hand!"
5d         He stretched it out, and it was restored
6a Pharisees went out of synagogue
6b                           and took counsel to kill Jesus
```

These correspondences tie the sections together; in each part, for example, there is a movement into or out of the synagogue. At the same time, many of the correspondences contrast Jesus with the Pharisees and thus emphasize the element of conflict; his entrance into the synagogue at the beginning, for example, is opposed to their exit at the end, and his intention of "giving life" on the Sabbath is contrasted to their plot to kill.

3:1–4: scene-setting and challenge. The passage begins with Jesus entering the synagogue—presumably the one in Capernaum (2:1), presumably on the same Sabbath as in the previous passage, and presumably in the company of his disciples (cf. 3:7), although none of these circumstances is stated explicitly. On the level of source reconstruction the singular verb "he entered," along with the lack of specificity about date and locality, suggests that the story was at first independent of its present context; Jesus really was alone in the original story (see the Introduction to 2:1–3:6). But on the level of Markan intention the singular verb reflects the progression from the question of the disciples' Sabbath observance in 2:23–28 to the question of Jesus' own Sabbath observance here.

The presence of a man with a "withered" hand (see the NOTE on "withered" in 3:1) sets up the issue that is to be the main theme of the narrative:

will Jesus now follow up his claim to be lord of the Sabbath (2:28) by using that day for healing in a public place, and thus come into open conflict with the Pharisees? The situation is graver than that in 2:23–28, not only because it is Jesus' own behavior that is at issue but also because of the public setting and the impression that both the Pharisees' opposition to Jesus and his violation of their sensibilities are premeditated from the start.

The Pharisees are described as "watching closely" (*paretēroun*) to see if Jesus will heal on the Sabbath. This same verb is used in Ps 36:12 (one of only two LXX usages), where it is sinners who lie in wait for the righteous person, to slay him (cf. Ps 129:3)—a portrayal similar to the description of the Pharisees' plot at the end of our passage (3:6). Through the intertextual echo with Psalm 36, then, the same Pharisees who have objected to Jesus' eating with "sinners" (2:16) are now revealed to belong in the camp of sinners themselves. Jesus seems to divine supernaturally (cf. the NOTE on "And he said to them" in 3:4) their intention of finding a way to accuse him of violation of the Sabbath law, which forbade "work" on that day (Exod 20:10). Despite this awareness, and the peril that such a legal charge might theoretically entail (see the NOTE on "so that they might bring charges against him" in 3:2), Jesus nevertheless goes ahead and lays the groundwork for the healing, telling the crippled man to come forward to the center of the synagogue and thus setting up an open confrontation with the Pharisees; as Dewey puts it (*Debate*, 104), his action amounts to "a virtual taunt." Immediately, however, he heads off the Pharisees' anticipated objection with the question, "Is it permissible to do good on the Sabbath or to do evil, to save life or to kill?" This question places the Pharisees in a quandary, since according to their own principles, the necessity of saving life overrules the imperative of Sabbath observance (see the NOTE on "to save life or to kill" in 3:4).

The problem for the exegete is that, at least on the surface, the question is not one of saving life; the man with the "withered" hand is not in mortal danger, and if Jesus waits a few hours to allow the Sabbath to end before performing the cure, he will not be killing him. Here as elsewhere, however, Jesus reinterprets Old Testament or Jewish principles in an apocalyptically intensified manner (cf. 10:2–9 and see Gnilka, 1.127). Just as, in the first two antitheses in the Sermon on the Mount (Matt 5:21–30), the Matthean Jesus equates anger with murder and lust with adultery, so here the Markan Jesus makes withholding the cure of the man's paralyzed hand, even for a few hours, tantamount to killing him, and performing the cure immediately tantamount to saving his life (cf. Vermes, *Religion*, 22 n. 14). For Mark's Jesus, the eschatological war is already raging, and on that battlefield every human action either strikes a blow for life or wields one for death; the cautious middle ground, upon which one might wait a few minutes before doing good, has disappeared. And if Jesus is "the holy one of God," whose holiness implies the apocalyptic destruction of demons and disease (cf. 1:24), then his Sabbath-day healing of the man with the paralyzed hand is a fulfillment rather than an infraction of the commandment to "remember the Sabbath day and keep it holy" (Exod 20:8; cf. Neh 13:22).

The Pharisees cannot either disavow their principle of saving life on the Sabbath or go along with Jesus' radicalization of it. They are silent—ominously so, because disputants who have lost face by being reduced to speechlessness in public are liable to become dangerous enemies (cf. the NOTE on "they were silent" in 3:4).

3:5–6: Jesus' reaction, his cure, and the Pharisees' reaction. One might now expect Jesus to perform the cure, since he has cleared the way for it by silencing the Pharisees; but instead Mark raises the narrative tension further by a delay that also provides a rare insight into Jesus' inner state: he is angered at the Pharisees' "hardness of heart." The most famous biblical exemplar of hard-heartedness is the Pharaoh of the exodus story (see Exod 7:3, 13, 22; 8:15, etc.), and it may well be that Mark intends his readers to link the Pharisees with the Egyptian king, especially since the Greek words "Pharaoh" and "Pharisee" are so close to each other (*Pharaō/Pharisaios*). This would be a tremendously ironic linkage, since in Jewish sources from the Bible onward Pharaoh is the prototypical enemy of God's people and representative of ungodliness (cf. Aberbach, "Pharaoh"), whereas the Markan Pharisees present themselves as the spiritual guardians of the nation. Pharaoh's hardness of heart was, from one point of view, his own fault (Exod 8:11, 28; 9:34; cf. Ps 95:8; Eph 4:18), but it was also willed by God (Exod 7:3; 9:12; 11:10; 14:4, 8, 17; cf. Isa 6:10 and see Räisänen, *Hardening*, 52–56). There is the same curious duality in Mark's conception of hardness of heart: it is both a sin that angers Jesus (3:5; 8:17–18) and an affliction for which he grieves (see the NOTE on "grieved" in 3:5), and elsewhere in Mark it can visit even those who are well intentioned (see 6:52; 8:17–18 and cf. Taylor, 223). Pharaoh's obduracy, moreover, ultimately led to the revelation of God's glory (see Exod 10:1–2; 14:4, 17; cf. Rom 9:17–18), and Mark probably thinks that the Pharisees' hardness of heart has a similarly salvific effect: it causes them to plot Jesus' death, but that death becomes the occasion for God's self-disclosure (cf. 15:37–39).

Despite the hint of sadness in Jesus' response to the Pharisees' obduracy, his main concern is not with them but with the disease-stricken man; and in the climax of the passage he turns away from them to the man and heals him. He does so in a clever way that eludes the charge of performing work on the Sabbath; rather than touching the afflicted limb (cf. 1:31, 41), he commands the man to stretch it out himself, and when he does so, it is miraculously healed by the eschatological power of God ("was restored" is a divine passive).

Bested again, the Pharisees "go out"—perhaps, in view of 3:31–35 and 4:10–12, a significant verb implying self-exclusion from the divine presence (cf. John 13:30)—and conspire with the Herodians to put Jesus to death. Contrary, then, to the Pharisees' principle of saving life on the Sabbath and their professed concern for that day's sanctity, they themselves desecrate the Sabbath by using it to plot Jesus' murder (for a similarly ironic combination of ritual piety with murder, see John 18:28). In retrospect, then, Jesus' challenge in 3:4 ("Is it permissible to do good on the Sabbath or to do evil, to save life or to kill?") becomes not just a question of abstract principle but an expression of his clairvoyant insight into the evil the Pharisees are already plotting against him (cf. 3:2) and the way it negates their own moral code.

The root of this perversion is suggested by the correspondence between the final clause, "in order that they might destroy him" (*hina apolesōsin auton*) and 1:24, where the demons have asked Jesus whether he has come (*ēlthes*) to destroy them (*apolesai hēmas*). The end of the passage, then, brings the Markan audience back to what the author of 2 Thess 1:7 calls "the mystery of iniquity": those who oppose to the point of murder Jesus' acts of power and mercy do so not only through their own choice but also because God's mysterious will has placed them on the side of the devil in the eschatological battle. Thus a few verses before the Pharisees' accusation that Jesus exorcises through Satan's power (3:22), attentive readers already know that it is not he but they who are actually the devil's tools.

The initiation of the plot against Jesus' life ends the controversy section in 2:1–3:6 on a somber note. The powers that will drive Jesus to death are beginning to materialize; near the beginning of his ministry, the end is already in sight. But this very fact seems to give a new urgency to his mission. The next passage will highlight the eschatological gathering of "all Israel" to Jesus and his renewed success in the battle against the demons.

SECOND MAJOR SECTION
(MARK 3:7–6:6a)

◆

INTRODUCTION: THE STRUGGLE INTENSIFIES

Following the initial series of conflicts between Jesus and his human opponents, which culminates in the decision of the Pharisees to do away with him
(3:6), both sides begin to mobilize their forces for the coming struggle. After a
transitional passage describing Jesus' intensifying popularity and summarizing
his increasingly powerful ministry of healing (3:7–12), Mark portrays him in-
stituting a core group of twelve disciples who will be his constant companions
until the debacle of his final night (3:13–19). The opposition, however, is also
mobilizing, gaining in vociferousness and penetrating even into Jesus' family
circle (3:20–35); indeed, almost this entire section of the Gospel is bracketed
by stories of opposition to Jesus from his relatives and townsfolk (3:20–21, 31–
35 and 6:1–6a). The "official" opposition is also busy; the decision to destroy
Jesus in 3:6 is soon followed by an accusation that, were it sustained, would
carry the death penalty (see Exod 22:18 and Lev 20:27; cf. *m. Sanh.* 7:4, in
which possession of a familiar spirit and sorcery are capital offenses).

Does such growing opposition falsify the gospel message that in Jesus' ministry "the time has been fulfilled and the dominion of God has come near"?
The parable chapter (4:1–34) grapples with this important issue with images
that suggest that the opposition experienced by God's royal power does not
negate that power's hidden presence in the world. This assertion is then sub-
stantiated by the most powerful miracles yet portrayed in the Gospel: Jesus
demonstrates his command over the forces of nature (4:35–41), over a fiercer
concretion of demonic antagonism than any yet encountered (5:1–20), and
even over death (5:21–43).

All of these miracles, as well as those in 3:7–12; 6:31–44; 6:45–52, and
6:53–56, picture Jesus in a boat, and Keck ("Mark 3:7–12") has suggested that
they were part of a pre-Markan "boat cycle" (see the similar theory of Pesch,
1.277–81):

3:7–12	Summary: Jesus' healings, preparation of boat
4:35–39	Calming of sea
5:1–20	Exorcism of Gerasene demoniac
5:21–43	Healing of Jairus' daughter and woman with hemorrhage

6:31–44   Feeding of five thousand
6:45–52   Walking on water
6:53–56   Summary: Jesus' healings

This is an attractive theory. It helps explain the oddities that the boat that is readied for Jesus is never actually used in 3:7–12 and that the next episode begins without transition with his ascent of a mountain; according to Keck's theory, the superfluous boat is a relic of the pre-Markan collection. The putative cycle is symmetrical, being framed by two summary passages and two sea miracles, and the stories share distinctive motifs besides the boat (the description of illnesses as "afflictions," the crowd thronging Jesus, and people falling down before him and touching him). But a problem is posed by the parallels between some of the Markan passages and John 6, since these parallels extend into the doublet in Mark 8, suggesting that if there was a pre-Markan source, it did not end at 6:56 (see Schnackenburg, *John*, 1.28; Brown, 1.238):

Miraculous feeding: John 6:1–13; Mark 6:34–44 (cf. 8:1–10)

Walking on water: John 6:16–21; Mark 6:45–52 (cf. 8:13)

Return to western shore: John 6:24–25 (Capernaum); Mark 6:53 (Gennesaret)

Demand for a sign: John 6:30; Mark 8:11

Remarks on bread: John 6:35–59; Mark 8:14–21

Confession of Peter: John 6:68–69; Mark 8:29

Passion theme; betrayal: John 6:70–71; Mark 8:31–33

Therefore, while Keck's theory has a certain appeal, it cannot be regarded as certain (for criticisms of Pesch's similar theory, see Neirynck, "L'Évangile").

In any case, whether or not Mark got his sea stories from a pre-Markan boat cycle, they are suitable for this section of the Gospel, since the sea is an appropriate setting for epiphanies, and this section presents Jesus increasingly as an epiphany of God himself: he stills the unruly waters, walks upon the sea, and identifies himself with the formula "I am," as God himself does in the Old Testament (4:35–39; cf. 6:45–52). Mysteriously, however, the miracles in this section fail to convince people that Jesus has been sent by God; indeed, they cause some to ask him to leave their shores (5:17) and become a cause for offense for his own townspeople (6:1–6). The section thus ends, like 2:1–3:6, on a depressing note: Jesus' power is limited by his hometown's lack of faith in him, and he himself is taken aback by this skepticism. Even as Jesus' miracles are growing in grandeur, the hard-hearted human resistance to interpreting them as signs of his divine commission is also growing. "The mystery of the dominion of God" is beginning to emerge in all its paradoxicalness (cf. 4:11).

THE SPREADING IMPACT OF JESUS (3:7–12)

3 [7]And Jesus, together with his disciples, withdrew to the sea; and a great crowd from Galilee followed—and from Judaea [8]and from Jerusalem and from Idumaea and from Transjordan and from the region around Tyre and Sidon, a great crowd that had heard the things he had done came to him. [9]And he told his disciples to prepare a boat for him because of the crowd, so that they might not crush him; [10]for he had healed many people, so that as many as had afflictions fell upon him in order to touch him. [11]And the unclean spirits, whenever they beheld him, fell down before him and yelled out, saying, "You are the Son of God!" [12]And he sharply rebuked them, in order that they might not make him known.

NOTES

3 7. *withdrew.* Gk *anechōrēsen.* Most of the NT usages of this verb refer to a withdrawal from danger or other undesirable circumstances (see e.g. Matt 2:12, 13, 14, 22; John 6:15), but the word can also indicate mere departure (e.g. Matt 9:24) or search for privacy (e.g. Acts 23:19; 26:31; cf. BAGD, 63). Withdrawal from danger would certainly fit our context, where a murderous conspiracy has been mentioned in the previous verse, and Jesus could be presumed to know about it through his supernatural insight (cf. 2:8; 3:2, 4–5).

followed. Gk *ēkolouthēsen.* Western and Caesarean witnesses lack this singular verb, other witnesses change it to a plural and/or add the word "him," and there is a great variation in word order (see Metzger, 79–80). These variations and omissions are probably due to the awkwardness of the word, which breaks up the description of localities and is reiterated by the phrase "came to him" in 3:8; it is likely, therefore, to be original.

7–8. *from Judaea and from Jerusalem and from Idumaea and from Transjordan and from the region around Tyre and Sidon.* Gk *apo tēs Ioudaias kai apo Hierosolymōn kai apo tēs Idoumaias kai peran tou Iordanou kai peri Tyron kai Sidōna.* Jerusalem was in the northernmost part of the province of Judaea, Idumaea was to the south of Judaea, and Transjordan and Tyre/Sidon were to the east and west respectively; there is a rather similar description of the localities from which Jews came up to Jerusalem at Pentecost 4 B.C.E. in Josephus (J.W. 2.43; Ant. 17.254), though Tyre and Sidon are not mentioned. The order north-south-east-west, though usual today, was rare in biblical times (but cf. Ezek 48:16–17); initial orientation was usually toward the east before the discovery of magnetic north in the twelfth century C.E. (cf. Drinkard, "Direction"). On the significance of the list of localities, see the COMMENT on 3:7–10.

8. *a great crowd . . . came to him.* Gk *plēthos poly . . . ēlthon pros auton.* The phrase for "great crowd" repeats that of 3:7, but in the reverse order; "came to" similarly repeats "followed" in a slightly different form. In the introduction to the COMMENT I explain this repetition as a typical Markan framing device

for a redactional insertion (cf. 2:5–10; 3:14–16; 4:31–32). In fairness, however, I should mention that after a parenthetical remark an author can resume *his own* narrative thread with a similar repetition; a splendid example is provided in Joseph Conrad's *Nostromo*, part 2, chapter 8: *"The short flare of a match* (they had been kept in a tight tin box, though the man himself was completely wet), *the vivid flare of a match*, disclosed to the toiling Decoud the eagerness of his face . . ." (emphasis added).

9. *so that they might not crush him.* Gk *hina mē thlibōsin auton. Thlibein* means literally "to press upon, to crowd, to exert pressure upon," but it can also mean metaphorically "to oppress, afflict" (cf. BAGD, 362). In the latter sense it is used in the NT especially for the persecution of Christians as a sign of the end (see e.g. 1 Thess 3:4; 2 Thess 1:6–7); Mark uses the cognate noun *thlipsis* ("tribulation") in the same way in 13:19, 24 (cf. 4:17). The *thlipsis* that threatens Jesus here, therefore, may anticipate his later suffering in the passion narrative, which is in a sense the eschatological tribulation (see Allison, *End*).

10. *afflictions.* Gk *mastigas.* Literally, the word means a whip or a lash, but it is already used in Homer and later Greek writers in the metaphorical sense of a suffering sent by God (see BAGD, 495).

fell upon. Gk *epipiptein.* The word can be used of an eager embrace (e.g. Acts 20:10, 37), but also in a hostile sense for an attack (e.g. Josh 11:7; 2 Kgdms 17:9; see LSJ, 651; M-M, 243). Significantly, *epipiptein* can also be used for a disease attacking a person (e.g. Hippocrates *Airs Waters Places* 3); in our passage, then, those who have been attacked and lashed by disease (see the NOTE on "afflictions") in their turn attack Jesus in their eagerness to be healed.

11. *whenever they beheld him, fell down before him and yelled out.* Gk *hotan auton etheōroun, prosepipton autō kai ekrazon.* The form of these clauses (*an* + imperfect in protasis, imperfect in apodosis; see GLOSSARY) is the Koine Greek method of rendering past general supposition; see Burton, §315. A repeated series of encounters between Jesus and the demons, then, is presupposed.

You are the Son of God! Gk *Sy ei ho ʾhuios tou theou.* Reploh (*Lehrer*, 40) thinks that the demon here, as in 1:24 and 5:7, invokes Jesus' identity in order to ward off his exorcistic attack, but this interpretation is unlikely, since the demon does not beg Jesus to desist, as the spirits do in the other two passages; see the APPENDIX "The Messianic Secret Motif."

COMMENT

Introduction. The controversy about Jesus' healing on the Sabbath and the consequent pact between the Pharisees and the Herodians to do away with him (3:1–6) is followed by a passage emphasizing the other side of the response to Jesus: crowds flock to him from all points of the compass, people beg him to heal them, and demons acknowledge his sovereignty (3:7–12). The human and demonic reactions to Jesus are linked by the use of similar verbs: the human sufferers *fall upon* him in their agitation to touch him, and the unclean spirits *fall before* him blaring out his divine identity. The quick and dramatic succession of these two falling groups contributes to the sense of Jesus' awesome sovereignty and power in the midst of a chaotic situation. Mark seems to be operating here with a conception very much like that of the pre-Pauline hymn in Phil 2:10–11: the knees of both earthly and unearthly creatures are beginning to bow before Jesus, and even the mouths of the demons are confessing his eschatological lordship.

The core of this scene is pre-Markan; Keck ("Mark 3:7–12") notes the five Markan *hapax legomena* (see GLOSSARY) in 3:7ab, 9–10, as well as the grammatical roughness of the additional place-names in 3:7c–8 and the unusualness of crowds rather than disciples "following" Jesus. Mark is probably responsible for the additional localities (from Judaea on); they occur between two instances of "a great crowd followed/came to him," and such repetition is a favorite Markan device for framing redactional insertions (cf. 2:10; 3:16; 4:32). Mark may also have inserted the *gar* ("for") clause in 3:10a, which uses typical vocabulary ("many," "healed"), and he is probably responsible for the concluding verses, 3:11–12, which are a classic example of the Markan messianic secret motif (cf. especially 1:34). The verbs in these verses are in the imperfect (contrast the aorists in the preceding verses), suggesting a desire to generalize in view of the overall Markan story; the concluding command to be silent, moreover, contains typical Markan vocabulary (*polla* ["sharply"] and *phaneron* ["known"]; cf. Räisänen, 169).

In its present form this generalized description and 1:45, which also emphasizes the flocking of crowds to Jesus from everywhere, seem designed by Mark to frame the controversy section in 2:1–3:6. As Dewey ("Tapestry," 228) puts it, "The resumption of the earlier narrative in effect brackets the controversies for later development, while resuming the story of Jesus' popularity." The passage alternates between descriptions of Jesus' activity and descriptions of the reaction to him from human beings and demons. These reactions hold center stage, yet the whole narrative is so structured that the actions of Jesus frame it:

3:7a	Jesus crosses sea with disciples
3:7b–8	Huge crowd follows him
3:9	Jesus tells disciples to ready a boat
3:10	because all the sick are thronging him
3:11	Unclean spirits do obeisance and confess his identity
3:12	Jesus sharply rebukes them

The function of the passage is both to summarize and cap what has gone before and to form a transition to what follows. On the one hand, the healings and exorcisms recall those that have previously occurred (1:21–34, 40–45; 2:1–12; 3:1–5), and the silencing of the demons echoes similar incidents in 1:25

and 1:34. Moreover, although the positive response to Jesus here contrasts with the negative response in the preceding portion of the Gospel, the atmosphere of battle has not been left totally behind. The passage contains an extraordinary number of words that imply forceful, even violent behavior: the multitudes threaten to *crush* Jesus, *falling upon* him in their frenzy to be healed of the afflictions that have *lashed* them (see the NOTE on "afflictions" in 3:10); the demons *fall down* before him with a *yell*; and Jesus *sharply rebukes* them. On the other hand, certain themes are so heightened that they imply discontinuity from what has preceded: the gathering of Galileans to Jesus in 1:45 has become a muster from all parts of Palestine and even beyond its borders, the single day of healing in Capernaum in 1:21–34 has become a general ministry of healing, and the crowds around Jesus have grown so large that he runs the risk of being crushed (cf. Koch, *Bedeutung*, 168). Mark introduces at this point, moreover, a new mode of transport, the boat, which will play a significant role in the subsequent narrative (cf. 4:1; 5:2, 21; 6:32, 45, 54).

The passage can be divided into two parts: the human reaction to Jesus (3:7–10) and the demonic reaction (3:11–12).

3:7–10: the human reaction. After the implied threat from the Pharisees and Herodians, Jesus withdraws to the seashore and is followed by a huge crowd from all parts of Palestine and even beyond. Such a far-flung movement toward Jesus near the beginning of his ministry is historically dubious, and it is probably for this reason that Matt 4:25 eliminates the reference to Tyre and Sidon (cf. Reploh, *Lehrer*, 38). The Markan list of localities appears to be arranged in three pairs: (1) Judaea and Jerusalem, which seems to be a fixed phrase for Mark (cf. 1:5 and contrast Matt 3:5, which logically turns the phrase around), (2) Idumaea and Transjordan, and (3) Tyre and Sidon. Reploh (*Lehrer*, 38) thinks the point is that people are streaming to Jesus from all regions in which Jews were represented; the Idumaeans had been (forcibly) converted to Judaism under the Hasmonaeans, and there were substantial Jewish minorities in many of the Transjordanian cities and in Tyre and Sidon (see Schürer, 2.3–6, 85–184; 3.1.14–15). But Mark may also wish to suggest that people from predominantly Gentile areas are beginning to be attracted to Jesus; the six place-names represent an increasing sociological distance from Judaism, which may be why Judaea is mentioned first. Judaea and Jerusalem were traditional, uncontestedly Jewish areas, Idumaea had been conquered and converted by Jews, and the Transjordan was part of the Israelite inheritance in the biblical conquest tradition (see Num 32:33–42) but had long since fallen into Gentile hands. Tyre and Sidon, however, had never been part of Israel. The list may thus be partly designed to foreshadow the post-Easter expansion of the news about Jesus into Gentile areas and would be especially suggestive if Mark's predominantly Gentile community were itself situated in one of the areas listed near the end (Transjordan or the Tyre/Sidon region; see the INTRODUCTION).

The huge crowd he has attracted threatens to crush Jesus, so he tells the disciples to prepare a boat in case it is needed as a means of escape. Ironically, then, having eluded the threat posed by the Pharisees and Herodians, Jesus is immediately endangered again—by his own followers! Though the crowd's attitude toward Jesus is positive, there is an undertone of threat, which is reinforced by the use of the aggressive verb "fell upon" in the next verse (see the NOTE on this verb in 3:10). Thus, as in 1:36 (cf. the NOTE on "hunted . . . down" in that verse), a positive reaction to Jesus contains undercurrents that point toward later estrangement and even hostility (cf. 15:11–15). This interpretation is reinforced by the fact that the verb for "crush," *thlibein*, has implications of eschatological distress and may foreshadow Jesus' suffering and death as the afflictions of the end-time (see the NOTE on "so that they might not crush him" in 3:9).

3:11–12: the demonic reaction. The reaction of human sufferers to Jesus is immediately paralleled by a demonic reaction, and this similarity reinforces the Markan connection between physical illness and exorcism (see the COMMENT on 1:29–31 and on 1:40–42 and cf. Broadhead, *Teaching*, 89). The unclean spirits' acknowledgment of Jesus' status as Son of God and Jesus' squelching of this acknowledgment also reflect major Markan concerns. Mark now specifies what it is that Jesus has previously forbidden the demons to divulge (cf. 1:34), namely his identity as the Son of God. This is the most important and adequate title for Jesus in the Gospel, and its usage here represents the climax of the passage—a point paradoxically confirmed by Jesus' suppression of it. This is the second Markan usage of the concept of divine Sonship, the first being the voice from heaven in 1:11, which provides a significant comparison and contrast:

1:11	*3:11*
You are my beloved son	You are the Son of God
in you I have taken delight	

The demons are conspicuously *not* pleased with Jesus, and he is *not* beloved by them. The contrast hints at the forces of hatred that will eventually drive Jesus to his death. In its context the demonic confession also gives the lie to the scribes' subsequent slander that Jesus casts out demons by Beelzebul (3:22), for here the spirits acknowledge that, far from being in collusion with them, Jesus is in the process of vanquishing them by the power of God. It is significant that Jesus' divine Sonship is correlated with his effective opposition to the power of Satan. In Mark's conception, then, "Son of God" is not simply a title for Jesus as the human Messiah—indeed, there seems to have been no general expectation in Judaism that the Messiah would be an exorcist (see Twelftree, *Exorcist*, 182–89)—but a designation suggesting that he participates in God's sovereignty over evil supernatural forces (cf. Phil 2:9–11).

The Markan Jesus does not allow the demons' acknowledgment to continue unchecked but forbids them to make him known. This ban does not make much sense on a historical level, since according to v 11 the demons are crying out persistently (see the NOTE on "whenever they beheld him") and loudly, and in such a case it is likely that someone besides Jesus would hear them (cf. Reploh, *Lehrer*, 41). The prohibition, rather, reflects Mark's messianic secret motif, according to which Jesus' divine Sonship is hidden from human knowledge until the crucifixion and resurrection can make clear the exact way in which it is to be understood (see the APPENDIX "The Messianic Secret Motif"). Moreover, it is not for the demons or even an angel from heaven to proclaim the message of Jesus' divine Sonship and what it means for the cosmos (cf. Gal 1:8). That place of honor is reserved for human beings; in the next passage a core group of them will be chosen for the task.

THE COMMISSIONING OF THE TWELVE
(3:13–19)

3   [13]And he went up the mountain and called to himself those whom he himself wanted, and they came away to him. [14]And he appointed twelve, in order that they might be with him and that he might send them out to preach [15]and to have authority to cast out demons. [16]And he appointed the Twelve, and he gave Simon the name Peter; [17]and James the son of Zebedee and John, James' brother—and he gave them the name Boanerges, that is "sons of thunder"; [18]and Andrew and Philip and Bartholomew and Matthew and Thomas and James the son of Alphaeus and Thaddaeus and Simon the Kananite—[19]and Judas Iscariot, who also betrayed him.

NOTES

3   13. *called to himself.* Gk *proskaleitai*, the middle form of *kalein*, "to call" (cf. the NOTE on "called" in 1:20), compounded with *pros*, "to."

14. *appointed.* Gk *epoiēsen.* The use of *poiein* for "to appoint" is unclassical, reflecting a Semitism found in the LXX (e.g. 1 Kgdms 12:6; 3 Kgdms 13:33) and elsewhere in the NT (e.g. Heb 3:2; Rev 5:10; cf. Taylor, 230). The root meaning of the verb is "to do," "to make," or "to create," and it is prominent in Genesis 1; on the possible relevance of this creation nuance for our passage, see the COMMENT on 3:13–15.

twelve. Gk *dōdeka.* On the eschatological significance of this number, see the COMMENT on 3:13–15. Bultmann (345–46) questions the historicity of the Twelve; he sees the group as a retrojection of an institution that arose in the early church as the latter began to appropriate the structures of Judaism. But Jesus himself, as well as the early church, could have been influenced by Jewish models of community structure. It is hard to see the Twelve as the creation of the early Christian community, since the group does not play a significant role in the church's continuing life, fading from view after the resurrection appearances (1 Cor 15:5) and the replacement of Judas by Matthias (Acts 1:15–26). The membership of Judas in the original group of twelve, moreover, was an embarrassment for the church (cf. the attempt to explain it as a fulfillment of scripture in Acts 1:16–17), and it is therefore implausible that the church would have remembered him as "one of the Twelve" (Mark 3:19) had he not in fact been one.

Some manuscripts (e.g. ℵ, B, C*) add "whom he also named apostles" here. Although these are strong witnesses, other good manuscripts (e.g. A) leave the words out, and one manuscript (W) places them differently. This variation suggests that the reference to apostles is not part of the original text but an assimilation to Luke 6:13 (cf. Matt 10:2); it is easy to see why a later scribe, influenced by the developing church's emphasis on apostolic office (see Betz, "Apostle," 309–11), might introduce the reference to apostles, but difficult to see why a later scribe would deliberately omit it. Elsewhere in Mark, "apostle" appears only once, in 6:30, where it does not have its later technical significance but simply means a person sent out (cf. 6:7).

16. *And he appointed the Twelve.* Gk *kai epoiēsen tous dōdeka.* These words are missing in some manuscripts (e.g. A, C², D, L, Θ) but this is probably because of the awkward way in which they repeat 3:14.

gave . . . the name. Gk *epethēken . . . onoma,* a phrase repeated in 3:17. In the ancient world renaming or bestowal of a nickname or epithet was a common phenomenon, and often represented a recognition of a distinctive feature of a person's personality or appearance (see G. Horsley, "Names"). In *'Abot R. Nat.* 18 (A), for example, R. Judah the Prince gives nicknames to several Tannaitic sages, calling R. Tarfon "a heap of stones": "When a person removes one, they all topple and fall over each other." The stone imagery here is similar to our passage, in which Simon is nicknamed Peter, "the rock." In our passage, however, the renamings probably imply a change of status rather than recognition of a preexistent character trait; in the Septuagint "gave the name" is used either for the naming of a child (Judges 8:31) or for a renaming that accompanies a transformed position (4 Kgdms 24:17; Neh 9:7; Dan 1:7).

Simon . . . Peter. Gk *tǭ Simōni Petron.* This name stands out not only because it is the first in the list of disciples but also because it does not fit grammatically with the other names (see Stock, *Boten,* 33–34). "Simon" (Heb *Šim⁽ôn*) is one of the most common Jewish names known to us from antiquity, whereas "Peter" (Gk *Petros*), which is the Greek form of the Aram *Kephā'* = "rock" (cf. Gal 2:9), does not seem to have been a proper name before Simon Peter. For him it was a nickname, like "Rocky," as is already suggested by the fact that it is translated (cf. Cullmann, *Peter,* 19–23). In Mark this nickname now replaces Peter's proper name, "Simon," which has been the invariable designation for him up to this point (1:16, 29, 36); only in 14:37 does the name "Simon" momentarily resurface, probably to hint at the danger of apostasy. Brown et al. (*Peter,* 90 n. 210) suggest that the nickname may originally have alluded to Peter's "tough" character. The early church associated it with his foundational role in its history (see Matt 16:18 and cf. Gal 2:9, where Peter is one of the "pillars" of the Jerusalem church), and this association could be related to the image of Abraham; cf. the COMMENT on 3:16–19.

17. *James . . . John.* Gk *Iakōbon . . . Iōannēn.* On the two sons of Zebedee, who together with Peter form an inner circle of three disciples in Mark (5:37; 9:2; 14:33), see the NOTE on "James the son of Zebedee and his brother John" in 1:19.

Boanerges, that is "sons of thunder." Gk *Boanērges, ho estin huioi brontēs.* *Boane-* may represent *běnê*, the Hebrew word for "sons of," but the rest of Mark's transliteration is puzzling, since *rges* does not correspond to the Hebrew or Aramaic words for "thunder"; the nearest Hebrew is *rᶜm*, which Jerome (on Dan 1:7) thought was the underlying word (see Lagrange, 66); the last letter, however, is a problem. Other possibilities are that *rges* renders a word for excitement (*rgz*), for commotion and anger (*rgš*), or for quaking (*rᶜš*; see Rook, "Boanerges"). On the negative nuance of the epithet, see the COMMENT on 3:16–19; Dahl, however ("Parables," 161), suggests that it could also hint that the brothers will be exposed to the eschatological thunderstorm, as will Jesus himself (cf. 10:38–40). The suggestion of a positive meaning is slightly supported by the similar name of an ancient Jewish town, *Běnê Běraq* = "sons of lightning," which like most town names probably has a positive nuance.

18. *Andrew.* Gk *Andrean.* Andrew is separated from his brother Peter and distinguished from the inner three, reflecting his obscurity in the tradition; see the NOTE on 1:16.

Philip . . . Simon. Gk *Philippon . . . Simōna.* None of the names between Andrew and Judas appears elsewhere in Mark's narrative, although *James the son of Alphaeus* may be the brother of "Levi the son of Alphaeus," who became a disciple of Jesus in 2:14. (Or is "Levi" in the latter verse a corruption of "Levite," and the person referred to perhaps the same?) *Thaddaeus* is replaced by Judas son of James in Luke 6:16 and Acts 1:13; for possible explanations, most of them highly speculative, see Taylor, 233–34.

Kananite. Gk *Kananaion.* Some have suggested that this epithet means "from Cana," a town mentioned in John 2:1; the second nu, however, is problematic for this explanation. Others have interpreted it as "Canaanite," but in Greek the word for "Canaanite" begins with a chi, not a kappa. A third theory is that it is a transliteration of Aram *qanʾān*, which means "zealous" or "zealot"; this seems, at least, to be Luke's interpretation, since he replaces *Kananaion* with *zēlōtēn*, the Greek word for "zealot" (cf. Acts 1:13).

19. *Judas Iscariot.* Gk *Ioudan Iskariōth.* On the many theories about Judas' epithet *Iskariōth*, see the survey in Brown, *Death,* 2.1410–16. As Davies and Allison point out (2.157), the three most common ones are (1) from the Heb *ʾîš Qěrîyyôt* = "man of Qerioth," a town in Judah near Hebron, (2) from the Aram *ʾišqaryāʾ* = "false one," and (3) from the Gk *sikarios* = "dagger-man, assassin," which became the name of one of the Jewish revolutionary parties, the Sicarii. In terms of the "historical Judas," it is impossible to decide among these interpretations, but in terms of Mark's understanding, the revolutionary interpretation seems most likely (see the COMMENT on 3:16–19). It is sup-

ported by several manuscripts of our passage (and of the Matthean and Lukan parallels) that read *Skariōth*, a term that like *sikarios* lacks the initial iota.

betrayed. Gk *paredōken.* The basic meaning of *paradidonai* is to transfer something or someone into the possession of another, usually without any nuance of treachery (see e.g. Luke 1:2; 1 Cor 11:2, 23; 1 Pet 2:23; cf. Popkes, "Paradidōmi," 18). But in the Gospels the word takes on a predominantly negative meaning through its association with Judas' deed and with similar acts of handing Christians over to the authorities (cf. 13:9, 11–12). Even here, however, it is sometimes unclear whether the one who delivers to suffering and death is a treacherous human being or, as in certain OT passages, God (cf. the NOTE on "handed over" in 1:14).

COMMENT

Introduction. The second major section in the Gospel, 3:13–6:6, begins, like the first, with a commissioning narrative (cf. 1:16–20): Jesus ascends a mountain, calls a group of disciples, and sets apart twelve of them for special tasks and fellowship. The passage concludes with a list of the Twelve.

This list of the Twelve probably came to Mark already connected with the story of their call; the latter is too short to have been transmitted independently, and if Mark had been composing the whole passage freely, he would have spoken of ascent of *a* mountain rather than ascent of *the* mountain, no mountain having previously been mentioned in the Gospel. (It may be that 3:13–19 was originally a pendant to the Transfiguration story in 9:2–8; this might explain not only the definite article in "*the* mountain," but also the name change of Simon to Peter, "the Rock," and of the sons of Zebedee to Boanerges, "the sons of thunder": the former reflects the building imagery in 9:5 [cf. Matt 7:24–25], and the latter the voice out of the cloud in 9:7.) The most obvious redaction by Mark himself occurs in 3:14–15, which is bracketed by two instances of the same short clause ("and he appointed twelve"), a common Markan device for resuming a narrative after an editorial insertion (cf. 2:10; 3:8; 4:32). The phrase "in order that they might be with him" may be original, since it fits in well with the setting, but the rest of 3:14–15 is probably editorial, since it contains typical Markan vocabulary ("preach," "authority," "cast out demons") and introduces a discordant note: Jesus calls the Twelve both to leave him and to remain with him. The list of the Twelve is basically traditional, but Mark may have added the portentous relative clause "who also betrayed him" in 3:19, which foreshadows the use of the same verb for Judas in 14:10–11, 18, 21, 42, 44.

The passage falls naturally into two parts: (1) Jesus' ascent of the mountain and summons of disciples (3:13–15) and (2) the list of the Twelve (3:16–19).

3:13–15: ascent and commission. The little narrative that precedes the list of the Twelve consists of two sentences of three clauses each, the one describing

Jesus' ascent of a mountain and summons of disciples, the other describing his institution of the Twelve. The relation between these two sentences is unclear. Is the commissioning of disciples from the mountaintop (3:13) the same as the appointment of the Twelve (3:14), or does Mark first describe the calling of a mass of disciples and then depict the selection of twelve of them for more intimate fellowship and a special mission? In view of other Markan passages implying a wider group of disciples accompanying the Twelve (4:10; 10:32), the latter alternative is preferable.

It is probable that, when Mark describes Jesus' ascent of "the" mountain, he has in mind Moses' ascents of Sinai throughout the Pentateuch (Exodus 19, 24, 34; Numbers 27; Deuteronomy 9–10, 32). As Allison (*New Moses*, 174–75) points out, in the Septuagint Mark's phrase *anabainein eis to oros* ("to go up the mountain") occurs twenty-four times, of which eighteen are in the Pentateuch, and most of the latter refer to Moses. Exodus 19:3 is a particularly interesting example, since two verses later it is prophesied that Israel will be God's treasured possession, and this is similar to the way in which the Markan Jesus chooses the Twelve for intimacy with himself and hence by implication with God. Another important Mosaic ascent occurs in Exod 24:1–4, where Moses ascends Sinai in the company of a group of priests and elders and sets up pillars symbolizing the twelve tribes; thus the Markan linkage between the ascent of the mountain, association with a group of leaders, and the number twelve also has a Mosaic parallel. Moreover, as Horbury ("Twelve") has shown, the twelve tribal leaders are often linked with Moses in biblical and postbiblical Jewish traditions (see e.g. Numbers 7; Josephus *Ant*. 3.47, 219–22; *Num. Rab*. 13.2). A Mosaic typology, therefore, is probably at least part of the background for the NT picture of Jesus surrounded by twelve disciples.

Before Mark describes the institution of the Twelve, however, he first depicts, in a deeply symbolic way, the commissioning of a larger body of disciples: Jesus ascends the mountain and calls to himself "those whom he himself wanted," and they come away to him. Both the middle voice of *proskaleitai* ("called to himself") and the pleonastic *autos* ("himself") emphasize Jesus' power of choice, which mirrors the sovereign electing power of God in the Old Testament (see e.g. Deut 7:6–8; Isa 41:8–10); in Isa 45:4, significantly, divine election is accompanied by a renaming, as in Mark. This divine call has its desired effect, for God's word does not return to him void (cf. Isa 55:11); those chosen follow Jesus up the mountain, "coming away" (*apēlthon*) from their previous pursuits. The verb "came away" is probably significant, since Mark could have simply said "came"; the use of the compounded form is perhaps a reminder that following Jesus means leaving other things behind (cf. 1:20).

But those who do so, Mark implies, discover something that makes up for any loss they may suffer, for they find themselves incorporated into an act of God that reconstitutes Israel and gives human history in general a fresh start. For Jesus' next action is to name twelve of his newly called disciples to a position of special intimacy and responsibility, and the number twelve awakens memories not only of Moses, the human leader who welded Israel into a nation, but also of deeply felt Jewish hopes for a renewal of the nation at the eschaton. Ten of the twelve Israelite tribes had disappeared as social units after the Assyrian invasion of the eighth century B.C.E., though some individual Jews such as Paul preserved memories of their affiliation to these tribes (see Rom 11:1; Phil 3:5). But many Jews in Jesus' time cherished hopes for the eschatological restoration of the Ten Lost Tribes (see e.g. *Sib. Or.* 2:170–76; *T. Jos.* 19:1–7; Josephus *Ant.*, 11.133; cf. Bergren, "People"). Twelve, then, was a number symbolizing the longed-for fulfillment of Israel's destiny in the end-time (cf. Sir 36:11; Ezek 45:8; *Pss. Sol.* 17:26–28; Matt 19:28), and it is no accident that the eschatologically oriented Qumran community was ruled by a council of this number (see 1QS 8:1). In another Qumran passage, the pesher on Isa 54:11–12 (4Q164), the twelve chief priests and the twelve tribal leaders of the renewed Israel are compared to stones in the eschatological Temple, and the stone symbolism here is similar to that in our passage, in which Simon is renamed Peter, "the Rock" (cf. 12:9–10 and see Flusser, "Qumran"). The eschatological nuance is further supported by Mark's repeated usage of *epoiēsen* (lit. "made") for "appointed," which may echo Genesis 1 and thus associate Jesus' appointment of the Twelve with the hope for a new creation (cf. the COMMENT on 7:35–37), and by the fact that the Twelve are instituted to proclaim the good news and to cast out demons, both of which activities are linked with the arrival of the new age in the Markan narrative (see e.g. 1:14–15, 24; 3:27; 7:24–30).

But the Twelve are not only summoned to perform acts of proclamation and exorcism; those acts flow out of a prior commission, the call to "be with Jesus." This tension between being with Jesus and being sent out by him is most simply resolved by interpreting 3:14 and 3:15 sequentially: *now* the disciples are with Jesus, but *later* he will send them out to preach and exorcise (cf. 6:7, 12–13). But Mark's odd formulation probably also contains another layer of meaning. Throughout the Gospel, Mark speaks of the disciples being with Jesus or his being with them (1:29; 2:19; 3:7; 4:36, 5:37, 40; 6:50; 8:10; 9:8; 11:11; 14:7, 14, 17, 18, 20, 33, 67), and many of these references seem to be redactional (cf. Stock, *Boten,* passim). In other cases Mark seems to have introduced references to the Twelve or to the disciples generally (e.g. 2:15; 3:20; 6:1; 11:11) or to have highlighted their presence rhetorically by his use of plurals (e.g. 11:15, 19, 27). These features have the effect of portraying Jesus as one who is almost constantly surrounded by a circle of disciples; he does not exist primarily as a solitary individual but as a being-in-community, and living the Christian life means "being with him." This portrayal of the life of discipleship as a communion with Jesus would undoubtedly resonate with the experience of Mark's community. In this light there is another way of reconciling the tension within 3:14: *now*, in the post-Easter period, it is possible *both* to be with Jesus *and* to be sent out by him; Mark, in fact, would probably say that any mission not rooted in "being with Jesus" is doomed to failure.

3:16–19: the list of the Twelve. After the heavily symbolic narrative about the call of disciples and selection of the Twelve, Mark appends a list of the latter.

Within this list the first three names are the most prominent; Simon (= Peter), James, and John all receive nicknames, and James and John usurp the place that would naturally fall to Peter's brother Andrew, who follows them. In the course of the Gospel these three disciples will become Jesus' most intimate companions (5:37; 9:2; 14:33; cf. 13:3). A group with the same names (though the identity of James was different) were "pillars" of the Jerusalem church (cf. Gal 2:9), and it is possible that the prominence of Peter, James, and John in the Gospel foreshadows this important post-Easter group.

But the portrait of a select group of three within a larger body of twelve may also have an eschatological significance, suggesting the patriarchs within the new Israel. Blenkinsopp (*Pentateuch*, 46–47) notes the 3 + 12 arrangement of the Latter Prophets in the Old Testament (Isaiah, Jeremiah, and Ezekiel + the Book of the Twelve), and he argues that this arrangement is meant to recall Abraham, Isaac, and Jacob + the twelve sons of Jacob/Israel and thus to symbolize "the totality of reconstituted Israel as the object of eschatological faith." It would be in line with this eschatological interpretation of the 3 + 12 organization that the Qumran council of twelve either included or was supplemented by a special group of three (see again 1QS 8:1 and cf. Bauckham, *Jude*, 75 n. 89). Strictly speaking, the Markan inner circle has a 3 + 9 organization rather than a 3 + 12 one, but the numbers three and twelve are the prominent ones in the Gospel.

The renaming of the three disciples reinforces the impression that our passage alludes to the eschatological rebirth of Israel under new patriarchs. In the Bible the bestowal of a new name is usually a means of indicating a change in status (see the NOTE on "gave . . . the name" in 3:16), and in Isa 62:5 and 65:15 the newness of this bestowed identity is related to the hoped-for renovation of all things and thus becomes a sign of an eschatological destiny (cf. Rev 2:17 and Swete, *Apocalypse*, 40–41). The well-known renamings of two of the patriarchs, Abram to Abraham and Jacob to Israel, are linked to their foundational significance in the history of Israel (Gen 17:5; 32:28). A comparison of Peter with Abraham, the ancestor of Israel, is particularly apt, since Simon's new name is *Petros*, which means "rock," and in Isa 51:1–2 Abraham is called the "rock" (*petra*) out of which the people of God is hewn (cf. Davies and Allison, 2.264). The epithet of James and John, "sons of thunder," may also have a positive eschatological nuance (see the NOTE on "Boanerges" in 3:17).

But the renamings may also hint at negative aspects of the inner three that will come to the fore later in the Gospel; if so, Jesus has foreseen these traits as he will later prophesy the Twelve's abandonment of him (cf. 14:27, 30). The rockiness of Peter, for example, could be related to the seed sown on rocky ground in the Parable of the Sower, which stands for hearers who receive the gospel message with joy but fall away when tribulation arises, as happens to Peter in 14:66–72 (the Greek term used in 4:16, *petrōdē*, is etymologically related to *Petros*; see Tolbert, 154–56). In a parallel vein Mark's biblically literate readers might associate Peter's rockiness with an Isaian text, Isa 8:14, which speaks of a stone of offense and a rock of stumbling (cf. Brown et al., *Peter*, 94 n. 218). Similarly, the epithet "sons of thunder" may hint at the hot temper that the sons of Zebedee will later display (9:38; cf. Luke 9:54). All is not well, then, in the eschatological Israel.

To be sure, these negative nuances are only dark undertones in the Markan picture, comparable to the human failings of the OT patriarchs, and they are not the last word about the three or about the Twelve in general (cf. 14:28). By the time Mark's hearers reach the end of his list, however, a darker order of reality has emerged, since the final name is "Judas Iscariot, who also betrayed him." The description of Judas is especially jarring because it comes close on the heels of Jesus' renaming of Peter, James, and John, in which he performs a role that is reserved for God or his angels in the OT texts. This juxtaposition adumbrates a central Markan paradox: although possessed of nearly godlike authority, the Son of Man—a title of majesty in Daniel 7— will be handed over to the evil will of human beings, delivered into the hands of sinners (see 9:31; 14:41). Judas, the instrument of this betrayal, is what Martyn (*History and Theology*, 27–30) calls a "two-level" character: on the one hand, he stands for the betrayer of the earthly Jesus, but on the other hand, he prefigures the betrayers of the Markan Christians to judicial inquiry and death, perhaps by their "brother" Christians (13:9, 11–12). Such a two-level role is especially likely because Judas' epithet "Iscariot" is similar to the name of the revolutionary party the Sicarii at whose hands the Markan Christians may have suffered (see the NOTE on "Judas Iscariot" in 3:19). For Mark's readers, then, the treachery of Iscariot may gain an added dimension of horror from the terror of the Sicarii.

But the somber note at the end of the list, with its foreshadowing of the violent Markan ending and its echoes of the violent Markan present, is not the predominant one in our passage. The main theme, rather, is the joyful one of being specially called by God's grace, chosen by Jesus to be with him, and personally enlisted in the apocalyptic war where battles are won by proclaiming good news and thereby shattering demonic structures of evil (3:14–15; cf. 1:39; 6:12–13). But those who wade into such apocalyptic warfare soon learn that in the melee of combat it is easy to become confused about the identity of the fighters; Satan can masquerade as a prince of light (cf. 2 Cor 11:14), divine confessions can be made by demons (cf. Mark 1:25, 34; 3:11; 5:7), and God's own agent can appear to be using Satan against demons (cf. 3:22). It is vital, then, to be clear about who is who and what is what. The next passage in the Gospel intends to impart such clarity.

WHICH SIDE IS JESUS ON? (3:20–35)

3 [20]And he went into a house. And a crowd gathered again, so that they could not even eat their food. [21]And his relatives, hearing about it, went out to seize him; for they said, "He has gone out of his mind."

²²And the scribes who had come down from Jerusalem said, "He has Beelzebul, and it's by the power of the ruler of the demons that he casts out demons." ²³And calling them to himself, he spoke to them in parables: "How can Satan cast out Satan? ²⁴If a dominion is divided against itself, nothing can make that dominion stand. ²⁵And if a household is divided against itself, nothing can make that household stand. ²⁶And if Satan has risen against himself and has become divided, he cannot stand, but is coming to an end. ²⁷But no one can enter into the strong man's house and plunder his things unless he first ties the strong man up—then he will plunder his house. ²⁸Amen, I say to you: all things will be forgiven to people, both their sins and the blasphemies that they blaspheme. ²⁹But whoever blasphemes against the Holy Spirit never gains forgiveness, but is guilty of an eternal sin" ³⁰(because they were saying, "He has an unclean spirit").

³¹And his mother and his brothers came, and standing outside they sent a message to him, calling him. ³²Now a crowd was sitting around him, and they said to him, "Look, your mother and your brothers and your sisters are outside looking for you." ³³And he answered and said, "Who are my mother and my brothers?" ³⁴And looking around at the group seated in a circle around him he said, "Look—my mother and my brothers! ³⁵For whoever does the will of God, that one is my brother and sister and mother."

NOTES

3   20. *he went.* Gk *erchetai.* Most texts have the plural *erchontai* ("*they* went home"), but this is probably a secondary scribal harmonization with the preceding list of disciples and the plural at the end of the verse (cf. Metzger, 81).

21. *his relatives.* Gk *hoi par' autou,* lit. "those from beside him." In classical Greek this term denotes envoys and ambassadors, but in the LXX and other Hellenistic literature it means either adherents and followers (e.g. 1 Macc 11:73; 12:27; 2 Macc 11:20) or parents and other relatives (e.g. Prov 31:21; Susanna 33; Josephus *Ant.* 1.193; cf. Taylor, 236). In the present case the familial interpretation seems to be demanded by the context, since *hoi par' autou* are *distinguished* from the disciples mentioned in the previous verse, and the same group seems to be referred to on the other end of the Markan "sandwich" as "his mother and his brothers" (3:31; cf. Crossan, "Relatives," 84–85). A close parallel is provided by 1 Macc 9:44, where א and V read *tois par' autou* but A has *tois adelphois autou,* "his brothers" (cf. K. Schmidt, 121). As Lane (138) notes, the change of our text to "the scribes and the rest" in D, W, and some old Latin manuscripts is evidence for scribal discomfort with the idea that Jesus' closest relatives considered him demented.

they said. Gk *elegon.* Some (e.g. Lagrange, 70) have suggested that the verb is being used impersonally, like the French *on disait,* "people were saying." As Best ("Mark III," 313) points out, however, if this were the meaning, the clauses in 3:21 would be in the reverse order ("and they were saying, 'He's gone out of his mind'; and his relatives . . . went out to seize him"). The subject of the Markan *gar* ("for") clauses, moreover, is usually found in the surrounding context; the strikingly parallel 14:1–2 provides an especially good illustration. The impersonal interpretation is primarily a scholarly attempt to protect Jesus' family from blame, similar in tendency to the textual variant discussed in the previous NOTE.

He has gone out of his mind. Gk *exestē*, lit. "he has stood outside" (of normal human sanity); cf. the modern slang expressions "beside oneself" or "out of it." The verb is a compounded form of *histēmi* = "stand," which is used in 3:24–26 of Satan's dominion; for Mark, then, the true instability resides not in Jesus' personality but in the devil's rule. In the next verse the scribes accuse Jesus of demonic possession; this juxtaposition is probably deliberate, since insanity was often attributed to demonic influence, as in John 10:20: "He has a demon and is insane." This Johannine passage, like ours, goes on to question whether Jesus, if he were possessed by a demon, would be able (*dynatai*) to perform miracles of healing. It is also interesting that, cross-culturally, people accused of being demon-possessed are often those who, like Jesus in our passage, are at variance with their nuclear families (see S. Davies, *Jesus*, 81–86).

Mark's readers might have been able to identify with the slurs against Jesus' sanity, since Christians were sometimes regarded as deranged; see e.g. Acts 26:24–25; 2 Cor 5:13; 1 Cor 14:23. The latter is particularly apposite because the charge of madness is related to extraordinary charismatic activity.

22. *the scribes who had come down from Jerusalem.* Gk *hoi grammateis hoi apo Hierosolymōn katabantes*. Since Jerusalem is situated in the Judaean hills, "to descend" is a natural verb to use for the scribes' journey, but the verb may also have symbolic overtones: the scribes' descent here contrasts with Jesus' recent (3:13) and future (9:2) ascent of a mountain and his future ascent to Jerusalem (10:32–33). In biblical texts descent is often a bad thing; see, for example, the Israelites' descent to Egypt (Isa 30:2; 31:1; 52:4, etc.) and the descent or fall of Satan and his angels from heaven (Gen 6:1–4; Isa 14:12; Luke 10:18, etc.). Jerusalem also has negative connotations in the Markan context (see the COMMENT on 3:22–26); this attitude is the opposite of the usual one in Judaism, where the city is revered as the epicenter of God's gracious dealings with humanity (cf. e.g. Isa 2:3, although contrast the anti-Jerusalem polemic of Jeremiah). A particularly illuminating contrast with the negative Markan picture of scribes descending from Jerusalem is provided by *Ep. Arist.* 32–39, in which the scribes who journey from Jerusalem to Alexandria to translate the Law possess a special authority because they come from the Jewish capital, just as the magnificent edition of the Torah that accompanies them, "coming from Jerusalem as it does, represents the authoritative original" (Müller, *Bible*, 53).

said. Gk *elegon hoti*, lit. "said that." The *hoti*, which is repeated after "he has Beelzebul," is superfluous in direct quotation, and although such superfluous *hotis* are common in Koine Greek (see the NOTE on 1:15), they may serve in the present instance both to separate the charges (Lane, 141) and to distance the narrator from them.

He has Beelzebul. Gk Beelzeboul echei. As the parallelism between the end of this verse and 3:23 makes clear, in Mark's interpretation Beelzebul = "the ruler of the demons" = Satan, though outside of the NT Beelzebul is not attested as a synonym for Satan (see Kruse, "Reich," 39). As Davies and Allison show, however, Satan had several aliases in Second Temple times, such as "Asmodeus" (Tob 3:8), "Belial" or "Beliar" (Jub. 1:20; Qumran literature; 2 Cor 6:15), and "Mastema" (Jub. 10:8; 11:5; 17:16; Qumran literature), and "Beelzebul" could certainly have been another (Davies and Allison, 2.195–96). As a matter of fact, the language for Mastema in Jubilees is very similar to that for Beelzebul in our passage; in Jub. 10:8 he is dubbed "the chief of the [evil] spirits," and in the Greek version of *Jub.* 17:16 he is called *ho archōn tōn daimoniōn*, "the ruler of the demons," exactly as Beelzebul is in Mark 3:22 (cf. Kollmann, *Jesus*, 178).

The name "Beelzebul" can be traced back to Ugaritic texts in which the Canaanite god Baal is known as *zbl ba'al* = "Exalted Baal"; the reverse form, *ba'al zbl*, would mean "Baal is raised" (see Held, "Root"). A similar OT name for a Philistine deity, Baalzebub = "lord of the flies" (2 Kgs 1:2 etc.), is probably a contemptuous deformation of this Canaanite divine title, like the transformation of *b'l* into *bšt* ("shame") in the names "Jerubbaal/Jerubbesheth" and "Ishbaal/Ishbosheth" (Judg 9:1; 2 Sam 11:21; 2 Sam 2:8 LXX/MT; cf. Bailey, "Jerubbesheth"). Hebrew speakers, similarly, may have connected the name "Beelzebul" with the Heb *zebel* = "dung." But in its four OT occurrences (1 Kgs 8:13; Isa 63:15; Hab 3:11; Ps 49:15) and in later Hebrew *zĕbûl* comes to mean "abode," and this etymology would fit Matt 10:25, "If they have called the head of the household Beelzebul . . ." (see Lewis, "Beelzebul"). This interpretation also goes well with the continuation of our passage, which speaks of the earth as Satan's house (3:25, 27); Satan, then, would be "the lord of the household" as "the ruler of this world" (cf. John 12:31, etc.).

Is it at all relevant for the name "Beelzebul," or merely a coincidence, that in Judg 9:28 Jerub*baal*'s name is followed by that of his officer *Zebul*?

it's by the power of the ruler of the demons that he casts out demons. Gk en tō archonti tōn daimoniōn ekballei ta daimonia. M. Smith (*Jesus*, 109) cites for comparison two passages from Eusebius on driving out one demon by another (*On Philostratus* 26 and *Praeparatio Evangelica* 4.23.1).

23. *calling . . . to himself. Gk proskalesamenos.* This verb usually takes for its object either the disciples (3:13; 6:7, etc.) or the crowds (7:14; 8:34), not enemies such as the scribes. Since, however, it has a nuance of imperious command (cf. 15:44 and see Lohmeyer, 77), and since it can be a legal term for the act of subpoenaing someone (see Acts 5:40), it is appropriate in the present polemical context.

in parables. Gk en parabolais. On the meaning of this phrase, see the NOTE on "in parables" in 4:2.

How can Satan cast out Satan? Gk *pōs dynatai Satanas Satanan ekballein.*
Jesus' rhetorical question seems to assume that exorcism is *prima facie* evidence of divine presence. A different view is implied by Matthew, who omits the rhetorical question from his parallel passage and includes in the Sermon on the Mount a denial that those who perform exorcisms but practice "lawlessness" (*anomia*) are really on God's side (Matt 7:21–23). This Matthean stance comes strikingly close to Jewish rejections of the charismatic Jesus because of his looseness about the Law (see the COMMENT).

24. *dominion.* Gk *basileia.* On the Jewish apocalyptic notion that the evil spirits exist in organized bands under the leadership of a demonic "prince," see e.g. *1 Enoch* 6:1–8 and cf. Russell, *Method,* 254–57; on the unity of this Satanic realm, see J. Smith, "Interpreting," 437, and Böcher, *Christus,* 162. Royal language can be used for the devil's relation to his subordinates and to human beings; see e.g. 4Q286 10 ii.1–13, which speaks of the dominion(s) of Belial and his lot, and *T. Dan.* 6:1–14, which speaks of the dominion of the enemy. In Mark's mind, therefore, the situation before the advent of the royal power of God (cf. 1:15) is not one in which royal rule is absent from the world but one in which the world is ruled by Satan. As Davies and Allison comment (2.336): "Over against the kingdom of God is the kingdom of Satan."

nothing can make that dominion stand. Gk *ou dynatai stathēnai hē basileia ekeinē,* lit. "that dominion cannot be made to stand." The aorist passive infinitive of *histanai* is used here and in 3:25, and many scholars (e.g. S. Porter, *Idioms,* 72) think that it is synonymous with the aorist active infinitive of the same verb, which is used in 3:26 and translated "stand." But if Mark meant the verbs to be synonymous, he would probably have used the active voice consistently throughout the passage. The verb in either the active or the passive voice can have the nuance of holding one's ground in the face of an assault (see Xenophon *Anabasis* 1.10.1; Eph 6:14; Rev 6:17; cf. BAGD, 382 [IId]).

25. *a household.* Gk *oikia,* the group of people living together in one house, usually members of the same family; *oikia,* then, can be equivalent to "family" (cf. 6:4; John 4:53; 1 Cor 16:15). On our text's alternation between a dominion's stability and that of a household, cf. 1 Sam 2:35, in which God through a prophet says that he will build for his faithful priest a "sure house" (*bayît ne'ĕmān*), i.e. an uninterrupted chain of descendants; the Targum changes this to "lasting dominion" (*malkû qayāmā'*). Contrary to Åalen ("Reign") and O'Neill ("Kingdom"), therefore, the alternation in our passage does not mean that the *basileia* ("dominion") of God is primarily conceived as a place; our passage 3:25 is not talking about the division against itself of a house as a physical object!

26. *And if Satan has risen against himself and has become divided.* Gk *kai ei ho Satanas anestē eph' heauton kai emeristhē.* Verses 3:23–26 seem to assume that Satan's dominion is still intact, but 3:27 portrays Satan as paralyzed. On the various unsatisfactory ways that exegetes have tried to reconcile this tension, see Marcus, "Beelzebul." One of the most frequent is the assertion that the passage is speaking about Satanic psychology rather than objective reality;

Satan would not even consider rising against himself, because he knows that such internal revolt would only lead to his own downfall. This suggestion, however, is rendered questionable by the use of the aorist indicatives *anestē* ("has risen") and *emeristhē* ("has become divided") in our verse, for these seem to point not to a course that Satan is presently contemplating and rejecting but to the refutation of the implication that Satan has in the past actually risen against himself. On the resolution of this tension on the level of the historical Jesus and of Mark, see the COMMENT on 3:22–26.

27. *no one can.* Gk *ou dynatai oudeis*, lit. "no one cannot," a typical Markan double negative; there is another at the beginning of our passage (lit. "they were not able not even to eat," 3:20).

the strong man's house. Gk *tēn oikian tou ischyrou*. In Semitic languages indefinite nouns or adjectives sometimes take the definite article, so that the putative Aramaic original may have simply meant "the house of *a* strong person" (see Black, 93–95). But for Mark, who writes in Greek, the definite article probably refers to Satan as a well-known figure. The parable seems to assume that, before Jesus appeared on the scene, Satan was the head of the household of this world, an identification perhaps already implied by the epithet "Beelzebul" = "lord of the abode" (see the NOTE on 3:22). In rabbinic parables, by contrast, it is more common to find God in the householder role (see e.g. *m. ʾAbot* 2:15; *b. Ber.* 50a; *Midr. Ps.* 3.3; cf. Flusser, *Gleichnisse*, 32 and 109 n. 8). Jesus was certainly aware of this conventional usage, as is clear from some of his own parables (cf. Matt 20:1, 11; 21:33; Luke 14:21; see Pfammatter, "*Oikodespotēs*," 2.495). The displacement of God by Satan as the head of the household in the present passage is in line with Mark's (and Jesus') apocalyptic view of the world as fallen under the dominion of demonic powers (cf. de Boer, *Johannine Perspectives*, 154–55, for a similar Johannine reversal of a Jewish convention: the "ruler of the world" is not God but Satan). Thus, as in the early modern European sources studied by Clark (*Thinking*, 420), "the possessed . . . become emblems, with the whole world reduced to their condition." God's sovereignty has been deeply disturbed, and only a violent divine invasion can restore it by ejecting the cause of the disruption.

things. Gk *skeuē*. Literally, a *skeuos* is an object of any sort, often a serving dish; the plural can simply mean "property." But the term is also used figuratively for the human body as the vessel of the Spirit (e.g. 2 Cor 4:7; Hermas *Man.* 5.1.2) or of an evil spirit, as in *T. Naph.* 8:6: "The devil inhabits him as his own vessel."

ties . . . up. Gk *dēsē*. In ancient demonological texts Satan and his demons tie people up and so oppress them (see e.g. Luke 13:16 and cf. the NOTE on "his tongue was unshackled" in 7:35), and the antidote to such binding is to tie the demon up oneself; to bind a demon, therefore, is to immobilize it and render it incapable of inflicting further damage (see e.g. *1 Enoch* 10:4; *Jub.* 5:6; 10:7–11) or even to destroy it (see *PGM*, 4.1245–48). One of the hopes for the coming of the new age in apocalyptic texts is that Satan himself will be bound and immobilized; see, for example, *T. Levi* 18:10–12; Rev 20:2–3; cf. Hiers, "Binding," 235–39.

28. *Amen*. Gk *amēn*, a transliteration of Heb *'āmēn*, which is derived from a root denoting truth, trustworthiness, or faithfulness, and is already used in liturgical settings in the OT (see e.g. Deut 27:15–26; 1 Chr 16:36). The Septuagint usually translates it as *genoito*, "Let it be" (see Schlier, "*Amēn*," 335–36). Outside of Jesus' sayings, the word is almost always used to confirm a previous statement (*T. Abr.* [A] 8:7 is the only significant exception, and this recension of *Testament of Abraham* has been influenced by the New Testament; see E. Sanders, "Testament," 879). In the Jesus tradition, however, "Amen" is used ubiquitously as an introduction (thirteen times in Mark), never as a confirmation. Jeremias (*New Testament Theology*, 35–36) argues that this unusual usage goes back to the historical Jesus and witnesses to his self-consciousness as an eschatological figure with unprecedented authority, so that he can assert in advance the absolute trustworthiness of his words. Recent challenges (see the summary in Chilton, "Amen," 1.184–86) have chipped away at the edges of Jeremias' thesis but left its essential core untouched; the ubiquity of the introductory usage in Jesus' sayings really does stand out, and there is no credible way to explain it apart from dominical origin (see Davies and Allison, 1.489–90).

to people. Gk *tois huiois tōn anthrōpōn*, lit. "to the sons of human beings." Q preserves the first part of this saying in a different version: "And every one who speaks a word *against the Son of Man* will be forgiven . . ." (Luke 12:10; cf. Matt 12:32). Both Mark and Q seem to be based on the same Aramaic saying of Jesus; Q has apparently taken *lĕ-bar 'ĕnāšā'* as a reference to *the* Son of Man, i.e. Jesus, whereas the Markan version has taken it to mean *a* son of man, i.e. a human being, and has changed the singular to the plural to avoid confusion. Altering Lindars (*Jesus*, 34–36) slightly, we may reconstruct the Aramaic original and the Q and Markan interpretations as follows:

	wĕ-	*kôl*	*dî*	*yōmar*	*millāh*
Q	and	everyone	who	says	a word
Mk		every	which	one says	thing,

	lĕ-bar 'ĕnāšā'	*yištĕbēq*	*lēh*
Q	against the Son of Man,	there will be forgiveness	to him
Mk	to mankind	there will be forgiveness	for it

31. *brothers*. Gk *adelphoi*. This term implies that after Jesus' birth his mother, Mary, conceived and bore other children, a view compatible with Luke 2:7 ("*firstborn* son") and with Matt 1:25 (Joseph and Mary did not engage in sexual intercourse with each other *until after* Jesus' birth). The official Roman Catholic position, however, maintains that Mary remained "perpetually virgin," and so since the fourth century Catholic theologians as well as some Protestants (including Martin Luther and John Calvin!) have argued that those

designated Jesus' "brothers" in NT texts were either cousins (Jerome) or step-brothers, children of Joseph by a previous marriage (Epiphanius; see recently Bauckham, "Brothers"). Today, however, most scholars, including an increas-ing number of Roman Catholics, advocate a literal interpretation of "brothers" (see e.g. Taylor, 247–49; Pesch, 1.322–25; Meier, *Marginal Jew*, 318–22).

This position is well founded, and the alternatives are unreasonable. With respect to the stepbrother hypothesis, in the New Testament outside of our passage and the parallel instance in 6:3, *adelphos* as a familial term almost al-ways means full brother; the one important exception is Mark 6:17//Matt 14:3, where it denotes a half brother, i.e. one who shares one biological parent, rather than a stepbrother, i.e. a brother by marriage, with no biological relat-edness. (Technically, Matthew's and Luke's references to Jesus' brothers are also an exception, since their accounts of Jesus' virgin birth mean that his brothers are actually half brothers; to outsiders, however, they would be full brothers.) There is, moreover, no independent evidence for a previous mar-riage of Joseph. With respect to the "cousin" hypothesis, there is only one OT text in which "brother" has this connotation (1 Chr 23:22), and here the meaning is elucidated by the immediate context, which is scarcely the case in Mark 3:31–35. Greek, moreover, has a perfectly good and unambiguous word for "cousin," *anepsios* (cf. Col 4:10), and this probably would have been used if "cousin" were meant. The application of the "cousin" thesis to Jesus in-volves a convoluted and improbable genealogy in which Mary's sister—also coincidentally named Mary—marries a man named either Clopas (John 19:25) or Alphaeus (Mark 3:18; cf. 6:3; 15:40). Finally, as Meier remarks (*Marginal Jew*, 1.323), the rhetorical impact of 3:35 is considerably weakened if *adelphos* is taken to mean "cousin."

calling. Gk *kalountes.* This syntactically redundant word is omitted in the Matthean and Lukan parallels, perhaps partly because of its use as a technical term for commissioning by God and Jesus (cf. Mark 1:20; 2:17, etc.). Mark may, however, include it to create a contrast with 1:19–20, in which Jesus "called" two brothers away from their family to follow him; in our passage, on the other hand, Jesus' natural family is trying to "call" him back to his blood relatives and away from his mission to his spiritual relatives.

32. *they said.* Gk *legousin.* Probably the subject is not the crowd, since it is difficult to picture them both blocking the access of Jesus' family and inter-ceding for them. The third plural, rather, is used impersonally here, and means "it was said"; as Swete (66) puts it: "The message is passed from one to another until it reaches Jesus."

and your sisters. Gk *kai hai adelphai sou.* These words are not in most early manuscripts, and Metzger (82) thinks they are a later interpolation, presum-ably to conform 3:32 with 3:35. If so, however, it is difficult to explain why they were not interpolated into 3:31 as well (see the United Bible Societies' majority opinion, ibid.). It is best, therefore, to regard them as original, and omitted by later scribes either intentionally, to match 3:33, or inadvertently, because of their multiple homoeoarcton and homoeoteleuton (*kai hoi adelphoi sou kai hai adelphai sou*).

33. *he answered and said*. Gk *apokritheis . . . legei*, lit. "having answering, he said." This is a common OT idiom (e.g. Gen 31:31, 36; Exod 4:1; Num 23:12) that is also used elsewhere in Mark (6:37; 7:28; 8:29, etc.).

35. *the will of God*. Gk *to thelēma tou theou*. The genitive *tou theou* (= "of God") could be either objective (that which God wishes to be done; cf. Rom 12:2; Eph 5:17; 1 Thess 5:18) or subjective (God's own action of willing or desiring; cf. Gal 1:4; Eph 1:11; 1 Pet 3:17). The usage with "to do" supports the objective nuance, but in view of the strong emphasis on predestination in the immediately following passage (4:1–20), a subjective nuance cannot be totally excluded: those who do God's will, do so through God's own initiative.

my brother and sister. Gk *adelphos mou kai adelphē*. For Mark's readers this phrase would probably echo the early Christian usage of "brother" and "sister" as terms for fellow Christians (see Rom 1:13; 16:1, etc.), especially in view of 10:29–30, where the terms are used in the description of the new family gained by those who leave their natural relatives for the sake of Jesus and the good news. As Lohmeyer remarks (81), the emphasis is on the relation between Christians being as close and indissoluble as that between people who come out of the same womb. The Christian usage was rooted in the OT employment of "brother" and "sister" as terms for fellow Israelites, i.e. the common descendants of Jacob/Israel (see e.g. Ps 22:22–23). The Christian idiom is even closer to that of the Dead Sea Scrolls, where "brother" is used for a fellow member of the elect community, which is the true Israel (see e.g. 1QS 6:10, 22; CD 6:20; 7:1–2; cf. Wilkins, "Brother").

my . . . mother. Gk *mētēr*. Jesus' father is not mentioned because he is absent from the scene, presumably because dead, but also perhaps because, in the eschatological family, God rather than any human being is his true father (see 14:36 and cf. Matt 23:9; see Brown et al., *Mary*, 53 n. 92). It is doubtful, however, that the tradition of the virgin birth is in view; Mark does not relate the circumstances of Jesus' birth, and if he believed that Jesus had been miraculously conceived, it is hard to imagine that he would have depicted Mary as sharing in the view that he was insane (cf. 3:21 and see Montefiore, 1.95–96).

COMMENT

Introduction. The ominous conclusion of the list of Jesus' twelve handpicked disciples with the name of Judas, his future betrayer, leads into a short series of interlocked stories that highlight the opposition to him both from his own family and from the scribes.

It is probable that Mark has been active in arranging and shaping these stories. There is, to be sure, a version of 3:22–27 in Q (Matt 12:25–29//Luke 11:17–22), and this fact suggests that even at the pre-Markan stage the Parable of the Divided Dominion (3:23–26) was combined with the Parable of the

Strong Man (3:27). In the Q version this combination of parables has been expanded with additional sayings (Matt 12:28, 30//Luke 11:20, 23), just as in Mark it has been extended with the saying about the unforgivable sin (3:28–30), though it is impossible to tell if the latter extension is to be attributed to Mark or to the pre-Markan tradition. What does seem fairly certain is that Mark himself is responsible for framing the whole complex about scribal opposition (3:22–30) between the stories that imply Jesus' alienation from his own family (3:20–21, 31–35); in order to do this, he has probably divided and sandwiched around the Beelzebul controversy a pre-Markan narrative in which Jesus' relatives decided he was crazy, went to fetch him, and were rebuffed in favor of those who sat around him listening to his word. This framing technique is typically Markan (cf. 2:1–12; 5:21–43; 6:14–29; 11:12–25; 14:54–72), and elsewhere, as here, it creates problems of narrative logic (cf. the introduction to the COMMENT on 2:1–12 and on 11:12–25). In Q the Beelzebul controversy begins with an exorcism, which provides a plausible motive for the scribes' charge of demonic complicity; it is hard to imagine that 3:22–26 ever existed as an independent pericope without some such beginning. But in Mark the scribes' charge is unmotivated because he has eliminated this introductory exorcism for the sake of his literary "sandwich" (cf. Hooker, 114–15). This editorial intervention has also created other narrative difficulties; the hostile scribes, for example, are among those thronging Jesus in the house, but they suddenly disappear after 3:30 (cf. K. Schmidt, 122).

Besides creating the sandwich structure, Mark is probably also responsible for some other editorial touches: the plural *"they* could not eat" in 3:20b (the disciples play no further role in the story, and the plural conflicts with *"he* went into a house" in 3:20a); the characterization of Jesus' opponents in 3:22a (cf. 7:1); 3:23, which contains typical Markan vocabulary ("calling to himself," "in parables," "can," "cast out") and is missing in the Q parallel; "but is coming to an end" in 3:26, which is also missing in Q and corresponds to Markan eschatology; and 3:30, which is a typical Markan explanatory clause. The double negatives in 3:20 and 3:27, "can" in 3:23–37, "outside" in 3:32, and "looking around" and "around him" in 3:34 may also reflect his editorial style; all are characteristic Markan vocabulary, and some are awkward, superfluous, and/or missing in Q (cf. Bultmann, 29–30; Brown et al., *Mary*, 52–53; and Hultgren, *Adversaries*, 102).

The present Markan composition is chiastically structured (see the GLOSSARY) around the Parable of the Strong Man in 3:27 (cf. Robbins, in Mack and Robbins, *Patterns*, 161–93 for a slightly different analysis):

3:20–21   Jesus' relatives
3:23–26   Charge of demonic agency
3:27   Parable of the Strong Man
3:28–30   Charge of demonic agency
3:31–35   Jesus' relatives

The centrality of the Parable of the Strong Man is no accident, since it lays bare the underlying cause of the opposition to Jesus both from his family and from the religious authorities: the ineradicable division and fierce enmity between him and the demonic forces that hold the human race in thrall and blind it to its true good.

3:20–21: *Jesus' family, Part I.* The passage begins with Jesus' entry into a house after his sojourn on the mountain with the newly formed group of the Twelve. The location of the house is not specified, but readers would probably assume it to be close to or in Nazareth, since Jesus' mother and brothers quickly appear. Jesus' presence immediately attracts a crowd, and he and the Twelve are so busy tending to them that they do not even have time to eat. In the pre-Markan story it was probably only Jesus who was thus overwhelmed (cf. 3:30a, "*He* went into a house"); Mark has included the disciples ("*they* could not even eat") in order to tie our story with the previous one by sustaining the image of the Twelve as a group chosen "in order that they might be with him" (3:14).

Jesus' family jumps to the conclusion that he is insane (3:21). It is difficult to fathom this surmise; just because Jesus is so popular that he is continually in demand, does that mean that he is mad? But the reaction is similar to that of other people in the Gospel who interpret Jesus' good deeds in a negative way; in the next verse the scribes will represent his exorcisms as evidence of demonic collusion, and in 6:1–6 his townspeople will acknowledge his miracles and wisdom but take offense at them. Mark would probably interpret all of these instances of unprovoked opposition as evidence of "the mystery of the dominion of God" (cf. 4:11); somehow such strange antagonism must serve God's purpose, because nothing else could explain it (cf. the COMMENT on 6:1–6a). In any case, Mark's unfavorable evaluation of Jesus' family for their rash verdict is reinforced by his apparently redactional juxtaposition of it with the similar opinion of Jesus' confirmed enemies, the scribes. Moreover, the family's act of trying to seize (*kratēsai*) Jesus, ostensibly in order to restrain him, foreshadows the usage of the same verb for the efforts of Jesus' enemies to arrest him (see 12:12; 14:1, 44–45).

These features mean that Mark is the harshest of all the Gospels in its depiction of Jesus' relation to his family, and it is interesting to speculate why. To some extent Mark's portrait of strained relations must be historical; it is probably not the sort of depiction that the church would have created out of thin air, since it seems to put both Jesus and his family in a dubious light. John 7:3, moreover, supports its central point by saying that Jesus' brothers did not believe in him. But Mark's added harshness still needs to be explained, and one popular theory has pointed to evidence that Jesus' family was influential in the pre–70 Jerusalem church (cf. Bauckham, *Jude*, 5–133), that Jesus' brother James was strongly identified with a strictly Torah-observant position (see Gal 2:12; Acts 21:18–25), and that Peter is associated with this Law-observant party in Gal 2:11–14. Jesus' family, then, and perhaps even the disciples, might represent the Torah-observant Jewish Christian church in Jerusalem against which Mark as an exponent of Torah-free Gentile Christianity was battling (see e.g. Trocmé, *Formation*, 130–37; Crossan, "Relatives," 110–13). Despite the lack of direct evidence for this thesis, it is noteworthy that 7:17–18 associates the disciples with the Pharisees' misunderstanding of Jesus' attitude toward the Law ("Are you also without understanding?").

A more important factor, however, is probably the alienation of some Markan Christians from their own family members (see Best, "Mark III," 317–18; Bauckham, *Jude*, 48–49); similarly, the accusation of Jesus' madness corresponds to aspersions often cast against the sanity of early Christians (cf. the NOTE on "He has gone out of his mind" in 3:21). This explanation is supported by the way in which, in the overall narrative of the Gospel, the references to Jesus' tension with his family in our passage and in 6:3 are bracketed between two references to *disciples* abandoning their families, 1:18–20 and 10:28–31. In the latter, Jesus lauds those who leave their families "for my sake and the gospel's," promising them that they will receive a new family "with persecutions"; the note of familial persecution here is further echoed in 13:12–13, where Jesus foretells that some of his disciples will be betrayed to death by their own relatives and "hated by all on account of my name." These prophecies probably reflect experiences of familial alienation and persecution common among early Christians, and hence the picture in 3:31–35 of Jesus' problems with his own family would likely produce a shock of recognition for some in the Markan community. It would also remind them of the eschatological aspect of their present situation, since apocalyptic texts portray alienation from family members as one of the end-time woes to be endured until God shortens the time and saves his people (13:13, 20; cf. e.g. Mic 7:6; *Jub.* 23:16; Matt 10:34–36//Luke 12:51–53; *m. Soṭa* 9:15). If even Jesus did not escape this eschatological trial, how much less can the Markan Christians expect to do so! Mark's readers, then, may feel that the picture of familial alienation in 3:20–21 is uncomfortably close to the bone—but also comfortingly so, since the person slandered, Jesus, is the one whom they know to have been vindicated by God.

3:22–26: the charge of demonic agency. Serious as the family's charge of insanity is, there is an added element of malice and threat in the immediately subsequent allegation of the scribes that he performs his exorcisms by Beelzebul; such accusations of sorcery potentially carried the death penalty (see the introduction to 3:7–6:6a). The negative characterization of the scribes is underlined by the fact that they have "come down from Jerusalem"; "descent" is often a negative concept in biblical texts, and in Mark Jerusalem is a place with an unfavorable connotation, since it is the city where Jesus will be condemned to death, beaten, and crucified, and which will be visited with destruction as a consequence (see 12:6–9; 13:1–2; cf. Sariola, *Gesetz*, 60, and the NOTE on "the scribes who had come down from Jerusalem" in 3:22).

The specific charge of the Markan scribes is that Jesus' miracle working ability, which they do not dispute, flows from a demonic source rather than a divine one; he casts out demons by Beelzebul, the ruler of the demons. For Mark's readers, this charge has been falsified since 1:24, where the demons themselves acknowledged that Jesus had nothing in common with them (cf. 5:7). The charge now receives more detailed refutation, however; perhaps this is because it is continuing to be heard in Mark's own day (cf. the later attestations in Justin, *Dialogue* 69; Origen *Against Celsus* 1.6; 8.9; *b. Sanh.* 43a; 107b; see M. Smith, *Jesus*, 45–67). It is an understandable charge given the moral ambiguity of miracles and other charismatic phenomena; Old Testament and Jewish traditions, therefore, attempt to provide criteria for distinguishing divine charismata from demonic ones. The basic guideline is that charismatic activity consistent with or confirmatory of the Law is sanctioned (see Urbach, *Sages*, 1.102–10), while charismatic activity that leads one away from the Law is discountenanced, labeled magic or demonism, and deemed to be worthy of death (see e.g. Deut 18:19–20 and Philo *Special Laws* 4.50–52 and cf. Garrett, *Demise*, 13–17). It was probably, therefore, partly Jesus' perceived looseness about the Law that caused the scribes to believe that his exorcisms and other healings must depend upon demonic influence (cf. Hooker, 116); in our Gospel, significantly, the scribal charge of demonic collusion in 3:22 follows the controversies with the scribes about the Law in 2:1–3:6.

The Markan Jesus rejects this accusation forcefully, summoning the scribes as if into a court of law to clear his name (see the NOTE on "calling . . . to himself" in 3:23). He fights back "in parables," the plural perhaps encompassing the individual comparisons within 3:24–27 (Divided Dominion and House, Strong Man's House) as well as the proverblike judgment in 3:28–30 (see the NOTE on "in parables" in 4:2). In this first Markan example of a discourse denoted "in parables," then, these parables are not timeless maxims but weapons of warfare, and this pattern will characterize Jesus' subsequent parabolic speech as well.

The parables are introduced by the rhetorical question "How can Satan cast out Satan?" (3:23), which seems to be based on the widespread assumption that the demonic realm is a tightly structured, indivisible whole (see the NOTE on "dominion" in 3:24). The absurdity of the scribes' charge is then further emphasized by the Parable of the Divided Dominion and House (3:24–26), which combines the image of a king's rule over his dominion (3:24) with that of a householder's rule over his household (3:25). This is a natural enough combination in a Hellenistic context, where the two spheres of authority were frequently linked (see e.g. 1 Pet 2:13–3:12 and cf. Balch, "Household Codes," 318).

The overall line of thought in 3:24–27, however, is hard to follow. Jesus begins by arguing contrafactually: if he were casting out demons by Satan, that would mean that Satan had risen against himself, that his dominion and household were divided, that his reign was coming to an end; but Satan's dominion is obviously not coming to an end, so Jesus' exorcisms do not indicate that Satan is fighting against himself (3:23–26). But by the time Mark's hearers encounter the Parable of the Strong Man (3:27), they will have to revise this initial impression; now it does indeed seem that Satan "cannot stand, but is coming to an end" (cf. 3:26), since the Strong Man parable portrays him as the fettered captive of a victorious Jesus (see the NOTE on "And if Satan has risen against himself and has become divided" in 3:26 and cf. C. F. Evans, *Luke*, 491). The situation presented by the Parable of the Divided Dominion and House, then, is *not* contrafactual but a portrayal of the way things actually are.

This tension may point, on the historical level, toward a development in the thought of Jesus; he may have started out as an exorcist and healer who had not yet drawn the conclusion that he or anyone else had overthrown Satan (cf. 3:23–26), but later he began to view himself as the effective opponent of Satan, the Stronger One whose exorcisms testified to his role as the spearhead of the inbreaking age of God's dominion (cf. 3:27 and see Marcus, "Beelzebul"). On the level of the Markan redaction, however, the two juxtaposed parables take on a different meaning; this transformation is assisted by the transition between them, the words "but is coming to an end" at the conclusion of 3:26, which may be Markan redaction. Now the Parable of the Divided Dominion and House is subordinated to the Parable of the Strong Man, which is the center of the chiasm that structures the entire passage. The rhetorical effect, therefore, is somewhat similar to that of 2:18–23, where the central verse, 2:20, is in tension with the rest of the passage but crucial for the meaning of the passage in its chiastic Markan form. The Parable of the Divided Dominion and House is retained because it is important to refute the scribal charge of demonic collusion, but its meaning shifts: now it establishes not *whether or not* Satan's dominion has fallen, but *in what manner* it has been devastated. It shows, in other words, that Satan's dominion is not *self*-destructing; it is, rather, being reduced by an outside force, the power of God acting through Jesus (see Barrett, *Holy Spirit*, 60).

3:27: *the Parable of the Strong Man.* The latter point is strikingly made in the high point of the passage, the Parable of the Strong Man (3:27). In a provocative manner that is typical of Jesus' parables, here he compares his own actions to those of a transgressive character, in this case a thief who breaks into a strong man's house, ties him up, and steals his goods (cf. Matt 24:43//Luke 12:39 and Luke 16:1–8; 18:1–8). In the implicit allegory that has been created by the narrative, Satan is the strong householder (cf. 3:25), Jesus is the Stronger One who has invaded his realm, trussed him up securely, and plundered his goods (cf. 1:7), and the latter are the human beings whom he had formerly possessed. Jesus' ability to do what no other force on earth can accomplish is underlined both by the double negative (see the NOTE on "no one can" in 3:27) and by the emphatic use throughout this passage of the verb *dynatai* ("can"), both of which are perhaps Markan touches. In the context the parable implies that Jesus' exorcisms demonstrate the end of the dominion of Satan (cf. 3:24) and the arrival of the dominion of God, an implication that is supported by *Jub.* 5:6, where the binding of the evil angels is parallel to their being "uprooted from all their dominion" (cf. *Jub.* 10:7–8), and is made explicit in the Q parallel (Matt 12:28//Luke 11:20), where Jesus interprets his exorcisms as a sign that "the dominion of God has come upon you."

Several Old Testament texts about God's liberating—and captivating— power probably underlie the vivid imagery of 3:27 (see Kruse, "Reich," 43–44). In Isa 49:24–25, for example, God takes spoils from a powerful opponent by rescuing his people from their captivity. According to one construal of Ps 68:19, moreover, when he ascended on high he took captivity captive and claimed human beings as his tribute (cf. Ibn Ezra). If this is the correct translation of the Psalm passage, it anticipates Mark 3:27 in its portrayal of a God who destroys the captivity of human beings by placing them in a higher captivity to himself. This, indeed, is the central theme of the exodus: God frees Israel from slavery to Pharaoh and Egypt so that they will freely become his slaves (Freedman).

In these Old Testament traditions the strong liberator is God himself, and it is possible that this is the original meaning of 3:27 in Jesus' mouth. In the Markan context, however, the juxtaposition with 3:22–26 secures an identification of Satan's antagonist as Jesus, and this identification is confirmed by the larger Gospel context, in which John the Baptist has identified Jesus as "the Stronger One" (1:7). Far from being in league with Satan, then, Jesus is the one who liberates human beings from his control. His exorcisms are a sign that God's new age is dawning and that he is the appointed agent for its advent (cf. *As. Mos.* 10:1); they are not just isolated instances of a powerful spirit besting other spirits but part of a decisive, coordinated attack on the entire structure of evil in the universe (see Lohmeyer, 79; Kee, "Terminology," 245; Forsyth, *Old Enemy*, 293–96).

3:28–30: *the saying about the unforgivable sin.* Having decisively refuted the accusation against him, Jesus now moves to the offensive; it is not *he* who has sinned by making a pact with Satan, as his enemies have charged, but *they* who have committed an unforgivable sin by their false accusation. Although the transition to this countercharge is a bit awkward (why does Jesus interrupt his own speech with "Amen"?), it still makes a certain amount of sense in the Markan context. The "Amen" is an implicit claim to high authority (see the NOTE on 3:28), and this claim flows not illogically from the picture in 3:27 of Jesus as the wielder of decisive supernatural power in the eschatological war against the Devil. Moreover, the promise of forgiveness of sins, which immediately follows the "Amen," can be taken as one of the fruits of the Stronger One's victory over Satan, who in Jewish and Christian traditions is pictured as "the accuser of our brothers and sisters, . . . who accuses them day and night before our God" (Rev 12:10, RSV alt.; cf. Job 1–2; *Jub.* 48:15–19; *Apoc. Zeph.* 3:8–9).

But this seemingly categoric promise of forgiveness ("*all* things will be for-given," 3:28) is immediately qualified: there will be no forgiveness for those who sin "against the Holy Spirit" (3:29). This qualification is not surprising in light of other ancient Jewish traditions. A rule may be stated categorically, then an exception adduced; *m. Sanh.* 10:1, for example, is parallel in both form and content: "All Israel has a share in the world to come . . . And these are they that have *no* share in the world to come . . ." (Danby trans., emphasis added). Judaism, moreover, knew of sins that were unforgivable; Sanders, for example, sums up the attitude in Tannaitic (early rabbinic) literature thus: "God has appointed means of atonement for every transgression, except the intention to reject God and his covenant." This intention is shown especially by profana-tion of the name of God (see e.g. 'Abot R. Nat. [A] 39), which was "the only transgression about which there was any doubt as to whether or not there was an appropriate means of atonement" (E. Sanders, *Paul*, 157–61). Mark 3:28–30 fits generally into this Jewish theology of atonement: all sins are forgivable ex-cept that of blaspheming against the Spirit, i.e. rejecting the ultimate revela-tion of God's will (in Jesus).

But what more precisely *is* for Mark the unpardonable sin, the blasphemy against the Spirit? This question and its existential counterpart, "Have I committed it?," have tortured sensitive Christians down through the ages; we need only recall the case of John Bunyan, who in his anguish confessed to an elderly fellow Christian "that I was afraid that I had sinned the sin against the Holy Ghost; and he told me, he thought so too" (*Grace Abound-ing*, §181). Pastors who counsel such troubled souls that, if they are worried about having blasphemed against the Holy Spirit, they probably have not done so, have good biblical grounds for their position. In the Markan con-text blasphemy against the Spirit means the sort of total, malignant opposi-tion to Jesus that twists all the evidence of his life-giving power into evidence that he is demonically possessed (see 3:22, 30); those guilty of such blasphemy would not be overly concerned about having committed it. This charge that Jesus is demon-possessed is "blasphemy against the Holy Spirit" because, in Mark's view, the true source of Jesus' exorcistic and miracle working power is not an unclean spirit but the Holy Spirit, the power of God's new age. To misconstrue this liberative divine action as a deed of the Devil is to demonstrate such a complete identification of the self with the forces of destruction, such a total opposition to the forces of life, that no fu-ture possibility of rescue remains. Putting our passage together with 2:6–10, it may be said that in Mark's view all blasphemies will be forgiven to hu-mans, "the sons of men"—except the blasphemy of saying that the forgiver, the Son of Man, stands on the wrong side of the divine/demonic divide. Ironically, therefore, it is actually Jesus' enemies, who accuse him of de-monic collusion, who are permanently wedded to Satan; as sometimes hap-pens in courtroom dramas, the plaintiffs turn out to be guilty of the charge they themselves have leveled at the defendant.

In the Gospel's life-setting, the charge of having committed the unpardonable sin may be common currency between the Markan community and its opponents. The passage shares vocabulary and themes with 2:6–10, in which Jesus is accused of blasphemy; 14:53–65, in which he is arraigned before a court and condemned to death on the same charge; and 13:9–13, in which members of the Markan community are haled before courts and condemned to death but upheld by the power of the Spirit. It is possible, then, that the Markan Jesus is arraigning the scribes on a charge of unforgivable blasphemy similar to the the charge of blasphemy that contemporary scribes are directing at Jesus and his followers in the Markan context. He thereby discloses an ironic truth that contradicts the community's immediate experience but witnesses to a deeper reality: it is the judges themselves who are guilty of blasphemy; soon they rather than the Markan Christians will be judged. Through our passage, then, what the Parable of the Strong Man portrays becomes reality: the seemingly powerful enemies are revealed to be helpless giants, symbolically immobilized, and rendered incapable of inflicting real harm.

3:31–35: Jesus' family, Part II. Having decisively put down his most virulent opponents, the scribes, the Markan Jesus now returns to the more intimate enemy, his own family, whose encounter with him had been interrupted by the scribes' intervention. Although the transition from 3:30 to 3:31 is rough, there is a certain oblique connection with the theme of demonic collusion in the previous sections (3:22, 30): if according to 3:35 Jesus' adherents are doers of God's will, then he himself must be a doer of it, and not on the side of Satan at all.

Jesus' mother and brothers, unfortunately, do *not* seem to be doers of God's will in this passage. As Magill points out (*Markan Controversy,* 216–17), the reader has recently learned that being with Jesus (3:14) and being against him (3:19) are not mutually exclusive; our passage reinforces this point by describing Jesus' relatives as *hoi par' autou* (lit. "those from beside him," 3:21) but depicting them as outsiders to his circle. This status is physically symbolized by the description of their "standing outside" (3:31), presumably outside of the house mentioned in 3:20. This placement is not a merely formal device but emblematic of their opposition to God's will (cf. 3:35); instead of responding to Jesus' call, they try to call him away from his mission (see the NOTE on "calling" in 3:31). Ironically, then, the same relatives who had said in 3:21 that Jesus was "standing outside" of normal human sanity (see the NOTE on "he has gone out of his mind" in 3:21) are now revealed to be the true outsiders; they are thus parallel to Jesus' opponents, who in the following chapter will be called "those outside" (4:11; cf. Pesch, 1.222). This description of familial opposition, like the one in 3:21, would probably reverberate loudly for the members of the Markan community; they, too, know how family concerns can tempt one to abandon one's mission, and have experienced the painful necessity of having to close one's ears to this siren song.

Told about the arrival of his mother and brothers, Jesus refuses to submit to their summons; instead he gestures with his eyes toward the crowd seated around him, declaring that his true mother, brothers, and sisters are those who do the will of God. The clear implication is that this crowd is made up of such obedient doers and that they belong to Jesus' true family. This point is reinforced intertextually by the descriptions of their sitting "around him" (*peri auton*, 3:32) or "in a circle around him" (*peri auton kyklǭ*, 3:34), which are reminiscent of OT portrayals of a patriarch surrounded by his children (cf. Ps 128:3 and Job 29:5 LXX, both of which use *kyklǭ*). Thus both the symbolism of the narrative setting and Jesus' concluding saying present him as the center of a new "family circle." Although it is not explicitly stated, this circle seems to be made up of those who listen to Jesus' teaching; when a crowd forms around Jesus elsewhere in Mark, it is usually to hear his word (cf. 2:2, 13; 4:1–2; 6:34; 8:33; 10:1)—unless they have come for healing, in which case they do not sit around quietly but throng about him madly. Mark 3:31–35, then, leads into the following chapter of the Gospel not only by its contrast between insiders and outsiders but also by its theme of hearing the word of God (4:1–20).

In his concluding pronouncement (3:35) Jesus declares that these doers of God's will are his brothers and sisters and mothers. The mention of Jesus' spiritual siblings would probably be particularly resonant for Mark's Christian readers, since early Christians referred to each other as brothers and sisters (see the NOTE on "my brother and sister" in 3:35). The picture of a new family, moreover, would probably fit in with the Markan community's sense of eschatological advent, since OT, Jewish, and Christian traditions looked forward to the restoration of the family as a sign of the end-time (see e.g. Mal 4:6; Sir 48:10; Luke 1:17), and Mark demonstrates his awareness of the eschatological dimension of the "new family" concept by his terminology in 10:30. It may not be coincidental, moreover, that Isa 49:18–21 and 60:4 express their hope for the eschatological restoration of the family in terms that are similar to the description of Jesus' glance in Mark 3:34: Zion is exhorted to *lift up her eyes, look around* (LXX: *kyklǭ*), and *see* her children restored to her.

But Jesus' vision of the group seated around him contains a dimension not present in these Isaian passages: his look is a creative one, not so much registering the existence of the eschatological family as calling it into being by a gaze that takes possession of people and thus decisively routs the power of the Devil (cf. Lohmeyer, 81, and the COMMENT on 1:16–18). Jesus' initiative, then, is strongly emphasized, as in the Flannery O'Connor story in which the piercing eyes of the Byzantine Christ tattooed onto the main character's back seize hold of him and transform him, against his will, into a Christian ("Parker's Back"). Yet this divine initiative includes rather than excludes human action, since according to 3:35 Jesus' "brothers and sisters and mother" are those who *do* the will of God by listening to Jesus' word (see the NOTE on "the will of God" in 3:35).

But if some humans, unlike the crowd seated around Jesus, do *not* hear God's word and thus do not do the divine will, whose fault is that? Is inattention to the word to be ascribed to culpable human negligence, Satanic interference, and/or a mysterious divine ordering of human affairs? The parables in the next chapter will explore this question as part of their explication of "the mystery of the dominion of God" (4:11).

THE PARABOLIC DISCOURSE
ABOUT THE DOMINION OF GOD
(MARK 4:1–34)

◆

INTRODUCTION

In Mark 3:24 the word *basileia*, "dominion," has appeared twice—the first appearances of the term after its initial usage in 1:15, where Jesus came into Galilee proclaiming the nearness of God's dominion. The usage in 3:24, however, has spoken of another dominion, which is opposed to that of God: the dominion of Satan, which according to 3:27 has been fatally weakened by the advent of "the Stronger One," Jesus. According to the context of the discussion in 3:27, evidence for Satan's disarmament can be seen in Jesus' exorcisms, which show that Satan's "house," the world, is being plundered of its human captives.

But is this really so? Has Satan really been disarmed? If so, why are there still so many realities in the world that seem to suggest the contrary? Why is the Markan community itself going through a tribulation unprecedented since the world began (13:19)? Why do some of the members of that community seem to be hated by the whole outside world (13:13), and why is this pressure from the outside matched by delusion, disillusion, and apostasy on the inside (13:6, 9–13, 22)? Does this sound like a world in which Satan is being deposed, or does it sound like one in which he still sits firmly and terribly on the throne?

These are issues addressed by the Markan parable chapter (Mark 4:1–34), which begins a few verses after the parable of Satan's house/dominion. The central, unspoken question that these parables answer, a question posed not only by 3:22–27 but also by other passages earlier in the narrative, is: what time is it in the world? Is it the time of Satan's dominion or the time of God's dominion? Is it the time of Jesus' absence from the Markan community, and therefore an epoch of mourning and steadfast endurance in the face of demonic assault (2:20; cf. 16:6)? Or is it the time of Jesus' presence with the community, and therefore an epoch of joy and celebration that God has extended his graceful rule into the earthly sphere (2:19; cf. 13:10–11)? Or is it, in some mysterious way, both (cf. John 16:20)? As we shall see, the last answer is the one toward which our chapter seems to point, centrally concerned as it is with "the mystery of the dominion of God" (see 4:11, 26, 30).

Within Mark, 4:1–34 is the longest discourse of Jesus aside from chapter 13, and it is a discrete unit bounded by a narrative introduction (vv 1–2) and a narrative conclusion (vv 33–34). The chapter is appropriately placed at this point in the narrative for two main reasons: (1) The previous section of the Gospel, from the beginning of chapter 2 to the end of chapter 3, has described the increasingly sharp division between Jesus and his opponents. By the end of Mark 3, they are accusing him of working his miracles by demonic agency, and he is accusing them of blasphemy against the Holy Spirit (3:20–30). The first half of the parable chapter (4:1–20) traces this division between insiders and outsiders, good soil and bad soil, back to God's will. (2) Immediately following the parable chapter, Jesus will make his first foray into Gentile territory (4:35–5:20). The second half of the parable chapter (4:21–32) prepares for this expansion of the good news by using dynamic images of the movement from darkness to light (4:21–22), the unpredictable growth of a seed (4:26–29), and the way in which a mustard seed blossoms into a huge shrub under whose branches the birds of the air can shelter (4:30–32).

The unit seems to be carefully constructed; Dupont ("Transmission," 206 n. 12), for example, discerns in it a simple but elegant chiasm (see the GLOSSARY):

A   Narrative introduction (vv 1–2)
B   Seed parable (vv 3–9)
C   General statement (vv 10–12)
D   Explanation of parable (vv 13–20)
C′   General statements (vv 21–25)
B′   Seed parables (vv 26–32)
A′   Narrative conclusion (vv 33–34)

This analysis has the advantage of placing at the center of the chiasm the explanation of the Parable of the Sower, which according to 4:13 provides the key to all the parables.

Despite this seemingly well thought-out structure, there is a major narrative glitch in the chapter. In 4:10 Jesus, after addressing the Parable of the Sower to the crowd, segregates himself with the disciples, and there is no subsequent indication that the audience has been widened again to include the crowd. When, therefore, the readers reach 4:33–34a and hear, "With many such parables he used to speak the word to them," their natural assumption will be that "them" refers to the disciples and that all of 4:11–32 has been private instruction to them. When, however, they continue to v 34b, they get a surprise, because here Mark says that, in *contrast* to Jesus' procedure with "them," he explained everything "to his own disciples." Apparently, then, the crowd is "them" and has heard at least some of the parables in 4:21–32, but Mark has forgotten to mention their reentry into Jesus' circle of hearers.

This problem may indicate a narrative seam, i.e. the adoption and somewhat clumsy editing of previous tradition. That such is the case is confirmed

by the circumstance that, in the present form of the chapter, the disciples'
question about the parables (4:10) receives two responses (4:11–12 and 4:13–
20). The first of these responses speaks about parables, plural, as the disciples'
question had done; the second, however, seems to presume that Jesus has
been asked only about the Parable of the Sower. The best explanation for
these "blanks" (see the GLOSSARY) in the Markan narrative would seem to
be that Mark himself is responsible for the insertion into its present context of
the "parable theory" (4:11–12), which is introduced by the frequently redactional formula *kai elegen autois* ("and he said to them"), as well as for the addition of 4:34b, which coheres with it. Mark has probably also introduced into
their present context the sayings about the lamp and the measure (4:21–25),
which appear in a different context in Q and, like 4:11–12, are introduced by
kai elegen autois and deal with the question of perception. He has also made
some minor editorial adjustments, such as changing "parable" in 4:10 to "parables" (cf. Jeremias, *Parables*, 14 n. 11).

The resultant collection, like biblical parables generally, performs an important narrative function. As Drury remarks with regard to 2:18–22, parables
create a break in a story, and a collection of parables can clarify a narrative's
overall thrust from a standpoint outside the narrative (*Parables*, 46). This is
even more the case with the large parable collection in 4:1–34. Offering relief
from the hectic pace of the overall Markan Gospel and from the increasing
tension that has characterized it since 2:1, this section slows the tale down,
filling the enlarged narrative space with a solemn commentary on what has
happened so far and what is still to come (see Rhoads and Michie, 44–45;
Drury, *Parables*, 49). The increasing opposition Jesus has been experiencing
in the Gospel, and the even greater opposition he will soon encounter, are
represented figuratively by the obstacles to growth in the Parable of the Sower,
the blindness and hiddenness in 4:10–12 and 4:21–22, and the smallness of
the mustard seed in 4:26–29. This opposition, however, is set into perspective
by being juxtaposed with the motifs of successful growth (4:8), eventual revelation and vision (4:21–22), and wondrous harvest (4:26–32). These positive
themes, too, point backward and forward in the narrative, recalling and anticipating Jesus' powerful teaching and miracle working, his verbal triumphs
over his opponents, and ultimately his resurrection.

The parables, indeed, like biblical parables generally (see the NOTE on "in
parables" in 4:2), set the previous narrative not only within the framework of
the portions of the story still to come but also within the larger epic of God's relationship with humanity from the beginning of creation until the end of history (cf. Drury, *Parables*, 68–69). A universal perspective is thus gained on such
troubling realities as Jesus' association with the dregs of society; the offense he
causes to religious leaders, his own family, and many of his compatriots; and
above all his ignominious suffering and death. Since all of these experiences of
Jesus have correspondences within the Markan situation, the parabolic discourse also grants to the Markan community a cosmic outlook on its own situation of suffering for the sake of Jesus and the good news: all appearances to the

contrary, the irresistible power of God is at work in the community and pushing toward full manifestation in the world: "first a shoot, then the ear, then full grain in the ear!"

THE PARABLE OF THE SOWER (4:1–9)

4 ¹And again he began to teach beside the sea. And there gathered to him the biggest crowd yet, so that he got into a boat and sat on the sea; and the whole crowd was by the sea on the land. ²And he was teaching them many things in parables, and he said to them in his teaching: ³"Listen! Look! A sower went out to sow. ⁴And it came to pass in the sowing that one part fell beside the way, and the birds came and ate it up. ⁵And another part fell into the rocky ground where it did not have much earth, and immediately it sprang up because it did not have depth of earth; ⁶and when the sun rose it was scorched, and because it did not have root it withered. ⁷And another part fell into the thorns, and the thorns came up and choked it, and it did not yield fruit. ⁸But other parts fell into the good earth, and they were yielding fruit, coming up and growing, and they were bearing thirtyfold and sixtyfold and a hundredfold." ⁹And he said, "The one who has ears to hear, let him hear!"

NOTES

4 1. *the biggest crowd yet.* Gk *ochlos pleistos.* In previous and subsequent sections of the Gospel the crowd is described merely as "great" (*polys*: 3:7–8; 5:21; 6:34; 8:1; 9:14; 12:37). The superlative *pleistos* is capable of meaning "very, very big," but in this case there is probably an intensification of the previous descriptions, in which the size of the group thronging about Jesus has been steadily increasing (1:33; 2:2, 13; 3:7–10, 20; see Fusco, *Parola*, 151–52).

sat on the sea. Gk *kathēsthai en tē thalassē.* Biblically literate readers might be reminded of the picture in Psalm 29 of God sitting in royal majesty on the waters and giving utterance to his earth-shattering voice: "The voice of the Lord is on the waters . . . The Lord sits enthroned on the flood; the Lord sits enthroned as king forever" (Ps 29:3, 10, NRSV alt.; cf. Drury, *Parables*, 49). If so, there is already a foreshadowing here of the central theme of the parable chapter, namely the kingly rule of God.

2. *in parables.* Gk *en parabolais. Parabolē* literally means "throwing alongside." In classical Greek literature the term designates a mode of speech distinguished by its power to convince. In Aristotle's *On Rhetoric* (2.1393b 3–7) this forceful speech is a clear means of communication, but after Aristotle, and especially in the LXX and Jewish apocalyptic literature, it becomes a term for a message, often encrypted in a comparison of some sort, that is difficult to comprehend and requires decipherment (see Cuvillier, *Concept*, 21–79). In the LXX it usually translates *māšāl,* a Hebrew term that may be etymologically related to the verb "to rule" (*mšl*) and therefore may from the beginning designate

the sort of authoritative speech that is characteristic of a ruler (see Cuvillier, *Concept*, 53); thus the intimate Markan connection between the "parable" and "the mystery of the dominion of God" (4:10–11; cf. 3:23–36; 4:26, 30) may (unintentionally?) mirror the very etymology of the Hebrew term. In the LXX *parabolē* can be used for a variety of forms of speech, from a short saying, proverb, byword, or riddle to an elaborate allegory or prophetic oracle (see the surveys in Drury, *Parables*, chapters 1–2, and Cuvillier, *Concept*, 49–65). As Drury points out, parables in the NT, as in the OT and apocalyptic Judaism, usually have to do with the divine action in history. Cuvillier (*Concept*, 195–96) calls attention to similar nuances in the Markan *parabolē*: it appears in different literary forms (usually a comparison or illustrative story, but a proverb in 7:17) and is a revelation that needs to be explained (see the COMMENT on 4:11–12) and that concerns God's reassertion of his dominion over the world (see the COMMENT on 4:3–8). He also notes that *parabolē* in Mark is both Christological and anthropological: Christological in its linkage with Jesus' assertion of his authority, anthropological in its association with humanity's rejection of that authority (see 3:22–30; 7:14–17; 12:1–12; cf. Cuvillier, *Concept*, 143–44, 168–69, 198).

3. *Listen! Look!* Gk *akouete, idou*. The awkward doubling of the verbs of perception corresponds to the parabolic form, which is verbal ("Listen!") and yet paints a picture ("Look!"). But it also corresponds to Mark's estimate of the supreme importance of this parable (cf. 4:13); since it is so important, its audience must exert both their sense of sight and their sense of sound in order to take it in.

4. *beside the way.* Gk *para tēn hodon*. Jeremias (*Parables*, 11–12) suggests that *para* should be translated "on" and that the parable describes a typical method of sowing in ancient Palestine, where plowing generally followed sowing (see e.g. *Jub.* 11:11, 24; *m. Šabb.* 7:2; *t. Šabb.* 4:12; *t. Neg.* 6:2; cf. Payne, "Order"). The farmer, then, might sow seed on the path that led through his field (or, as in the continuation, on stony or thorny ground), knowing that he would *afterward* plow up the ground and hope for a good harvest. It is doubtful, however, that *para* should be translated as "on," since it never seems to carry this meaning elsewhere (see Horman, "Source," 336 n. 32), and in Mark at least *para* + accusative always seems to mean "beside" (1:16; 2:13; 4:1; 5:21; 10:46); this includes 4:1, just three verses before 4:4. The Bartimaeus story, where the same phrase *para tēn hodon* occurs, favors the translation "beside": a beggar would sit *at the side* of the road, not *on* it. At the conclusion of this story, Bartimaeus moves from being a blind beggar *para tēn hodon* to being a sighted disciple of Jesus *en tę hodǫ* = "on the way."

8. *thirtyfold and sixtyfold and a hundredfold.* Gk *hen triakonta kai hen hexēkonta kai hen hekaton*. The yield was calculated by comparing the amount of seed sown with the amount of grain harvested; see e.g. *b. Ketub.* 112a: "One *se'ah* in Judaea yielded five *se'ah*: one *se'ah* of flour, one *se'ah* of fine flour, one *se'ah* of bran and one *se'ah* of cibarium." This Talmudic text, as well as ancient passages from non-Jewish sources (e.g. Columella *On Agriculture* 3.3.4; Cicero *Against Verres* 2.3.47), suggests that yields of thirty-, sixty-, and a hun-

dredfold would have been considered quite remarkable. Indeed, they would be extraordinary even in the twentieth century, in which yields of sevenfold to elevenfold are typical of countries using traditional cropping systems. If other ancient writers (e.g. Varro *On Agriculture* 1.44.2; Strabo *Geography* 15.3.11) occasionally describe yields of fifty- and one hundredfold or better, these reports are in the nature of tall tales told by foreigners returning from exotic locations (see McIver, "Hundred-fold"); similarly legendary are the hundredfold yields reported in Gen 26:12 and *Sib. Or.* 3:261–64. But these are still small potatoes, so to speak, compared to some apocalyptic and rabbinic descriptions of the incredible fruitfulness of the end-time, which mention yields of 1,000, 10,000, and even 150,000! (See Marcus, *Mystery*, 42–43.)

COMMENT

Introduction. After the claustrophobic atmosphere of the indoor scene in 3:20–35, the movement to the seashore at the beginning of the parable chapter comes as a relief; most of the parables in this chapter, including the first one, the Parable of the Sower, also have an outdoor setting.

The elaborate scene-setting in 4:1–2 seems to be largely Mark's own creation, since it is full of Markan redactional vocabulary ("again," "began to," "teach," etc.), and the emphasis on the crowd's huge size fits into a Markan progression (see the NOTE on "the biggest crowd yet" in 4:1). Within the parable itself, however, it is difficult to identify redactional features, though it is possible that the belated phrase "coming up and growing" in 4:8 and the imperative "listen" in 4:3, which makes for an awkward introduction (see the NOTE), are Mark's own additions. Apart from these features, the substance of the parable undoubtedly goes back to Jesus; it uses the sort of agricultural imagery with which he would have been familiar, and its very obscurity, which is acknowledged even by Mark (4:13), suggests that it was transmitted by the church not because its message was immediately clear but because it was revered as a word from Jesus.

The scene in its present form is structured in a series of alternations. In the stage-setting 4:1–2 a focus on Jesus alternates with a focus on the crowd (see the COMMENT on 4:1–2 below). Similarly, in the parable itself, the fate of each portion of seed is described in parallel fashion: we hear first of the seed falling into the ground, then of whether or not or in what way it grows. Moreover, sections in which the fate of the seed is depicted concisely (4:4, 7) alternate with sections in which it is described expansively (4:5–6, 8). These patterns of alternation perhaps mirror the cyclical nature of the agricultural processes that are described in the parable and throughout the chapter.

4:1–2: the scene-setting. The chapter begins with Jesus returning to the seashore he had last visited in 2:13. He begins to teach there, and his powerful word draws to him the biggest crowd he has yet attracted (see the NOTE on "the biggest crowd yet" in 4:1). The size and urgent interest of this crowd are emphasized by the circumstance that now Jesus is actually forced to use the boat that was prepared for him in 3:9 "so that they might not crush him," but that was not apparently employed earlier. The sense of drama is further heightened by the almost cinematic way in which the subject of the verbs alternates from Jesus to the crowd:

> *Jesus* begins to teach by the sea,
> > and a huge *crowd* gathers;
> *Jesus* is forced to move to a boat,
> > and the *crowd* stands on the seashore;
> *Jesus* teaches them in parables, and he says in his teaching . . .

Back and forth, back and forth, the camera shuttles between Jesus and the crowd; they face each other in a dramatic confrontation. As Jesus opens his mouth to teach in parables, then, an eschatologically decisive revelation of divine truth is about to be made. Matthew is in the spirit of Mark's dramatic introduction when he applies to the parable chapter the "prophecy" of Ps 78:2: "I will open my mouth in parables, I will utter things that have been hidden since the foundation of the world" (Matt 13:35, RSV alt.).

The significance of the scene is underlined by the repetition of words having to do with teaching (the verb *didaskein*, "to teach," is used twice, the noun *didachē*, "teaching," once). This concentration is matched only by the repetition of "teaching" words in the introduction to the exorcism at Capernaum in 1:21–22. There, however, the power of Jesus' teaching was immediately confirmed by an exorcism. Here the parabolic teaching itself must carry the burden of authentication.

4:3–8: *the Parable of the Sower.* The preeminent example of this teaching is now adduced: the Parable of the Sower. Later in the chapter the Markan Jesus will make the cruciality of this parable clear, saying that it is the key to all the parables (4:13). Already in 4:3, however, he calls attention to its importance by prefacing it with the second person imperative *akouete* ("Listen!"); this command will be paralleled at the end of the parable by another use of the same verb, *akoueto* ("let him hear!"). This crucial parable, then, is bracketed by exhortations to listen to its message.

But what is it that the Markan audience is supposed to hear in this critically important parable? Some clarification will be provided in the two comments on the parable, the saying about the mystery of the dominion of God in 4:10–12 and the allegorical interpretation in 4:13–20. Lacking these two explanations, however, Mark's hearers may for the moment feel as confused as the disciples initially do (4:10). It may be that this effect is intentional; as D. Stern (*Parables*, 75) shows in applying Sternberg's idea of narrative "gaps" to rabbinic parables, Jewish parables are often intentionally ambiguous; like biblical stories in general, they are "notorious for their sparsity of detail . . . And the resultant gaps have been left open precisely at key points, central to the discourse as a dramatic progression as well as a structure of meaning and value"

(Sternberg, *Poetics*, 191–92). These gaps challenge hearers to utilize all their exegetical resources in order to make sense of the narrative, and thus involve them actively in the struggle of interpretation.

In making such an attempt at narrative closure, Mark's readers would be aided by the fact that, in the Old Testament, fruitfulness is a standard image for the blessings of the "good time coming," the hoped-for new age (see e.g. Jer 31:12; Hos 2:21–22; Joel 2:22; Amos 9:13; Zech 8:12). In later apocalyptic traditions, moreover, visions of eschatological beatitude sometimes include enormous agricultural yields (e.g. *1 Enoch* 10:19; *2 Apoc. Bar.* 29:5; Irenaeus *Against Heresies* 5.33.3). Lack of fruitfulness, on the contrary, is characteristic of "the present evil age," in which the earth languishes under God's judgment (see e.g. Gen 3:17–18; Jer 8:13; Joel 1:12), and this sterility can be expressed by descriptions of abnormally low yields (see e.g. Isa 5:10). Thus contrast between the failed seed of Mark 4:4–7 and the marvelously successful seed of 4:8 would probably remind some Markan readers of the apocalyptic contrast between the sterility of the old age and the fruitfulness of the new age. This interpretation is supported by the fact that it is not unknown in apocalyptic Jewish texts for the eschaton to be described as the point at which good and bad seed will be harvested; *2 Apoc. Bar.* 70:2, for example, speaks of what will happen "when the time of the world has ripened and the harvest of the seed of the evil one and good ones has come" (Stone trans., *Fourth Ezra*, 95; cf. Matt 13:36–43). Although our parable speaks of seed sown on good or bad soil rather than of good or bad seed, the similarity of imagery is clear enough. The message of the parable, then, would seem to be that the hoped-for new age of the dominion of God is, in Jesus' ministry, arriving, despite all evidence to the contrary.

This interpretation is confirmed by the continuation of the parable chapter. Immediately after the Parable of the Sower, Jesus' disciples will ask him about "the parables"—especially, one would assume from the context, the Parable of the Sower. He will reply with the statement "To you has been given the mystery of the dominion of God . . . " One assumes from the progression that this reply, like their question, concerns the parables, especially the Parable of the Sower. Apparently, then, for Mark the Parable of the Sower imparts "the mystery of the dominion of God."

But to speak of the arrival of the dominion of God as a "mystery" implies that there is something elusive about it, and this implication dovetails with the characterization of the parable's message in the previous paragraph: God's new age is arriving, *despite all evidence to the contrary.* For the parable does not only describe successful seed; three-quarters of its space is devoted to unsuccessful seed. But what is this unsuccessful seed, this sign of old-age failure and weakness, doing in a parable about the advent of the dominion of God? Surely when God arrives on the scene, he should manifest his rule in power and success, not in failure and weakness! According to the standard OT and Jewish conceptions, he will swallow up death forever and wipe away the tears from all faces, eliminating every trace of the old age and bringing his glorious reign to the redeemed earth, where his ransomed people will sing for joy, and sorrow and sighing will flee away (cf. Isa 25:7–8; 35:8–10). When God's dominion arrives, all the weaknesses, failures, sins, and sufferings of the old age will be swept away by a cleansing, transforming, vivifying flood of divine power (see e.g. *As. Mos.* 10:1–3), and there will no longer be even a memory of "the former things," much less a vestige of them (see Isa 65:17).

It is especially significant that, in these conventional expectations, the hoped-for transformation of the world can be described through the image of the replacement of a bad field by a good field, as in 4 Ezra 4:26–29:

> The age is hurrying swiftly to its end. It will not be able to bring the things that have been promised to the righteous in their appointed times, because this age is full of sadness and infirmities. For the evil about which you ask me has been sown, but the harvest of it has not yet come. If therefore that which has been sown is not reaped, and if the place where the evil has been sown does not pass away, the field where the good has been sown will not come.

As Drury notes (*Parables*, 27), the basic images here are the same as those in Mark 4:3–8 and the Matthean Parable of the Weeds (Matt 13:24–30): sowing, an intermediate period of perplexity, harvest. These images are used in 4 Ezra to denote eschatological realities ("the age is hurrying swiftly to its end"), just as Mark's Parable of the Sower symbolically depicts "the mystery of the dominion of God." In both parables the sterility associated with the evil old age is contrasted with the fruitfulness associated with the coming age of God's glory, and each of these ages is associated with a field or a part of a field. In both cases, moreover, the idea of divine determinism undergirds the parable; things are unfolding as God has determined them in the mystery of his will (see the reference to "the mystery of the dominion of God" in Mark 4:11; and on 4 Ezra, see Stone, *Fourth Ezra*, 93–94). And in both texts the long seed parable is explicated by shorter seed parables later in the book (cf. Mark 4:26–29, 30–32; 4 Ezra 8:41; 9:31; cf. Drury, *Parables*, 28). Although 4 Ezra as a literary document postdates Mark (it comes from the end of the first century C.E.), its seed parables probably go back to earlier traditions, as is shown, for example, by their similarity to 1 Cor 15:35–50 (see Drury, *Parables*, 36–38). The striking similarities between 4 Ezra 4:26–29 and Mark 4:3–8, therefore, suggest that Mark is drawing on a standard apocalyptic metaphor: the new age will be like a miraculously fruitful field.

The differences between the two parables, however, are also striking. In 4 Ezra the bad field, the field in which bad seed has been sown, must first pass away before the good field, the field in which the good seed has been sown, can come into existence. In other words, and logically enough, *first* the old age must end; only *then* can the new age come. But in Mark, by contrast, the good and bad soils, symbolic of the new and old ages, mysteriously *coexist* alongside each other (cf. Matt 13:24–30). The new age, in other words, has arrived; the glorious, almost unbelievable yields ascribed to the good soil (see the NOTE on "thirtyfold and sixtyfold and a hundredfold" in 4:8) are testimony to its advent for those with eyes to see. But at the same time it has not come in such a way that it blasts away every vestige of the old age; the bad soil, symbolic of the sterility, weakness, and suffering of the old eon, still tenaciously persists in bringing forth its harvest of death. This strange coexistence of the new and old ages is, for Mark, "the mystery of the dominion of God." Because of this mysterious hiddenness, one needs the eyes of faith in order to discern the presence of God's reign; for as Martin Buber once put it, "The true victories, won in secret, sometimes look like defeats . . . In the limelight, our faith that God is the Lord of history may sometimes appear ludicrous; but there is something secret in history which confirms our faith" ("If Not Now," 238–39). For Mark this secret something is the cross, for it is there that the believer looks to see God's victory in an apparent defeat.

Despite our parable's clear-eyed reckoning with the continued existence of realities opposed to God's will, it is basically optimistic in tenor. The movement from unsuccessful to successful seed accentuates the positive, and the fruitful seed occupies the point of emphasis at the end. The positive tenor of the parable is reinforced by the fact that the unsuccessful seed is lost at progressively later stages of its growth, and by the increasing yield of the successful seed (see Dupont, "Semeur," 5–7). Moreover, the description of the yields from the good soil, with which the parable climaxes, hints at an unexpectedly gracious quality in the divine power that has been released into the world by Jesus' death and resurrection. Things do not unfold in the logical manner humans anticipate, as would be suggested by a straight linear progression of thirty, sixty, and *ninety* or even by a regular doubling of thirty, sixty, and *one hundred twenty*; there is, rather, an element of divine exuberance and even playfulness in the unanticipated leap at the end: the yield is thirty-, sixty-, and *one hundred*fold.

4:9: the exhortation to hear. Because of the mysteriousness of God's dominion, a special sort of perception is required to register its presence; the parable therefore concludes with another exhortation to hear, matching the imperative "Listen!" at its beginning (4:3). There is, however, a progression between these two uses of the verb *akouein:* now it is not *everyone* who is exhorted to listen; only "the one who has ears to hear—let *him* hear!" For not all can receive Jesus' strange message about the arrival of God's royal power in the midst of the sufferings and weakness of the old era; not everyone has ears to hear. The only ones who can hear this paradoxical message, rather, are those who have been granted the organ to do so by God; the author of the Qumran Hymns Scroll expresses a similar idea when he praises God for having "uncovered my ears to marvellous mysteries" (1QH 1:21; cf. 1QM 10:11).

The concluding exhortation thus forms an effective transition to the "parable theory" in 4:10–12 and the interpretation of the Parable of the Sower in 4:13–20. For it already hints at what those passages will spell out with relentless candor: God does not *intend* for everyone to receive his word, at least not at present, so it should come as no surprise if some people reject it. At the same time, however, the concluding exhortation would also reinforce the Markan audience's sense of gratitude at being given the grace to accept the divine message, and it would thus prepare them to hear as addressed to themselves Jesus' words to the disciples: "To *you* has been given the mystery of the dominion of God!" (4:11).

WHY JESUS SPEAKS IN PARABLES (4:10–12)

4   ¹⁰And when he was alone, those around him with the Twelve asked him about the parables. ¹¹And he said to them: "To you has been given the mystery of the dominion of God; but to those outside everything happens in parables ¹²in order that 'in their looking they may look but not *see*, and in their hearing they may hear but not understand; lest they turn and it be forgiven them.'"

NOTES

4   11. *has been given*. Gk *dedotai*. This is probably a divine passive (see the NOTE on 1:41); balancing God's action of blinding outsiders through parables is his action of revealing to insiders through parables the mystery of the dominion of God (see the COMMENT on 4:11–12). The mystery has been "given" in the Parable of the Sower, but the disciples do not understand it yet. This is similar to the situation in Dan 2:27–30, where Daniel says that, in King Nebuchadnezzar's parable-like dream, God has revealed and made known mysteries to the king—even though Nebuchadnezzar does not yet understand the dream, and will not do so until Daniel provides its interpretation.

the mystery. Gk *to mystērion*. Both Matthew (13:11) and Luke (8:10) read instead, "To you has been given *to know* the *mysteries* of the dominion of heaven/ of God," thus changing Mark's singular "mystery" to a plural and adding the verb "to know." This is one of the "minor agreements" between Matthew and Luke over against Mark, so called because they are relatively slight in extent and significance (as opposed to the major agreements that gave rise to the Q-hypothesis). For the various ways of accounting for the minor agreements, including discussion of the present passage, see the treatment of the minor agreements in the section on Gospel relationships in the INTRODUCTION.

On the word "mystery," see Brown, *Background*, and Marcus, "Mark 4:10–12," 563–67. The most significant background is in OT and apocalyptic Jewish passages where the strange way in which God deals with humanity renders that relationship a mystery that can only be fully fathomed at the eschaton. The Qumran scrolls are especially rich in such "mystery" language. At Qumran, as in our passage, the mysteries include that God forgives the sins of the members of the elect community (CD 3:18) while at the same time allowing, and even causing, outsiders to be led astray (1QH 5:36). Similar features are reflected in 2 Thess 2:7, which speaks of "the mystery of lawlessness," i.e. "the mysterious disposition of divine providence whereby evil is allowed to exist and work in the world" (Brown, *Background*, 39), and in Rom 11:25–26, where the *mystērion* is the strange way in which God first chooses Israel, then "hardens" Israel in disobedience, and finally brings Israel back into the covenant.

those outside. Gk *hoi exō.* Jesus has just retired with his followers to a private place, perhaps to a house (see the COMMENT); if so, this term refers on the most basic level to those outside the house. But the picture also has a symbolic resonance; "those outside" are people who stand outside the community of disciples, the circle of the saved (cf. 3:31–35). In the Pauline corpus "those outside" becomes a term for non-Christians (1 Cor 5:12–13; 1 Thess 4:12; Col 4:5; cf. 1 Tim 3:7; Rev 22:14–15; 2 *Clem.* 13:1); similarly, in a rabbinic text it is used for heretics (*m. Meg.* 4:8) and in a Pythagorean text for non-Pythagoreans (Iamblichus *Life of Pythagoras* 35.252).

12. *in order that.* Gk *hina.* This word is not a direct part of the quotation from Isa 6:9–10 that follows, though the basic idea is there in the OT text. It is not immediately clear whose purpose the *hina* clause indicates, that of Jesus, who is the speaker of the parables, or that of God. Probably we should think principally of God's purpose because of the background in Isaiah 6, where the divine intention to harden Israel's heart is announced to the prophet. It would be artificial and contrary to Markan theology, however, to create a sharp distinction between God's will and Jesus' on this matter.

There has been much discussion of the meaning of this *hina*, largely because of the theological difficulty it creates if, as is usually the case in Greek, it denotes purpose (a usage referred to by grammarians as "final"). Manson suggests that *hina* is a mistranslation of the Aram *dě* found in the Targum, which can mean not only "in order that" but also "who, that" (*Teaching*, 75–80). Jesus, therefore, was really speaking about people " *who* look and look without seeing, hear and hear without understanding," not about God's intention that they should do so. As M. Black points out, however (Black, 212–14), even the *dě* of the Targum, followed as it is by *dilĕma* (= "lest"), unambiguously suggests purpose.

Moreover, it is Mark's Greek and not some reconstructed Aramaic original that must be interpreted. Some, such as Peisker ("Konsekutives"), have observed that *hina* may be "consecutive," i.e. it may denote result rather than purpose (e.g. John 9:2; 1 Thess 5:4). The Markan Jesus, in other words, may be saying that his parabolic speech *has the result* of increasing people's incomprehension, not that it *aims* to do so. Chilton, similarly, notes that in our passage *hina* introduces an allusion to scripture, as it will later do in 9:12, and in the latter passage the *hina* seems to mean little more than "that," so that it may have the same nuance here (*Galilean Rabbi*, 93–94). But 9:12 is not an exact parallel to our passage, since there the *hina* is preceded by *gegraptai* ("it has been written"), making the meaning "that" obvious, whereas there is no such syntactic pointer in 4:12. Moreover, as with Manson's theory about the Aramaic, Peisker's and Chilton's theories about the Greek founder on the word that follows the *hina*, namely *mēpote* = "lest." While this word can upon occasion mean "perhaps" (e.g. 2 Tim 2:25), its normal meaning is "in order that . . . not" or "lest," and it strains credulity that two rare meanings should be assigned to *hina* and *mēpote* when their usual meanings yield good sense and correspond to their regular Markan significance (for *hina* cf. 1:38; 2:10; 3:2, 9–10, 12, 14, etc.; for *mēpote*, cf. 14.12, the only other Markan example). It is no accident, therefore, as C. A. Evans points out (*To See*, 95), that when Matthew and Luke want to lessen the severity of the Markan form of the saying, they both omit the *mēpote* clause, and Matthew changes *hina* to *hoti* ("because"). When all is said and done, then, *hina* in Mark 4:12 almost certainly means "in order that," *mēpote* means "lest," and the passage speaks of a deliberate divine intention that some people should misunderstand and be impenitent, as is also true in the Hebrew original of Isa 6:10 — distressing as these conclusions may seem. For further analysis, see Marcus, *Mystery*, 119–21, and C. A. Evans, *To See*, 92–99; cf. the discussion of the motif of hardness of heart in the COMMENT on 3:5–6.

in their looking etc. Gk *blepontes* etc. This is a truncated quotation from Isa 6:9–10, a text that is often quoted in the NT to explain that Israel's strange blindness to the gospel is a reflection of God's will (see John 12:40; Acts 28:26–27; Rom 11:8; cf. C. A. Evans, *To See*, for an overview of the text's usage in early Judaism and Christianity). As Schneck points out (*Isaiah*, 129), the Isaian passage as a whole fits well into the Markan context, since Isaiah 6 begins with the revelation of God enthroned in awesome splendor as the king of the cosmos; there is thus an intertextual connection with the Markan parable chapter's overarching theme of the dominion of God.

Mark's version of Isa 6:9–10 basically uses the same vocabulary as the LXX, even when the LXX differs from the MT, as in its transformation of *yd'* = "to know" into *idein* = "to see." It differs from both the LXX and the MT, however, in two ways that are similar to the Targum: the verbs in the first clause are third person rather than second, and the concluding clause speaks of being forgiven rather than of being healed (see Marcus, *Mystery*, 76, and C. A. Evans, *To See*, 92; for a helpful chart of the various versions, see Gnilka, *Verstockung*, 14–15). One Markan feature is a departure from *all* OT versions: Mark has reversed the order of hearing/seeing to seeing/hearing. This reversal may reflect the preoccupation with vision that will emerge later in the two Markan stories of the healing of blind men (8:22–26; 10:46–52), in the exhortations to "see" in chapter 13, and in the allusions to sight in the scene of Jesus' death (15:32, 35, 36, 39). The later position of the references to hearing also smoothens the transition to 4:14–20, where hearing becomes a major theme.

looking . . . look . . . see. Gk *blepontes . . . blepōsin . . . idōsin*. The first verb, "to look," usually denotes physical sight and is often opposed to being physically blind, whereas the second one, "to see," can be used, as here, for spiritual insight (cf. Marcus, *Mystery*, 104).

hearing . . . hear . . . understand. Gk *akouontes . . . akouōsin . . . syniōsin*. Here *akouein* ("to hear") is used for mere physical perception, as opposed to the

deeper level of insight connoted by *synienai* ("to understand"). This is similar
to the usage of *akouein* in 4:15, 16, 18, where a superficial hearing of God's
word does not lead to fruit-bearing; it is different, however, from 4:3, 9, where
the word (there translated "listen") is used for true insight. These different
senses of *akouein* result from the fact that Greek, like Hebrew, has only this
one word and its compounds to express the notion of hearing; in contrast,
there are a number of different verbs for seeing.

    turn. Gk *epistrepsōsin.* This verb renders Heb *šwb,* a verb that means liter-
ally to come back, but which is already used throughout the OT, especially in
the prophets, for what Martin Buber calls "the turning," i.e. the reorientation
of a person's whole life toward God (cf. Friedman, *Buber's,* 144). *Šwb* can also
be translated with *metanoiein,* "to repent," which appears in 1:15 and 6:12.

COMMENT

Introduction. Jesus now retires with his disciples to a private place, giving
these intrigued but mystified followers an opportunity to ask him about the
parable he has just uttered. His reply, in its strange harshness, is one of the
most formidable sayings in the entire New Testament.

    This "parable theory" passage has probably been inserted into its present
context by Mark himself (see the introduction to 4:1–34), though he has not
invented the saying but drawn it from a source; it contains an unusual number of *hapax legomena* (see the GLOSSARY), its content is similar to that of
the "Johannine thunderbolt" in Matt 11:25–26, and the scriptural citation
with which it concludes is close in form to the Targum, which is unusual for
Mark (see the NOTE on "in their looking" in 4:12). The one point at which
Mark's editorial hand is evident is in the reshaping of the description of the
addressees; the awkward phrase "those around him with the Twelve" sounds
like a composite description, and Best ("Use," 17–18) argues strongly that the
pre-Markan form of the saying mentioned only the Twelve ("and when he was
alone with the Twelve"); this would account for the fact that the verb "was" is
singular. The addition of "those around him" is plausibly explained as Mark's
attempt to compensate for the harshness of the outsiders' exclusion by widening the circle of the insiders. This widening is consonant with 3:13–14, where
the Twelve are part of a larger group of followers, and with 4:36, where Mark
has apparently broadened the group accompanying Jesus on his sea journey
(see the introduction to the COMMENT on 4:35–41).

    The structure of the passage reflects its message. Its first verse and a half al-
ternates between a focus on Jesus and a focus on the disciples; the strong link
between the two groups, and the implicit connection between both and God,
are emphasized by the phrases "those around him," "he said to them," and "the
mystery of the dominion of God." But the final verse and a half suddenly shifts
its focus to a third party, "those outside," who are portrayed as being alienated
from Jesus and the disciples (by their position outside the company) and from

God (by their blindness and deafness to his word and the fact that they are not forgiven by him). This negative aspect of Jesus' parabolic discourse is strongly emphasized by the disproportionate amount of space devoted to it.

4:10: the disciples' question. The discussion is initiated by Jesus' withdrawal to a private place (perhaps a house, because it is near the seashore; cf. 4:35). He is followed by a group that includes both the Twelve and another set of people, "those around him." The inclusion of the latter group would remind readers of the picture in 3:32 of the crowd of disciples, Jesus' true family, seated around him to listen to his word. "Those around him" in 4:10, accordingly, may be members of the crowd described in 4:1–2 who have been stimulated by Jesus' parable to inquire further and become his disciples (cf. 4:34, where the group from 4:10 is designated "his own disciples"). This sort of inquiring spirit was highly prized in apocalyptic circles; in the Hymns Scroll from Qumran, for example, the hymnist thanks God for his graciousness to "those that inquired of me" (1QH 4:23–24), whereas the author of the Community Rule denounces the wicked because they have not inquired of God or sought him (1QS 5:11–12). In Mark, similarly, the disciples' questions to Jesus represent a vital stage in their learning process (cf. 7:17; 9:11, 28; 10:10, 26), and it is a sign of serious spiritual impairment when they become afraid to ask them (9:32).

Mark's own community probably includes inquirers such as "those around Jesus" in 4:10 — auditors who have been stimulated enough by what they have heard of the good news to make the effort to learn more. It is therefore likely that the phrase would remind the Markan audience of their own situation. They, too, have become members of Jesus' true family (cf. 10:29–30), and they, too, in 4:11–12 and throughout the Gospel, hear the secret teachings withheld from outsiders. Mark's readers, therefore, would probably hear as addressed to *themselves* the great declaration of 4:11a, "To *you* has been given the mystery of the dominion of God."

4:11–12: Jesus' reply. The first part of Jesus' answer to the disciples' inquiry is a neatly balanced antithesis between the effect of his teaching on his disciples and its effect upon "those outside." Baird ("Approach," 201–7) has diagrammed this antithesis as follows:

the mystery of the dominion of God	all things
has been given	happen
to you	to those outside
(with explanations)	in parables

This diagram is helpful in showing the balance of the antithesis, but it should be altered in one respect. The disciples have asked Jesus about parables, and it therefore makes sense to conclude that *both* parts of his answer concern parables; the disciples, in other words, have been given the mystery of the dominion of God *in the parables*, especially in the Parable of the Sower. That parable, as we have seen in the COMMENT on 4:3–8, is about "the mystery of the dominion of God" because it portrays the unexpected way in which the new age has arrived without totally eradicating the old age (see also the NOTE on "the mystery" in 4:11). Thus the parentheses on the lower left of Baird's comparison should contain "in parables" rather than "with explanations"; the difference between the two groups is not that one gets parables while the other does not but that one gets parables in order to understand them whereas the other gets parables in order that they may be hardened in disbelief.

It has often been asserted (most cogently by Räisänen, chapter 3) that this "parable theory" is not consistently maintained in Mark's Gospel. In order to see the grounds for this assertion, the reader should consult figure 6, where I have tabulated the various Markan references to understanding and misunderstanding of parables. Räisänen asserts that Jesus does not always need to explain his parables and that their clarity runs counter to the implication of 4:34 that uninterpreted parables are incomprehensible; in 7:14–15, for example, Jesus preaches publicly in parables with the evident intention of being understood, and in 3:23–27 and 12:1–12 even his enemies seem to grasp the point of his parabolic speech. Verses 4:13a and 7:18a, moreover, seem to suggest that the disciples should be able to understand parables even without explanations.

Figure 6: Insiders and Outsiders

	Insiders	*Outsiders*
3:23–27		Jesus responds to scribes' charge of demonic collusion with Parables of Satan's Kingdom and Strong Man
4:1–2		Jesus teaches the crowd in parables
4:10	In private, "those around him with the Twelve" ask Jesus about the parables	
4:11–12	These disciples are told that they have been given the mystery of the dominion of God [in parables]	To outsiders all things happen in parables in order that they may look without seeing and hear without understanding, lest they turn and be forgiven

Figure 6: Insiders and Outsiders (continued)

	Insiders	Outsiders
4:13a	Disciples rebuked for not understanding Parable of Sower	
4:14–20	Disciples given explanation of Parable of Sower	
4:33–34	"All things" are explained to disciples	Those who are not disciples are taught solely in parables, "as they were able to hear"
7:14–15		Crowd exhorted, "Listen to me, all of you, and understand," and given Parable of Digestion
7:17	In private, disciples ask Jesus about Parable of Digestion	
7:18a	Disciples rebuked for not understanding Parable of Digestion	
7:18b–23	Disciples given explanation of Parable of Digestion	
12:1–9		Jesus addresses Parable of Vineyard to his enemies
12:12		Jesus' enemies perceive that Parable of Vineyard is directed against them, and try to arrest him
13:28	In private, Jesus addresses Parable of Fig Tree to four disciples, who are exhorted to "learn" it	

But the "parable theory" is not as inconsistent as Räisänen asserts. All Markan parables have *some sort* of explanation; the Parable of the Vineyard in 12:1–9 is interpreted by the scriptural citation from Ps 118:22–23 in 12:10–11, the parables about Satan in 3:23–27 are elucidated by the saying about blasphemy against the Holy Spirit in 3:28–30, and the Parable of the Fig Tree in 13:28 is clarified by Jesus' saying about his return in 13:29. The rebukes that Jesus administers to the disciples in 4:13a and 7:18a for not understanding uninterpreted parables should not necessarily be taken at face value; a reprimand, rather, can have a pedagogical purpose, and this may well be the case in Mark. Lemcio ("Evidence") has discerned what he calls a "dialogue form" in 4:1–20; 7:14–23, and 8:14–21: ambiguity, incomprehension, surprised or critical rejoinder, and explanation. In this form, which Lemcio traces back to the OT (e.g. Ezek 17:1–24; Zech 4:2–14), hearers cannot really be expected to understand the initial statement, which is ambiguous, and the revealer's rebuke actually functions to call them to attention and introduce the full explanation.

As for the comprehension of parables on the part of Jesus' enemies, they may grasp the substance of the parables he enunciates in 3:23–27 and 12:1–11, but it is doubtful that this sort of superficial knowledge is really what Mark means by "understanding." The citation of Isa 6:9 in Mark 4:12, correspondingly, concedes to the outsiders a superficial form of perception—they do "look" and "hear"—but it denies to them the deeper sort of insight that is designated by "seeing," "understanding," and "turning." Mark's "parable theory," then, is fairly consistent: Jesus uses parables to enlighten his disciples, appending explanations to assist them; to outsiders, however, he often withholds explanations, and even when he does provide them, he does so in a way that is deliberately off-putting and thus poses an obstacle to true understanding.

This resolutely hostile treatment of "those outside" is the chief difficulty of the passage. According to 4:11b–12, it is not God's intention that Jesus' parables should enlighten the outsiders but that they should blind them, choke off their understanding, and prevent their attainment of repentance and forgiveness—a theory that commentators have termed "cruel," "perverse," and "monstrous" (see C. Moore, "Mk 4,12," 335–36). To compound the difficulty, this part of the passage is particularly accented; as Fusco notes ("Accord," 355), it is much longer than the earlier part about the privilege of the insiders, and within it the stress falls on the last and most difficult clause, "lest they turn and it be forgiven them," which is rhetorically emphasized by its position at the end and its departure from the parallelism of the first two clauses in 4:12 (see H. Koester, "Test Case," 44). A comparison with the related saying in Matt 11:25–26 highlights this point. As in our passage, this saying mentions that God has hidden his mysteries "from the wise and discerning," but it does so only in order to accentuate the miracle that God has now revealed them "to babies." In our passage, however, the negative side of revelation dominates. But why should God, or Jesus (on this ambiguity, see the NOTE on "in order that" in 4:12), *want* people not to understand his word, *want* them to reject it and therefore to be condemned? Is the God in whom Mark believes so

radically different from the one described in 1 Tim 2:4, who "desires all people to be saved and to come to a knowledge of the truth" (RSV alt.)?

The idea that the gods or God sometimes act arbitrarily in ways inimical to human well-being is very widespread in the history of religions; the hostile gods can even interfere in human cognition, as happens not only in our quotation drawn from Isaiah but also in the story of the deceitful spirit dispatched by God in 1 Kgs 22:19–23 or in Euripides' statement that "those whom God wishes to destroy, he first deprives of their senses" (Fragment, Greek Iambic; cf. Boswell, Life, 2.468 n. 1). On one level such conceptions flow from the inescapable conclusion that, if God is in control of the world, he must somehow be responsible for misfortunes such as insanity as well as for good things (see Isa 45:7). In the OT this recognition of divine sovereignty is combined with a view of God as inscrutable, holy, awe-inspiring, and transcendent, a consuming fire whom no human can see and live (cf. Exod 33:20). Hard-to-understand actions such as striking dead the hapless Uzzah in 2 Sam 6:6–7 are manifestations of the eerie, threatening, primordial force that is the reverse side of this holy God's mysterious power of fascination (see Otto, Idea). In later OT texts this idea of God's terrible and fascinating holiness is enriched by notions of his involvement in history, his judgment of human evil, and his commitment to his people. Pharaoh is punished for refusing to release Israel from its captivity in Egypt, and this punishment is his own fault because he has hardened his heart against God's will, but it is also his misfortune because God has hardened his heart in order to show forth his glory by delivering Israel from slavery (Exod 4:21; 7:3; 9:16; see Räisänen, Hardening).

Our text in its Markan context shows the same sort of duality. "Those outside" are, in line with common usage and with the larger Markan context, not just people who happen to be outside of the house where Jesus is presently closeted with his disciples, but Jesus' opponents, people who have deliberately excluded themselves from the circle of salvation by their attitude of hostility to Jesus (see the NOTE on "those outside" in 4:11). The blind hatred and hardheartedness that these opponents have been manifesting toward Jesus has been growing in the past two chapters of the Gospel (see particularly 3:5), so that in a way their condemnation to blindness and obduracy in 4:12 is just a ratification of a process already in motion. As Schneck notes (Isaiah, 125–27), this pattern is similar to that in the Isaian source for Mark 4:12, since in Isaiah 6 the condemnation of the people to blindness, deafness, and hard-heartedness follows several chapters describing their resistance to the bearer of God's word. But there is no escaping God's responsibility even for the Markan opponents' initial antagonism toward Jesus; Mark has strongly implied that its origin is demonic (see the COMMENT on 3:28–30), and in Mark's world demons do not do their work without God's permission (see 5:13a).

This stress that God is responsible for evil probably reflects the situation of Mark's community. As with the other quotations of Isa 6:9–10 in the New Testament, it stems from a desire on the part of early Christians to trace back to

God's will the perplexing rejection of the gospel by the Jewish people as a whole (see Gnilka, *Verstockung*). That rejection induced a deeply disturbing case of cognitive dissonance among Christians such as the members of the Markan community: Israel had been expected to welcome her Messiah with open arms, yet Jesus was the Messiah and Israel had rejected him. For the Markan Christians this rejection was made even more painful by the communal violence of the Jewish War. The sharp dualism of Mark 4:11–12, then, probably reflects the Markan community's bitter experiences of powerlessness, marginalization, and persecution even to the point of death. They have proclaimed the good news, as Jesus has told them they must; but the end result has been that they have become "hated by all for the sake of my name" (13:9–13). In such situations of persecution, a theology of apocalyptic determinism functions to assure the hard-pressed faithful that their suffering does not signal a loss of divine control; Drury (*Parables*, 53) appositely compares the expression of this theology in the book of Revelation: "The time is near. Let the evildoer still do evil, and the filthy still be filthy, and the righteous still do right, and the holy still be holy" (22:10–11, RSV).

But is this reference to divine determinism of evil Mark's final utterance on the subject of the extent of revelation? In Isaiah, Mark's source, a whole series of later texts (29:18, 24; 32:3; 35:5) implies that the new age will bring a reversal of the sentence of insensibility found in Isaiah 6, and Isa 32:3 even uses the same rare word found in 6:10 ($\check{s}^{cc}$ = "smeared over") to describe what will *no longer* be true of the eyes of those living in the messianic era. In Mark, similarly, the purpose clause in 4:12 ("in order that . . . they may . . . not see") is taken up by the purpose clauses in 4:21–22 ("in order that it may be put on the lampstand"; "in order that it may be made manifest"; "in order that it might come to manifestation"). The hiding of truth described in our passage, then, in the end must serve the revelation of truth; for Mark as for Isaiah, human blindness, deafness, and condemnation will not have the last word.

But they certainly have the last word in *our* passage. And although the next pericope, the allegorical interpretation of the Parable of the Sower, will note that some people *do* hear God's word, it will also reinforce the "parable theory" by reminding Mark's readers that many are simply unable to do so.

THE INTERPRETATION OF THE PARABLE OF THE SOWER (4:13–20)

4 ¹³And he said to them, "Don't you know this parable? How then will you know all the parables? ¹⁴The sower is sowing the word. ¹⁵And these are the seeds beside the path, where the word is sown: they who, when they hear, immediately Satan comes and takes away the word that has been sown in them. ¹⁶And these are the seeds sown in the rocky ground: they who, when they hear the word, immediately receive it with joy, ¹⁷and do not have root in

themselves but are temporary and, when tribulation or persecution on account of the word arises, immediately fall away. [18]And others are the seeds sown among the thorns; these are they who hear the word, [19]but the cares of the age and the deceitfulness of wealth and desires for other things enter into them and strangle the word, and it becomes unfruitful. [20]And these are the seeds sown in the good earth: they who hear the word and accept it and bear fruit thirtyfold, sixtyfold, and a hundredfold.

NOTES

4   13. *How then . . . ?* Gk *kai pōs.* In 4 Ezra 4:2, 10–11; 5:40 and in *T. Job* 38:5 we meet a similar form: "You don't understand X? How then will you understand Y, which is greater?" (cf. Drury, *Parables,* 25).

14. *is sowing.* Gk *speirei.* The results of this sowing are interpreted in the subsequent verses as events presently occurring in the Markan environment (e.g. people apostasizing), and the unambiguously continuous translation "is sowing" is thus better than the possibly punctiliar "sows." Cf. Theophylact's comment on our parable (*PG* 123.797): "But the Son of God never ceases to sow in our hearts."

the word. Gk *ton logon.* In the background is the vital OT concept of God's word (cf. Brown, "Parable," 261). The Old Testament, however, does not usually speak of "the word" absolutely (though cf. Jer 7:1) but of "the word *of the Lord,*" "the word *of God,*" or similar construct formulations (cf. W. Schmidt et al., "*Dābar,*" 111–15). The absolute usage of the term in a technical sense, however, is frequent in early Christian literature (besides our passage and parallels, see Mark 2:2; 16:20; Luke 1:2; Acts 4:4; 6:4; 8:4; 10:44; 11:19; 17:11; 19:20; Gal 6:6; Col 4:3; 2 Tim 4:2; 1 Pet 2:8; 3:1; cf. Kittel, "*Legō,*" 115). The lack of a qualifier may reflect a deliberate ambiguity about whether the word's proclaimer is God, Christ, or the Christian preacher (see the COMMENT on 4:13–14).

In this verse the seed is identified with the word, and 4:15 twice speaks of the word being sown; furthermore, in the references to "the word" in 4:16, 18, 19, and 20, it is clear that the seed is being allegorized. On the other hand, 4:15, 16, 18, and 20 speak of human beings as "those sown," implying that the seed is different kinds of people rather than the word. Fourth Ezra 9:31; 8:41 has a similar alternation between seed as God's law and seed as human beings (see Marcus, *Mystery,* 48). This kind of plasticity in interpretation is very common in OT, Jewish, and NT parables; cf. Drury, *Parables,* 18–19 and passim.

15. *the seeds beside the path.* Gk *hoi para tēn hodon,* lit. "those beside the path"; similarly in 4:16, 18, and 20.

they who, when. Gk *kai hotan akousōsin,* lit. "and when they hear." Mark's grammar is very rough here and in the other equations in 4:16, 18, and 20; the grammar has been cleaned up by Matthew and Luke in their parallels, and it has been necessary to smoothen it out a bit in the translation so as to make the English comprehensible.

Satan comes. Gk *erchetai ho Satanas.* Satan disguises himself as a bird in several Jewish texts; see *Apoc. Abr.* 13:3–8; *b. Sanh.* 107a and cf. *Jub.* 11:11, in which Mastema = Satan sends birds to eat seed sown in the earth.

17. *root in themselves.* Gk *rizan en heautois.* The "rootlessness" of the wicked is a commonplace in Jewish literature (e.g. Sir 23:25; 40:15; Wis 4:3), but it is striking that in our passage those who apostasize are said to have no root *in themselves*; it would be more usual for a Christian writer to say that apostates are not rooted in God or Christ (cf. Col 2:7; Eph 3:17). As Swete (75) points out, the Markan image probably has to do with the mixed metaphor by which the hearer of the word is both plant and soil (see the NOTE on "the word" in 4:14); his roots, therefore, are within himself. But the phrase may also indicate that Mark has a rudimentary theology of the self and that the command in 8:34 to deny oneself exists in dialectical tension with the idea that those who follow Jesus find their true selves (cf. Francis, *Jesus*).

temporary. Gk *proskairoi,* a word that literally means "lasting only for a time" (cf. BAGD 715). In the apocalyptic Markan context the word would be linked with the contrast between *ho kairos houtos,* the present age which is rapidly coming to an end, and *ho aiōn ho erchomenos,* the coming, eternal age of God's glory (cf. 10:30 and the NOTE on 1:15). Similarly, Paul in 2 Cor 4:18 contrasts *proskaira,* temporary, visible things belonging to the present age, with *aiōnia,* eternal, invisible things belonging to the age to come (cf. Pseudo-Clementine *Homilies* 2.15: "The present world is *proskairos,* the coming one is eternal").

fall away. Gk *skandalizontai.* It is hard to find a one-word equivalent for this resonant Greek verb, which will reappear in 6:3; 9:42–47, and 14:27–29. It is cognate with the noun *skandalon,* from which we get "scandal." The basic image is of being enmeshed in or falling into a trap (see Stählin, "Skandalon," 339–40), and the word group often has connotations of idolatry, apostasy, and/ or eschatological ruin in the OT prophets and the NT (see e.g. Wis 14:11; Zeph 1:3 [Sym.]; Matt 13:41; Rev 2:14). It can also, as in 6:3, suggest taking or causing offense—often with eschatological consequences (e.g. 9:42–47).

18. *sown among the thorns.* Gk *eis tas ankanthas speiromenoi.* According to *Ecclesiastes Rabbah* on 4.14, the Evil Inclination "entangles people as if among thorns" (Soncino trans.).

19. *the age.* Gk *tou aiōnos.* Implicit is the Jewish apocalyptic contrast between "this age" (*ho aiōn houtos*) and "the age to come" (*ho aiōn ho erchomenos;* cf. 10:30; 1 Cor 1:20, etc.).

COMMENT

Introduction. After defining the theme of the Parable of the Sower as "the mystery of the dominion of God" in 4:10–12, the Markan Jesus now gives the parable an interpretation that specifically allegorizes some of its major terms.

Mark is probably not responsible for this allegory; it seems, rather, to have been part of the tradition he received (see the introduction to 4:1–34). The only recognizably Markan feature is 4:13b ("How then will you know all the parables?"), since it expresses the characteristic Markan reproach of the disciples and implies that, in explaining the Parable of the Sower, Jesus unlocked "all the parables." This theme is consonant with the Markan comment in 4:34b that Jesus explained "all things" to his own disciples.

It is a matter of dispute whether the rest of the interpretation was an original part of the parable or whether it came in at a post-Jesus, pre-Markan stage. The dogmatism of older exegetes such as Jülicher (*Gleichnisreden*), who maintained that allegory was always a sign of secondary growth, has been exploded by Brown ("Parable"), Drury (*Parables*), and Stern (*Parables*), who point out that parables in the OT, Jewish apocalyptic literature, and rabbinic texts often include allegorical explanations. As noted by Davies and Allison (2.376), moreover, a division of humanity into four types of hearers may have been a Jewish commonplace (cf. *m. 'Abot* 5:10–15), so it is not impossible that Jesus allegorized his parable in this way. But against the originality of the allegorical interpretation is its absence from the *Gospel of Thomas*, as well as certain discontinuities between the explanation and the parable itself. The explanation, for example, is more pessimistic in tone; as Kuhn points out (*Sammlungen*, 114), the descriptions of failed seed in 4:15–19 are considerably expanded from the original parable, whereas the description of successful seed remains about the same size. Some of the explanation's vocabulary, moreover, is endemic to early Christianity; this includes the absolute use of "*the* word" (see the NOTE on 4:14) and expressions and concepts with which the word is linked: "receiving the word with joy," "persecution on account of the word," falling away on account of the word, and the word bearing fruit (see Acts 17:11; Col 1:6, 10; 1 Thess 1:6; 2:13; 2 Tim 1:8; 2:9; Jas 1:21; 1 Pet 2:8 and cf. Jeremias, *Parables*, 77–78). The weight of the evidence, then, points to the explanation being the work of the early church, at least in its present form.

The structure of this interpretation corresponds closely to that of the parable itself; each part is allegorized, section by section, almost as the *pěšārîm*, the biblical commentaries at Qumran, move verse by verse through OT passages (cf. Pesch, 1.242). The interpretation can be divided into three sections: preliminaries (4:13–14), the unproductive soils (4:15–19), and the good soil (4:20).

4:13–14: the rebuke of the disciples and the meaning of the seed. The passage begins with two preliminaries, the rebuke of the disciples and the interpretation of the seed. The rebuke of the disciples for not understanding the Parable of the Sower seems harsh; the parable, after all, is really obscure, and if twenty centuries of commentators have been baffled by it, how can the disciples be expected to grasp it immediately? The rebuke, however, should probably not be taken literally; like the imperative "Listen!" in 4:3, to which it is parallel, it has a pedagogical purpose, namely to call Jesus' audience, and by implication the Markan hearers, to attention (cf. the COMMENT on 4:10–12). Still, there is an undertone of warning here; even if the disciples are insiders to Jesus' circle (4:11a), they seem to be in jeopardy of falling into the same blindness that afflicts "those outside" (cf. 4:11b–12; 7:18; 8:14–21).

The rebuke to the disciples foreshadows the main theme of the allegorical explanation, namely the obstacles to perception of "the word." This theme is introduced by the allegorical identification of the seed in the parable as "the word." It is puzzling that the explanation goes on to interpret every other major element of the parable—the kinds of soil, the factors that inhibit the seed's growth, and the results of the sowing—with the conspicuous absence of the sower himself. Why is his identity not specified? As I have suggested elsewhere (Marcus, "Blanks"), this absence is probably an intentional "gap" in the narrative—a point that has been left obscure to engage the reader's attention and thought and to point to the central concern of the parable (on "gaps," see the COMMENT on 4:3–8). For in the apocalyptic Markan worldview, the identity of the sower of the word of God is not a simple matter, since proclamation is not an autonomous human action in which a person merely decides to open his mouth and form words about God; it is, rather, a complex act in which divine and human factors are inextricably and confusingly mixed together. On one level, that is to say, the Markan sower/proclaimer is God himself, as in the many OT passages that speak of the powerful divine word. On a second level the sower is Jesus, as in the Markan passages in which Jesus teaches, speaks, or proclaims the word (2:2; 4:33; 8:32; 9:10; 10:22, 24; 11:29; 13:31; 14:39). On a third level the sower is the preachers of the Markan community, whose proclamation of the good news (8:35; 10:29; 13:10; 14:9) will continue Jesus' own announcement of it (1:14–15). Jesus' words, then, are not just *his* words but God's, and they will become the words of the Markan community. The blending of these three aspects of the proclaimed word is made clear by 13:11: when the Markan Christians are called upon to bear witness to their faith, "it will not be you who are speaking, but the Holy Spirit"—the Spirit that is God's breath, but equally, according to 1:8, a baptismal gift of Jesus. Thus 4:14 does not just describe something that happened once upon a time, back in the bygone era of the historical Jesus, but something that continues to happen in the Markan present, as the Markan community carries on Jesus' proclamation of his word, even beyond his own death: "The sower *is sowing* the word" (see the NOTE on "is sowing" in 4:14).

4:14–19: the allegorization of the unproductive soils. But if the word is so mighty that it can transcend death, if it has the power of God and of Jesus behind it, why does it so often seem to fall on deaf ears? This is the problem taken up in the major portion of the explanation, the allegorization of the seed that falls on unproductive soil in 4:14–19. This allegorization reveals that, just as the proclamation of the word is a complex process in which human and superhuman factors are confusingly intertwined, so the reception of the word is a fusion of the human, the demonic, and the divine.

Each of the three unproductive soils is described in the same pattern:

"these are the seeds sown" + LOCATION +
"they who, when they hear" + RESULT

The very regularity of this pattern suggests that the failure of the word to come to fruition is the fulfillment of a divine plan, and this suggestion is reinforced by the implicit logic of the parable: soil is the way it is, presumably because God has made it that way; people are either able or unable to hear, depending on how God has fashioned them (cf. 4:33, "as they were *able* to hear"). Contrary to the way the Parable of the Sower is often interpreted, then, its message is not "Become good soil!" Good soil is good soil, and bad is bad; the ground cannot change its own nature. The image, indeed, seems to be deliberately chosen for its passivity.

Human beings, to be sure, do act; the descriptions of the second and fourth soils (4:16–17, 20) particularly emphasize the importance of the human action of receiving and holding fast to the word. But these more anthropologically framed descriptions alternate with the descriptions of the first and third soils (4:15, 18–19), which are frankly demonological. The Devil is explicitly mentioned in 4:15. Here there is no room for an act of the human will; Satan *immediately* comes and attacks the soil, removing the seed before it has a chance to germinate. Similarly, in 4:18–19 the "concerns of the age," the preoccupations that arise out of and wed a person to the dying eon, do not permit people a choice but rather *enter into* them like demons and usurp their ability to make a decision for God (see Kuhn, *Sammlungen*, 116–19, and Fusco, *Parola*, 329–31). As is often the case in apocalyptic writings, then, the boundary between the exercise of the human will and the influence of supernatural powers is blurred; as a character in one of William Faulkner's novels puts it, human beings are "all mixed up in the same luck and destiny and fate until cant none of us tell where it stops and we begin" (*Mansion*, 374).

These descriptions of seed going astray would be of great interest to the Markan community, since some of its own former members have probably apostasized (see the INTRODUCTION). The sketches of the second and third soils, the rocky ground and the thorny one, are probably especially resonant, as their very length suggests. Probably some within the Markan community have *not* been rooted enough in the faith to withstand the pressure when persecution has arisen on account of the word, have *not* been able to endure to the end, and so to be saved (13:13); perhaps others have been lured away by wealth and other worldly concerns. They have turned out to be *proskairos*, "temporary," when the going got rough (4:17). It is noteworthy that in 4 Macc 15:2, 8, 23, as in our passage, this term has a profound martyrological nuance: a mother sacrifices the temporary, this-worldly (*proskairos*) safety of herself and her seven sons, letting them and herself be martyred in order to save them all for eternal life with God. In contrast, those described in our passage give up the spiritual fruitfulness associated with the new age for a temporary, this-worldly escape from persecution.

Faced with such defections, our passage implicitly exhorts the Markan audience to hold on, to continue listening to God's word, not to fall away, and so to show that they are indeed good soil. It also implicitly comforts them: if many are rejecting their proclamation, this rejection does not mean, as they might be tempted to think, that the word they have listened to and proclaimed is not God's word. Indeed, it is precisely *because* it is God's word that the reaction is sometimes so brutal and swift, that Satan swoops down like a bird of prey to snatch it out of people's hearts (cf. Gen 15:11 and *Apoc. Abr.* 13:3–8). For the word is not only a message *about* the new age but also God's instrument for liberating humanity and thus *bringing in* the new age (cf. Isa 61:1–4)—and that is why the old-age powers that hold humanity captive are so concerned to strangle it (cf. 4:19).

4:20: the allegorization of the good soil. Paradoxically, then, even the fierce resistance provoked by the Markan community's proclamation of the Christian message is good news, because it reveals that the word is powerful and having an effect, that it is shaking up the demonic forces that formerly held sway over the earth. But it is even better news for the Markan community to be told that despite all such opposition the word is actually finding an entrance into human hearts and that some hearers are prepared and able to listen to it, to receive it, to permit it to fructify their lives—and to let everything else go. In this regard, it is significant that, in the interpretation of the last, productive soil, the pattern of description changes from that which prevailed in the previous three soils. Now *akouein* ("to hear") is no longer a subordinate aorist subjunctive or a subordinate aorist participle, as it had been in the descriptions of the previous types of hearers, but has become a present indicative that is the main verb of the clause. This grammatical change implies that the people who are being described here really *hear* the word, listen to it continually, allow themselves to be broken apart and put together again by the word as a growing plant shatters and transforms the earth in which it is sown; it no longer occupies a secondary place in their lives but has moved to the very center of their existence.

The allegorical interpretation of the Parable of the Sower, then, extends the message of the parable itself. That message, as we have seen, is that the dominion of God has arrived on the scene in Jesus' ministry, despite all appearances to the contrary; the new age has broken in, but in a mysterious way that does not eradicate every trace of the old age. The allegorical interpretation expresses an epistemological corollary of the hiddenness of this advent: some can discern God's advent in Jesus' life, death, and resurrection, but many cannot. Yet even this blindness of the many "outsiders" must reflect God's will (cf. 4:11b–12).

And it is not God's will that his dominion should be hidden forever. Indeed, as the second half of the parable chapter will make clear, Mark believes that the opposite is true: darkness will soon give way to light, and indeed the darkness even *serves* the light. That paradoxical point is a principal theme of the next passage.

THE PARABLES OF THE LAMP AND
THE MEASURE (4:21–25)

4   ^{21}And he said to them, "Does the lamp come in order that it may be put
under the bushel or under the bed? Doesn't it come in order that it may be
put on the lampstand? ^{22}For there is nothing hid, except in order that it may
be made manifest; nor has anything become hidden, but in order that it
might come to manifestation. ^{23}If anyone has ears to hear, let him hear!"
^{24}And he said to them, "Pay attention to what you hear! With what measure
you measure, it will be measured to you—and more will be added to you.
^{25}For, the one who has—more will be given to him; and the one who does not
have—even what he has will be taken away from him.

NOTES

4   21. *Does the lamp come . . . the lampstand.* Gk *erchetai ho lychnos . . . tēn
lychnian.* The definite articles are a bit awkward and may translate original
Semitisms (see Black, 68–70), but they also immediately alert the Greek
reader to the symbolic character of the speech here, as does the strange image
of the lamp *coming.* Mark does not explicitly designate the figures of speech
in 4:21–22 and 4:24b–25 as parables, but that is probably what he considers
them to be, since like his other parables they are figurative comparisons having to do with God's action in history (see the NOTE on "in parables" in 4:2).
As Pesch (1.248) points out, moreover, the call to attention in 4:23, which refers to 4:21–22, has been applied to the Parable of the Sower in 4:9; cf. Jeremias, *Parables*, 91.
   Does . . . Doesn't? Gk *mēti . . . ouch. Mēti* indicates that the first question
expects a negative answer and *ouch* that the second question expects a positive answer.
   22. *has . . . become.* Gk *egeneto.* In the pre-Markan version of 4:22 the two
parts of the saying were probably synonymous; cf. the Q version, "Nothing is
covered that will not be revealed, and hid that will not be known." Most exegetes think that the two parts of Mark's version are also synonymous; *egeneto,*
then, would have to be a timeless aorist, rather than referring to the past, as
aorist indicatives normally do. But if Mark had intended *egeneto* to have a
present meaning, he probably would have left it out altogether, as Q did. It is
better, therefore, to conclude that *egeneto* refers to the past. Verse 4:22, then,
may be paraphrased: "Just as, in the past (during Jesus' lifetime?), nothing was
hidden except in order to become manifest, so it is in the present: all the hiddenness of the current age will ultimately serve the purpose of revelation."
   24. *more will be added.* Gk *prostethēsetai,* lit. "it will be added."
   25. *what he has.* Gk *ho echei.* Luke 8:18 changes this to "what he *seems* to
have," thus dealing with the problem of how a person can both have and not
have. Cf. Chrysostom (cited in Aquinas *Catena Aurea* 2.81), who says that he

"has a lie." In terms of Markan dualism we may think of one who has "the things of human beings" but not "the things of God" (8:33).

COMMENT

Introduction. After interpreting the Parable of the Sower allegorically (4:13–20), the Markan Jesus now imparts four more parables: the Lamp, the Hidden and the Manifest, the Measure, and Having and Not Having (see the NOTE on "Does the lamp come . . . the lampstand" in 4:21 on why these images deserve to be called parables). These parables, with their emphasis on revelation and the necessity of paying attention to it, extend the allegory's theme of the word and its hearers.

Mark is probably responsible for combining four originally independent sayings here and for placing them in their present context; the sayings are scattered in Q, and Mark could have inserted them here to balance his inserted comments on the purpose of revelation in 4:11–12. He is probably also responsible for various other touches: the four appearances in 4:21–22 of the word *hina,* "in order that," which also appears significantly in 4:11–12; the strange terminology of the lamp "coming" in 4:21; the verb "has become" (*egeneto*) in 4:22; the awkward clause, "Pay attention to (*blepete,* lit. "see") what you hear!" in 4:24a; and the clause "and more will be added to you" in 4:24. All of these are differences from the Q versions (see figures 7–9), and all of them, as we shall see, fit in with Markan theology (cf. Marcus, *Mystery,* 129–40).

The resultant Markan composition divides naturally at 4:24. Each half of the complex consists of a pair of parables (4:21–22 and 4:24b–25) which is introduced by the formula "and he said to them." In each case the second parable explains the first and is in the form of a *gar* ("for") clause. The two pairs are welded together by a central pair of commands to hear (4:23, 24a). The structure of the two sections, then, is fairly symmetrical:

4:21a	"And he said to them"			A
4:21b		Parable of Lamp		B
4:22			Explanatory parable (*gar*)	C
4:23			Exhortation to hear	D
4:24a	"And he said to them"			A′
4:24b			Exhortation to hear	D′
4:24c		Parable of Measure		B′
4:25			Explanatory parable (*gar*)	C′

The similarity in structure between the two parts reinforces the connection between their themes: the coming transition from hiddenness to revelation (4:21–23) and the anthropological corollary of that transition, the necessity of attentive listening (4:24–25).

Figure 7: The Parable of the Lamp and the Lampstand

Mark 4:21	Luke 8:16	Luke 11:33 (Q)	Matt 5:15 (Q)	Thomas 33
Does the lamp come in order that it may be put under the bushel	For no one having lit a lamp covers it with a vessel	No one having lit a lamp	Neither do they burn a lamp and put it under the bushel	For no one lights a lamp and puts it under the bushel
		puts it in a hidden place		nor does he put it in a hidden place
or under the bed? Doesn't it come in order that it may be put on the lampstand?	or puts it under a bed but on a lampstand	but he puts it on the lampstand	but on the lampstand	but he puts it on the lampstand
	in order that those going in	in order that those going in	and it gives light to all in the house	in order that everyone going in and coming out
	may see the light	may see the brightness		may see its light

Figure 8: The Saying about Hiddenness and Manifestation

Mark 4:22	Luke 8:17	Luke 12:2 (Q)	Matt 10:26 (Q)	Thomas 5	Thomas 6
For there is not anything hid except in order that it may be made manifest	For there is not anything hid that will not become manifest	And nothing is covered that will not be revealed	For nothing is covered that will not be revealed	And what is hid from you will be revealed to you	For there is nothing hid that will not be made manifest
nor has anything become hidden	nor hidden	and hid	and hid		and there is nothing covered
but in order that it might come to manifestation	that will not be known and come to manifestation	that will not be known	that will not be known		that will remain without being revealed

Figure 9: The Parable of the Measure

Matthew 7:2 (Q)	Luke 6:38 (Q)	Mark 4:24
For with what measure you measure it will be measured to you	For with what measure you measure it will be measured again to you	With what measure you measure it will be measured to you and more will be added to you

4:21–23: the movement from hiddenness to revelation. The Parable of the
Sower and its interpretation have portrayed the dominion of God as a hidden
reality; the good soil, i.e. attentive hearers of God's word, bears witness to the
advent of the new age, but the unproductive soil, i.e. hearers who do *not* accept the word, provides evidence of the endurance of the old age. The beginning of the present passage, however, asserts forcefully that this mysterious
hiddenness of God's dominion will not go on forever; if covert action is God's
modus operandi in the present, he will soon manifest his power openly. There
is also a history-of-religions connection between the interpretation of the Parable of the Sower, with its focus on the fate of "the word," and the present passage, with its imagery of the lamp; God's word (*logos*), according to Ps
119[LXX 118]:105, is "a lamp (*lychnos*) to my feet, and a light to my path"
(RSV), and in ancient Jewish iconography the lampstand, the *menorah*, is often associated with the shrine of God's word, the Torah (see Goodenough,
Jewish Symbols, 4.71–98). The link between word and lamp is further assisted
by the closeness in sound between *logos* and *lychnos*. The transition to our
passage from the interpretation of the Parable of the Sower, then, is a natural
one; the "coming" of the lamp is equivalent to the falling of the seed of the
word on the various kinds of "soils."

But if the lamp is a symbol for God's word, what the Markan Jesus says at
the beginning of our passage is a significant qualification of the statement
about parable purpose in 4:11–12: even if in the short term God intends
"those outside" to misunderstand his parabolic word, the lamp/word does not
come to be hidden forever, but to be put on a lampstand, i.e. to be publicly
manifested (4:21). The link between the two passages is strengthened by the
fact that the *hina* ("in order that") of 4:12 is now repeated in 4:21–22 four
times. Mark himself is probably responsible for these four striking *hinas*.

But why did the earlier passage speak of a deliberate veiling of the truth if
the truth is meant to come out? Jesus responds in 4:22a that even obscurity
serves the purpose of disclosure: "For there is nothing hid, except in order
that it may be made manifest" (4:22a). But this comforting assertion immediately raises another question: what sense does it make to *hide* something if
one intends to make it known? The Q and *Gospel of Thomas* versions of this
saying (see figure 6) are more logical than the Markan form; according to
them, there is nothing hidden *that will not* be known. This is a commonsense
observation frequently found in the wisdom tradition: a secret cannot be kept
forever; everything hidden will eventually be revealed; what is said in secret
places will be shouted from the rooftops (see Eccl 10:20; Luke 12:2–3; *m.
'Abot* 2:4). The Markan idea of hiding *in order to* reveal, however, is paradoxical—almost as paradoxical as the idea of speaking to crowds *in order that* they
might not understand (4:11–12).

In the overall Markan context these two paradoxical ideas are probably related to each other and to the messianic secret motif (see the APPENDIX
"The Messianic Secret Motif"). God's word, uttered by Jesus, is misunderstood by his opponents—misunderstood in the existential sense of being re-

jected, not allowed to penetrate, or emptied of its force (e.g. 7:8–9, 13; 8:38; 11:29–33; 12:13). This rejection of the word leads inexorably to Jesus' death, a result that, from the divine perspective, is necessary (8:31; 9:31; 10:33–34); he is killed by those who cannot grasp his identity and who look and look but never see, hear and hear but never understand (see the echoes of 4:12 in the uses of the verbs "to see" and "to hear" in the trial and death scenes in 14:64; 15:32, 35, 36). But in this divinely willed death, which is caused by the spiritual blindness and deafness of human beings, a new age of revelation begins; after Good Friday and Easter Sunday Jesus' identity as Messiah and Son of God, which was hidden from all during his earthly lifetime, becomes the open proclamation of the Markan community (see the COMMENT on 9:9–13). The obscurity of the word thus ultimately serves the purpose of its revelation by leading to Jesus' revelatory death; what was hidden was hidden only *in order that* it might come into the light.

If this interpretation is correct, then 4:21–22 pictures the Markan present as an epoch of revelation: the lamp of God's word has come into the room and is casting its light into every dark crevice (cf. 1 John 2:8). At the same time, however, hiddenness continues to be a factor in the present (see the NOTE on "has . . . become" in 4:22); the dominion of God over the world through Jesus is still a hidden dominion, and there are still many who oppose the word of the gospel. But this blind opposition, too, must ultimately serve the purpose of revelation; even the persecution that the Markan community faces for the sake of the good news (8:35; 10:29) will become an occasion for that news to spread (see 13:9–13). Because of the continuing hiddenness of God's dominion, however, Mark's hearers must be called to attention, and so it is logical that the first section of our passage ends with an exhortation to hear (4:23). Here, as in 4:3, 9, which this verse repeats, the verb *akouein* ("to listen, hear") is a present imperative, suggesting the necessity of a continuous turning to the divine word.

4:24–25: the necessity of listening. This wake-up call is then repeated and reinforced by the exhortation that introduces the second half of the complex, "Pay attention to [lit. "see"] what you hear!" (4:24a). As in 4:3 and 4:12, the sense of hearing is doubled by the sense of sight, suggesting that what is called for is an involvement of the whole person with all his faculties. Another significant aspect of the wording here is the call to pay attention, not to *how* one hears, as in Luke 8:18, but to *what* one listens to. For in a world that is still, in some sense, Satan's house and dominion (cf. 3:23–26), not all the voices that may be heard *ought* to be heard (cf. 5:36, where Jesus ignores what is said about Jairus' daughter being dead). There is abroad in the world not only the word of God but also a deceitful, Satanic word claiming to be God's word and capable of leading astray even the elect (cf. 13:5–6, 22–23). To listen to this Satanic word is, ultimately, to lose one's "root in oneself" (4:17), indeed, in a real sense, to die (cf. 4:15–19). On the other hand, to listen to God's word about his coming world, which is already the secret reality of *this* world, is, ultimately, to flourish—even though one may lose one's life in the process (cf. 4:20; 8:35).

This point is reinforced by the parable about the measure in 4:24b and the parable about having and not having in 4:25. Each of these parables employs divine passives ("will be measured" and "will be added" in 4:24b and "will be given" and "will be taken away" in 4:25), and this prominence of divine passives rhetorically reinforces the theme of the parable chapter, the hidden action of God in the world. As was the case in 4:22, both of these parables are common-places that are given a characteristic Markan twist having to do with perception.

The first parable, the saying about measuring, uses an image found fre-quently in ancient literature to express the thought—especially beloved by Christian preachers on Stewardship Sunday—that one will receive back what one gives out to others (see the Q parallel, Matt 7:2//Luke 6:37-38; cf. Prov 11:24; Cicero *Orations* 2.65 [261]; 2 Cor 9:6-12). Mark, though, following in the footsteps of some Qumran texts (e.g. 1QS 8:4; 1QH 14:18-19), reapplies the metaphor of the measure to epistemology: people will receive insight accord-ing to the measure of their attentiveness. There is something deliberately par-adoxical about the application of the measure image to perception, since measuring is an action that one does for the benefit of *others*, but Mark refers it to listening, which is an action that one does for *oneself*. In his view, appar-ently, one has an obligation not only to others but also to oneself, and that ob-ligation is discharged by a turning of the self to God's word.

The divine response to this turning is not a matter of strict tit-for-tat, since the Markan Jesus adds—in what may be a Markan touch—that attentive lis-teners will receive even *more* than they are actually entitled to: "and more will be added to you." This basic idea is similar to one that is often expressed or im-plicit in rabbinic literature (e.g. *Pesiq. Rab Kah.* 5:6; *Cant. Rab.* 5.2.2; *Pesiq. R.* 44:9): if a person takes a tiny step toward God, God will more than match his movement (see Schechter, *Aspects*, 327). One of Emily Dickinson's poems (no. 323) superbly expresses this idea of divine overcompensation:

> As if I asked a common Alms,
> And in my wondering hand
> A Stranger pressed a Kingdom
> And I, bewildered, stand—

Nor, in the Markan passage, is the divine blessing of additional understand-ing to be understood exactly as a *reward* for human attentiveness. To ward off such a misapprehension, Mark immediately invokes another proverbial idea (see e.g. Terence *Phormio* 1.1.7-8; Juvenal *Satires* 3.208-9; cf. Lindeskog, "Logia-Studien," 149), the mordant observation that the rich get richer and the poor get poorer, which has been expressed unforgettably in our century by Billie Holiday's song "God Bless the Child":

> Them that's got shall get,
> Them that's not shall lose:
> So the Bible says,
> And it still is news.

In the Markan context, however, as sometimes happens in rabbinic literature, this acerbic social comment becomes a further meditation on the strangeness of God's way of dealing with the human capacity or incapacity to hear his word. Lindeskog ("Logia-Studien," 148–53) compares passages in rabbinic literature that, like our text, use the idea of the rich getting richer as a metaphor for the way in which God "gives wisdom to the wise" (Dan 2:21). In *Eccl. Rab.* 1.7, for example, the Danielic verse is explained by the example of a rich man who would rather lend money to a rich man than to a poor man. In Mark's view, then, those graced with insight into the mystery of the dominion of God will be given more comprehension; those not given insight will have taken away from them even the knowledge that they do have (cf. Rom 1:18–32). We are back to the harsh dualism of 4:10–12, which resembles 4:25 even structurally:

Mark 4:11–12	*Mark 4:22*
to you	the one who has
has been given the mystery of the dominion of God	it will be given to him
but those outside	and the one who does not have
look without seeing, hear without understanding, lest they be forgiven	even what he has will be taken away from him

In both cases we move from a statement about the "in" group, which is given insight by God, to a statement about the "out" group, whom God desires to blind and condemn.

This determinism is apocalyptic, as can be seen by comparing it with the larger context of the scriptural passage to which *Midraš Qohelet* refers, Dan 2:20–22:

> . . . to [God] belong wisdom and might. He changes times and seasons; he puts down kings and sets up kings; he gives wisdom to the wise and knowledge to those who have understanding; he reveals deep and mysterious things; he knows what is in the darkness, and the light dwells with him. (RSV, alt.)

Here, as in Mark 4:21–25, we find in an eschatological context (cf. 2:44–45) the themes of making the wise wiser, the revelation of secrets, and God's power to establish and undermine whom he will, as well as light imagery. These are not just formal parallels, but reflect the apocalyptic stance of Mark, one that he shares with Paul: at the moment of crisis when the power of God's new eon breaks into the world, it brings eschatological insight to those chosen to be its recipients, but an eschatological judgment of blindness on those predestined to be in the enemy ranks (cf. 1 Cor 1:18–19; on the relation of Mark to Paul, see the discussion of Mark's place in Christian life and thought in the INTRODUCTION).

Thus, after raising the eschatological curtain momentarily in 4:21–22 to allow a glimpse of the end, a universe filled with light, Mark abruptly lowers it again in 4:25. The vision of ultimate revelation fades, and we are back to the picture that has dominated the parable chapter from its inception to 4:20: a portrayal of a world on the brink, divided by God's baffling will into colliding realms of light and darkness, of divine and demonic sovereignty. This withdrawal from the vision of ultimacy disclosed momentarily in 4:21–22 prepares the way for more discussion in 4:26–32 of hiddenness and its relation to revelation.

TWO MORE SEED PARABLES (4:26–34)

4   ²⁶And he said, "The dominion of God is like this: as if a man should throw seed on the earth, ²⁷and should sleep and rise night and day, and the seed should sprout and grow up—how, even he does not know. ²⁸All by itself the earth yields fruit—first a shoot, then an ear, then full grain in the ear. ²⁹But when the condition of the fruit allows it, immediately he sends forth the sickle, for the harvest has come."

³⁰And he said, "How shall we form a likeness for the dominion of God, or in what parable shall we put it? ³¹It is as a mustard grain, which, when it is sown on the earth, is smaller than all the other seeds on earth, ³²but when it is sown, it grows up and becomes bigger than all other shrubs and puts out large branches, so that the birds of heaven can lodge under its shadow."

³³And with many such parables he used to speak the word to them, as they were able to hear. ³⁴Indeed, without a parable he did not speak to them; but privately, to his own disciples, he explained everything.

NOTES

4   26. *as if.* Gk *hōs,* lit. "as." This corresponds to Heb/Aram *lĕ,* which is often used to introduce parables; see the NOTE on "it is" in 4:31.

27. *sleep and rise night and day.* Gk *katheudē̢ kai egeirētai nykta kai hēmeran.* The order of words here follows the Jewish mode of reckoning, where a "day" begins at sunset, as in the recurrent formula in Genesis 1, "And there was evening and there was morning, one day (a second day, etc.)."

sprout. Gk *blastą̄.* In a Jewish context this word might have a messianic nuance. In Zech 3:8; 6:12 the Messiah is called "the sprout" (*ṣemaḥ*) of the Davidic line (cf. Jer 23:5–6; 33:14–16), and this terminology also appears in the Qumran literature (e.g. 4QpGenaᵃ 5) and the fifteenth benediction of the Amidah (see Kimelman, "Messiah," 315–16). Although the LXX does not render *ṣemaḥ* in the biblical passages with a cognate of *blastan,* elsewhere it uses *blastan* to translate the cognate verb *ṣmḥ* (Judg 16:22; 2 Kgdms 23:5; Eccl 2:6; Isa 55:10).

29. *But when the condition of the fruit allows it.* Gk *hotan de paradoi ho karpos,* lit. "but when the fruit allows." This subordinate clause invokes the

apocalyptic concept of the eschatological measure: certain things must happen before the end can come, and the sum of those things (their "measure") is now almost full (see the COMMENT on 4:26–29; would the Markan audience have already been reminded of the notion of the measure by the use of the cognate verb in 4:24?). *Paradoi* is from *paradidonai*, "to hand over" or "to permit." This verb is used elsewhere in the Gospel for the handing over of John the Baptist (1:14), Jesus (14:10–11, 18, 21, 41–42, 44), and Markan Christians (13:9, 11–12) to judicial inquiry and death; the implied agent is both God and the human beings who accomplish his will (see the NOTE on "handed over" in 1:14 and Marcus, *Way*, 173 n. 71 and 188). Verse 4:29 may imply that these "handings over" are filling up the eschatological measure; see the COMMENT.

he sends forth the sickle, for the harvest has come. Gk *apostellei to drepanon, hoti parestēken ho therismos.* This seems to echo Joel 4:13 LXX (ET 3:13): *exaposteilate drepana, hoti parestēken trygētos* ("send forth sickles, for the harvest has come"). The context speaks of God's destruction of the surrounding nations who gather together against Israel, so that foreigners will never again pass through Jerusalem (Joel 3:11–21). The Markan context, on the other hand, seems to point toward the opposite attitude, namely solicitude for Gentiles (see the NOTE on "lodge under its shadow" in 4:32). Is this a deliberate intertextual reversal of the text from Joel?

30. *How shall we form a likeness for the dominion of God.* Gk *pōs homoiōsōmen tēn basilian tou theou.* This is very similar to a common introduction to rabbinic parables, *lěmah hādābār dômeh* = "To what is the matter like?" (see Jeremias, *Parables*, 100–1). The first person plural verbs ("How shall *we* form a likeness . . . in what parable shall *we* put it?") may simply be "literary plurals" that associate Mark's readers with the attempt to form an image of God's dominion (see BDF, §280), but they could also be intended to link Jesus' parabolic discourse with the disciples, who will continue Jesus' teaching (cf. 6:30 and the COMMENT on 4:13–14).

31. *It is as.* Gk *hōs*, lit. "as," the beginning of many rabbinic parables (see the NOTE on "as if" in 4:26). The comparison is usually not just to the object that is immediately mentioned (here the mustard grain) but to the whole situation described in the parable (see Jeremias, *Parables*, 100). In the present case, however, there is also a sense in which for Mark the dominion of God is like a mustard seed—which, in the larger context of Mark 4, is a symbol for the word (see 4:14). For the dominion of God is like the word: paltry in appearance, but hiding a tremendous divine potency behind its apparent insignificance.

is smaller than all the other seeds. Gk *mikroteron on pantōn tōn spermatōn*, lit. "being smaller than all the seeds." The grammar is awkward, not only because the participle *on* should be a finite verb (to which it has been changed in our translation) but also because its gender, which should really be masculine (corresponding to *kokkō* = "grain"), has been attracted into the neuter of the following *spermatōn* = "seeds." This grammatical awkwardness perhaps reinforces the parable's point: the mustard is so insignificant that it cannot even retain its gender!

The parable's statement is not horticulturally exact; the orchid seed, not the mustard, is the smallest (Trever, "Mustard"), and perhaps this is why the other Gospels do not reproduce this Markan clause. The mustard seed is chosen because of its commonness and the contrast with the largeness of the grown plant.

32. *bigger than all other shrubs.* Gk *meizon pantōn tōn lachanōn*, lit. "bigger than all the shrubs." Funk ("Looking-Glass") and Scott (*Jesus*, 71–73) argue that the point of the parable is not the mustard plant's extraordinary size but rather its ordinariness. Mark deliberately alters his source, Ezek 17:23, so that the reference is no longer to a great *tree* but only to a rather large *bush.* (This point, however, is lost in Q, which changes the bush back into a tree, following the OT model but contradicting horticultural reality.) The dominion of God, then, is not like a towering cedar but like a humble mustard plant. Scott concludes that the parable makes fun of the exaggerated expectations of the apocalyptic tradition and "carries with it the threat that the Kingdom may be so ordinary that it will be missed." This interpretation, however, does violence to the actual rhetoric of the parable, in which the overwhelming contrast (reinforced by the Markan redaction emphasizing the smallness of the seed) is between the tiny seed and the huge plant. True, the mustard plant may not be big in comparison with a cedar tree, but that is not the plant with which it is being compared; *Mark's* point is that the mustard plant, with its large branches, is "bigger *than all other shrubs*," and immensely larger than the tiny seed from which it starts. The mustard plant was chosen as the central image for the parable not because it was not a cedar but because it was so well adapted to the contrast between small beginnings and large outcomes (cf. Gundry, 233–34).

the birds of heaven. Gk *ta peteina tou ouranou.* In Ezek 31:6 LXX this phrase is used as a symbol for "all the multitudes of the nations," and in Theodotion's later Greek translation of Dan 4:18, a similar phrase is used as part of an image for Nebuchadnezzar's dominion "to the ends of the earth" (see the discussion of these passages in the COMMENT on 4:30–32). These intertextual linkages suggest that the birds in our parable may symbolize Gentiles, an idea that is made plausible by the explicit identification of the two in later Jewish texts (*1 Enoch* 90:30; *Midr. Ps.* 104:10).

lodge under its shadow. Gk *hypo tēn skian autou . . . kataskēnoun.* The verb for "to lodge" here, *kataskēnoun* (lit. "to pitch one's tent"), is also used in Zech 2:11 LXX and some manuscripts of *Joseph and Aseneth* 15:6 to speak of the eschatological gathering of Gentiles to the God of Israel. While Jeremias (*Parables*, 147) goes beyond the evidence when he says (on the basis of the *Joseph and Aseneth* passage alone!) that *kataskēnoun* is "an eschatological technical term for the incorporation of Gentiles into the people of God," it is true that the later rabbis spoke of Gentile converts to Judaism as people who had come to dwell "under the wings of the Shechinah" (see Moore, 1.330). This image goes back to Ps 91:1–4, which may be in the background, since that psalm, like our parable, speaks of dwelling beneath God's shadow as a symbol of divine protection.

33. *as they were able to hear.* Gk *kathōs ēdynanto akouein*. In the pre-Markan parable collection the audience here was limited to the disciples (see the introduction to 4:1–34), and "as they were able to hear" meant "according to their God-given ability to hear." The Markan redaction, however, has drawn the crowd of "outsiders" mentioned in 4:11–12 into the audience, and for *them* the meaning of the phrase must be "according to their *inability* to hear with true understanding."

COMMENT

Introduction. Mark ends his parable chapter with two more seed parables: the Seed Growing by Itself (4:26–29) and the Mustard Seed (4:30–32). These parables are followed by a short concluding statement about Jesus' general practice of teaching the crowd in parables and explaining the parables privately to his disciples (4:33–34).

The two seed parables were probably part of a pre-Markan parable collection, which concluded with something like 4:33–34a; v 4:34b, therefore, is probably Mark's own editorial contribution (see the introduction to 4:1–34). Mark may have made a few minor changes in the parables as well, especially in the Parable of the Mustard Seed (4:30–32; see figure 10 for a comparison of the versions in Mark, Q, and *Thomas*). For example, the introductory formula, with its repetition and its first person plural verbs, reflects Mark's love for duplicate expressions (see Neirynck, *Duality*) and his desire to associate the disciples with Jesus (see the COMMENT on 4:13–14); he may be entirely responsible for the second half of the verse, which is not present in Q or in *Thomas* and which drives home the Markan point that Jesus' teaching was *in parables*. Moreover, 4:31–32a is awkward because of the repetition of "when it is sown" (absent in Q and *Thomas*) and the difficult grammar of the clause about the smallness of the seed (also probably absent in Q). It is likely that Mark himself has introduced this awkward clause along with the second instance of "when it is sown"; as Crossan notes ("Seed Parables," 256–57), he often repeats a clause after making a redactional insertion (cf. 2:5, 10; 3:7–8, 14–16). Mark may also be responsible for the words "all" and "can" (*dynasthai*) in 4:32, both of which are frequently redactional words and are not present in Q. There is, however, no direct literary relationship between Mark and Q, since other differences between the two versions do not seem to be redactional (see Tuckett, "Mark and Q," 172–74).

The structure of the two parables is similar. Each begins by comparing the dominion of God to a seed planted in the ground and ends by describing the final, full-grown state of the seed, which corresponds to the full, public manifestation of that dominion. But within this overall similarity, the two parables have differing emphases: the Parable of the Seed Growing by Itself focuses more on the interim stage of growth, whereas the Parable of the Mustard Seed concentrates on the difference between the initial stage of sowing and the final stage of fruit-bearing. The Parable of the Seed Growing by Itself, moreover, has much to say about the activity (and inactivity) of the sower, who is not mentioned in the Parable of the Mustard Seed.

4:26–29: *The Parable of the Seed Growing by Itself.* The previous passage has emphasized both the inevitability of the public manifestation of the dominion of God (4:21–22) and the present hiddenness of this dominion: some can hear, and "have" its secret, while others cannot, and do not "have" (4:24–45). The dominion of God is thus mysteriously present, but hidden—a point that develops the main theme of the previous passage, the interpretation of the Parable of the Sower (4:13–20).

The present parable continues this theme by emphasizing that the manner of the growth of God's dominion eludes comprehension and is beyond human power to control. All that the farmer does is cast the seed into the ground and wait; the seed germinates and develops by itself, even while he is sleeping, and he has no idea how it grows (4:27). The parable seems purposely to ignore all the human activities that are necessary for successful agriculture, such as tilling the ground and weeding the field, in order to make this point. The parable thus joins a theological battle that has mobilized Jewish thinkers from Jesus' time until the present: is the coming of final redemption dependent on God's will alone, or is it somehow contingent on human action (see Scholem, "Messianic Idea," and Ravitzky, *Messianism*, 19–22)? Our parable enters this debate strongly on the side of divine determinism, which should come as no surprise after 4:11–12 and 4:13–20; the emphasis on human ignorance and lack of control is similar to that in the famous Talmudic saying "Three things come unawares: the Messiah, a found object, and a scorpion" (b. *Sanh.* 97a; Scholem trans.). In the Markan context this emphasis on lack of human control may be particularly directed against Jewish revolutionaries who are trying to "force the end" by their military efforts against Rome (cf. Dupont, "Semence," 375 n. 28).

Although the farmer is not ultimately responsible for the seed's growth, he does do one thing, and that is to cast the seed into the ground (4:26b). This action would probably have important resonances for the Markan community as well. For a few verses previously Mark has identified the seed as "the word," and with this identification in mind the Markan community would probably hear the parable as an encouragement to those concerned about the incomplete success of the proclamation of the good news about Jesus. To such Christians the parable says: what God does with his word is *his* business; it is only for the preacher to cast the seed into the waiting ground, not to dictate in what way or at what pace it will bear fruit. Ultimate success is assured, but the precise modalities of its realization are known only to God.

For the real causative agent of the word's fruition is not the farmer who plants the seed but the ground, which "by itself" (*automatē*) brings the plant

Figure 10: The Parable of the Mustard Seed

Mark 4:30–32	Luke 13:18–19 (Q)	Matthew 13:31–32 (Q)	Thomas 20
How shall we form a likeness for the dominion of God or in what parable shall we put it?	What is the dominion of God like and to what shall I liken it?	The dominion of heaven	
It is as a mustard grain which, when it is sown on the earth,	It is as a mustard grain which taking, a man threw into his garden	is as a mustard grain which taking, a man sowed in his field	It is as a mustard seed
being smaller than all the seeds on the earth and when it is sown		which is smaller than all the seeds	smaller than all seeds but when it falls on tilled earth
it grows up and becomes bigger than all the shrubs	and it grew and became a tree	but when it grows it is bigger than the shrubs and becomes a tree	
and puts out large branches so that the birds of heaven can lodge under its shadow	and the birds of heaven lodged in its branches	so that the birds of heaven come and lodge in its branches	it produces a large branch and becomes a shelter for the birds of heaven

forth and causes it to develop until it is ready for harvesting. The Greek term *automatē*, from which we get "automatic," is frequently used in the OT and later Jewish texts to refer to that which is worked by God alone; in Lev 25:5, 11, for example, it designates crops that grow up in the sabbatical year and thus display God's sovereign care for his people. *Automatē*, moreover, often has a nuance of the miraculous; in 4 Kgdms 19:29, for example, it is part of a divine sign of deliverance from the Assyrian foe, and in several passages in Philo's *On the Creation* (40–43, 80–81, and 167) it is used for the paradisiacal conditions of Eden (see Stuhlmann, "Beobachtungen," 154–56, and Klauck, *Allegorie*, 221–22). It is thus appropriate that Mark uses it to describe the divinely energized, miraculous growth that is creating the new Eden: the spread of the good news about Jesus, which is calling into existence a world in which God is truly king.

This "automatic" growth of the dominion of God unfolds in discrete stages: "first a shoot, then an ear, then full grain in the ear" (4:28b). This description is similar to what is described in several Jewish apocalyptic texts (see Dahl, "Parables," 147–48, 164–65, and Marcus, *Mystery*, 185–89):

(1) Time is divided into "times" (see e.g. CD 16:2–4; 4 Ezra 3:14; 4:36–37; 11:44; 2 *Apoc. Bar.* 48:2–3; 54:1).
(2) These times are directed by God, so that they occur in an orderly progression (4 Ezra 4:36–37; 2 *Apoc. Bar.* 48:2; 1QpHab 7:12–13).
(3) Because of this orderliness, the progression of the times can be compared to natural phenomena such as the growth of seed (2 *Apoc. Bar.* 22:5–6; 4 Ezra 5:46–49; 1 *Enoch* 5:1–2; 1QH 12:4–18).
(4) Each "time" has its own peculiar character, including its own mixture of hiddenness and revelation (1QS 8:3–4; 9:20; 1 *Enoch* 91:11; 93:10).
(5) When the eschatological measure is filled, the end will come swiftly (4 Ezra 4:36–37, 4:40–43; 2 *Apoc. Bar.* 22:5–6; 1 *Clem* 23:4–5; cf. Stuhlmann, *Mass*).

The similarities of these apocalyptic conceptions to Mark 4:26–29 are obvious. In the latter, too, history is divided into discrete stages ("first . . . then . . . then") under the direction of God (symbolized by the "automatic" earth), and the image for these stages is an orderly growth that occurs in the natural sphere. Each stage contains a different degree of approximation to the final crop and therefore a different degree of hiddenness; the shoot is still quite far from that of the mature plant, but the ear is closer. When this process of unfolding is finished, but not before, the end will come suddenly. It may even be that our parable's progression of shoot→ear→full grain corresponds, in Mark's mind, to three identifiable phases in the unfolding of the divine dominion: Jesus' earthly ministry, the post-Easter epoch of the church, and the eschaton. Things are not as hidden in the post-Easter epoch as they were in the lifetime of Jesus; Jesus' identity, for example, which had to be kept secret during his lifetime (1:25, 34; 3:11–12, etc.) is revealed after the resurrection (9:9). A further revelation will occur at the eschaton, when not just the chosen but *all* "will see the Son of Man coming in clouds with great power and glory" (13:26).

In any case, whether or not Mark's audience would link the discrete stages described in 4:28 with the development from Jesus to the church to the Second Coming, by the time they reached the final verse they would know that it was describing the end of all things, the apocalyptic conclusion when Jesus will return on the clouds as the eschatological judge, the Son of Man. For the harvest pictured here is a standard OT, Jewish, and NT image for the Last Judgment (see Isa 17:5–6; 18:5; Micah 4:12; Matt 3:12; Rev 14:15; 4 Ezra 4:28–37; 2 *Apoc. Bar.* 70:2), and one OT usage of this image, Joel 3:13 (MT and LXX 4:13), seems to be deliberately echoed in the ending of the parable, "he sends forth the sickle, for the harvest has come" (see the NOTE on these words in 4:29).

The signal for this climactic event is, according to 4:29a, the full development of the fruit on the grain stalk. Mark is employing here the well-known Jewish concept of the eschatological "measure" (see number 5 above and cf. the NOTE on "But when the condition of the fruit allows it" in 4:29). Events are filling up the time, which is thought of as comparable to a container; when the container is full, the end will come suddenly and irrevocably. This notion of the eschatological measure is extensively developed elsewhere in Mark. A divine necessity (*dei* = "it is necessary") demands that certain events occur before the eschaton can come: Elijah must first come (9:11–13); the Son of Man must suffer, die, and rise again (8:31; 9:31–32; 10:32–34); the disciples must face suffering and persecution themselves (13:9–13); many must be led astray (13:21–22); the "abomination of desolation" must occur (13:14); judgment must come on the Temple and the Jewish leaders (12:1–12; 13:2); and the Gospel must be preached to all nations (13:10). Knowledge of one's position on this eschatological timeline is vital: "Do not be disturbed; these things must occur, but the end is not yet" (13:7). But since "these things" have, from the perspective of the Markan community, *already* occurred, the end cannot be far away!

Thus, while even the Markan Christians cannot plumb the nature of the miraculous divine power that is at work, they can see God's dominion unfolding before their eyes and moving rapidly to its consummation. The ear has already taken shape; just a few more grains need to be formed, and then the Son of Man will send in the sickle.

4:30–32: the Parable of the Mustard Seed. But in the meantime, until the eschaton, the dominion of God will continue to exist in a state of hiddenness that makes it mysterious (4:11), not readily apparent (4:3–8), and difficult to describe. The introduction to the Parable of the Mustard Seed emphasizes this difficulty strongly: "How shall we form a likeness for the dominion of God, or in what parable shall we put it?" (4:30). Although this introductory question is close to a later rabbinic idiom (see the NOTE on "How shall we form a likeness for the dominion of God" in 4:30), the doubling of the question is unusual (see McArthur, "Parable," 200 n. 6), and here it is probably intended to hint at the elusiveness of the dominion of God (Schweizer, 103).

This point is strongly made in the body of the parable, which places great stress on the tiny size of the mustard seed that symbolizes the initial inconspicuousness of God's dominion (4:31). Although mention of a mustard seed would have made the point by itself, since this seed was proverbial for its smallness (see e.g. *m. Nid.* 5:2 and *b. Ber.* 31a), Mark highlights the motif further by introducing the awkward phrase "is smaller than all the other seeds on earth" (see the NOTE on this phrase in 4:31). In this insertion we perhaps sense one aspect of the beleaguered Markan community's self-image: confronted with the hostility of society and the power of antagonistic authorities, it does not feel itself to be strong, but "smaller than all the other seeds on earth."

But the Markan community would probably also identify with the description of the huge size of the full-grown mustard plant at the end of the parable (4:32), both as a promise for the future and also, in a way, as an experience of the present. As a hope for the future, the description of the huge mustard plant corresponds to the glory that the community can expect at the eschaton; if the final stage of the seed described in 4:26–29 is symbolic of the Second Coming, so must be the full development of the mustard plant. At the eschaton, then, the puniness of the Markan community will be replaced by grandeur and its suffering by joy.

But there is also a sense in which the Markan community would probably feel that it was *already* participating in the glory of God's dominion on earth, as symbolized by the grown mustard seed. *Already* it finds that its weakness becomes the arena in which God's strength is displayed, that its suffering becomes the occasion for joy. This interpretation of the parable's end is supported by passages from Ezekiel and Daniel that form the background to the Markan picture of birds nesting in branches:

Ezekiel 17:23 LXX

I will plant it [the cedar = restored dominion of David], and it shall bear a shoot (*blaston*), and it shall yield fruit (*poiēsei karpon*), and it shall become a great cedar. And every bird shall rest beneath it, and every fowl shall rest under its shadow (*kai pan peteinon hypo tēn skian autou anapausetai*).

Ezekiel 31:6 LXX

In his [Pharaoh's] boughs all the birds of heaven (*panta ta peteina tou ouranou*) made nests, and under his branches (*kladōn*) all the beasts of the plain bred, and in his shade (*skią*) all the multitude of the nations dwelt.

Daniel 4:18 (21) Theodotion; cf. 4:9 (12)

Under it [the great tree = King Nebuchadnezzar] the wild beasts lodged, and in its branches (*kladois*) the birds of heaven dwelt (*ta ornea tou ouranou kateskēnoun*).

These passages draw on the widespread ancient Near Eastern image of the "cosmic tree" to describe a worldwide empire (cf. Zimmerli, *Ezekiel 2*, 146–47), and they have numerous points of contact with our parable and with the Seed Growing by Itself: the vocabulary is similar, and in all five passages a king or his dominion is compared to a shoot that grows up, bears fruit, and puts forth branches that shelter birds. It is therefore relevant for the decipherment of the Parable of the Mustard Seed that these OT passages use "birds of heaven" as a symbol for Gentiles (see the NOTE on "lodge under its shadow" in 4:32). The picture in 4:32 of "the birds of heaven" gathering under the shelter of the ripe mustard plant, therefore, would likely remind the Markan audience of their own situation, in which the good news is being proclaimed to all nations (13:10) and many people, especially Gentiles, are becoming followers of Jesus (see the discussion of the Markan setting in the INTRODUCTION).

Mark, then, would probably expect his readers to link the final state of the mustard seed with both the eschaton and the present state of his community and to conclude that, as the seedlike hiddenness of Jesus' earthly ministry and ignominious death has now given way to the plantlike revelation of the Christian mission, so the seedlike hiddenness of the present situation of suffering will soon give way to the plantlike revelation of the parousia. And since Mark has identified the seed with the divine word (4:14), the parable's end suggests the loftiest estimation of the word imaginable: not only is it the means of *describing* the new creation, the dominion of God, but it is also the very instrument for *bringing it into being*, since the huge plant grows out of this tiny seed. Despite the difficulty of describing the dominion of God (4:30), therefore, the word is designed not only to convey ideas about it but also to make it present.

4:33–34: the conclusion of the parable chapter. But in the current divided age the word accomplishes this task only among the small band of Jesus' followers; its true meaning, like the dominion of God itself, is hidden from the vast majority of people. This hiddenness has its pedagogical corollary in the esotericism of Jesus' teaching, which is reemphasized in the conclusion to the parable chapter (cf. 4:10–12). Not all are able to hear the word with understanding (cf. 4:9, 13–20, 23), and this division between those who understand and those who do not must reflect God's will (cf. again 4:10–12). Indeed, the linkage between "can" in 4:32 and "were able" in 4:33 (the same word in Greek) suggests that, if people are able to hear God's word (4:33), this is only because God has liberated them for such hearing by causing his royal power to break forth from heaven and to spread across the face of the earth (4:32).

But not all have experienced that power—not yet. After the magnificent vision of eschatological consummation presented by the ending of both parables, Mark again withdraws into the dualism of 4:10–20 and 4:24–25. He concludes the parable chapter by reminding his readers that Jesus explained the secret sense of his parables only to "his own disciples"; all others, by implication, were left in the dark.

Indeed, Mark's sense of darkness is even more brooding than that. The next passage will take place literally in the dark; and the disciples themselves will seem to participate in the darkness.

JESUS OVERPOWERS A STORM (4:35–41)

4 [35]And that day, as evening was coming, he said to them: "Let's go to the other side." [36]And sending the crowd away, they took him off, when he had gotten back in the boat and other boats were with him. [37]And a great windstorm arose, and the waves were breaking into the boat, so that the boat was beginning to fill with water. [38]And he was in the stern, sleeping on a cushion. And they woke him up and said to him, "Teacher, don't you care that we're about to die?" [39]And he roused himself and rebuked the wind, and said to the sea, "Silence! Shut up!" And the wind died down, and there was a great calm. [40]And he said to them, "Why are you cowardly? Don't you have faith yet?" [41]And they feared a great fear and said to each other: "Who then is this?—for even the wind and sea obey him!"

NOTES

4 35. *that day, as evening was coming.* Gk *en ekeinę tę hēmerą opsias genomenēs.* A typically Markan double time notice; see Neirynck, *Duality,* 47–48.

36. *when he had gotten back in the boat.* Gk *hōs ēn en tǭ ploiǭ,* lit. "when he was in the boat." This clause is often translated as "as he was, in the boat," but the meaning of "as he was" is unclear—"without going ashore" (Swete, 84)? Or "without delay" (Lohmeyer, 90)? It is better to recognize that Gk *hōs,* like Aram *kad,* can mean not only "as" but also "when," and that the meaning is that Jesus has returned to the ship after disembarking from it in 4:10.

in the boat. Gk *en tǭ ploiǭ.* In 1986 the hull of a first-century fishing boat, probably similar to the one Mark's readers would have in mind, was discovered intact in the Sea of Galilee. It was 26½ feet long, 7½ feet wide, and 4½ feet high; the boat's fore and aft sections (the latter is where Jesus is sleeping in our story) were probably originally decked in (see Wachsmann, "Boat," and cf. the NOTES on "in the stern" and "a cushion" in 4:38).

other boats were with him. Gk *alla ploia ēn met' autou.* These additional boats play no further role in the story; why are they mentioned? Lohmeyer (90) emends the text to "other boats were *not* with him," suggesting that the absence of other vessels to come to the rescue heightens the danger to Jesus and his disciples. Theissen (102) arrives at a similar result via a different route: in the pre-Markan story the other boats were sunk by the storm, thus magnifying the danger to Jesus and the Twelve. But if the Jonah typology is central here (see the COMMENT on 4:37–39), the other boats' safety rather than their peril could be the point; cf. *Pirqe R. El.* 10:6–7, where other boats accompany that of Jonah and are untroubled while Jonah's craft is battered by the storm. The other boats also allow Mark's readers to imagine themselves in the story; see the COMMENT on 4:35–36.

38. *in the stern.* Gk *en tę prymnę*. The sort of boat envisaged in the story would have had a large stern platform, which was the helmsman's station, underneath which there was an area protected from the elements. This is where Jesus is pictured as sleeping; see Wachsmann, "Boat," 33.

a cushion. Gk *to proskephalion*, lit. "*the* cushion." On the Semitic tendency to use the definite article with indefinite nouns, see the NOTE on "the strong man's house" in 3:27. It is possible, however, that the use of the definite article indicates that the cushion is part of the boat's equipment, perhaps a sandbag used for ballast; see Wachsmann, "Boat," 33.

Teacher. Gk *Didaskale.* This may seem at first to be an unusual way for the disciples to address Jesus at this moment, when they stand in need of a miracle rather than of instruction. For Mark, however, teaching and power are inextricably intertwined (cf. 1:22, 27).

we're about to die. Gk *apollymetha.* This verb occurs three times in an almost identical form in the LXX of Jonah (*mē apolōmetha* = "in order that we not die"; 1:6, 14; 3:9), where it expresses the leitmotiv of the entire book, escape from destruction at the hand of God.

39. *And he roused himself and rebuked the wind.* Gk *kai diegertheis epetimēsen tǭ anemǭ.* On the exorcistic nuance of *epitiman*, see the COMMENT on 1:23–26; the Aramaic counterpart, *g⁽r*, is used in an exorcistic context in the spell in Naveh and Shaked, *Amulets*, Amulet 1:8–10, where it is combined with the invocation "In the name of I-am-who-I-am."

Stories of miraculous rescue at sea abound in ancient literature, partly because ancient navigation was such a risky business. Theissen (101–2) helpfully divides such stories into two categories: (1) those such as Mark 6:45–52, in which the epiphany of a god brings rescue from the outside and (2) those such as the present story and Acts 27, in which "the rescue depends on the numinous power of a person present in the ship." In the first category belong rabbinic stories in which a Jew, caught in a life-threatening storm at sea, prays to God and is saved when the storm miraculously stops (e.g. *b. B. Meṣ.* 59b; *y. Ber.* 13b). In the second category belongs the description in Philostratus' *Life of Apollonius of Tyana* (4.13) of how people ask to join Apollonius' ship because they believe that he is more powerful than storms.

said to the sea, "Silence! Shut up!" Gk *eipen tę thalassę, Siōpa, pephimōso.* The second verb here is another form of the passive of *phimoun*, which is addressed to the unclean spirit in 1:25; see the NOTE there.

In 2 Macc 9:8 Antiochus Epiphanes, whose epithet means "the god made manifest," displays his hubris by attempting to command the sea, which in the Old Testament is the prerogative of God alone (e.g. Job 26:11–12; Ps 104:7; Isa 51:9–10; in a similar situation King Canute of England used the occasion to prove to his courtiers that he had no divine powers). In the view of the author of 2 Maccabees, the tyrant's horrible death is a fitting recompense for such pretension to godlike status. This passage suggests, perhaps, how some non-Christian Jews would have reacted to the sort of high Christology enshrined in our story; cf. the COMMENT on 4:37-39 and on 2:6-10a. See however *Pesiq. R.* 36:1, which quotes Ps 89:25 to refer to the Messiah controlling the flow of seas and rivers.

died down. Gk *ekopasen.* The same verb is used for the calming of the sea in the Jonah story (Jonah 1:11-12 LXX).

40. *Don't you have faith yet?* Gk *oupō echete pistin.* This probably implies that, at some later time, the disciples will have faith; cf. 8:17, 21 and Philostratus *Life of Apollonius of Tyana* 1.23: "You have not become a philosopher yet (*oupō philosopheis*), . . . if you are afraid of this sort of thing (*ei dedias tauta*)."

In our passage faith seems to have two aspects. On the one hand, it is a trust *like* Jesus', a basic confidence in God's provident care, the sort of trust that Jesus shows by sleeping through the storm (4:38; cf. Wellhausen, 37). There are several OT texts (e.g. Pss 3:5; 4:8; Prov 3:24) in which sleeping peacefully is a sign of trust in the protective power of God (see Nineham, 146), and one of these passages, Prov 3:25, goes on to exhort the reader not to be afraid of the storm that strikes the wicked; cf. 1QH 6:25, in which survival of the eschatological hurricane is coupled with faith in God. On the other hand, faith is also a trust *in* Jesus; by the end of our passage, *pistis* has come to mean a perception of his cosmic stature, and the consequent conviction that nothing bad can ultimately happen to the person who is with him (4:40; cf. Lohmeyer, 91-92, who aptly sums up the message of the passage with a reference to John 16:33). In the progression from 4:38 to 4:40, then, we move from seeing Jesus as an example of *pistis* to seeing him as the object of it.

41. *they feared a great fear.* Gk *ephobēthēsan phobon megan.* The same idiom is used in the Jonah story, though the grammar is slightly different (*ephobēthēsan . . . phobǭ megalǭ,* Jonah 1:16 LXX). The cognate accusative is probably a Semitism or Septuagintism (see Maloney, *Semitic Interference,* 185-90). Two sorts of fear are common in biblical narratives, and both are illustrated in our passage. The fear (*phobos*) mentioned in the present verse is the proper response to a manifestation of the divine, whereas the quailing before the storm found in the previous verse (*deiloi* = "cowardly") is reprehensible.

for. Gk *hoti.* The Greek is awkward; it is possible that the *hoti* reflects Aram *dě,* which means "for, because" but can also be used for the relative pronoun (cf. Black, 71-72). Originally, then, the exclamation may have read, "Who is this, whom even the wind and the sea obey him?," which is good Aramaic syntax.

even the wind and sea obey him. Gk *kai ho anemos kai hē thalassa hypakouei autǭ.* The vocabulary and theme here are similar to those of the recently published Qumran fragment 4Q521, which includes the line: "[The hea]vens and the earth will obey His Messiah" (Eisenman and Wise trans.; cf. Puech,

"Apocalypse"). The root used for "obey" here, *šmᶜw*, literally means "hear" or "listen" and thus is similar to Mark's *hypakouei*, which is a compounded form of *akouein*, which also means "to listen." The Peshitta, and the Hebrew translations of Delitzsch and the UBS Committee, all translate *hypakouei* here with a form of *šmᶜ*.

COMMENT

Introduction. Having used parables of Jesus to describe the royal power of God in 4:1–34, Mark now hints at the relation of that power to Jesus himself in an evocative narrative of rescue at sea. If the parables are stories that speak of an action of God that is imperceptible to unspiritual eyes because it is hidden under an appearance of weakness, our passage displays a Jesus apparently overcome by exhaustion and indifferent to the fate of his disciples, but in reality their savior from the demonic forces that threaten them. Thus a strong connection is suggested between the dominion of God as presented by the parables and the identity of Jesus as presented by the Markan narrative, and from this point on, the narrative will focus ever more strongly on the latter theme.

As indicated in the introduction to the COMMENT on 3:7–12, our story may have originally been part of a pre-Markan cycle of boat miracles and related stories that lies behind 3:7–12; 4:35–5:43; 6:31–56, and perhaps other Markan narratives (see the introduction to 3:7–6:6a). Mark 4:36 follows on logically from 3:7–12: Jesus has ordered the disciples to make a boat ready, in case the crowd begins to crush him; now the disciples, perhaps panicking at the press, dismiss the crowd and spirit Jesus away in the boat. According to this reconstruction, the introductory verse of the present passage, 4:35, would be a Markan link with the parable chapter, which Mark has introduced into its present position; this link transfers the initiative for Jesus' first journey to a Gentile area from the disciples to Jesus. Mark may also be responsible for the word *oupō* = "not yet" in 4:40, since this word refers to the larger Markan narrative (cf. its repetition in 8:17, 21), and for the displacement of the verse from its previous position before 4:39. In the present story the rebuke of the disciples for their fear comes improbably late, *after* the miracle has already been accomplished (see Lohmeyer, 91); the Markan displacement of it to the aftermath of the miracle highlights the theme of lack of faith and contributes to his darkening portrait of the Twelve (cf. 4:13). It is also possible that "Teacher" in the previous verse is Mark's contribution, since it reflects an important Markan theme and fits rather oddly into the storm situation (see the NOTE on "Teacher" in 4:38).

The passage in its present form falls into three parts: a stage-setting introduction (4:35–36), the description of the storm and Jesus' conquest of it (4:37–39), and an interpretative conversation (4:40–41). After the introduction, the passage is structured around three instances of the word *megas* = "great" in 4:37, 39, and 41:

4:37   a great storm (*lailaps megalē*) arose

4:39   there was a great calm (*galēnē megalē*)

4:41   they feared a great fear (*phobon megan*)

The repetition of *megas* implies that the disciples are threatened by a devastating superhuman power, but that a greater power than it comes upon the scene in the person of Jesus, who conquers it and inspires overwhelming awe. The message is thus very similar to 3:27: the Strong Man's grip on the cosmos has been broken, because a Stronger One has come. This similarity to the Strong Man parable is no accident, since our narrative is in some ways like an exorcism, as is especially clear from 4:39.

4:35–36: introduction. After finishing his parabolic revelation, the latter half of which emphasizes the irresistible expansion of God's dominion and hints at the inclusion of non-Jews in it (4:21–32), the Markan Jesus proposes to the disciples that he and they make their first trip "to the other side"—that is, to the predominantly Gentile Decapolis region on the far shore of the Sea of Galilee. The linkage with the parable chapter's themes of Gentile inclusion and a wider view of God's purposes is reinforced by the Jonah typology that permeates our passage (see below on 4:37–39), since the issue of Gentile salvation is central to the book of Jonah. Jonah was imprisoned in the "great fish" because he did not want to give the pagan Ninevites the opportunity to be saved from destruction, and later Jewish sources emphasize what a great honor God conferred on them by overruling this objection, since a prophet of the true God had never before been sent to "the nations of the world" (Ginzberg, 6.349 n. 27). Perhaps in the pre-Markan form of the story, Jesus was initially reluctant to journey to a Gentile region, as Jonah was (cf. 7:24–30); the Markan redaction, however, has changed this attitude, making the initiative for the trip his rather than the disciples' (see the discussion of the prehistory of the passage above).

This linkage of our passage with the Gentile mission is in line with a tradition of exegesis from Tertullian onward (*On Baptism* 12) that has seen the little group in the boat with Jesus as a symbol of the church. This line of interpretation is supported by the odd detail in 4:36, "and other boats were with him." In its Markan context this detail recalls 3:14, in which the Twelve were chosen "in order that they might be with him," and 4:10, in which the circle of disciples was widened to include "those around him with the Twelve" (cf. Gnilka, 1.193). Whatever the function of the other boats in the pre-Markan narrative (see the NOTE on "other boats were with him" in 4:36), for Mark they are probably there to hold the larger group of disciples that has been in view since 4:10, and they are thus an invitation to Mark's audience to read themselves into the narrative (see the COMMENT on 4:10–12).

4:37–39: Jesus' conquest of the storm. That invitation would become nearly irresistible in the next and climactic section, which describes the storm and

Jesus' conquest of it. A tempest arises; the waves are breaking into the boat; already it is filling with water and presumably beginning to sink (4:37). Living in the midst of such tribulation as had never been (13:19), with the storm of civil war and persecution breaking upon them from all sides (13:9–13), the members of the Markan community must have felt at times much like this, and their inclination to identify with the disciples' crisis would have been encouraged by the tendency of apocalyptic texts to use a storm at sea as a symbol of the terrors of the end-time (Dan 7:2–3; 1QH 3:6–18; 6:22–25; 7:4–5; cf. *T. Naph.* 6). The persecution experienced by the Markan community, moreover, seems to have been related to its mission to the Gentiles (see 13:9–13), thus forging a link between the community's situation and that of the disciples buffeted by the waves on a journey "to the other side." We may well hear an echo of the community's sense of desperation, therefore, in the anguished appeal of the disciples: "Teacher, don't you care that we're about to die?" (cf. 13:20).

The description of the storm at sea would probably also remind some Markan readers of the biblical story of Jonah. Cope (*Matthew*, 96–97) has noted the similarities between the two narratives:

(1) departure by boat
(2) a violent storm at sea
(3) a sleeping main character
(4) badly frightened sailors
(5) a miraculous stilling related to the main character
(6) a marveling response by the sailors

These overlaps do not relate just to shared themes but also to common vocabulary (see the NOTES on "we're about to die" in 4:38, "died down" in 4:39, and "they feared a great fear" in 4:41). Moreover, the third element in Cope's list actually fits Jonah's situation better than it does Jesus'; Jonah's sleeping through a storm in the hold of a seafaring vessel is plausible, but "the sleeping of Jesus stretched out on the deck of a small fishing boat on the Sea of Galilee through a storm so violent as to imperil boat and crew is not at all credible" (Cope, *Matthew*, 97; on the size of Jesus' vessel, see the NOTE on "in the boat" in 4:36). This suggests a literary relationship between the two stories and raises a question about the historicity of our passage, at least in its present form.

Cope's list of parallels between Jonah and Jesus could even be expanded. Jewish legends, for example, describe Jonah threatening the sea monster Leviathan with eschatological destruction (e.g. *Pirqe R. El.* 10; *Tanḥuma* on Leviticus, 8), and Jonah is sometimes identified with the widow's son whom Elijah resuscitated in 1 Kings 17, and on this basis he is said to have entered Paradise alive (Ginzberg, 6.351 n. 38). Our story, similarly, portrays Jesus as the eschatological conqueror of the sea, which is personified (Jesus "rebukes" it), and there is perhaps a hint of his resurrection in the use of the verb *egeirousin* for the disciples' rousing of him (4:38).

But any readers sensitive enough to pick up such parallels would also recognize that there are significant differences between Mark 4:35–41 and the Jonah story. Unlike Jonah, Jesus is not fleeing from God but actively involved in the accomplishment of his will. The disciples, moreover, do not ask Jesus to intercede with God, as happens in Jonah 1:6, but call upon him to save them as the distressed sailors of Ps 107:23–30 call upon the Lord (see Batto, "Sleeping," 174). While he is similar to Jonah, then, the Markan Jesus is, as Pesch (1.269) puts it, also greater than Jonah (cf. Matt 12:41//Luke 11:32), and in an essential way more like God than like Jonah.

Indeed, even the sleeping of Jesus is part of his likeness with God. In ancient Near Eastern myths the supreme deity is often portrayed as sleeping as a sign of his sovereignty: there are no enemies powerful enough to disturb his slumber (see Batto, "Sleeping," 159–64). Old Testament adaptations of this idea, however, turn God's sleeping into a cause for concern; Israel calls on him to awaken, arise, and come to his people's aid. The Psalmist, for example, invokes God in these terms:

Rouse yourself! Why do you sleep, O Lord?
Awake, do not cast us off forever!
   (Ps 44:23–24; cf. 35:23; 59:4)

This passage was well known, since it played a prominent role in the liturgy of the Second Temple; because of their daily recitation of it, the Levites were called "the wakers" (cf. *b. Soṭa* 48a). The widespread image of the sleeping God, then, combines the notion of omnipotence with that of apparent indifference, and both ideas seem to be important in our passage: Jesus demonstrates his sovereign power over the elements, thus answering his disciples' complaint that he is unconcerned about their fate.

Nor is this the only way that the Jesus of our passage is like the God of the Old Testament and Jewish traditions. For the latter, like the Markan Jesus, battles and triumphs over the power of the sea, which he "rebukes." Isa 51:9–10, for example, combines a call on God to awake with a reminder of his primeval battle against the personified ocean, and God rebukes the sea in Job 26:11–12, several Psalms (18:15; 104:7; 106:9), and Isa 50:2. Based on such OT texts, an Aramaic exorcistic spell uttered "in the name of I-am-who-I-am" (cf. Exod 3:14) calls for God to rebuke (*gʿr*) evil spirits (Naveh and Shaked, *Amulets*, Amulet 2:7–10), and in other Aramaic spells the linkage of the verb "rebuke" with the primordial divine conquest of the sea becomes clear (see the COMMENT on 1:23–26).

The Markan Jesus is also similar to the OT God in other ways. Like God in Psalm 46, he is "Israel's" helper, who is in their midst and works wonders through his word, and because of whom they should not fear though the waters of the sea be troubled. (The Matthean parallel seems to develop the likeness to Psalm 46 even further by introducing an earthquake: Matt 8:24; cf. Ps 46:2). Zech 2:10–3:2, moreover, speaks of God dwelling in the midst of his people, rousing himself, and rebuking Satan, all of which correspond to elements in Mark 4:35–41. (Both of these passages, by the way, are frequently used in later Aramaic magical texts, increasing the likelihood that they are alluded to in our passage; see Naveh and Shaked, *Magic Spells*, 25, 52, 177, and 240). If our passage, then, reflects the persecution being experienced by the Markan community, it also perhaps reflects one of the causes of that persecution, namely a high Christology that goes a long way toward equating Jesus with the OT God and thus lays the community open to Jewish charges of blasphemy (cf. 2:7). At the same time, however, the passage hints at the source of the community's perseverance in the face of this furious reaction: the conviction that the one in whom they have believed is the all-powerful one who is able to calm every threatening wave.

Jesus displays this power at the climax of the passage, his command to the wind and sea in 4:39. This command is reminiscent of that issued to the unclean spirit in 1:25; in both passages the demonic power is rebuked (*epetimēsen*) and told to be silent in rude terms ("Shut up!"; cf. Naveh and Shaked, *Magic Spells*, 93, in which there is a linkage between exorcism and rebuking the sea). Thus, if the waves beating on the little boat are symbolic of the persecution being experienced by the Markan community, that persecution is shown by the linkage with 1:25 to have its source in Satan's implacable hostility to Jesus' mission. But our passage also reveals that this Satanic hostility is ultimately unavailing. So it is not only our passage's description of the terror experienced by the little group of tempest-tossed disciples that corresponds to the experience of the Markan community but also its portrayal of the effect of Jesus' word: "And the wind died down, and there was a great calm."

4:40–41: conclusion. The passage ends with a dialogue between Jesus and the disciples that reinforces the impression of his awesomely high identity, which the disciples are having difficulty in grasping. After conquering the external threat, Jesus turns to the internal one, his followers' unbelief, asking his companions in the boat why they are so cowardly and whether they do not yet believe. The language of this reprimand would, again, resonate in the persecuted Markan community, since the call not to be afraid and to have faith is reminiscent of the language of martyrdom (cf. John 14:27; 2 Tim 1:7, and especially Rev 21:8, which conjoins *deilos* and *apistos*, "cowardly" and "faithless"). Jesus' question in a way responds to the anguished question put by the disciples in 4:38:

4:38 "Teacher, don't you care that we're about to die?"

4:40 "Why are you cowardly? Don't you have faith yet?"

The human challenge to God, "Don't you care?," is met by the divine challenge to the human being, "Why are you cowardly?" These are both real questions because both reflect realities—on the one hand the desperate human situation, on the other hand the divine assurance that "all shall be well and / all manner of thing shall be well" (T. S. Eliot, "Little Gidding," 5, quoting

Julian of Norwich). The ultimate issue at stake in any given circumstance is which of these two realities will turn out to be determinative.

The disciples respond to Jesus' question about their cowardice and lack of faith with a third question, one that is similar to that asked by the crowd after the first great Markan exorcism in 1:21–28 ("What is this?"/"Who is this?" and a reference to the submission [*hypakouein*] of the demonic power; cf. Batto, "Sleeping," 174–75). This linkage with the earlier passage should come as no surprise, given the likeness that has already been noted between Jesus' rebuke of the sea and his reprimand of the Capernaum demon. But there has also been a progression beyond the earlier passage: the impersonal choral reaction to Jesus' first exorcism in Capernaum, "*What* is this?" (1:27), has now been sharpened to the personal question "*Who* is this?" If the Capernaum exorcism was the first great demonstration of the truth of Jesus' assertion that the dominion of God had drawn near (1:14–15), it is now becoming clearer and clearer that that dominion is concretized in Jesus himself.

The disciples' question is followed by the exclamation "For even the wind and sea obey him!," with which the passage concludes. This acclamation suggests at least part of Mark's answer to the "Who is this?" question, since a fragmentary text from Qumran, 4Q521, prophesies that, at the end appointed by God, heaven and earth will obey *his* Messiah (see the NOTE on "even the wind and sea obey him" in 4:41). This fragment continues a line of development begun by Deut 18:18 and passing through Mark 9:7 and Acts 3:22–23, which indicate that the eschatological prophet will be obeyed. But in both 4Q521 and Mark 4:41 this idea has been magnified, because now obedience is rendered to the Messiah not only by human beings but also by inanimate powers. The one so acknowledged is not just a human but a cosmic figure; if he is the Messiah, he is a Messiah who bears the marks of divinity.

Who this is, then, is the bringer of a new world, who, like the creator God in ancient Near Eastern myths and poetic OT texts, defeats a demonic sea monster and thus brings a new order, a cosmos, into being (see Isa 51:9–10; Job 26:10–13; Ps 104:5–9; cf. Anderson, *Creation*, 1–52, 74–89). Yet this victory has, in Mark, a curiously provisional character. In our story Jesus exorcises the roaring, Satanic power of the sea, but in the next passage this evil power reappears on dry land in the form of a screaming demoniac, only to be driven back into the sea in the herd of pigs (cf. Batto, "Sleeping," 175). By the time Jesus again crosses the sea, in 6:45–52, the water has reverted to its demonic character and must be subdued by a renewed epiphany of the godlike Jesus.

This continual shuttling of the demons back and forth between sea and land contributes to the audience's perception of evil's restless, questing nature, and also to the impression that Jesus has not yet unsheathed the weapon that will deliver the final deathblow against it. Jesus wins all of his encounters with the opposition, but they appear ultimately to be inconclusive. A final reckoning, a decisive battle, looms in the future.

JESUS HEALS A DEMONIAC IN A
GENTILE REGION (5:1–20)

5 ¹And they came to the other side of the sea, to the region of the Gerasenes. ²And he came out of the boat, and immediately there came out from the tombs to meet him a man in an unclean spirit ³who had his dwelling among the tombs, and no one had ever yet been able to tie him up for long, not even with a chain—⁴for he had often been tied up with fetters and chains, but the chains had been torn apart by him and the fetters had been smashed, and no one had the power to subdue him. ⁵And he was in the tombs and in the mountains continuously, night and day, shrieking and cutting himself with stones. ⁶And seeing Jesus from far away, he ran up and threw himself down before him, ⁷and shrieking with a loud voice he said, "What do I have to do with you, Jesus, Son of the Most High God? I adjure you by God: Don't torture me!" ⁸(For Jesus had said to him, "Let the unclean spirit come out of the man.") ⁹And Jesus asked him, "What is your name?" And he said to him, "My name is Legion, for we are many." ¹⁰And they pleaded with him greatly not to send them out of the land.

¹¹Now there was a large herd of pigs grazing on the mountain. ¹²And the demons pleaded with him, saying, "Send us into the pigs, so that we may enter them." ¹³And he permitted them; and the unclean spirits came out and entered the pigs—and the whole herd, about two thousand of them, rushed headlong over the cliff into the sea, and choked to death in the sea!

¹⁴And those who had been grazing the pigs ran away and spread the news in the city and the villages. And people came to see what had happened; ¹⁵and they came to Jesus, and they beheld the one who had been demonized for so long, sitting, clothed, and sane, the man who had had the legion of demons. And they were afraid. ¹⁶And the eyewitnesses described what had happened to the demoniac, and the story of the pigs. ¹⁷And the townspeople began to plead with him to go away from their region.

¹⁸And as he was getting into the boat, the former demoniac began to plead with him that he might be with him. ¹⁹And he didn't permit him, but said to him, "Go to your house, to your people, and announce to them what great things the Lord has done for you, how he has had mercy on you." ²⁰And he went out and began to proclaim in the Decapolis what great things Jesus had done for him; and everybody was amazed.

NOTES

5 1. *they came.* Gk *ēlthon.* The plural is to include the disciples in the story, though they play no role in the subsequent narrative and were probably absent in the originally independent tale (cf. Bultmann, 344–45).

Gerasenes. Gk *Gerasēnōn.* Some texts read "Gadarenes" and others "Gergesenes." "Gerasenes," however, has the best external attestation (early Alexandrian and Western manuscripts) as well as being the most difficult text and therefore likely to be original. The difficulty has to do with Transjordanian geography. Gerasa, on the site of modern Jerash in Jordan, was one of the Decapolis cities (see the NOTE on "the Decapolis" in 5:20), and it was situated thirty-seven miles southeast of the Sea of Galilee. This is a difficult setting for our story, in which the pigs run over the cliff and fall into the sea. Because of this difficulty, Matt 8:28 probably moves the story to Gadara (though the Matthean verse is textually uncertain as well), which was another city of the Decapolis five miles southeast of the lake and possessing territory running up to the lake itself. The Markan manuscripts that read "Gadarenes" are probably an assimilation to this Matthean correction. "Gergesenes," the most poorly attested of the readings, is also the most geographically plausible one, if Gergesa is correctly identified with Kursi, which is on a plateau on the east bank of the Sea of Galilee (see Guelich, 275). But this means that later scribes would have had good reason for substituting it for the geographically inaccurate "Gerasenes" (cf. Metzger, 23–24 and 84).

Although "Gerasa" is difficult geographically, it is appropriate symbolically, since the Hebrew root grš means "to banish" and is a common term for exorcism (see Derrett, "Spirit-Possession," 287).

2. *tombs.* Gk *mnēmeiōn.* As Bratcher (55) notes, "People were often buried in cave-like openings dug into the rock, big enough for a person to enter on foot, and usually high enough inside to allow a person to stand upright. Such a place would provide shelter for a man who had no other place to live." Tombs, however, were ritually impure places because of the presence of dead bones (see the Mishnah tractate *Oholot* and Matt 23:27). This impurity made a graveyard an ideal dwelling place for "unclean spirits."

a man in an unclean spirit. Gk *anthrōpos en pneumati akathartǭ.* The delay of the subject until the end of the sentence builds up the suspense. On the phrase, see the COMMENT on 1:23–26. Although later in the present chapter, *en* ("in") is reduced to the general idea of association or accompaniment (5:25; see Zerwick, §116), in our story the theme of bondage to the demon suggests that the *en* should be taken more literally: the man has been swallowed up by his possessing spirit. To be sure, at the end of the story the spirit will come out of the man, not the other way around (5:13), but we should not look for too much consistency when dealing with things as ambivalent and protean as demonic spirits.

The possessed man would probably be understood by Mark's readers as a Gentile. The land to the east of the Sea of Galilee was predominantly inhabited by Gentiles, though some Jews lived there. In 5:7, moreover, the man uses a term for God that was typically employed by Gentiles when referring to the God of Israel (see the NOTE on "Son of the Most High God"). The association of the possessing spirits with pigs in 5:11–13 also suggests a Gentile context, since these animals were unclean in Jewish eyes, a fact well-known even in non-Jewish circles (see Whittaker, *Jews,* 73–80).

3. *who had his dwelling among the tombs* etc. Gk *hos tēn katoikēsin eichen en tois mnēmasin* etc. Derrett, noting the graveyard setting and the demo-

niac's self-mutilation, suggests that his state reflects a mourning ritual that has gone out of control ("Spirit-Possession," 287). The demoniac could also be a former magician; in a Talmudic passage "he who consults with the dead" (Deut 18:11) is interpreted as a person "who spends the night in a cemetery, so that an unclean spirit may rest upon him," thus enabling him to predict the future (*b. Sanh.* 65b; cf. *b. Ḥag.* 3b).

to tie . . . up. Gk *dēsai.* These attempts may reflect not only an effort to prevent the demoniac from harming himself but also magical practices; Geller ("Theurgic," 143–44) notes that Aramaic and Mandaic incantation bowls often portray fettered, shackled, or hobbled demons. Demons themselves "bind" people (see the NOTE on "ties . . . up" in 3:27), and so our passage may contain an element of irony: the world's method for dealing with those whom Satan has enchained is to tie them up further.

for long. These words are not present in the text, but they are implied by the next verse, which does indeed speak of the man being tied up.

4. *had been torn apart by him . . . had been smashed.* Gk *diespasthai . . . syntetriphthai.* The use of the passive voice here is odd and striking; the thought could have been expressed more smoothly by the active, "he had shattered the chains and smashed the fetters." Mark perhaps chooses the passive because the man is not in control of his life but the victim of external forces. We might almost speak of "demonic passives" here, the mirror image of the divine passives employed elsewhere in the Gospel (see the NOTE on "be cleansed!" in 1:41).

no one had the power to subdue him. Gk *oudeis ischyen auton damasai.* This clause is linguistically as well as thematically reminiscent of the Strong Man parable in 3:27; both use *oudeis* = "no one," both speak of binding in the context, and the verb *ischyen* = "had the power" here is cognate to *ischyron* = "the strong man" there. The implication is that the possessed man in our passage derives his supernatural strength from the Strong Man, Satan. There is also perhaps an echo of 1:12–13, where Jesus is with the wild animals, having apparently tamed their feral nature by his eschatological power.

5. *shrieking.* Gk *krazōn.* This verb can be used for articulate speech (cf. 3:11; 5:7, etc.), but also for sounds made "when one utters loud cries, but no words capable of being understood" (BAGD, 447 [1]); cf. 9:26 and the variant reading in 15:39, where it is used for Jesus' death-cry.

7. *What do I have to do with you.* Gk *ti emoi kai soi.* On the idiom, see the NOTE on "What do we have to do with you" in 1:24.

Son of the Most High God. Gk *huie tou theou tou hypsistou.* This phrase occurs in Luke 1:32 and in the related but fragmentary Qumran 4Q246. The reference in the latter is probably to a Jewish messianic figure (see J. J. Collins, "Messiahs," 293–95).

As a term for God, "Most High" has roots both in the OT, where it originally reflected a Canaanite divine name (cf. Gen 14:18–20), and in Greek religion, where it was a common designation for Zeus (see e.g. Pindar *Nemean Odes* 1.60; 11.2; one of the gates of Thebes was called *Hypsistai* from Zeus' temple there: LSJ, 1910). The epithet was thus both Jewish and cosmopolitan, and so was ideally suited to be a name for God in Diaspora Judaism, where it is often found in synagogue inscriptions. For similar reasons, Gentiles typically use it to refer to Israel's God in biblical and intertestamental literature (see e.g. Num 24:16; 1 Esdras 2:2; Dan 3:26; 4:2; 2 Macc 3:31; 3 Macc 7:9), so that in our passage it is appropriately employed by a Gentile demoniac (Nineham, 153). A particularly close parallel to our passage is provided by Acts 16:17, where a Gentile girl with a demonic "spirit of divination" refers to Paul and his companions as "servants of the Most High God." These exorcistic usages of "Most High" may reflect its employment in Psalm 91, a text that from its inception was used as a charm against evil spirits (see Burrelli, *Psalm 91*).

The "Most High God" in OT and Jewish texts is associated not only with Gentiles but also, more particularly, with the sovereignty of the God of Israel over the whole earth, even Gentile realms (Deut 32:8; Dan 4:17). This sovereignty was already established by a primordial triumph over anti-God powers (Isa 14:12–15; cf. Deut 32:7–8), but it was reasserted by subsequent divine defeats of those powers' human exponents, i.e. the armies of the Gentiles, in holy war (Gen 14:10; Pss 9:3; 47:2; 83:18; 3 Macc 6:2; 1QH 6:33). Our passage may reflect this background: by casting out the legion of demons, the "Son of the Most High God" is subduing a hostile Gentile territory through a saving act of holy war. The theme of God's holy war victory is also associated with the "Most High God" title in 2 Sam 22:14, and here the larger context is significant: in 22:18 David praises God for delivering him "from my strong enemy, from those who hated me; for they were too mighty for me."

I adjure you by God. Gk *horkizō se ton theon*. Today's English Version gives a nice paraphrase: "For God's sake, I beg you . . . " "To adjure" is standard exorcistic terminology, but it is usually employed by the exorcist rather than by the demon (see Kee, "Terminology," 241). Koch (*Bedeutung*, 55–61) acknowledges this point, but in his treatment of 1:24 argues inconsistently that it would be nonsensical to put exorcistic terminology into the mouth of a demon. But there is an element of deliberate parody in the demon's invocation of God and its usage of exorcistic terminology, as well as in its plea that Jesus not torture it.

Don't torture me! Gk *mē me basanisēs*. Philostratus (*Life of Apollonius of Tyana* 4.25) provides a striking parallel in which a demon begs an exorcist not to torture it (*mē basanizein*). But *basanizein* is also used for the eschatological torment of demons in Rev 20:10. Matthew, therefore, is probably just developing Mark's thought when he has the demons speak of Jesus torturing them *before the time* (Matt 8:29; cf. Nineham, 153).

8. *had said*. Gk *elegen*. On this usage of the imperfect for a pluperfect, see Zerwick, §290.

9. *What is your name?* Gk *ti onoma soi*. In magical contexts, knowing the name of a god or demon grants power over it; cf., for example, *T. Sol.* 2:1 and *PGM* 4.3037–39: "I adjure you, every demonic spirit, to say what sort you are."

Legion. Gk *Legiōn*. The demon employs a Roman military term. A legion at full strength consisted of about 5,000 soldiers (see Kennedy, "Roman

Army," 5.789–90), but they were rarely if ever at full strength; an average head count was 3,600, which brings the number closer to that of the pigs drowned in 5:13. According to Wellhausen (39), the demon's reply is a clever evasion, since it reveals not its name, which could be magically manipulated, but only its number. But since Jesus' exorcism succeeds, it is hard to follow Wellhausen's exegesis.

10. *pleaded.* Gk *parekalei.* Mark uses the imperfect, which indicates repeated or continuous action, evidently because these pleas are unsuccessful and therefore repeated; in 5:12 the tense switches to the aorist, because that plea is granted (see MHT, 3.65). As Kollmann ("Schweigegebote," 271) points out, demonic pleas to God or to exorcists are common in ancient literature; in *T. Sol.* 2:6 and *b. Pesaḥ.* 112b, for example, demons beg to be allowed to remain at large.

out of the land. Gk *exō tēs chōras.* The translation attempts to capture two nuances of *chōra:* a region, especially the rural region surrounding a city (see the NOTE on 1:5), and dry land as opposed to the sea (see e.g. Acts 27:27). As in the Parable of the Strong Man in 3:27 and the Parable of the Vineyard in 12:7, Jesus' enemies desire to stay in possession of the territory they hold.

12. *so that we may enter them.* Gk *hina eis autous eiselthōmen.* The generally burlesque atmosphere of the story (see the COMMENT on 5:1–10 and on 5:11–13) suggests that the request may contain a sexual innuendo, a possibility supported by the way in which the pigs seem to go mad when the demons enter them; "pig," moreover, could be a slang term for female genitalia (e.g. Aristophanes *Acharnenses* 773; cf. Derrett, "Spirit-Possession," 290).

13. *rushed headlong over the cliff into the sea, and choked to death in the sea!* Gk *hōrmēsen . . . kata tou krēmnou eis tēn thalassan, . . . kai epnigonto en tȩ thalassȩ.* The interpretations of this ending to the exorcism proper are, if not "legion," at least numerous. Some scholars see it merely as a dramatic demonstration of the demons' eviction from the man or of the destructive nature of demonic powers. Others think it indicates that Jesus has tricked the demons, either because they are destroyed along with the pigs or because they are deprived of their new, porcine lodgings (see Bultmann, 210). Bauernfeind, however, thinks that the demons are tricky rather than tricked (*Worte,* 41–44); elsewhere in the NT the possessed always do the will of their possessor, so it is unlikely that the death of the pigs is unintended by the demons. Rather, by destroying the herd of pigs, the demons have caused Jesus to be rejected in Gerasa and have forced him to leave the area. Against this exegesis, however, the demons seem to be thwarted in their desire to stay in the Gerasene land, at least in their present form, and thus it is likely that Jesus has tricked them (cf. the COMMENT on 5:11–13). They will, however, immediately assume a different form and launch a counterattack (see the COMMENT on 5:14–17).

14. *people came.* Gk *ēlthon,* lit. "they came," one of Mark's many impersonal plurals (cf. Black, 126–28). Here and in 5:12, 15, 17, the subject is not specified, and it is left up to the reader's wit to decide whether "they" are the demons, the pig herders, or the townspeople. As Black remarks, this lack of

clarity about the subject is characteristic of Semitic narrative; he gives a good parallel from *Lam. Rab.* 1:31.

15. *who had been demonized for so long*. Gk *ton daimonizomenon*. "For so long" is not explicit in the Greek, but duration is implied by the present participle *daimonizomenon* (see Zerwick, §371).

they were afraid. Gk *ephobēthēsan*. This word can indicate a natural or even commendable religious awe, as in 4:41; 5:33, and 6:20. It can also, however, suggest a culpable timorousness, as in 5:36; 6:50; 9:32; 10:32; 11:18, 32; 12:12, and 16:8. In our passage as in 16:8 the meaning of the term has probably changed from the positive to the negative form of fear in the development from the pre-Markan to the Markan tradition. But what does Mark think the townspeople are afraid of? Some have speculated that their fear has to do with the economic loss Jesus' healing has brought about (two thousand pigs represented a substantial fortune; see e.g. Guelich, 284). But in the story it is the townspeople, not the herders, who ask Jesus to leave, and no hint is given that they are the owners of the pigs. It would be more in line with the rest of the story and with the overall Markan narrative to suggest that the townspeople, like the scribes in 3:22–30, interpret Jesus' exorcism as the work of the devil.

17. *the townspeople began to plead with him to go away from their region*. Gk *ērxanto parakalein auton apelthein apo tōn horiōn autōn*, lit. "they began to plead"; see the NOTE on 5:14. This repudiation, which may well be a Markan addition (see the introduction to the COMMENT), is an unusual ending for a miracle story; such stories usually end with acclaim, not rejection. Theissen (72) says that he knows of no analogies from outside the NT, and even within the NT he can cite only distant parallels (Mark 3:6; John 5:16; Acts 16:19–23). The more usual pattern is represented by John 4, which is strikingly parallel to our pericope except for the ending: in both passages Jesus performs a miracle in a deserted, non-Jewish region; those affected by the miracle go into town and tell others about it; the latter come out to the site of the miracle and are awestruck by what they see. In John, however, the onlookers' reaction to Jesus is positive, which is natural; in our passage, on the contrary, their reaction is negative, which is unnatural. On the way in which this negative reaction reflects the Markan situation, see the COMMENT on 5:14–17.

19. *Go to your house*. Gk *hypage eis ton oikon sou*. Some, following Wrede (140–41), see this as a command to keep the healing secret, since elsewhere in Mark the house is a place of secrecy (5:38–43; 7:17, 24; 8:26; 9:28, 33?; 10:10). The man's subsequent proclamation therefore becomes an act of disobedience similar to 1:45 and 7:36. Up to this point in the Gospel, however, the house has been a place of publicity rather than of secrecy (1:29–34; 2:1–2, 15; 3:20), and Wrede's interpretation of 5:20 would be more compatible with the contrastive *ho de* ("but he"; cf. 1:45; 7:36) than with the normally copulative *kai* ("and he"; see R. Lightfoot, *History*, 89). Moreover, the meanings of *apangeilon* ("announce") and *kēryssein* ("to herald forth") are too similar for the second to be seen as a betrayal of the first. The man interprets Jesus' command expansively but not wrongly.

20. *the Decapolis.* Gk *tę̄ Dekapolei.* A group of ten cities (the literal mean-ing of "Decapolis") east of the Jordan and the Sea of Galilee and known for their Hellenistic culture. Though earlier historians supposed that these cities constituted a kind of confederacy, more recent investigations have shown that they were not in any sense a politically coherent unit. Rather, "their unity comes from their Hellenistic character, which distinguished them sharply from neighboring populations, Jews to the W, Nabataeans to the S, highland tribes or seminomads to the N" (Rey-Coquais, "Decapolis," 2.119).

COMMENT

Introduction. After the tempestuous boat ride of 4:35–41, Jesus reaches his destination, the other side of the Sea of Galilee, a region populated mainly by non-Jews (see the NOTE on "a man in an unclean spirit" in 5:2). He is imme-diately confronted by a shrieking demoniac, whom he frees from his terrible affliction after a dialogue with the possessing spirits. He is not so successful, however, in his encounter with the demoniac's neighbors, who end up asking him to leave their region.

There are several features in the story that suggest that it is not an original unity but has grown by a process of accretion that has left some loose ends dangling (see Bauernfeind, *Worte,* 34–35; Pesch, "Markan Version"). In its present form, for example, the story is generally positive about non-Jews; the Gentile demoniac whom Jesus delivers from his affliction ends up becoming a missionary of sorts and proclaiming what Jesus has done for him throughout the predominantly pagan region of the Decapolis, causing everyone there to be amazed. Some of the story's elements, however, seem to reflect an origin in a chauvinistic Jewish environment; it implicitly links unclean spirits with what are for Jews unclean places (graveyards), unclean people (Gentiles), and unclean animals (pigs), and it describes with relish the death of the latter. It is even possible that the story, or parts of it, originally had nothing to do with Jesus (see Nineham, 154).

Mark himself is probably responsible for some of the loose ends in the present form of the tale, though most of it is pre-Markan. The *gar* ("for") clause in 5:8, for example, though confusing in its present sequence, corresponds to Mark's typical style and to one of his characteristic themes: the inserted clause makes it clear that the initiative for the exorcism comes from Jesus (cf. the COMMENT on 1:16–18, on 3:31–35, and on 5:25–34 and the introduction to the COMMENT on 4:35–41). Mark may also be responsible for some or all of the conclusion of the story in 5:17–20. The demonstration of cure and the awed reaction of the spectators in 5:15–16 would make a suitable ending for an exor-cism story, whereas the last four verses relate to repeated themes in the Markan macrostructure (the rejection of Jesus, the proclamation of the good news, and the irresistible spread of Jesus' fame) and are full of Markan vocabulary (e.g. "began," "plead," "go away," "get in," "be with him," "allow," "do," "proclaim," "Decapolis," "everybody").

In its present form the story is a minidrama in four acts: Jesus' initial encounter with the demonized man (5:1–10), the transfer of the demons to the pigs (5:11–13), the townspeople's reaction (5:14–17), and the man's promulgation of the news of the miracle (5:18–20; cf. Taylor, 277). The first three "acts" demonstrate features typical of an exorcism story: the initial meeting with the demoniac (5:1–2), the description of his dangerous condition (5:3–5), the demon's recognition of the exorcist (5:6–8), the exorcism itself (5:9–13a), the demonstration of the demon's departure (5:13b–15), and the impression on the spectators (5:15 end; cf. Bultmann, 210). There are several repetitions here: the confrontation with the demon (5:2, 6), the description of the illness (5:2–3, 4–5), and the demon's cringing request (5:7, 10, 12). These may be signs of the growth of the tradition in the pre-Markan stage, but they may equally reflect a storyteller's enjoyment of the details of an exciting tale (cf. Dibelius, 76–77).

While there is probably some sort of historical event at the root of this story, it has been embellished not only by the storyteller's art but also by Old Testament motifs. Some features of the story, for example, are reminiscent of Isa 65:1–7 MT, in which Yahweh reaches out to a people who had not sought him and who sit in tombs, eat swine's flesh, and revile him upon the hills (cf. 5:5; see Gnilka, 1.203–4). Other features seem to echo Ps 68:6 LXX: "God makes the solitary dwell in a house (cf. 5:19), leading forth mightily them that have been bound (cf. 5:4), and also them that behave rebelliously and that dwell in tombs" (cf. 5:2–3). Still other features of our passage and its predecessor (4:35–41) recall Ps 65:7–8, which speaks of God stilling the sea's roaring and the madness of the peoples, and of a revelation of his signs to the ends of the earth (see Nineham, 152). But the most pervasive echoes are of the story of God's defeat through Moses of the Egyptian army at the Reed Sea in Exodus 14–15 and related passages (cf. Derrett, "Contributions," 6–8). Both are stories in which God displays his mercy on his people and his incomparable power over his enemies, and both climax in a scene in which a multitude is drowned; there are, besides, several verbal echoes of the Septuagint version of the Exodus tale (see figure 11). The applicability of the Exodus story to the present context is confirmed by an exorcistic spell, *PGM* 4.3036–37, which invokes the god "who saved his people from Pharaoh" and occurs right before a striking parallel to Mark 5:9 (see the NOTE on "What is your name?" in 5:9). Our passage, then, seems to cast Jesus in a Moses-like role as an incomparable conduit of divine power, while at the same time hinting at an extension of the divine sovereignty beyond the Israel that Moses founded.

5:1–10: the initial encounter with the demonized man. Upon Jesus' alighting from the boat, a demoniac immediately pops into view with terrifying, supernatural swiftness, like the monster in a horror movie. The confusion of identity between the demonic parasite and its human host is at once suggested by the phrase "a man in an unclean spirit" (see the COMMENT on 1:23–26): the man's identity has been swallowed up by the demon's, so that he speaks with the demon's voice, tries to protect the demon from eviction from his own body,

Figure 11: OT Background to the Gerasene Exorcism

Mark 5:1–20	*Exodus 14:1–15:22 LXX and Related Passages*
5:1: They came to the other side of the sea (*thalassa*)	14:22: Israelites pass through the sea (*thalassa*; cf. 15:16)
5:3–4: No one had been able (*edynato*) to tie him up; no one had the power (*ischyen*) to subdue him	14:28; 15:4; 15:6, 13: The power (*dynamis*) of Pharaoh is destroyed; the power (*ischys*) of God is glorified
5:7: "Son of the Most High God (*tou theou tou hypsistou*)"	15:2: "This is . . . my father's God, . . . and I will exalt (*hypsōsō*) him"
5:13: The pigs . . . choked to death in the sea	14:28–30; 15:19: The Egyptians are drowned
5:14: Those who had been grazing the pigs ran away (*ephygon*)	14:27: The Egyptians ran away (*ephygon*)
5:15, 17: And they were afraid (*kai ephobēthēsan*) . . . and they began to plead with him to go away	15:14–15: The nations heard and shook (Codex A + MT; other LXX mss. read "were angry") . . . Trembling took hold of them (cf. 15:16: Let trembling and fear [*phobos*] fall upon them)
5:19: "Go . . . and announce (*apangeilon*) . . . what great things the Lord has done for you" (*hosa ho kyrios soi pepoiēken*; cf. 5:20: He began to proclaim in the Decapolis what great things Jesus had done for him)	14:31: Israel saw the great hand, the things that the Lord had done to the Egyptians (*ha epoiēse kyrios tois Aigyptois*; cf. 9:16: "For this reason I have kept you alive, . . . in order that my name might be announced [*diangelę̄*] in all the earth")

and becomes the demon's instrument for his own torture. This phrase is one of a number of similarities between our passage and 1:21–28: in both the possessed man appears suddenly, is termed "a man in an unclean spirit," asks "what do I/we have in common with you, Jesus?," and goes on to refer to Jesus with a title that uses the genitive "of God." Moreover, as the exorcism in chapter 1 was placed in a cosmic context by the preceding description of Jesus' struggle with Satan (1:12–13), so the present exorcism is placed in a cosmic context by the preceding description of Jesus' godlike conquest of the demonic sea (4:35–41). Thus it is hardly accidental that, just as the first narrative in Jesus' public ministry in a Jewish region was a description of an exorcism, so is the first narrative of his ministry outside of Palestine (see D. Schmidt, 72). For Mark Jesus' exorcisms are the essence of his ministry (see the introduction to the COMMENT on 1:21–28).

The terrible plight of this particular demoniac is brought out by the description of his condition in 5:3–5, which as Nineham (150) notes is given in unusual detail. He lives in a deserted, unclean place, among the graves; no one can chain or tame him; he spends night and day howling through the tombs and the hills and cutting himself with stones. The overall impression is of a person who has lost control of himself and is at the mercy of destructive outside forces; his neighbors, too, are totally unable to help him. Mark underlines this incapacity by the striking pileup of negatives in 5:3b, which might literally be translated "and not with a chain no longer could nobody tie him up" (cf. Porter, *Idioms*, 284), and by the awkward use of the passive voice in 5:4 (see the NOTE on "had been torn apart by him . . . had been smashed"). The motif of human incapacity is then driven home by another negative statement, "and no one had the power to subdue him" (5:4 end), which is linguistically and thematically reminiscent of the Strong Man parable in 3:27 and thus suggests that the ultimate source of the man's bondage is Satan himself (see the NOTE on "no one had the power to subdue him" in 5:4).

Besides stressing the magnitude of the power that possesses the man, 5:3–5 also emphasizes its malevolent destructiveness. This is most obvious from the description of the demoniac shrieking and cutting himself with stones, but it is also aided by the depiction of his alienation from other human beings, whose only response to his plight is to try to chain him up; of his sleeplessness; and of his forced inhabitation in terrifyingly desolate places where no sane person would choose to live. His dwelling among tombs, moreover, suggests that his demons are impelling him toward death, as will become clear when they enter the pigs and drive them over a cliff; as is typical of sadistic tormentors, however, they prefer to keep the man alive for further torture rather than to kill him outright.

There is thus an element of burlesque comedy when the demons, as part of their negotiations with Jesus, plead with him not to torment them and back up this plea by invoking God himself (5:7 end). Very religious demons indeed, and very brazen, to plead for mercy when they have shown none; like typical bullies, they can dish it out but can't take it. Their absurd plea for mercy is accompanied by the demoniac's running forward, throwing himself on the ground before Jesus, and asking what he, "Son of the Most High God," can have to do with a demon. These actions and words suggest a curious and somewhat eerie mixture of avoidance and attraction. Despite the demoniac's plea for mercy, he does not adopt the obvious expedient of avoiding Jesus but instead seems to seek him out; yet when he addresses Jesus he pleads with him to leave him alone. Is the demoniac's approach and obeisance an indication that, at some level, the lost human being trapped inside the destructive forces is still aware of his plight and wants to be liberated (cf. Derrett, "Spirit-Possession," 290)? Or do the demons experience a "fatal attraction" for their eschatological destroyer? Or are they, with the cunning servility of a Uriah Heep, prudently acknowledging the superior force of their opponent while casting about for a way to outwit and defraud him? Perhaps all three elements are present, corresponding to the divided nature of "a man in an unclean spirit" and the demons' typical combination of slyness and stupidity (cf. the COMMENT on 1:23–26 and 1 Cor 2:6).

In any event, as Derrett has correctly emphasized ("Spirit-Possession"), 5:7–13a is the sort of bargaining session that is typical of encounters between exorcists and demons. The first move initially seems to be that of the demons, who try to ward off Jesus' anticipated assault with defensive measures by putting forth a leader who not only invokes God and pleads for mercy but also attempts to weaken Jesus by making a magical use of his name and honorific title, "Jesus, Son of the Most High God" (5:7; see the NOTE on "What is your name?" in 5:9). The title itself, however, suggests Jesus' unlimited power (see the NOTE on "Son of the Most High God" in 5:7) and thus foreshadows the successful conclusion of the exorcism, in which Jesus will do what no human has been able to accomplish (cf. the reference to 2 Sam 22:14–18 in the NOTE on "Son of the Most High God" in 5:7). Mark, moreover, reinforces this emphasis on Jesus' sovereignty by immediately correcting the pre-Markan story's impression that the demon had made the first move; rather, Mark suggests by means of a redactional insertion (5:8), Jesus inaugurated the encounter by telling the spirit to come out.

Jesus now presses his advantage home by reversing the "hold" that the demon had attempted to secure over him by asking it *its* name (5:9); the demon replies, seemingly without attempting to resist (resistance would be futile), "Legion, for we are many." This name and its interpretation emphasize the sheer magnitude of the Satanic force with which Jesus is confronted and which he successfully vanquishes; if at the climax of the story the evil spirits occupying the man transfer themselves into two thousand pigs and drive them to their deaths, the conqueror of such a prodigious force must be powerful indeed. This point is reinforced in the next verse, in which the word *polloi* ("many") is deliberately repeated when the demons beg Jesus *polla* ("greatly"); the repetition suggests that, although the demons are so numerous, they are no match for Jesus, but are reduced to desperate pleading.

The demons' self-identification may also have a political nuance, since "legion" was a Latin military term (see the NOTE on "Legion" in 5:9), and the narrative may have originally been a satire on the Roman military presence in the east. The demonic, unclean Romans, like imperialists everywhere, do not want to be dislodged from the land they have occupied (5:10), and "the story symbolically satisfies the desire to drive them into the sea like pigs" (Theissen, 255–56). This interpretation is aided by the fact that the wild boar was the emblem of the Roman legion stationed in Palestine, and Jewish sources as old as *1 Enoch* 89:12 identify the boar with Esau, who became a symbol of Rome (see Ginzberg, 5.294 n. 28). As Myers points out (*Binding*, 192–94), the narrative thus reflects the connection between Roman imperialism and what Frantz Fanon called the "colonization of the mind" of subjugated peoples, and the exorcism story points toward the longed-for expulsion of the Roman power; as happens elsewhere in apocalyptic movements, the liberation of the possessed becomes a symbol for the anticipated redemption of the world (see Clark, *Thinking*, 420). It is not clear if Mark himself is a party to such anti-Roman sentiments, but the portrayal of Jesus as the conqueror of a legion of demonic foes fits into the overall Markan concept of the Messiah as God's holy warrior.

5:11–13: the transfer of the demons to the pigs. This concept continues to dominate the next section of the story, which describes the transfer of the legion of demons into a herd of pigs and their stampede to death. As Derrett notes ("Contributions," 5–6), several of the verbs used here have a martial nuance (*pempein* ["send"], *epitrepein* ["permit," "command"], and *hōrman* ["rush headlong"]). Even the sexual innuendo in "so that we may enter them" (see the NOTE on this phrase in 5:12) is compatible with this military interpretation, since ancient armies, like modern ones, were famous for rape (see Brownmiller, *Against*, 31–113).

Realizing that, despite their huge numbers, they are hopelessly outmatched by Jesus, the demons next try to negotiate a way out of their predicament by pleading with him to allow them to enter the pigs (5:12). Jesus gives them leave (5:13a), and it seems for a moment that the two parties have come to a mutually amicable agreement; the demons will leave the man, as Jesus wants, but they will not have to leave the Gerasene "land," as they want. But the comedy concludes when the demons, upon entering the pigs, find themselves incapable of controlling them and send them careening over a cliff into the sea (5:13b). This gruesomely funny conclusion emphasizes the destructiveness of the demons as well as their shortsightedness: incapable of restraining their brutal rage, they unintentionally destroy their new lodgings and so thwart their own desire to stay on Gerasene soil (5:10). Jesus has outwitted them; like Pharaoh's army, they, or rather their swinish hosts, have met a watery death through God's will and the mediation of his human agent.

5:14–17: the townspeople's reaction. Yet the expulsion of the spirits from the possessed man does not mean the end of demonic opposition to Jesus; it now resurfaces, but in a subtler form. The pig herders flee before the manifestation of God's dominion, going into the town and spreading the news of the miracle. The townspeople come out to see for themselves, and having observed the cured man, they are overcome with fear. In the pre-Markan story this was probably the sort of praiseworthy awe that is a standard part of the conclusions of miracle stories; in Mark, however, it has become a culpable fear that causes the townspeople to drive Jesus from their shores (see the NOTE on "they were afraid" in 5:15). This negative reaction is not exactly what one would expect from the narrative so far, from previous reactions of Markan crowds to Jesus' miracles (1:28; 2:12) or from parallel miracle stories elsewhere (see the NOTE on "the townspeople began to plead with him to go away from their region" in 5:17). It is probably related to the developing Gospel theme of opposition to Jesus and is not accidentally placed after the sentence of blindness in 4:11–12 has been pronounced. It also probably relates to the rejection experienced by

Mark's own community. The members of that community know firsthand that the marvels Jesus performs on behalf of suffering humanity sometimes lead, paradoxically, to persecution for the sake of his name.

In the Markan form of the story, which has been shaped by this experience of persecution, the reaction of the hostile townspeople to Jesus mirrors that of the demons in a remarkable way. Like the demons, they are initially drawn to Jesus, almost against their will (5:6, 14–15). Like the demons, however, their overriding reaction is one of fear (5:7, 15 end), which causes them to plead (*parakalein*) that Jesus depart or leave them alone (5:7, 10, 17). The demons desire to stay in possession of the territory (5:10), and so their human agents evict Jesus from it (5:17). As often in Mark, then, the human opposition to Jesus reflects the demonic one, which is implied to be its source (see the introduction to 2:1–3:6). Though the demons have been bested in their direct encounter with Jesus, they, or their relatives, seem to have succeeded in a subtle counterattack. This feature of the story, too, would probably reverberate with the Markan community's experience; some at least of their missionary failures result not from faulty evangelistic techniques but from the fact that Satan swoops down and takes away the sown word before it can take root (cf. 4:15).

5:18–20: the making of a missionary. Jesus' rejection by the Gerasenes is not the last word in our story, just as the fruitlessness of the sown seed is not the last word in the Parable of the Sower (cf. 4:20) or, presumably, in the Markan situation. As opposed to the townspeople's plea for Jesus to depart and leave them alone, the former demoniac pleads (again *parakalein*) "that he might be with him" (5:18), an obvious echo of 3:14. This man, then, wishes to be a disciple of Jesus.

Jesus, however, refuses his request (5:19); it is interesting that this refusal contrasts not only with Jesus' assent to the request of the townspeople that he depart (5:17) but also with his acquiescence to the plea of the demons that they be allowed to depart (5:12–13). It is not necessarily a sign of grace, then, but may be the opposite, when Jesus accedes to a request, and it is not necessarily a sign of divine disapproval, but may be the opposite, when he refuses one. In this particular case Jesus does not consent that the man should be numbered among the Twelve, the constant companions of his earthly ministry, who are destined to become the initial witnesses of his resurrection (16:7; cf. Schmahl, *Zwölf*, 56–57). Rather, he commissions him for a task more suited to his own situation: to return to his home and his own people and to proclaim to them from his own experience the great things the Lord has done (5:19).

Those people are, presumably, Gentiles like the former demoniac himself (see again the NOTE on "a man in an unclean spirit" in 5:2), and his announcement of Jesus' mighty act on his behalf becomes for Mark the first proclamation of the good news about Jesus on Gentile soil and an anticipation of the spread of the gospel into the wider world after Easter (see 13:10). It thus symbolizes a significant transition in Christian history, and this may help to explain Jesus' command that the man not follow him back to Palestine but stay in his own Gentile region (see R. Lightfoot, *History*, 89–90). It may also illuminate the story's replacement of the injunction to secrecy that prevailed in the previous section of the Gospel (cf. 1:25, 34, 44; 3:12) with a direction to tell the news (see D. Schmidt, 74): the "messianic secret" is broken because the story points toward the post-Easter period of open revelation.

The Markan wording for the man's fulfillment of his commission also suggests post-Easter realities. Verse 5:20 is significantly different from the phrasing of the commission itself in 5:19, where Jesus tells the man to spread the news about what great things *the Lord* has done for him. The man, on the contrary, proclaims what great things *Jesus* has done for him. This alteration of the object of proclamation from "the Lord" to "Jesus" expresses an important Markan insight about the role and identity of Jesus in relation to God: where Jesus acts, there God is acting. This does not mean that, for Mark, Jesus *is* God (cf. 10:18; 12:35–37; 13:32), but neither can the two be absolutely separated (see the COMMENT on 1:1–3). As R. Lightfoot puts it, in Mark's view the benefits of Israel's God are conferred through Jesus; "therefore the God of Israel is glorified, when Jesus is proclaimed" (*History*, 90). The conclusion of the pericope, then, gives added force to the demon's earlier acclamation of Jesus as the Son of God Most High.

Thus Jesus' initial rejection in Gerasa does not stop the good news from going forth and electrifying the countryside; the last words of the passage are "everybody was amazed" (5:20). The story as a whole, then, illustrates the Gospel's theology of the cross, as experienced within the Markan community: the advent of God's eschatological healing power provokes a vicious counterattack, but even this counterattack ultimately serves God's cause by providing an arena for his grace to manifest itself in the midst of persecutions (cf. 10:30). Just as the hostility of Pharaoh did not thwart God but actually furthered the announcement of his glory in all the earth (Exod 9:16), so the hostility of the demons and of demon-inspired people has not impeded the proclamation of the great things God has done through his eschatological agent, Jesus.

In the next passage, in which a dead girl will be raised to life, it will become clear just how amazing, just how discontinuous with the sad, predictable course of affairs in the dying old world, is the eschatological power of the rejected Jesus—a power still coursing through the persecuted Markan community.

JESUS HEALS A WOMAN AND RAISES A GIRL TO LIFE (5:21–43)

5 [21]And when Jesus had again crossed over to the other side, a great crowd gathered together around him, and he was beside the sea. [22]And there came one of the rulers of the synagogue, whose name was Jairus, and seeing him he

fell at his feet [23]and pleaded with him urgently, saying, "My little daughter is about to die; come and lay your hands on her, so that she'll be cured and start to live again." [24]And he went off with him, and a great crowd followed him and was pressing against him.

[25]And a woman who had a flow of blood for twelve years, [26]and had suffered many treatments from many doctors, and had spent all her money on them and hadn't benefited a bit but had rather gotten worse, [27]heard about Jesus and came behind him in the crowd and touched his garment. [28]For she said, "Even if I just touch his clothes, I'll be cured." [29]And immediately the fountain of her blood dried up and she knew in her body that she had been healed of her scourge. [30]But immediately Jesus, knowing in himself that power had gone out of him, turned in the crowd and said, "Who touched my clothes?" [31]And his disciples said to him, "You see this crowd pressing against you and you say, 'Who touched me?'" [32]But he continued looking around to see the woman who had done this. [33]And the woman, fearing and trembling, knowing what had happened to her, came and fell down before him and told him the whole truth. [34]And he said to her, "Daughter, your faith has saved you. Go in peace and be well from your scourge."

[35]While he was still speaking some people came from the house of the synagogue ruler saying, "Your daughter has died. Why bother the teacher any more?" [36]But Jesus, ignoring what had been said, said to the synagogue ruler, "Don't be afraid, just keep on believing." [37]And he didn't let anyone follow him except Peter and James and John, James' brother. [38]And they went into the house of the synagogue ruler, and he saw the commotion made by the people weeping and wailing loudly, [39]and as he entered he said to them, "Why are you making a commotion and weeping? The child hasn't died but is sleeping." [40]And they laughed at him. But he, throwing them all out, took with him the father of the child and the mother and his companions and went in where the child was. [41]And taking the child's hand he said to her, "*Talitha koum*," which is translated, "Girl, I say to you: Rise!" [42]And immediately the girl arose and began walking around—for she was twelve years old. And immediately they were greatly amazed. [43]And he commanded them urgently that no one should know this, and said that she should be given something to eat.

NOTES

5 22. *one of the rulers of the synagogue*. Gk *heis tōn archisynagōgōn*. The *archisynagōgos* did not have the plethora of jobs associated with a modern-day rabbi but was simply the leader of worship services (see Schürer, 2.432–36). There might be more than one at a single synagogue (see Acts 13:15), but Mark's phrase *"one of the . . . "* may also be intended to emphasize that not all of the Jewish authorities were opposed to Jesus (cf. Nineham, 157). This is similar to the point made by the phrase "one of the scribes" in 12:28–34 and the reverse of the point made by the reference to Judas as "one of the Twelve"

in 14:10, 43: among Jesus' intimate companions there was one who betrayed him, but among the Jewish authorities there was one, a sympathetic scribe, who praised him and another, Jairus, who threw himself at his feet and begged for his help.

Jairus. Gk *Iairos.* Most of Mark's minor characters, including the two females healed in our story, are anonymous. The inclusion of Jairus' name, therefore, may mean that it is significant; it could be the Greek transliteration either of *Yāʾîr* = "he enlightens" or of *Yaʿîr* = "he awakens" (see Guelich, 295). Either name would be appropriate for Jairus, since his *seeing* of Jesus is emphasized in our verse, and Jesus "awakens" his daughter from the sleep of death in 5:39–43.

23. *is about to die.* Gk *eschatōs echei,* an idiomatic expression close to the Latin *in extremis* and meaning literally "has it terminally."

come and lay your hands on her. Gk *hina elthōn epithēs tas cheiras autē̦,* lit. "in order that coming you may lay your hands on her," but the *hina* + second-person construction is probably imperatival, as in 10:51 and 12:19 (cf. Rochais, *Récits,* 58). There is a close parallel to this request, as well as to the description a few verses later of the woman with the flow of blood, in the *Genesis Apocryphon* from Qumran:

Mark 5:23, 26	Genesis Apocryphon 20:20–22
Jairus asks Jesus to come and lay his hands on his daughter, "so that she'll be cured and start to live"	Pharaoh's friend asks Abraham to come and pray for Pharaoh, "and lay my hands upon him so that he would live"
The woman with the flow of blood has "suffered many treatments from many doctors, . . . and hadn't benefited a bit but had rather gotten worse"	All his doctors and wizards were unable to heal Pharaoh

Fitzmyer notes (*Genesis Apocryphon,* 140) that the *Genesis Apocryphon* passage is the first attestation of a Jewish rite of healing by the laying on of hands, but he also notes a Markan difference from the *Apocryphon:* neither here nor in any of the other NT passages in which Jesus lays hands on people does he pray over them.

be cured. Gk *sōthē̦,* lit. "be saved." The same verb is used in 5:28, where it is translated in the same way, and in 5:34, where it is translated literally. The root meaning of *sō̦zein* is deliverance from danger or suffering; in our passage, as frequently in the larger Greco-Roman world, it means release from chronic or life-threatening illness, sometimes by miraculous means, and can simply be translated "cure" (see Foerster and Fohrer, "*Sō̦zō*"). In Jewish contexts, however, the term and its various Hebrew counterparts often have a wider horizon, connoting a deliverance not only of individuals but of the elect people as a whole; it is frequently stressed that only God can accomplish this deliverance (see e.g. Ps 44:1–8; Isa 43:11; 45:21; 63:9; Hos 14:3). In proto-apocalyptic and apocalyptic literature, this salvation becomes an eschatological event that ushers in a new age in which all threats are removed (e.g. Isa 45:22; Tob 14:7 א; 1QM 4:13 and frequently in the Dead Sea Scrolls). These eschatological connotations characterize the use of the term elsewhere in Mark (8:35; 10:26; 13:13, 20).

start to live again. Gk *zēsē̦*, lit. "live." Some have taken "be cured and live" as a hendiadys (see GLOSSARY), but Rochais (*Récits*, 59) cogently argues that the words have distinct nuances and that the aorist *zēsē̦* is inceptive: the father asks for healing for his daughter because she has her whole life in front of her.

25. *a woman who had a flow of blood.* Gk *gynē ousa en rhysei haimatos*, lit. "a woman being in a flow of blood"; cf. the similar construction "a man in an unclean spirit" in 1:23; 5:2, though there the expression should be taken more literally (see the NOTE on "in" in 1:23). The woman's bleeding is probably vaginal; if it had been, say, "a little bleeding at the nose" (cf. van der Loos, *Miracles*, 510 n. 1), Mark would not have been so shy about specifying its location. Moreover, the linguistic background for the present phrase and for "the fountain of her blood" in 5:29 lies in statutes in Leviticus regarding the ritual uncleanness incurred by the menstruant (*niddâ*) and the woman with a vaginal discharge outside of her period (*zābâ*, lit. "oozer"; see Lev 12:7; 15:19–33; 20:18; cf. Selvidge, "Mark 5:25–34," and S. Cohen, "Menstruants"); the Mishnah has a tractate devoted to each, with the *zābâ* being treated along with her male counterpart. As Cohen points out ("Menstruants," 288–89), two third-century Christian documents, the *Epistle to Basilides* of Dionysius of Alexandria (chapter 2) and the *Didascalia Apostolorum* (chapter 26), confirm this diagnosis by treating the woman as akin to a menstruant. It is impossible to be certain whether the woman's ailment is an abnormally heavy monthly flow (menorrhagia) or a chronic light hemorrhage (see van der Loos, *Miracles*, 509–10; Gundry, 279), but in view of the narrative's emphasis on her immediate knowledge of the cure (5:29), a chronic condition is more likely; she is therefore, in Jewish terms, a *zābâ* (see Cohen, "Menstruants," 278–81).

As a *zābâ* the woman would probably have been quarantined, since *zābôt* and *niddôt* seem to have been treated in this way in Second Temple and later Judaism (see e.g. 11QTemple 45:7–17; 46:16–18; 48:14–17; Josephus *Ant.* 3.261; *m. Nid.* 7:4; cf. Milgrom, *Leviticus*, 1.765). Cohen, to be sure, argues that the quarantine of *zābôt* and *niddôt* began only in the sixth or seventh century, when it is attested in the *Beraita de Nidda*; he cites our passage in support of this argument, since the story does not indicate that the woman, though clearly a *zābâ*, is regarded as impure or suffers isolation. The surreptitiousness of the woman's approach to Jesus, however, is probably an indirect indication that she is ritually unclean and is violating a taboo by being out in public; Cohen can make his case, moreover, only by dismissing the passages from the Temple Scroll as utopian, deemphasizing *m. Nid.* 7:4, and virtually ignoring *Ant.* 3.261. Furthermore, as he notes with surprise, Dionysius and

the *Didascalia* were already debating during the third century whether or not
menstruating women should be kept out of church, at least three centuries
before the *Beraita de Nidda*; the most logical explanation of this debate is that
the Christian authors disagreed about whether or not Old Testament/Jewish
law was binding on Christians, as Cohen himself states (290). But if that is the
case, it is likely that the debate reflects actual Jewish practices.

As in many other ancient and modern societies, such restrictions on bleeding
women were based on the fear generated by the belief that blood contains life
(see Lev 17:10–14; Deut 12:23); in *b. Pesaḥ.* 111a the opinion is even expressed
that proximity to a menstruating woman can cause death, and similar appre-
hensions were current in the non-Jewish world, even among educated people
(e.g. Pliny *Natural History* 7.64; cf. Theissen, 134). A less drastic possible consequence of contact with a menstruant, but one that is relevant for our story, is
that it might cancel a charismatic individual's miraculous power; cf. the deliberately exaggerated story in *Hekhalot Rabbati* 18 (third–fourth century C.E.), in
which a rabbi on a heavenly tour, and thus engaged in "magic," is immediately
brought down to earth by another rabbi placing on his knees a piece of wool
that had been touched very slightly by a menstruating woman who had been
declared pure by a majority of the rabbinical court (cf. Scholem, *Gnosticism*,
10–12; Gruenwald, *Apocalyptic*, 164)!

In Jewish sources menstruation is sometimes viewed as a curse for Eve's sin;
like the other judgments on Adam and Eve, however, it will be removed in the
age to come (*b. 'Erub.* 100b; *'Abot R. Nat.* 42 [B]; *Tanḥuma* on Lev 15:25; cf.
Ezek 36:16, 25; *Gen. Rab.* 20.5).

26. *had suffered many treatments from many doctors.* Gk *polla pathousa
hypo pollōn hiatrōn.* This is an ironic comment, since doctors are supposed to
alleviate suffering, not increase it. As Lohmeyer (101) points out, attitudes toward doctors in ancient Jewish and Christian sources vary, from high praise
(e.g. Sir 38:1–15) to mockery or scathing criticism (*m. Qidd.* 4:14 even says
that the best doctor is worthy of hell!). Mark leans toward the negative end of
this spectrum. His remark that the woman has not benefited from the doctors
is similar to Tob 2:10 and *1QapGen* 20:20 (cf. Pesch, 1.302 n. 22; on the latter
passage, see the NOTE on "come and lay your hands on her" in 5:23). The remark that the woman has only gotten worse due to the doctors' ministrations,
however, is not just a literary trope; a glance through *b. Šabb.* 110ab will
make clear that some ancient treatments for menstrual disorders were of the
sort that were as likely to harm as to help the patient (e.g. frightening her or
feeding her grain found in a mule's dung).

27. *heard about Jesus.* Gk *akousasa peri tou Iēsou.* That the woman only
hears about Jesus, whereas Jairus *sees* him (5:22), may reflect her ostracism
from society because of ritual impurity (see the NOTE on "a woman who had
a flow of blood" in 5:25).

touched his garment. Gk *hēpsato tou himatiou autou.* Freedman intriguingly
suggests that the woman touches only Jesus' garment in order to avoid passing

her ritual impurity on to him (cf. the NOTE on "a woman who had a flow of blood" in 5:25). But although impurity contracted through contact with clothes is less serious than impurity contracted through contact with flesh (see Lev 15:7 and cf. Milgrom, *Leviticus*, 1.914), it is still defiling; otherwise the instruction to wash one's clothes would be senseless (Lev 15:11, 21–22, etc.; cf. *m. Kelim* 27–28 on the impurity of clothes).

28. *Even if I just touch his clothes, I'll be cured.* Gk *ean hapsōmai kan tōn himatiōn autou sōthēsomai.* For belief in the power of magicians to stop abnormal vaginal bleeding, cf. the Jewish magical spell "for menstruation, that it should cease" in Geniza 23.2.5–11 (Naveh and Shaked, *Magic Spells*, 220–21). The idea of the healing effect of contact with a holy man's garments, even without his conscious intention, is repeated in 6:56 and extended in Acts 19:12, where handkerchiefs and aprons taken from Paul's body have the power to heal. These passages seem to presuppose that there is a sort of power resident in the holy person's body that can be stored, tapped, or even transferred to other physical objects (see Davies and Allison, 2.129). The germ of such ideas is already present in the Old Testament, as Gundry (280) points out; in 2 Kgs 13:20–21, for example, a corpse that is cast into Elisha's tomb miraculously revives when it touches his bones, and in Exod 17:11–12 the position of Moses' hands determines whether or not the Israelites prevail in battle. But in our passage the idea has been extended from the holy person's body to his garments.

29. *scourge.* Gk *mastix*, literally a whip, but the term can be used figuratively for the lashing of disease.

31. *You see*, etc. Gk *blepeis* etc. Lane (193) is eager to excuse the disciples' apparent impertinence; their retort "reflects an awareness that their immediate mission was to assist a girl who was dying, and delay could be fatal." The disciples' words, however, do not focus on the problems that delay might cause but on the impossibility of locating the person who has touched Jesus in the huge crowd. If anything, their response reflects the theme of their incomprehension, which will become increasingly important in this section of the Gospel (6:52; 7:18; 8:4, 14–21).

32. *continued looking around to see the woman who had done this.* Gk *perieblepeto idein tēn touto poiēsēsan.* The last three words literally mean "the one having done this," but the definite article is feminine. Lane (193 n. 50) argues that the gender is related from the narrator's perspective, not Jesus'. But since elsewhere in Mark Jesus is assumed to be clairvoyant (e.g. 2:8; 3:5; 5:30; 8:17), and since this clairvoyance is linked with verbs of seeing (2:5; 6:48; 12:15), it is better to conclude that the emphasized expression "continued looking around to see" is another example of the supernaturally penetrating gaze of Jesus, and that for Mark Jesus does indeed know the gender of his accoster.

33. *fearing and trembling.* Gk *phobētheisa kai tremousa.* As Lohmeyer (130) points out, this reaction is natural in the situation, but fear is also the standard biblical response to a theophany (an appearance of God) from Genesis onward

(e.g. Gen 15:12; 28:17; Judg 6:22–23). The combination "fear and trembling" occurs in a theophanic context in 4 Macc 4:10; and in Phil 2:12, which implies the presence of God in the Christian community, the phrase is linked with salvation, as in our passage.

the whole truth. Gk *pasan tēn alētheian*. This phrase is at home in judicial proceedings, just as today witnesses are sworn to tell "the truth, the whole truth, and nothing but the truth"; our exact phrase occurs in trial settings in Isocrates *Antidosis* 50; Plato *Apology* 17b; and Lycurgus *Leocrates* 32 (cf. also Josephus *J.W.* 7.31). The last two passages are particularly significant, since the *Apology* is the defense speech of Socrates, the prototypical martyr for the truth, and the passage from Lycurgus concerns judicial inquiry to establish by torture the facts of a case. These judicial and martyrological resonances may be important for the usage of the phrase in our story (see the COMMENT on 5:25–34).

34. *Daughter.* Gk *thygatēr*. The woman is not related to Jesus, and she is not necessarily younger than him; in the OT and later Jewish traditions "my daughter" is a typical respectful and affectionate mode of address to females regardless of age or family relationship (see e.g. Ruth 2:8; 3:10). But for Mark's readers Jesus' address to the woman may also involve the concept of the Christian community as a new family (cf. 10:29–30 and see the COMMENT on 5:25–34).

your faith has saved you. Gk *hē pistis sou sesōken se*. *Pistis*, "faith," implies not just intellectual assent but emotional involvement and commitment and is sometimes better translated by "trust." The formula "your faith has saved you" occurs here and in Jesus' address to blind Bartimaeus in 10:52; Luke also includes it in two non-Markan stories (Luke 7:50; 17:19). Marshall (*Faith*, 108) is probably right that for Mark the question "Faith in Jesus or faith in God?" is a false dichotomy; the woman, and Jairus in 5:36, have faith both in God and in Jesus, for they rely on the power of God working through Jesus.

In the Greco-Roman world it is common for healing miracles to be linked with faith, as for example in Lucian of Samosata *False Philosopher* 13: "You presumably do not believe (*pisteuein*) in the gods either, if you really think that healings cannot be brought about through sacred names." There is also, however, a *difference* between the motif of faith/belief in the Synoptics and in other Hellenistic stories of healing miracles (including those in the Fourth Gospel): in the latter, faith does not lead to miracles, but the other way around (see John 1:50; 2:11, etc. and cf. Theissen, 130–32, 140). On the other hand, in Hellenistic passages in which people are exhorted to take courage, hope, etc. as a necessary condition for cure by the gods, the language of faith/ trust is not used. Neither are there exact Jewish parallels to the idea of saving faith. The closest approach comes in apocalyptic and proto-apocalyptic traditions, where people are exhorted to trust or have faith, and promised that if they do so they will be rescued from dangers (see e.g. Isa 28:16; Hab 2:4); here, however, the language of salvation is not used. Later in our own Gospel, in a similarly apocalyptic context, Jesus will speak of being saved but not of faith, though the necessity of faithfulness will be implied: "He who endures to the end will be saved" (13:13).

Where one *does* find the idea of saving faith explicitly mentioned is in early Christian texts, particularly in the Pauline and Deutero-Pauline correspondence (Rom 1:16; 10:9–10; 1 Cor 1:21; Eph 1:13; 2:8; 2 Tim 3:15) and in Luke-Acts (Luke 8:12, 50; Acts 14:9; 15:11; 16:31); see also 1 Pet 1:5, 9; Jas 2:14; 5:15; Heb 11:7, and the inauthentic Mark 16:16. This evidence points toward the idea of saving faith being rooted more in the life of the early Christian church than in the ministry of the historical Jesus. "Your faith has saved you" may, as a matter of fact, be a baptismal formula, as Braumann ("Schuldner," 490) and Wilckens ("Vergebung," 418–22) have argued. One of the passages linking salvation and faith mentions baptism (Mark 16:16), another has frequently been identified as a baptismal confession (Rom 10:9–10), and several others have clear baptismal associations (Luke 7:50; Acts 17:31; Eph 1:13; Heb 11:7). This baptismal interpretation of the formula is also supported by its use in later church history; both Tertullian (*On Baptism* 12:8) and Cyprian (*Treatise on Re-baptism* 18) cite it in the context of discussions of baptism.

Go in peace. Gk *hypage eis eirēnēn*, lit. "go into peace," a literal translation of the Hebrew *saʿ lĕšālôm*, which is a traditional OT and Jewish departure formula (Judg 18:6 etc.) subsequently taken up by the early church (Acts 16:36; Jas 2:16). But in the eschatological Markan context this ordinary greeting would take on added dimensions; the *eis* = "into" is construed more literally and the formula becomes an invitation to the woman to depart into the fullness of well-being, the *šālôm*, associated with the new age (cf. Foerster, "*Eirēnē*," 405–8, 412–15).

be well from your scourge. Gk *isthi hygiēs apo tēs mastigos sou*. Some scholars think that this promise has been introduced secondarily, since it comes awkwardly late in the story, *after* the woman has been cured; C. F. Evans (*Luke*, 391), for example, suggests that it has been inserted to qualify the original story's impression of "automatic healing." But the words may express the wish that the woman may *remain* free of the affliction from which she has just been freed; it would then correspond to Jesus' later command that an exorcised spirit never return to its former host (cf. 9:25).

35. *the house of the synagogue ruler.* Gk *apo tou archisynagōgou*. In Greek the word "house" is absent, but the use of a genitive to indicate "the house of" is a Greek idiom (see Robertson, 502).

saying. Gk *legontes hoti*, lit. "saying that," but as the *hoti* introduces direct discourse, it is not translated. This "*hoti* recitative" is quite characteristic of Koine Greek (see the NOTE on "and saying" in 1:15) and has already occurred previously in our passage, in 5:23; cf. the COMMENT on 5:35–43.

Your daughter has died. Gk *hē thygatēr sou apethanen*. While Jesus has been healing and conversing with the woman, Jairus' daughter has died. It is interesting that, in the Lazarus story in John 11, which is parallel in general theme and vocabulary to the story of the girl's resuscitation (sleep, awakening, resuscitation of a dead person), there is a similar element of delay: Jesus deliberately waits two days after hearing that Lazarus is ill, thus allowing him time to die.

36. *ignoring.* Gk *parakousas.* This verb has three basic meanings: (1) overhear, (2) ignore, and (3) disobey (BAGD, 619). Either of the first two is possible here, but as Guelich (291) notes, all seven LXX instances and the only other NT one (Matt 18:17) mean "ignore." This meaning is also consonant with the emphasis on faith in the passage, since in Jairus' case faith means ignoring the reality of death to cling to Jesus' promise of resurrection (on the resurrection language in our passage, see the COMMENT on 5:35–43).

Don't be afraid. Gk *mē phobou.* It is possible that the negated present imperative implies that Jairus has already begun to be anxious (see the next NOTE)—as would only be natural (see Rochais, *Récits*, 62).

keep on believing. Gk *pisteue*, a present imperative. The present imperative implies linearity, and a plausible interpretation of this element is that Jairus has already displayed faith in his initial approach to Jesus and is now urged to maintain that trust even in the face of death (see Marshall, *Faith*, 95–96).

38. *he saw.* Gk *theōrei.* As Rochais notes (*Récits*, 64), the singular verb is surprising after the plural "they went." It may reflect an earlier version of the story in which Jesus was unaccompanied by disciples (see the introduction to the COMMENT). It also makes sense, however, as part of the general emphasis in the passage on Jesus' perception (see the COMMENT on 5:25–34).

the commotion made by the people weeping and wailing loudly. Gk *thorybon kai klaiontas kai alalazontas polla*, lit. "commotion and people weeping and wailing greatly." These are probably professional mourners rather than friends and relatives of the dead girl, since Jesus throws them out but takes the parents with him when he goes in to heal her (5:40).

39. *hasn't died but is sleeping.* Gk *ouk apethanen alla katheudei.* Rationalistic critics in the nineteenth and twentieth centuries seized on this declaration in support of their theory that the girl was in a coma, so that Jesus' subsequent resuscitation of her was plausible and supernatural agency did not need to be invoked (see Strauss, *Life*, 478–79, for a sampling of such explanations). Possible support for this position is provided by *Life of Apollonius of Tyana* 4.45, in which the biographer Philostratus leaves open the possibility that a girl seemingly raised from the dead by Apollonius was still alive, though the doctors declared her dead (see the NOTE on "*Talitha koum*" in 5:41). But the miraculous element is impossible to eliminate completely from our story; even if the girl were in a coma, it would still be a miracle that Jesus knew in advance that she would be healed. Moreover, Jesus' statement that she is not dead but sleeping is probably not a reference to a comatose state but a usage of the common biblical and Jewish metaphor of death as a form of sleep (cf. the usage of this same metaphor in the story of Lazarus in John 11:5–16 and see again the COMMENT on 5:35–43).

40. *went in where the child was.* Gk *eisporeuontai hopou ēn to paidion.* The existence of a separate bedroom is testimony to Jairus' wealth; most Palestinian dwellings from this time were poor, one-room affairs (cf. Marshall, *Faith*, 95).

41. *Talitha koum.* The retention of Aramaic here is partly for effect: the exotic foreign words increase the sense of mystery about the miracle that is about to occur. Cf. Lucian of Samosata's reference to the tendency of faith healers to use *rhēsis barbarikē,* "foreign language" (*False Philosopher* 9). The only other healing story in which Jesus' words are rendered in Aramaic is the narrative about the deaf-mute in 7:31–37; in both cases, as Mussies ("Use," 427) points out, the Aramaic words are the verbal counterpart to the non-verbal healing action (cf. the NOTE on "Ephphatha, that is, 'Be opened!'" in 7:34), and in both cases the healing takes place in seclusion. This combination of the motifs of seclusion and mysterious words is probably not accidental; Theissen (140–42, 148–49) notes that in the magical papyri, injunctions to silence frequently occur before or after occult formulae, in order to guard their secrecy (*PGM,* 1.40, 130, 146–47, etc.). Also strikingly parallel to our narrative is Philostratus' story of the resuscitation of a dead girl by Apollonius of Tyana: "He simply touched her and said some secret words to her and woke her from seeming death" (*Life of Apollonius of Tyana* 4.45). Not only does this tale share with ours the motif of secret words, but it also includes the pattern of the healer touching a dead girl and thus "awakening" her. The combination of motifs is so close that it is hard not to agree with Pesch (1.310) that our story reproduces typical techniques of ancient faith healing. (Meier [*Marginal Jew,* 2.580] raises the possibility that Philostratus is plagiarizing the Gospels, but admits that he cannot establish the probability of this supposition.)

Rise! Gk *egeire.* On the "resurrectional" nuance of this word, see the COMMENT on 5:35–43. Jas 5:15 promises that "the prayer of faith will save the one who is sick, and the Lord will raise him up." There is a remarkable closeness here to the overall story in Mark 5:21–43: one sick person is saved (= cured) by faith, and another is raised up. As Rochais suggests (*Récits,* 60), Mark's juxtaposition of these two tales may hint that, on the way to the final "healing" of humanity at the resurrection, people already see the power of death driven back when Jesus heals them of their illnesses.

42. *they were . . . amazed.* Gk *exestēsan.* There is perhaps a deliberate half-pun between this word (which can also mean "to go out of one's mind"; see the NOTE on "He has gone out of his mind" in 3:21) and the word for "arose," *anestē.* The words sound similar and are both compounded forms of the word "to stand": the girl stands up, and this causes the onlookers to "stand outside" of their everyday reactions to events.

twelve years old. Gk *etōn dōdeka.* In the present Markan composition Jairus' daughter is linked in a strange way with the woman with the flow of blood, who has been ill for twelve years; as Bengel puts it, for these two females "the beginning of misery and the beginning of life happened at the same time" (*Gnomon* on Mark 5:42). The two stories may originally have been brought together partly because they both mentioned twelve years (see the introduction to the COMMENT).

43. *said that she should be given something to eat.* Gk *eipen dothēnai autę phagein.* Rochais (*Récits,* 70) is one of a number of commentators who thinks

that here, as in Luke 24:41–43, the meal is to prove that the girl is not a phantom. The features that make this explanation certain in the Lukan postresurrectional meal, however, are lacking here, and it is more likely that it is simply to confirm the healing and strengthen the patient who has returned from death's door.

COMMENT

Introduction. After exorcising the Gerasene demoniac, Jesus crosses back to the "Jewish" side of the Sea of Galilee, where he performs two more miracles of healing, the cure of a woman with a twelve-year "flow of blood" and the raising to life of a twelve-year-old girl, the daughter of the synagogue president, Jairus.

The story of the healing of Jairus' daughter surrounds that of the healing of the hemorrhaging woman in a typical Markan "sandwich" arrangement: the Jairus story is begun (5:21–24), interrupted by the story of the woman (5:25–34), and then concluded (5:35–43). This "sandwich" is probably a Markan creation, like similar structures elsewhere in Mark (cf. 2:1–12; 3:20–35; 6:14–29; 11:12–25; 14:1–11; 14:54–72); each story is a self-contained unit, and there are significant stylistic differences between them: the one about Jairus is composed of short sentences dominated by the historical present, whereas the one about the woman is made up of long sentences filled with participles and dominated by the aorist (see Guelich, 292). Mark may have found one or the other of the stories in the pre-Markan boat cycle, if there was such a thing (see the introduction to 3:7–6:6a), and he may have brought it together with the other narrative partly because both mentioned a time span of twelve years, partly because the intercalation of the story of the hemorrhaging woman allows time for Jairus' daughter to die (for a similar use of time in Markan "sandwiches," see 6:14–29 and 11:12–26). Mark may also be responsible for other redactional touches, such as the introduction of the disciples into the story in 5:31 and/or 5:37 (see the NOTE on "he saw" in 5:38) and the injunction to be silent in 5:43a. The latter contains typical Markan redactional vocabulary ("commanded," "stringently," "no one") and is illogical in the narrative context: how can the girl's healing remain a secret when a crowd has witnessed Jairus' request, the messengers' report that the girl has died, Jesus' encouragement to Jairus to believe in spite of her death, and his entry with Jairus into the house (see Wrede, 50–51, and Räisänen, 162)? As we will see, however, the command makes *theological* sense in the overall Markan framework.

In their present form the two stories are tied together by common vocabulary and themes (see Marshall, *Faith*, 93–94). In both, the petitioner desires "salvation" (5:23, 28, 34) and falls at Jesus' feet (5:22, 33). In both, the person healed is called a "daughter" (5:23, 34, 35); in the one case the "daughter" has been ill for twelve years, in the other she is twelve years old (5:25, 42). The condition of the two female sufferers, moreover, is similar in that both have been rendered ritually unclean, the one by a menstrual disorder, the other by death. Yet in both cases this uncleanness is boldly ignored, in the one case by the woman, who touches the garment of Jesus, in the other case by Jesus, who touches the girl's corpse. Fear, moreover, is mentioned in both healings (5:33, 36), and faith is a factor in both (5:34, 36).

5:21–24: Jairus' request. Jesus' return to Palestine from the predominantly Gentile area of the Decapolis is greeted by two of the standard characters whom he regularly encounters there: a Jewish crowd and a Jewish leader. This time, however, in contrast to the usual pattern (2:6–12; 11:18; 12:12; 14:1–2), the response of the crowd and that of the leader are not opposed to each other: the crowd flocks to Jesus (5:21), and the synagogue ruler, Jairus, impelled by the life-threatening illness of his daughter, throws himself at his feet (5:22). Thus, in spite of the general rejection that Jesus will experience in his homeland, and upon which he will comment sadly in the next passage (6:4), there is at least *one* among the Jewish elite who has been led by a combination of insight and desperation to seek his help (see the NOTE on "one of the rulers of the synagogue" in 5:22). This man, in contrast to the other Jewish leaders, really *sees* Jesus (*idōn*, 5:22)—the first instance of the language of perception that will permeate the story (see Marshall, *Faith*, 96).

Even more important to the story than Jairus' position as a Jewish leader is his position as a father, which comes to expression in his forceful ("urgently") and heart-wrenching request on behalf of "my little daughter," who, he believes, "is about to die" (5:23). This father is, as a matter of fact, the first of three parents who request healing for their children in the next few chapters of the Gospel (cf. 7:26–27; 9:17–24). As S. Anderson ("Exegetical Study," 25) points out, in all three cases the sick cannot request healing for themselves (one is near death, one is mute, and one is possessed), and in all three cases the parent perseveres in spite of the temptation to give up. This motif of parents having faith on behalf of their children may well have reminded readers in the early church of the practice of intercessory prayer.

Jairus' request expresses both the urgency of his situation and his trust in Jesus to relieve it. It is broken into three parts, each part introduced either by *hoti* (usually = "that," but here untranslated; see the NOTE on "saying" in 5:35) or by *hina* (lit. "in order that," but untranslated before "come"). The segments of the request, then, are uttered in staccato fashion, like three gasps delivered in one breath (see Marshall, *Faith*, 95). In the first segment Jairus describes the imminence of his daughter's death, a description that lends the narrative greater tension when the healing is subsequently delayed. In the second he requests Jesus' healing touch, thus prefiguring a major theme in the narrative as it unfolds (cf. 5:27, 41). In the third he expresses his confidence that Jesus can heal his daughter, that through him she may "be cured and start to live."

The word for "be cured" here is *sōthę̄*, which literally means "be saved." This language of salvation, which reappears in the story of the woman in 5:34, has both a surface meaning and a deeper theological significance. The root meaning of the verb is to rescue from danger. On the surface this means release from chronic or life-threatening illness, a common enough nuance of the term in the larger Greco-Roman world. At a deeper level, however, and in line with biblical and postbiblical Jewish expectations and with the overall Markan narrative, it means eschatological deliverance by God from the sufferings of the end-time (13:13, 20) or of the realm of the dead (8:35; 10:26; cf. the NOTE on "be saved" in 5:23 and Marshall, *Faith*, 96). It will soon become apparent that it this deeper sort of definitive, eschatological salvation that is necessary in the present situation, since Jairus' daughter is not just *in extremis* but dead.

Jesus signifies his acquiescence to Jairus' request by going with him (5:24), and the stage seems to be set for an impressive healing: the huge crowd that throngs about them will witness the girl restored to life and will praise Jesus for performing yet another miracle.

5:25–34: the healing of the woman with the hemorrhage. But before Jairus' daughter can experience "salvation," she will first experience death; and the need of another woman for cure will provide the occasion for her to do so. The rush to reach Jairus' daughter before she dies is slowed by what Marshall calls a "tormenting delay." This delay is occasioned by a woman whose dire straits are emphasized in 5:26–27 by the series of seven participles describing her condition, a sequence that "conveys to the audience the relentless compounding of the woman's need over a twelve-year period" (Marshall, *Faith*, 104).

This woman is at the opposite end of the social, economic, and religious spectrum from Jairus. While he is a male leader, she is a nameless woman; while he is a synagogue official, she is ritually unclean and thus excluded from the religious community; while he has a family and a large household, she must presumably live in isolation because of her condition; while he is rich, she is impoverished by payment of doctors' fees (Marshall, *Faith*, 97, 104). But now their fortunes seem to be suddenly reversed, for his loss of time becomes her gain: the same crowd that has slowed Jesus' progress toward his daughter's deathbed offers her the opportunity to be healed. Earlier, in 2:2–4, such a crowd was an obstacle to healing, but here it provides a chance for the woman to make contact with Jesus without being observed.

This surreptitious behavior is made necessary by her medical condition, which is apparently chronic vaginal bleeding that would render her perpetually unclean and make her a source of defilement to anyone with whom she came into physical contact, and which would thus normally prevent her from appearing in public (see the NOTE on "a woman who had a flow of blood" in 5:25). Her dilemma, therefore, is profound: according to her conception (which Jairus apparently shares: 5:23), one must come into physical contact with a healer in order to be cured by him. But she is unclean, and her touch defiles, and therefore there is a danger that any physical contact she may have with the healer will annul his miracle working power and wreck the whole effort (see again the NOTE on "a woman who had a flow of blood" in 5:25). And even if she is willing to proceed in the hope that this will not happen, how can she induce the healer to touch her and thus defile himself?

Her solution is simple but audacious: instead of asking Jesus to touch her, *she* touches *him*, before he is aware of what has happened. Indeed, the moment of contact is grammatically highlighted by the fact that the word "she touched" is the first finite verb after the series of seven participles: "And a woman *being* in a flow of blood for twelve years, and *having endured* many treatments from many doctors, and *having spent* all her money on them and not *having benefited* at all but rather *having gotten worse*, *having heard* about Jesus and *having come* behind him in the crowd, **touched** his garment." The word "touched" thus gains extraordinary intensity as the climax of the string of participles.

By making this illicit contact with Jesus, the woman in our story displays the same sort of bold, risk-taking attitude that will be shown by the Syrophoenician woman in 7:24–30. These two plucky women, the first a Jew and the second a Gentile, form a divine counterpoint to the demonic impetuosity of Herodias and Salome in the intervening story in 6:17–28, and Mark seems to have deliberately juxtaposed the four female characters in order to bring out the similarities and contrasts among them. Another and even closer parallel is with the sinful woman in Luke 7:36–50; as Wilckens ("Vergebung") points out, the motifs in the two stories are remarkably similar:

A woman hears about Jesus (Mark 5:27; Luke 7:37).

She comes to Jesus from behind and touches him (Mark 5:27; Luke 7:38–39).

She is healed/forgiven without Jesus' intention (Mark 5:29–30; Luke 7:44).

Jesus turns to look at her (Mark 5:30; Luke 7:44).

She throws herself at his feet (Mark 5:33; Luke 7:38).

He dismisses her with the words "Your faith has saved you; go in peace" (Mark 5:34; Luke 7:50).

This striking parallel makes especially relevant for our story Wilckens' conclusion that the Lukan narrative was originally a tale of conversion that was transmitted in the context of Christian baptism ("Vergebung," 421). Our story, too, would make sense in such a context, as we shall see in what follows.

The woman with the hemorrhage touches Jesus' clothing, and immediately something like an electric shock courses through her body, drying up "the fountain of her blood" (5:29). In contrast, then, to the twelve-year-long failure of the doctors, who relied on human wisdom or human sham, the divine power breaking forth from Jesus heals her on the spot. This eruption of curative energy simultaneously deals with the problem of defiling contact; as Davies and Allison put it (2.130), "Instead of uncleanness passing from the woman to Jesus, healing power flows from Jesus to the woman." Thus the healing, like the ones in 1:40–45 and 5:35–44, involves the touching of a ritually unclean person and thus the transcendence of Levitical purity restrictions. It is perhaps relevant in this regard that in Num 5:1–4 God commands Moses to remove from the Israelite camp (1) the person with scale-disease, (2) the *zāb* or "oozer" (see the NOTE on "a woman who had a flow of blood" in 5:25), and (3) anyone who is unclean by contact with a corpse. In the course of Mark's Gospel, Jesus treats nearly the same three categories of sufferers in exactly the same order: a man with scale-disease (1:40–45), a *zābâ* (5:25–34), and a corpse (5:35–43).

He can do so because his healing power is the power of God's new age, and the coming of the eschaton has ramifications for the interpretation and even the substance of the Law (see the COMMENT on 7:17–19). This eschatological dimension of the story is indicated by the repeated use of the verb *sǭzein* ("to save/cure"), a word with strong eschatological connotations in Mark (see the NOTE on "be cured" in 5:23), and by Old Testament and Jewish backgrounds that look forward to the end of menstruation in the age to come (see the NOTE on "a woman who had a flow of blood" in 5:25). No wonder, then, that the effect on the woman of the healing touch is so overwhelming; she has experienced in her body the power of God's new age.

The woman instantly realizes that she has been cured. Indeed, her subjective experience of the various stages in the healing is emphasized throughout the story in a way that is unprecedented in the Gospels. We are informed about her initial hearing of the news about Jesus, which corresponds to Jairus' initial seeing of him (5:27); about the thoughts that motivate her approach ("Even if I just touch his clothes . . . ," 5:28); about her internal experience of the healing itself ("she knew in her body that she had been healed," 5:29b); and about her reaction to the miracle ("fearing and trembling, knowing what had happened to her," 5:33). Since faith is a form of knowledge, it is not coincidental that the same intertwined stories that contain this abundance of epistemological language also prominently feature the theme of faith, and that it is particularly conspicuous in the story of the woman, where the declaration "your faith has saved you" forms the climax of the story.

This stress on the woman's perception is coupled with an emphasis on that of Jesus; in the moment after the woman touches him, he *knows* in himself that power has gone out of him (5:30), and he immediately turns around to identify her. Both the disciples' subsequent question ("You *see* this crowd pressing against you . . . ?") and the narrator's description of Jesus' further investigation ("he continued *looking* around to *see*") maintain the extraordinary pileup of epistemological language and the concentration on Jesus' perception; Mark's grammar, moreover, suggests that Jesus supernaturally perceives the gender of the person who has touched him (see the NOTE on "continued looking around to see the woman who had done this" in 5:32). Thus at this crucial point in the narrative the focus suddenly shifts from the human perception of Jesus to Jesus' perception of humans; the change in perspective is similar to Paul's correction of himself in Gal 4:9: "Now, however, that you have come to know God, or rather to be known by God . . ." What is important is not so much how people see Jesus but how Jesus sees them.

Jesus, therefore, ignores the disciples' dense and somewhat sarcastic question as to how they can be expected to identify his accoster in the huge throng (5:31) and eagerly continues seeking the person whose need has caused her to reach out to him. Mark's audience would probably relate personally to this feature of the story: their longing for Jesus, ardent though it may be, can never be as passionate as his desire to establish a relationship with them (see Francis, *Jesus*). It is, moreover, significant that Jesus "looks around to see" the woman, a feature that would probably remind Mark's readers of Jesus' riveting, supernatural, discipleship-creating gaze elsewhere in the Gospel (see 1:16, 19; 2:14 and cf. 12:34).

Though the woman does not respond to this gaze by becoming a follower in the way that the brothers in chapter 1 or the tax collector in chapter 2 do, the story is told in such a way that it would probably remind Mark's readers of their own entry into the Christian faith. Fearing and trembling, knowing what has happened in her, the woman, after an initial hesitation, comes forward, throws herself at Jesus' feet, and tells him "the whole truth" (5:33). The situation is probably similar for the Markan Christians: they, too, are aware that a miracle "has happened in them" and that they can never be the same again; they therefore find themselves impelled to overcome their timidity, demonstrate their devotion to Jesus, and tell "the whole truth." The example of the woman, then, may function as an encouragement to the members of the Markan community to profess their faith in Jesus boldly and not to hold back out of fear of the consequences. As we know from passages such as 8:38 and 13:9–13, those consequences could be severe, including trial and even execution; there must have been a strong temptation to hide one's association with Jesus, as Peter himself will do later in the Gospel (14:53–72). The fact that the term "the whole truth" is at home in judicial settings supports this "two-level" reading of the woman's experience (see the NOTE on "the whole truth" in 5:33).

It is also supported by the conclusion of this part of the story, in which Jesus reassures the woman, whom he calls "daughter," that her faith has saved her and tells her to depart in peace (5:34). As Miller points out (*Mark's*), in the Markan context this benediction implies that the woman has become part of the new family around Jesus, who are connected to him through their actions of doing the will of God (3:35; cf. 10:28–30). "Your faith has saved you," moreover, is probably a baptismal formula (see the NOTE on "your faith has saved you" in 5:34). Hearing Jesus' concluding benediction on the woman he has healed, therefore, Mark's readers may well have been reminded of the time when their own faith "saved" them from the world of death and set them on the path toward eschatological *šālôm* ("peace, wholeness"). The story of the woman with the menstrual disorder, then, is their story. They have been touched by the power of God and separated from the faceless crowd by their fearful and wonderful knowledge of what has happened to them through Jesus; through Jesus' help and gentle prodding they have found the courage to confess this truth and to enter the Christian community. In baptism Jesus has turned to them and confirmed that, through their faith in him, they now stand within the sphere of the new age; when persecution, apostasy, and death threaten to engulf them, their faith will save them. Whether they live or die, therefore, they will "go into the peace" of the new age (see the NOTE on "go in peace" in 5:34).

5:35–43: the raising of Jairus' daughter. But Jesus' eagerness to establish a personal relationship with the woman he has healed seems at first to have had a tragic consequence. Already upon reading 5:30, the audience might feel concern for Jairus' daughter: if Jesus' power has gone out of him, how will he be able to heal the mortally ill girl? And now an even greater problem presents itself: messengers coming from Jairus' house inform the synagogue ruler that, while Jesus has been searching for, finding, and conversing with the woman, Jairus' daughter has died (5:35). Their message is introduced by a *hoti* recitative (see the NOTE on "saying" in 5:35) and provides an artful and pathetic contrast with the previous instance of this form in 5:23:

5:23 "My little daughter is about to die."

5:35 "Your daughter has died."

Previously, when Jairus made his request for aid, there was still a basis for hope; now there seems to be none. A similar contrast will be present a few verses later, when the adverb used in 5:38 to describe the mourners' loud wailing, *polla*, will be the same one that was employed in 5:23 to describe Jairus' urgent summons of Jesus (there translated "urgently"). The contrast is again a depressing one: the time for emergency medical procedures is past; now it is time to call in the professional mourners. "Why bother the teacher any more?" the messengers add cruelly. The girl's death thus challenges Jesus' credibility sharply: why, readers might wonder, has he been wasting his time on a woman whose illness was not life-threatening, thus allowing the life of the young girl to slip away? Is his sense of triage so amiss? In the world, sadly, it is often true that one person benefits only at the expense of the others, as contemporary debates about medical priorities painfully illustrate.

But a different logic prevails in the kingdom of God, a logic in which what is good for one person is also good for his or her neighbor (cf. Dante, *Purgatorio* 15.49–57). If the woman has been freed from her twelve-year-long affliction, that does not mean that the girl's life must come to an end at twelve years. She, too, can be healed; there is more than enough eschatological power to go around. Consonant with this kingdom logic, the messengers' words of negation carry, contrary to their intention, a promise. For they refer to Jesus as "the teacher," and that noun and its cognate verb have spoken from the beginning of the Gospel of his heaven-sent authority and wonder-working power, which is potent against all the forces of evil (see 1:21–22, 27; 4:38; 6:2; 9:17, 38; cf. Marshall, *Faith*, 97). In accordance with the promise implicit in the word "teacher," Jesus calls Jairus to trust in Jesus' vivifying power even at the moment when Jairus' daughter's death is staring him in the face, just as Jesus himself ignores the message that the patient has slipped away (cf. the NOTE on "ignoring" in 5:36).

The two men proceed to the house where the dead girl is lying. As they proceed, there is a progressive narrowing of the group around them (see Broadhead, *Teaching*, 109). This sort of restriction of the audience for a miracle is attested not only in Mark (7:33; 8:23) but also elsewhere in the NT (Acts 9:40), in the OT (1 Kgs 7:19; 2 Kgs 4:33), and frequently in Hellenistic miracle stories (e.g. Lucian of Samosata *False Philosopher* 16; *PGM* 3.616–17; cf. Theissen, 61). As Davies and Allison note (2.132), the common motive for the restriction is a feeling akin to that expressed in Matt 7:6: certain doctrines and practices are too holy for general publicity. Consequently, Jesus leaves the crowd behind when he goes with Jairus to the place of death, and of his disciples he takes only the "Big Three," Peter, James, and John (5:37). These are the same three followers who will be given a foretaste of Jesus' resurrection glory at the Transfiguration (9:2) but will also be called upon to share in his suffering in Gethsemane (14:33). Thus the raising of Jairus' dead daughter is implicitly related to Jesus' own death and resurrection (see Marshall, *Faith*, 99).

Arriving at Jairus' house, Jesus visually absorbs the sight of the mourners bewailing the dead girl (5:38). But he refuses to accept their interpretation of the situation. Instead he strides boldly into the situation (see *eiselthōn*, "as he entered," which is redundant but emphatic after *erchontai*, "they went," in the previous verse) and utters a pregnant sentence that seems to run counter to the evidence of everyone's senses: "Why are you making a commotion and weeping? The child hasn't died but is sleeping." This assertion makes use of the common OT, Jewish, and NT metaphor of death as a form of sleep. Death, then, is not the end of life but only an interim state of waiting before the final resurrection at the end of time (see e.g. Dan 12:2; 1 Cor 15:6; 1 Thess 5:10). In view of this coming eschatological fact, which is even now beginning to invade the present, death becomes not the ultimate reality but only the penultimate one (see Gnilka, 1.221). Jesus' words, then, are an example of eschatological irony. This is not, like most irony, a contrast between two static realms of appearance and of truth but a way of seeing that looks beyond present appearances to the coming eschatological situation and interprets the present on the basis of the future (see Marcus, *Mystery*, 113).

But Jesus' eschatologically ironic statement that the girl is only sleeping is greeted by the professional mourners, the experts on death, with derision (5:40a). They know full well that the girl is dead and that dead people don't come back to life! This skepticism may mirror that of some in the Markan environment, perhaps even that of some prospective followers of Jesus (cf. 9:10). The early Christians' belief in the resurrection induced puzzlement in their contemporaries, since many people were inclined to doubt life after death, and those who accepted it generally looked forward to the immortality of the soul rather than the resurrection of the body (see MacMullen, *Paganism*, 53–56). It is no surprise, therefore, to find Paul instructing the Thessalonians concerning "those who have fallen asleep," i.e. those who have died (note the similarity to the "sleep" vocabulary of our passage), linking their imminent resurrection with Christ's already accomplished one and contrasting this assurance of resurrection with the uncertainty of "those who have no hope" (1 Thess 4:13–14). Indeed, the Christian belief in the resurrection could induce ridicule among outsiders (see Acts 17:32), and for Mark's readers this ridicule may reverberate in the derisive reaction of the mourners to Jesus' statement that the girl has only fallen asleep (see Rochais, *Récits*, 65). It is appropriate that such representatives of the unbelieving world should be banished before the miracle of resurrection takes place.

Jesus, therefore, ejects the mourners from the house, leaving only himself, the three disciples, and the parents of the girl to witness the final act of the drama. The strong verb used for this ejection, *ekbalōn*, is also employed throughout the Gospel for the exorcism of demons (1:34; 3:15, 23, etc.); Mark may therefore wish to imply that Jesus' miracles of healing are part of his eschatological warfare against demonic powers, including "the last enemy," death (see 1 Cor 15:26). The reduction of the audience by the ejection of the mourners increases the sense of mystery and drama in the story, and that sense is further built up by the progressive approach to the inner sanctum, the awesome place where death holds sway (cf. Marshall, *Faith*, 91). The news of the girl's decease had first reached the protagonists when they were still far off from the house (5:35). A few moments later they *arrived* (*erchontai*) there and viewed the mourning activities, apparently from the outside (5:38). Then they *entered* (*eiselthōn*) the house and conversed with the mourners (5:39–40a). Now the little party *enters* (*eisporeuetai*) the room where the girl is lying dead (5:40b). The emphasized progression of the group underlines that the healing takes place in a hidden place and increases the tension to the breaking point.

This tension is dispelled in a flash. Jesus enters the room in which death has established its outpost, and without further ado he launches his attack against it, taking the dead girl by the hand and commanding her to rise (5:40b–41). The reader, especially with 5:27–29 in mind, would probably understand Jesus' grasp of the girl's hand as a bestowal of life force. His order to her to awake would be understood in a similar way, as a supernaturally powerful utterance that accomplishes what it commands; Jesus speaks to her as though she were alive—and lo and behold, she *is* alive! As in the "awakening" of Lazarus in John 11:43, then, a personal address calls the sleeper back from the realm of the dead. The impressiveness of Mark's description is increased by the fact that he renders Jesus' words in the original Aramaic (see the NOTE on *"Talitha koum"* in 5:41); their translation into Greek, besides making them understandable to readers not conversant with Aramaic, also adds a final moment of delicious suspense to the long-drawn-out story. But the suspense is quickly banished: the girl immediately gets up and begins to walk around, as though pulled up from the realm of death and restored to the land of the living by Jesus' strong, Orpheus-like grasp (5:42a; see Miller, *Mark's*).

Mark apparently wants his readers to link this rescue from death with Jesus' own resurrection. There are, to be sure, differences between the two events: the resuscitated girl, like Lazarus (cf. John 12:10), will die again, whereas the resurrected Jesus will not (cf. Rom 6:9). But the analogy seems to be more important to Mark. Jesus tells the girl to "rise" (*egeire*), just as he will "be raised" from the dead (*ēgerthē*, 16:6), and she "arises" (*anestē*), just as he will arise (*anastēsetai*) from death after three days (8:31; 9:31; 10:34). Since these two verbs and their cognate nouns were so commonly used for Jesus' own resurrection in early Christianity generally (see *BAGD*, 70, 214–15), Mark's readers would immediately grasp the implication that the power by which Jesus raised the dead girl was the same eschatological power through which God later raised him from the dead. This sort of linkage is made explicit in a later Aramaic magical bowl that juxtaposes the magician's invocation of Jesus' power to heal his client with a reference to God's resurrection of Jesus (Bowl 17:4, 6; Naveh and Shaked, *Magic Spells*, 120–21). And within Mark itself this connection between magical power and resurrection will be confirmed in the next chapter, when King Herod will assert that Jesus is John the Baptist raised from the dead, and that is why "the powers are at work in him" (6:14). It is further supported by a fragment from Qumran that says that someone, either God or the Messiah, will at the eschaton "heal the sick, raise the dead, and preach good news to the poor" (4Q521 1:12)—a description that corresponds roughly to Jesus' actions in Mark 5:21–43 and 6:1–6.

The link between our story of the "raising" of a dead girl and Jesus' own resurrection helps to explain the command to silence that concludes the story (5:43); despite the narrative problem it creates (see the introduction), this prohibition makes sense in the overall logic of Mark's messianic secret motif. For if the healing of Jairus' daughter foreshadows Jesus' resurrection, that healing is, in a sense, premature at this point in the story. It must therefore remain a secret until Jesus himself has arisen, just as the Transfiguration, which shows Jesus in his resurrection glory, must stay under wraps until the Son of Man has risen from the dead (9:9).

Even within the Markan Gospel, which is so full of accounts of the wondrous works performed by Jesus, our passage is an incomparable demonstration of his power and authority. It is difficult to see how anyone could react to a personage so manifestly graced by God and benevolently disposed toward suffering humanity except with reverent awe and grateful homage. Amazingly, however, many people will react in a different way. In the next passage, as a matter of fact, Jesus' own townspeople will reject him, not *in spite of* the wonders he performs but precisely *because of them*.

JESUS IS REJECTED IN HIS HOMETOWN (6:1–6a)

6 ¹And he went out from there and came to his hometown, and his disciples followed him. ²And when the Sabbath had come he began to teach in the synagogue. And many people, when they had heard him, were amazed, saying, "Where does this man get these things from? What wisdom has been given to him! And such works of power are performed by his hands! ³Isn't this the carpenter, the son of Mary and the brother of James and Joses and Judas

and Simon? And aren't his sisters here with us?" And they were scandalized by him. ⁴And Jesus said to them, "A prophet is not dishonored, except in his hometown and among his relatives and in his own household." ⁵And he could not do any work of power there, except that he laid hands on a few sick people and cured them. ⁶ᵃAnd he was dumbfounded at their lack of faith.

NOTES

6 1. *hometown.* Gk *patrida.* Although in classical Greek *patris* usually means "fatherland" (it is cognate to "father," *patēr*), in its NT usages it seems always to mean "hometown" (see Lohmeyer, 111 n. 1, and cf. the Peshitta on our passage). This meaning is particularly clear from Luke 4:23, where the inhabitants of Nazareth want Jesus to repeat in his *patris* the miracles he has performed in Capernaum, another Galilean city, and from Heb 11:14–16, where *patris* is parallel to *polis* (= "city"). But the paternal link is still present; it is ironically significant that in Jesus' *patris* (6:1, 4) he is referred to by his mother's name rather than, as is usual in Jewish texts, by his father's name (see the NOTE on "the carpenter, the son of Mary" in 6:3).

2. *What wisdom has been given to him! And such works of power are performed by his hands!* Gk *tis hē sophia hē dotheisa toutǭ kai hai dynameis toiautai dia tōn cheirōn autou ginomenai.* As Marshall (*Faith,* 192) points out, the passive form of the word for "given" (*dotheisa;* cf. the "divine passive" *dedotai* in 4:11) and the phrase "by his hands" suggest that the townspeople think that Jesus' talents do not have their origin on the human level, i.e. that he is being used as the channel for some supernatural power. Cf. 6:14: "The powers (*dynameis*) were at work in him." On the question of the nature of these powers, see the COMMENT on 6:1–3.

Guelich (309) and Marshall (*Faith,* 192) point out that wisdom and might (*ischys*) are ascribed to the future Davidic ruler in Isa 11:2 and that Isaiah's wisdom terminology is repeated in the description of the Messiah in Pss. Sol. 17:23. In the larger context of both the Isaian and the *Psalms of Solomon* passages, however, the Davidic ruler's wisdom is used not only to save Israel but also to smite its enemies; for Mark, on the other hand, the wise Messiah is rejected by his own people, especially by those in his own hometown, but accepted by Gentiles (cf. 7:24–30; 13:10; 15:39).

3. *the carpenter, the son of Mary.* Gk *ho tektōn ho huios tēs Marias.* In Jewish sources the father's name is normally used to identify the son even when the father is dead (see e.g. Do'eg son of Joseph in *b. Yoma* 38b and Jesus son of Jesus in the Babatha archive; cf. Ilan, "Man," 23 n. 3). Contrary to this custom, Jesus is designated by his mother's name rather than his father's. Both Matthew and Luke revert to the usual pattern, Luke 4:22 reading "the son of Joseph" (cf. John 6:42) and Matt 13:55 "the son of the carpenter." Some manuscripts of our passage, such as p⁴⁵, conflate our text with Matthew's to produce "the son of the carpenter, the son of Mary," but the external evidence is overwhelmingly in favor of the reading chosen.

Why then does Mark choose to identify Jesus by a matronymic rather than a patronymic? Ilan ("Man") has shown that a matronymic could be used when the mother's pedigree was superior to the father's, but that can scarcely be the case here, since Davidic descent was the most important of all, and Jesus was a Davidide on his father's side (see the genealogies in Matthew and Luke and early passages such as Rom 1:3), a fact of which Mark himself seems to be aware (see 10:48; 11:10; cf. Bauckham, "Brothers," 698–99). Bauckham thinks that "son of Mary" distinguishes Jesus from his "brothers," who in Bauckham's view are sons of Joseph by a previous wife, but in that case the brothers' mother would need to be specified too; lacking such an identification, the natural assumption is that the men listed after Jesus have the same mother as he does. (On the meaning of "brother," see the NOTE on "brothers" in 3:31.) Freedman suggests that perhaps they did all have the same mother, Mary, but that Joseph had a previous or subsequent marriage and that Jesus and his brothers (and sisters) therefore needed to be distinguished from the children of Joseph's other wife or wives. But in that case Mary should be mentioned *alongside* of Joseph, not *instead of* him.

These alternate theories being found wanting, and given the hostile nature of the confrontation, it is likely that the use of Jesus' mother's name is a slur against his legitimacy, as Stauffer ("Jeschu") and S. Wilson (*Strangers*, 188) among others argue. This aspersion would correspond to the tendency in later Jewish traditions to portray Jesus as a bastard (see e.g. Origen *Against Celsus* 1.28–32, 39, 69; *b. Sanh.* 67a), a pattern that may already be reflected in John 8:41. Ilan, though disagreeing with this exegesis, cites an interesting parallel, the derogatory designation of Titus as "the son of Vespasian's wife" in *'Abot R. Nat.* 7 (B), which implies that he is illegitimate (see Ilan, "Man," 42–43 n. 86, and cf. Saldarini, *Fathers*, 68 n. 15). McArthur ("Son of Mary") argues against the implication of illegitimacy in Mark 6:3 that "son of Mary" is an informal reference, not a formal genealogical expression, and that there is nothing necessarily unusual or derogatory about an identification by the mother's name in such informal contexts (cf. e.g. 1 Kgs 17:17; Acts 16:1). But Mark 6:3 comes closer to being a genealogical formula than the parallels cited because of the extensive list of other male family members. McArthur's theory, moreover, does not explain the apparent embarrassment of Matthew and Luke at Mark's term or reckon with the hostile context of our passage and the evidence for a trajectory of Jewish aspersions against Jesus' birth.

The church's eventual response to the charge of illegitimacy was the assertion of Jesus' virginal conception (cf. esp. Matt 1:18–20; Luke 1:34–35), so that God became, in a more or less literal sense, his father. Mark, however, gives no explicit indication of knowing this tradition.

James and Joses and Judas and Simon. Gk *Iakōbou kai Iōsētos kai Iouda kai Simōnos.* As Lohmeyer (110) points out, all of Jesus' brothers have the names of biblical patriarchs: James = Jacob is the father of the twelve tribes, and the other names are those of three of Jacob's sons, Joses = *Yôsi* being an abbreviation for Joseph.

were scandalized. Gk *eskandalizonto.* On this verb, see the NOTE on "fall away" in 4:17. The cognate noun is used by Paul in Rom 9:33 in a quotation from Isa 8:14, which speaks of God becoming a "stone of stumbling and a rock of offense (*skandalou*)" to Israel. Paul significantly reapplies this oracle to Israel's lack of faith in Jesus (cf. 1 Cor 1:23), thus offering a close parallel to our passage.

4. *And Jesus said to them.* Gk *kai elegen autois ho Iēsous.* This clause often introduces Markan redaction (e.g. 4:11, 21, 24), and Gnilka (1.232) thinks it does so here as well. This, however, is questionable, since our narrative is a "pronouncement story," and removing 6:4 eliminates the pronouncement; without Jesus' saying about a prophet being without honor, the townspeople's rejection of him would be very baffling indeed. Gnilka's assertion that 6:4 is addressed to the disciples is also questionable; a reader would naturally suppose that the undefined "they" in our verse is the same as the undefined "them" in the previous verse, namely the Nazarenes.

A *prophet is not dishonored,* etc. Gk *ouk estin prophētēs atimas,* etc. Jesus here uses a proverbial saying which is widely attested in Greco-Roman literature; see, for example, Plutarch *De Exilio* 604D: "You would find that the most sensible and wisest people are little cared for in their own hometowns (*en tais heautōn patrisin*)."

In our passage Jesus implies that he is a prophet, whereas in 6:15 and 8:28 "prophet" seems to be an inadequate term for him. On a historical level this tension may point up the distance between the historical Jesus' own self-evaluation as a prophet and the higher view of him held by the early church, but one must also make sense of the tension as part of Markan theology: for Mark Jesus is a prophet, but also more than a prophet (cf. Matt 11:9//Luke 7:26). Here the particularly salient feature of the prophetic typology is rejection by one's own people; biblical prophets were not only seers who sometimes foretold the future but also, and more importantly, figures who declared God's will for his people and consequently were often spurned by them (cf. e.g. 2 Chr 24:19; 36:15–16; Neh 9:26; Jub. 1:12). This theme of prophetic rejection is extensively developed in the New Testament, especially in Q (see e.g. Matt 5:12//Luke 6:23; Matt 23:37//Luke 13:33–34; Acts 7:52; 1 Thess 2:15). The Markan form of this saying puts more emphasis on familial rejection than the parallels in the other Synoptics, John, and Papyrus Oxyrhynchus 1, a fragmentary second- or third-century C.E. text that includes eight dominical sayings in Greek (see chart p. 377 and cf. Fitzmyer, "Oxyrhynchus"). Matthew and Luke may have eliminated the reference to familial tension ("and among his relatives" + "in his house" in Luke) either inadvertently, by haplography (homoeoteleuton—repetition of *autou* = "his"), or deliberately, out of respect for Jesus' family. But it is also possible, in view of its absence from John and Papyrus Oxyrhynchus, that it is redactional in Mark (see the COMMENT on 3:20–21 and the introduction to the COMMENT on 6:1–6a).

Mark 6:4	Matthew 13:57	Luke 4:24	John 4:44	POxy. 1:5
a prophet is not dishonored	a prophet is not dishonored	no prophet is acceptable	a prophet	not acceptable is a prophet
except in his hometown	except in his hometown	in his hometown	in his own hometown	in his hometown
and among his relatives				
and in his house	and in his house		does not have honor	
				nor does a doctor make cures
				on those who know him

6a. *he was dumbfounded.* Gk *ethaumazen.* Guelich (312) aptly comments: "Jesus' amazement expresses his humanness, the very issue that had blinded those who knew him best!" (cf. 6:3). For other intimations of a limitation on Jesus' knowledge, see 5:41; 13:32; 14:36, and 15:34.

COMMENT

Introduction. Having returned to Jewish Galilee from the Gentile Decapolis in 5:21, and after performing a notable double miracle in 5:21–43, Jesus now comes home to Nazareth, the city where he was raised. Though the passage begins on a promising note, with his townspeople voicing their amazement at the wonders he has performed, it suddenly modulates into a minor key and ends with Jesus himself expressing amazement—at his neighbors' rejection of him.

This unexpected swerve toward negativity convinces most exegetes that our story is not an original unity; as Wellhausen (43) already remarked, astonishment (6:2) and scandalization (6:3) are not the same thing, and it is difficult to comprehend the transformation of the one into the other without an intermediate incident. Exegetes, however, are divided as to whether ours is a positive story that has been darkened or a negative story that has been lightened (see Grässer, "Mark VI.1–6a," 7). The former seems more likely, since the negative elements fit into the developing Markan theme of the opposition to Jesus, which is slowly gathering steam in this section of the Gospel (cf. 5:17; 7:1–13; 8:11–15), and therefore some of them (e.g. the end of 6:3 and some or all of 6:5–6a) are probably due to Markan redaction. Mark has probably also added the reference to the disciples at the end of 6:1, since they play no role in the subsequent story; Mark may have introduced them here with an eye to their subsequent mission in 6:7–13 (see Gnilka, 1.228). And he is probably also responsible for the phrase "and among his relatives and in his own household" in 6:4, which is missing from the parallel forms of the "prophet without honor" saying but fits the

Markan theme of familial tension (see the COMMENT on 3:20–21 and the NOTE on "prophet" in 6:4 and cf. Grässer, "Mark VI.1–6a," 16).

In its present form the passage divides naturally in the middle, after 6:3. Verses 6:1–3 describe Jesus' return to Nazareth and activity in the synagogue there, and the people's ambivalent reaction. Verses 6:4–6a describe Jesus' reaction to their reaction, which is also ambivalent: he is nonplussed, yet he still performs a few miracles in Nazareth. The clauses that conclude the two sections summarize their respective themes: "they were scandalized by him" (6:3) and "he was dumbfounded at their lack of faith" (6:6).

6:1–3: the reaction to Jesus in his hometown. Jesus returns to his hometown and gets off to an auspicious start: he teaches the people in the synagogue and they are amazed, marveling at his wisdom and mighty works (6:1–2). Anyone who remembers the Gospel's initial miracle, the exorcism in 1:21–28, would immediately recognize a likeness:

Mark 1:21–28	*Mark 6:1–6*
1:21: And on the Sabbath he went into the synagogue and immediately began to teach	6:2a: And when the Sabbath had come he began to teach in the synagogue
1:22: And the people were amazed at his teaching . . .	6:2b: And many people, when they had heard him, were amazed,
1:27a: "What is this? A new teaching with authority!"	6:2c: saying, "Where does this man get these things from? What wisdom has been given to him!"
1:27b: "He even gives orders to the unclean spirits, and they obey him!"	6:2d: "And such works of power are performed by his hands!"

The striking similarity leads the reader to anticipate that our passage, like that in chapter 1, will end on a positive note, for example with a remark about the spread of Jesus' fame (cf. 1:28). Indeed, such a reaction would be expected even if the parallels to 1:21–28 did not exist, solely on the basis of the way the story has developed in the first two verses of chapter 6. The Nazarenes' reaction has been described with the verb "to be amazed" (*explēssesthai*), which previously (1:22) and subsequently in the Gospel (7:37; 10:26; 11:18) is always a positive term. They have, moreover, referred to Jesus' teaching as a demonstration of *wisdom*, which hardly seems like a negative characterization. Even the mention of Jesus' family members in the first part of 6:3 could easily fit into a positive evaluation of him: "This kid has grown up right here in Nazareth, under our very noses, in a family we all knew—and we never guessed what fantastic things he was capable of!"

The narrative, then, makes an unexpected swerve at the conclusion of 6:3. Suddenly, the people are *offended* at Jesus rather than taking pride in him, and Jesus subsequently sums up their attitude as one of "dishonor" (6:4). This is an appropriate term to use, because they have implicitly acknowledged that he has done things worthy of praise, not reviling; if they subsequently turn against him, the reversal suggests a deliberate insult. But what is behind this hostility? Two recent developments in Mark's narrative help to account for it.

First, we have heard in 4:11–12 of a divine intention that outsiders to the Christian community (with whom Jesus' family was paralleled by the "outsider" language in 3:31–32) should look and look without seeing, hear and hear without understanding. Thus a perception of Jesus' striking words and deeds ("looking" and "hearing") may lead not to faith but to rejection of him ("not seeing," "not understanding") by an uncanny but irreversible outworking of the divine will. The unexpected and apparently unmotivated opposition in 6:3–6, then, may show that the somber divine determinism of the parable theory is beginning to work itself out within the Markan narrative (cf. Grässer, "Mark VI.1–6a," 14).

Secondly, and even more ominously, the townspeople's reaction to Jesus in 6:2–3 is similar to the scribes' reaction to him in 3:20–30: they acknowledge that his works do not result from human agency (see the NOTE on "What wisdom has been given to him!" in 6:2), but they refuse to ascribe them to God. In the dualistic worldview of the Gospel, that leaves only one possibility, namely that Jesus works his miracles through Satan—a charge that is itself, in Mark's view, based on Satanic influence (see the COMMENT on 3:28–30). Therefore the hometown crowd's swift and puzzling swerve from admiring amazement to offense at Jesus' marvelous works may suggest that an unhealthy, eerie, even demonic influence is at work among them.

6:4–6a: Jesus' response. Jesus responds to this local hostility by applying a traditional maxim to himself: a prophet is dishonored only in his own hometown. Contrary, then, to his townspeople's implicit charge that he teaches and heals by demonic power, he suggests that their negative reaction actually proves the opposite—that he is a rejected prophet, and thus on the side of God (see the NOTE on "prophet" in 6:4). As elsewhere in the Gospel, then, the savagery of the opposition to Jesus actually demonstrates that he is God's agent (cf. 1:21–28; 5:1–20).

The Markan form of the "prophet without honor" saying emphasizes more than any of the parallels the element of familial rejection; a prophet is disdained not only in his hometown but also "among his relatives and in his own household" (6:4b; see the NOTE on "prophet" in 6:4). This added stress, which seems to be redactional, probably reflects the Markan community's own experience of familial rejection, a probability that is increased by the fact that Mark has taken care to brushstroke the disciples into this scene in 6:1. Following in Jesus' painful footsteps, the Markan community, too, has been dumbfounded by familial rejection of the message that makes such eminent good sense to them and has transformed their lives (cf. 10:28–30 and 13:12–13). They, too, know what it is like to go through periods when the world-rectifying

power of the divine redemption, which their faith tells them has erupted decisively into the world in Jesus, seems strangely and disturbingly absent; they,
too, have encountered places where the prevailing skepticism or hostility has
meant that they "could not do any work of power" (6:5a).

Reacting to this sort of mystifying rejection, the Markan Jesus experiences a
mood swing of his own at the end of the passage: despite his pronouncement
in 6:4, which seems to accept local opposition as inevitable, he ends up astonished by the lack of faith he finds in his hometown (6:6a). But why should he
be amazed? Not only has he just acknowledged that a prophet's rejection is
unavoidable, but opposition to him is nothing new in the Gospel.

But if Jesus has experienced opposition before in the Gospel, it has usually
come either from demoniacs (1:24; 5:7) or from the religious authorities (2:1–
3:6 etc.). On another occasion he was asked by the populace of a city to depart
from their shores (5:17), but this occurred in a Gentile region. He has not yet
experienced communal rejection in a Jewish region, as he does now—a
wholesale turning against him in Galilee, the heartland of the Gospel, and in
his own hometown. Communal rejection *there* is not expected; for how can
the Messiah, the King of Israel, be rejected by his own people (cf. 15:32)? Yet
that is exactly what will happen later in the narrative, and our passage foreshadows this eventuality. The repudiation of Jesus by the overwhelming majority of the Jewish community, indeed, was a problem that exercised early
Christian thinkers greatly (cf. Romans 9–11), and the Markan Jesus' shock at
his reception in Nazareth probably reflects the church's astonishment at this
strange lurch in salvation history (cf. the NOTE on "were scandalized" in 6:3).
As Marshall (*Faith*, 195) puts it, "By placing this episode after a series of dramatic miracles (4:35–5:43), Mark shows how the powerful Son of God who
calms storms, expels demons, banishes diseases and raises the dead, is finally
checkmated by entrenched unbelief in his hometown."

To correct Marshall, however, it might be better to speak of Jesus' power
being "checked" than of it being "checkmated" in Nazareth by the people's
lack of faith. Jesus does, after all, perform a few miraculous healings there
(6:5b), and even a few miracles are sufficient to bear witness to the advent of
the new age. The opposition that God's dominion is suffering does not cancel
belief in it but rather testifies to its provocative power and demands a continual exercise of patient, hopeful, eschatological insight on the part of those
who have heard the rumor of its arrival. For those with eyes to see, however,
wonders are still occurring, and they are wondrous enough. Already the following passage will drive this point home.

THIRD MAJOR SECTION
(MARK 6:6b–8:21)

◆

INTRODUCTION: FEASTS

The third major section of the Gospel begins, like the first two, with a commissioning of disciples (6:7–13; cf. 1:16–20; 3:13–19), which follows a transitional summary of Jesus' movement and activity (6:6b; cf. 1:14–15; 3:7–12). This time, in contrast to the two previous occasions, the disciples actually go out and do something, namely proclaim repentance, cast out demons, and heal the sick (6:12–13). They are also prominent in the two feeding miracles, acting as intermediaries between Jesus and the hungry crowds and conveying the crowds' concerns to him and his nourishment to them (6:35–43; 8:5–8). But despite this increasing participation in Jesus' ministry, the disciples also display a decreasing spiritual IQ, asking stupid questions, doubting Jesus' capacity to save, and even demonstrating the quality of "hard-heartedness," which has previously been ascribed to Jesus' enemies, the Pharisees (6:35–37, 52; 7:17–18; 8:14–21; cf. 3:5). If the Twelve are model disciples, they are prototypes of fallibility as much as of obedience.

The focus of this section, however, is not so much on them as it is on Jesus, especially in his capacity as a provider of food. Not only does he feed the multitudes on two separate occasions (6:30–44; 8:1–9), but he also discusses food twice with the disciples (7:17–23; 8:14–21) and once with an unnamed Gentile woman (7:24–30); the evangelist, moreover, chimes in on the same theme with the remark that the disciples "did not understand about the loaves" (6:52). The feast that Jesus provides in the first feeding miracle, moreover, seems to be deliberately juxtaposed with the banquet scene in Herod's palace, which climaxes with the grisly sight of John the Baptist's head on a plate (6:14–29). The theme of food, then, dominates this section from first to last; Jesus provides "bread from heaven" (cf. John 6:31–33 etc.), implicitly assuming the mantle of Moses, the distributor of manna. Not everyone, however, can recognize him for who he is, and some people prefer "the leaven of malice and evil" to his "unleavened bread of sincerity and truth" (cf. 1 Cor 5:8).

But despite such dark undertones, this is generally a sunny part of the Gospel. The disciples go out and work miracles, and they can barely contain their joy at their success (6:12–13, 30). Jesus twice provides food in a desert place, and even the descriptions of the leftovers emphasize the motifs of fullness and superabundance (6:43; 8:8). The new-age power of the gospel breaks out of the confines of old-age dietary regulations and ethnic exclusivism (7:1–30). The choral acclamation at the end of the miracle story in 7:31–37, which seemingly comes out of nowhere to echo Genesis 1 and to suggest God's eschatologically creative act, could easily stand as the caption over this entire section of the Gospel: "He has done all things well." If the section also contains somber hints that this demonstration of divine goodness comes at a heavy price (6:14–29), perhaps because of human blindness (6:52; 8:14–21), these counterpoints do not efface its overwhelmingly positive thrust. For here even the references to human blindness seem to point hopefully toward a future day of revelation: "Do you not *yet* understand?" (8:21).

THE DISCIPLES ARE SENT OUT ON A MISSIONARY JOURNEY (6:6b–13)

6   ⁶ᵇAnd he made a circuit of the villages in that area, teaching. ⁷And he summoned the Twelve and began to send them out two by two, and gave them authority over unclean spirits, ⁸and instructed them that they not take anything for the way except a staff—no bread, no provision bag, no small change for the money belt—⁹"but have your sandals strapped up, and don't put on two tunics!" ¹⁰And he said to them: "Into whatever house you go, there remain until you leave that place. ¹¹And whatever place does not accept you or hear you, when you leave there shake off the dust from under your feet, as a witness against them." ¹²And they went out and proclaimed that people should repent, ¹³and they cast out many demons and anointed many sick people with oil and healed them.

NOTES

6 6b. *in that area.* Not explicitly stated, but implied; cf. 1:38.

7. *began to send them out.* Gk *ērxato autous apostellein.* Mark loves the construction "began to" + infinitive, which occurs twenty-six times in his Gospel; most of these instances are omitted by Matthew and Luke, who obviously felt that Mark's "began to" was *beginning to* be redundant! For Dalman (*Words*, 26–28) this usage of "began to" is simply a Semitic idiom, but Hunkin ("Pleonastic," 395–402) argues that the redundant usage of "began to" is not particularly Semitic but a mark of popular, episodic narrative of many sorts; he cites, for instance, several examples from Xenophon (cf. Reiser, *Syntax*, 43–45). One may also question whether the usage of *ērxato* in passages such as ours is entirely redundant. To be sure, there are Markan instances in which *ērxato* seems to mean only "that the person in question has been doing something else, and that his activity now takes a new turn" (BAGD, 111 [2β]; see e.g. 1:45; 2:23; 4:1). But our passage is an ideal scene foreshadowing the post-Easter missionary activity of the apostles and the later church (see the COM-

MENT on 6:8–9 and on 6:10–11), and therefore there is a sense in which it describes the "beginning" of an activity that will continue after the resurrection (see the COMMENT on 1:1). In favor of this interpretation is the verbal link between 6:7 and 3:14–15, where the Twelve were chosen to preach and cast out demons but did not yet take up these offices. Now, however, the moment has arrived for them to *begin* doing so (cf. Reploh, *Lehrer*, 54).

two by two. Gk *duo duo*. The sending out of the Twelve in pairs, which is also implied in the list in Matt 10:2–4, corresponds to the practice of the later church (see Acts 13:1–3), but it is uncertain whether the church continued Jesus' custom or whether the later practice was read back into Jesus' ministry. In either case the measure had pragmatic advantages such as increased security (cf. Tob 5:4–22 and passim), but it probably also reflected a Jewish practice of sending out official representatives in pairs (see e.g. *b Sanh.* 26a and 43a and cf. Jeremias, "Paarweise," 136–38). This Jewish practice, in its turn, probably reflects the OT stipulation that two witnesses are required to establish legal testimony (Deut 17:6; 19:15; cf. Hooker, 155). This explanation would cohere with the larger context in our passage, which refers to the disciples' "witness" (6:11).

8. *staff*. Gk *rabdon*. Staffs were used both for walking on rough terrain and for defense against wild animals, bandits, and so on (see D. Schmidt, 79); their defensive function makes our passage similar to Josephus' report (*J.W.* 2.125) that the Essenes took nothing but a weapon when they went on a journey. The walking staff, along with the provision bag (see the next NOTE), was associated with the wandering Cynic philosophers, who were numerous in the first century; Epictetus, for example, quotes the popular opinion that the distinguishing marks of a Cynic are "his provision-bag and his staff and his big mouth" (Arrian, *Discourses of Epictetus* 3.22.50; cited in Downing, *Christ*, 48).

provision bag. Gk *pēran*. This was usually made of leather and carried food and other necessities for a journey (see e.g. Jdt 10:5). It became a standard part of the equipment of wandering Cynics and was linked with the Stoic/Cynic ideal of self-sufficiency (see e.g. Diogenes Laertius 6.85 and Pseudo-Diogenes, *Epistles* 30.4). This linkage may be part of the reason for the Markan Jesus' rejection of the provision bag: the Christian missionary is not self-sufficient but empowered by God.

small change. Gk *chalkon*. These were copper coins of the lowest value.

9. *but have your sandals strapped up*. Gk *alla hypodedemenous sandalia*, lit. "having bound sandals under [your feet]." As Lohmeyer (114) notes, the phrase suggests continual readiness for departure; this strengthens the possible allusion to Exodus 12, on which see the COMMENT on 6:8–9. The switch from indirect to direct discourse adds liveliness to the narrative.

two tunics. Gk *duo chitōnas*. The *chitōn* was a long tunic worn as an undergarment and reaching to the knees or ankles; two *chitones* might be worn in layers by people going on journeys, perhaps for warmth at night (see Josephus *Ant.* 17.136 and cf. Rebell, "*Chitōn*," 468). Cynics typically wore a *doubled* cloak, so it might be suspected that Mark's *single* tunic is intended to trump

Cynic austerity; the Cynic cloak, however, was not a *chitōn* but a *tribōn*, a poor person's garment that was humbler than a *chitōn* (Musonius Rufus 19).

10. *remain until you leave that place*. Gk *menete heōs an exelthēte ekeithen*. This is different from the behavior advocated in *Didache* 11–13, where visiting apostles are to be put up for one or two days at the most; anyone who wishes to stay longer thereby shows that he is a false prophet (11:5)! As Guelich (322) points out, however, the Markan passage seems to envisage a community-founding visit, whereas the *Didache* passage is addressed to established churches. Perhaps the *carte blanche* of the dominical commandment in our passage gave rise to the abuses countered by the *Didache*.

11. *shake off the dust from under your feet*. Gk *ektinaxate ton choun ton hypokatō tōn podōn hymōn*. Strack-Billerbeck (1.571) asserts that Jews returning to the Holy Land from abroad would shake off the dust of the unclean pagan lands in which they had been sojourning, but the passages they cite (e.g. *m. Ohol.* 2:3; *b. Ber.* 19b) do not support this assertion. Rather than implying a rejection of Gentile impurity, the action of shaking off dust seems to symbolize a desire to break communion with someone, as in the related action of shaking out garments in Neh 5:13 and Acts 18:6 (cf. Cadbury, "Dust and Garments," 270–71). The basic idea is that the disciples are henceforth to have nothing at all to do with the places that have rejected them (but contrast 5:16–20, where Jesus is rejected in Gerasa but his "messenger" is received).

as a witness against them. Gk *eis martyrion autois*. Grammatically, *autois* could be either a dative of advantage or of disadvantage; theoretically, therefore, the meaning could be "as a witness *for their benefit*," as seems to be the case in 1:44. Taylor (305) thinks that the dative is one of advantage in our passage as well; the shaken dust is "intended to provoke thought and to lead men to repentance." But *martyrion* + dative normally has a negative nuance outside of the NT, where it usually denotes incriminating evidence against a defendant (cf. 13:9 and see Guelich, 77), and the present context supports this negative reading: shaking the dust off one's feet is a response to rejection, and it implies a desire to separate oneself from the locality in which the rejection has been experienced (see the previous NOTE).

13. *anointed . . . with oil*. Gk *ēleiphon elaiǭ*. Anointing with oil, usually olive oil, was widely practiced in antiquity for medicinal purposes (see e.g Isa 1:6; Luke 10:34; Josephus *J.W.* 1.657). Jesus himself is never described as healing by anointment with oil, but the early church did so, as is shown by our passage and Jas 5:14–15 (cf. Matt 6:16–18 and see Finn, "Anointing"). This practice was probably influenced by the tradition of medicinal anointing in the environment, although James emphasizes that it is not the oil itself that is efficacious but the "prayer of faith" that accompanies it. It is unclear what relation there was between the custom of anointing the sick and the later church's practice of baptismal anointing, which in its turn recalls Jesus' anointing with the Holy Spirit at his baptism (Acts 4:27; 10:38); did early Christians think that anointing the sick "worked" because it reactivated the spiritual anointment they had received at baptism?

many sick people . . . healed. Gk *pollous arrōstous . . . etherapeuon.* Mark seems to contrast deliberately the disciples' successful outreach here with Jesus' ineffective mission to his hometown in the immediately preceding passage: Jesus could perform no miracle in Nazareth except for laying his hands on *a few sick people* (*arrōstois*) and *healing* (*etherapeusen*) them (6:5), but the Twelve anoint *many sick people* (*arrōstous*) with oil and *heal* (*etherapeuon*) them. This contrast may be meant to emphasize that, just because one missionary has failed in a particular spot, that does not necessarily mean that others will fail there—even if the first missionary was Jesus himself! The principle, then, might be similar to John 14:12: after the resurrection Jesus' disciples will do even greater works than Jesus himself did during his earthly ministry.

COMMENT

Introduction. The account of Jesus' rejection by his hometown (6:1–6a) is followed by a brief description of his further teaching in the area (6:6b) and a more extended account of his dispatch of the Twelve on a missionary journey (6:7–13). In a typical Markan "sandwich" this description of the missionary journey is interrupted for the story of John the Baptist's death (6:14–29), then completed by the account of the return of the Twelve from their journey (6:30). The latter begins the transition to the story of the Feeding of the Five Thousand (6:31–44). The verb "to teach," *didaskein*, forms an inclusion (see the GLOSSARY) around this whole "sandwich" (6:6b, 30; see Reploh, *Lehrer*, 51–52).

The "sandwich," like most if not all of the Markan intercalations, is probably Mark's editorial creation (cf. 2:1–12; 3:20–35; 5:21–43; 11:12–25; 14:54–72), and he seems to have played a major role in shaping the wording of our pericope as well. For example, the "frame" of the passage, vv 7 and 12–13, closely reproduces the language and themes of 3:13–15, and when two such widely separated pericopes are so close linguistically, redactional activity is probable (see Reploh, *Lehrer*, 50). As for the specific instructions enclosed by this frame, there is an alternate form in Q (Luke 10:1–16; see figure 12) which is more expansive, especially about the way in which missionaries are to behave in the houses they visit (Luke 10:4–7); on this subject the Markan directive (6:10) is short to the point of being cryptic and conveys the impression of being boiled down from something like the Q version. The Markan form is more lenient to the disciples than the Q one, since Mark allows them the walking staff and sandals that are forbidden in Q (Luke 9:3; Matt 10:10//Luke 10:4); Mark, on the other hand, seems more pessimistic about their chances of meeting with a positive reception, since he concentrates more on the possibility of rejection. These differences may well reflect Markan editing, since the staff and sandals correspond to the Exodus typology that pervades this section of the Gospel (see the COMMENT below on 6:8–9), and the rejection motif fits the Markan situation. Also perhaps Markan are the phrase "for the way" (*eis hodon*) in 6:8, which is not present in Q and fits in with the Markan "way" theme, and the

Figure 12: Missionary Instructions

Mark 6:8–11	Luke 9:3–6 (Mark + Q)	Matthew 10:5–15 (Mark + Q)	Luke 10:2–12 (Q)
and he instructed them that they not take anything for the way except a staff— no bread, no provision bag,	And he said to them, "Don't take anything for the way, neither a staff nor a provision bag, nor bread, nor silver,	He instructed them and said, "Don't acquire gold or silver or small change for your money belts or a provision bag for the way	And he said to them, ... "Don't carry a purse or a provision bag
no small change for the money belt— "but have your sandals strapped up, and don't put on two tunics!"	nor two tunics each.	or two tunics or sandals or a staff.	or sandals . . .
And he said to them, "Into whatever house you go,	And into whatever house you go,	And into whatever village you go, find out who in it is worthy and remain there until you go. And go into the house and greet it. And if the house is worthy, let your peace go out to it.	Into whatever house you go, first say, 'Peace to this house.' And if a son of peace is there, your peace will rest on him. If not, it will return to you. Remain in that house,
there remain until you leave that place.	there remain and leave from there.		

Figure 12: Missionary Instructions (continued)

Mark 6:8–11	Luke 9:3–6 (Mark + Q)	Matthew 10:5–15 (Mark + Q)	Luke 10:2–12 (Q)
			eating and drinking their food
			for the worker is worthy of his wages.
			Do not move from house to house.
			And into whatever city you go and they accept you, eat the things they set before you . . . .
And whatever place does not accept you or hear you,	And as many as do not accept you,	And whoever does not accept you or hear your words,	And into whatever city you go and they do not accept you
		go out of that house and that city	go out into its boulevards and say,
when you leave there shake off the dust from under your feet,	go out from that city and shake off the dust from your feet	and shake off the dust from your feet.	'Even the dust of your city that sticks to our feet,
as a witness against them."	as a witness against them."		we wipe it off against you . . . ,'
		Amen I say to you, it will be easier for the land of Sodom and Gomorrah in the day of judgment than for that city."	It will be easier for Sodom 'on that day' than for that city."

non-Q phrases "or hear you" and "as a witness against them" in 6:11, which also cohere with Markan motifs (cf. 4:1–34 and 1:44; 13:9). With such drastic redactional intervention being apparent, Guelich (319) is justified in his assertion that the passage is substantially a Markan creation.

. In its present form the passage is divided into three parts: the introduction to the commissioning (6:6b–7), the instructions for missionaries (6:8–11), and the description of the successful mission (6:12–13). The first and third parts parallel each other; Jesus' peripatetic teaching corresponds to the disciples' missionary preaching, and his empowerment of them to cast out unclean spirits corresponds to their performance of exorcisms and healings. The middle part, which consists of missionary instructions, is subdivided into directives for the road (6:8–9) and for the house (6:10–11). This order is logical; first Jesus tells his disciples how to get to where they are going, then what to do when they get there.

6:6b–7: introduction. The passage begins with the transitional notice about Jesus' circuit of Galilean villages (6:6b); despite the rejection he has encountered in his Galilean hometown (6:6a), he does not give up on the region but continues on a redemptive round of teaching. He even commissions the Twelve to extend his work, sending them out two by two, a procedure that itself implies official representation (see the NOTE on "two by two" in 6:7), and giving them authority over unclean spirits (6:7). The connection between sending out and endowment with authority makes sense in a world in which it was believed, according to a later rabbinic formula, that "a person's representative (*šālîaḥ*, lit. 'sent-out-one') is as the person himself" (*m. Ber.* 5:5). This idea of representation leads to some remarkable parallels between Jesus and the Twelve: Jesus' teaching (6:6b) is mirrored in the teaching of the Twelve (6:30; cf. 6:12), and their proclamation of repentance in their inaugural mission (6:12) reflects his emphasis on repentance in his initial proclamation of the good news (1:14–15). Their preaching and wonder-working (6:13), moreover, are the means for *his* name becoming known (6:14)—presumably because their actions are carried out "in his name" (cf. 9:38–39). And just as his first major actions in both Jewish and Gentile regions were powerful exorcisms (1:21–28; 5:1–20), so he accords pride of place in his missionary instructions to the disciples' expulsion of evil spirits.

6:8–9: instructions for the road. The fact that the Twelve have received an endowment of spiritual power from Jesus indicates that God is on their side, and so they need not worry about how they are to support themselves along the way; the same God who has given them dominion over superhuman foes will certainly supply their physical needs (cf. Matt 6:25–34). Correspondingly, Jesus' first set of instructions to them about their missionary trip concerns not so much what they *should* bring but what they need not: no bread, no provision bag, no money, and only the clothes on their backs. Presumably, their needs for food and shelter will be catered to by those who receive their mes-

Figure 13: Cynic vs. Exodus Background for Missionary Discourse

Mark 6:8–9	*Luke 10:3 = Q*	*Cynics*	*Exodus story*
staff	no staff	staff	staff (of Moses, and of Israelites in Exod 12:11)
no bread		bread	no bread (instead, bread from heaven)
no bag	no bag	bag	
no money in belt		no money	cf. Exod 12:11: loins girded
sandals	no sandals	no sandals	sandals (Exod 12:11; Deut 29:5)
single tunic		doubled cloak	single garment (Deut 8:4; 29:5)

sage. But in a deeper sense the disciples will be looked after by God, and in this regard it is significant that there are strong overlaps between the Markan description of their equipment and OT portrayals of the gear of the Israelites whom God led out of Egypt and sustained in the desert for forty years. As the Markan missionaries will not need to bring bread with them, so the Israelites did not need to take bread because manna rained down on them from heaven (Exodus 16). As the Markan missionaries are enjoined to take only one suit of clothing, so the wandering Israelites did not need to replace their garments, since they were supernaturally preserved from deterioration (see Deut 8:4; 29:5; cf. *Deut. Rab.* 7.11; Justin *Dialogue* 131). Moreover, three of the items mentioned in Mark 6:8–9 — clothes, bread, and sandals — also come together significantly in Deut 29:5–6, and sandals are again mentioned in the instructions for eating the Passover in Exod 12:11, along with a fourth item from Mark 6:8–9, the walking staff. And the staff is also reminiscent of the famous magical staffs of Moses and his assistant and older brother Aaron (Exodus 4, 7–8; Numbers 17; cf. Toombs, "Rod"). Thus, although some recent exegetes have stressed the overlaps between Jesus' missionary charge and the practice of the wandering Cynic philosophers (see the NOTES on "staff" and "provision bag" in 6:8), there are more extensive parallels with the Exodus tradition (see the comparison in figure 13).

If these Exodus parallels are deliberate — and the fact that Mark is responsible for some of them suggests that they are — Mark probably wishes to imply that the disciples' missionary journey will be a participation in the new exodus inaugurated by Jesus (see the COMMENT on 1:1–3). The Twelve will not need to take along with them the usual travel kit, because they will be entering into this divine act of eschatological liberation, and the God of the exodus and of Jesus Christ will sustain them along the way. This would be an important message for the members of the Markan community, because they would probably identify with the Twelve; indeed, our passage seems to be shaped in such a way as to encourage such an identification. Everything that would reveal a concrete setting is omitted; readers are given no information about where the disciples are sent or where Jesus stays or what he does in the interim. The tradition hands on only those details that would also hold good for the situation of post-Easter missionaries (see Wellhausen, 44, and Lohmeyer, 141). In the light of this doubling with the post-Easter situation, the note in 6:7 that Jesus *"began to* send out" missionaries becomes doubly significant; not only does this phrase designate the inception of the Twelve's mission, but it also suggests that that mission will be continued by the church, including the Markan community (see the NOTE on "began to send them out" in 6:7).

6:10–11: instructions for the house. The church's likeness with Jesus in his divine empowerment almost means likeness with him in the rejection he experiences from "this generation" (cf. 8:12; 9:19). For in line with "the mystery of the dominion of God," the arrival of the new age does not immediately flatten all opposition; God's designated agents, rather, mysteriously suffer outrage from inimical forces (see the COMMENT on 4:10–12). And so the Twelve must be alerted not only to the power they will hold in their hands but also to the opposition they will face from their contemporaries. This opposition is the main theme of Jesus' concluding instructions (6:10–11). Wherever the disciples are accepted, there they should remain, but wherever they are rejected, they should abandon the town or village after performing a prophetic action that anticipates the judgment that God will send on it (see Reploh, *Lehrer*, 53, 58). This reaction may seem extreme, but it should be remembered that the rejection in view is not just a polite unwillingness to listen but active persecution and even murder (cf. 13:9–13). This sort of antagonism is so deep-seated that it seems to be endemic to the locality itself ("whatever *place*"); Markan readers might well be reminded of the bad soil in the Parable of the Sower, which would not allow the word to bear fruit (4:5–7, 15–19).

In response to this deeply "grounded" repudiation, the missionaries are told, appropriately enough, to shake the *dust* from their feet as they depart—a sign that they are to reject the place as completely as it has rejected them. The very difficulty of the act envisaged—dust is not so easily removed, especially from sandaled feet that have been walking on unpaved Middle Eastern roads— hints at the depth of feeling that evokes it. Not even the tiniest reminder of the place that has rejected the missionaries is to remain with them; they must assiduously purge themselves of every trace of it and depart, not giving their persecutors another thought. God himself will see to the latter on the day of judgment, when the very dust will cry out "as a witness against them" (cf. Luke 19:40; Jas 5:3). These instructions, again, transcend the narrative frame of the story; the Twelve themselves are not described as meeting with any opposition on this particular journey. But in the post-Easter period they, and the Markan missionaries who follow in their wake, will confront intense opposition (see again 13:9–13), and our passage anticipates and responds to this experience of rejection.

   6:12–13: the successful mission. The sobering suggestion of future judgment at the end of the missionary instructions aids the transition to the concluding Markan description of the mission of the Twelve. Listening to the word from and about Jesus is such a vital matter that its rejection leads to eschatological judgment; it is therefore of the utmost importance to repent, i.e. to turn away from the opposition to God that is characteristic of humanity in the old age and to turn with all one's being to the inbreaking power of the new age (6:12), which is demonstrated in the disciples' many exorcisms and healings (6:13; cf. 1:15). In view of those miracles, the mission of the Twelve, which anticipates the outreach of the Markan community, would appear to be a brilliant success. But the passage's gloomy anticipation of future rejection (6:11), as we have just seen, also reflects Markan realities. These two themes may perhaps be unified by the observation that, in Markan theology, the word is proclaimed all the more forcefully, and God's power manifested all the more intensely, in the midst of persecution (cf. 13:9–13). The vivifying power of the resurrection, which is foreshadowed in the disciples' miraculous works and effective preaching, flows out of the rejection, suffering, and death of Jesus, which is continued in the persecutions of the early church.
   This point is reinforced by the very structure of the Markan missionary journey, which interposes our next pericope, the story of the execution of John the Baptist, between the two halves of the miraculous, life-giving journey of the Twelve. John the Baptist's execution, however, foreshadows the crucifixion of Jesus. Jesus' death on the cross, then, is the basis for the life-giving power of the gospel.

THE MARTYRDOM OF JOHN THE BAPTIST
(6:14–29)

6[14]And King Herod heard about it, for Jesus' name had become well known, and people were saying that John the Baptist had been raised from among the dead, and on account of that the powers were at work in him. [15]But others said that he was Elijah. And still others said that he was a prophet, like a prophet in the Scriptures. [16]But Herod, when he heard these opinions, said, "The one I myself beheaded, John, has been raised."
   [17]For Herod himself had sent out and arrested John and bound him in prison on account of Herodias, the wife of his brother Philip, because he had married her. [18]For John had said to Herod, "You're not allowed to marry your brother's wife." [19]And after that Herodias had it in for him and wanted to kill

him, but she wasn't able to. [20]For Herod was afraid of John, knowing that he was a righteous and holy man, and he protected him; and when he listened to him he was greatly perplexed, and yet he listened to him eagerly.

[21]But an opportune day arrived for Herodias when Herod, for his birthday, made a feast for his lords and military commanders and the magnates of Galilee; [22]and his daughter Herodias came in, danced, and pleased Herod and his guests. The king said to the girl, "Ask of me whatever you want, and I will give it to you." [23]And he swore to her, "Whatever you ask of me, I will give it to you, up to half my kingdom." [24]So she went out and said to her mother, "What shall I ask for?," and she said, "The head of John the Baptizer." [25]So she went in to the king with haste and immediately made her request, saying, "I want you to give me immediately, on a platter—the head of John the Baptist!" [26]And although he became very sad, still because of his oaths and his guests he didn't want to deny her. [27]So immediately the king sent one of his bodyguards and commanded him to bring him his head. And he went away and beheaded him in prison [28]and brought his head on a platter and gave it to the girl, and the girl gave it to her mother. [29]And his disciples heard about it and came and took up his corpse and buried it in a tomb.

NOTES

6 14. *King Herod.* Gk *ho basileus Herōdēs.* This is Herod Antipas, the ruler of Galilee and the Transjordanian region of Perea from the death of his father, Herod the Great, in 4 B.C.E. until his exile in 39 C.E. Despite Mark's terminology, Antipas was not actually a king but a tetrarch (= "ruler of a fourth part"), i.e. a puppet ruler appointed by the Romans, who had removed royal sovereignty from the Jews after the death of Herod the Great. Mark's reference to him as a "king" could be a simple mistake or reflection of popular custom; Hoehner (*Herod,* 150) compares the way in which Hyrcanus II is called "ethnarch" by the Romans but "king" by the Jews in the writings of Josephus. But see also the COMMENT on 6:14–16.

heard about it. Gk *ēkousen.* Heard about what? In the present context the reference is apparently to the activities of Jesus' disciples. But 6:14 may incorporate a pre-Markan tradition that had a different context such as a report about Jesus' miracles; Herod goes on to speculate about the source of Jesus' power, not the disciples' (see Dibelius, *Überlieferung,* 82–83).

people were saying. Gk *elegon,* lit. "they were saying," an example of an impersonal usage of the third person plural, which is frequent in Mark (see the NOTE on "people came" in 5:14). Some very good manuscripts (א, A, C, etc.) read *elegen,* "he was saying," attributing this opinion to Herod (cf. 6:16, where he reiterates it). But *elegon* (read by B, W, and important Old Latin witnesses) is the more difficult text, since with that reading the subject jumps confusingly, but in a way consonant with the liveliness of Markan narrative, from Herod to an undefined plural entity (cf. Lohmeyer, 115 n. 4).

from among the dead. Gk *ek nekrōn*, lit. "from among the dead people," i.e. from the realm of the dead.

on account of that the powers were at work in him. Gk *dia touto energousin hai dynameis en autǭ*. The word translated "powers," *dynameis*, is also used in 6:2, 5, where it is translated "works of power"; it is thus strongly associated with miracles in this section of Mark (cf. 5:30; 9:39). But there is no other evidence that John the Baptist had a reputation as a wonder-worker, and indeed John 10:41 seems to imply that he was not. Bultmann (*John*, 394 n. 4) nevertheless thinks that the Johannine statement is polemical and that John was remembered in some circles for miracles. But it is more likely that the emphasis here is on the transformation wrought by his supposed resurrection (cf. John 14:12 and Rev 13:3–4 and see Lohmeyer, 116). M. Smith (*Jesus*, 33–34) thinks that Herod is identifying Jesus as a necromancer, one who works miracles through the spirits of dead people, but as Davies and Allison point out (2.468), elsewhere in the NT "raised from the dead" has nothing to do with necromancy.

15. *a prophet, like a prophet in the Scriptures.* Gk *prophētēs hōs heis tōn prophētōn*, lit. "a prophet, like one of the prophets." There were other "prophets" in first-century Palestine (see the survey in Horsley and Hanson, *Bandits*, and cf. Wellhausen, 46). The second phrase, "like one of the prophets," distinguishes Jesus from these contemporary prophets and links him with *the* prophets, i.e. those of the Old Testament, whose line was considered to have ceased, only to be renewed at the eschaton (cf. 1 Macc 4:46; 14:41; cf. Sommer, "Did Prophecy?").

16. *The one I myself beheaded.* Gk *hon egō apekephalisa*. Actually, Herod's dirty work was done by his bodyguard (6:27). Rulers are responsible for the executions they order, so Herod's statement is in a way true, but the superfluous and perhaps boastfully emphatic *egō* ("I myself") fits in with the passage's stress on the hollowness of Herod's royal pretensions (see the COMMENT on 6:14–16).

has been raised. Gk *ēgerthē*. This is a divine passive (see the NOTE on 1:41); to the human act of wickedness is opposed a divine act of vindication. Mark, then, puts in Herod's own mouth the fundamental thought of martyr theology (see Ernst, *Johannes*, 29), which is classically expressed by the contrast in the book of Acts: "*You* killed him . . . but *God* raised him up" (Acts 2:23–24; 3:15, etc.). For Herod, however, the assumed divine miracle of John's resurrection is a cause not for celebration but for terror; as Euthymius comments: "The murderer fears the one he has murdered. That's the way it is with the evil man" (cited by Lohmeyer, 117 n. 2)—a principle well illustrated by Macbeth's horror at Banquo's ghost. Berger (*Auferstehung*, 17–22) takes our passage as evidence of a Jewish belief in a dying and rising eschatological prophet. Although there is little corroboration for this specific idea (see Davies and Allison, 2.468), the general phenomenon of popular expectation of the return from the dead of an important leader is attested in the first century; see,

Figure 14: Simplified Herodian Family Tree

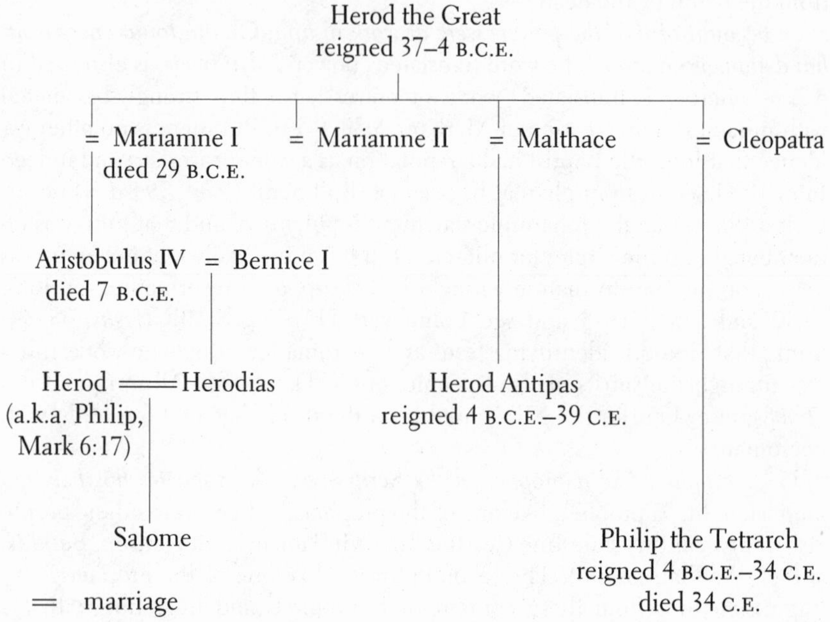

Herod the Great
reigned 37–4 B.C.E.

```
       = Mariamne I        = Mariamne II    = Malthace        = Cleopatra
         died 29 B.C.E.


    Aristobulus IV  = Bernice I
    died 7 B.C.E.


     Herod ====Herodias              Herod Antipas
    (a.k.a. Philip,                reigned 4 B.C.E.–39 C.E.
     Mark 6:17)


          Salome                          Philip the Tetrarch
                                        reigned 4 B.C.E.–34 C.E.
     ==  marriage                             died 34 C.E.
```

for example, the belief that the emperor Nero had returned (Tacitus *Histories* 2.8; Dio Chrysostom *Orations* 21.10; *Sib. Or.* 4.119–24, etc.; see Griffin, "Nero," 1080).

17. *sent out.* Gk *aposteilas*, the verb that is used for Jesus' sending out of messengers to heal and proclaim good news in the previous story (6:7), and one that is cognate with "apostles" in the following story (6:30). This contrast between the two sendings-out is part of a motif of demonic caricature that runs through the passage; see the COMMENT on 6:21–28.

on account of. Gk *dia.* Herod is so favorably disposed toward John in Mark's account (see the COMMENT on 6:17–20) that it is even possible, as Freedman suggests, that this *dia* indicates that Herod arrests John in order to protect him against Herodias' murderous resentment (cf. 6:19–20). The Baptist's confinement in Herod's dungeon means that he is not susceptible to assassination by others and can only be executed by Herod's express order (cf. 6:27).

Herodias, the wife of his brother Philip, because he had married her. Gk *Hērǭdiada tēn gynaika Philippou tou adelphou autou, hoti autēn egamēsen.* The Herodian family tree is quite complicated, since Herod the Great had ten wives and numerous offspring, many of whom intermarried with each other. Figure 14 diagrams the relationships relevant to our passage. Herodias was a granddaughter of Herod the Great. Her first husband was a son of Herod the Great (hence her uncle); his name, according to Josephus, was also Herod; Mark, however, calls him Philip, perhaps confusing him with Philip the Tetrarch, Herodias' son-in-law. (Luke seems to be aware of this error, since he drops the name "Philip" in Luke 3:19.) Herodias divorced this Herod and then married his half brother Herod Antipas, who was her uncle too. (She seems to have liked uncles and men named Herod—and there were a lot of both around, thanks to Herod the Great.) Thus Salome, Herodias' daughter by her first marriage, was at the same time Antipas' niece (on her father's side), his grandniece (on her mother's side), and his stepdaughter. On Mark's possible mistake about Salome's name and relationship to Antipas, see the NOTE on "his daughter Herodias" in 6:22.

18. *You're not allowed to marry your brother's wife.* Gk *ouk exestin soi echein tēn gynaika tou adelphou sou.* Lev 18:16 and 20:21 forbid a man to have sexual intercourse with his brother's wife, though Deut 25:5–10 commands it when the brother has died without leaving a son. Later Jewish law specifies that the prohibition includes the wife of a half brother, as in the present case (see *b. Yebam.* 55a). It is interesting that the Damascus Document of Qumran forbids marriage with a niece (CD 5:8–11), which would also apply in the present case (see the previous NOTE), though this is not the stated reason for the denunciation (against M. Black, *Scrolls*, 123).

In a Greco-Roman context John's fearless denunciation of Herod would be seen as an expression of *parrēsia*, boldness in speech, one of the most revered virtues in the hierarchical and often repressive Hellenistic world (cf. Schlier, "*Parrēsia*"). Mark's readers would have experienced a vicarious thrill in hearing about such a bold and subversive act, but they also would have been keenly aware that it exposed its perpetrator to the risk of swift and effective revenge.

20. *he was greatly perplexed.* Gk *polla ēporei.* Two letters separate this reading from *polla epoiei,* which is supported by a broad range of Greek and versional witnesses and is thought by some to reflect an Aramaic original meaning "he heard him often" (e.g. MHT, 2.445–46; BDF, §414[5]). But *polla ēporei* also has weighty witnesses and uses *polla* in a typically Markan way to mean "greatly." *Ēporei,* moreover, must be reckoned the more difficult reading; if Herod was so confused by the Baptist, why did he keep listening to him (cf. Wellhausen, 46; Metzger, 89)?

21. *But an opportune day arrived for Herodias when.* Gk *kai genomenēs hēmeras eukairou hote.* Herodias is not actually mentioned in the Greek, but in view of her desire to do John in (6:19), the reference can only be to her.

for his birthday, made a feast. Gk *tois genesiois autou deipnon epoiēsen.* Both the rabbis (e.g. *m. 'Abod. Zar.* 1:3) and the church fathers (e.g. Origen *Commentary on Matthew* 10.22) deprecated birthday parties, especially for kings, as pagan, idolatrous celebrations, and they were not observed in ancient Judaism (see *EncJud,* 4.1054).

for his lords and military commanders and the magnates of Galilee. Gk *tois megistasin autou kai chiliarchois kai tois prōtois tēs Galilaias.* The first term, *megistanes* = "lords" or "great ones," denotes the inner circle of Herod's government; cf. Dan 5:23 LXX, which uses the word in a similar context. The second term, *chiliarchoi* ("military commanders"), literally means "leaders of a thousand [soldiers]," though by the first century the number of men could be considerably less; in today's terms the *chiliarchos* would be equivalent to a major or colonel. The third group, the *prōtoi tēs Galilaias* = "magnates [lit. "first men"] of Galilee," is vaguer, denoting not an official governmental or military body but the aristocracy of the region (see Hoehner, *Herod*, 102 n. 3 and 119 n. 3).

22. *his daughter Herodias*. Gk *tēs thygatros autou Hērǫdiados*, the reading of important manuscripts (א, B, D, etc.), which make Herod Antipas the dancing girl's father and give her the same name as her mother, Herodias (which is not so implausible in a family in which so many of the males were named Herod). If this is the original text, however, it is one of a number of inaccuracies in the passage (see the introduction to the COMMENT). The girl was actually named Salome, and Herod Antipas was her uncle, her father being another Herod, his half brother, whom our story wrongly calls Philip (see Josephus *Ant.* 18.136 and cf. the NOTE on 6:17). Mark, then, may have confused the two Herods, or he may have used "daughter" imprecisely for "stepdaughter." One can easily understand why a later scribe would have tried to straighten things out by changing the reading *autou* to *autēs*, then adding a *tēs* to make it clear that "Herodias" is the name of the mother rather than the name of the daughter, as in the other major reading (A, C, K, etc.; cf. Matt 14:6). The reading chosen, which makes the performer of the dance that titillates Herod and his guests into Herod's own daughter, accords with the story's general atmosphere of wild abandon.

danced. Gk *orchēsamenēs*. For some (e.g. Taylor, 315) the impropriety of a young girl dancing before a group of men at a feast is a major obstacle to accepting the historicity of Mark's account. But while there are several legitimate grounds for doubting Mark's accuracy (see the COMMENT), this is not one of them, since the Herodian household in general and Antipas in particular were scarcely paragons of Jewish virtue (see e.g. Josephus *Ant.* 18.36–38; *Life* 65).

pleased. Gk *ēresen*. In the Septuagint this verb often has connotations of arousing or satisfying sexual interest (see e.g. Gen 19:8; Judg 14:1A, 14:3A, 14:7A; Esth 2:4, 9; Job 31:10 and cf. 1 Cor 7:33–34). The verbal similarity to Esther 2:9, *kai ēresen autǫ to korasion* ("and the young girl pleased him"), is particularly striking, especially because the "him" in question, King Ahasuerus, ends up promising Esther half his kingdom (see the next NOTE). In our passage the all-male audience and the extraordinary promise to which Herod is driven are evidence for a similar sexual connotation.

The king said. Gk *eipen ho basileus*. The clause lacks Mark's typical "and" (*kai*) or any other conjunction; this asyndeton (see GLOSSARY), which makes the clause emphatic, perhaps underscores Herod's sexual excitement (see the COMMENT on 6:21–28).

23. *Whatever you ask of me, I will give it to you, up to half my kingdom*. Gk *ho ti ean me aitēsęs dōsō soi heōs hēmisous tēs basileias mou*. In Esth 5:3 King Ahasuerus says, "What do you want, Esther? And what is your request? [Ask for] up to half of my kingdom (*heōs tou hēmisous tēs basileias mou*), and it shall be yours." The parallel embraces not only the specific wording but also

the motif of the king repeatedly urging a young girl to make a request. Though Ahasuerus is a more positive figure than Herod in the Bible itself, later Jewish tradition besmirches his character; see, for example, the derogatory interpretations of his name in *Esth. Rab.* 1:1–3, *Exod. Rab.* 2.2–3.

25. *went in to the king with haste and immediately made her request.* Gk *eiselthousa euthys meta spoudēs pros tēn basilea ̜tēsato,* lit. "going in immediately with haste to the king made request." From this word order, "immediately" would seem to modify "going in" rather than "made request," but this may be an example of Mark's tendency to introduce "immediately" prematurely (see the NOTE on "And as he was coming up out of the water, he immediately" in 1:10).

Here and in the preceding verse, *aitein* ("to ask for, request") is used by the girl in the middle voice, whereas in 6:22–23 it had been used by Herod in the active. This shift may imply that the girl sees herself as standing in a business relationship with Herod (see BDF, §316[2]); he has promised her something in return for her erotic dance, and he is obligated to fulfill this promise.

27. *one of his bodyguards.* Gk *spekoulatora,* a Latin loanword originally meaning "spy" or "scout." From its origins, then, the term has a nuance of skulduggery. Here it does not denote an official executioner but a bodyguard who can be dispatched on all sorts of dirty business. As Hoehner notes, quoting Sherwin-White (*Herod,* 119–20 n. 3), it is used in Tacitus (*Histories* 1.24–25; 2.73) for "a special body of imperial guards who tend to appear in moments of military intrigue."

28. *brought his head on a platter and gave it to the girl,* etc. Gk *ēnengken tēn kephalēn autou epi pinaki kai edōken autēn tọ korasiọ.* Besides gratifying a sadistic whim, the production of the head also provides convincing proof that John has been killed.

COMMENT

Introduction. The story of the missionary journey of the Twelve (6:12–13, 30) is interrupted for a flashback about the execution of John the Baptist by Herod Antipas (6:17–29; on this Herod, see the NOTE on "King Herod" in 6:14). As Luke senses (Luke 3:19–20), the proper place to describe the circumstances of John's imprisonment would be before Jesus' ministry has gotten started; if Mark has instead intercalated his long account of it and of John's death into a spot where they do not chronologically belong, he must have some narrative reason for doing so. On a crude rhetorical level the flashback gives the disciples time to go out and come back again (see Bultmann, 301–2). But the intercalation of the story of the Baptist probably also has a deeper purpose; it points to the paradox that the miraculous successes of Christian missionaries are made possible by the suffering death of Jesus, to which the death of the Baptist points.

The story probably existed in substantially its present form before it was incorporated into Mark; in contrast to most other Markan passages, it makes no use of the historic present but is told exclusively in the imperfect and aorist, although the pluperfect would have been more appropriate to its present context (Lohmeyer, 117). Moreover, at least one of its features, the description of John as a "righteous and holy man" (6:20), is in tension with Markan theology elsewhere (cf. 2:17; 10:18). Only the bulk of the transition in 6:14–16 (cf. the similarity to 8:27–28) and a stray phrase here and there, such as "he listened to him eagerly" in 6:20 (cf. 12:37), can safely be attributed to Mark.

Form-critically, our narrative is a tale of martyrdom, comparable to the influential stories of the executions of the Maccabean martyrs (2 Macc 6:18–31; 4 Macc 5:1–6:30), the description of Stephen's murder in Acts (Acts 6:8– 7:60), or the rabbinic account of R. Akiba's death (b. Ber. 61b). It is a superb example of the genre; the grisly tale is suspensefully told, with plentiful use of the tricks of the storyteller's trade. In terms of its structure it is one of the most elaborate unified compositions outside of the passion narrative, matched only by the story of the Gerasene demoniac in 5:1–20, and it is the only one in which the focus of attention is on someone other than Jesus. After the transition in 6:14–16, the main part of the story unfolds in two scenes: the arrest and imprisonment of John (6:17–20) and the events at Herod's birthday party (6:21–28). The burial of John's body by his disciples (6:29) forms a coda.

6:14–16: transition. The transition from the account of the disciples' missionary journey to the flashback about John the Baptist is provided, none too smoothly, by Herod's assertion that Jesus is John raised from among the dead (6:14–16). This awkward transition (Herod hears about the disciples but comments about Jesus) may reflect an earlier version of the story in which he actually heard something about Jesus (see the NOTE on "heard about it" in 6:14) — perhaps an uncomplimentary remark that Jesus had made about him or his family (cf. 8:15; Luke 13:32), one that reminded him of John. In the Markan context, however, this transition drives home the point of the previous passage: the disciples' activity is an extension of Jesus' own (cf. "gave them authority" in 6:7), so that their success redounds to his glory (cf. Reploh, Lehrer, 55–56).

The recipient of the report about Jesus is called King Herod throughout the story (6:14, 22, 25–27). The title "king" is technically inaccurate (see the NOTE on "King Herod" in 6:14), but its repeated usage here is probably not just a Markan mistake. It is, rather, an example of the evangelist's irony, for it is prominent in a passage in which Herod is outwitted and manipulated by two women and hamstrung by his own oath and his fear of losing face before his courtiers (cf. J. Anderson, "Dancing Daughter," 127). Throughout the passage, moreover, we see that this supposed "king" is not even in control of himself, much less of his subjects; he is, rather, overmastered by his emotions, which swing wildly from superstitious dread (6:14, 16) to awe, fascination, and confusion (6:20), to a sexual arousal that seems to border on insanity (6:22–23), to extreme depression (6:26). In this context his pretensions to royal authority (6:16, 27) appear almost farcical; Herod is one who merely *appears* to rule (cf. 10:42), whereas actually his strings are pulled by others. This ironic portrait of "King" Herod is Mark's version of a common antityrannical theme, the germ of which is present in the Old Testament (e.g. Pharaoh, Ahasuerus in Esther, the king in Daniel) but that is more explicitly developed in the Greco-Roman sphere from Plato to the Cynics and Stoics: the tyrant is not a true king but a slave to his own passions (Plato *Republic* 9.573b–580a, 587b–e), and his claim to sovereignty is belied by his inability to enforce his will and avoid what he hates (Arrian, *Discourses of Epictetus* 1.19.2–3; cf. 1.24.15–18 and Schlier, "*Eleutheros,*" 493).

Corresponding to the inadequacy of Herod as king, the opinion he expresses about Jesus' identity is also inadequate, and the other two estimates sampled in the passage are similarly faulty. Jesus is neither John the Baptist raised from the dead, nor Elijah, nor merely a prophet. All three opinions, to be sure, are on the right track to the extent that they place Jesus in the class of eschatological figures, but all three contain an element of miscalculation. Mark's readers, for example, know that Jesus is not John, since John and Jesus were alive at the same time; John, rather, was Jesus' forerunner (cf. 1:2–8; 9:11–13). With respect to Elijah, Mark has already linked this OT figure not with Jesus but with John (1:2–8), and he will shortly drive this identification home (9:11–13). And, while Jesus has indirectly referred to himself as a prophet in 6:4, in a subsequent passage closely related to ours he will imply that "prophet" is an insufficient valuation of him (8:27–30). While the title is accurate so far as it goes, it does not fully grasp Jesus' identity (there is a similar ambiguity about the titles "Son of David" and "Messiah"; cf. 8:27–30; 12:35–37; 14:53–65).

Although the evaluation of Jesus as a reincarnation of John the Baptist is clearly mistaken in Mark's eyes, Herod reiterates it, thus further undermining his royal pretensions to omnipotence and omniscience. Jesus, he stubbornly insists, is John, "the one I myself beheaded" (see the NOTE on this clause in 6:16). This insistence leads into the account of how that beheading took place.

6:17–20: arrest and imprisonment. The flashback begins with the story of John's arrest, which merges into an account of his death. We are in the unusual position of possessing a narration of these events independent of the Gospels, that of the Jewish historian Josephus in *Antiquities of the Jews* (18.116–19); interestingly, Josephus, like the Gospels, describes John's death in a flashback (cf. Hoehner, *Herod*, 111–12). Several of the other details of these two accounts, however, conflict. Mark, for example, implies through the presence of Galilean notables (6:21) that John was executed in Herod's official palace in Tiberias in Galilee; Josephus, however, locates the execution far away in Herod's fortress at Machaerus in southern Perea, on the eastern shore of the Dead Sea. There are also discrepancies about the names of the daughter of Herod's wife Herodias and of her former husband (see the NOTES on "Herodias, the wife of his brother Philip, because he had married her" in 6:17 and "his daughter Herodias" in 6:22). Most striking, however, is the disparity concerning Herod's attitude toward John and the motivation for John's arrest and execution. Mark presents Herod as positively inclined toward John; he is only manipulated into killing him by the scheming of Herodias and the en-thralling dance of her daughter. Josephus, however, says that Herod arrested and executed John because he feared he would start a revolution.

These two accounts really cannot be reconciled with each other, despite the efforts of scholars such as Taylor (311) to do so: "Political ends and the anger of an insulted woman cannot be regarded as mutually exclusive." But this argument ignores the fact that the attitude toward John ascribed to Herod in the two accounts is entirely different: in Mark he wants to *protect* him (see 6:20 and cf. the NOTE on "on account of" in 6:17), whereas in Josephus he wants to *kill* him. Of the two accounts, Josephus' seems to be more reliable historically. Mark's is gossipy and sensational, like a contemporary soap opera or the outpourings of the tabloid press, whereas the atmosphere of cold political calculation in Josephus is intrinsically more credible. It corresponds to early Christian apologetic, moreover, to portray rulers as favorably inclined toward Christian heroes, as Mark does, whereas in reality they may have been less friendly; the same tendency can be observed in the depictions of Pontius Pilate in the Gospel passion narratives. While Mark's story has a historical core, then—John was executed by Herod and this execution was popularly connected with Herod's marital arrangements (see Josephus *Ant.* 18.109–16)—this core has been greatly embellished by folkloristic features and theological tendencies.

One of those tendencies is a concern to emphasize the likeness between John and Jesus. As Gnilka points out ("Martyrium," 83), the phrase "in prison" frames the entire story of the Baptist (6:17, 27), and his incarceration and fettering in a gloomy dungeon (cf. "bound him" in 6:17) contrasts sharply with the Herodian court's atmosphere of luxury and unrestraint, which eventuates in his execution. The contrast thus foreshadows Jesus' subsequent statement that "they did to [John] whatever they wanted" (9:13)—a characterization that also applies to Jesus himself (cf. 9:31; 14:41). The arrest (*ekratēsen*) and binding (*edēsen*) of John in 6:17, moreover, look forward to the arrest (*ekratēsan*) and binding (*dēsantes*) of Jesus in 14:46 and 15:1.

But if Mark's Baptist points toward Jesus, he also has a unique role to play in the redemptive drama—that of Elijah. According to Mark, the catalyst for "their" desire to kill John is supplied by his denunciation of Herod's marriage to Herodias (6:17–18), which violates the injunction of the OT law against marrying the wife of one's brother (Lev 18:16; cf. Lev 20:21 and see the NOTE on "You're not allowed to marry your brother's wife" in 6:18). John thus appears as an Elijah-like figure, zealous for the Lord and his Law (cf. 1 Kgs 19:10, 14) and willing to risk the wrath of a king in order to press the Law's imperious claims (cf. 1 Kgs 21:17–24; cf. 2 Chr 21:12–19). More dangerously still, he, like Elijah, antagonizes the king's wife, who therefore seeks his death (6:19; cf. 1 Kgs 19:2). The Elijan echoes are probably not fortuitous, because Mark elsewhere identifies the Baptist with Elijah (1:2–8; 9:11–13).

As the story unfolds, however, we see that there is one major obstacle to the queen's revenge—the divided mind of the dictator himself (6:20). Despite the insult to himself from John's denunciation and despite the fear that John inspires in him, Herod listens to him eagerly—forceful testimony to the power of the divine word (cf. "receive the word with joy" in 4:16). Even in Herod's fascination with John, however, there is a sinister undertone, since the strange mixture of fear of, and attraction to, a holy man is reminiscent of the demon's response to the "Son of the Most High God" in 5:6–7.

Despite this demonic parallel, for the moment Herod's desire to protect John sets up a hurdle against Herodias' ambition to kill him. The rest of the story describes the devilishly clever way in which she overcomes that hurdle.

6:21–28: *Herod's birthday party.* The opportunity comes on the festive occasion of Herod's birthday party, and the account of the way in which Herodias seizes it is superbly told. As Gnilka points out, for example ("Martyrium," 83), the scene is enlivened by the entrance, exit, and reentrance of the daughter (6:22, 24, 25) and the constant change of subject (king → girl → mother → girl → king → executioner). The verbs "ask for" and "give," which epitomize the action, stand out by their constant repetition. Another important term is *eukairou* ("opportune"), which occurs significantly near the beginning; in the overall Markan context, this adjective anticipates Judas' search for an opportunity (*eukairōs*) to betray Jesus in 14:41—one more parallel between their deaths (cf. J. Anderson, "Dancing Daughter," 120–21). But *eukairou* also recalls *euangelion* ("good news") and *kairos* ("time") in 1:14–15 and anticipates the cognate verb *eukairoun* ("had a chance") in 6:31; the opportune time of 6:21, then, is a counterweight to the fulfilled time announced by Jesus and an example of a motif of demonic caricature that pervades the passage (see below and the NOTE on "sent out" in 6:17).

The opportunity for Herodias' diabolical plot to be executed is provided by the dance of her daughter, which is probably meant to be understood as sexually provocative in nature (on the girl's name and the nature of her dance, see the NOTES on "his daughter Herodias" and "danced" in 6:22). The long periodic sentence in 6:21–22 builds up tension through a series of participles, a tension that is finally (and erotically!) released through the finite verb "pleased" near its end. Herod's lecherous impatience is underlined by the asyndeton (see GLOSSARY) of his speech to the girl in 6:22b and by the repetition and expansion of his promise to her in 6:23.

But there is more to the story than lechery; it also contains some significant biblical echoes, especially of the book of Esther (cf. Aus, *Water*). "The girl pleased him" and "up to half my kingdom," for example, are nearly exact quotations from Greek Esther (see the NOTES on "pleased" in 6:22 and "Whatever you request of me, I will give it to you, up to half my kingdom" in 6:23). It is interesting, moreover, that the late *Esther Rabbah*, perhaps reflecting earlier traditions, describes the head of the former queen being brought in to the king on a platter (4.9, 11) and is thus parallel to the gory conclusion of our story. To be sure, there are also some significant differences between Esther and Mark, the most important being that Herod and Herodias' daughter are negative characters whereas King Ahasuerus and Esther are positive, but the contrast may be deliberately ironic: whereas Esther saved God's people through her ability to please men, Herodias' daughter uses the same talent to bring about the death of God's prophet (see J. Anderson, "Dancing Daughter," 128).

Besides the similarities between the Markan tale and the biblical book of Esther, there are also some significant nonbiblical parallels to the banquet scene. In the apocryphal Jewish book of Judith, for example, a woman uses her attractiveness to beguile a man and cut off his head. In several non-Jewish stories, moreover, a king is forced, against his own true desire, to grant a favor at a banquet. Herodotus (*Histories* 9.108–13) describes how Xerxes was constrained, by the Persian custom that at royal banquets every favor asked must be granted, to accede to his wife Amestris' desire that her own sister-in-law be turned over to her; Amestris subsequently tortured and maimed this rival, just as Herodias uses the opportunity provided by Herod's banquet to have her enemy murdered (cf. Gnilka, "Martyrium," 88). Josephus, similarly, recounts an incident in which the emperor Caligula, pleased by a banquet that Agrippa I had arranged in his honor, insisted that Agrippa ask him for a favor; when the favor turned out to be the rescinding of Caligula's own order to erect his statue in the Jerusalem Temple, he was forced to accede because he, like Herod in our story, "regarded it as unseemly to break his word before so many guests" (Josephus *Ant.* 18.289–304). Livy, moreover, in recounting the life of Crassus, recoils at the horror of staining a feast with the blood of an innocent man to gratify the whim of a prostitute (*History of Rome* 39.43), and Plutarch describes the bringing of the head of an enemy to a king at a feast (*Parallel Lives, Crassus* 33.1–3; cf. Hoehner, *Herod*, 165–67).

Our scene, then, contains numerous traditional and folkloristic elements, which is one of the reasons for questioning its historicity. These elements, moreover, are combined in such a way that they become vehicles for Markan concerns. The tension builds as the dancing girl, promised her heart's desire by the excited king, goes out to seek her mother's advice as to what her heart should desire (6:24a). The reader who has been following the thread of the story has perhaps anticipated that, whatever Herodias suggests, it will not spell good news for the imprisoned John. This impression is confirmed by the quick, almost reflexive manner in which, without batting an eyelash, Herodias answers, "The head of John the Baptizer" (6:24b). This instantaneous reply may, as Taylor suggests (316), imply premeditation, but it may also imply that the cunning demonic forces that have been working for John's downfall have now at last sprung their trap.

The daughter's reentry to the banqueting hall sets the stage for the climactic scene. Her delayed response to Herod in 6:25 makes skillful use of narrative delay to keep the king guessing until the end, building up suspense to her shocking request: "I want you to give me, immediately, on a platter—the head of John the Baptist!" The platter, incidentally, had not been mentioned by Herodias, and is her daughter's own macabre touch; apparently, Herodias' gift for creative improvisation in sadism is either hereditary or contagious. The daughter also seems to have a gift for extortion; the voice of the verb "ask/make request" in 6:24–25 implies a reminder to Herod that they have a deal (see the NOTE on "went in to the king with haste and immediately made her request" in 6:25). In the larger context of the Gospel these two daringly evil female figures, Herodias and her daughter, are bracketed by two daringly positive female figures, the woman with the hemorrhage (5:24–34) and the Syrophoenician woman (7:24–30; note the common usage of the word "daughter" in all three stories); the four women, then, represent heroines of the faith and their demonic counterparts.

The moment of truth and the climax of the scene have now arrived. In the crucial test of his soul, Herod must decide between saving face and saving John's head; between the good opinion of his noble guests, who expect their royal patron to fulfill his promises no matter what, and his awe of John; between gaining the world and gaining his soul (8:36). For it is not a foregone conclusion, even now, that John must die. Herod could refuse the horrible request; he is, after all, supposedly "the king." But the same divided mind that formerly preserved John's life now condemns him to death; although Herod is depressed at the idea of acceding to the murderous petition to dispatch John, he is afraid to refuse it "because of his oaths and his guests." Herod, then, lets John die, and thus shows himself to be among those in whom, despite their attraction to God's dominion, the concerns of this age end up choking the word (4:19).

The banquet ends in a scene of Gothic horror. There are overtones of cannibalism, for John's head is brought into the feast on a serving platter. The grotesque manner in which it is then passed around makes a striking contrast to the chain of transmission in the immediately following passage, which will also describe a kind of feast. There the miraculously multiplied loaves, which probably symbolize eucharistic bread, will be passed from Jesus to the disciples to the crowd (6:41; cf. 8:6 and see Fowler, *Loaves*, 86); here the Baptist's head is passed around on a platter from executioner to daughter to mother. Moreover, the verb that will be used for the true king's commanding the crowds to sit down, *epetaxen*, is exactly the same one that is used in our passage for the false king's commanding his henchman to execute John (6:27, 39). The element of caricature that we have observed throughout our narrative, then, pervades it to the end, and the connections with the Feeding of the Five Thousand suggest that it is meant to be seen as a kind of demonic eucharist. That this interpretation is plausible is indicated by the medieval practice of venerating a devotional image of John's head on a platter as a type of the eucharist (see Stuebe, "Johannisschüssel," 6–7, and J. Anderson, "Dancing Daughter," 127).

6:29: John's burial. The bizarre tale ends with John's burial. This is an odd ending for a martyrdom story, and it matches other anomalous features of the narrative. Overall, John plays an extraordinarily minor role in the story of his death. In the whole long narrative he is the subject of a verb only in 6:18, elsewhere merely receiving the action of others (Herod, Herodias, Salome, the executioner); as Dibelius points out, moreover (*Überlieferung*, 78–79), apart from 6:18 the living Baptist never puts in an appearance at all—only his severed head materializes at the end of the scene! In contrast to other examples of the martyrdom story, Mark provides no interpretative scene in which John confronts his persecutors and prophesies divine judgment on them with his dying breath, as in 2 and 4 Maccabees, the Stephen story in Acts, or the story of R. Akiba in *b. Ber.* 61b. Nor does he explicitly hold John's martyrdom up as a model for imitation or otherwise attempt to make sense of it, as occurs even in Josephus' account of the Baptist, where the historian vindicates John by asserting that Herod's military defeat by Aretas was a punishment for his execution (see Gnilka, "Martyrium," 84–85). In Mark, rather, John is simply murdered—an event that occurs, untypically for a martyrdom, offstage—and his disfigured body is buried by his disciples. Readers may well wonder about the missing element of divine compensation for the outrage John has suffered.

In the overall context of the Gospel the compensation comes with the vindication of that other rejected and grotesquely murdered figure, to whom the Gospel so resolutely subordinates John: Jesus himself. As we have noted along the way, there are numerous parallels between the Baptist, as he is presented in our passage, and Jesus (cf. Ernst, *Johannes*, 28–29). Each is "eagerly heard" (see 6:20; 12:37) and becomes the object of the curiosity of a leader (6:12; cf. 15:9–10, 14–15), who tries unsuccessfully to save him (6:20; cf. 15:4, 9–14). Each, however, falls victim to his enemies' murderous intention (6:19; cf. 3:6; 14:1, etc.), is arrested and bound (6:17; cf. 14:46; 15:1), and is ignominiously executed and buried (6:27–29; cf. 15:16–47). Somehow, then, in Mark's conception, the compensation for John's sufferings—and, we may add, for the sufferings of all whose injuries go unavenged in this world (cf. 9:42–49)—is mysteriously wrapped up with the vindication of Jesus, the rejected stone, whom God has now made into the keystone of a new Temple (12:11–12).

Thus the end of our passage comes full circle from its beginning. It starts with Herod recognizing a likeness (in his mind an identity) between John the Baptist and Jesus on the basis of their shared charismatic power. It ends with John's execution and burial, which points toward a far more significant likeness in persecution and death. Yet out of death comes new life, as readers will be reminded in the following scene of miraculous divine provision in a desolate wilderness (6:30–44).

JESUS FEEDS FIVE THOUSAND MEN (6:30–44)

6 ³⁰And the apostles congregated before Jesus and told him all that they had done and taught. ³¹And he said to them, "Come by yourselves privately to a deserted place and rest up a little." For there were many people coming and going, and they didn't even have a chance to eat. ³²So they went away in a boat to a deserted place privately. ³³But they were seen going, and many peo-

ple found out about it, and they ran together to the spot on foot and got there before them. [34]And when he got out of the boat Jesus saw a great crowd, and he took pity on them, for they were like sheep not having a shepherd, and he began to teach them many things.

[35]And since the hour was already late, the disciples came to him and said, "This place is deserted, and the hour is already late. [36]Send them away, so that they may go into the neighboring villages and towns and buy themselves something to eat." [37]But he answered and said to them, "Give them something to eat yourselves." And they said to him, "What do you want us to do? Shall we go out and buy two hundred denarii worth of bread and and give it to them to eat?"

[38]And he said to them, "How many loaves do you have? Go and see." And they found out and said, "Five, and two fish." [39]And he commanded them to make them all recline eating-group by eating-group on the green grass. [40]So the people reclined cluster by cluster in groups of a hundred and in groups of fifty. [41]And taking the five loaves and the two fish, and looking up into heaven, he said the blessing and broke the loaves, and kept giving them to his disciples, in order that they might distribute them; and the two fish he divided among them all. [42]And they all ate and were satisfied; [43]and they took up twelve baskets full of bread fragments and fish. [44]And there were five thousand men who ate the loaves.

NOTES

6   30. *apostles.* Gk *apostoloi,* lit. "those sent out." On the principle of representation embodied in this term, see the COMMENT on 6:6b–7.

31. *privately to a deserted place.* Gk *kat' idian eis erēmon topon.* This is one of Mark's typical doubled expressions (see Neirynck, *Duality,* 95), and it expresses two of his characteristic themes: the seclusion of Jesus with the disciples (4:10, 34, etc.) and sojourn in the wilderness (1:12–13, 35, 45; cf. Mauser, *Christ*). Both phrases recur in 6:32, and "deserted place" also appears in 6:35. Since Wellhausen (48), the suggestion has frequently been made that Jesus' withdrawal from public activity was motivated by his fear that Herod Antipas, who linked him with John the Baptist (6:14–16), would treat him in the same brutal way he had treated John. But nothing is said about such a motivation in our passage, and it seems more in keeping with the sequence of events and with Markan theology in general to suggest that John's death prompts Jesus to devote more concentrated attention to the disciples who will take his place after his own death (see Davies and Allison, 2.486).

many. Gk *polloi.* This favorite Markan word occurs six times in the first six verses of our passage. Besides the present instance, in 6:33 *many* people (*polloi*) see Jesus and the disciples going away, in 6:34 Jesus sees a *great* (*polyn*) crowd and begins to teach them *many things* (*polla*), and in 6:35 both the narrator and the disciples say that the hour is *late* (*pollē*). Most of these instances of the word emphasize the greatness of the need Jesus confronts; the reference in 6:34 to the many things Jesus teaches points to the sufficiency of his response to this challenge.

33. *they were seen.* Gk *eidon auton*, lit. "they saw them," another example of the third person plural used impersonally (cf. 1:22, 32; 2:3; 3:32; 5:14; 6:14).

34. *like sheep not having a shepherd.* Gk *hōs probata mē echonta poimena.* Mesopotamian kings already described themselves as shepherds of their people (see e.g. *Code of Hammurabi*, Prologue i), and in the OT and later Jewish literature both God and human leaders are pictured as shepherds who should lead and care for their flock (see Vancil, "Sheep"). As Levenson points out, moreover (*Death*, 144), in the OT and later Jewish traditions, "two shepherds in particular, Moses and David, are noteworthy for the transition they made from the literal to the metaphorical forms of their vocation" (see e.g. Ps 78:70–72 and *Exod. Rab.* 2.2–3). Our passage thus strengthens the impression that Jesus is both the Davidic Messiah (cf. *Pss. Sol.* 16:23–46, in which the Messiah is termed a shepherd) and a Mosaic figure.

It is the latter, Mosaic aspect of the shepherd image that is most emphasized in our passage. Admittedly, the "sheep without a shepherd" phrase is not limited to Moses in the OT but becomes a proverbial metaphor for the people suffering either through lack of strong leadership (Num 27:17; 1 Kgs 22:17// 2 Chr 18:16; Jdt 11:19) or through evil rulers (Ezek 34:8; Zech 10:2), and both nuances may apply in the present case. But the phrase most closely echoes Moses' words in Num 27:17, and in moving from an allusion to Moses to a reference to Jesus' teaching, Mark is probably drawing on a Jewish tradition that sees the Torah, the teaching of Moses, as the divine response to the dilemma of the shepherdless sheep of Israel (see Ps 119:176; Philo *Posterity and Exile of Cain* 67–69; *2 Apoc. Bar.* 76:13–14; cf. Lohmeyer, 124 n. 6).

In Num 27:17, Moses' request that God appoint a shepherd in his place is answered by God pointing to Joshua (Greek *Iēsous* = Jesus), "a man in whom is the Spirit." In light of this sequence, one wonders whether a Joshua/Jesus typology may be at the back of Mark's mind: Jesus, too, is a successor of Moses in whom God's Spirit dwells (see 1:9–11 and cf. Heb 4:8, where the Joshua/Jesus typology is played upon). Joshua, moreover, was remembered as one like Moses (see Allison, *New Moses*, 23–28), and in the remainder of the feeding narrative Jesus will act like Moses.

35. *since the hour was already late.* Gk *ēdē hōras pollēs genomenēs*, a genitive absolute construction that is probably a Markan redaction. Mark uses the genitive absolute frequently for time indications (14:17; 15:33, 42; 16:2), and most of these usages have symbolic connotations, as does also the time notice in 1:35. *Pollēs* (= "late" here), moreover, is a favorite Markan word (see the NOTE on "many" in 6:31), and it is missing in Matthew, Luke, and John. Its presence in Mark creates a temporal difficulty: after it is already late, Jesus has time to arrange the huge crowd in ordered ranks, to feed them bread and fish, to have the massive amount of leftovers collected, to send the disciples away, to dismiss the crowd, to climb a mountain, and to pray—all before it gets dark! (cf. 6:47; see Brown, 1.253).

37. *Give ... yourselves.* Gk *Dote ... hymeis.* The second person plural pronoun is not necessary to indicate the number and person of the addressees, since these are already defined by the second person plural imperative verb ("Give!"). Although such superfluous pronouns are sometimes present without any great emphasis in Koine Greek (see Robertson, 676–77), in this case the pronoun is probably emphatic (see the COMMENT on 6:35–37), as is commonly true in the OT (see Gesenius, §135.1).

What do you want us to do? Not present in the Greek, but added in the translation to indicate the sarcastic nature of the following question; the idea of the disciples having half a year's wages to spend on food for the crowd (see the next NOTE) is clearly absurd.

two hundred denarii. Gk *dēnariōn diakosiōn.* As Lohmeyer (126 n. 6) points out, according to Matt 20:1–16 a denarius is a typical day's wages, and in Luke 10:35 the Good Samaritan pays the innkeeper two denarii for an overnight stay. The Scholars Bible therefore rightly paraphrases two hundred denarii as "half a year's wages."

38. *How many loaves do you have?* Gk *Posous artous echete.* Despite the similarity to the manna miracle (see the COMMENT on 6:38–42), the analogy is imperfect, because the food does not come out of nothing; the disciples provide the basic "raw material," which is miraculously multiplied. This feature derives from a different OT source, the stories about Elijah and Elisha in 1 Kgs 17:8–16; 2 Kgs 4:1–7, and especially 2 Kgs 4:42–44 (cf. the introduction to the COMMENT).

loaves ... Five. Gk *artous ... pente.* The five loaves of bread may be related to the Law of Moses, the Pentateuch (which in Hebrew is called the Ḥûmāš, which like "Pentateuch" means "five-part book"). Following the lead of Prov 9:5 (cf. Deut 8:3), postbiblical Judaism developed bread or manna into a symbol for the Torah (see Philo *On the Change of Names* 259–60; *Gen. Rab.* 43.6; 54.1; 70.5; cf. Borgen, *Bread,* 114), and this may be part of the symbolism here (see the COMMENT on 6:38–42).

and two fish. Gk *kai duo ichthyas.* The fish play a comparatively minor role in the story; the previous discussion has concerned only bread (6:37), and in 6:38a Jesus has asked only how many loaves the disciples have, not how many fish (though the total of seven may be significant; see the NOTE on "the two fish he divided among them all" in 6:41). This concentration on the bread is probably due to its more important symbolism (see the previous NOTE and the COMMENT on 6:38–42).

39. *to make them ... recline.* Gk *anaklinai;* cf. *anepesan* = "reclined" in 6:40. In the ancient world, banqueters normally reclined on banqueting couches, but in the Jewish sphere the reclining posture was especially associated with Passover (cf. 14:18 and see Jeremias, *Eucharistic Words,* 48–49, and Bokser, *Origins,* 130 n. 48). Thus the references to reclining may be part of the Passover typology of our passage (see the COMMENT on 6:38–42).

eating-group by eating-group. Gk *symposia symposia,* lit. "eating group eating group"; the distributive repetition is a Semitic idiom that recurs in 6:40

("cluster by cluster"; see Black, 124). The NT *hapax legomenon* (see GLOS-SARY) *symposion* literally means "drinking together" and originally designated a drinking party; it then came to mean a dining room or banquet. Greco-Roman symposium literature, of which Plato's *Symposium* is the most famous example, combines the banquet setting with a philosophical discussion. Mark uses the term here in a transferred sense to refer to companies of diners (see M-M, 598). In view of the Passover/exodus features of our narrative, it is perhaps significant that in Hellenistic times the Passover seder assumed many characteristics of a Greek symposium (see Stein, "Influence").

on the green grass. Gk *epi tǭ chlōrǭ chortǭ.* In Palestine grass grows in the desert only in springtime, and the parallel in John 6:4 sets this miracle during Passover, a spring festival. The green grass may be part of the Passover/exodus typology of the passage rather than a personal reminiscence (against Taylor, 321). Blooming grass, like the Passover/exodus typology in general, points forward to an expected eschatological recapitulation of the exodus events (see Gnilka [1.260]), who cites Isa 35:1–2 and *2 Apoc. Bar.* 29:5–8). In an interesting article, moreover, Allison ("Psalm 23") analyzes the reference to the grass and several other motifs in the story (the shepherd, satisfaction of wants, reclining, even perhaps the seaside setting) as allusions to Psalm 23. This suggestion supports the thesis of an eschatological orientation to the story since, as Allison notes, early Christian references to Psalm 23 (Rev 7:17; *1 Clement* 26) are eschatological. This orientation is shared by some rabbinic interpretations of Psalm 23 (*Gen. Rab.* 88.5; *Exod. Rab.* 25.7; 50.5; *Num. Rab.* 21.21).

40. *cluster by cluster.* Gk *prasiai prasiai,* lit. "cluster cluster," another distributive doubling (see the NOTE on "eating-group by eating-group" in 6:39). Like *symposia symposia* in 6:39, this is a NT *hapax legomenon* (see the GLOS-SARY) and a usage unprecedented in Greek. A *prasia* is literally a garden bed, and Mark uses the term to suggest the regularity of the arrangement of the groups (M-M, 533). This agricultural image invites comparison with rabbinic texts in which pupils are compared to plants arranged in lines before their teacher and thus, as Bolyki puts it, "rooted in the tradition" (e.g. *y. Ber.* 4:1 end; see Bolyki, "Menge," 23–24). In the Hymns Scroll from Qumran, significantly, the elect community of the end-time is pictured as a garden, a "shoot of the eternal planting" that miraculously springs up in the desert (1QH 8:5–11).

in groups of a hundred and in groups of fifty. Gk *kata hekaton kai kata pentēkonta,* lit. "by hundred and by fifty." The declining order of the numbers is unusual (contrast e.g. 4:8, 20) and suggests some particular history-of-religions background, which is provided by the OT references to Israel arranged in military camps of one hundred and of fifty in the desert (Exod 18:21, 25; Deut 1:15); note that in the last-named passage the reference to these camps is combined with a mention of the heads of the (twelve) Israelite tribes, thus creating a linkage with the twelve baskets in our story (6:43). The numbers are thus part of the exodus typology of the passage. At Qumran this exodus ordering is reproduced both in the regulations for the present life of the community (1QS 2:21; CD 13:1; 1QSa 1:14–15) and in those for eschatological holy war (1QM 4:1–5), implying that the communal life of the sect foreshadows the life of the new age (cf. Tagawa, *Miracles*, 138–39).

At the corresponding point in his version of the feeding story, John has the number five thousand (John 6:10), which is a hundred times fifty. It is unclear whether the Johannine tradition has multiplied out the Markan tradition's hundred and fifty or whether Mark or his source has factored out the five thousand of the pre-Johannine story.

41. *taking the five loaves* etc. Gk *labōn tous pente artous*. The phrasing here, and in the parallel account in 8:6, is similar to that of the narratives of the Last Supper in 14:17–23 and parallels, and is probably meant to remind readers of the Eucharist (see figure 15 and cf. the COMMENT on 6:38–42). Boobyer ("Eucharistic") disputes this, pointing out that there are no fish at the Last Supper and there is no wine at the miraculous feeding; neither does the latter contain any reference to Jesus' body. The parallels that do exist, he asserts, result not from a special link with the Eucharist but from a general connection with ancient Jewish meals, such as the one described in Acts 27:35. As Davies and Allison (2.481) argue, however, the connection of the feeding stories with the Last Supper is much closer than that with other meals (see figure 16). Tagawa (*Miracles*, 136–37), moreover, notes that Matthew and Luke are freer in their editing of the rest of the Markan story than they are in their redaction of 6:41–42 (see figure 17), and he plausibly relates this greater exactitude to the relatively fixed form of the eucharistic liturgy.

said the blessing. Gk *eulogēsen*, lit. "blessed." But whom or what does Jesus bless, God or the bread? Mark ambiguously leaves the object unexpressed. The traditional Jewish grace before meals blesses God, "who brings forth bread from the earth" (cf. *m. Ber.* 6:1), and this nuance is suggested by the preceding words, in which Jesus looks up into heaven. The following words, however, might suggest that Jesus blesses the loaves ("he blessed and broke the loaves") or even that his blessing is the means for their multiplication (see Dibelius, 90). It seems impossible to choose between these alternatives.

In Judaism there is, in addition to a short grace before the meal, also a longer series of four benedictions after it. The first three of these benedictions are among the most ancient prayers of the Jewish liturgy (see Millgram, *Jewish Worship*, 292–94). Parts of this *Birkat Hamazon* are suggestively similar to the themes of our story and those of the related feeding in 8:1–10, for they call God the shepherd of Israel, emphasize his compassion, and invoke his mercy on "the kingdom of the house of David your anointed." The grace after meals at Qumran (4Q434a), similarly, emphasizes eschatological consolation ("As a man consoles his mother, so will he [God] console Jerusa[lem]"). Graces, indeed, are a natural context for ideas about "tasting" the bliss of the age to come.

broke the loaves, and kept giving them to his disciples. Gk *kateklasen tous artous kai edidou tois mathētais autou.* In a notorious piece of rationalization, the nineteenth-century critic H. E. G. Paulus argued that nothing truly supernatural is being described here; some members of the crowd, having secretly

Figure 15: The Eucharistic Act

Mark 6:41	Mark 8:6	Mark 14:22	Luke 22:19	1 Cor. 11:24
and taking the five loaves (*artous*)	and taking the seven loaves (*artous*)	taking bread (*arton*)	and taking bread (*arton*)	he took bread (*arton*)
he blessed (*eulogēsen*)	giving thanks (*eucharistēsas*)	blessing (*eulogēsas*)	giving thanks (*eucharistēsas*)	and giving thanks (*eucharistēsas*)
and broke (*kateklasen*)	he broke (*eklasen*)	he broke (*eklasen*)	he broke (*eklasen*)	he broke (*eklasen*)
and gave to the disciples	and gave to his disciples	and gave to them	and gave to them	

brought food with them, were shamed by Jesus' example of openhearted generosity into sharing it with the others. Strauss (*Life*, 507–19) demolished this and other rationalistic explanations by demonstrating that they simply do not correspond to the Gospel story. As Strauss showed, the "mythical" element is not so easily removed from the story; Jesus' miraculous provision of bread, for example, reflects expectations for a renewal of the manna miracle in the age to come (see e.g. 2 *Apoc. Bar.* 29:8; *Mekilta* on Exod 16:25; *Eccl. Rab.* 1:9; *Tanḥuma* on Exod 16:33). This manna symbolism would cohere with the Passover setting of the miracle (see the NOTE on "on the green grass" in 6:39), since the manna is associated with Passover in passages such as Josh 5:10–12 and the *Mekilta* on Exod 16:1 (see Gärtner, *John 6*, 18–19).

Our passage also reflects eucharistic terminology, as the parallel with Mark 14:22 shows (see the NOTE on "taking the five loaves" above and the COMMENT on 6:38–42); perhaps the disciples do not perform a similar mediating role with respect to the fish because fish do not play a role in the Eucharist. The word for "giving," *edidou*, unlike the other verbs in the passage, is in the imperfect tense, perhaps to indicate the repetition of the action because the supply of eucharistic loaves is never exhausted (see Schweizer, 139). Cf. John 6:34: "Lord, give us this bread always."

the two fish he divided among them all. Gk *tous duo ichthyas emerisen pasin.* The vision of the new age in 2 *Apoc. Bar.* 29:3–8 combines a prophecy that "the treasury of the manna will come down again from on high" with a description of the sea monster Leviathan—a sort of huge fish—becoming a meal for the remnant of Israel (cf. 4 Ezra 6:52; see Davies and Allison, 2.481–82). This passage has several other noteworthy parallels to our story: the revelation of the Messiah, the marvelous fruitfulness of the ground (cf. the NOTE

Figure 16: The Feeding of the Five Thousand and Other Meals

Mark 6:35–42 (Feeding of 5,000)	Mark 14:17–23 (Last Supper)	Acts 27:35 (Non-Eucharistic Meal)
the hour being late . . .	evening having come . . .	
they reclined . . .	as they were reclining . . .	
taking loaves (*artous*)	taking bread (*arton*)	taking bread (*arton*)
he blessed (*eulogēsen*)	blessing (*eulogēsas*)	he gave thanks (*eucharistēsen*)
And broke the loaves	he broke	and breaking
and gave to the disciples	and gave to them	
. . . they all ate	. . . they all drank	

on "on the green grass" in 6:39), and the statement near the end that "those who are hungry will enjoy themselves" (cf. Mark 6:42). The fish may also be part of the exodus typology in our passage; see *Sipre* on Num 11:22 (95), in which Miriam's well, which followed the Israelites, provided them with fish during their wilderness wanderings. It is more difficult to explain why there are *two* fish, but it is probably significant that the number of loaves plus the number of fish adds up to seven, the number for divine perfection, which reappears in the second feeding miracle in the seven baskets of leftovers (8:8; cf. Schmithals, 1.325–26).

Mark does not specify whether the fish that are miraculously produced are raw, dried, or cooked, but they are probably the same sort as those that the disciples have brought along and that Jesus has divided, i.e. the salted and dried fish that were a favorite provision for journeys (cf. John 6:9, which uses the term *opsaria* = "dried fish"; see Hastings, *Dictionary*, 267, and Brown, 1.233).

43. *twelve*. Gk *dōdeka*, i.e. one basket for each disciple. But the number twelve also has important symbolic associations within Judaism, being especially linked with the twelve tribes of Israel and therefore with the concept of the eschatological fullness of the people of God; see the COMMENTS on 3:13–15 and 8:17–21.

baskets full of bread fragments. Gk *klasmata . . . kophinōn plērōmata*. The term for "basket," *kophinos*, is a different one from *kanoun*, the usual word for a basket in Attic Greek and the LXX; it also differs from *spyris*, the word used in the parallel story in 8:8. *Kophinos* seems to designate a kind of basket particularly associated with Jews; Juvenal twice satirizes Jewish travelers with their *kophinoi* (*Satires* 3.14; 6.542), and a related word, *qûpāh/qūpā'*, is present in Rabbinic Hebrew and Aramaic (see Jastrow, 1337). The word for

Figure 17: The Feeding of the Five Thousand in the Synoptics and John

Mark 6:32–44	*Matthew 14:13–21*	*Luke 9:10–17*	*John 6:1–15*
Jesus and disciples go away in a boat to a deserted place privately	Jesus withdraws in a boat to a deserted place privately	Jesus withdraws privately to a city called Bethsaida	Jesus goes away across the sea of Galilee
"They" run on foot from all the cities and get there first	The crowds follow him on foot from all the cities	The crowds follow him	A great crowd follows him . . .
Jesus sees a great crowd and has compassion on them, for they are like sheep without a shepherd, and he begins to teach them many things	Jesus sees a great crowd and has compassion on them	Jesus receives them and speaks to them about the dominion of God	Jesus lifts up his eyes and sees a great crowd coming toward him
	and heals their sick	and those that have need of care he heals	Cf. 6:2: They follow because they have seen the signs he has performed for their sick
Because of late hour, disciples ask Jesus to send people away to buy food	Because of late hour, disciples ask Jesus to send crowds away to buy food	Because of late hour, Twelve ask Jesus to send crowd away to buy food	Jesus to Philip: "Where will we get loaves for them to eat?"
Jesus: "Give them something to eat yourselves!"	Jesus: "They don't have to go away; give them something to eat yourselves!"	Jesus: "Give them something to eat yourselves!"	
Disciples: "Shall we go buy 200 denarii worth of bread . . .?"			Philip: "200 denarii worth of bread wouldn't be enough to feed them"
Jesus: "Go see how many loaves you have."			
Disciples: "Five, and two fish (*ichthyas*)"	Disciples: "We have only five loaves and two fish (*ichthyas*)"	Disciples: "We don't have more than five loaves and two fish (*ichthyas*); do you want us to go and buy food for the whole people?" . . .	Andrew: "There's a boy here who has five barley loaves and two fish (*opsaria*), but what's that for so many?"

Mark 6:32–44	Matthew 14:13–21	Luke 9:10–17	John 6:1–15
Jesus commands disciples to make the people recline (anaklinai) eating-group by eating-group on the green grass	Jesus commands disciples to make the people recline (anaklithēnai) on the grass	Jesus tells disciples, "Make the people recline (kataklinate) by fifties"	Jesus tells disciples, "Make the people sit down (anapesein)"; there is a lot of grass in the place
They sit down (anepesan) plot by plot, by hundreds and by fifties		They do so, and sit them all down (kateklinan)	The men, about 5,000 in number, sit down (anepesan)
Jesus takes five loaves and two fish (ichthyas), looks up to heaven, blesses (eulogēsen),	Jesus takes five loaves and two fish (ichthyas), looks up to heaven, blesses (eulogēsen),	Jesus takes five loaves and two fish (ichthyas), looks up to heaven, blesses (eulogēsen) them,	Jesus takes loaves, gives thanks (eucharistēsas),
breaks loaves and gives them to disciples to distribute to them,	breaks and gives the loaves to the disciples, and the disciples to the crowds	breaks and gives them to the disciples to distribute to the crowd	and distributes them to the guests
and divides the two fish (ichthyas) among them all			and likewise of the fish (opsarion) as much as they wanted
They all eat and are satisfied	They all eat and are satisfied	They eat and are all satisfied	When they are full, Jesus says to the disciples:
They take up twelve baskets full of fragments, and of the fish	They take up the excess (to perisseuon) of the fragments, twelve baskets full	The excess (to perisseusan) of their fragments is taken up, twelve baskets	"Gather together the excess (ta perisseusanta) fragments . . ."
Those who eat are 5,000 men	Those who eat are about (hōs) 5,000 men, excluding women and children	Cf. 9:14: There are about (hōs) 5,000 men	Cf. 6:10: The men are by number about (hōs) 5,000

"full of," *plērōmata*, actually means "fullnesses" and helps to convey the idea of eschatological completion that is so central to Mark's understanding of the feeding (cf. the COMMENT on 8:17–21).

44. *five thousand.* Gk *pentakischilioi.* As Lohmeyer (125) points out, this is an astoundingly huge number, considering that cities such as Capernaum and Bethsaida contained approximately two or three thousand inhabitants. The five thousand men may be related to the five loaves of bread. An army of five thousand men appears in Josephus *Life* 212–13, perhaps reflecting the military organization in the biblical passages about the exodus mentioned in the NOTE on "in groups of a hundred and in groups of fifty." It is probably just coincidence, however, that Acts 4:4 gives the number of Christians as five thousand; cf. the COMMENT on 8:17–21.

men. Gk *andres.* Not the word for "human beings," *anthrōpoi,* but the word for adults of the male gender; cf. Matt 14:21, which adds "apart from women and children" (cf. Exod 12:37 and the censuses in Numbers 1 and 26, which only count males who bear arms, though women and children are present). Mark probably does not wish to imply that only the men ate while the women and children went hungry. Either he wants to convey the impression that there were no women or children present, or he is echoing the OT passages by only counting the men; in view of the strong exodus typology of our passage, the latter is more likely.

the loaves. Gk *tous artous.* Some ancient texts omit these words, perhaps because of haplography (homoeoteleuton: *phagontes tous artous*), perhaps because of the awkwardness that the fish are not mentioned (see Metzger, 92). It is also possible, however, that the words have been added by a later scribe to enhance the eucharistic symbolism of the passage; the external evidence is about evenly balanced.

COMMENT

Introduction. After the long digression about the death of John the Baptist, Mark resumes the thread of his narrative with a description of the return of Jesus' disciples from their missionary journey (6:30). Overwhelmed by the crowds Jesus has attracted, the disciples depart with him for a private retreat in a desert location; the crowd, however, gets wind of the planned retreat and beats them to the spot (6:31–33). There Jesus displays his compassion by teaching them, thus meeting their spiritual needs (6:34), and then by miraculously providing food, thus meeting their physical needs (6:35–44).

Mark has apparently inherited the outline of this resonant story from a traditional source that also included the ensuing passage. In Mark 8 and John 6 we encounter the same sequence of miraculous feeding (6:30–44; cf. 8:1–9; John 6:1–15), sea-crossing (6:45–51; cf. 8:10; John 6:16–21), and allusion to bread (6:52; cf. 8:14–21; John 6:22–59), and John 6:1–13 contains features similar to both Markan feeding stories (see figure 20 in the COMMENT on 8:1–9). Since John seems to be literarily independent of the Synoptics (see the INTRODUCTION), these common features and this common sequence are best explained by shared dependence on a pre-Gospel source; thus Fowler (*Loaves*, 89–90) is probably mistaken in his argument that Mark himself has composed our story on the model of the traditional story of the feeding of the four thousand in 8:1–9.

But Fowler is correct that certain features of the narrative seem to reflect Markan redaction. The transitional passage in 6:30–34, for example, is full of typically Markan vocabulary (e.g. "in the boat," "privately," "deserted place," "many"), syntactical features (e.g. the *gar* clause in 6:31), and themes (e.g. Jesus expresses his compassion by *teaching*; cf. Reploh, *Lehrer*, 51). Similarly, the way in which Jesus asks the disciples to feed the multitudes (6:37a) and uses them as his intermediaries (6:41) reflects the stress throughout this section of the Gospel on their participation in his authority (6:6b–13, 14, 30), while the sarcastic tone of their question in 6:37 corresponds to the Markan theme of apostolic misunderstanding, especially in this section of the Gospel (6:52; 8:4, 14–21). It is noteworthy that several of these features are absent in John 6 and/or the Matthew/Luke parallels (see figure 17), absences that support the theory of Markan editing (perhaps Matthew and Luke know an alternate version of the story that is in some ways similar to John). Other Markan features that are unmatched in John and may represent Markan redaction include the symbolic notice about the lateness of the hour in 6:35 (see the NOTE on "since the hour was already late" in 6:35), the lovingly described detail of the seating arrangements in 6:39–40, which has vivid apocalyptic connotations, and the words "full of" in 6:43, which has a similar nuance (see the NOTE on "baskets full of bread fragments" in 6:43).

As Theissen (103–6) has shown, our story fits into a standard form, the "gift miracle," in which needed material goods are provided in astonishing ways; similar stories are told about Elijah and Elisha in 1 Kgs 17:8–16 and 2 Kgs 4:1–7, 42–44, about Jesus in Luke 5:1–11, and about R. Ḥanina ben Dosa in *b. Taʿan.* 24b–25a. In all of these stories, as in ours, the miracle is a spontaneous act of generosity, not a response to a request from a person in need, and the mechanism by which it transpires is left obscure, only the subsequent abundance demonstrating its occurrence. The vocabulary and sequence of events are especially close to those in the story about Elisha in 2 Kgs 4:42–44 (the comparison is expanded from Davies and Allison, 2.482):

Elisha takes bread and ears of grain	Jesus takes bread and fish
Elisha commands: "Give to the men, that they may eat"	Jesus commands: "Give them something to eat"
Servant asks skeptically how he is to feed a hundred men	Disciples ask skeptically how they are to feed the crowd
Elisha repeats the command	Jesus commands disciples to sit the people down

Servant sets food before the people   Disciples distribute food to the
                                           people
The people eat and food is left over   The people eat and food is left over

These parallels are especially interesting because of the other similarities be-
tween Elisha and the Jesus of the Gospels (cf. the NOTE on "the holy one of
God" in 1:24 and the COMMENT on 1:5–6 and 6:48–50). As Freedman points
out, these include the fact that, just as Elisha succeeds Elijah, so Jesus succeeds
John, whose death has been narrated in the previous passage and who is an
Elijah-like figure. Jesus' name and Elisha's, moreover, are similar; both com-
bine a word for God with the root $y\check{s}^c$ ("to save") or $\check{s}w^c$ ("to help"; cf. Brown,
Birth, 131).

Narratives about miraculous feedings, however, are not stories confined to
antiquity. Martin Buber, for example, retells a Hasidic tale about R. Elimelekh
of Lizhesnk (d. 1786), who was in the habit of feeding fifteen Hasidim in his
house. One day forty showed up, and R. Elimelekh's wife fretted: "We hardly
have enough for fifteen!" R. Elimelekh, however, prayed fervently, and then
invited everyone to come and eat; and "when the forty had eaten all they
wanted, the bowls and platters were still full" (Tales, 1.259–60).

Our story is artistically told, with especially effective use of repetition. At the
beginning the repeated phrases "deserted place" and "privately" and the sixfold
usage of polys (= "great, many, late") set the stage and emphasize the greatness
of the need with which Jesus is confronted (6:31–35). In the middle the two usages of the word "buy" highlight the disciples' wrongheaded response to this
need. At the end the repeated usages of "bread" and "fish" (five each in 6:37,
38, 41, 43, 44) and the two usages of "to give" (6:37, 41) mark the true solution
to the need. And phagein (= "to eat"), which expresses the theme and major
problematic of the narrative, occurs throughout (6:31, 36, 37[2x], 42). The narrative falls naturally into four sections: the transitional stage-setting (6:30–34),
the description of the problem (6:35–37), the feeding itself (6:38–42), and the
concluding notes about the amount of leftovers and the number of people fed,
which confirm the magnitude of the wonder (6:43–44).

6:30–34: transitional stage-setting. The story begins with an implicit comparison and contrast between the disciples of John the Baptist, sadly taking up
his disfigured body for burial, and the disciples of Jesus, returning from their
missionary tour in triumph to tell Jesus what they have done and taught
(6:30)—a comparison not entirely favorable to the latter group. Nevertheless,
two details cast Jesus' disciples in a more favorable light. This is the only Markan passage in which they are termed "apostles" (apostoloi; see the NOTE on
"apostles" in 6:30) and the only instance in which someone other than Jesus is
said to teach, and the coincidence of these features is probably deliberate: the
Twelve have been able to teach and perform miraculous works precisely
because they are Jesus' sent-out-ones, who have been endowed with his own

eschatological authority, which transcends even that of the Baptist (cf. 6:6b–13 and 1:7–8 and see Ambrozic, "New Teaching," 132). Perhaps partly because of this apostolic authority of the disciples, the crowds in 6:33 are described as anticipating the arrival not just of Jesus but of "them."

These crowds have eagerly, almost desperately, pursued Jesus and the Twelve into their wilderness retreat (6:33). Wellhausen (47–48) points out the historical difficulties posed by this part of the narrative: the crowd of thousands somehow finds out Jesus' secret destination and reaches it more quickly via the roundabout land route than the compact group of Jesus and his disciples can reach it via a water route, though the latter is presumably more direct. In this case, as in the similar use of the pursuit theme in 1:35–36, we are probably dealing with a theological motif rather than with a historical memory; the crowd's hunt for Jesus underlines the spiritual hunger and hope he has stirred up in them.

Jesus proceeds to meet this hunger and hope, and the way in which he does so is part of the pronounced Mosaic typology of our passage and of this section of the Gospel (cf. the introduction to 6:6b–8:21); this typology also includes the repeated references to the wilderness location (6:31, 32, and 35), the description of the crowd arranged for the meal (6:39–40), and the numerical symbolism in 6:38, 40, and 43–44 (see below). Mark says that the crowds pursuing Jesus are "like sheep not having a shepherd" (cf. Num 27:17) and that when Jesus sees them, he is moved to compassion (*esplachnisthē*) upon them (6:34). As Davies and Allison note (2.479), throughout the Synoptic tradition this verb is typically and naturally associated with miracles (e.g. most manuscripts of Mark 1:41; Mark 8:2//Matt 15:32; Mark 9:22; Matt 14:14; Matt 20:34; Luke 7:13). In our passage, however, Jesus' compassion does not immediately lead him to perform a miracle but to teach them—a typically Markan fusion of the motif of wonder-working power with that of teaching (cf. 1:26–27). Jesus' compassionate response to the crowd, moreover, implicitly places him on a par with Moses, who taught Israel in the wilderness and whose teaching (Torah) was compared to bread and was the gracious divine response to the wandering of the shepherdless Israelite "sheep" (see the NOTES on "like sheep not having a shepherd" in 6:34 and on "loaves . . . five" in 6:38). Similarly, in our passage, Jesus sees the spiritual darkness of the people, has compassion upon them, and expresses this compassion in the most effective way possible—by teaching them.

6:35–37: *the people's hunger.* The satisfaction of the people's spiritual hunger still leaves their physical bellies empty, and our story is far from discounting the importance of this physical need or of the miraculous act that meets it (cf. Schmithals, 1.321). The deed is occasioned by the disciples approaching Jesus with the suggestion that the time has arrived to dismiss the crowd, seeing that the hour is already late (6:35–36). The reference to the lateness of the hour, which has no counterpart in the Johannine parallel and probably represents

Markan redaction (see the NOTE on "since the hour was already late" in 6:35), has the symbolic purpose of showing that time is running out and that only divine intervention can save the day; as one of Emily Dickinson's poems (no. 623) puts it:

It was too late for Man—
But early, yet, for God—

On one level the disciples' suggestion that Jesus dismiss the crowd reflects a commendable regard for the people's well-being, comparable to Jesus' own concern about the disciples' hunger in 6:31; and the solution is similar, namely to send them away so that they may eat. On a deeper level, however, the proposed solution reflects the Twelve's ignorance of Jesus' power, as if they believed on the one hand that it was fine for him to be concerned about the edification of the masses but on the other hand that there was no alternative to letting the people fend for themselves when it came to important practical matters such as food.

Jesus' response, however, calls the disciples back to their apostolic mission: "Give them something to eat yourselves" (6:37a). The stressed word "yourselves" (*hymeis*) contrasts with the disciples' suggestion that the people be dismissed to seek food "for themselves" (*heautois*, also emphatic). The people are neither to be thrown back upon their own resources nor to be made the recipients of an unmediated miracle from Jesus; they are, rather, to be fed by the disciples as mediators of Jesus' power. This is a natural enough response for Jesus to make after the way in which the disciples have entered into his charismatic ministry in 6:6b–13, 30; the Markan Jesus' point, then, is similar to St. Teresa of Avila's: "God has no hands but our hands."

Mysteriously, however, the disciples react to this challenge with disbelief and even sarcasm (6:37b; see the NOTE on "What do you want us to do?" in 6:37). Like the skeptical reactions of the people involved in certain OT feeding miracles (Num 11:13, 21–22; 2 Kgs 4:42–43), this response is the narrator's literary device for ironically highlighting the extraordinary nature of the wonder that is about to be accomplished. But it is also a further sign of the disciples' misunderstanding of Jesus. The repetition of the word "buy" accentuates this theme; the disciples are still looking, as they were in 6:36, to normal human means, to buying and selling, to alleviate the crowd's problem; now, however, the misunderstanding is even worse, as the progression from alarm to sarcasm suggests. Thus this section of the story ends on a note of spiritual deficiency that corresponds to, but is even more distressing than, the material deficiency that has occasioned it.

6:38–42: *the feeding*. Jesus, however, ignoring the disciples' sarcasm, tells them to see how many loaves they have (6:38a), and this reference to the food that will provide the "raw material" for the miracle foreshadows the imminent reversal of the situation of dearth. Bread and fish were the staples of most

Galileans, as passages such as Matt 7:9–10 illustrate (cf. Davies and Allison, 2.489), but these foods probably also have a symbolic significance. Bread was a symbol of the Torah (see the NOTE on "loaves . . . five" in 6:38), and miraculously produced bread, the manna, was associated with Israel's wilderness wanderings; fish, moreover, could be linked with the wilderness trek on the basis of Num 11:22b ("Shall all the fish of the sea be gathered together for them, to suffice them?" [RSV]; see *Sipre* on this passage and cf. Wis 9:12). Thus when Jews speculated about the eschaton, which they often imagined as a new exodus, they frequently looked for a renewal of the gift of the manna (see the NOTE on "broke the loaves, and kept giving them to his disciples" in 6:41) and sometimes for a miraculous fish dinner (see the NOTE on "the two fish he divided among them all" in 6:41). In view of this pervasive new exodus typology, it is probable that the five loaves are related to the five books of Moses, the Torah or teaching of God, which Jews considered to be his greatest gift to humanity (see the NOTE on "loaves . . . five" in 6:38). As in the reference to Jesus as a compassionate shepherd in 6:34, he is being presented in 6:38 as a revealer of divine truth who is on a par with Moses. The symbolism of the loaves and fish, therefore, points toward the feeding as an eschatological wonder that recalls and surpasses the revelatory miracles performed by Moses in the wilderness.

The Mosaic and eschatological symbolism continues in the account of the disposition of the crowd for the meal (6:39–40). In a description that, in contrast to the Gospel parallels, lingers lovingly over these details (cf. Lohmeyer, 127), Mark has Jesus commanding the disciples to make the people sit down in eating-groups (*symposia*) on the green grass; the people obey by sitting down in discrete, ordered groups (*prasiai*, "clusters") of one hundred and of fifty. These numbers are again reminiscent of the exodus (Exod 18:21, 25), but they also point forward to the hope for a new exodus by a renewed Israel, as the Qumran literature shows (see the NOTE on "in groups of a hundred and in groups of fifty" in 6:40). Similarly, the first term for the seated crowd, *symposia*, has a traditional linkage with Passover, and the second, *prasia*, connects with Jewish ideas concerning the renewed Israel as the eschatological planting of God (see the NOTES on "eating-group by eating-group" in 6:39 and "cluster by cluster" in 6:40). Bolyki ("Menge") discerns a progression in the transformation of the people from an *ochlos* or disorganized crowd (6:34) to a *symposion* or table fellowship (6:39) to a *prasia* or organized group (6:40). The syntax itself suggests such a movement toward increasing order, as *ochlos* becomes *symposia symposia* becomes *prasiai prasiai kata hekaton kai kata pentēkonta*. When the God of the new exodus manifests himself, Mark implies, human disorder is transformed into organic, paradisiacal order. A character in Toni Morrison's *Beloved* (272–73) describes the transformative power of love in similar terms: "She gather me, man. The pieces I am, she gather them and give them back to me in all the right order."

Having seated and created order among the people through the mediation of the disciples, Jesus proceeds to feed them (6:41–42). The description of the feeding is later echoed in striking detail in the narrative of the Last Supper (Mark 14:17–23; see figure 15), and it is highly probable that Mark sees the miraculous feedings here and in 8:1–10 not only as reminiscent of the exodus but also as anticipatory of the Last Supper and hence of the Christian Eucharist (cf. the NOTE on "taking the five loaves" in 6:41). Bread is central to the Eucharist, and while fish is not, it became a standard symbol for Christ himself in the early church (see Quesnell, *Mind*, 268–70). As Gerhardsson (cited in Davies and Allison, 2.494) points out, the linkage of our story with the Eucharist would have been especially clear to early Christians, whose eucharistic celebrations included a full meal (see e.g. 1 Cor 11:20–34). Brown (1.247) notes awareness of the linkage in second-century catacomb art, where the feeding stories are used to represent the Eucharist. The Passover and eschatological nuances of our story, moreover, are compatible with this eucharistic interpretation, since the early church regarded the Last Supper as a Passover and the Eucharist as a foretaste of eschatological fulfillment (cf. Mark 14:12, 25; 1 Cor 11:26).

In the feeding of the people, as in their seating, the disciples play a noteworthy mediating role: Jesus gives the broken bread to *them*, and *they* give it to the people (this motif is even more stressed in Matt 14:19 but absent in John 6:11). Although previously, therefore, the disciples had sardonically rejected Jesus' command, "Give them something to eat yourselves" (6:37), they actually fulfill it in 6:41 — but only because Jesus has first given to them (note the repetition of *didonai* = "to give"). Despite their thickheadedness and even their disparaging sarcasm toward the Shepherd of Israel, then, the Twelve remain his disciples and coworkers, who can again be taken back into communion with him and used by him (cf. 14:27–28; see Schmithals, 1.326). The combination of negative and positive aspects in the portrayal of the disciples in our passage is part of a general Markan ambiguity that puts the emphasis on their apostolic calling despite their human waywardness.

Receiving Jesus' bread from the disciples' hands and the fish directly from Jesus himself (see the NOTE on "broke the loaves, and kept giving them to his disciples" in 6:41), the assembled multitudes all eat and are satisfied (6:42), and there is much food left over (6:43). It is difficult for modern-day readers who live comfortably in the first world and have never gone hungry to imagine the impact these statements may have had on some of their first hearers, who may have known hunger frequently; it is not for nothing that one of the most frequent biblical images of the bliss of the age to come is a *banquet*, in which the participants will be able to eat as much as they wish (see e.g. Isa 25:6–9). As Theissen (103) notes, the biblical stories in which nourishment is miraculously supplied "illustrate problems of human labour, the problem of how to get food to live and wine to feast." It is important not to spiritualize away this materialistic dimension of our story, the way in which it presents Jesus as a provider who meets people's need and longing for physical food. This is true even if the narrative is a foreshadowing of the Christian Eucharist, since, as we have seen, the Eucharist was a real meal in the earliest church.

This is not, however, to deny the symbolic dimension that we have seen all through the passage. Even the notice "And they all ate and were satisfied" recalls the description of the promised land at the end of the exodus journey ("And you shall eat and be full," Deut 8:10), and thus may be part of the Moses/exodus typology of our story (cf. D. Schmidt, 83).

6:43–44: the confirmatory conclusion. The story ends with two numbers that confirm the magnitude of the miracle: twelve baskets of fragments are taken up, and five thousand men are fed (see the NOTE on "men" in 6:44). Twelve is a resonant number associated with Israel and the hope for a renewed Israel at the eschaton (see the NOTE on "twelve" in 6:43), and five, as we have already noted, is particularly linked with Moses, the giver of the "bread" of Torah. It may be, then, that these concluding numbers would have reminded Mark's readers again that Jesus was a Moses-like figure giving a new Torah to a renewed Israel.

The pronounced Mosaic and eschatological features of our passage may have had a topical relevance for Mark and his community in their proximity to the Jewish War. Josephus describes Moses- and Joshua-like prophets of a revolutionary bent who led their followers out to the wilderness and promised to work wonders there, apparently basing their hopes on the biblical prophecies of a new exodus (*J.W.* 7.437–442; *Ant.* 20.97–99, 167–72, 188; see D. Schwartz, "Temple"). Our story, then, presents Jesus as the realization of these hopes: he is the expected revealer and shepherd of the people who will lead them to final victory. Yet he fulfills these expectations in a way that breaks the expected pattern, throwing a banquet rather than raising an army; at the conclusion of the story, moreover, the disciples gather up the remaining bread, whereas in the exodus story (Exod 16:19–20) the people were stringently warned *not* to collect the leftovers of the manna (cf. Davies and Allison, 2.482–83). The latter difference may symbolize the continuity of the eucharistic miracle into the Markan present; the leftover bread is collected so that the church may be fed from the overflowing baskets of Jesus' multiplication of the loaves. If Jesus, then, fulfills the Mosaic model, he also transcends it.

This point will be reinforced in the next story (6:45–52), which on the one hand will recall a theophany to Moses, but which on the other hand will present Jesus not in the Mosaic role but in the divine one.

JESUS WALKS ON THE SEA (6:45–52)

6   [45]And immediately he made his disciples get into the boat and go before him to the other side, toward Bethsaida, while he himself sent the crowd away. [46]And having dismissed them, he went away to the mountain to pray. [47]And when evening had come, the boat was in the middle of the sea, and he alone was on the land. [48]And seeing them making tortuous progress in their rowing—for the wind was against them—at around the fourth watch of the night

he came toward them, walking on the sea, and intended to pass them. [49]But they, seeing him walking on the sea, thought that he was a ghost, and they cried out—[50]for they all saw him, and were disturbed. But he immediately spoke with them and said to them, "Be brave, I am here; don't be afraid!" [51]And he came up to them, into the boat, and the wind died down, and they were greatly amazed within themselves; [52]for they did not understand about the loaves, but their heart was hardened.

NOTES

6   45. *go before him.* Gk *proagein,* lit. "to go before" or "to proceed"; the "him" is not explicitly stated, but can be supplied from the following "while" clause and the parallel with "to pass by them" in 6:48 (cf. BAGD, 702[2b]).

toward Bethsaida. Gk *pros Bēthsaida.* Bethsaida, which was in what is now the Golan Heights on the east bank of the Jordan near where it enters the Sea of Galilee from the north, was a Hellenistic city with some Jewish inhabitants (cf. John 1:44). The destination is problematic, however, since at the end of the journey Jesus and the disciples do not dock at Bethsaida but at Gennesaret on the west bank (6:53), reaching Bethsaida only in 8:22. Some (e.g. Swete, 129–30) think the disciples are blown off course by the storm, but such a detour is not mentioned, and at the end of our story the wind dies down, presumably allowing them to head back toward the original destination even if they had been deflected (see Gnilka, 1.266). For other solutions to the discrepancy, see the NOTES on "intended to pass them" in 6:48 and "crossing over, they came to land at Gennesaret" in 6:53, and the COMMENT on 6:53–56.

while he himself sent the crowd away. Gk *heōs autos apolyei ton ochlon.* The Markan Jesus first dismisses his disciples, then the crowd; one might have expected the reverse, on the supposition that Jesus could have used the disciples' help in seeing the crowd off. Perhaps, however, that is just the impression Mark wishes to ward off, in a story that emphasizes Jesus' initiative, volition, and sovereign power (see the introduction to the COMMENT and the COMMENT on 6:48–50).

46. *having dismissed them.* Gk *apotaxamenos autois.* As Lohmeyer (132) points out, it is not entirely clear whether Jesus here dismisses the disciples or the crowd. One assumes, however, that it is the crowd, since their dismissal has just been mentioned at the end of the previous verse and since Mark is here creating, rather clumsily, a parallel to 4:36, where the crowd was dismissed (cf. the introduction to the COMMENT).

went away to the mountain to pray. Gk *apēlthen eis to oros proseuxasthai.* The use of the definite article suggests that this is a special mountain with symbolic importance. Schmithals (1.333) and others think that it is the mountain of the resurrection, as in Matt 28:16, and that our story is a displaced resurrection narrative. While 6:45–52 does have some features in common with a resurrection appearance (see the COMMENT on 6:48–50), it is more likely, in view of the the exodus imagery that runs through this story (see the COM-

MENT on 6:48–50 and 6:51–52) and the other two Markan mountain narratives (3:13–19 and 9:2–8), that a linkage is being made with Exod 24:15, 18, in which Moses goes up on "the mountain" (= Mount Sinai) in order to commune with God. In some Jewish traditions Moses was deified by his communion with God on Sinai (see e.g. Ezekiel the Tragedian *Exagōgē* 68–81, and Philo *Life of Moses* 1.155–58; cf. Meeks, "Moses"); is it just a coincidence that in the remainder of our narrative Jesus shows himself to be godlike (see the COMMENT on 6:48–50)?

48. *seeing.* Gk *idōn*. Throughout the Gospel, Mark puts special emphasis on Jesus' "seeing," his piercing glance that is especially directed at disciples (1:16, 19; 2:14; 3:34; 8:33; 10:14, 23), potential disciples (10:21; 12:34), and other objects of his compassion (2:5; 5:32; 6:34; cf. the COMMENT on 1:16–20). In 2:5 and 5:32 *idein* has a connotation of supernatural insight, and that is the case in our passage as well because of the darkness ("when evening had come") and the distance between Jesus and the disciples ("the boat was in the middle of the sea"; cf. Pesch, 1.360); John 6:19 is accurate when it gives the distance to the midpoint of the "sea" as twenty-five to thirty stadia = three or four miles.

making tortuous progress in their rowing. Gk *basanizomenous en tǭ elaunein*, lit. "being tortured in the rowing." *Basanizein* can have a nuance of eschatological tribulation (Rev 9:5; 11:10; 12:2, etc.; cf. Schenke, *Wundererzählungen*, 250 n. 766). It is also frequently used for judicial torture and is attested in this sense in Jewish and Christian stories of martyrdom (e.g. 2 Macc 7:13; 4 Macc 6:5; *Mart. Pol.* 2:2). The word for "rowing," *elaunein*, can have a nuance of persecution (e.g. Homer *Odyssey* 5.290; Sophocles *Oedipus the King* 28; see LSJ, 529 [I4]).

the fourth watch of the night. Gk *tetartēn phylakēn tēs nyktos*. Roman custom divided the time from 6:00 P.M. to 6:00 A.M. into four "watches" (cf. e.g. Diodorus Siculus 19.26.1; Josephus *Ant.* 18.356), and Mark reflects this division not only here but also in 13:35. The watch in our passage is the last one, which ends with dawn. In the OT (e.g. Exod 14:24; Ps 46:5; 130:6; Isa 17:14), in Jewish traditions (e.g. *Joseph and Aseneth* 14:1–2; *Bib. Ant.* 42:3), and in the NT (e.g. Mark 16:2) dawn is the time of God's help, because it is the point at which light chases away darkness.

walking on the sea. Gk *peripatōn epi tēs thalassēs*. This *could* mean "walking *by* the sea" (cf. John 21:1), and the early-nineteenth-century commentator H. E. G. Paulus thought that our miracle story arose from precisely this philological error. This rationalizing line of interpretation is continued by Taylor (327): "The action of Jesus in wading through the surf near the hidden shore was interpreted as a triumphant progress across the water." But as Strauss already pointed out (*Life*, 500), such explanations do not correspond to the narrative, in which the disciples are not near the shore but in the middle of the sea (for a survey of other opinions about the historicity of the narrative, see Davies and Allison, 2.498–500).

intended to pass them. Gk *ēthelen parelthein autous*. *Ēthelen* can also mean "wanted" or "was willing." The same verb appears in John's version of our story

Figure 18: Jesus' Walk on the Sea and the Stilling of the Storm

John 6:16–21 (Walking on Sea)	*Mark 4:35–41 (Stilling of Storm)*	*Mark 6:45–52 (Walking on Sea + Stilling of Storm)*
16–17a: When evening comes, the disciples go down to sea (on their own initiative), get into a boat, and start across toward other side of sea, to Capernaum	35: When evening comes, Jesus says to the disciples, "Let us go across to the other side"	45: Jesus compels the disciples to get into boat and precede him to other side of sea, to Bethsaida
	36: Sending the crowd away, the disciples take Jesus off with them in the boat	46: Having dismissed the crowd, he goes up to the mountain to pray
17b: After dark, Jesus still has not come to them		47: When evening comes (cf. John 6:16), the boat is in midsea (cf. John 6:19a), but Jesus himself is alone on the land
18: The sea rises because of a strong wind	37: A great storm of wind arises and the waves beat on the boat	48a: Jesus sees the disciples making little progress because wind is against them
19a: When they have gone 25–30 stadia (= 3–4 miles) they see Jesus walking on the sea		48b: He comes to them at the fourth watch of night, walking on the sea

John 6:16–21 (Walking on Sea)	Mark 4:35–41 (Stilling of Storm)	Mark 6:45–52 (Walking on Sea + Stilling of Storm)
	38: The disciples say to Jesus: "Don't you care that we're about to die?"	48c: Jesus wants (ēthelen; cf. John 6:21) to pass them by
19b: They are frightened	[cf. v 41]	49: When they see him walking on the sea they think he is a ghost and cry out in fear
		50a: For all see him and are disturbed
20: He says to them, "I am here; don't be afraid"	[cf. v 40]	50b: He says to them, "Be brave! I am here; don't be afraid!"
21a: They are willing (ēthelon) to take him into the boat	39: He rebukes the wind, and it dies down	51a: He goes into the boat, and the wind dies down
	40: He says to them, "Why are you cowardly?"	51b–52: They are greatly amazed because they don't understand about the loaves
	41: They are terrified	

(6:21) but in a more logical context (see figure 18): Jesus' reassurance overcomes the disciples' fear that he is some sort of spirit, and they are *willing* (*ēthelon*) to take him into the boat. But in our passage Jesus' desire to pass his disciples on the sea is puzzling, and has been a notorious crux of interpretation (for a survey, see Snoy, "Marc 6,48"): if Jesus' sea walk is motivated by his concern for his disciples, as implied by 6:48a, and if he starts out coming toward them, as described in 6:48b, why does he then attempt to pass them in 6:48c? Not surprisingly, the Matthean parallel omits this puzzling element, and modern explanations have ranged from the psychologically subtle (the text describes the disciples' subjective impression of Jesus' intention, not his actual purpose—Cranfield, 226) to the psychologically incredible (Jesus wants to beat the disciples to the opposite shore in order to surprise them—Wellhausen, 52). None of these psychologizing interpretations, however, has any purchase in the text.

Rather, the background to this strange feature of the narrative is to be found in Exod 33:17–34:8, where God reveals his glory to Moses by *passing by* him; this tradition became so important that it was reworked in the story of God's self-revelation to Elijah in 1 Kgs 19:11–13 (see Heil, *Jesus Walking*, 69–71). Under the impact of these passages the verb *parelthein* ("to pass, to pass by") became almost a technical term for a divine epiphany in the Septuagint; in Dan 12:1 and Gen 32:31–32 LXX, for example, it was inserted into contexts that lacked it in the MT. (Interestingly, the Genesis text, like Mark 6:48, combines an epiphanic usage of *parelthein* with a symbolic reference to dawn.) Mark, similarly, has introduced the motif of Jesus "passing by" into the narrative of the walking on the water because of its epiphanic connotation, but since he needs to end the story by having Jesus united with the disciples in the boat, he writes only that Jesus *wanted* to pass them, not that he *did* so.

Rau ("Markusevangelium," 2122–24) seeks to supplement this Old Testament/Christological explanation of "intended to pass them" with an ecclesiological one. He points out that the intended original destination of the trip is Bethsaida, a predominantly Gentile city on the east bank of the Jordan (see the NOTE on "toward Bethsaida" in 6:45). The narrative, then, is alluding to Jesus' desire to lead the Markan community into a mission in non-Jewish areas (cf. 13:10), but this intended expansion of their outreach is temporarily checked by the disciples' fear. But if the Markan community is already predominantly Gentile and situated outside of Palestine (see the discussion of the Markan community in the INTRODUCTION), this interpretation does not hold. Moreover, neither here nor elsewhere in the Gospel (4:35–5:1; 7:24, 31) do the Markan disciples complain about being sent to non-Jewish areas; their only reluctance arises from the stormy sea they encounter on the way.

50. *were disturbed.* Gk *etarachthēsan.* On the usage of this verb in Psalm 77, see the COMMENT on 6:48–50. *Etarachthēsan* is also applied to sea waters in Psalm 45 LXX (Psalm 46 MT), and this psalm has several other contacts with our passage: God's salvation in the morning, his wonders, "I am God" (*egō eimi ho theos*), and "we shall not be afraid" (*ou phobēthēsometha*). On the usage of this Psalm in Aramaic magical texts, see the COMMENT on 4:37–39.

I am here. Gk *egō eimi*, lit. "I am." The word "here" is absent in the Greek, but it is important to retain the "I am" structure, and the sense of divine presence in the passage (see below) means that "*I am here*" is certainly not a distortion of the meaning. On the simplest level *egō eimi* merely means "it's me" or "I'm the one," with the emphasis on the pronoun (cf. Mark 13:6; Matt 26:22, 25; John 9:9; Acts 10:21). But it can also have what Brown (1.533–58) calls "a solemn and sacral use" in the OT, Jewish literature, the NT, Gnosticism, and non-Jewish Greek religious writings. The OT texts in which God identifies himself by means of *egō eimi* (Exod 3:14; Deut 32:39; Isa 41:4; 43:10–11; cf. Isa 47:8, 10) are the most important background for the weighty NT usages of the phrase (besides our passage, cf. especially John 8:58 and 18:6); this background is especially relevant for our passage because so many other features of the pericope are evocative of the OT God (walking on the waters, passing by, reassuring adherents, conquering the storm; see the NOTE on "intended to pass them" in 6:48 and the COMMENT on 6:48–50). These OT texts are all based on Exod 3:14, in which God reveals that his name is *egō eimi ho ōn*, "I am the One who is," a name denoting his active, upholding, uncircumscribed, everlasting presence, which allows no rival force to withstand it (cf. Childs, *Exodus*, 61–70). This mysterious divine name was used by some Jews for magical purposes (see e.g. Naveh and Shaked, *Amulets*, 45, 51, 55), including the calming of storms (see *b. B. Bat.* 73a).

51. *within themselves.* Gk *en heautois.* As Swete (132) puts it, these words indicate that "the astonishment did not express itself in words" (cf. 2:8; 5:30).

52. *for they did not understand about the loaves.* Gk *ou gar synēkan epi tois artois.* The Qumran text 1QH 3:13–15, like our verse, connects eschatological storm-at-sea imagery with the theme of human bewilderment: "Their wise men are for them like sailors in the deep, for all their wisdom is destroyed because of the roaring of the waters" (Dupont-Sommer trans.). Nevertheless this verse dealing with incomprehension is itself difficult to understand; it would make much more sense at the end of the previous narrative, which dealt with the multiplication of the loaves. Taylor (331) projects his perplexity about the verse onto Mark himself, saying that it "possibly . . . reveals an embarrassment on the part of the narrator"—a remark that *certainly* reveals exegetical embarrassment on the part of the commentator! It is possible that at least part of its purpose is to link readers with the disciples in temporary befuddlement in order to promote their identification with the Twelve (cf. the introduction to the COMMENT on 8:14–21).

O'Callaghan ("Papyri") has argued that the fragmentary Qumran ms. 7Q5 contains a quotation from Mark 6:52–53. This identification, however, is doubtful; see Stanton, *Gospel Truth*, 20–32.

their heart was hardened. Gk *ēn autōn hē kardia pepōrōmenēn.* Although from time to time Mark ascribes a special role to certain of Jesus' followers such as Peter, James, and John, he often treats the disciples as an undifferentiated group. This is well illustrated here, where the many disciples are said to share a single, hardened heart. But why does Mark speak here of their hardened heart rather than of their blinded eyes (cf. 4:12; 8:18)? The latter would seem at first to be more appropriate, since they suffer more from an inability to perceive ("they did not understand") than from an unwillingness to do so. But the motif of the hardened heart fits with the other echoes of the exodus story here, since it is very prominent in Exodus, where God hardens Pharaoh's heart (cf. Exod 7:3, 13, etc.; cf. the COMMENT on 3:5–6). Israel, too, is charged in the OT with stony-heartedness (see Ezek 11:19) or tough-heartedness (Deut 29:18), and the *idea* of hardening their heart is present in the famous passage in Isa 6:9–10 ("make the heart of this people fat"), but the specific *vocabulary* of the hardened heart is usually reserved for Israel's enemies (see, however, Isa 63:17).

COMMENT

Introduction. The feeding of five thousand people with five loaves of bread and two fish is followed by an even more amazing miracle, Jesus' defiance of the law of gravity by walking on the Sea of Galilee. There is continuity between these two miracles, since the sea passage extends the exodus typology of the multiplication story.

These passages were probably already linked in the pre-Markan tradition, as their combination in the Gospel of John suggests (see the introduction to the COMMENT on 6:30–44). John's version of our story, however, is less elaborate than Mark's (see figure 18); the element of the miraculous is more muted, since Jesus does not demonstrate supernatural vision (6:48a) or calm the storm (6:51b), nor does John seem to share Mark's concern to refute the charge that the disciples experienced a hallucination (Mark 6:49–50a; cf. Brown, 1.253–54).

Why this Markan difference? Several of the elements of Mark's narrative are similar to features of his earlier sea story in 4:35–41 (see again figure 18):

(1) Jesus' compulsion or initiative
(2) dismissing the crowd
(3) "when evening had come"
(4) dangerous wind
(5) Jesus' volition ("Don't you care?"/wanted to pass them by)
(6) Jesus rebukes disciples for their fear or commands them not to be afraid.
(7) Jesus causes wind to die down.
(8) at end of story, disciples react with terror/astonishment.

Significantly, numbers 1, 2, 5, 7, and 8 are missing from John; the suspicion arises, then, that Mark has combined a simpler walking-on-water story, like John's, with elements of his own earlier stilling-of-the-storm. Other typically Markan elements not present in the Johannine parallel, and perhaps attributable to Markan editing, are the ascent of the mountain in 6:46 (cf. 3:13; 9:2); praying alone in 6:46 (cf. 1:35; 14:32–36); Jesus' "seeing" the disciples in 6:48a (cf. the NOTE on "seeing" in 6:48); the symbolic time-notice in 6:48b (cf. the NOTE on "since the hour was already late" in 6:35); the *gar* ("for") clause in 6:50a, with the favorite Markan word "all"; and the emphasis on the misunderstanding of the disciples in 6:52. Mark also emphasizes Jesus' volition a number of times (*compelling* the disciples to depart, *dismissing* the crowd, *wanting* to pass the disciples by—all absent from John), and these features may also represent Markan redaction. Mark's reworking of the story that has come down to him, then, seems to have been substantial; it was very important to him to emphasize certain theological, and especially Christological, aspects of this tale.

This redactionally crafted narrative is carefully structured. Its main action is encapsulated in a chiasm:

6:45   Jesus makes disciples get into boat
6:48a   He sees them struggling in their rowing on sea
6:48b   In fourth watch he comes over sea to them
6:49–50   They see him and are disturbed
6:51   He gets into boat

Appropriately, the midpoint of the chiasm, the description of Jesus' journey across the waters (6:48b), is also the dramatic center of the narrative. The chiastic structure also highlights the importance of the Markan theme of seeing by paralleling Jesus' vision of the disciples (6:48a) with their vision of him (6:49–50). The prominence of this theme reflects the form of the story, which is an epiphany, a genre that Heil (*Jesus Walking*, 8) defines as "a sudden and unexpected manifestation of a divine or heavenly being experienced by certain selected persons, in which the divine being reveals a divine attribute, action or message"; the motif of perception, then, is intrinsic to it. In our particular case, as we have noted, the epiphany is elaborated with elements drawn from a narrative of rescue at sea. Such a mixture is not unprecedented; Theissen (101) points to classical Greek, Hellenistic, and NT narratives in which a rescue at sea is accomplished through the epiphany of a god (*Homeric Hymns* 33.12; Aristedes *Hymn to Serapis* 33; Acts 5:17–25; 12:3–19).

The narrative falls into three fairly equal parts. Verses 6:45–47 lay the groundwork for the miracle by establishing the setting: the disciples in the middle of the sea, Jesus on the shore. The central section, 6:48–50, describes the extraordinary epiphany of Jesus upon the water, the disciples' terrified reaction to it, and Jesus' symbolically loaded identification of himself in response. The narrative concludes in 6:51–52 with Jesus' reunion with the disciples in the boat, which is accompanied by another miracle (the sudden calming of the wind), another dumbfounded reaction from the disciples (amazement), and the narrator's editorial comment on this response ("for they did not understand . . ."). The drama revolves around Jesus' separation from the disciples; in the beginning he compels them to go before him across the water (6:45), while in the middle *he* tries to go before *them* (6:48). Only at the conclusion is the tension caused by this separation somewhat dissipated as Jesus is reunited with the disciples in the boat (6:51); even then, however, the resolution is incomplete because they remain spiritually alienated from him: "for they did not understand about the loaves, but their heart was hardened" (6:52).

6:45–47: *transitional stage-setting*. Jesus sets in motion the chain of events that will lead to the miracle by dispatching the disciples to the other side of the Sea of Galilee (6:45)—a redactional feature that is not present in the Johannine parallel, where the disciples depart of their own volition. Thus the subsequent miracle has been initiated by Jesus' action; as in the later stories of the triumphal entry (11:1–7) and preparation for the Last Supper (14:12–16), Jesus has foreseen and planned the subsequent course of events. There is, as Davies and Allison (2.501) point out, an "edifying lesson" for Mark's community in this feature: though they may run into danger because of their obedience to Christ's command, he will ultimately save them.

After the disciples have departed, Jesus dismisses the crowd (6:46a), something that the disciples had asked him to do ten verses earlier. Their request has now been granted, but according to Jesus' timetable rather than their own—again, an important lesson for the Markan church. Jesus then goes up "the mountain" in order to pray (6:46b; cf. 1:35), a feature that is probably meant to be understood as reminiscent of Moses, and this typology continues the Mosaic symbolism that dominated the preceding passage about the feeding of the five thousand (see the NOTE on "went away to the mountain to pray" in 6:46).

The stage-setting is completed by the note that, by the time evening comes, the boat has reached the middle of the sea, while Jesus himself is on the dry land, alone (6:47). The disciples are thus cut off from Jesus by a great distance; it seems impossible that he should see their distress from miles away in the dark, much less come to their rescue across the roaring sea. Yet, in what follows, that is exactly what will happen: he will see them, he will come to them (cf. Boring, *Sayings*, 202). Regarded in this way, the scene would doubtless have a symbolic resonance for a Markan community that sometimes feels separated from Jesus (cf. 2:20) and prays for his presence (cf. Lohmeyer, 133, and Schmithals, 333).

6:48–50: *epiphany*. With his piercing, supernatural vision (see the NOTE on "seeing" in 6:48), Jesus detects the plight of his lonely, beleaguered followers, straining at the oars in the midst of the windswept sea (6:48a). This description, too, would be resonant for Mark's readers. Because of the biblical linkage of the stormy sea with death (see e.g. 2 Sam 22:5; Cant 8:6–7; Ps 69:2–3; Jonah 2), it became in Jewish apocalyptic literature a standard image of the climactic distress of the end-time, as is illustrated by several passages from the Qumran Hymns Scroll (1QH 3:6, 12–18; 6:22–25; 7:45) as well as by NT passages such as Luke 21:25 (cf. Heil, *Jesus Walking*, 22). A contrary wind can also be a symbol of eschatological distress (see Matt 7:25, 27). And since the word for "making tortuous progress" can be used of eschatological tribulation, and since it and the word for "rowing" can have nuances of judicial torture and persecution (see the NOTE on "making tortuous progress in their rowing" in 6:48), the distress of the Markan disciples at sea would probably remind the Markan community of the eschatological affliction and bewilderment they themselves were experiencing in the wake of the persecutions associated with the Jewish War. Because of the identification with the disciples' situation that such associations would induce, it is probable that Mark's readers would have heard the narrative of Jesus' miraculous appearance over the storm-tossed waters, like the earlier sea story in chapter 4, as carrying a profound message of hope for themselves (see the COMMENT on 4:37–39 and on 4:40–41). This message would be symbolically reinforced by the fact that the miracle happens in the fourth watch of the night (3:00 to 6:00 A.M.), the time when darkness is beginning to loosen its grip over the earth, in accordance with the common biblical theme of God's help arriving at dawn (see the NOTE on "the fourth watch of the night" in 6:48).

At this time of dawning victory, Jesus comes striding across the foaming sea to the disciples (6:48b). This is the turning point of the entire narrative, as is shown by the fact that the verbal tense suddenly shifts from the aorist to the historical present (*erchetai*, lit. "comes") and the point of view from the perspective of Jesus to that of the terrified disciples. While there is a remote biblical analogy to Jesus' amazing feat in the story of the axhead that Elisha caused to float (2 Kgs 6:1–7), it is even more similar to acts of levitation that were claimed for sorcerers and other wonder-workers in Hellenistic antiquity (see e.g. Lucian *Lover of Lies* 13; PGM 1.121; cf. M. Smith, *Jesus*, 120), and this impression is confirmed by the disciples' anxiety that Jesus may be a ghost (see Lohmeyer, 135).

In the OT-saturated atmosphere of our narrative, however, more is involved in Jesus' walking on the waters than just an astounding feat of magic. For Jesus' passage through the sea is reminiscent of the Israelites' crossing of the Sea of Reeds in the exodus and thus continues the Passover/exodus/Moses typology that characterized the preceding narrative, in which Jesus like Moses provided bread, as well as the beginning of our story, in which Jesus like Moses ascended "the mountain." As Brown notes (1.255), the Passover Haggadah (*Dayyenu* section) and later rabbinic texts closely connect the gift of the manna with the Israelites' crossing of the sea, so this is a natural connection to make. The crucial point in that crossing, moreover, occurred "in the morning watch" (Exod 14:24), just as our miracle does. Furthermore, Psalm 77:20 says that, in the exodus crossing, God's way was on (or in) the sea, and the Septuagint translation of this psalm (76:16 LXX) speaks of the waters seeing God and being disturbed (*etarachthēsan*), the same verb that is used in Mark 6:50 for the disturbance of the disciples (the Targum, like Mark, transfers the disturbance from the waters to "the peoples"; cf. Davies and Allison, 2.505). And Jesus' self-identification formula, "I am here" (*egō eimi*), has strong connections with Passover; it is dwelt upon in the Haggadah ("I, the Lord, I Am and no other"), and one of the biblical "I am" passages, Isa 51:6–16, is a Jewish lectionary reading (*haptārā*) for the holiday. "I am" is also the interpretation of the divine name that God revealed to Moses at the burning bush (Exod 3:14) and is part of the Ten Commandments that he gave to him on Sinai (Exod 20:2; Deut 5:6). Thus the Mosaic and exodus echoes in our passage are unmistakable.

But these nuances do not mean that Jesus is just being compared to Moses here; the more important analogy is that which exists between the Markan Jesus, on the one hand, and the God who spoke and revealed himself to Moses, on the other. For in the OT and some later Jewish texts it is consistently God or his wisdom who walks on the waters of the sea and tramples its waves, thus demonstrating that he and no other is divine (see e.g. Job 9:8; Hab 3:15; Ps 77:19; Isa 43:16; 51:9–10; Sir 24:5–6). Similarly, in the OT and Jewish traditions it is God alone who can rescue people from the sea (Ps 107:23–32; Jonah 1:1–16; Wis 14:2–4, etc.; cf. Davies and Allison, 2.503). This interpretation is confirmed by the otherwise puzzling note about Jesus' intention to *pass* the disciples, which is reminiscent of the striking and important description of God revealing himself as he passes before Moses in Exod 33:17–34:8 (see the NOTE on "intended to pass them" in 6:48). In this OT text God's "passing by" is accompanied by his proclamation of his own identity as a gracious and merciful deity (Exod 34:6); in our narrative, similarly, Jesus identifies himself by saying "*I am here*" and compassionately comes to the aid of his disciples. The link between our passage and Exodus 33–34 becomes even clearer when it is recalled that the name which God proclaims in Exodus 34:6 when he passes by, "Yahweh," is etymologically explained in Exod 3:13–14 as deriving from the verb "to be," thus forging a connection with the *egō eimi* of Mark 6:50. Although, therefore, Mark never explicitly says that Jesus is divine, he comes very close to doing so here, and this high evaluation of Jesus is consonant with indicators elsewhere in the Gospel (cf. e.g. 4:35–41; 14:61–62).

Yet, precisely at this most "divine" moment in the Markan Jesus' life, he also displays his humanness, for his will seems momentarily to be thwarted. He *wishes* to pass the disciples by for their own good, to give them a full revelation of his identity, but he cannot do so because of their terror and incomprehension (cf. 6:5); he is called back to earth by the necessity of ministering to them. There is, perhaps, another spiritual lesson here for the Markan community: Jesus' followers' fear may stand in the way of a full divine self-disclosure to them, but the good news is that Jesus will come to them even when they are afraid.

Despite this qualification, the overwhelming impact made by our narrative is an impression of Jesus' divinity, and it is precisely this divine quality that will enable him to conquer death, his own and that of his followers; this conquest, which will ultimately be accomplished through his resurrection, is foreshadowed by our narrative as well. As we have already noted, there is a strong OT association between waters, especially the waters of the unruly sea and death; this association is reflected in Mark's narrative itself in 10:38–39, which speaks allusively of death as a form of baptism, and elsewhere in the NT in Rev 15:2, where those who stand on the crystal sea are martyrs who have triumphed over death (cf. Lohmeyer, 135). With this association in mind, Jesus' walking on the sea becomes symbolic of his conquest of death, a symbolism that seems to be picked up in the retelling of the story in *Odes Sol.* 39 (cf. Dibelius, 277–78). This interpretation is supported by the numerous parallels between our passage and resurrection appearance accounts, especially that in Luke 24:36–43:

(1) epiphany of Jesus, who appears suddenly after long separation from disciples (Mark 6:48; Luke 24:36)
(2) Disciples think Jesus is a ghost (Mark 6:49a; Luke 24:37b).
(3) Disciples are afraid (Mark 6:49b; Luke 24:37a) and troubled (Mark 6:50; Luke 24:38a).
(4) Jesus tells them not to be afraid (Mark 6:50b; Luke 24:38).
(5) He says, "I am here" (*egō eimi*; Mark 6:50b; Luke 24:39).
(6) Disciples are astonished (Mark 6:51; Luke 24:41a).
(7) reference to food (Mark 6:52a; Luke 24:41b)
(8) hardened/doubting hearts (Mark 6:52b; Luke 24:38b)
(9) stress that Jesus is not a ghost (Luke 24:39; implied by Mark 6:50a)

Although some of these parallels are common to theophanies in general, the list is so long and striking that it does not seem to be fortuitous, especially since some of the corresponding elements, such as the denial that Jesus is a ghost and the progression from fear to astonishment, are particularly appropriate in a resurrectional context. The motifs of doubt and hardness of heart, moreover, appear frequently in resurrection narratives (Matt 28:17; Luke 24:11; John 20:24–29; Mark 16:11–14). Mark, then, may very well have elaborated his walking-on-the-sea story not only with elements drawn from his earlier sea story (see the introduction to this COMMENT) but also with features borrowed from resurrection appearance narratives; indeed, it is even possible that the walking-on-the-sea story originally *was* a resurrection narrative (cf. Madden, *Jesus' Walking*). In either case it is probable that Mark means the tale to be understood as a symbolic portrayal of Jesus' conquest of "the last enemy" (cf. 1 Cor 15:26). Not even the waters of death can put a stop to the compassion of Jesus (cf. Cant 8:6–7); in spite of distance, in spite of death, he will come to the disciples whom he loves and whose predicament he sees.

The disciples, however, are apparently not yet ready for this revelation; they cry out in fright, thinking that Jesus is a ghost (6:49). Besides its allusion to doubt about the reality of the resurrection, this feature may have an existential resonance for Mark's readers, who are probably being tempted by the persecution they suffer to think that they have placed their trust in a hallucination or a phantom without power to save. Mark, however, quickly disposes of such doubts. His addition of the *gar* ("for") clause in 6:50a subtly undermines the possibility that the appearance of Jesus is a hallucination; *all* of the disciples see the figure walking on the water, so if it is a delusion, it is a rare case of mass psychosis (an argument that Paul uses with respect to a resurrection appearance in 1 Cor 15:6).

The climax of the passage immediately follows as the Markan Jesus reasserts his identity, prefacing this reassertion with a pleonastic formula, "he immediately spoke with them and said to them," that emphasizes the reestablishment of communication after absence and highlights the cruciality of what is being communicated. Jesus is with the disciples again, he speaks to them again, and his words back up the sheer wonder of his renewed presence with the sovereign announcement "Be brave, *I am here*; don't be afraid!" (6:50b). This reassurance also shows that Jesus is not a ghost, for ghosts generally try to frighten people rather than calming their fears. Jesus' consoling, empowering words also reinforce the connection the story has forged between him and the OT God, both because of the divine connotations of the *egō eimi* formula (see the NOTE on "*I am here*" in 6:50) and because, throughout the Old Testament, including the exodus narrative (Exod 14:13), God calls his people to cast aside their fear (see D. Schmidt, 84).

6:51–52: conclusion. This sophisticated web of biblical allusions, however, seems again to be lost on Jesus' thickheaded disciples, for Mark concludes his passage with the editorial remark that they did not understand because their heart was hardened (6:52). This remark follows the denouement of the story, in which Jesus gets into the boat, the wind eerily dies down, and the disciples are greatly astonished (6:51). Such astonishment would make a good ending for a miracle story, and indeed the story probably *did* end this way at the pre-Markan stage: Jesus again demonstrated his mastery over nature by rescuing the disciples from the storm, and they responded with appropriate wonder. Mark's addition of 6:52, however, has transformed this appropriate astonishment into a reprehensible incomprehension, thus expressing the typical Markan theme of apostolic misunderstanding (cf. 16:7–8, where a similar transformation of theophanic wonder seems to have taken place). Even more threatening to the disciples, in a story replete with exodus allusions, is the specific reference to their hardened heart. In this chapter of the story of the new exodus, Jesus' disciples not only appear thickheaded, faithless, and fearful, like Israel in the desert, but almost begin to approximate the image of Israel's hard-hearted opponent, Pharaoh (cf. Exod 7:3, 13, 22; 8:15, etc. and the NOTE on "their heart was hardened" in 6:52).

Equally surprisingly, Mark does not say that the disciples' problem is incomprehension about the sea-walking that has just taken place but misunderstanding about the *loaves*, thus somehow linking the Twelve's perceptual difficulty in our story with their obtuseness in the previous one (cf. 6:35–37). The key to the interpretation of this cryptic remark must therefore lie in themes that these two passages share (see Lohmeyer, 134). The most obvious similarity is that both pericopes portray Jesus saving the day when human resources are at an end, but this cannot be the whole answer, since it still does not explain why the reference is to incomprehension of the *loaves* rather than a misunderstanding about the present story. Quesnell, in a full-length monograph devoted to Mark 6:52 (*Mind*), seems to be on the right track when he argues that the allusion to the loaves is a eucharistic one, since the previous story about the multiplication of the loaves foreshadows the Lord's Supper (cf. the COMMENT on 6:38–42). This exegesis coheres with my exegesis of the present passage, since I have emphasized that one of the major themes of our story is the way in which Jesus miraculously makes himself present to the Markan community across the gulf of death; if Mark's eucharistic theology was anything like that in Pauline circles (cf. 1 Cor 10:2–4, 16–17; 11:17–12:31), he would have thought that Jesus' presence was communicated by the distribution of the eucharistic bread, which made the Lord's body an active reality among the members of the church (cf. 14:22; for other theories about 6:52, see the NOTE on "for they did not understand about the loaves" there).

As we have seen, both this eucharistic theme in the multiplication story and several motifs in our sea-walking passage hark back to the exodus narrative of the Old Testament. In both passages, in accordance with this exodus background, Jesus appears at some points as a man subordinate to God, similar to Moses "the servant of God" (cf. Num 12:7; Heb 3:5); he looks up to heaven in a gesture of dependence as he breaks the mannalike bread (6:41), and he ascends "the mountain" in order to commune with God (6:46). Yet, especially in the present passage, this Moses-like role sometimes gives way to scenes in which Jesus assumes the character of the God of the exodus himself (cf. the NOTE on "went away to the mountain to pray" in 6:46 for a precedent for this transition in certain traditions about Moses himself). This combination of Jesus' continuity with and transcendence of the human Mosaic image provides an appropriate prolegomenon to the controversy with the scribes and Pharisees that will shortly follow (7:1–23), for there Jesus will both affirm his conformity with the spirit of one of the Ten Commandments, the command to honor parents (7:9–13), and abrogate the letter of what was to Jews a basic prescription of the Mosaic Torah, the taboo on ritually impure food (7:19).

MORE AND MORE HEALINGS (6:53–56)

6 ⁵³And crossing over, they came to land at Gennesaret, and docked. ⁵⁴And when they got out of the boat he was immediately recognized, ⁵⁵and people ran through that whole region and began bringing the sick on pallets to wherever they heard that he was. ⁵⁶And wherever he went, into villages or cities or hamlets, they laid the sick down in the marketplaces and pleaded with him to let them touch just the fringe of his garment; and as many as touched him were cured.

NOTES

6 53. *crossing over, they came to land at Gennesaret.* Gk *diaperasantes epi tēn gēn ēlthon eis Gennēsaret*, lit. "crossing over to land they came to Gennesaret." The Greek is ambiguous; "to land" could go either with "crossing over" or with "they came."

"Gennesaret" was not the name of a village but of the 3½-mile-long plain on the western shore of the Sea of Galilee between Tiberias and Capernaum (see Edwards, "Gennesaret"); it is a Greek rendering of the Hebrew name for the "sea," *Kinneret*, which is derived from the Hebrew word for "lyre," *kinnôr*, and refers to the harplike shape of this body of water (cf. the NOTE on "the Sea of Galilee" in 1:16).

Why do Jesus and the disciples land at Gennesaret, when they had set out for Bethsaida (6:45)? If we reject the unlikely theory that they were blown off course (see the NOTE on "toward Bethsaida" in 6:45), we must search for some redactional explanation of the discrepancy. Hooker (171), noting that Bethsaida is next mentioned in 8:22, after another miraculous feeding (8:1–9) and another sea crossing (8:10), suggests that Mark has split up the original connection between 6:32–52 and 8:22–30 by his insertion of 6:53–8:21, which provides an alternate version of some of the same material. One problem with this theory, however, is that John's Gospel supports an original connection between the stories of the feeding of the five thousand and the walking on the water, on the one hand, and the landing at Gennesaret (rather than Bethsaida), on the other; in the Johannine parallel the boat sets sail for and lands at Capernaum, which is on the Gennesaret plain (John 6:17, 24). If, as I have argued, John is literarily independent of Mark (see the discussion of Gospel relationships in the INTRODUCTION), this would seem to suggest that in the pre-Gospel tradition the walking on the water was followed by a landing on the western side of the lake (Gennesaret or Capernaum) rather than on the eastern side (Bethsaida). Even the Johannine tradition, however, is equivocal about the location of the landing, since 6:23, 25 imply that it occurred across the sea from Tiberias, i.e. on the eastern shore. It may be that both Mark and John, each in his own way, have combined two versions of the same cycle.

and docked. Gk *kai prosōrmisthēsan.* These words are omitted by Codex D, perhaps by homoeoarcton (*kai prosōrmisthēsan kai exelthontōn*).

54. *he was immediately recognized.* Gk *euthys epignontes auton*, lit. "immediately recognizing him, they ran . . ." This is another example of the third person plural used impersonally for the passive (cf. 1:22, 32; 2:3; 3:32; 5:14; 6:14, 33).

56. *pleaded with him to let them touch.* Gk *parekaloun auton hina . . . hapsōntai*, lit. "pleaded with him in order that they might touch." From the grammar, the subject would at first seem to be those who bring the afflicted to Jesus, since they are the subject of the preceding verb ("they laid"), but the continuation ("and as many as touched him were saved") makes it clear that the suppliants are the sick themselves (on Mark's tendency to leave subjects confusingly undefined, see the NOTE on "people came" in 5:14). Their plea contrasts with other instances in which people ask Jesus to heal them by his touching *them* (5:23; 7:32; 8:22), but it is also different from 5:25–34, where the woman with the hemorrhage touches Jesus without his consent. The picture in the present passage is unrealistic: in pandemonium such as is being described, people would probably either touch without asking permission, as

the woman with the hemorrhage did, or shout out a request for direct healing, not a request for permission to touch in order to be healed. Besides, it would be difficult for invalids to get close enough to Jesus to touch him in the crowd that would almost surely surround him.

the fringe of his garment. Gk *tou kraspedou tou himatiou autou.* The word translated "fringe" here, *kraspedon*, could mean a hem, but it is also the word used in the plural in the Septuagint (Num 15:38–39; Deut 22:12) and the NT (Matt 23:5) for the tassels (*ṣîṣîyôt*) worn by Jewish males at the four corners of their garments to remind them of God's commandments. Since the commandment to wear these fringes is a biblical one, it is to be expected that most Jewish males would have complied, and *Ep. Arist.* 158 and some Talmudic passages (e.g. *b. Taʿan.* 22a; *b. Menaḥ* 43a) suggest that even Gentiles could recognize Jews by their tassels (though no non-Jewish source confirms this; see Cohen, "Those Who Say," 7–8). Some Talmudic passages (e.g. *b. Menaḥ* 43b–44a) ascribe cosmic symbolism and near-magical powers to the fringes, and it is possible that some such ideas underlie our story. It is also perhaps relevant, given the exodus symbolism of the two previous passages, that the fringes are especially associated with the memory of the departure from Egypt (see Num 15:37–41 and *Sipre* on Num 15:38 [§115]).

were cured. Gk *esǫzonto,* lit. "were saved"; see the NOTE on "be cured" in 5:23.

COMMENT

Introduction. The eventful, revelatory journey of Jesus and the disciples across the Sea of Galilee ends with them docking at the plain of Gennesaret, on the western side of the lake. Here Jesus is again mobbed, as on previous occasions (1:45; 3:7–12; 6:33), by a horde of sick people who have heard about his healing power and are desperate to appropriate it for themselves.

The landing at Gennesaret creates a narrative problem, since the disciples had set out not for Gennesaret but for Bethsaida (6:45). Mark seems to be combining traditions, and to be doing so somewhat awkwardly (see the NOTE on "crossing over, they came to land at Gennesaret" in 6:53). This awkwardness suggests that the "summary passage" in 6:53–56 has a traditional basis, as is also indicated by the uncharacteristic absence of the themes of Jesus' teaching (cf. 2:1–2, 13; 4:1–2, etc.) and of exorcism (cf. 1:32–34, 39; 3:11–12; cf. Egger, *Frohbotschaft,* 136). The narrative, therefore, may well have been part of a pre-Markan source. Nevertheless, the passage has been heavily reworked by Mark, as can be seen from the abundance of Markan vocabulary (e.g. "immediately," "began to," "villages" and "cities," impersonal plural), and it is really impossible to discern its original contours beneath the Markan revision.

The passage in its present form is characterized by a great sense of movement and excitement, comparable, in a way, to that which will later inform the narrative of Jesus' triumphal entry into Jerusalem (11:8–10). The impression of dynamism, and of the universal impact of Jesus' presence, is emphasized by the pervasive use of the imperfect tense and the repeated relative clauses ("wherever they heard," "wherever he went," "as many as touched"; cf. Guelich, 355; Egger, *Frohbotschaft*, 135). The climax is reached at the very conclusion of the passage, for only there is the problem of sickness that has pervaded it finally addressed with a swift and decisive resolution: "And as many as touched him were cured."

6:53–56: *the healings at Gennesaret.* Jesus' spreading fame is emphasized from the beginning of the passage; no sooner have he and the disciples landed in Gennesaret and moored their boat there than they are recognized, and the excitement begins (6:53–54). The picture conveyed is that, from the moment of Jesus' landing, the same numinous power that he just displayed in walking on the water begins to radiate out and convulse the entire countryside, as people rush about frantically to drag their invalid friends and relatives to spots where, rumor has it, he will pass by (6:55). The following half-verse (6:56a), in a typically Markan manner (see Neirynck, *Duality*; Egger, *Frohbotschaft*, 135), repeats and extends this thought, and this entire central section of the passage emphasizes by its repetition and chiastic arrangement the helpless condition of those who supplicate Jesus; like the paralytic in 2:1–12, they cannot even approach him by themselves, but need to be carried:

> people . . . began bringing the sick on pallets
>   to wherever they heard that he was.
>   And wherever he went, into villages or cities or hamlets,
> they laid the sick down in the marketplaces

The dramatic climax of the passage immediately follows this chiasm: as the storm of divine grace roars through each town square, the invalids who have been placed there plead, with touching humility, to be allowed to touch just the fringe of Jesus' garment (6:56b). This picture of invalids requesting permission to touch the clothing of the passing healer is somewhat unrealistic (see the NOTE on "pleaded with him to let them touch" in 6:56) and may very well be symbolic: faith reaches out to touch Jesus, but even this outreach proceeds only by his authorization. As Davies and Allison point out, moreover (2.129), our text continues a development begun in two recent healing stories: in 3:7–12 people touched *Jesus*, in 5:21–34 the woman touched only Jesus' *garment*, and in our passage people touch only *the fringe of his garment*. This progression in reticence may have to do with the increasingly lofty portrayal of Jesus in the Gospel; our passage, after all, immediately follows one in which Jesus has been portrayed in a godlike form (see the COMMENT on 6:48–50), and the two passages are linked in that both describe Jesus "passing by" (explicitly in 6:48, implicitly in to "touch just the fringe of his garment" in 6:56). As in the previous story, this "passing by" turns out to be a revelation of divine grace and power, for the appeals made by the sufferers do not go unanswered: "and as many as touched him were cured" (6:56c).

Our pericope prepares for the ensuing controversy with the Pharisees and scribes about the tradition of the elders and the commandment of God (7:1–23), subtly undermining the position that Jesus' opponents will express, namely that he and his disciples are culpable renegades from authoritative tradition. By its demonstration of Jesus' raw charismatic power, it shows that, unless one assumes that he performs his miracles by demonic agency (cf. 3:22–30), one will be forced to conclude that he works them by the power of God and that any tradition that sets itself up against him is suspect. Moreover, if, as seems likely, the miracle working "fringe" of Jesus' garment is the *ṣîṣîyôt* enjoined on Jewish males in the Old Testament (see the NOTE on "the fringe of his garment" in 6:56), then our passage portrays Jesus as an observant Jew even to the tassels of his garment (cf. Booth, *Jesus*, 31). But if, according to Num 15:39, the fringe is a constant reminder to Jews in every generation to observe "all the commandments of the Lord," it is also a perpetual warning "not to follow after your own heart and your own eyes, after which you are inclined to stray" (RSV alt.). The reference to the fringe of Jesus' garment, then, provides a fitting transition to a passage in which he will set the divine commandment over against traditions of human beings whose hearts have strayed from God.

JESUS ARGUES WITH THE PHARISEES ABOUT SCRIPTURE AND TRADITION (7:1–15)

7 ¹And the Pharisees, and some of the scribes who had come from Jerusalem, gathered together before him. ²And when they saw that some of his disciples were eating loaves of bread with impure, that is unwashed, hands — ³for the Pharisees, and all the Jews, unless they first wash their hands with the hand shaped into a fist refuse to eat, since they hold fast to the tradition of the elders; ⁴nor, when they come from the marketplace, do they eat unless they immerse; and there are many other customs which they have received to preserve, immersions of cups and of pitchers and of copper utensils and of beds — ⁵and the Pharisees and the scribes asked him, "Why don't your disciples walk according to the tradition of the elders? — but they eat bread with impure hands."

⁶And he said to them, "Isaiah did a good job of prophesying about you hypocrites; as it has been written: 'This people honors me with their lips, but their heart stands far off from me; ⁷they worship me pointlessly, teaching as divine teachings the commandments of human beings.' ⁸You forsake the commandment of God and hold fast to the tradition of human beings."

⁹And he said to them, "You do a good job of annulling the commandment of God, so that you may establish your tradition. ¹⁰For Moses said, 'Honor your father and your mother,' and 'The person who curses father or mother, let him be executed.' ¹¹But *you* say, 'If a person says to his father or mother, "Whatever of mine you might have benefited from is *korban*, that is, a gift to God"' — ¹²you no longer allow him to do anything for his father or mother, ¹³thus voiding the

word of God for the sake of your tradition which you have passed down. And you do many similar things of this sort."

[14]And summoning the crowd again he said to them, "Listen to me, all of you, and understand: [15]There is nothing from outside of a person which, when it goes into the person, is able to defile him; but the things that come out of the person are the ones that defile the person."

NOTES

7   1. *gathered together.* Gk *synagnotai*, the same verb that is used with a positive nuance in 2:2; 4:1; 5:21; 6:30. In our passage, however, it gains a more sinister connotation from being ascribed to a part of the Jewish leadership, the Pharisees, who have sworn to destroy Jesus (3:6), and the listing of *two* groups gathered together, the Pharisees and scribes, adds to the impression of hostile bands ganging up against him (cf. 3:6). For the scriptural background of the verb, see the COMMENT on 7:1–5.

2. *some of his disciples.* Gk *tinas tōn mathētōn autou.* Does this imply that some others of Jesus' disciples *do* wash their hands before eating, or just that the ones whom the Pharisees happen to see do not? If the former is the case, the passage may reflect the presence within the Markan church of Jewish Christians who are inclined to adopt Pharisaic traditions such as handwashing (cf. the COMMENT on 7:14–15 and on 7:17–23).

loaves of bread. Gk *artous*, lit. "the breads." This plural is a bit awkward in the context; the singular *arton* would be more natural (cf. Matt 15:2). The plural is probably employed to forge a connection with 6:30–44, 52.

impure. Gk *koinais*, lit. "common." The more natural term would be "unclean" (*akathartos*), which Mark uses frequently elsewhere (1:23, 26, 27; 3:11, etc.), but perhaps he wishes to restrict that word to unclean *spirits*. The present terminology is found only in Diaspora Jewish texts (e.g. 1 Macc 1:47, 62; Josephus *Ant.* 11.346) and in the NT, though it is similar in semantic range to the Hebrew root *ḥll*, which means "to render profane" or "to pollute" (cf. BDB, 320). The Diaspora Jewish and NT usage of "common" as a synonym for "impure" stems from the fact that both words are the opposite of "holy," which means "separated from the profane realm" (see Hauck, "*Koinos*," 790–91, 797, and cf. the NOTE on "the holy one of God" in 1:24).

3. *for the Pharisees, and all the Jews.* Gk *hoi gar Pharisaioi kai pantes hoi Ioudaioi.* "All the Jews" is not strictly accurate, although the Pharisees seem to have had a great influence on the population even before the assumption of leadership by their successors, the rabbis, after the war of 66–72 c.e. (see the APPENDIX "The scribes and the Pharisees"). Even after the war, however, Pharisaic purity regulations were not universal; rabbinic traditions themselves complain about the deficient purity of the *'am hā'āreṣ*, the "people of the land" (see Schürer, 2.386–87, 396–400). On the other hand, in the Diaspora handwashing before prayer seems to have been frequent among Jews and may help explain why ancient Diaspora synagogues were generally located near wa-

ter; the Jewish work *Epistle of Aristeas* (305) even approximates the language of our passage by saying, "Following the custom of *all the Jews*, they washed their hands in the sea in the course of their prayers to God" (cf. *Sib. Or.* 3.591–93 and E. Sanders, *Jewish Law*, 228, 260). And if Jews washed their hands before or during prayer, and prayed before eating, then they would have washed their hands before eating. Although handwashing was not universal, therefore, it was widespread and was probably a "boundary marker" by which Jews both identified themselves and were identified by outsiders as being set apart from their neighbors (see Dunn, *Jesus*, 48). Moreover, some of the other washings listed in the next verse—of cups, pitchers, and copper utensils—were biblical requirements (see the NOTE on "immersions of cups and of pitchers and of copper utensils" in 7:4) and therefore would have been generally observed. "All the Jews" also prepares for the polemical language of the citation from Isa 29:13 in 7:6, which speaks of the vain worship not of selected individuals but of "this nation" (see Berger, *Gesetzauslegung*, 486). Mark's statement, then, does not necessarily reflect a faulty knowledge of Judaism (as asserted, for example, by Niederwimmer, "Frage"). And while his need to inform his readers about Jewish customs suggests that at least some of them are non-Jewish, it does not necessarily mean that all of them are, or that he himself is, as is shown again by the parallel to *Ep. Arist.* 305 (see the discussion of Markan authorship and setting in the INTRODUCTION).

with the hand shaped into a fist. Gk *pygmē*, the dative form of the word for "fist" (from which our English word "pugilist" is derived). This is a perplexing expression, and it is no wonder that some texts have omitted it and that others, including ℵ, have replaced it with the more comprehensible term *pykna* (= "often" or "thoroughly"). Several explanations of the more difficult text have been proposed:

(1) "up to the fist or wrist"; cf. *m. Yad.* 2:3: "The hands . . . are rendered clean [by the pouring over them of water] up to the wrist" (see Edersheim, *Life*, 2.11).
(2) "with a fistful of water"; cf. *m. Yad.* 1:1: "[To render the hands clean] a quarter-*log* [= the bulk of an egg and a half] must be poured over the hands" (see Hengel, "Mc 7.3").
(3) "with a cupped hand" (the position in which modern religious Jews hold their hands while they wash them; see S. Reynolds, "PYGMI").

The last explanation is the one adopted in my translation, since it is the closest to the literal meaning of *pygmē*. But in the end what Swete (136) said in 1898 still holds true: "It must be confessed that no explanation hitherto offered is wholly satisfactory."

the tradition of the elders. Gk *tēn paradosin tōn presbyterōn.* Josephus (*Ant.* 13.297) uses similar terminology in writing about the Pharisees, who, he says, "had passed down (*paredosan*) to the people certain regulations handed down by former generations and not recorded in the Law of Moses." Josephus adds that these regulations are rejected by the Sadducees, who hold that only the regulations written in Scripture, not those "from the tradition of the fathers" (*ek paradoseōs tōn paterōn*), need to be observed (cf. also Gal 1:14). It is recognized in rabbinic texts that the particular tradition in view in our passage, handwashing by laypeople, is not explicitly commanded in the Bible (e.g. *b. Ber.* 52b: "The washing of hands for secular food is not from the Torah").

In the OT and early Jewish texts "elder" is a general term for a prominent person whose wisdom matches his age (see Campbell, *Elders*), and in rabbinic traditions it is often nearly synonymous with "scribe" or "scholar" (see Bornkamm, "*Presbys*," 659–61). The idea of a linkage with former ages is intrinsic in the present usage of the word, and it is remarkable that Mark concedes to the Pharisees such a presumably positive connection with venerable tradition. Later in the Gospel, however, the word will gain a more sinister overtone when another kind of elder, the prominent members of the Sanhedrin who are neither chief priests nor scribes (8:31; 11:27; 14:43, 53; 15:1), conspire to take Jesus' life. The word for "tradition," *paradosis*, can likewise be a positive term in the NT (cf. 1 Cor 11:2), but it takes on a dark overtone in our Gospel, since the cognate verb *paradidonai* is used frequently for the handing over or betrayal of John the Baptist, Jesus, and the Christians to suffering and death (1:14; 3:19; 9:31; 10:33; 13:9–12; 14:10–44; 15:1–15).

4. *nor, when they come from the marketplace, do they eat unless they immerse.* Gk *kai ap' agoras ean mē baptisōntai ouk esthiousin*, lit. "and from the market unless they immerse they do not eat." In the market one might inadvertently come into physical contact with unclean persons or foods (cf. Strack-Billerbeck, 2.14), making "the human swarm of the marketplace" into a nest of ritual contagion (cf. Dillon, "Authority," 108). Although there is no fixed rabbinic requirement for immersing oneself after a trip to the market, there is one rabbinic story in which descendants of Aaron do so (*y. Šeb.* 6:1, 36c; see Büchler, "Law," 38–39). As A. Baumgarten points out ("Associations"), this passage helps explain ours, since the Pharisees aspired to live like priests, and they may have been stricter about immersions etc. than most later rabbis were (cf. the reference to immersion before eating in Luke 11:38 and the APPENDIX "The Scribes and the Pharisees").

On the texts that read "sprinkle" rather than "immerse," see the NOTE below on "and of beds."

immersions of cups and of pitchers and of copper utensils. Gk *baptismous potēriōn kai xestōn kai chalkiōn*. As E. Sanders points out (*Jewish Law*, 261), the washing of certain kinds of containers and utensils, which can contract ritual impurity, is a biblical requirement (e.g. Lev 11:32; 15:12), though the particular way in which this would have been done would have been regulated by the Pharisaic tradition (see the Mishnaic tractate *Kelim* = "Vessels" and cf. the polemic of Matt 23:25–26).

and of beds. Gk *kai klinōn*. These words are absent in some very old and respected manuscripts (p[45], ℵ, B, L), but the witnesses for their inclusion are also powerful (A, D, K, W, etc.). It is possible that they have dropped out inadvertently (double homoeoteleuton), but more likely that their exclusion (or addition) is deliberate. Two of the important witnesses for omission (ℵ and B) also read "sprinkle" (*rhantisōntai*) rather than "immerse" (*baptisōntai*), though they still retain the noun "immersions" (*baptismous*). We really have a choice, then, between the following two texts:

> unless they immerse . . . immersions of cups and of pitchers and of copper utensils and of beds
>
> unless they sprinkle . . . immersions of cups and of pitchers and of copper utensils

Of these texts the second certainly paints the more plausible picture, since the immersion of beds is hard to imagine. For this very reason, however, we may suspect that the first is the original text, which a later scribe altered; this seems more likely than that a scribe created the strange picture of immersed beds under the sole influence of Leviticus 15 (cf. Metzger, 93–94), which speaks of beds becoming unclean but does not say how they are purified. If the reading "and of beds" is original, it bears witness to a gap in Mark's knowledge about Pharisaic practice, or to a passing phase of Pharisaic zealousness, or to the sharp edge of Markan sarcasm, and it is really impossible to decide among these options. Even if the sarcastic interpretation is the correct one, however, this does not necessarily mean that Mark is a Gentile (against Sariola, *Gesetz*, 57, 61); Jews themselves are capable of bitter irony against their fellow Jews, as the Qumran scrolls abundantly attest (on the question of Mark's ethnicity, see the discussion of the author in the INTRODUCTION).

5. *Why don't your disciples.* Gk *Dia ti ou . . . hoi mathētai sou*. It seems strange to some, such as Bultmann (18), that Jesus is questioned not about his own failure to wash his hands but about the disciples' omission to do so, when he would presumably fail the same test of ritual hygiene. (If he was rigorous about handwashing, he probably would have imposed the same regimen on his disciples, or at least would not have defended them when their failure to wash was challenged.) Bultmann thinks that the anomaly shows that the controversy arose only in the post-Easter church, but Daube ("Responsibilities") counters that in antiquity a master was responsible for the behavior of his followers. This explains why Jesus would have to defend his disciples' practice, but not why his own goes unchallenged. Both Bultmann and Daube may be right: a question about handwashing already arose in Jesus' ministry, but our story has been shaped by post-Easter concerns (cf. the COMMENT on 2:15–17 and the NOTE on "your disciples" in 2:18).

walk. Gk *peripatousin*. In the OT and later Judaism, "to walk" is a standard metaphor for "to live in a certain way," "to carry on one's life before God" (see e.g. Ezek 36:25–27). Out of this metaphor develops the rabbinic term *halakhah*, which literally means "walking" and is used for the behavioral as opposed to the narrative aspect of divine revelation.

6. *hypocrites.* Gk *hypokritōn.* In classical Greek this word usually designates a play actor (see BAGD, 845); for some of the Markan connotations, see the COMMENT on 7:6–13. A. Baumgarten (*"Paradosis,"* 70–71) calls attention to the similar condemnation of the Pharisees in Josephus *Ant.* 17.41, a section dependent on the anti-Pharisaic Nicolaus of Damascus; they are "a group of Jews priding itself on its adherence to ancestral custom and pretending (*propoioumenon*) to observe the Laws of which the Deity approves." Here the linkage with ancestral tradition, the insinuated contrast with God's laws, and the implication of hypocrisy ("pretending") are comparable to our passage. Also similar to our text are passages in the Dead Sea Scrolls in which the "seekers after smooth things," who are probably the Pharisees, are accused of being hypocrites (*n῾lmym*) and of practicing an exegesis rooted in *šryrwt lb* ("stubbornness of heart"), which in the Qumran literature means following the desires of one's own heart as opposed to the law of God (see 1QH 4:7–15 and cf. Mark 7:7–8). But in the Gospels the "hypocrisy" of the Pharisees is usually demonstrated by their making the Law more severe than it is in the OT (see e.g. Matt 23:4), while in the Dead Sea Scrolls the Pharisees are charged with a hypocritical quest for easy interpretations, i.e. being too lenient in their exegesis of the Torah (CD 1:18; 4QpNah 1:2, 7, etc.; cf. Matt 5:20). In general, in ancient Jewish and Christian contexts a "hypocrite" is a person whose interpretation of the Law differs from one's own.

6–7. *This people honors me with their lips,* etc. Gk *Houtos ho laos tois cheilesin me timą,* etc. This quotation is almost identical to the Septuagint of Isa 29:13, and the few minor differences fit the verse grammatically into the Markan context.

10. *Honor your father and your mother.* Gk *Tima ton patera sou kai tēn mētera sou.* This follows the Septuagint also (Exod 20:12//Deut 5:16 LXX). As Berger (*Gesetzauslegung,* 288) points out, in some Jewish texts, as in Mark, the fourth commandment is interpreted in terms of material support of parents (see e.g. *b. Qidd.* 31b, " 'Honor' means that he must give him food and drink, clothes and cover him, lead him in and out"; cf. Sir 3:3, 8, 12–16; Philo *Decalogue* 113–18).

The person who curses. Gk *ho kakologōn,* a citation of Exod 21:17//Lev 20:9, basically following the Septuagint (see the next NOTE). But, wrong as it may be to withhold material support from one's parents (and it was a special hardship in the days before Social Security), how is it equivalent to *cursing* them? As Fitzmyer notes (*"Qorbān* Inscription," 99), in the Mishnah *qônām,* a synonym for *qorbān,* is used in curses (see e.g. *m. Ned.* 4:6; 8:7). But our passage may also be an example of the sort of eschatological sharpening of the Torah that is attributed to Jesus elsewhere in the Synoptic tradition (cf. the COMMENT on 3:1–4); just as being angry or refraining from performing a cure is equivalent to murder, so withholding support from parents is equivalent to cursing them.

let him be executed. Gk *thanatǭ teleutatō,* lit. "by death let him die." As happens here, the Septuagint often renders the Hebrew infinitive absolute by means of a cognate dative (see Conybeare and Stock, *Grammar* §61). Mark seems to be conflating the verb used in Exod 21:16 LXX (21:17 MT), *teleutan*, with the form used in Lev 20:9 LXX, the third person singular imperative.

11. *korban, that is, a gift to God*. Gk *korban, ho estin dōron*. The words "to God" are not present in the Greek, but that is the sense. *Korban* is a transliteration of a Hebrew and Aramaic word for a sacrifice or offering, derived from the root *qrb* = to bring near. A close Aramaic parallel to our passage has come to light in the inscription on the Jebel Hallet et-Turi ossuary near Jerusalem: "Everything that a person will find to his profit in this ossuary is an offering (*qorbān*) to God from the one within it." As A. Baumgarten points out ("*Korban*," 6, 7, 16), here the implication is that the contents of the ossuary are to be treated *as if they were* an offering to God, i.e. as unavailable for any other use (cf. *y. Ned.* 1.4, "*Qorbān*, that is, like a *qorbān*"). It is not implied that they *are* an offering, since presenting to God the ritually unclean bones from an ossuary would be unthinkable. Similarly, in our passage, the person declares that any material support he might have given his parents is *korban*, i.e. pledged to God—not that he necessarily intends to *deliver* it to God but that he wants to remove it from his parents.

12. *you no longer allow him to do anything*. Gk *ouketi aphiete auton ouden poiēsai*. According to Num 30:2–4, any vow made to the Lord is permanently binding, and Philo says that this includes cases in which a man devotes his wife's sustenance to a sacred purpose, or a father his son's, or a ruler his subjects' (*Hypothetica* 7:4–5; cf. A. Baumgarten, "*Korban*," 8). Interestingly, however, Philo does *not* include the case of a son's pledging of his parents' sustenance; is this because of the perceived conflict with the commandment to honor parents? As Berger (*Gesetzauslegung*, 493–94 n. 3) points out, Josephus (*Ant.* 5.169), who claims to have been a Pharisee, opposes the fulfillment of antisocial vows. We have no direct evidence for judging the attitude of the Pharisees to vows, but their successors, the rabbis, agreed with Josephus and the Jesus of the Gospels: vows are not binding if made for an unworthy purpose, and avoidance of the necessary support of parents would fall into this category. The sort of abuse mentioned here is specifically forbidden in the third century by the Mishnah, which says that the imperative to honor parents overrules any vow (*m. Ned.* 9:1).

Klausner (*Jesus*, 290) mentions three possibilities for resolving the contradiction between our passage and later rabbinic practice: (1) Mark's charge against the Pharisees is a slander, (2) Pharisaic stringency on vows was subsequently relaxed by the rabbis, (3) a Pharisaic *permission* for the son to withhold help from his parents in certain cases is being misinterpreted as a *command* that the help be withheld. Of these possibilities the second seems most likely, especially in view of S. Cohen's depiction of the movement from Pharisaic sectarianism and stringency to rabbinic inclusiveness and leniency ("Yavneh"). It is also possible, however, that a Pharisaic ruling is being conflated with a priestly one, since priests would have had a motive for insisting that vows to the Temple be

honored (cf. A. Baumgarten, *"Korban,"* 14. n. 54). In our passage Jesus is arguing not just with Pharisees but also with scribes, and the latter may well have
been priests (see the APPENDIX "The scribes and the Pharisees").

15. *There is nothing from outside of a person*, etc. Gk *ouden estin exōthen tou
anthrōpou*, etc. This is the ultimate answer to the question of the Pharisees and
scribes as to why Jesus' disciples eat with unwashed hands (7:5). It seems to be
assumed that the Pharisees think that unwashed, ritually impure hands transmit their impurity to the food they touch and that this food, when eaten, in turn
transmits its impurity to the eater; Jesus counters by saying that external things
like unwashed hands have no power to transmit defilement (see Hübner,
Gesetz, 159; Poirier, "Why," 226–27). The problem with this interpretation,
which appears to be implicit in Mark's story, is that, according to the rabbis of
the Mishnah, hands cannot convey defilement to ordinary food, only to holy
food, i.e. that which priests eat (see Booth, *Jesus*, 173–87). As Hübner points
out, however (*Gesetz*, 163–64), it is uncertain to what extent the rabbinic
theory of degrees of impurity prevailed among the pre-70 Pharisees; they may
well have had a more undifferentiated and therefore more restrictive view of
uncleanness prior to Yavneh (cf. the reference to Cohen in the previous NOTE).
This seems more likely than Booth's suggestion (*Jesus*, 189–203) that the Pharisees viewed handwashing as a supererogatory action and that they were merely
urging Jesus and his disciples to strive for the same high standard of piety they
themselves had attained. The hostile atmosphere of our dialogue undermines
this irenic interpretation, and the Pharisees in our story seem to view handwashing as a requirement, not as a work of supererogation. Cf. *m. 'Ed.* 5:6–7,
where R. Eliezer b. Enoch is placed under a ban because he casts doubt on the
sages' teaching concerning the cleansing of hands.

Matthew's version of the saying in Mark 7:15 is less radical than Mark's:

Matthew 15:11	*Mark 7:15*
It is not what goes into the mouth	There is nothing from outside of a person which, when it goes into the person,
that defiles a person	is able to defile him
but what comes out of the mouth	but the things that come out of the person
that defiles the person	are the ones that defile the person
15:20: but to eat with unwashed hands does not defile a person	7:19: declaring all foods clean

Matthew lacks Mark's sweeping clause, "There is nothing which is able," and
he omits Mark's editorial conclusion that, by his saying, Jesus was declaring all
foods to be clean. Instead, in his narrative Jesus limits the implications of the
saying to the conclusion that eating with unwashed hands does not defile a per-

son. This toning down may reflect Matthew's Law-observant, Christian Jewish perspective (see Overman, *Matthew's Gospel,* and Saldarini, *Community*).

to defile. Gk *koinōsai,* lit. "to make common." This is the verbal form of the word translated "impure" in 7:2, 5; see the NOTE on "impure" in 7:2.

In some old manuscripts (A, D, K, etc.), along with the majority of witnesses, 7:15 is followed by 7:16, "If anyone has ears to hear, let him hear!" But this verse, as Metzger (95) points out, is absent from some important Alexandrian witnesses (ℵ, B, L, etc.), and it was probably not in the original manuscript. It is easy to understand why a scribe, noticing the formal similarity to 4:3–20, would have inserted it between the "parable" in 7:15 and the explanation in 7:17–23, but it is difficult to see why a scribe would have deliberately omitted it if it was original; neither is there any indication of haplography through homoeoarcton or homoeoteleuton. As Gundry (367) points out, moreover, the absence of a Matthean parallel here weighs against originality in Mark, since Matthew seems fond of the saying, retaining it in Matt 13:9//Mark 4:9 and adding it in Matt 11:15; 13:43.

COMMENT

Introduction. Jesus' striking demonstration of miraculous healing power on the predominantly Jewish west bank of the Sea of Galilee (6:53–56) is followed by an argument between him and two related groups of Jewish leaders, the Pharisees and some scribes (see the APPENDIX "The Scribes and the Pharisees"). The passage is loosely linked with what precedes it by the theme of touching (cf. 6:56), which is implicit in the controversy about unwashed hands, and by the plural "loaves of bread" in 7:2, which recalls the loaves of 6:30–44 and 6:52 (see the NOTE on "loaves of bread" in 7:2).

Mark 7:1–23 is a section that has grown over time. The awkward, intrusive comments in 7:3–4 and the end of 7:19, which the translation renders with dashes and parentheses respectively, seem to be the work of a later editor, probably Mark himself. Every significant word or phrase of 7:14 is special Markan vocabulary, and the first part of the verse is especially similar to 8:34; this verse, too, is Markan redaction. Also shaped by Mark is the transition to the scene of private instruction with the disciples in 7:17–18a; this transition contains several typically Markan motifs (withdrawal from the crowd into a house, private instruction, disciples' incomprehension) and is especially close to 4:10–20, where we encounter the same pattern: segregation with the disciples for instruction, disciples' questions about a "parable," Jesus' rebuke of their incomprehension, and his explanation (4:10). Some of the vocabulary of the saying in 7:15, which is repeated in 7:18, may be Markan ("nothing . . . but," "is able," "outside"). There is a broad consensus among exegetes that these are Markan features; here, however, the consensus ends (for a detailed survey, see Sariola, *Gesetz,* 23–52).

Many, however, are of the opinion that the primitive core of the passage is contained in 7:1–2, 5, and 15: Jesus, when asked why his disciples ate with unwashed hands and thus violated Pharisaic teaching, responded by saying that what comes from outside of a person does not defile, but that what comes from inside does. This is the only real response in our complex to the question that the Pharisees pose in 7:5, the other two replies (7:6–8 and 7:9–13) being the sort of excoriation that is easily attributable to early Christian polemic. Subsequently (perhaps at the pre-Markan stage), this mini-controversy was expanded by scriptural arguments against the Pharisaic tradition (7:6–8, 9–13), by an explanation that shifted the point of the controversy to the question of eating nonkosher food (7:18b–19), and by a list of the evils that issue from the heart (7:20–23). Finally, Mark came along and added the editorial touches mentioned in the previous paragraph.

In its present form the passage is structured in a series of questions and answers:

A 7:1–5: Pharisees and scribes *ask* Jesus why his disciples violate the tradition and eat with impure hands.

B   7:6–8: He *says* to them that their tradition is mere human teaching, quoting an OT passage (Isa 29:13).

B   7:9–13: He *says* to them that they violate another OT passage (Exod 20:12//Deut 5:16) by their *korban* practice.

C   7:14–15: He *says* to the crowd that nothing from outside a person is able to defile that person.

A′ 7:17: In the house his disciples *ask* him about the parable.

B′   7:18–19: He *says* to them that it is not external things that defile a person.

B′   7:20–23: He *says* that the truly profaning things come from inside a person.

It can be seen that there is a rough parallelism between 7:1–15 and 7:17–23: each section begins with a question, which then receives two related answers; this is also the pattern in 2:23–28 (cf. Sariola, *Gesetz*, 86). The parallelism is broken by 7:14–15, the third answer to the first question, which addresses a different group from the first questioners, namely the crowd, and which prompts the second question from a third group, namely the disciples.

This COMMENT will be divided into four sections: the Pharisees' challenge (7:1–5), Jesus' first scriptural rebuttal (7:6–8), his second scriptural rebuttal (7:9–13), and his pronouncement about purity (7:14–15).

7:1–5: the Pharisees' challenge. The passage begins with introductory verses that lay the groundwork for the subsequent debate, in typical controversy story fashion, by introducing Jesus' opponents, the Pharisees and scribes, and their objection to the eating practices of Jesus' disciples. Already attentive readers might discern an implicit threat in the description of the Pharisees and scribes in 7:1, since it shows them gathering together (*synagontai*) against Jesus and notes that the scribes have come down from Jerusalem. The verb "to gather together" is used in Ps 2:2 LXX for the way in which the rulers muster their forces against the Lord and his anointed one (*christos*); its use here, therefore, may be a subtle reminder of scriptural prophecies of opposition to God's Messiah from those in authority. In two other psalms, moreover, the same verb is used for the wicked conspiring against the righteous to take his life (31[LXX 30]:13 and 35[LXX 34]:15). And the fact that the scribes who interrogate Jesus come down from Jerusalem marks them as originating from the center of the opposition, the city where Jesus will eventually be executed, and their journey as being the opposite of his God-willed ascent from Galilee to Jerusalem (see the NOTE on "the scribes who had come down from Jerusalem" in 3:22).

After a long parenthesis in which Mark explains, presumably for the benefit of the non-Jewish section of his Christian audience, that the Pharisees' opposition to Jesus is based on "the tradition of the elders" (7:2–4), he describes the way in which their hostility solidifies into a challenging question about ritual purity: "Why don't your disciples walk according to the tradition of the elders? — but they eat bread with impure hands" (7:5). Handwashing is not a biblical requirement for laypeople; in the OT only priests are required to wash their hands before offering a sacrifice (Exod 30:18–21; 40:31; cf. also Lev 15:11). The Pharisees, however, in their tradition, appear to have extended the requirement of handwashing to the laity, on the theory that every Jew should live as a priest and every Jewish home should become like the Temple (see the APPENDIX "The scribes and the Pharisees"). It is this tradition that forms the basis for their challenge to Jesus.

7:6–8: Jesus' first scriptural rebuttal. On the principle that the best defense is a good offense, the Markan Jesus responds to the Pharisees' hostile, challenging query not with a direct answer but with an attack on his interlocutors and on the concept of tradition that undergirds their question. This attack consists of two parts, 7:6–8 and 7:9–13, each of which consists of the formula "and he said to them," a scriptural refutation, and a conclusion contrasting the commandment or word of God with the Pharisaic tradition.

This attack would probably be heard by Mark's readers as supplying the answer to arguments they were hearing from the Pharisees and scribes of their own time (see Marcus, "Scripture"). In order to understand it, it is vital to dig behind the Markan polemic and to try to reconstruct what these contemporary opponents were saying. The Pharisees in the Markan environment, for example, certainly would not have agreed with the Markan Jesus' charge that their tradition represented a betrayal of the commandments of God found in their Bible, the Old Testament (cf. 7:8–9, 13). The Pharisees, rather, believed that the tradition permitted them to *fulfill* God's ancient commandments correctly. In their understanding, indeed, the tradition was not opposed to revelation but a part of it that had been handed down orally from Sinai through an unbroken human chain to the Pharisees themselves (see above all *m. 'Abot* 1, which probably goes back to the first century; cf. Herr, "Continuum," 50). This feeling of connection with ancient revelation is what has given Rabbinic

Judaism, the successor to Pharisaism, its great sense of continuity down to the present day. As Tevye the dairyman says in the musical *Fiddler on the Roof*: "And how do we keep our balance? I can tell you in one word: tradition!"

In line with such a philosophy, it would have been easy for the Pharisees to turn some of the major arguments in 7:6–13 around and to use them against Jesus and the Christians—so easy, in fact, that we may suspect that the Pharisees were actually the first ones to employ them. It was, after all, a basic principle of God's written word, the Torah delivered to Moses, that Israel was "to make a distinction between the unclean and the clean, and between the living creature that may be eaten and the living creature that may not be eaten" (Lev 11:47). Anyone who did what the Markan Jesus does in our passage, denying this dietary distinction and declaring all foods to be permissible (7:19), would immediately be identified as a seducer who led the people's heart astray from God (cf. 7:6) and from the holy commandment he had given to Moses (cf. 7:8, 9, 13). The Markan Jesus, then, rather than the Pharisees, might easily be accused of substituting human commandments, i.e. his own precepts, for the clear teaching of God, and thus of falling under the condemnation of Isa 29:13 (cf. Mark 7:7–8). This is especially likely because Isa 29:13 is alluded to in apocalyptic texts that prophesy an end-time apostasy in which many Jews will prefer the commandments of human beings to the divine, Mosaic laws and will thereby make themselves impure like the heathen (*T. Asher* 7:5; *T. Levi* 14:4). This charge could easily have been applied by more zealous Jews to Jewish Christians such as Mark, who countenanced the violation of the food laws and the rupture of the dividing wall between God's people and the impure Gentiles, and such a charge would have been an especially serious matter in the context of the Jewish revolutionaries' holy war against the Romans, in which anti-Gentile feeling ran high and transgressions of ritual purity were probably perceived as a threat to the entire war effort (cf. Schwier, *Tempel*, 55–74, 90–101).

The Markan Jesus responds to the Pharisees' question about handwashing by giving his own interpretation of the important verse Isa 29:13 (Mark 7:6b–7). This scriptural polemic is introduced by a specific mention of Isaiah's name (7:6a), which would probably have reminded Mark's readers of the other explicit mention of that prophet in the scriptural citation at the very beginning of the Gospel (1:2–3), where the way of Jesus is significantly linked with the way of God (see the COMMENT on 1:2–3 and cf. Marcus, "Mark and Isaiah"). Jesus, then, is on the side of God, not an apostate from God's way; any tradition that opposes him is taking its cues not from the deity but from the disloyal opposition to him.

The Markan Jesus hammers this point home by his citation of Isa 29:13 (7:6b–7), which he interprets as a prophecy of the "hypocrisy" of the Pharisees and scribes, who substitute human commandments for the divine teaching—thus perhaps turning around the charge being made against the Markan Christians themselves. In the Markan view, as Gnilka remarks, this "hypocrisy" is not conscious dissimulation but the reflection of a deep malady that results in a tragic split between claim and reality. The heart has strayed from

God, and the people have fallen under the sway of a human tradition that has emptied the divine word of its force and blinded its possessors to God's true will (cf. 4:11–12); therefore when Jesus' disciples show signs of a similar tendency, he will say to them, "Are you also *without understanding?*" (7:18).

But the fact that the Pharisees' opposition to Jesus is based at least in part on a perceptual distortion does not blunt the sharpness of his assault on them. One of the weapons he deploys is irony; 7:6b in its Markan context suggests a connection between Isaiah's denunciation of those who honor God with their *lips*, on the one hand, and the Pharisees' obsession with what passes the lips, i.e. food, on the other (7:6b; see Donahue, "Mark 7:1–23," 3). More substantively, Jesus deflects the Pharisees' charge that he violates "the tradition of the elders" by contrasting their keyword "tradition" with the command of God and by linking it with the merely human realm through the following contrasts:

7:8   "the tradition of human beings" vs. "the command of God"

7:9   "your tradition" vs. "the command of God"

7:13 "your tradition which you have passed down" vs. "the word of God"

These contrasts transform the Pharisaic term "the tradition of the elders" (7:3) into a negative category. "The elders" are revealed to be merely human beings, and in the apocalyptic Markan worldview, to take one's cues from human beings is to oppose the will of the holy God whose eschatological power is now revealing itself through Jesus' teaching (cf. 8:33; 10:9; 11:27, 30, 32; 12:4, where the antithesis between God and human beings is repeated; see Berger, *Gesetzauslegung*, 486; Sariola, *Gesetz*, 58).

7:9–13: Jesus' second scriptural rebuttal. Jesus repeats the charge that the Pharisaic tradition opposes God's commandment at the beginning of the second set of biblical citations and commentaries in 7:9–13, where the command to honor parents (Exod 20:12//Deut 5:16) is referred to. Mark 7:6–10 is thus a chiasm (see the GLOSSARY):

7:6–7 OT citation

7:8   opposition of Pharisaic tradition to God's commandment

7:9   opposition of Pharisaic tradition to God's commandment

7:10   OT citations

The central point of this chiasm is the antithesis between the Pharisaic tradition and the divine will—a point that is repeated again for good measure in 7:13.

Although Wellhausen (54) claims that 7:9–13 is merely a repetition of the charge in 7:6–8, the structure is actually more of a spiral: the accusation of "hypocrisy" is repeated and then demonstrated with a pointed example. The Markan Jesus elaborates the antithesis between the Pharisaic tradition and

God's commandment by zeroing in on a specific example of a Pharisaic tradition that empties the word of God of its force, a legal fiction by means of which a grown-up child's obligation to support his parents, might be avoided through the invocation of a binding vow (*qorbān*; see the NOTE on "*korban*, that is, a gift to God" in 7:11). There are historical problems with this indictment, since there is no other evidence that the Pharisees advocated such a practice; indeed their successors, the rabbis, specifically opposed it. It may be, however, that the rabbis' attitude represents a modification of Pharisaic stringency (see the NOTE on "you no longer allow him to do anything" in 7:12).

Jesus opposes to this putative Pharisaic casuistry the Torah's injunction that children are to honor their parents (Exod 20:12//Deut 5:16), conflating it with the scriptural warning that the person who curses his/her parents should be put to death (Exod 21:17//Lev 20:9). Dishonoring of parents, then, is in principle a capital matter according to the Torah, yet the Pharisees facilitate it by their *korban* practice; that institution, then, and what it reveals about Pharisaic corruption, become Exhibit A in the Markan Jesus' riposte to the Pharisees' charge that his disciples have culpably ignored their venerable tradition. This tradition is not to be honored, Jesus responds, since far from being a necessary elaboration of God's word, as the Pharisees would have it, it has become a subversion of that word, in this case by aiding and abetting filial greed. Indeed, since the word for "tradition," *paradosis*, can also have the meaning "betrayal" (see the NOTE on "the tradition of the elders" in 7:3), it may be that Mark's usages of this term in 7:8–13 suggest not only the obvious meaning conveyed in my translation but also a deeper, ironic significance: "You forsake the commandment of God and hold fast to the betrayal (*paradosis*) of human beings" (7:8); "You do a good job of annulling the commandment of God, so that you may establish your betrayal" (*paradosis*; 7:9), "thus voiding the word of God for the sake of your betrayal (*paradosis*), by means of which you have betrayed" (*hē paredōkate*; 7:13).

7:14–15: Jesus' pronouncement about purity. Rhetorically powerful as Jesus' equation of the Pharisaic tradition with a betrayal of the word of God is, however, it still does not answer the specific question that touched off the whole discussion, namely the reason for his disciples' failure to wash their hands before eating. Perhaps part of the reason that Mark's readers need an answer to this question is the presence within their community of Jewish Christians who are inclined to follow Pharisaic practices (see the NOTE on "some of his disciples" in 7:2 and the COMMENT on 7:17–19). Therefore, although Jesus earlier avoided defending his disciples' neglect of handwashing when the Pharisees pressured him to do so, he now summons a different audience, the crowd (7:14), and utters a gnomic saying that explains it: "There is nothing from outside of a person which . . . is able to defile him; but the things that come out of the person are the ones that defile the person" (7:15). Thus Jesus strikes at the root of the Pharisaic challenge, namely the presumption that touching an external thing such as bread with another external thing such as an unwashed hand can defile the bread, which in turn can defile its eater (see the NOTE on "There is nothing from outside of a person" in 7:15).

Mark considers this saying, which he calls a parable in 7:17, to be the climax of our passage and the central point of the whole complex in 7:1–23. He has highlighted its importance, as Wellhausen (55) points out, by providing it with an attention-grabbing introduction in 7:14, "Listen to me, all of you, and understand." This introduction is similar to, though more elaborate than, the introduction to the Parable of the Sower in 4:3 ("Listen! Look!"), which Mark also considers to be a hermeneutical key (see 4:13); moreover, as with the Parable of the Sower, our "parable" is followed by esoteric instruction, for the disciples' ears only, that unlocks its mysteries. These features contribute to the impression that it touches on a matter of vital importance for the Markan community.

Jesus' assertion that it is not external things but internal ones that defile a person occurs in a less radical form in Matt 15:11 (see the NOTE on "There is nothing from outside of a person" in 7:15), and it also seems to be reflected in Rom 14:14 ("I know and am persuaded in the Lord Jesus that nothing is impure [*koinon*] in itself"), where Paul uses it as part of his discussion of the role played by Jewish scruples about food in the relations between the various house-churches in the Roman Christian communion. It is possible that it is being invoked here as part of a similar debate within the Markan community (see Räisänen, "Mark 7.15"; Dunn, *Jesus*, 49–50; Donahue, "Mark 7:1–23"). The saying itself, however, is ambiguous; its original message may not have been so different from that of the prophets, who railed against their fellow Israelites' preoccupation with external ritual rather than justice, and even proclaimed that God despised their sacrifices and festivals—without thereby intending to abolish those ceremonies (e.g. Amos 5:21–57; Hos 6:6; Isa 1:11–17). Similarly, Jesus' saying, in line with the Semitic idiom of dialectical negation, may originally have meant something like, "A person is not *so much* defiled by what enters him from outside as by what comes from within" (see Kruse, "Dialektische Negation," and Westerholm, *Jesus*, 83). This would be comparable to the way in which Philo says that the true defilement is injustice and impiety (*Special Laws* 3.208–9) yet still advocates literal observance of the ritual regulations of the Torah (*Migration of Abraham* 89–94). The spiritualization of the idea of ritual impurity, then, does not necessarily imply abrogation of the literal purity laws of the OT; in Judaism, rather, spiritualization and literal observance can go hand in hand (cf. Barclay, *Jews*, 176–80), and this may even be how the Christian Jew Matthew understands the present saying (see the NOTE on "There is nothing from outside of a person" in 7:15).

On the other hand, our saying is also capable of a more radical interpretation, and this seems to be the direction in which it is taken by Mark. After all, although "it is not what goes into the mouth . . ." *may* mean "it is not so much what goes into the mouth . . . ," it may *also*, and more naturally, mean "it is not what goes into the mouth"! But what becomes of the Jewish dietary laws if it is immaterial what enters the mouth? They would seem to be negated in principle, along with the foundation of the entire Jewish purity system, the assumption that external realities can defile human beings (cf. Riches, *Jesus*, 135–38).

External things, Jesus asserts, cannot render anyone unclean; rather, he adds, in the sort of reversal of received wisdom and common sense that is typical of him, it is paradoxically what comes from *within* a person (*ta ek tou anthrōpou ekporeuomena*) that defiles him or her (7:15b). In the Markan context the usage of the word *anthrōpos* ("person," "human being") here binds the conclusion of Jesus' response to its earlier parts:

7:7   They worship me pointlessly, teaching as divine teachings the commandments of human beings (*anthrōpōn*).

7:9   You forsake the commandment of God and hold fast to the tradition of human beings (*anthrōpōn*).

7:11 But you say, "If a person (*anthrōpos*) says to his father or mother . . . "

7:15 There is nothing from outside of a person (*anthrōpou*) which, when it goes into the person, is able to defile him; but the things that come out of the person (*anthrōpou*) are the ones that defile the person (*anthrōpon*).

The constant recourse here to the word *anthrōpos* can scarcely be accidental. Mark's point seems to be that human traditions, no matter how laudable their original intention may have been, end up suffocating revelation because of a basic warp in the *anthrōpos* that corrupts everything he or she touches—including the word of God. In the next passage Jesus will explicate this propensity to evil by identifying the human heart rather than unclean food as the fountainhead of corruption in the universe.

The Markan Jesus' radical statement that nothing external can defile, then, has implications that transcend a critique of the Pharisaic custom of handwashing. Rather, as he will make clear in the private explanation that follows (7:17–23), it raises unsettling questions about the status of the Law of Moses itself.

What Really Defiles a Person (7:17–23)

7 [17]And when he went into a house, away from the crowd, his disciples asked him about this parable. [18]And he said to them, "Then are you also without understanding? Don't you know that anything from outside that goes into a person cannot defile him, [19]because it doesn't go into his heart but into his stomach, and goes out into the latrine?" (declaring all foods clean). [20]And he said, "What comes out of a person—that is what defiles the person. [21]For from within, from the heart of human beings, the evil thoughts come out: sexual sins, robberies, murders, [22]adulteries, actions motivated by greed, wicked actions; deceit, indecency, an evil eye, abusive speech, arrogance, foolishness. [23]All of these evil things come out from within and defile the person.

NOTES

7   17. *parable*. Gk *parabolēn*. The saying in 7:15 is unlike most of the other Markan parables, which are illustrative stories or comparisons; it still, however, falls within the range of meaning of Heb *māšāl*, since it is a proverb or riddle (see the NOTE on "in parables" in 4:2). For Mark, moreover, it is also a parable precisely because it requires interpretation (see the COMMENT on 4:11–12).

19. *declaring all foods clean*. Greek *katharizōn panta ta brōmata*. The grammar is awkward, since the subject to which the participle *katharizōn* refers, Jesus, is not mentioned in close proximity to it. This awkwardness causes some scholars to suggest that the phrase is an ancient marginal gloss that has been incorporated into the manuscript; others think that our participle refers to the latrine, which disposes of all foods (cf. KJV; see Schmithals, 1.350). The participle, however, is in the wrong case to agree with "latrine," and there is no manuscript evidence to support the theory of a gloss. The grammatical clumsiness, in any case, is no greater than that in 7:1–5, where a Markan insertion is responsible for it, and our phrase, too, is probably editorial.

There is a striking terminological parallel to this editorial remark in Rom 14:20: *panta men kathara* ("all things are pure"). But does this mean that Mark knew Paul? Paul seems here to be quoting a pre-Pauline slogan; though he agrees with it (Rom 14:14), he did not make it up. The parallel, therefore, may merely mean that Paul moved in the same sort of circles that Paul did, namely those of Gentile Christians who did not feel themselves bound by the Jewish Law. Cf. the discussion of Mark's relation to Paul in the section of the INTRODUCTION on the place of Mark in Christian life and thought.

Katharizein literally means "to purify or cleanse." In the LXX it can be used in cultic contexts either for an act of making something pure (e.g. Exod 29:36–37) or for the *declaration* that something has already been made pure (e.g. Lev 13:6, 23). On its meaning in our passage, see the COMMENT on 7:17–19.

20. *What comes out of a person—that is what defiles the person*. Gk *to ek tou anthrōpou ekporeuomenon, ekeino koinoi ton anthrōpon*. As the following verse makes clear, Jesus is speaking of the sorts of moral failing that proceed from the human heart, but the imagery in our verse suggests excretion, especially in view of the reference to latrines in the previous verse. Some OT authors (Prov 30:12; Ezek 4:12–15) and some later Jewish groups, such as the Essenes (Josephus *J.W.* 2.147–49; cf. CD 10:10–11; 11:2), considered excretion to be ritually defiling, though this was not the usual Jewish view (see A. Baumgarten, "Temple Scroll").

21. *sexual sins*. Gk *porneiai*, the plural of a general term for disapproved forms of sexual intercourse. Our passage begins with the Pharisees accusing Jesus' disciples of infringing "the tradition of the elders" because they eat with unwashed, impure hands (7:2, 5); it ends with Jesus identifying the real cause of impurity as the evil thoughts of the heart, listing sexual sin as the first of these "thoughts." This juxtaposition is of psychological interest, since Freud

saw compulsive handwashing as a symptom of an anxiety rooted in sexual guilt (see e.g. Breuer and Freud, *Studies*, 327 n. 1).

21–22. *robberies, murders, adulteries, actions motivated by greed.* Gk *klopai, phonoi, moicheiai, pleonexiai.* As Berger points out, these are violations of the Decalogue (*Gesetzauslegung*, 478). Similarly, as Wibbing notes (*Tugendkataloge*, 32), in the vice catalogues in the *Testaments of the Twelve Patriarchs* some of the offenses listed are violations of the Decalogue. Others, however, such as deceit and arrogance—which are also mentioned by Mark—are more general vices (see *T. Isa.* 7:2–4; *T. Gad* 5:1; *T. Reub.* 3:2–7).

22. *indecency.* Gk *aselgeia.* As Taylor (346) points out, this term, like its English counterpart, often has a sexual connotation, but with the additional nuance of open flaunting.

an evil eye. Gk *ophthalmos ponēros.* This term can denote stinginess, as in Deut 15:9; covetousness, as in Prov 28:22; or jealousy, as in Sir 14:8; Matt 20:15. In any case, as Davies and Allison point out (1.640), "an evil eye" is the opposite of generosity (cf. *m. ʾAbot* 5:13). Given the context in Mark 7:17–23, "evil eye" here probably does *not* suggest putting a hex on someone, as in ancient and modern superstitions.

abusive speech. Gk *blasphēmia*, lit. "speaking badly." This word is also used in 3:28 and 14:64, where it is translated "blasphemy," i.e. abusive speech directed at God, but in the present context, where all the other sins are social ones, verbal abuse of one's fellow humans is probably meant. The focus thus shifts from the evil eye, which envies the neighbor, to the evil tongue, which reviles him or her.

COMMENT

Introduction. Having made a pronouncement that cuts the ground out from under any system of ritual purity and impurity (7:15), Jesus withdraws with his disciples, who ask for enlightenment about this revolutionary "parable" (7:17). Mark himself is probably responsible for transforming the present passage, in which Jesus gives his answer, into an address to insiders (see the introduction to the COMMENT on 7:1–15), but this explanation probably already existed in some form in the pre-Markan tradition, since Mark himself has to make an awkward insertion in order to gloss it ("declaring all foods clean" in 7:19).

In its present form, the explanation falls into three parts: (1) the disciples' question (7:17), (2) Jesus' first response (7:18–19), and (3) his second response (7:20–23). Jesus' two responses have some parallel elements; both begin with the narrator's "and he said," and both end with a sentence that gives prominence to the word *panta* ("all") and thus emphasizes the universality of the assertion. These two responses take up the halves of the saying in 7:15 in order; the first part, 7:18–19, explains why what goes into people cannot defile them, while the second part, 7:20–23, catalogues the things that come out of people and leave defilement in their wake.

7:17–19: the disciples' question and Jesus' first response. The passage begins with Jesus' entry into a house with his disciples (7:17), thus leaving behind the crowd to which he addressed his statement about what really defiles (7:14–15). The disciples immediately ask about the meaning of this "parable" (for the reason that Mark calls it a parable, see the NOTE on "parable" in 7:17).

In the first part of his reply (7:18–19a) the Markan Jesus, after a characteristic rebuke of the disciples' incomprehension (cf. 4:13, 40–41; 8:17–21, 33), moves to dispel it by asserting that external things cannot defile a person, since they pass through the body without leaving a trace. This rather crude, physical refutation of the idea that foods convey ritual impurity is probably not meant to be understood as an exact analysis of the situation but as another parable, a "parable of digestion," as Drury calls it (*Parables*, 61). It is useful for Mark primarily because of its picture of foods bypassing the heart in favor of the stomach; in the second part of Jesus' response he will focus on the heart as the true source of impurity. In any event, the Parable of Digestion certainly would not have convinced a Torah-observant Jew, and Mark seems to be aware of its limitations, since he immediately moves the argument onto another plane with his redactional comment "declaring all foods clean" (7:19b), which emphasizes not the physical process of digestion but Jesus' authority to redefine ritual purity.

But on what basis does he redefine it? As the NOTE on "declaring all foods clean" in 7:19 makes clear, *katharizōn . . . brōmata* might mean "declaring that all foods had *always* been clean"; Jesus would then be acting the part of a sage or philosopher, ripping apart the veil of illusion and error that had deluded literal observers of the food laws and revealing the underlying reality that had always been there, namely that no food is unclean. The logic of 7:19a might go along with this interpretation, since it points to the way in which digestion has *always* worked in the world. But *katharizein* is never used in ritual contexts in the OT to mean "declaring that something has always been clean"; besides, if all foods had always been pure, why had Moses, whose authority Jesus accepts (cf. 7:18), said that some foods were impure?

It is better, therefore, to interpret *katharizōn panta ta brōmata* as "declaring that all foods had *now* become pure." In Mark's view Jesus' saying about purity in 7:15 is a performative pronouncement, one that *accomplishes* the purification it announces, like the heavenly voice telling Peter about the acceptability of eating nonkosher food in Acts 10:15, which uses language comparable to that in our passage: "What God has cleansed (*ekatharisen*) you must not make impure (*sy mē koinou*)." In the same manner Jesus in our passage is not just holding a mirror up to nature, depicting what has always been the case, but actually *changing things* by his apocalyptic pronouncement that all foods are (now) clean. In a biblical context such a change in the purity of foods is not without precedent; after all, from the postdiluvian period to the giving of the Law of Moses, all animals could be eaten (Gen 9:3), although before then Adam and his descendants appear to have been vegetarians (Gen 1:29; cf. *b. Sanh.* 57a–b; *Gen. Rab.* 34.13–14), and after that certain animals were disallowed.

The explicit revocation of the OT kosher laws ascribed to Jesus by Mark in 7:19b probably goes beyond what the historical Jesus actually did; it needs to be borne in mind that "declaring all foods clean" is *Mark's* interpretation of Jesus' statement in 7:15, not Jesus', and that Matthew seems to have a much less radical interpretation of the dominical saying (see the COMMENT on 7:14–15). The judgment that all foods could be eaten was only hammered out by Christians when the entry of growing numbers of Gentiles into their communities made a decision on the issue imperative, and it was taken only after much reflection and debate and even, according to those involved, divine revelation (see e.g. Gal 2:11–16 and Acts 10:1–11:18). When Paul, therefore, used terminology very much like that of Mark and said in Rom 14:20 that "all things [i.e. all foods] are clean" (cf. the NOTE on "declaring all foods clean" in 7:19), he was expressing a postresurrectional insight that was still very much a matter of debate within the church of his time (see Räisänen, "Mark 7.15," 145). It may still have been an issue within the Markan church (against Sariola, *Gesetz*, who claims that the Law is no longer a problem for Mark and his addressees), since the Markan disciples question Jesus about his statement privately, and his response begins, "Then are you also without understanding? Don't you know . . . ?" This sort of private instruction is often a Markan device for addressing issues that have arisen in the evangelist's own day (cf. 4:10–20; 9:28–29; 13:3–37), and the reproach "are you *also* without understanding?" suggests that ritual purity is a bone of contention not only between the Markan community and the Pharisees but also within the community itself (cf. the NOTE on "some of his disciples" in 7:2 and the COMMENT on 7:14–15).

Mark 7:1–23, then, is what Martyn (*History and Theology*, 27–30) calls a "two-level narrative": Jesus' saying questioning the power of externals to defile, which was initially directed against the Pharisaic tradition of handwashing, was later expanded into a challenge to the dietary regulations of the written Law itself. This proleptic abrogation of the OT food laws, laws that divided Jews from Gentiles, is very significantly placed before a section of the Gospel in which Jesus feeds Gentiles (7:24–8:10). It immediately precedes a passage in which a Gentile woman's witty repartee with Jesus overcomes his reluctance to "feed" impure Gentile "dogs" (7:24–30), and it comes shortly before he miraculously satisfies the hunger of four thousand people, who probably are to be understood as Gentiles (8:1–10). Mark 7:15 as interpreted by 7:19, therefore, points the way forward for the church in its relation to the world: the dividing wall of hostility between Jews and Gentiles represented by the OT food laws has now, in the end-time, been breached, and within the Christian community all God's children may enjoy the bread of life together (cf. Eph 2:14–15; John 6:51).

7:20–23: *Jesus' second response*. Having declared all foods clean and thus having shown that there is no longer anything external to human beings that can defile them, the Markan Jesus goes on to identify the real source of defilement: the human heart itself. It is not what goes into people but what comes out of them that defiles (7:20); the anthropological pessimism and scatological imagery here are similar to that in the Qumran Hymns Scroll, where the Hymnist refers to himself as "a source of uncleanness and of vile filth" (1QH 12:25; cf. the NOTE on "What comes out of a person—that is what defiles the person" in 7:20).

The catalogue of representative offenses that emerge from the heart, which now follows (7:21–23), belongs to a fixed literary genre within the NT, the "vice catalogue" or "vice list." Indeed, as is clear from the charts provided by Wibbing (*Tugendkataloge*, 86–89), if cognate words are counted, only two of the items in our list, "evil thoughts" and "an evil eye," do not form part of similar lists within the NT (Gal 5:19–21; Col 3:5–8; 1 Pet 4:3, 15, etc.). These NT vice catalogues borrow a popular literary form from the larger world; such lists were common in Stoic writings, other works of Greco-Roman popular philosophy, and Diaspora Jewish circles influenced by Hellenistic philosophy. The Alexandrian Jewish philosopher Philo, for example, has one vice catalogue that consists of 150 items (*Sacrifices of Abel and Cain* 32)! As Wibbing has shown, however, ever closer parallels are to be found in literature that stems from Palestinian Judaism (*Jubilees, 1 Enoch*) or is closely related to it (the *Testaments of the Twelve Patriarchs; Did.* 5:1; cf. *Tugendkataloge*, 30–42). The closest parallels of all lie in a passage from one of the Dead Sea Scrolls, 1QS 4:9–11, where the effects of "the spirit of deceit" on humanity are said to include "greed, . . . irreverence, deceit, pride and haughtiness of heart, . . . appalling acts performed in a lustful passion, filthy paths for indecent purposes, an abusive tongue, [and] blindness of eyes." All of these items have more or less exact correspondences in the Markan list (cf. Wibbing, *Tugendkataloge*, 43–61, 91–94). In this Qumran parallel, however, the catalogue of offenses has its positive counterpart in a catalogue of manifestations of goodness (1QS 4:6–8), and the same holds true for many of the other parallels, including some in the NT; Paul, for example, details not only "the works of the flesh" but also "the fruit of the Spirit" (Gal 5:22–23; cf. 1 Cor 3:12–14). It is perhaps a reflection of Mark's dark view of human possibilities that such a positive list is lacking not only here but elsewhere in his Gospel.

In any case, Mark's catalogue of human offenses is incorporated into a truly hellish picture, in which the interior of the human being is depicted as a Pandora's box, a cave of malignancy out of which hordes of demonlike evils emanate. Even this catalogue of offenses, however, has a certain structure to it, like Dante's *Inferno*; a series of seven offenses in the plural, usually implying "cases of" (MHT, 3.28) and consisting mostly of prosecutable crimes outlawed by the Decalogue (7:21–22a), is followed by a series of seven offenses in the singular, most of which are of a more abstract nature (7:22b; cf. Berger, *Gesetzauslegung*, 478).

At the head of the list stands *hoi dialogismoi hoi kakoi* = "evil thoughts." The grammar suggests that all the other evils are in apposition to this overarching category, since *hoi dialogismoi hoi kakoi* precedes the verb *ekporeuontai* ("come out"), whereas all the other evils follow it. *Hoi dialogismoi hoi kakoi* appears to be the Markan counterpart to the biblically rooted rabbinic conception of *yēṣer hārā'* "the Evil Inclination," a phrase that can sometimes appear in the plural. This inclination is the inner enemy of God lodged within the human heart (Gen 6:5; 8:21; cf. Mark's "from the heart of human beings"), a wild force that propels people willy-nilly into actions that are opposed to God's will (cf. Marcus, "Evil Inclination in James" and "Evil Inclination in Paul"). Nor is it by chance that, after this global category, the first specific misdeeds to be mentioned are sexual sins; in Hellenistic popular philosophy these sins were the premier example of the chaotic, ungovernable aspect of human nature, which precipitously pursues its own desires and is blind to its own true good, and in Judaism these sins were frequently associated with the promptings of the Evil Inclination (see Marcus, "Evil Inclination in James," 616). After sexual sins, the following four offenses (robberies, murders, adulteries, and actions motivated by greed) are all infractions of the Decalogue; the final plural, *ponēriai* = "wicked actions," would seem to be somewhat superfluous after the preceding itemization and may have been added simply to bring the number to seven and to make the transition to the more abstract group of seven that follows. That group refers more often to internal dispositions than it does to external actions, though they are the sort of dispositions that would necessarily issue in destructive actions (cf. Wibbing, *Tugendkataloge*, 58–59). It, too, contains a certain amount of structure; for example, "indecency," which implies open flaunting of morals, immediately follows "deceit," which implies secret mischief.

It is usually difficult to tell to what extent, if any, such catalogues of offenses reflect actual problems that have risen among the addressees of the work (see Barclay, *Obeying*, 150–55). Nevertheless, in the present case it is probably significant that the Markan Jesus, who begins his speech by rebuking the disciples for their lack of understanding (7:18), concludes his catalogue of offenses with "foolishness" (7:22 end), a problem that consistently afflicts the disciples (see e.g. 4:13; 6:52; 7:18; 8:14–21). This emphasis on the disciples' misunderstanding, in turn, probably corresponds to Mark's evaluation of his own church community: some within it are desperately in need of instruction about the basics of the Christian life, including perhaps the unimportance of ritual purity.

The disciples, in any event, do not stand apart from the group of humans whose hearts pour forth evil into the world (cf. 8:33); the problems that are analyzed in our passage are general human ones that cut across any artificial division between church and world. It is not insignificant, then, that the very last word in our passage is *anthrōpos* ("person" or "human being"; 7:23 end), which as we have seen is a keyword throughout 7:1–15 (cf. the COMMENT on 7:14–15). This word also occurs in 7:18, 20 (2x), and 21 ("anything from outside that goes into *a person*"; "what comes out of *a person*—that is what defiles *the person*"; "from the heart of *human beings*"). *Anthrōpos*, then, turns up five times in our short passage, and puts in an extraordinary eleven appearances in 7:7–23. The basic problem Christians should be concerned about,

Mark seems to be saying through this striking pileup, is not how or what one should eat but the internal corruption of the *anthrōpos*. It is this malignancy that chokes the life out of tradition, turns it into an enemy of God, contorts it into a way of excusing injustice, and blinds those afflicted by it to their own culpability for the evils that trouble the world.

The passage ends up on a deliberately paradoxical note, the repetition and expansion of the second half of the purity saying from 7:15 that it is only what comes out from the inside that defiles a person (7:23). Notions of pollution, however, generally involve the opposite, a concern for things that enter the inside from the outside (see Douglas, *Purity*). How then can what comes out from the inside of human beings pollute them? Only, perhaps, if a human being is essentially a being in relationship with others, so that what ruins relationships also destroys something that is essential to the soundness of the individual.

The Markan Jesus, then, turns the whole notion of pollution upside down, and he does so by means of the same sort of apocalyptic inversion by which he declares unclean food to be clean. For people unready to accept the claim that Jesus was God's eschatological envoy, such inversions would have seemed like invitations to moral disorder and would have appeared to fall under the denunciation of Isaiah, who vilifies those who call evil good, put darkness for light, exchange bitter for sweet, and are wise in their own eyes (Isa 5:20–21). The Markan Jesus, then, breaks out of the boundaries imposed by tradition, law, and even logic; the challenge he poses is whether people will continue to take their point of departure from those boundaries, or whether they will learn to see things through his eyes.

The following passage, appropriately enough, takes place on a boundary, the border between biblical Israel and the Gentile world, and it concerns Jesus' relationship to a woman who is, from the Jewish point of view, beyond the pale. Remarkably enough, in view of what has just been said about submission to Jesus' judgment, this woman takes issue with Jesus' initial statement to her—and is commended for it!

JESUS GRANTS A GENTILE WOMAN'S REQUEST FOR HEALING (7:24–30)

7 ²⁴And he got up from there and went away to the region around Tyre. And he went into a house and didn't want anyone to know it, but he was unable to escape notice. ²⁵Rather, a woman whose daughter had an unclean spirit immediately heard about him and came and fell down at his feet. ²⁶(This woman was a "Greek," a Syrophoenician by race.) And she asked him to cast the demon out of her daughter. ²⁷But he said to her, "Let the children first be satisfied; for it is not right to take the children's bread and throw it to the dogs." ²⁸But she answered and said to him, "Lord, even the dogs under the table eat from the children's leftovers." ²⁹And he said to her, "Because you have

said this, go—the demon has gone out of your daughter." [30]And she went away to her house and found her child cast onto her bed, with the demon gone out of her.

NOTES

7   24. *the region around Tyre.* Gk *ta horia Tyrou.* Some manuscripts read "the region around Tyre and Sidon." While it is possible that the shorter reading results from an accidental omission of *kai Sidōnos* because of the repetition of *kai* that immediately follows, it is more probable that the longer reading is an assimilation to Matt 15:21 and Mark 7:31 (cf. Metzger, 95). As Theissen (*Gospels*, 72–80) points out, there was bad blood between the Tyrians and the Galileans, partly because much of the agricultural produce of Jewish Galilee ended up in Gentile Tyre, the main urban area near Galilee, while the Jewish peasants often went hungry. When Jesus speaks, therefore, about the unfairness of taking bread out of the mouths of the (Jewish) children and giving it to the (Gentile) dogs, his statement may partly reflect the socio-economic tension between the two communities.

25. *unclean spirit.* Gk *pneuma akatharton.* As Focant notes ("Mc 7,24–31," 48), at the conclusion of the pericope this spirit is twice referred to as a "demon" (7:29, 30). It is possible that Mark has substituted the term "unclean spirit" at the beginning of the passage to make a link with the impurity theme of the previous section (7:1–23).

26. *Greek.* Gk *Hellēnis.* This term definitely does not mean "of Greek ancestry," since Mark immediately adds that the woman is "a Syrophoenician by race." The term "Greek" here is the functional equivalent of "Gentile," as in Rom 1:16; 1 Cor 1:22–24; note especially the similarity of Mark 7:27–28 to the idea and language of Rom 1:16. The more frequent NT term for Gentiles is *ethnē* (lit. "nations"), but this word is not used in the singular with the meaning "Gentile." "Greek" may also mark the woman out as a Greek-speaker and thus perhaps as a member of the upper crust of Phoenician society (see Theissen, *Gospels*, 69–70); if so, this is one of a number of similarities between her and the apparently wealthy woman in 5:24–34 (see the introduction to the COMMENT). Mark may wish to imply that the conversation between Jesus and the woman was carried on in Greek (though a "Syrophoenician" would probably have been capable of conversing in Aramaic); on the extent of Jesus' knowledge of Greek, see Porter, "Use," and for Mark 7:26 in particular pp. 149–50.

Syrophoenician. Gk *Syrophoinikissa.* Hengel (*Mark*, 29, 137–38) thinks that this term distinguishes Phoenicians living in the Roman province of Syria from Phoenicians living in the area around Carthage (Libyphoenicians) and that it therefore points away from the vicinity of Palestine as the place of the Gospel's composition; if Mark had lived near Palestine, "Phoenician" would have sufficed. It is also possible, however, that "Syrophoenician" connotes a native of the Phoenician section of Syria as opposed to the Coele-Syrian section, or that it designates a descendant of Phoenicians who had intermarried with Syrians (see Theissen, *Gospels*, 245–47; Marcus, "Jewish War," 445–46).

27. *children*. Gk *tekna*. The word derives from *tiktein* = "to beget, give birth to" and thus designates "the child from the standpoint of origin" (Oepke, "*Pais*," 638). On the Jews as God's children, see, for example, Deut 14:1; Isa 1:2; *m. 'Abot* 3:15.

first. Gk *prōton*. The neuter singular form of this word is always used in Mark for events on the eschatological time line: the coming of Elijah before the Messiah (9:11–12), the binding of Satan before the despoiling of his "house" (3:27), Jesus' ministry to his fellow Jews before the Gentile mission (7:27), and the expansion of the gospel beyond Israel before the eschaton (13:10). Only after these events have occurred in their divinely ordered sequence can the end come: "*first* a shoot, *then* an ear, *then* full grain in the ear" (4:28).

The word *prōton*, and the thought behind it, are similar to those of Paul in Rom 1:16 and Romans 11: Jesus came for the Jews first, but also for the Gentiles. But just as, in the previous Markan passage, it was uncertain whether Mark's Pauline-sounding formulation meant that he knew Paul or whether it just meant that he moved in the same circles that Paul did (see the NOTE on "declaring all foods clean" in 7:19), so here it is uncertain whether Mark is in contact with Paul or merely with the sort of tradition that Paul picked up. Werner, for example (*Einfluss*, 203), thinks that "to the Jew first" in Rom 1:16 is a pre-Pauline slogan, since it contradicts Paul's usual missionary practice. On Mark's "Paulinism," see the discussion in the section of the INTRODUCTION on the place of Mark in Christian life and thought.

dogs. Gk *kynariois*. The regular term for "dog" is *kuōn*, and *kynaria* is technically a diminutive, but this does not necessarily mean that Jesus is referring affectionately to the woman or her daughter as "little dogs" or "pups" (against the translation of Rhoads, "Syrophoenician," 356–57). In Koine Greek the diminutive is often indistinguishable in meaning from the regular form (e.g. *paidas/paidia* = "children," *ploion/ploiarion* = "boat"), and the normal term for "little dog" is not *kynarion* but *kynidion* (see Burkill, "Development," 170; Pokorny, "Puppy," 324). *Kynarion* can be employed with no diminutive force at all (e.g. Plutarch *Aratus* 7:3; see BAGD, 457). As Rhoads acknowledges, the diminutive form may be used here simply to match that of the word for "daughter," *thygatrion*, in 7:25, which is also diminutive.

Although it may come as a shock to readers in our canine-loving society, the OT/Jewish tradition generally thinks negatively about dogs; as Turner remarks, "The biblical writers . . . seem unfamiliar with any kind of warm personal relationship between a dog and its master" ("Dog"). To call someone a dog, therefore, was an insult (see e.g. 1 Sam 17:43; Isa 56:10–11). This negative imagery is related to the fact that the dogs pictured in the Bible and in Jewish tradition are generally the wild, scavenger sort rather than the domestic variety (see e.g. *m. Kil.* 8:6; cf. *Joseph and Aseneth* 10:14, which contrasts the two types). Such wild dogs lived outside of cities (cf. Rev 22:15) and ate carrion, including the flesh of unclean animals and even human beings (cf. Exod 22:31; 1 Kgs 4:11); dogs, therefore, are often associated with uncleanness (see *b. B. Qam.* 83a). The New Testament continues this negative attitude; what is holy should not be thrown to the dogs, who are associated with pigs (Matt 7:6) and are often a symbol for opponents and heretics (2 Pet 2:22; Phil 3:2; Rev 22:15, etc.; see Theissen, *Gospels,* 62 n. 1). In Rev 22:15 the "dog" is an outsider to the community of God's grace, an idolater whose life is based on a lie. Such NT symbolism probably develops a Jewish association between dogs and Gentiles; cf. already *1 Enoch* 89:42, 46, 47, 49, in which dogs are symbols for Philistines. Feldmeier ("Syrophönizierin," 218) notes that the association between dogs and Gentiles is particularly prominent in contexts having to do with the necessity of separation from non-Jews (see e.g. *Pirqe R. El.* 29: "He who eats with an idolater is like him who eats with a dog"), and this consideration may be relevant to the present context (see the introduction to the COMMENT).

It would be an exaggeration, however, to say that the image of the dog is *always* negative in the OT/Jewish tradition. Friendly dogs, for example, appear in some manuscripts of Tob 6:1 and 11:4 and in *b. 'Abod. Zar.* 54b. Domestic dogs, moreover, can symbolize righteous Gentiles. *Midr. Ps.* 4.11, for example, like our passage, compares Gentiles to dogs at the eschatological banquet; in both passages the dogs get to eat, but do not dine as sumptuously as the invited guests or family do. It is possible, then, that "dogs at the banquet" was a fixed image for the participation of righteous Gentiles in the eschatological blessings of Israel. Indeed, the Syrophoenician woman's self-description as a dog that is within the house, but that is in a position inferior to that of the children, corresponds to the way in which Gentile sympathizers with Judaism ("God-fearers") were regarded by some Jews (see e.g. *1 Enoch* 50:2 and *Mekilta* [on Exod 22:20]; cf. Reynolds and Tannenbaum, *Jews and God-Fearers,* 48–66, and S. Cohen, "Crossing," passim). It is striking, therefore, that the term "Greek," which is used of the woman in 7:26, is also a frequent designation for God-fearers in Josephus, Acts, and the Gospel of John (Josephus *Ag. Ap.* 2.133; *Ant.* 3.217; *J.W.* 7.45; Acts 14:1; 16:1, 3; 17:4, 12; 18:14; John 12:20; see de Boer, "God-Fearers," 68–69). Does Mark perhaps wish to suggest that the Syrophoenician woman is a God-fearer? Interestingly, in the Pseudo-Clementine *Homilies* (13.7.3) she is described as a proselyte to Judaism; cf. *b. Pesaḥ.* 112b, where R. Judah the Prince's reference to "a Syrian woman" is interpreted as an allusion to a proselyte.

28. *answered and said.* Gk *apekrithē kai legei.* This OT formula usually introduces words of Jesus himself in Mark (3:33; 6:37; 9:19, 10:3, 24, 51, etc.) and often expresses the main point of the passage (e.g. 8:29; 11:14, 22). In the OT and later Judaism, as in our pericope, bright women occasionally overcome male figures in argument. The wise woman of Tekoa in 2 Samuel 14, for example, maneuvers King David into reversing his banishment of Absalom, and Hauptman ("Images," 202) describes rabbinic passages in which

women outwit male figures. The tradition she cites from *b. 'Erub.* 53b is particularly close to ours in its general pattern (statement by girl, response by rabbi, witty and conclusive retort by girl). R. Joshua introduces this anecdote with the remark "No one has ever gotten the better of me except a woman, a little boy and a little girl."

Lord. Gk *kyrie.* Some texts read *nai* = "yes" before *kyrie,* but this is probably an assimilation to Matt 15:27 (see Metzger) which would also appeal to later scribes because it tones down the woman's impudence. *Kyrie* may be an example of Markan double entendre; the woman addresses Jesus deferentially as "sir," but *kyrios* is also the divine title "Lord," a meaning with which Mark is familiar (1:3; 12:29–30, 36; 13:20) and upon which he plays in other passages about Jesus (2:28; 5:19; 11:3, 9; 12:36–37; 13:35).

the children's leftovers. Gk *tōn psichiōn tōn paidiōn.* The term for "children," *paidia,* is a different word from *tekna,* the word Jesus uses in 7:27, but the same one as is used for the woman's daughter in 7:30. The variation may be simply for stylistic reasons, but it may also be an attempt to help the woman's case by switching to a Greek term that puts less emphasis on origin (see the NOTE on "children" in 7:27 and cf. Baudoz, *Miettes,* 300–1). Rhoads ("Syrophoenician," 357–58) is probably overreading when he asserts that the diminutive form of *paidiōn* connotes fondness; Mark never uses the absolute form of *pais,* and he has a predilection for diminutives that are synonymous with absolute forms (see the NOTE on "dogs" in 7:27).

For Baudoz (*Miettes,* 303, 382) the phrase "the children's leftovers" implies that the children themselves, out of their affection for the dogs waiting under the table, intentionally give their leftover bread to them; Matt 15:27, in significant contrast, speaks only of the leftovers that happen to *fall* from the table. If Baudoz is right, Mark's formulation may reflect his view that Jewish Christians, the first people to be "fed" by Jesus with the bread of the gospel, should then turn around and spread it not only among themselves but also among the Gentiles.

29. *Because you have said this.* Gk *dia touton ton logon,* lit. "because of this word."

30. *cast.* Gk *beblēmenon,* the perfect passive participle of *ballein* ("to cast, throw"), the verb whose compounded form *ekballein* ("to cast out") is used for exorcising demons in 1:34, 39; 3:15, etc.

her bed. Gk *tēn klinēn,* lit. "the bed." "Her" may be understood from the context, though it is also possible to take this as an instance in which the definite article is understood indefinitely ("a bed"), in line with Semitic idiom (cf. the NOTE on the "strong man's house" in 3:27).

COMMENT

Introduction. The progression from 7:1–23 to 7:24–30 is a logical one: having challenged not only Pharisaic purity regulations but also the Old Testament dietary laws that separated Jews socially from Gentiles, the Markan Jesus is now positioned to respond favorably to a Gentile woman's plea for the healing of her demon-possessed daughter. Already Chrysostom (*Homily on Matthew* 52.1) noticed that this sequence corresponds to that in Acts 10, in which Peter's vision about the permissibility of eating unclean food paves the way for his acceptance of a Gentile into church. Our story is thus about transcendence of Jewish particularism, and looks forward to the increasingly Gentile church of Mark's own day. Yet the narrative chooses an odd way to express this point, for it has Jesus himself at first refuse to heal the unclean Gentile "dog."

Scholars have adopted various methods of explaining this oddity and our passage's mixture of genres (miracle story with controversy narrative). As Focant notes ("Mc 7,24–31"), some (e.g. van Iersel, Kertelge) have suggested that the story was originally a "pure" miracle to which the dialogue in 7:27–28 was added, others (e.g. Lohmeyer, Burkill) have argued that the miracle story has grown out of the dialogue, and still others (e.g. Bultmann, Schenke) assert that the dialogue and the miracle story have always belonged together (for a more exhaustive survey, see Baudoz, *Miettes*). Focant himself adopts the third view because of the implausibility of the first two; why, he asks, would anybody create or shape a story in such a way that the point of view voiced by Jesus ended up being refuted? This same point suggests the basic historicity of the narrative (see Feldmeier, "Syrophönizierin"). Even those who argue for its essential unity and historicity, however, usually admit that it contains some Markan touches. Verse 24, for example, is full of Markan vocabulary and is very much like 10:1, a redactional linking verse; it contains, moreover, characteristic Markan motifs such as the house as a place of concealment (cf. 7:17) and the Markan secrecy motif (see Burkill, "Congruence," 24). Likewise redactional is 7:27a ("let the children first be satisfied"), which is somewhat in tension with 7:27b: if it is wrong to give the children's bread to dogs, what difference does it make whether or not the children have been fed yet? This half-verse seems to recall early Christian views of salvation history, and it fits into the general pattern of events in this section of Mark: first a feeding of Jews (6:30–44), then a feeding of Gentiles (8:1–9).

In its present form the story is effectively narrated. It is framed by the verb "went away" (*apelthein*, 7:24, 30) and unified by verbs of entering and exiting (7:24, 29, 30), by various forms of "to cast, throw" (7:26, 27, 30), and by the nouns "daughter" (7:25, 26, 29), "unclean spirit/demon" (7:25, 26, 29, 30), and "child" (7:27, 28, 30). In the overall Markan context it forms an inclusion with the narrative of the woman with the hemorrhage in 5:21–43. The latter is, like the heroine of our story, an anonymous, plucky, ritually unclean woman who "hears about Jesus" and receives healing from him, and is coupled with a younger girl (Jairus' daughter, the Syrophoenician's daughter) who is healed. These two female combinations surround a more sinister mother/daughter combination, Herodias and her daughter (6:14–29). It is hard to believe that this arrangement is accidental.

7:24–26: setting the stage. The stage for the crucial encounter with the Syrophoenician woman is set by Jesus' entry into the region of Tyre, an area inhabited primarily by Gentiles, where he tries unsuccessfully to remain hidden
(7:24). This is the Markan Jesus' first entry into a Gentile area since he was
asked to leave the Decapolis after exorcising the Gerasene demoniac (5:1–20),
and Rhoads ("Syrophoenician," 361–62) connects his desire to escape notice to
that previous experience, which discouraged him from further contact with
non-Jews. But why, if Jesus was so discouraged about non-Jews, would he
bother to go to a Gentile region at all? His continual rejection among *Jews*,
moreover, has not deterred him from continuing to teach, preach, and minister
among *them*. It seems unlikely, then, that the Markan Jesus' attempt to shun
publicity reflects a desire to avoid Gentiles. Rather, the hiding motif here primarily serves to demonstrate his charismatic power, which *cannot* be hidden —
a point that will quickly be reiterated in 7:36 (cf. the APPENDIX "The Messianic Secret Motif").

Not that the setting in a Gentile region is irrelevant; three of the four passages in which Jesus unsuccessfully tries to hide, or to forbid disclosure of what
he has done (5:19–20; 7:24, 36–37), have to do with Gentiles, and the fourth
(1:40–45) involves transgression of a Jewish purity regulation. This combination of the motifs of Gentiles and inability to hide is probably not coincidental;
Jesus' glory cannot remain a secret for the same reason that the good news will
not stay permanently bottled up within Israel: "The word of God is not
chained" (2 Tim 2:9; cf. Luz, "Secrecy," 79). Both motifs speak of the explosive,
boundary-effacing power of the God who reveals himself in Jesus. This movement beyond the boundaries of Israel, however, itself has Old Testament precedent; Elijah performed a miracle for a Gentile woman in the Tyre/Sidon
region (1 Kgs 17:8–16; cf. Luke 4:25–26), and this miracle is especially relevant
because Jesus and John the Baptist echo the activities of Elijah and Elisha in
Mark (see the NOTES on "Look, I am sending my messenger before your face"
in 1:2, "passing by" in 1:16, "the holy one of God" in 1:24, and "intended to
pass them" in 6:48, and the COMMENT on 1:5–6; on 1:12–13; on 1:19–20,
and the introduction to the COMMENT on 6:30–44).

Because of this explosive power of the news about Jesus, the Gentile Syrophoenician woman "hears about him" (*akousasa . . . peri autou*), approaches,
and throws herself at his feet in an attitude of self-abasement and supplication
(7:25). This description is very close to that of the woman with the hemorrhage in 5:27, 33, who "heard about Jesus" and "came and fell down before
him." The likeness between the two women is increased by the fact that the
Syrophoenician, being a Gentile, is ritually impure, like the hemorrhaging
woman (see the NOTE on "Greek" in 7:26 and cf. Alon, "Levitical Uncleanness"); her daughter, moreover, has an unclean spirit (see the NOTE on "unclean spirit" in 7:25). Yet, despite her impurity, the Syrophoenician, like the
woman with the hemorrhage, hopes for healing from Jesus. Mark's audience
would presumably share this trust, not only because they are Christians but

also because elsewhere in Mark, when people in need hear about Jesus and come to him, he invariably heals them (cf. 3:8; 5:27; 6:55; 10:47).

7:27–28: *the amazing dialogue.* The woman's hope that her daughter will be healed, and the reader's, seem to be dashed by Jesus' response. Using terminology that was as insulting in ancient times as it is today, Jesus says in effect that his ministry is limited to God's children, the Jews, and does not extend to Gentile "dogs" like the Syrophoenician woman and her daughter (7:27; see the NOTES on "children" and "dogs" in 7:27). This statement is an extreme example of the ethnocentrism that characterized some, though by no means all, Jewish teachers (see Feldmeier, "Syrophönizierin," 218–19, for an overview). As the Jewish scholar Klausner says with justifiable bitterness, "If any other Jewish teacher of the time had said such a thing Christians would never have forgiven Judaism for it" (*Jesus*, 294). The Christian exegete Theissen adds that the saying is morally offensive, as though a doctor should refuse to treat a foreign child; and he points out the incongruity that Jesus couches his refusal to help a child in a parable about the necessity of attending to children (*Gospels*, 61, 65).

Despite the offensiveness of the saying, the most straightforward reading of it on the historical level is a literal one: Jesus was initially inclined to refuse the woman's request, and his subsequent decision to heal her represented a change of mind. Some exegetes have attempted to evade this conclusion with rationalizations; Taylor, for example, hypothesizes that in 7:27 Jesus was talking to himself, not to the woman. In a similar vein, Filson suggests that his facial expression or tone of voice tipped the woman off that his refusal was not final (*Matthew*, 180), and Hassler ("Incident") speculates that he may have winked!

If we are not prepared to go along with such rationalizations—and nothing in the text supports them—then we must accept that 7:27 as spoken by the historical Jesus was meant as a refusal, probably because he viewed his mission as limited to Israel (cf. Matt 10:5–6). Indeed, Rhoads ("Syrophoenician," 361–62) thinks that this is also its meaning for Mark; Jesus only changes his mind about ministry to Gentiles after his encounter with the Syrophoenician woman, whereupon he immediately demonstrates his new attitude by going "through the middle" of the Decapolis, a Gentile region (7:31). But the ending of the passage creates problems for this interpretation; does "because you have said this" (7:29) imply "because you have changed my mind"? Possibly, but in the Markan context it seems more likely to mean "because you have passed the test." Elsewhere in Mark, Jesus often ascribes healing to people's persistent faith (2:5; 5:34; 10:52; cf. Matt 15:28). Two chapters later, moreover, Jesus will heal a demon-possessed child whose parent has interceded for him (9:14–29). As in our passage, the parent's request for healing is not immediately fulfilled; Jesus instead makes an initial response that sounds like a refusal (9:19a) but that turns out to be a ploy designed to evoke a significant expression of faith on the part of the parent (9:24; cf. also Matt 8:5–13//John 7:46–54). This is also probably the Markan meaning here; whatever their significance for the historical Jesus, in Mark's plot the words in 7:27 are in the nature of a test of faith (see Pokorny, "Puppy," 328). Luther, then, may be on the right exegetical track when he uses our passage as the basis for a moving exhortation to Christians to persist in trusting God even when he seems to turn his back on them; they must learn to see the "yes" hidden in his "no" (WA 17/2.200–4).

But even if Mark understands Jesus' words in 7:27 as a test, he also takes them seriously as an outline of salvation history up to his own day. For in Mark's view, which is shared by other early Christian writers, God's children, the Jews, had in the economy of salvation to be "fed" with the food of the gospel first, before the Gentiles could be nourished by it (cf. Rom 1:16; Acts 13:46 and see the NOTE on "children" in 7:27). On the level of the Markan narrative this salvation-historical progression is reproduced by the order of the accounts of miraculous feedings: *first* five thousand Jews are satisfied (6:30–44), *then* four thousand Gentiles are fed (8:1–9). But since, as Mark knows, the Jews have by his own time for the most part rejected the Christian message, and since Gentiles have shown themselves to be more receptive to it, the "first," Jewish Christian epoch referred to in 7:27 has now given way to the Gentile Christian epoch referred to in 13:10, in which the good news is being preached to all nations (see the NOTE on "first" in 7:27 and cf. Pokorny, "Puppy," 332). Mark 7:27a, then, may speak not of a live option but of a lost opportunity, much as the speech of Paul and Barnabas in Acts 13:46 does: "It was necessary that the word of God should be spoken *first* (*prōton*) to you. Since you reject it, . . . we are now turning to the Gentiles" (cf. 18:6).

But just as the Paul and Barnabas of Acts are found preaching in a synagogue a few verses after this passage (Acts 14:1), so there is a certain ambiguity in Mark as well. By using the word *tekna* in 7:27a, the Markan Jesus seems to accept the point of view that the Jews are God's children, and nowhere else does he deny this identification or transfer it to the Gentiles. There is apparently, then, an exceptionally close, familial relationship between Jesus, who is secretly God's son, and the Jews, whom he acknowledges as God's children — even if *they* do not acknowledge *him*. But children do not cease to be children simply because they disobey their parents' wishes.

Jesus' statement in 7:27, therefore, is important, both as a test and as an expression of the Markan view of salvation history; but the woman's response to it in 7:28 is even more important. The significance of this response is grammatically signposted by the use of the biblical formula "answered and said" to introduce her words and by the switch into the historical present (the phrase is literally "answered and *says*," the only historical present in the passage). As Rhoads remarks ("Syrophoenician," 361), the woman "steals the scene"; her retort to Jesus is a delightful mixture of respectful address ("Lord"), seeming acceptance of an inferior position ("dogs"), and daring repartee. There is a certain analogy to the occasional OT or rabbinic tale in which a woman wins an argument against a respected leader or teacher by sheer force of wit (see the NOTE on "answered and said" in 7:28).

The woman accomplishes her rhetorical coup by entering Jesus' metaphor, taking up the canine image that he had used against her and subtly shifting it to her own advantage (see Pokorny, "Puppy," 328). As Swete (149) notes, this reversal gives added meaning to the introductory formula "answered and said": "Her saying was in the strictest sense an answer: she laid hold of Christ's word and based her plea upon it." The woman's response transforms the dog of Jesus' metaphor, which is presumably a street dog that lives outside the house, into a domestic dog that resides inside the house (on these two types of dog, see the NOTE on "dogs" in 7:27). The dog, therefore, though admittedly in a position inferior to that of the children, is still part of the "household of faith" (cf. Gal 6:10). As Euthymius paraphrases her reply: "Since then I am a dog, I am not a stranger" (Swete, 149).

There is also another dimension to the woman's response, one that would not be accessible to her as a character in the story but that would be appreciated by readers attentive to the overall flow of the Markan narrative. In its reference to the leftovers eaten by the dogs, the woman's response recalls the account of Jesus' feeding of five thousand of his fellow Jews, at the conclusion of which twelve baskets full of bread were collected (6:43). The Jewish "children," then, have *already* been fed by Jesus, and there is plenty of food left over for the Gentile "dogs" (see Pokorny, "Puppy," 334). They, too, will presently be fed by Jesus (8:1–9).

7:29–30: *denouement*. Jesus responds to the woman's audacious stroke with a reply beginning, "Because you have said this, go . . . " (7:29a). This is another fine example of the rhetorical art of the narrative, for these words could momentarily be construed as a final rebuff, as though Jesus were punishing the woman's impudence by dismissing her. But the tension is quickly resolved by Jesus' concluding statement that "the demon has gone out of your daughter" (7:29b). Hearing this joyful news, the woman returns home and finds the girl cast onto her bed (7:30), presumably having been thrown there by the cast-out demon (cf. 7:26) in a departing demonstration of malice (cf. 1:26; 9:25; see the NOTE on "cast" in 7:30).

The story of the Gentile woman from the Tyre region who wrests a blessing from Jesus is remarkable in more than one way. Not only does it present the only example in the Gospels of a person who wins an argument with Jesus, but it also portrays a Jesus who is unusually sensitive to his Jewish countrymen's claims to salvation-historical privilege and unusually rude about the position of Gentiles: the Jews are God's children, and their needs come first; compared to them, non-Jews are just "dogs."

There is nothing quite like this elsewhere in the Gospel. Indeed, it is somewhat surprising in a Gospel that pictures Jesus as in constant conflict with the leaders of Judaism and that has just depicted him challenging the basis of its communal life, the Law (7:19); that portrays Judaism itself as an old wineskin incapable of accommodating the new wine of the gospel (2:21–22); that foreshadows and foretells the destruction of Judaism's central institution, the Temple, and of those who control it (11:12–25; 12:1–9; 13:1–2; 15:38); and that depicts the Jewish multitude as joining with their leaders in calling for Jesus' crucifixion (15:11–14). Elsewhere in the Gospel, moreover, the Markan Jesus shows great solicitude for Gentiles, as in the continuation of our own passage and in 7:31; 13:10, and 15:39.

This exceptional emphasis is perhaps illuminated by the physical setting of our passage in the region around Tyre and the putative setting of our Gospel in the tumult surrounding the Jewish War of 66–73 C.E. For the Tyrian region was one that was badly hit by the Jewish/Gentile tension that led up to and accompanied that war (see Theissen, *Gospels*, 77–78). Josephus reports that the Tyrians were among the Jews' bitterest enemies (*Ag. Ap.* 1.70) and cites pogroms going back to the the first century B.C.E. (*Ant.* 14.313–21). During the Jewish War, Tyrian Gentiles killed a considerable number of their Jewish neighbors and imprisoned the rest in chains (*J.W.* 2.478), and a Tyrian army burned the Jewish fortress of Gischala. This poisonous atmosphere may well have infected the fledgling Christian church in Tyre, the majority of whose members were probably Gentiles; Acts 21:3–4 presents the Tyrian Christians as begging Paul not to go up to Jerusalem.

It may be significant, then, that Mark retains the pre-Markan localization of our story in the Tyrian region, and adds a half-verse (7:27a) that emphasizes the precedence of the Jews in God's plan of salvation. He may feel that Christian communities in this region, where Gentile (including perhaps Gentile Christian?) animosity against Jews runs high, need to be sharply reminded of God's continuing favor for his ancient people. Theology is always shouting into the wind, and in Tyre the wind may be blowing in an anti-Jewish direction; the Christians in Tyre, therefore, may need to hear a clear message about the Jewish "first" (cf. Schmithals, 1.354).

Yet there is no doubt that, from Mark's perspective, the future of the Christian movement lies largely in the Gentile world. In the next passage this future will be foreshadowed as Jesus makes a triumphal tour of Gentile regions on the border of Palestine.

JESUS HEALS A DEAF-MUTE (7:31–37)

7 [31]And he came out again from the region of Tyre and went through Sidon to the Sea of Galilee, going through the middle of the Decapolis region. [32]And they brought to him a man who was deaf and could scarcely speak, and they began to plead with him to put his hand on him. [33]So taking him away from the crowd privately, he thrust his fingers into his ears, spat, and touched his tongue, [34]and looking up to heaven he sighed and said to him, "*Ephphatha*," that is, "Be opened!" [35]And his ears were opened, and his tongue was unshackled, and he spoke normally. [36]And he commanded them not to tell anyone; but the more he commanded them, all the more greatly did they spread the news. [37]And they were exceedingly astonished, saying, "He has done all things well. He makes both the deaf to hear and the mute to speak."

NOTES

7 31. *came out again from the region of Tyre and went through Sidon to the Sea of Galilee, going through the middle of the Decapolis region.* Gk *palin exelthōn ek tōn horiōn Tyrou ēlthen dia Sidōnos eis tēn thalassan tēs Galilaias ana meson tōn horiōn Dekapoleōs.* Tyre and Sidon are in Lebanon, and it is perhaps significant that both Isaiah 35, which is alluded to at the end of our passage (see the COMMENT on 7:35–37), and Isa 29:17–19 mention Lebanon in the context of a divine cure for deafness.

If Mark's wording is meant to describe a direct journey, it implies that Sidon and the Decapolis are on a line from Tyre to the Sea of Galilee. This is scarcely the case; the Sea of Galilee is southeast of Tyre, but Sidon is north of Tyre and the Decapolis region is mostly east of the Sea of Galilee (of the ten cities, only Scythopolis is west of it). Mark's notice, then, is comparable to a description of an American trip from Portland to Denver via Seattle and the Great Plains or a British trip from Liverpool to London via Glasgow and Norfolk. Many have taken the verse as evidence that Mark is not a native of Palestine, but since the geographical knowledge of nonspecialists was even more faulty in antiquity than it is today, this is not necessarily the case (see Hengel, *Mark*, 148 n. 51). Moreover, as Lang ("Über Sidon") and Theissen (*Gospels*, 243–45) have argued, Mark may be deliberately constructing for Jesus a tour of Gentile areas abutting Palestine—perhaps regions where there are Christian communities in his own day. Acts 21:3–6 and 27:3, for example, describe Christian communities in Tyre and Sidon, and there was also an important Christian center in Damascus, which is counted as part of the Decapolis in Pliny's *Natural History* (5.16.74). Theissen points out that 7:31 and the other major Markan geographical "error," the implication in 5:1 that Gerasa is near the Sea of Galilee (cf. 5:13), share several features: they relate to the part of Syria neighboring Palestine, they foreshadow the movement of the gospel to the Gentiles, and they are found at the beginning of a pericope, where one normally expects redactional activity. These similarities may well reflect the location of Mark's audience; as Theissen puts it, "Jesus' long detour over Sidon and the Decapolis in Mark 7:31 would have led him into the neighborhood of Markan Christianity."

32. *they brought.* Gk *pherousin.* As in 7:36–37 and elsewhere in Mark (1:22, 32; 2:3, etc.), this is an impersonal use of the third person plural.

deaf. Gk *kōphon.* As Taylor (353) points out, the original meaning of this word is "blunt" or "dull." It is probably not accidental that the deaf man is a Gentile (see the NOTE on "came out again from the region of Tyre" in 7:31), since Gentiles are associated with deafness in several passages from the OT prophets (Isa 42:17–19; 43:8–9; Mic 7:16) because of their presumed insensitivity to God's word.

could scarcely speak. Gk *mogilalon,* lit. "difficult of speaking." This NT *hapax legomenon* (see GLOSSARY) is probably an allusion to Isa 35:6 LXX, where the word appears for the only time in the OT. As BAGD (525) notes, the ancient versions interpret this word to mean "lacking all power of speech," which corresponds to the Hebrew *'illēm* of Isa 35:6 and is supported by 7:37, where mutes (*alalous*) are mentioned. But the more literal interpretation of *mogilalos* is supported by "spoke normally" in 7:35.

33. *thrust.* Gk *ebalen*, lit. "threw, cast," the word whose compounded form is used for casting out demons in 1:34, 39; 3:15, etc., and whose uncompounded form has just been used in the previous passage for the girl cast onto her bed by the exorcised demon (7:30). Hull (*Hellenistic Magic*, 83) suggests that Jesus thrusts his fingers into the man's ears in order to create a passageway through which the evil spirit causing the deafness may exit.

spat. Gk *ptysas*, lit. "having spat." Mark does not say *where* Jesus spits. There seem to be three possibilities: (1) He spits on the ground as a sign of contempt for the evil spirit that is afflicting the man (see the previous NOTE and the NOTE on "his tongue was unshackled" in 7:35). (2) He spits on his fingers, with which he subsequently touches the man's tongue. (3) He spits in the man's mouth (cf. *t. Sanh.* 12:10, where R. Aqiba anathematizes magicians who spit on a wound). Of these possibilities, number 2 seems the most likely, since Jesus' fingers have just been mentioned, whereas the ground and the mute's mouth have not.

Spittle was extremely popular as a folk remedy in antiquity and was even highly regarded by "professional" physicians (see e.g. Galen *Natural Faculties* 3.7; on the continuation of such superstitions into modern times, see Opie and Tatem, *Dictionary*, 373–74). The spittle of famous or charismatic personalities was especially prized; Tacitus (*Histories* 4.81) and Suetonius (*Vespasian* 7) tell a story about a blind man who begged the emperor Vespasian to heal him with his spittle. The idea of its medicinal effectiveness was widespread among Jews as well; in *b. B. Bat.* 126b, for example, R. Ḥanina sends people in need to his son, "for he is a first-born, and his saliva heals." Some rabbis, however, opposed the use of spittle because of its magical associations (see the reference to *t. Sanh.* 12:10 in the previous paragraph and cf. Preuss, *Medizin*, 321–22).

What is the basis for this ancient belief in the curative power of spittle? Eitrem (*Notes*, 56–57) points out that spittle, like every bodily secretion, was considered to be a vehicle for a supernatural power that could be either beneficent or harmful; the Assyrians, for example, knew both a "saliva of life" and a "saliva of death." Spittle itself, then, was primarily neither positive nor negative but "power-laden" (Ritner, *Mechanics*, 87). The belief in its life-giving and curative properties was probably aided by its visual similarity to semen as well as "the instinctive habit of licking wounds and the weak antibacterial properties of saliva" (*Mechanics*, 78–80). The belief in spittle's destructive capacity, conversely, was aided by its similarity in appearance to urine and to snake's venom. It is this negative side that is emphasized in the OT references, where spittle is linked with madness (1 Sam 21:13) and worthlessness (Isa 40:15) and is seen as a transmitter of impurity (Lev 15:8; Ritner, *Mechanics*, 90); basing itself on Lev 15:8, an anonymous opinion in the Talmud (*b. Nid.* 55b) declares spittle to be unclean. Both positive and negative aspects of spittle are probably involved in our story. Since Jesus is a figure who is saturated with the Spirit

(1:9–11), the spittle that comes out of his body is charged with his holiness and is destructive to the demonic force that binds the tongue of the mute (see the NOTE on "his tongue was unshackled" in 7:35). There may also be an element of sympathetic magic: spittle passes from Jesus' properly working tongue to the mute's deformed tongue and thus restores the latter.

34. *sighed.* Gk *estenaxen.* Taylor (355) asserts that "only a love for the bizarre . . . will find in the groaning of Jesus anything other than a sign of His deep feeling and compassion for the sufferer." But sighing, like spitting and the usage of exotic foreign words, was a standard part of ancient magical technique; see, for example, the charm from the great Paris Magical Papyrus (suppl. gr. 574): "After reciting this, throw incense on the fire, sigh, and descend [from the roof]" (cited by Bonner, "Thaumaturgic Technique," 172).

Scholars disagree about the function of Jesus' sighing. Hull, for example, thinks that it works by sympathetic magic; Jesus is imitating both the hoped-for restoration of speech and the ejection of the indwelling demon (*Hellenistic Magic,* 84). Lohmeyer (150), on the other hand, hypothesizes that it signifies the entrapment of the wonder-worker's own powerful spirit within his earthbound body; cf. *PGM* 4.537, in which the magician is instructed to inhale deeply three times in order to gather his radiant breath (cited by Gnilka, 1.297). But sighing may also indicate the magician's reliance on a source of power outside himself/herself, for example a demon (demons sigh according to *T. Sol.* 5:12–13; see Bonner, "Thaumaturgic Technique," 174) or the divine Spirit (cf. Rom 8:26: "The Spirit himself intercedes for us with sighs too deep for words"; see Eitrem, *Notes,* 54–55). This last theory garners support from the immediate Markan context, since Jesus' sighing directly follows his raising his eyes to heaven in an attitude of supplication to God. Jesus' sigh may also suggest struggle with a demonic obstacle; cf. 8:11–12, in which he will sigh again as a result of Pharisaic "testing," a word with a Satanic nuance (see 1:13). Moreover, if a demon can sigh when it wrestles with an exorcist (cf. again *T. Sol.* 5:12–13), then it makes sense for an exorcist to sigh as he struggles with a demon.

"Ephphatha," that is, "Be opened!" Gk *Ephphatha, ho estin dianoichthēti.* Black (234) and others have argued that *ephphatha* is a transliteration of an Aramaic word, *'eppataḥ,* which is the *Ithpěʿel* or *Ithpaʿal* imperative of *ptḥ.* The more usual form would be *'etpataḥ,* but the *taw* has apparently been assimilated to the *peʾ/phe'.* This analysis, however, has been challenged by Rabinowitz ("Be Opened"), who prefers to derive *ephphatha* from a Hebrew word, *hippataḥ,* which is the *Niphʿal* imperative of the same root. But Black's Aram *'eppataḥ* is closer to Mark's *ephphatha* than Rabinowitz's Heb *hippataḥ* is, and Rabinowitz's main argument, the lack of attestation for the assimilation of the *taw* in Western Aramaic, has been challenged by Wilcox, who points to the interchange of the forms *'etpataḥ* and *'eppataḥ* in the Neofiti and Vat. Ebr. 440 manuscripts of the fragmentary Targum on Gen 49:1 ("Semitisms," 998–99).

Both the Jews and the more numerous Gentiles in the Syrian Decapolis region spoke a dialect of Aramaic, so there is nothing unusual about Jesus' use of that language here. But Mark's retention of the Aramaic term in his narrative still needs to be explained, since he generally translates Jesus' words into Greek; he probably keeps the Aramaic here, as he does in 5:41, because of the popular belief in the power of Jesus' original words (see the NOTE on "*Talitha koum*" in 5:41). In dependence on our passage, the churches in Milan and Rome from early times performed in their baptismal liturgies a ceremony known as *Apertio* ("Opening"), in which the bishop applied his spittle to the candidate's nose and ears and said "*effeta*" (see Swete, 152). The placement of this rite immediately before the renunciation of the devil suggests that it had an exorcistic significance (cf. Hippolytus *Apostolic Tradition* 20.8), and this interpretation is confirmed by the words that accompanied it in the Roman rite: "Flee, demon; for the judgment of God has come near" (see Dölger, *Exorzismus*, 131). The retention of the Aramaic word *effeta* in the Latin ceremony supports the theory that words in the original language were considered to be especially potent.

35. *his ears were opened.* Gk *ēnoigēsan autou hai akoai.* This is part of an allusion to Isa 35:5 (see the NOTE on "could scarcely speak" in 7:32 and the COMMENT on 7:35–37), a text that the Targum interprets as God's enablement of his people to hear the words of the prophets. The connection made in the larger Markan context between the opening of ears and the hearing of the divine word (cf. 8:18) may be partially influenced by this sort of Jewish exegesis of Isaiah 35.

his tongue was unshackled. Gk *elythē ho desmos tēs glōssēs autou,* lit. "the bond of his tongue was released"; cf. the English expression "tongue-tied." In Mark this is most probably exorcistic terminology; the magical papyri attest spells for binding the tongue of an enemy and thus making him or her mute (see Deissmann, *Light,* 305–7). Almost identical terminology, which definitely is exorcistic, is used in Luke 13:16; on the exorcistic nuance of "binding and loosing" terminology in general, see Hiers, "Binding."

36. *all the more greatly.* Gk *mallon perissoteron,* lit. "more more-exceedingly," one of Mark's characteristic double expressions. *Perissoteron* is cognate with *hyperperissōs,* the word translated "exceedingly" in the next verse.

37. *exceedingly.* Gk *hyperperissōs,* lit. "superexceedingly," an over-the-top adverb that Doty ("Amazed," 50) calls a "double superlative" (cf. the cognate verb in Rom 5:20; 2 Cor 7:4). Thus both usages of the *periss-* root in 7:36–37 are greatly heightened ones, corresponding to the unprecedented nature and huge significance of the event that has just taken place (see the next NOTE and the COMMENT on 7:35–37).

He has done all things well. Gk *kalōs panta pepoiēken.* This clause echoes the Septuagint version of Gen 1:31, in which at the end of the sixth day of creation God sees all the things (*ta panta*) that he has made (*epoiēsen*) and concludes that they are very good (*kala lian*). This Genesis verse was well remembered in later Judaism; it may already be echoed in Exod 2:2, where Moses' mother sees "that he is good"; later rabbis, at any rate, saw a Genesis allusion in this Exodus passage (see e.g. *Exod. Rab.* 1.20 and cf. Allison, *New Moses,* 203). Sirach 39:16

also echoes Gen 1:31 verbally, as does the Septuagint of Qoh 3:11: "He has made (*epoiēse*) all things (*ta sympanta*) beautiful (*kala*) in their time" (cf. *Gen. Rab.* 9.2, which cites this verse in its comment on Gen 1:31). The wide influence of Gen 1:31 increases the likelihood that at least some of Mark's readers would have recognized the Genesis allusion in 7:37.

He makes both the deaf to hear and the mute to speak. Gk *kai tous kōphous poiei akouein kai alalous lalein.* This is an allusion to Isa 35:5–6, verses that are also alluded to in Luke 7:22 (cf. the COMMENT on 7:35–37 and the NOTES on "could scarcely speak" in 7:32 and "his ears were opened" in 7:35).

COMMENT

Introduction. Having acceded to a request by a Gentile woman to cast a demon out of her daughter, Jesus now goes on a tour of Gentile regions (see the NOTE on "came out again from the region of Tyre" in 7:31), during the course of which he heals a man who is deaf and can scarcely speak. Besides this connection with the previous story on the basis of the Gentile theme, there are also far-reaching parallels between our narrative and a later Markan healing, the cure of the blind man from Bethsaida in 8:22–26 (cf. Taylor, 368–69):

Mark 7:31–37	*Mark 8:22–26*
description of trip	*description of trip*
and they brought him (*kai pherousin autǭ*) a deaf man	and they brought him (*kai pherousin autǭ*) a blind man
and they beseeched him that (*kai parakalousin auton hina*) he lay his hand on him	and they beseeched him that (*kai parakalousin auton hina*) he touch him
and taking (*apolabomenos*) him away from the crowd privately	and taking (*epilabomenos*) his hand he led him out of the village
he put his fingers into his ears and spitting (*kai ptysas*) he touched his tongue	and spitting (*kai ptysas*) on his eyes, he put his hands on him
and looking up (*kai anablepsas*) to heaven he [Jesus] said . . .	and looking up (*kai anablepsas*) he [the blind man] said . . .
healing	*healing*
and he commanded them not to tell anyone	and he sent him back to his house saying, "Do not even go into the village"

These striking similarities suggest to some scholars (e.g. Gnilka, 1.296) that the two passages originally belonged together. Since, moreover, what they describe corresponds to Isa 35:5–6—the eyes of the blind are opened, the ears of the deaf are unstopped, and the tongue of the mute is released—an allusion to this verse may have concluded this putative combination (part of this allusion is still visible in 7:37). Mark may have split the two stories apart because he wanted to make them serve two different functions within his narrative, the healing of the blind man to comment on the disciples' spiritual state and the healing of the deaf-mute to foreshadow the church's mission, in which Gentiles' ears are opened to hear Jesus' word and their tongues loosened to spread the news about him (cf. 13:10; cf. Baudoz, "Mc 7,31–37"). Other probable Markan redactional touches include parts of 7:31, which contains characteristic redactional vocabulary ("came out," "again," "region," "Sea of Galilee"), and 7:36b, which uses *kēryssein* and describes the witnesses' inability to contain themselves, as in the redactional 1:45 and 5:20. "Them" in 7:36a may also be Mark's word, since the presence of witnesses clashes with the implication of private healing in 7:33 (see Theissen, 150).

The story falls into five unequal sections: the transitional scene-setting in 7:31, the request for healing in 7:32, the description of the healing technique in 7:33–34, the cure itself in 7:35, and the reaction to the cure in 7:36–37. As can be seen from the amount of space devoted to them, the emphasis falls on Jesus' method of healing and the reaction of the crowd.

7:31–34: scene-setting, request, and Jesus' healing technique. After his encounter with the Syrophoenician woman, Jesus' tour of Gentile regions (7:31) apparently brings him to the notice of other people in need, including the friends or relatives of a man who is deaf and has a severe speech impediment. They bring the man to Jesus with the plea that he administer a healing touch (7:32); as in 2:3–5, the fact that the man cannot come to Jesus and make his request himself emphasizes his helplessness.

Jesus responds by taking the man aside privately (7:33). This motif of secrecy, which is reinforced in 7:36a, is frequently found in ancient miracle stories, and it is of a piece with Mark's retention of Jesus' words of healing in the original Aramaic: both features enhance the atmosphere of mystery in the narrative (see the NOTE on *"Talitha koum"* in 5:41).

In line with this atmosphere, our passage, like its companion piece in 8:22–26, concentrates heavily on the method employed in the healing, graphically describing Jesus' actions of spitting, sighing, and sticking his fingers in the deaf man's ears (7:34). Nineham (204) intriguingly suggests that this description may have been intended for the instruction of Christian healers. This possibly pedagogic description is emphasized not only by its length but also by its chiastic arrangement:

A   And he *thrust* his fingers into the man's ears
B   And *having spat* he *touched* the man's tongue
B'   And *having looked up* to heaven he *sighed*
A'   And he *said*, "Be opened!"

Here the two actions at the beginning and end (AA′), the thrusting of Jesus' fingers into the man's ears and his command that those ears be opened, are indicated by finite verbs, and the actions correspond to each other (Jesus' fingers symbolically open the man's ears). In the center of the chiasm, similarly, the clauses have a parallel structure (aorist participle + aorist indicative) and perhaps correspond to each other thematically as well (Jesus' sigh may mimic the desired termination of the man's muteness; see the NOTE on "sighed" in 7:34). These stressed magical manipulations, and similar ones in 8:22–26, are probably a large part of the reason that Matthew omits both stories in his retelling of Mark.

Both here and in 8:22–26, however, these healing details do not just awaken exotic interest but also echo larger Markan themes. For example, the thrusting of Jesus' fingers into the man's ears, his use of spittle, and his sighing all have exorcistic connotations (see the NOTES on "thrust" and "spat" in 7:33 and "sighed" and "'Ephphatha,' that is, 'Be opened!'" in 7:34), thus linking our story with the exorcisms that so dominate the first half of Mark. This demonic dimension of the story is further reinforced by the fact that, in Mark's other narrative of the healing of a deaf-mute, the condition is explicitly ascribed to a demon (9:17, 25; cf. Schmithals, 1.360). Thus, as in 1:21–31, an exorcism (7:24–30; cf. 1:21–28) is followed by an exorcism-like healing (7:31–37; cf. 1:29–31). The exorcistic dimension is never far below the surface in our Gospel; if the Markan Jesus is creating a new world by "doing all things well" (7:37), a major aspect of this act of new creation is his triumph over Satanic evil, which recapitulates God's primordial victory over demonic chaos "in the beginning." This new creation is also a new exodus, and the exodus theme is central in this part of the Gospel (see the introduction to 6:6b–8:21); it may therefore be relevant for our passage that Jewish healers apparently linked the curative properties of saliva with Exod 15:26, "I will put none of the diseases upon you which I put upon the Egyptians" (t. Sanh. 12:10; 'Abot R. Nat. 36 [A]).

Two other aspects of Jesus' use of spittle may also be relevant. First, it was considered by some Jews to be unclean (see the NOTE on "spat" in 7:33). The Markan Jesus' employment of it, therefore, may be connected with the impurity theme that has been explicit in the discussion in 7:1–23 and implicit in the story of the Syrophoenician woman in 7:24–30; as in 1:40–45, 5:1–13, and 5:21–43, then, Jesus' healing technique brings him dangerously close to ritual defilement. Second, and even more threateningly, his use of spittle ironically foreshadows the way in which his enemies will later spit at *him* (14:65; 15:19; cf. 10:34). This connection may suggest that Jesus' curative power is somehow related to the salvific effect of his suffering, just as the "raising" language in the healing in 5:35–43 pointed forward to his resurrection.

But the end of this section also guards against a misconception. The fact that Jesus cures the man's hearing by sticking his fingers in his ears and eliminates his muteness by transferring some of his saliva to the man's tongue (see the NOTE on "spat" in 7:33) might suggest that his body had intrinsic healing properties. But the next verse immediately qualifies this impression by emphasizing the way in which he looks up to heaven, invoking God's power, right before the miracle occurs (7:34a); the word of healing that accompanies this gesture, moreover, is a divine passive ("Be opened!"; 7:34b). Thus Mark preserves an ambiguity we have noticed elsewhere (see the COMMENT on 1:2–3; 2:10b–12; 5:18–20): Jesus is the agent in the miracle, which is somehow connected with his own fingers going into the man's ears and his own spittle touching the man's tongue; yet ultimately the healing act is performed by God, and only takes place after Jesus has invoked God's power.

7:35–37: healing and acclamation. Once that invocation has taken place, the healing immediately ensues; the man's ears are opened and his tongue is unshackled (two more divine passives; 7:35ab), and he speaks like a normal human being (7:35c). Again, these events are probably meant to be understood not only literally but also symbolically. The motif of the opened ear, for example, is used in Jewish texts as a symbol for revelation; the Hymnist of Qumran praises God for having opened his ears to marvelous mysteries (1QH 1:21), and the Targum interprets the opening of deaf ears in Isa 35:5, one of the biblical verses alluded to in Mark 7:37, as enabling the people to hear the words of the prophets. As the NOTE on *Ephphatha* in 7:33 points out, moreover, this "opening" symbolism was continued in the *Apertio* ceremony of ancient baptismal liturgies based on our passage. The opening of the man's ears, therefore, is probably meant to be understood as a symbol of the way in which a person is made receptive to the Christian message by a divine act of enablement (see the COMMENT on 4:9). Similarly symbolic is the "unshackling" of the man's tongue, which empowers him to join with his companions in proclaiming what Jesus has done; this feature continues the exorcistic imagery of 7:33–34 (see the NOTE on "his tongue was unshackled" in 7:35) and points forward to the deliverance of Gentiles from their captivity to demons into the joyful liberty of the proclamation of the gospel. Mark's audience, then, would probably identify strongly with the healed man in our story; they, too, had once been deaf to God's word, but Jesus has opened their ears and freed their tongues to proclaim his glory. This application of our healing story to the situation of Christians in general, as well as its allusion to Isa 35:5–6, is familiar from Charles Wesley's hymn "O for a Thousand Tongues to Sing":

Hear him, ye deaf; his praise, ye dumb,
Your loosened tongues employ:
Ye blind, behold your Savior come;
And leap, ye lame, for joy!

Oddly enough, however, Jesus initially forbids the healed man and the helpers who had brought him to Jesus to employ their loosened tongues in this laudatory manner (7:36a); but they immediately go out and proclaim what has happened anyway, and the more Jesus tries to suppress them, the more they disobey (7:36b). Are they really to be blamed for this disobedience? Some scholars, such as Schweizer (155) and Watson ("Social Function," 52), think so; the violation of Jesus' explicit order is an obvious sin, and the choral acclamation of Jesus to which it leads ("He has done all things well . . . ") is an expression of uncomprehending wonder. It is hard to follow this line of reasoning, however, since 7:37 corresponds so closely to the faith of the early church in general and to that of Mark in particular, as we shall see in a moment (cf. Räisänen, 152). Rather, the point of the ban and its violation seems to be that the spread of the good news about Jesus is an act of God, and no one can stop it—not even Jesus himself! (It may be, as I suggest in the introduction to the COMMENT, that the ban on speaking in 7:36a is part of the story Mark has inherited; he has expanded it by his addition of 7:36b without smoothing out all the lumps.)

For it is hard to imagine the Markan audience overhearing what the onlookers say in 7:37 without assenting enthusiastically: "He has done (*pepoiēken*) all things well. He makes (*poiei*) both the deaf to hear and the mute (*alalous*) to speak (*lalein*)." The importance of this double use of *poiein* is underlined by the tenses Mark uses for it. The first instance is in the perfect (*pepoiēken*, "he has done"), the weightiest of all Greek tenses, since it expresses a past action that continues to have effects in the speaker's present (see Fanning, *Verbal Aspect*, 103–20). This nuance of present effect is underlined by the second instance, the present tense *poiei* ("he makes") in 7:37b, whose implication of continuing activity probably resonates for Mark's readers in their own time: Jesus is *still* working miracles of revelation, *still* loosening tied-up tongues.

This point is reinforced by the linkage with 5:19–20, the only other Markan passage in which Jesus' miracles are indicated by *poiein* (cf. Schmithals, 1.360). Mark 5:19–20 is a passage that, like the present one, portrays a healed person's disobedience of Jesus' command to silence, a disobedience that leads to the spreading of Jesus' fame in a Gentile area and that thus foreshadows the church's proclamation of the good news about Jesus "to all the nations," which will be described in 13:10–11. Our pericope itself is connected with 13:10–11 by the usage of *lalein* ("to speak"), which will reappear in the later passage three times: "When they hand you over and lead you up to trial, do not be concerned what you are to say (*laletēte*), but whatever is given you in that hour say (*laleite*), for it is not you who are speaking (*hoi lalountes*), but the Holy Spirit." Mark 7:31–37 and 13:10–11, then, are probably meant to be mutually illuminating: in their future trials the Christians will be given powerful words of testimony to speak, just as in the past Jesus unlocked the lips of the mute man, so that he and his friends ended up being powerful witnesses to what Jesus had done for them.

But Mark 7:37 does not just relate our story of healed deafness and muteness to the movement out into the Gentile world in the Markan present; it also relates the narrative to the Old Testament, so that even the outreach to the non-Jewish world is shown to reflect the Jewish Scriptures. The double use of *poiein* calls to mind Gen 1:1–2:3, where the verb is repeatedly used for God's creative act; nor is this echo accidental, since Mark 7:37, with its reference to Jesus doing all things *well* (*kalōs*), seems explicitly to echo Gen 1:31, where God sees all the things that he has *made* (*epoiēsen*), and pronounces them very *good* (*kala*; cf. the NOTE on "He has done all things well" in 7:37). This Genesis connection is reinforced by the fact that Mark has also used *poiein* earlier in his Gospel, in 3:14–16, to allude to the opening chapter of Genesis (see the COMMENT on 3:13–15), and it becomes even more plausible in view of the exorcistic features of our passage and the frequent mobilization of creation imagery in Aramaic exorcistic texts (see Naveh and Shaked, *Amulets*, 83, 159, 223–24). And the use of *lalein* recalls Isa 35:5–6, which prophesies deaf people hearing and mute people speaking. In Isaiah this passage is part of a description of the transformed world that will greet Israel's return to Zion; when that great event takes place, the blind will see, the deaf will hear, the lame will leap, and the mute will sing for joy. These two biblical backgrounds are closely related to each other and to the sense of eschatological advent that permeates Mark, for in Isaiah the miraculous renewal of nature, which includes the healing of the blind and the deaf, is a sign that now as "in the beginning" a new world is being born (cf. Isa 43:14–21). This theme of new creation pervades Mark's Gospel elsewhere, being especially concentrated in the Markan prologue (see the introduction to 1:1–15).

Mark gives a characteristic twist, however, to this Old Testament theme of new creation. For he presents a rather different picture from that in Isaiah 35 itself, where part of God's means for the renewal of creation is his vengeance against Israel's enemies (Isa 35:4) and his exclusion of unclean people from the Holy Way that leads to the promised land (35:8; so J. K. Riches orally). These exclusionary Isaian features come to the fore in some later interpretations of Isaiah 35, for example in 1QM 14:4–8, where Isaiah's dream of cosmic renewal, which includes the opening of the mouth of the mute, also involves destruction of the demonically inspired Gentiles who oppress Israel. It may not be an accident, then, but a deliberate inversion of a common pattern—one that is perhaps known to Mark from the propaganda of the Jewish revolutionaries—that Mark's own allusion to Isaiah 35 occurs precisely in the context not of the destruction of demonic Gentiles but of Jesus' ridding a Gentile of his demonic impairment and of the Gentile's consequent joyful praise of Jesus—a praise that reverberates in Mark's own predominantly Gentile Christian community. Mark's exegetical procedure here, then, is similar to that of the Lukan Jesus, who in his inaugural sermon quotes Isaiah's joyful oracle about release for the captives, sight for the blind, and liberty for the oppressed, but tellingly leaves off the Isaian reference to God's day of vengeance on the heathen (Luke 4:18–19; cf. Isa 61:1–2).

The allusions to Genesis 1 and Isaiah 35, then, reiterate a common Markan theme: Jesus' healings are important not just as testimonies to his charisma or to his skill at magic but as signs that by God's will a new world of plenitude and blessing is miraculously springing into existence through him. In the next passage this truth will be driven home as, for the second time in Mark's narrative, food for the hungry appears out of nowhere.

WILDERNESS FEEDING, TESTING, AND INCOMPREHENSION (8:1–21)

◆

INTRODUCTION

A new literary subunit within 6:6b–8:21 begins in 8:1 with the biblical formula "In those days." This subunit comprises the story of the feeding of the four thousand (8:1–9), the Pharisees' demand for a sign from heaven (8:10–13), and the discussion with the disciples about leaven and bread (8:14–21). The unit is bound together by a couple of sea-crossings (8:10, 13) and the theme of bread (8:1–9, 14–21). In 8:22 a new unit begins, with the first of the two healings of blind men (8:22–26 and 10:46–52) that frame the entire central section of the Gospel (8:22–10:52).

Our subunit has a common Old Testament background in the exodus narratives. As we have noted in the COMMENT on 6:30–44, that first Markan narrative of miraculous feeding already recalls the manna miracle of Exodus 16. The likeness is even stronger in the feeding in 8:1–9, and the exodus echoes continue in the following Markan passage, the Pharisees' demand for a sign (8:10–13), and in Jesus' subsequent warning about leaven (8:14–21). Besides being influenced by Exodus 16 and the immediately following account of the testing of Moses at Massa and Meribah in Exod 17:1–7, these passages also seem to echo the doublet of the manna tradition in Numbers 11, where Moses is challenged to provide meat rather than bread; Num 14:21–23, where God swears that the wilderness generation that has tested him will not enter Canaan; and two Psalm texts that recall these Pentateuchal texts, Ps 78:17–20 and Ps 95:7b–11. These parallels are charted in figure 19, which the reader is invited to study carefully. Perhaps the most striking verbal echoes are between Mark 8:10–13 and the latter half of the Septuagint version of Psalm 95 (94:7–11 LXX):

Today, if you hear his [God's] voice, do not *harden your hearts* as in the provocation, as at the day *of testing in the wilderness* (*peirasmou en tē erēmō*), when your fathers *tested* (*epeirasen*) me, tried me and saw my works. For *forty years* I was angry with *that generation* (*tē geneą ekeinę*), and I said, "They always stray in *their heart* (*tē kardią*), and they have not known my ways." As I said in my wrath, "[May I perish] *if they shall enter* (*ei eiseleusontai*) my rest."

Figure 19: Exodus Background to Mark 8:1–21

Mark 8:1–9: miraculous provision of bread in the wilderness	*Exodus 16 and related exodus traditions: miraculous provision of bread in the wilderness*
8:1: In those days . . .	2 *Apoc. Bar.* 29:8: And it will come to pass *at that time* that the treasury of manna will come down again from on high, and they will eat of it *in those years*.
8:4: "Whence (*pothen*) will anyone (*tis*) be able (*dynēsetai*) to get the loaves (*artous*) to satisfy these people here in the wilderness (*en tē erēmō*)?"	Exod 16:3 LXX: "Would that we had died in Egypt . . . when we ate bread (*arton*) to the full. For you have led us into this wilderness (*eis tēn erēmon tautēn*) to kill this whole assembly with hunger."
	Ps 78(LXX 77):19–20: "Will God be able (*dynēsetai*) to prepare a table in the wilderness (*en tē erēmō*)? . . . Is he able (*dynatai*) to give bread (*arton*)?"
	Num 11:13–14 LXX: "Whence (*pothen*) will I get meat to give to all this nation? . . . I will not be able (*ou dynēsomai*) to bear this nation alone."
	Num 11:18 LXX: "Who (*tis*) will feed us with meat?"
8:7: And they had a few small fish.	Num 11:22: "Or shall all the fish of the sea be gathered together for them, to suffice them?"
	Sipre on Num 11:22 (§95): Miriam's well, which followed the Israelites in the wilderness, provided them with fish.
Mark 8:10–13: testing of Jesus by demand for a miraculous sign	*Exodus 17:1–7 and related exodus traditions: testing of Moses and God by demand for a miraculous sign*
8:11: The Pharisees came out . . . seeking from him a sign (*sēmeion*) from heaven, testing (*peirazontes*) him.	Exod 17:2 LXX: "Why do you revile me, and why do you test (*peirazete*) the Lord?"

Figure 19: Exodus Background to Mark 8:1–21 (continued)

	Mekilta on Exod 17:2: pun between "test" (*těnasûn*) and "sign" (*nēs*); quarreling with Moses is quarreling with God.
	Exod 17:7 LXX: And he called the name of that place, Testing (*Peirasmos*) . . . because they tested (*peirazein*) the Lord, saying, "Is the Lord among us, or not?"
	Ps 78(LXX 77):17–18: They provoked the most high in a waterless place and tested (*exepeirasan*) God in their hearts.
	Ps 95(LXX 94):8–9: the day of testing (*peirasmou*) in the wilderness when your fathers tested (*epeirasan*) me . . .
8:12a: He sighed in his spirit and said, "Why does this generation (*hē genea hautē*) seek a sign (*sēmeion*)?"	Ps 95(LXX 94):10: I was vexed with that generation (*tē geneą ekeinē*).
8:12b: "[May I perish] if (*ei*) a sign will be given to this generation (*tē geneą tautē*)."	Num 14:21–23: Truly, as I live, . . . all those men who have seen . . . my signs (LXX *sēmeia*), . . . and yet have tested (LXX *epeirasan*) me now these ten times, [may I perish] if they shall see the land which I swore to their fathers.
	Ps 95(LXX 94):11: Therefore I swore in my anger, [May I perish] if (*ei*) they will enter my rest.
8:13: And he left them . . .	Deut 32:20 LXX: I will turn my face from them, and I will show what will happen to them in the last days, for they are a perverse generation (*genea*).
Mark 8:14–21: discussion about leaven, hardened hearts, remembering, and numbers	Passover/exodus associations of leaven, hardened hearts, remembering, numbers
8:15: "Beware of the leaven (*zymēs*) of the Pharisees and the leaven of Herod."	Exod 12:15; 12:19; 13:6–7, etc.: Passover = the feast of unleavened bread; the house is purged of leaven before the feast begins.

Figure 19: Exodus Background to Mark 8:1–21 (continued)

	m. Pesaḥ. 3:1, a list of things that must be removed on Passover: "These are subject to a 'warning.'"
8:17: "Has your heart (kardia hymōn) been hardened?"	Ps 95:8, 10: Do not harden your hearts (kardias hymōn) . . . They are a people who err in heart (kardiạ).
8:18: "Don't you remember?" (ou mnē-moneuete)	Exod 12:14: "This day shall be a memorial (mnēmosynon) for you."
	m. Pesaḥ. 10:5 etc.: Passover especially associated with remembering
8:19: Feeding of five thousand; twelve baskets left over	Exod 15:27a: Elim—twelve springs of water
	Philo Life 1.189 and Mekilta on Exod 15:27a: These twelve springs symbolic of the twelve tribes of Israel.
	Exod 24:15–18: God calls to Moses on seventh day; he is on Mount Sinai for forty days.
	Exod 16:35 (cf. Num 14:33–34): Israelites ate manna for forty years.
	Ps 95:10: For forty years I loathed that generation; cf. Hebrews 3–4, which links the "rest" spoken of in Psalm 95 with that of the seventh day.
8:20: Feeding of four thousand; seven baskets left over	Exod 12:15, 19, 13:6–7: Passover lasts for seven days.
	Exod 15:27b: Elim—seventy palm trees; Philo Life 1.189 and Mekilta on Exod 15:27b: these trees symbolic of seventy elders; cf. discussion of symbolism of seventh day in Philo Life 1.205–7.

In common with Mark 8:10–13 is the theme of testing (*peirasmos, peirazein*), the term "this/that generation," and the Semitic idiom whereby the divine wrath is expressed by means of a clause beginning with *ei* (see the NOTE on "God forbid that a sign should be given" in 8:12). Furthermore, the mention of the wilderness (*en tē̦ erēmō̦*) provides a linkage with Mark 8:1–9, and the terminology of the hardened heart provides a linkage with Mark 8:14–21. A strong case, then, can be made for the assertion that OT and Jewish traditions about the feeding with manna, the testing at Meribah, and related stories have influenced the development of Mark 8:1–21.

Who is responsible for the arrangement of material in 8:1–21, which contributes to the exodus typology? In John 6, as Brown (2.238) points out, we encounter a sequence of material very similar to that in Mark 8:1–33 (and to the Markan doublet in 6:30–52):

John 6:1–15 (cf. Mark 8:1–9)	feeding of multitude
John 6:16–21 (cf. Mark 8:10, 13)	sea-crossing
John 6:22–59 (cf. Mark 8:14–21)	discussion about bread
John 6:30 (cf. Mark 8:11–12)	demand for a sign
John 6:60–69 (cf. Mark 8:27–30)	Peter's confession
John 6:70–71 (cf. Mark 8:31–33)	passion theme; betrayal

Though the Johannine order is slightly different from the Markan one (the demand for a sign is included in the discussion about bread, rather than preceding it), the same basic structure is visible. John, however, lacks the highly developed Markan parallels with the "testing" traditions in Exodus 17 and Psalms 78 and 95; he uses the verb *peirazein*, for example, not for the Pharisees' testing of Jesus but for Jesus' testing of his own disciples (John 6:6)! It seems likely that both Mark and John inherited a sequence of traditions that begins with a miraculous feeding and that this sequence was loosely based on traditions about the wilderness generation, but that each has developed this sequence in his own way to reflect his own characteristic concerns.

JESUS FEEDS FOUR THOUSAND PEOPLE (8:1–9)

8 ¹In those days, when there was again a big crowd and they did not have anything to eat, he summoned his disciples and said to them, ²"I take pity on the crowd, for they have remained with me for three days, and they don't have anything to eat. ³And if I send them home without eating, they will faint on the way; and some of them have come from a distance." ⁴And his disciples answered him, "Where will anyone be able to get the loaves to satisfy these people here in the wilderness?"

⁵ And he asked them, "How many loaves do you have?" And they answered, "Seven." ⁶And he commanded the crowd to sit down on the ground. And tak-

ing the seven loaves, and giving thanks, he broke them and gave them to his disciples so that they might distribute them; and they distributed them to the crowd. [7]And they had a few small fish. And he said the blessing over them and told the disciples to distribute them as well. [8]And they ate and were satisfied, and the disciples took up seven large baskets full of bread fragments. [9]And there were about four thousand people; and he sent them away.

NOTES

8 1. *In those days.* Gk *en ekeinais tais hēmerais.* On this eschatological formulae, see the introduction to the COMMENT on 1:9–11. *2 Apoc. Bar.* 29:8 uses similar formulae to describe the expected renewal of the manna in the new age: "And it will come to pass *at that time* that the treasury of manna will come down again from on high, and they will eat of it *in those years.*" On the miraculous feedings as recapitulations of the manna miracle, see the COMMENT on 6:38–42.

2. *for three days.* Gk *hēmerais treis.* This nominative phrase is unusual, because Greek usually puts words for extent of time in the accusative. The construction could be a Semitism (see Doudna, *Greek,* 74–76), but such constructions also occur in papyri (cf. MHT, 2.447). "Three days" is not always an exact phrase in biblical and Jewish literature; it can simply indicate a short period of indeterminate length (see e.g. Hos 6:2; Josephus *Ant.* 8.408; *Bib. Ant.* 56:7; Acts 28:7, 12, 17; cf. J. Bauer, "Drei Tage").

3. *And if I send them home without eating, they will faint on the way.* Gk *kai ean apolysō autous nēsteis eis oikon autōn, eklythēsontai en tē hodǭ.* The language here may be influenced by Ps 107:2–5, which speaks of those who wandered *in desert places* and whose souls *fainted* within them because of *hunger* and thirst.

some of them have come from a distance. Gk *tines autōn apo makrothen hēkasin.* In view of the wilderness setting, it is odd that only *some* of the crowd is described as coming from a distance, but there is probably a symbolic reason for the remark. In the Old Testament, non-Jewish nations are often described as "far away" (Deut 28:49; 29:22; 1 Kgs 8:41, etc.), whereas Israel is "near" to God (e.g. Ps 148:14). In ancient Judaism, therefore, to make a Gentile into a proselyte was to bring him or her near to God (e.g. *Mekilta* on Exod 18:5), and Eph 2:13 reapplies this proselyte terminology to Gentiles who become Christians (cf. Acts 2:39; 22:21; see Lincoln, *Ephesians,* 138–39, and Guelich, 404).

Danker ("Mark 8:3") points to the way in which our verse verbally echoes the Septuagint of Josh 9:6, 9, and he sees this echo as supporting the identification of the recipients of the second Markan feeding as Gentiles. In Joshua 9 the speakers are the Gibeonites, who are Hivites (Josh 9:7), one of the "seven nations" that according to Deut 7:1–2 are to be exterminated by the invading Israelites. The Gibeonites, however, escaped destruction through a ruse involving loaves of bread, which was revealed after three days (Josh 9:5, 12, 16). It is possible that our story's symbolism of seven (loaves, baskets of leftovers) and its reference to three days echo this OT narrative.

4. *Where will anyone be able to get the loaves to satisfy these people here in the wilderness.* Gk *pothen toutous dynēsetai tis hōde chortasai artōn ep' erēmias,* lit. "From where will anyone be able to satisfy these people with loaves . . . ?" On the similarity of this question to the Israelites' complaint in Exod 16:3, see the introduction to 8:1–21. The *Mekilta* on this passage highlights the difficulty of finding food and thus increases the similarity with Mark when it speaks of the wilderness as "a desolation where there is nothing." The disciples, therefore, play the role of the murmuring Israelites here, although in the next passage the Pharisees will do so (see the end of the COMMENT on the present pericope). But such fluidity of roles is no problem in biblical typology (cf. Allison, *New Moses,* 94–95).

Dynasthai, "to be able," is a significant verb in Mark, where it often refers to Jesus doing what no other human being, but only God, can do (2:7; 3:27; 5:3; 9:3, 22–23, 28–29; cf. 10:26; 15:31).

6. *giving thanks.* Gk *eucharistēsas.* This word, from which we get the term "eucharist," is used in the account of the Last Supper in Luke 22:19 and 1 Cor 11:24, though in Mark's own Last Supper scene Jesus uses the nearly synonymous *eulogēsas* ("blessing"), which matches his other feeding account (see figure 15 in the NOTES to 6:30–44). Both words can translate the Heb/Aram *brk* (see Jeremias, *Eucharistic Words,* 175), and the two feeding stories may have been influenced by variant traditions of the Last Supper. On the ambiguity about whether Jesus blesses the bread or God, see the NOTE on "said the blessing" in 6:41.

gave them to his disciples so that they might distribute them; and they distributed them to the crowd. Gk *edidou tois mathētais autou hina paratithōsin, kai parethēkan tǭ ochlǭ.* As noted in the COMMENT on 8:5–7, these clauses emphasize the disciples' mediation of Jesus' grace, and may reflect the post-Easter situation in which the Twelve and other Christian leaders officiated at the Eucharist. Matthew emphasizes apostolic mediation even more strongly, for in the distribution of the bread in both of his feeding miracles we read that Jesus "gave to the disciples, and the disciples to the crowds" (Matt 14:19; 15:36). In John, on the other hand, the disciples play no role at all in the distribution of the bread and fish; this could either be because John's high Christology and democratic ecclesiology have focused the entire feeding action in Jesus or, more likely, because Mark has heightened the role of the disciples over against the pre-Markan tradition he shares with John (see the introduction to the COMMENT section).

7. *a few small fish.* Gk *ichthydia oliga. Ichthydion,* like other Koine diminutives (see the NOTE on "dogs" in 7:27), can mean the same as the nondiminutive form (see e.g. *Barn.* 10:5, 10), but its combination here with *oliga* ("a few") suggests that it may be a true diminutive. On the nature of these fish, see the NOTE on "the two fish he divided among them all" in 6:41.

8. *the disciples took up.* Gk *ēran,* lit. "they took up." Mark's propensity for impersonal third person plurals creates confusion.

seven. Gk *epta.* Some exegetes (e.g. Pesch, 1.404) have claimed that this number supports the identification of the recipients as Gentiles, since the Gentiles were divided by Jews into seventy nations (see e.g. the seventy shepherds in the Animal Apocalypse in *1 Enoch* 83–90 and cf. Ginzberg, 5.194–95 n. 72 for rabbinic references). Upon Gentiles, moreover, were imposed seven Noachide commandments (see e.g. *t. ʿAbod. Zar.* 8:4; *b. Sanh.* 56ab), and according to some scholars, they were represented in the early church by the seven "Helle-nist" deacons of Acts 6, a rival leadership group to the "Hebrew" Twelve. See also the reference to the "seven peoples of futility" in 1QM 11:8–9.

A special connection of the number seven with Gentiles, however, is hard to prove. Seven is the most important number in the Bible and early Jewish texts, and most of its appearances have nothing to do with Gentiles, as an examina-tion of the three full pages devoted to it in the index to Ginzberg will demon-strate. As for the seven deacons of Acts, they hardly represent Gentiles, and only in an extended sense the mission to the Gentiles (cf. Guelich, 407–8). The seven Noachide commandments are a more promising link with Gentiles and form a nice contrast with the five books of Moses, which could be related to the five loaves in the other feeding. The better contrast, however, would have been between seven loaves for the Noachide commandments and ten loaves for the Decalogue. Moreover, there is no first-century evidence for a Jewish belief in *seven* Noachide commandments (the first attestation, *t. ʿAbod. Zar.* 8:4, is dated to the first half of the second century C.E. at the earliest; see Bockmuehl, "Noachide," 88–89).

Rather than being associated particularly with Gentiles, the number seven in Mark may simply have its usual Jewish nuance of fullness, which goes back to the Genesis account of the seven days of creation—a passage alluded to at the end of the previous Markan pericope (7:37). For Mark the association is especially with *eschatological* completeness and new creation, as in Revela-tion, where a complex series of sevens symbolizes both eschatological judg-ment (seven seals, seven bowls, seven trumpets) and eschatological grace (seven lampstands, seven stars, seven churches, seven spirits of God). In this association of seven with eschatological completeness, Revelation follows very much in the tradition of the Old Testament, where the time until the es-chatological change is often reckoned as seventy years (Jer 25:11–12; 29:10; Zech 1:12; 7:5) or "seventy weeks of years" (Dan 9:24). Mendels (*Rise*, 386) thinks it may be no accident that the Bar Kokhba Revolt broke out in the seventh decade after the first Jewish revolt of 66–73 C.E., and some such nu-merology may also have helped catalyze the first revolt, which forms the back-ground for our Gospel (e.g. it erupted at the beginning of the seventh decade after the assumption of direct Roman rule of Judaea in 6 C.E.). Mark's symbol-ism of seven may also go along with the Mosaic and Passover typology of our passage; Passover is a festival lasting seven days (Exod 12:14), and Moses spent six days on Mount Sinai before ascending further to receive the Torah on the seventh (Exod 24:16; cf. "after six days" in Mark 9:2).

large baskets. Gk *spyridas.* The *spyris* was a large mat basket for provisions; the one used in Acts 9:25 is big enough to carry a person (see Cranfield, 257). The word does not have the special association with Jews that its counterpart in 6:43, *kophinos*, does.

9. *four thousand*. Gk *tetrakischilioi*. This number occurs several times in biblical and Jewish sources. In 1 Sam 4:2 the Philistines kill four thousand Israelites, and in 1 Chr 23:5 the Temple has four thousand gatekeepers and four thousand musicians. Both Philo (*Every Good Man Is Free* 75) and Josephus (*Ant.* 18.20) mention that the Essenes numbered more than four thousand. Acts 21:38 describes four thousand "assassins" joining an Egyptian revolutionary. Because of the exodus typology of our passage, it is interesting that Ginzberg (3.236) mentions a legend according to which each of the four groups of tribes occupied an area of four thousand cubits, but the source cited (*Yal.* 1.426) is so late that it is shaky evidence for our period. Also intriguing, because of the expectation of the regathering of the Ten Lost Tribes in a new exodus, is the statement in Jer 52:30 that the number of Babylonian exiles was 4,600 — but 4,600 is not four thousand. It is difficult to find a common denominator in these biblical and Jewish usages; four thousand seems merely to be a round number for a large group (see Quesnell, *Mind*, 273).

Because of the difficulty of determining a specific meaning for four thousand, some scholars have reduced the symbolism of four thousand to that of four (such a reduction is not totally implausible in view of Revelation 7, where the twelve thousand "sealed" servants of God are obviously related to the twelve tribes of Israel). Those who have done so have generally seen the number as a reference to the Gentiles, who are presumed to be people who come from the four corners of the earth or the four winds. The association between the number four and the Gentiles, however, is not particularly prominent in Jewish sources or in the New Testament, and the Q passage often quoted in its support, Matt 8:11–12//Luke 13:28–29, is probably an allusion to the ingathering of Israel, not to the inclusion of Gentiles in the kingdom of God (see Allison, "Who Will Come").

COMMENT

Introduction. The transition from the story of the healing of the deaf-mute in 7:31–37 to the story of the feeding of the four thousand in 8:1–9 is partly accomplished through intertextual connections. We have seen that the biblical allusions in 7:37, which are to Gen 1:31 and Isa 35:5–6, suggest that Jesus' healings are part of a creative feat comparable to the primordial act of creation and that they signal the advent of God's new age. It is probably no accident, therefore, that the first words of the new pericope are the eschatological formula "in those days" (see the NOTE on "In those days" in 8:1). Moreover, the second of the two passages alluded to in Mark 7:37, Isa 35:5–6, occurs in a context that speaks of the wilderness rejoicing and miraculously blossoming (Isa 35:1–2, 6–7); this context may be partly responsible for Mark's placement immediately afterward of a passage about a miracle in the wasteland. Mark highlights this desert location with the disciples' stage-setting question, "Where will anyone be able to get the loaves to satisfy these people here in the wilderness?" (8:4).

This question, however, poses one of the main exegetical issues of our passage: how could anyone who, like the disciples, had shortly before seen Jesus' miraculous feeding of five thousand people in the wilderness (6:30–44) doubt his ability to feed four thousand people in the same way? The disciples' question, rather, sounds like the reaction of people who have never witnessed such an event, and indeed such questions are a frequent feature of miracle stories, where they function to highlight the unprecedented nature of the wonder that is about to occur (see e.g. Gen 17:17; 18:12; Mark 5:35; 16:3; Luke 1:18, 34; John 6:5, 9; 11:37). This "knot" in the narrative, together with the striking parallels between the two passages, suggests to many commentators that 6:30–44 and 8:1–10 are variant accounts of the same event, both of which Mark has inherited from tradition.

But not all scholars agree. In the introduction to the COMMENT on 6:30–44 we have noted that Fowler (*Loaves*) thinks that Mark has created the feeding of the five thousand on the model of the feeding of the four thousand. Donfried ("Feeding Narratives"), on the other hand, asserts the reverse, pointing to what he considers to be the pervasiveness of Markan duplicate expressions throughout 8:1–9. Against both theories is the fact that the literarily independent Gospel of John (6:1–14) parallels *both* Markan stories, suggesting that both existed in pre-Markan tradition (see figure 20 and the NOTE on "giving thanks" in 8:6). Nor, so far as Donfried's argument is concerned, are the majority of examples he cites really duplications; nor is it safe to assume that the oral tradition lacked all repetition.

This is not to deny that Mark has done some editing in 8:1–9, as he has in 6:30–44. He has probably written the first part of 8:1, which contains many Markan features, such as "in those days" (cf. 1:9; 13:17, 24), *palin* ("again"), the genitive absolute construction, "a big crowd," and *proskaleomai* ("summoned"; cf. Fowler, *Loaves*, 47–51). He may also be responsible for the clause about members of the crowd coming from a distance in 8:3, which fits into his evident desire to present the recipients of this feeding as Gentiles (see the NOTE on "some of them have come from a distance" in 8:3), and for the notes about the disciples' agency in 8:6–7, which are not in the Johannine parallel and go along with Mark's conception of the disciples as people chosen "in order that they might be with him" (3:14).

The overall structure of our passage is very similar to that of 6:30–44, with the exception of the stage-setting and description of the seating of the crowd, which are both less elaborate than those in the earlier story. The narrative falls into three main parts: the description of the problem, namely the lack of food and the distance from a source of it (8:1–4), the feeding itself (8:5–7), and the concluding notes about the amount of leftovers, the number of people fed, and Jesus' dismissal of the crowd (8:8–9). A rough chiasm can be observed; it would be perfect were it not for the separate multiplication and distribution of the fish in 8:7, which is probably a Markan addition (it is not a separate action in Mark 6:30–44 or John 6:1–15):

8:1a	Large crowd present	
8:2b–3		Nothing to eat
8:4		Disciples' question: how feed so many?
8:5–6a		Multiplication of loaves
8:6b		Disciples' instrumentality in distribution
8:7		Multiplication and distribution of fish
8:8		They ate and were satisfied; quantity of leftovers
8:9	Four thousand in crowd; he sent them away	

8:1–4: the problem. Somewhat unusually for Mark, our passage does not begin with a change of location on the part of Jesus and the disciples. One assumes, therefore, that the setting is still the Decapolis region of the previous passage, an area dominated by Gentiles. A crowd of these Gentiles congregates around Jesus, and he has compassion on them, which he expresses by bringing their need for food to the attention of his disciples (8:1–2a). In our story, then, as in John 6, but differently from Mark 6, Jesus takes the initiative in helping the crowd by making the disciples aware of their problem. The comment in John 6:6 that Jesus was thereby testing his disciples conveys the sense of Mark's narrative as well.

Specifically, the Markan Jesus mentions that the crowd has been with him in the wilderness for three days and now has nothing to eat (8:2b). The motif of the three days emphasizes the magnitude of the emergency, and it may be related to the biblical tradition that God helps his people on the third day or after three days (see e.g. Hos 6:2; cf. Lehmann, *Auferweckt*, passim). But in the Markan context it may also be intended to foreshadow God's display of eschatological saving power "on the third day," i.e. at Jesus' resurrection (cf. the COMMENT on the "raising" of Jairus' daughter in 5:35–43).

Mark further emphasizes the problem faced by the stranded crowd when he has Jesus mention that, if he sends the people away without food, they may faint on the way, "for some of them have come from a distance" (8:3). This clause, which may be editorial, supports the claim made by some scholars that those fed in our passage are non-Jews and that the passage continues the Gentile theme found in 7:24–30 and 7:31–37. For from the Jewish point of view Gentiles were people who were "far away" from God, and some early Christian texts reflect this image (see the NOTE on "some of them have come from a distance" in 8:3). This perception of a Gentile theme in 8:1–9 is not necessarily incompatible with the assertion that our passage has important Old Testament background of the passage in the traditions about the miraculous feedings of the *Israelites* in the wilderness, since some (admittedly late) Jewish traditions assert that the pagans knew about the Jews' manna and wished to partake of it (see Ginzberg, 3.45; 6.18 n. 103), and in any case biblical typology can be very elastic (cf. the NOTE on "Where will anyone be able to get the loaves to satisfy these people" in 8:4). Matthew, who does *not* seem to think that those fed in our passage are Gentiles, chooses to omit the words about the people coming from a distance (see Davies and Allison, 2.563–64).

Figure 20: The Markan and Johannine Feeding Miracles

Mark 6:34–45	Mark 8:1–9	John 6:5–16
He saw a great crowd	When there was again a great crowd	Lifting up his eyes and beholding a great crowd
	and they didn't have anything to eat	
and had pity on them	Jesus: "I have pity on the crowd,	
Since the hour was already late		
his disciples said: "Send them away . . . that they might buy something to eat"	for they have been with me for three days and they haven't had anything to eat	Jesus to Philip: "Whence (pothen) shall we buy loaves in order that these people may eat?"
	And if I send them away hungry to their houses, they will faint on the way	
	For some of them have come from a distance."	
		This he said, testing (peirazōn) him, for he himself knew what he was about to do.
Jesus: "You give them something to eat"		
Disciples: "Shall we buy 200 denarii worth of bread and give them to eat?"	Disciples: "Whence (pothen) will anyone be able to satisfy these people with loaves here in the wilderness?"	Philip: "200 denarii worth of loaves would not suffice them, so that each should get a little"
Jesus: "How many loaves do you have?"	Jesus: "How many loaves do you have?"	

Figure 20: The Markan and Johannine Feeding Miracles (continued)

Mark 6:34–45	*Mark 8:1–9*	*John 6:5–16*
Disciples: Five, and two fish (*ichthyas*)	Disciples: Seven	Andrew: "A boy here has five barley loaves and two prepared fish (*opsaria*), but what are these among so many?"
And he commanded them to seat (*anaklinai*) the people on the green grass	And he commanded the crowd to sit (*anapesein*) on the ground	And he said, "Make the people sit down (*anapesein*)"
		And there was much grass in the place
		So the men (*andres*) sat down (*anepesan*),
		about 5,000 in number
And taking the five loaves and the two fish,	And taking the seven loaves	So Jesus took the loaves
Looking up into heaven		
he blessed (*eulogēsen*)	and giving thanks (*eucharistēsas*)	and giving thanks (*eucharistēsas*)
And broke (*kateklasen*) the loaves	He broke (*eklasen*)	He meted out (*diedōken*)
And gave to the disciples	And gave to his disciples	
so that they might distribute (*paratithōsin*) to them	so that they might distribute (*paratithōsin*)	
	and they distributed (*parethēkan*) to the crowd	to those reclining
	And they had a few small fish (*ichthydia*)	
And he divided the two fish (*ichthyas*) among them all	And blessing them he said to distribute these also	and of the prepared fish (*opsariōn*) as much as they wanted

Figure 20: The Markan and Johannine Feeding Miracles (continued)

Mark 6:34–45	Mark 8:1–9	John 6:5–16
And they all ate and were satisfied (*echortasthēsan*)	And they ate and were satisfied (*echortasthēsan*)	And when they were full (*eneplēsthēsan*)
		he said to his disciples, "Gather together the remaining (*perisseusanta*) fragments . . . "
And they took up twelve baskets (*kophinōn*) full (*plērōmata*) of fragments and fish	And they took up seven large baskets (*spyridas*) full (*perisseumata*) of fragments	So they gathered together and filled twelve baskets (*kophinous*) of fragments from the five barley loaves
And the eaters were 5,000 men	And there were 4,000	(See above: 5,000)
He made the disciples embark,	And he sent them away	(At evening disciples go down to sea and embark)
while he sent the crowd away	And immediately getting into the boat with his disciples he went away	Jesus goes off to mountain alone

The disciples, however, respond to Jesus' compassionate hint that he means to do something for the Gentile crowd with a skeptical question: "Where will anyone be able to get the loaves to satisfy these people here in the wilderness?" (8:4). This question, which as we have noted is illogical in view of the disciples' knowledge of the previous miraculous feeding, serves a number of purposes. As we have seen, it emphasizes the impressiveness of the miracle that will ensue by underlining its difficulty. It also contributes to the exodus typology that runs through our passage and this entire section of the Gospel, since it has striking verbal parallels to the references to Israel's wilderness wanderings in Ps 78:19–20 and Num 11:13–14 (see figure 19 in the introduction to 8:1–21). Thematically, too, it reproduces Old Testament patterns, since in the Pentateuch the Israelites doubted and grumbled even after God had saved them miraculously at the Sea of Reeds and had sustained them with manna in the wilderness, and partly for this reason there are in the Pentateuch two accounts of miraculous feeding in the wilderness (Exodus 16; Numbers 11), just as there are in Mark.

But the disciples' question is also important precisely because its incredible obtuseness fits into a developing Markan theme. The same twelve disciples who ask it have recently seen Jesus work just the sort of miracle that they now declare to be impossible (6:30–44), and Mark subtly reminds his readers of this previous feeding by beginning the passage with the words "In those days, when there was *again* a big crowd . . ." (8:1a). Even a comparison between the numbers involved in our story and those involved in the earlier feeding underlines the disciples' dullness, since they have previously seen five thousand people fed with five loaves; it is ludicrous, therefore, for them to panic now, when they have started out with a greater number of loaves (seven) and are confronted by a smaller crowd (four thousand; see Lührmann, 135). In our passage, then, Mark lays the groundwork for Jesus' diatribe in 8:14–21 on the subject of apostolic understanding.

Yet the words put into the disciples' mouths are not just an expression of culpable misunderstanding. For, on a deeper level, and in a symbolic, almost Johannine manner, they express a universal human question and striving: where, in the vast desert of this world, is the spiritual nourishment to be found that can meet the hunger of the multitudes? Who can provide such "bread of life"? This sort of interpretation of the feeding miracle is compatible not only with the treatment of the incident in the Fourth Gospel but also with its development in Mark 6:30–44, where Jesus' teaching is a prominent motif (6:34), and with the recollection of both feedings in 8:14–21, where leaven and bread are linked with misunderstanding and spiritual blindness.

8:5–7: the feeding itself. The disciples' question is quickly answered: *Jesus* can provide bread in the wilderness, for he has a source of power that is given to him not by human beings but "from heaven" (cf. 11:30).

The feeding itself is described in much the same terms as were used for that in 6:30–44, and like the previous feeding it both recalls the exodus and anticipates the Christian Eucharist and the messianic banquet (cf. the COMMENT on 6:38–42 and the NOTE on "giving thanks" in 8:6). Every year at Passover Jews remembered the way in which God had provided manna in the wilderness out of nothing, just as Jesus does in our passage, and they looked for a renewal of this manna miracle and for a great feast, sometimes to be hosted by the Messiah, in the age to come (see e.g. Isa 25:6–8; 1 Enoch 62:12–14; 2 Apoc. Bar. 29:1–4; Matt 8:11–12//Luke 13:28–29; cf. D. E. Smith, "Messianic Banquet"). Christians interpreted Jesus' feeding miracles as a partial fulfillment of these hopes, and they also saw them as pointing forward both to their own eucharistic celebrations and to "the marriage supper of the Lamb" in the kingdom of God (Rev 19:9)—a combination that is not surprising, since the Eucharist was conceived both as a recapitulation of the exodus and as an anticipation of the messianic banquet. A fish dinner was also part of some Jewish memories of the exodus and of expectations for the age to come, and fish became a standard part of Christian eucharistic iconography (cf. the NOTE on "the two fish he divided among them all" in 6:41). Our passage, then, reinforces the exodus, eucharistic, and eschatological nuances of the first feeding.

It is also like the first passage in its emphasis on the important role played by the disciples. Jesus first asks them how many loaves they have (8:5); hearing their response, he commands the crowd to sit on the ground (8:6a), then says grace and distributes the loaves through the disciples (8:6b). Finally, he blesses and distributes the fish as well (8:7). As compared to the previous feeding narrative, our passage denies to the disciples the task of seating the multitude, but it emphasizes more strongly their instrumentality in distributing the food: Jesus gives the loaves "to his disciples so that they might distribute them; and they distributed them to the crowd" (8:6b) The disciples play the same intermediary role in the distribution of the fish (8:7b). This mediation probably has something to do with the eucharistic symbolism of the distribution (see the NOTE on "giving thanks" in 8:6); it may well reflect the post-Easter situation in which the Twelve and other church leaders officiated at the Eucharist. Mark, therefore, is not totally negative about the disciples, even in a passage in which they display truly monumental stupidity, and this is a significant hint about his view of their future: despite their foibles, they will be used by Jesus to transmit the gift of God to the multitudes.

8:8–9: *aftermath*. The passage concludes with brief comments about the satisfaction of the crowd, the amount of the leftovers (seven baskets), the number of eaters (four thousand), and Jesus' dismissal of the crowd. The numbers have attracted a great deal of attention from scholars, and some think that they indicate that the crowd is to be understood as a Gentile group. While it is probably true that our passage *does* imply a feeding of Gentiles, it is questionable whether this conclusion is greatly supported by the symbolism of seven and four thousand (see the NOTES on "seven" in 8:8 and "four thousand" in 8:9). The more important of these two numbers is seven, which is highlighted by its three occurrences in our passage (8:5, 6, and 8) and which will be stressed again in 8:20. And seven does not seem to be *particularly* associated with Gentiles, either in Jewish sources or in Mark. If it has any special associations in our passage, it is with the notion of eschatological fullness and with the identification of Jesus as a Mosaic figure.

The feeding of the four thousand, then, is, for those with eyes to see, a "secret epiphany" revealing that, through Jesus, God's eschatological power is beginning to flood the wilderness of this world. The doors of heaven have been opened (cf. 1:10) and, as happened once under Moses, the treasury of the manna is coming down again from on high (cf. *2 Apoc. Bar.* 29:8). It is all the more ironic, then, that in the very next passage Moses' self-proclaimed disciples, the Pharisees, will challenge Jesus to perform a sign from heaven and will thereby unwittingly reprise the role of the murmuring Israelites in the wilderness.

JESUS IS PUT TO THE TEST BY
THE PHARISEES (8:10–13)

8 ^{10}And immediately he entered the boat with his disciples and went to the region of Dalmanutha. ^{11}And the Pharisees came out and began to dispute with him, seeking from him a sign from heaven, testing him. ^{12}And he sighed in his spirit and said, "Why does this generation seek a sign? Amen, I say to you, God forbid that a sign should be given to this generation." ^{13}And he left them and again entered the boat and went away to the other side.

NOTES

8 10. *the region of Dalmanutha.* Gk *ta merē Dalmanoutha,* lit. "the parts of Dalmanutha." Unfortunately, no locality of this name is known from ancient sources. Nestle ("Dalmanutha") suggests that the name arises from Mark's misunderstanding of the Aramaic phrase *dî* ("which") + *lĕ* ("belonging to") + *mĕnātāh* ("the portion"), i.e. "which belongs to the territory of," which corresponds to the preceding words in Greek (*ta merē*). It is also possible, however, that Mark knows of a town that has left no other trace in the sources. Matt 15:39 replaces Dalmanutha with another name, but the Matthean manuscripts are divided as to what it is; some change the location to Magdala, a town on the northwest shore of the Sea of Galilee, while others change it to Magadan, which like Dalmanutha is unknown (see Strange, "Dalmanutha"). In any case, Mark locates Dalmanutha on the western, more Jewish shore of the lake; the Pharisees are there, and the subsequent crossing removes Jesus to Bethsaida, on the eastern shore (8:13, 21).

11. *dispute . . . seeking.* Gk *syzētein . . . zētountes.* The word translated "seeking" is the uncompounded form of the verb translated "dispute." The latter, *syzētein,* is used without the nuance of hostility in 1:27 and 9:10, but with the nuance of debating in the present passage and in 9:14, 16; 12:28.

sign. Gk *sēmeion.* In the Old Testament and Jewish traditions it is not always a mark of disobedience to God to request a sign. Gideon famously "laid a fleece before the Lord" in order to ascertain whether or not God had chosen him as his instrument of military deliverance (Judg 6:36–40), and Hezekiah asked for and received a sign that he would be healed of his grave illness, apparently without censure from the biblical narrator (2 Kgs 20:8–11). God, moreover, positively *insisted* that Ahaz ask for a sign from heaven to confirm that he would deliver Judah (Isa 7:10–12); here it was an act of disobedience for the proud king to refuse to test God.

But elsewhere in the tradition skepticism is expressed about signs, and there is a more negative attitude toward humans who request them. In Deut 13:1–5, for example, a sign-working prophet who preaches apostasy is to be put to death, and the New Testament, including Mark, describes false prophets who work signs and wonders (Mark 13:22; Rev 13:13). The rabbis were divided on the subject of signs. On the one hand, some approved even of the signs requested by the wicked, and cited the examples of Hezekiah and other heroes of the faith for the principle that, if signs were permissible to the righteous, they were all the more so to the wicked (see e.g. *Exod. Rab.* 9.1). But other rabbis viewed signs as evil and interpreted Hezekiah's request for one as a sin (*b. Sanh.* 104a). In Mark 8:10–13 Jesus seems to belong to the antisign camp, and Mark describes the Pharisees' request for a sign as a "testing," a term that has a demonic overtone (see the NOTE on "testing" below).

To be sure, later in the Gospel the Markan Jesus himself will respond positively to his disciples' request to tell them the sign that the eschatological events are about to occur (Mark 13:4–31). But these are two different kinds of signs; that demanded in 8:11–13 is an authentication that Jesus is telling the truth, whereas that requested by the disciples in chapter 13 is a clue concerning the eschatological timetable (on these two types of signs, cf. Gray, *Prophetic Figures*, 123–30). Both types of signs appear in the famous and funny story in *b. Sanh.* 98a in which R. Yose b. Qisma's disciples first ask him what the harbinger of the Messiah's coming will be, then request a sign that his words are true. Here the eschatological sign requested is related to the coming of the Messiah, and other rabbinic traditions suggest that the Messiah himself is supposed to produce authenticating signs (see e.g. the story about Bar Kokhba in *b. Sanh.* 93b). The latter expectation may be partly based on a coalescence of the figure of the Messiah with that of the Prophet-like Moses (see e.g. *Eccl. Rab.* 1:9) and the memory that Moses had worked confirmatory miracles (cf. Martyn, *History and Theology*, 106–11, and Allison, *New Moses*, 85–90). It is probable that this coalescence was already beginning in the first century; it is assumed by NT passages such as Acts 3:17–26 and John 1:43–51; 6:14–15, and may be reflected in the references to an Egyptian prophet who promised a sign reminiscent of Moses' successor, Joshua, and intended to set himself up as king (see Josephus *J.W.* 2.261–62; *Ant.* 20.169, and Acts 21:38). The popular expectation that the Messiah would be a Mosaic figure who would work signs, then, is probably part of the background to the Pharisees' demand in Mark 8:11, especially in view of the strong Mosaic typology of this section of the Gospel. (Gray [*Prophetic Figures*, 125–28, 137, 141–42] is skeptical about the Mosaic dimension of the Jewish sign prophets, but the combination in Josephus' descriptions of these prophets of the motifs of liberation, miracles, wilderness location, and divine providence recalls his narratives about Moses.)

from heaven. Gk *apo tou ouranou.* "From heaven" could be taken literally (cf. Matt 24:30; Luke 21:11, 25; Rev 12:1, 3; 15:1), or it could be a circumlocution for "from God." The circumlocution interpretation seems more likely, since it is supported by the passive *dothēsetai* ("will be given") in 8:12, which implies divine agency, and by the parallel in 11:30–31, where an almost identical phrase is used as a periphrasis for God, and the context, as in our passage, has to do with the authority of Jesus. Gibson ("Jesus' Refusal," 43) attempts to dissociate our passage from 11:30–31 by pointing out that the latter employs *ex ouranou* rather than *apo tou ouranou*, but this slight difference is well within the normal range of Markan stylistic variation. Gibson also argues that, if *apo tou ouranou* in our passage meant "from God," it would be superfluous and redundant, since "it was of the very nature of 'signs' to be 'from God.'" According to 13:22, however, signs and wonders can be produced by false Christs and false prophets.

Davies and Allison (2.580) also argue for the literal interpretation, since for them it helps to explain the paradox that the Pharisees demand a miracle after one has just been performed: the feeding of the four thousand happened *on earth* (cf. 8:6), while the Pharisees are asking for a sign *from heaven*. In private correspondence Allison also points to Matt 24:24–30, where there seems to be a contrast between signs on the earth and a definitive cosmic sign from heaven. But in the next verse of the present passage Jesus seems to be discussing not atmospheric signs in particular but divine harbingers in general: *no* sign of any sort will be given "to this generation" (8:12).

testing. Gk *peirazontes.* This multilayered word combines nuances of examination, temptation, and provocation. On its background in the account of the "testing" of God by the Israelites at Massa and Meribah in Exod 17:1–7 and related traditions, see the introduction to 8:1–21. The plausibility of this typology is increased by the prominence of the Massa-and-Meribah tradition in later Old Testament, early Jewish, and early Christian retellings. The story was important enough to be mentioned several times subsequently in the Pentateuch (Deut 6:16; 9:22; 33:8) and in Ps 95:7–11. As the introduction to 8:1–21 and figure 19 there show, moreover, the themes and even the vocabulary of these retellings of the Massa story, particularly of Psalm 95, are echoed in our passage (testing in the wilderness, "this generation," oath formula with "if . . ."). And Hebrews 3–4 demonstrates that the account of the Massa-and-Meribah incident in Psalm 95, which conflates Massa and Meribah with the judgment of Israel at Kadesh in Numbers 14, was of interest to first-century Christians (cf. Lane, *Hebrews*, 1.85).

Besides invoking the story of Massa and Meribah, "testing" here may also have a demonic nuance. In Matt 4:3 and 1 Thess 3:5 Satan is "the tester" or "tempter" (*ho peirazōn*), and some Jewish traditions linked Satan with the testing of God in the wilderness (see e.g. *b. Šabb.* 89a; *Exod. Rab.* 43.1; *Pirqe R. El.* 45). Jesus' sigh in the next verse also supports the Satanic interpretation (cf. the NOTE on "sighed" in 8:12). In the Q passage Matt 4:5–7//Luke 4:9–12, interestingly, two of Satan's "tests" are challenges that Jesus prove his divine sonship by performing miraculous signs, one of which is turning stones into *bread*. Jesus responds with a quotation of Deut 6:16, which is a reference to the incident at Massah and Meribah (see Lövestam, *This Generation*, 24). There is thus a traditional connection between the testing of Jesus, the person of Satan, bread, and the Pentateuchal story about the testing of God at Massa and Meribah.

It is also interesting that John includes the word *peirazōn* in his account of miraculous feeding (John 6:6), whereas Mark uses it in the passage that follows one of the feedings. This coincidence may be explained by John's awareness of the Mosaic background to the feeding story (cf. his allusion to the "murmuring" traditions in 6:41, 43, 61). In John, however, the image is used differently: the people are not testing Jesus, but Jesus is testing them! This idea also has background in the wilderness traditions (see Exod 20:20).

12. *sighed*. Gk *astenaxas*, lit. "having sighed." The same verb is used in the exorcism-like healing in 7:34, where it seems to suggest a struggle with a demonic obstacle (see the NOTE on "sighed" in 7:34); it probably has a similar Satanic nuance here (see the NOTE on "testing" in 8:11).

this generation. Gk *hē genea hautē*. As Lövestam shows in an excellent short monograph ("This Generation," 8, 13, 18, 22), the primary background to this repeated NT phrase lies in OT and Jewish traditions about the evil generations of the flood and of the wilderness. The latter is the more important background, since most of the NT occurrences of "this generation" verbally echo Deut 1:35 and 32:5, 20 (Matt 16:4; Mark 8:38; 9:19; Matt 17:17//Luke 9:41; Matt 12:39//Luke 11:29; Acts 2:40). One similarity to Jewish traditions about the flood, however, is that Noah, like Jesus here, is not considered to belong to the "generation" in which he lives (see e.g. *Gen. Rab.* 30.1 and *Midr. Ps.* 1.12 on Psalm 1:6).

God forbid that a sign should be given. Gk *ei dothēsetai . . . sēmeion*, lit. "if a sign will be given." The Q parallel (Matt 12:39//Luke 11:29) reads, "No sign will be given" (*sēmeion ou dothēsetai*). The Markan version articulates the same thought through an abbreviated form of a Semitic expression (cf. Gen 14:23; Deut 1:35; Ps 95:11, etc.) whereby a speaker implies a curse upon himself if something should happen or should be allowed to happen (the expanded form of the idiom is seen in 2 Kgs 6:31: "So may God do to me, and more, if the head of Elisha son of Shaphat stays on his shoulders today"; see Lane, 278). The vocabulary and effect are similar to those of the "Valley Girl" expression "As if!"

Despite his statement that no sign will be given to "this generation," in 13:22 the Markan Jesus prophesies that false Christs and false prophets will arise and give signs that will deceive even the elect. According to 13:30, moreover, these deceitful signs will happen within "this generation." The contradiction may be resolved, however, by recognizing that *dothēsetai* ("will be given") in 8:12 is a divine passive (see the GLOSSARY), as is the same word in 4:25. *God* will not give authenticating signs on demand through Jesus, but the false prophets will give deceitful signs, and will be followed by the masses; cf. John 5:43.

COMMENT

Introduction. After performing his second miraculous feeding, Jesus crosses the sea, presumably reentering Jewish territory (see the NOTE on "the region of Dalmanutha" in 8:10), where he confronts the Pharisees again. This time the latter hostilely demand a miraculous sign from him—presumably to authenticate the sovereign, Moses-like legislative authority he arrogated to himself in their last encounter (7:1–15; on the expectation that the Messiah would be a Moses-like figure who would perform miracles, see the NOTE on "sign" in 8:11). Jesus refuses and departs.

The passage has a number of peculiarities. It is short, its ending is anticlimactic, and it describes a puzzlingly brief and inconsequential trip: Jesus crosses the sea, exchanges three sentences with the Pharisees, then immediately crosses back. The Pharisees' demand for a sign is also unusual, since in the Old Testament, Jewish traditions, and the New Testament, signs are most frequently requested or given in order to confirm explicit or implicit claims that have previously been made (see e.g. Judg 6:36–40; 2 Kgs 20:8–11; Isa 7:10–12; John 2:18–19; 6:30–31, *b. Sanh.* 98a; cf. Linton, "Demand"); this is true even in the Q parallel to our passage (Matt 12:38–42//Luke 11:29–32). In our story, however, the Pharisees demand a sign without Jesus having made any claim in the immediate context. The genre is anomalous as well. The passage cannot really be classed as a controversy narrative or pronouncement story (against Taylor, *Formation*, 78–79). Jesus' reply, unlike that in the Q parallel, is not the sort of conclusive, theologically loaded riposte one usually associates with such controversy narratives: how is it a convincing response to a demand for a sign merely to say that no sign will be given? Our story, then, gives the impression of being a fragment of an originally longer tale, perhaps one more like Q, although Mark is probably not literarily dependent on Q (see Tuckett, "Mark and Q," 158–62, and Gibson, *Temptations*, 156–57; cf. the discussion of Gospel relationships in the INTRODUCTION). Mark himself may be responsible for truncating the tale, for reasons that will be suggested at the end of this COMMENT.

Mark may have shaped the story in other ways as well. The "framework" verses 8:10, 13 employ characteristic Markan vocabulary ("immediately," "entered," "boat," "with the disciples," "again," "went away," "the other side") and therefore were probably heavily edited by the evangelist, though the motif of a sea-crossing was probably already present in the pre-Markan narrative, as it is there in the literarily independent John 6 (see the introduction to 8:1–21). It is probable, moreover, that it is Mark himself who has turned Jesus' interlocutors in 8:11 into Pharisees, Jesus' constant enemies in the Gospel; Luke 11:29 (Q) and John 6:22–59 lack the reference to them. Indeed, the entire first half of verse 11 is probably from the evangelist, given its typical Markan vocabulary ("came out," "Pharisees," "began to"). The redundant phrase "testing him" at the end may be his as well (cf. the references to Pharisees testing Jesus in 10:2 and 12:15).

In its present form the passage is chiastically structured:

8:10   Jesus enters boat and goes to Dalmanutha (across the Sea of Galilee)
8:11   Pharisees come out and test him by demanding a sign
8:12a   Jesus sighs and asks why "this generation" demands a sign
8:12b   Jesus rejects demand for a sign
8:13   Jesus enters boat and goes to other side of sea

The center of the chiasm is not the refusal of the sign but the question of why it has been demanded. Mark thus focuses attention again on "the mystery of the dominion of God," the perplexing conundrum of why God's eschatological power, instead of overwhelming all opposition, meets with skepticism and rejection from "this generation" (cf. the COMMENT on 4:3–8).

8:10–13: the request for a sign and its rejection. The passage begins with Jesus crossing the sea back into Jewish Galilee; there the Pharisees "come out" to dispute with him (8:10). Though "to come or go out" (*exerchesthai*) is a common enough verb in Mark, and it can be used with reference to Jesus (1:35, 38; 4:3, etc.) or other positive characters (2:12; 6:12, etc.), its usage with respect to the Pharisees may be meant to link them with the "outsiders" of 4:11 (cf. the COMMENT on 3:31–35). This symbolic nuance of "came out" would fit with the blindness the Pharisees display in our passage, which recalls that of the outsiders in 4:12 (looking without seeing, hearing without understanding).

This blindness is reflected in the Pharisees' demand that Jesus perform a miraculous sign (8:11), in spite of the fact that he has just performed a notable one, the feeding of the four thousand. Mark gives no indication, to be sure, that the Pharisees have seen that feeding, but they certainly know about other miracles of Jesus, for example his exorcisms, which they have hostilely misinterpreted as evidence of demonic collusion in 3:22. But just as in that earlier Markan passage Jesus turned the Pharisees' charge round and showed that it was *they*, not he, who were guilty of "blasphemy against the Holy Spirit" and thus on the side of Satan (3:28–30), so in our passage Mark unmasks the Pharisaic hostility to Jesus as an instance of demonically inspired "testing" (see the NOTES on "testing" in 8:11 and "sighed" in 8:12).

In seeking a sign despite the existence of previous signs, the Markan Pharisees undermine their own legitimacy not only through their illogic but also through their demonstration that they are the spiritual heirs of the disobedient wilderness generation, who rejected Moses by demanding signs even after they had seen astounding ones in Egypt and on the Reed Sea (see Lövestam, *This Generation*, 24). We have noted in the introductions to 6:6b–8:21 and to 8:1–21 that the wilderness traditions of the Pentateuch and their Jewish interpretations provide significant background to the present section of the Gospel (6:6b–8:21). In the preceding Markan narrative, the feeding of the four thousand (8:1–9), the manna story of Exodus 16 was particularly reflected. That Exodus story is immediately followed by the narrative of Israel's "testing" of Yahweh at Massa and Meribah (Exod 17:1–7), and the latter seems to be especially reflected in our passage. Both LXX Exod 17:2, 7 and Mark 8:11, for example, use the verb *peirazein* for the testing of God or his agent by the disobedient people (cf. the cognate noun *peirasmos* in Exod 17:7, which is the translation for "Massa"). In both cases the "test" is a demand for the performance of a miraculous sign; Moses is cajoled to produce water in the midst of a parched wilderness, in order to prove that God is with the Israelites (see

Exod 17:7), while Jesus is challenged to accomplish a wonder that will authenticate his authority (cf. 11:28). Some rabbinic traditions, moreover (e.g. *Sipre* on Num 11:22 [§95]), suggest that the people's request for a sign was disingenuous and was really designed to rid them of Moses' authority; the Pharisees' demand in Mark 8:11 seems to be similarly mischievous, as is indicated by the possibly redactional concluding phrase, "testing him." There seems to be little doubt, then, that in the first thirteen verses of chapter 8 the Markan narrative is following the order of events in Exod 16:1–17:7, first describing a miraculous feeding in the wilderness, then depicting a culpable testing by the demand for a sign. A small but possibly significant difference between Exod 17:1–7 and Mark 8:10–13, however, may reflect Mark's high estimation of Jesus. In Exodus it is God who is tested, not Moses, although the people's carping at Moses is a sign of their disobedience to God, and some later rabbinic traditions (e.g. *Mekilta* on Exod 17:2) use the wording of Exod 17:2 to make the point that quarreling with Moses is equivalent to quarreling with God. In Mark, however, Jesus himself is tested and thus assumes the role of God in the Exodus narrative.

Jesus responds to the Pharisees' "test," their hostile demand for a sign, by sighing (8:12a), which is a further hint at the demonic nature of the request (cf. 7:34), and by asking rhetorically, "Why does this generation seek a sign?" (8:12b). Here the point is not that signs should never be requested. It is, rather, that it is fruitless for *the Pharisees* to demand them, since their hostility to God's eschatological action in Jesus marks them out as belonging to "this generation" and therefore as being the recipients of his wrath, not of his gracious revelation (on the ambivalent biblical attitude to signs, see the NOTE on "sign" in 8:11). The term "this generation," significantly, has its primary biblical background in the stories about the wilderness generation that struggled against Moses (see the NOTE on "this generation" in 8:12). Like that evil generation, which perished in the wilderness and never attained the promised land, the Pharisees and their followers will not receive what they request. On the contrary, Jesus swears that a sign will never be given (*dothēsetai*) to them, just as in Num 14:21–23 and Psalm 95 God, in response to the Massah incident and other "tests" (cf. *b. ʿArak.* 15a), pronounces judgment with the same sort of oath formula on the wilderness generation, which is termed "this generation" in Psalm 95 (cf. the NOTE on "God forbid that a sign should be given" in 8:12). The attentive reader of Mark might also recall the usage of *dothēsetai* ("will be given") in 4:25 and add the corollary that even what this generation "has" will be taken away from it by divine judgment, just as the rabbis concluded that the wilderness generation had no portion in the world to come (*m. Sanh.* 10:3; cf. Hebrews 3–4). In token of this coming judgment, Jesus abruptly breaks off his conversation with the Pharisees and departs (8:13), as God in Deut 32:20 LXX (B) turns his face away from the perverse wilderness generation to show what will happen to it in the last days (cf. Lövestam, *This Generation*, 25–26).

The strongly developed exodus typology of Mark 8:1–9 and 8:10–13 would probably reverberate loudly in the setting of Mark's Gospel in close proximity to the Jewish War of 66–73 C.E. As Barnett ("Sign Prophets") and Gray (*Prophetic Figures,* 112–44) have discussed, the period from 40 to 70 C.E. was studded with appearances of "sign prophets": Theudas, during the procuratorship of Cuspius Fadus (44–48 C.E.; Josephus *Ant.* 20.97–99); unnamed "deceivers" during the procuratorship of Antonius Felix (52–60 C.E.; Josephus *J.W.* 2.258–59; *Ant.* 20.167–68); an Egyptian prophet during the same period (*J.W.* 2.261–63; *Ant.* 20.169–72; Acts 21:38); another "deceiver" during the procuratorship of Porcius Festus (60–62 C.E.; *Ant.* 20.188); and a "false prophet" who appeared when the Temple was already on fire on the tenth of Ab in 70 C.E. (*J.W.* 6.284–86). These prophets seem to have harked back to the exodus experiences of Israel and to have promised to perform "signs of deliverance," tokens showing that God was about to redeem Israel as he once had done under Moses. This association with Moses helps to explain why most of the sign prophets appeared in the wilderness, as Jesus does in 8:1–9 and throughout the Gospel. The eschatological frenzy that the sign prophets whipped up probably made a large contribution to the revolt against Rome that forms the background to Mark's Gospel; indeed, this thirst for an exodus-like deliverance was so unquenchable that even the sight of the Temple in flames could not destroy it.

Against this backdrop of Jewish sign-prophecy, Jesus' statement and action in our passage take on a special resonance (cf. Gibson, *Temptations,* 186–89). Like the sign prophets, the Markan Jesus uses the exodus typology. But he deliberately develops a different side of it—not the promise of an exodus-like deliverance that will be accompanied by the destruction of pagan oppressors but the judgment against a "generation" of Jews who recapitulate the faithlessness and rebelliousness of the Israelites who fell in the wilderness. No true divine sign will be given to "this generation"—the generation that stretches from the time of Jesus to the destruction of the Temple, the generation of the sign prophets with their delusive promises of divine deliverance for Israel (cf. 13:22). This background in late Second Temple Jewish sign-prophecy may help explain why Mark truncates our passage and avoids any positive reference to authenticating miracles such as "the sign of Jonah"—to do so would be too much like the revolutionary sign prophets.

If this reconstruction is accepted, the way in which Mark has reshaped the wilderness stories has a further significance. In Exodus itself the people who are fed with manna are the same people who are judged for demanding a sign and thereby "testing" Moses and God. Grace and judgment, therefore, belong together. Mark, however, creates a division, even a geographical partition, between the story of grace and the story of judgment; the narrative of the feeding of the four thousand, which foreshadows the eucharistic meals of the church (8:1–9), is separated by a sea-crossing (8:10) from the narrative of the Pharisees' testing of Jesus (8:11–13). The group that foreshadows the church, then, receives grace, whereas the Jewish leaders are subject to judgment; the Old Testament nexus between grace and judgment has been loosened.

Loosened, but not entirely sundered. For in the next passage (8:14–21) the Markan Jesus will turn his criticism searingly against his own disciples.

JESUS REBUKES HIS DISCIPLES FOR MISUNDERSTANDING (8:14–21)

8 ^{14}And they had forgotten to take loaves of bread, and except for one loaf they did not have any with them in the boat. ^{15}And he commanded them, saying, "Look! Beware of the leaven of the Pharisees and the leaven of Herod!" ^{16}And they were reasoning among themselves that he had said it because they had no loaves. ^{17}And when he knew it he said to them, "Why are you reasoning that I said it because you had no loaves? Do you not yet perceive or understand? Has your heart been hardened? ^{18}Having eyes, do you not see, and having ears, do you not hear? And don't you remember? ^{19}When I broke the five loaves among the five thousand, how many baskets full of bread fragments did you take up?" They said to him, "Twelve." ^{20}When I broke the seven loaves among the four thousand, how many big baskets full of bread fragments did you take up?" And they said, "Seven." ^{21}And he said to them, "Do you not yet understand?"

NOTES

8 14. *except for one loaf.* Gk *ei mē hena arton.* Räisänen (202) argues against a symbolic interpretation of this phrase, asserting that "there is no emphasis at all in the text on the note about the 'one loaf'"; Mark emphasizes not what the disciples *do* have in the boat but what they do not. But the "not . . . except" construction after a negative usually puts special emphasis on the excepted thing (cf. e.g. Matt 11:27; 12:4; 16:4; Mark 6:4; John 3:13); anyone, for example, hearing a story beginning, "When I came to this country I didn't have any resources except my two strong hands and my own common sense" would immediately expect to hear how strong hands and common sense won the day.

15. *Beware of the leaven.* Gk *blepete apo tēs zymēs.* "Leaven," *zymē* (Heb *ḥāmēṣ*), is not synonymous with yeast (Heb *śĕ'or*), which in ancient times was rare; dough, rather, was leavened by mixing into it a small amount of the previous week's dough, which had been kept back for that purpose, rather as some people today make homemade yogurt with a live culture from the previous batch. "Leaven," then, can be more or less synonymous with "leavened bread" (see Lev 7:13), as in the common phrase "to eat leaven" (cf. Rabinowitz, "Ḥameẓ"). This equation probably carries over to our passage, where the leaven of the Pharisees and of Herod is contrasted with the bread Jesus has miraculously provided.

In ancient Israel all leaven in the house was destroyed at the beginning of the yearly festival of unleavened bread, which was later merged with Passover; Mitton ("Leaven") suggests that this was because using leftover dough as leaven ran a risk of bacterial infection, but since most harmful organisms would be killed in baking, this explanation of the festival's origin is doubtful (thanks to Dr. John Karkalas, former Lecturer in Food Science at the University of Strathclyde, for discussing the health issues with me). Leaven is, however, associated in rabbinic texts with the Evil Inclination (see e.g. *Gen. Rab.* 34.10, but cf. already 1 Cor 5:6–8), perhaps because of its ability to permeate the whole lump (cf. Matt 13:33//Luke 13:21; Rom 11:16; 1 Cor 5:6; Gal 5:9). In some contexts this association takes on an eschatological coloring: the leaven is symbolic of the evil of the old age, and its purging is symbolic of the longed-for eschatological redemption (see e.g. Ezekiel the Tragedian *Exagōgē* 189–90, and Targum 2 to Esth 3:8, cited in the following NOTE; cf. Jacobson, *Exagoge*, 129; Bokser, *Origins*, 120 n. 13). The Mishnah expresses the basis of this symbolism succinctly: "[On Passover one eats] unleavened bread—because they were redeemed" (*m. Pesaḥ.* 10:5). In the New Testament itself, 1 Cor 5:6–8 probably incorporates a tradition from a Jewish Christian Passover Haggadah in which leaven and its removal at Passover were symbols of the corruption of the last days and of God's final deliverance of his people from this corruption through Jesus, the Passover lamb (cf. Jeremias, *Eucharistic Words*, 59–60).

Despite these common metaphorical usages of "leaven," the disciples' misunderstanding of Jesus' warning as a reference to literal leaven is natural enough, especially in the exodus/Passover context of this section of the Gospel (on this context see the introductions to 6:6b–8:21 and to 8:1–21). *M. Pesaḥ.* 3:1 demonstrates that a "warning" (*azhārāh*) about leaven could be issued in connection with Passover. In the Jerusalem Talmud, moreover, there is a discussion about the permissibility of eating the leaven of Samaritans immediately after Passover (*y. Šeb.* 8:8). Similar doubts might have been raised about the leaven of the Herodians, who were descended from Edomites (cf. Josephus *J.W.* 1.123) and thus, like the Samaritans, half-breeds from the Jewish point of view.

of the Pharisees and the leaven of Herod. Gk *tōn Pharisaiōn kai tēs zymēs Hērōdou.* Matthew and Luke seem not to understand Mark's phrase; Matt 16:6, 11–12 changes it to "the leaven of the Pharisees and the Sadducees" and interprets it as the teaching of these two sects, whereas Luke 12:1 limits it to "the leaven of the Pharisees" and interprets it as hypocrisy.

An intriguing parallel to the warning against "the leaven of Herod" is provided by the late Targum 2 to Esth 3:8: "Just as we remove the leaven, so may the evil rule be removed from us and may we be freed from this foolish king" (cited by Jacobson, *Exagoge*, 129).

16. *that he had said it because they had no loaves.* Gk *hoti artous ouk echousin.* "That he had said it" has been supplied in the translation to make sense of the context; the original says literally, "And they were reasoning among themselves because (or that) they had no loaves." Some good texts (א, A, C, L, W, etc.) read *echomen*, "we have," and in this case the *hoti* would introduce direct

speech, "And they reasoned among themselves, 'We have no loaves.'" But *echousin*, which is attested by p[45], B, W, etc., is probably original; the change to *echomen* seems influenced by a desire to smooth out the text as well as by the parallel in Matt 16:7 (see Metzger, 98). On other possible translations of the *hoti*, see Taylor, 366.

17. *when he knew it.* Gk *gnous.* In 2:6–8, as here, people *dialogizontai* ("reason, dispute") in or among themselves, Jesus perceives it (*epignous/gnous*), and he asks, *ti dialogizesthe* ("Why are you disputing/reasoning?"). The parallel may suggest that in our passage, as in 2:8, Jesus' insight into what is being said or thought is supernatural.

Do you not yet perceive or understand? Gk *oupō noeite oude syniete.* The form and content of this double question are reminiscent of those of the double question in Isa 40:21, "Do you not know? Have you not heard?," which is repeated in Isa 40:28. The context in this Isaian passage is significantly close to the Markan one, for it speaks of God's sovereignty and power, including his ability to *give strength to the weary* as a sign of eschatological redemption (Isa 40:29). These are the themes of the two Markan feeding miracles, which are recalled in the two questions that follow in Mark 8:19–20.

On the meaning of *oupō*, see the NOTE on "not yet" in 8:21.

19–20. *five . . . five thousand . . . twelve . . . seven . . . four thousand . . . seven.* Gk *pente . . . pentakischilious . . . dōdeka . . . hepta . . . tetrakischilious.* See Quesnell, *Mind*, 270–74 for a survey of scholarly opinion on the significance of these numbers; for a more recent attempt to crack the code, see Drury, "Mark," 414–15. Fascination with numbers is not limited to biblical authors, but has been shared by many people down to the present day; see, for example, Samuel Beckett's comment on James Joyce: "Why, Mr. Joyce seems to say, should there be four legs to a table, and four to a horse, and four seasons and four Gospels and four Provinces in Ireland? Why twelve Tables of the Law, and twelve Apostles and twelve months and twelve Napoleonic marshals and twelve men in Florence called Ottolenghi?" ("Dante," 21). To which Beckett's biographer responds, "Those not as obsessed by the significance of numbers as Beckett or Joyce might well reply, 'Why not?'" (Cronin, *Beckett*, 96). Mark, however, seems to belong in the number-obsessed camp, since he has Jesus highlight them in this evidently redactional passage. On twelve and seven as the more meaningful numbers here, and for their significance, see the COMMENT on 8:17–21. Is it just a coincidence, or a part of Markan numerology, that "seven" is the last word in 8:20, which is the seventh question in the passage?

20. *When I broke the seven loaves among the four thousand.* Gk *hote tous hepta eis tous tetrakischilious,* lit. "when the seven among the four thousand." The ellipsis, however, is perfectly clear; Mark is simply reproducing colloquial speech.

21. *not yet.* Gk *oupō.* NEB, JB, and Kelber (*Mark's Story*, 41) translate this word, which is repeated from 8:17, as "still not," but "not yet" is more accurate (see BAGD, 593). The difference, though seemingly small, is significant, since *oupō* implies that the disciples *will* eventually understand.

COMMENT

Introduction. As in 7:1–23, the Markan Jesus turns from an argument with the Pharisees to a private session with his own disciples. But as happened there (7:18a), he now encounters in those disciples a spiritual insensitivity that is in some ways comparable to that of his confirmed adversaries. The extended criticism of the disciples in our passage is an expansion of the Markan editorial remark in 6:52 that "they did not understand about the loaves, but their heart was hardened" and of the short rebuke of them for their lack of understanding in 7:18a.

Most critical scholars, even those such as Taylor who are interested in ascribing as much historicity as possible to Mark's narratives, tend to regard this one as basically a Markan composition. The latter half of it recalls, in order, the details of the two Markan stories of miraculous feeding (6:30–44 and 8:1–9), even down to the numbers fed and the different terms used for the baskets and the bread fragments. Moreover, it emphasizes throughout one of Mark's favorite themes, the incomprehension and fallibility of the disciples (cf. 4:13; 6:52; 7:18; 8:31–33; 9:6, etc.), and demonstrates Mark's characteristic preoccupation with seeing (8:22–26; 10:46–52; 13:2, 5, 9, 23, 33), hearing (4:3, 9, 10–20, etc.), and understanding (4:12; 7:14). The only part of the passage that is safely ascribed to tradition is the saying about leaven in 8:15 (cf. Räisänen, 200), and even there it may be wondered whether Mark has introduced the reference to the Pharisees, Jesus' stereotypical enemies in his Gospel, into a dictum of Jesus that originally dealt only with "the leaven of Herod" (for the historical Jesus' negative attitude toward Herod Antipas, cf. Luke 13:31–32).

In terms of structure the passage divides naturally into two parts, the stage-setting introduction in 8:14–16 and Jesus' interrogation of the disciples in 8:17–21. The latter section is unified by an inclusion, the question "Do you not understand?" (8:17b, 21), and it is bound together with the introduction by the repetition of the thought and vocabulary of 8:14, 16 in 8:17a. The passage ends very strikingly with a question of Jesus (cf. 3:4; 12:37), which simultaneously points to the disciples' present incomprehension and hints at their future enlightenment.

8:14–16: introduction. The scene takes place in the boat, crossing from Dalmanutha, somewhere on the western shore of the Sea of Galilee (8:10), to Bethsaida, on the northeastern shore (8:22). The disciples, we are told, have forgotten to take loaves of bread with them (8:14a), a statement that is immediately qualified by the clause "and except for one loaf they did not have any with them in the boat" (8:14b). Despite Räisänen's objections (see the NOTE on "except for one loaf" in 8:14), this otherwise superfluous clause, which highlights the one loaf, probably has symbolic significance; if it did not, Mark would presumably have been satisfied with saying that the disciples had forgotten to take bread (8:14a). It is likely that the symbolism is eucharistic; we know from 1 Cor 10:17 that "one loaf" could be used of the bread at the

Lord's Supper, and in Mark's Gospel Jesus' miraculous feedings, which will be linked with the disciples' concern about bread in 8:19–20, seem to foreshadow the Eucharist (see the COMMENT on 6:30–44 and 8:1–9 and cf. Quesnell, *Mind*, 230–39). Thus the bread that Jesus has provided in his feedings, and of which but a single loaf is left with the disciples in the boat, points forward to the bread Jesus provides to the Markan community in the Eucharist, which is "bread of life" for all who come to him (cf. John 6:35). For Mark's readers, then, our passage would be reminiscent of 4:35–41: the anxiety of the disciples is needless; they have Jesus with them "in the boat," which may be a symbol of the church, and that is all they need (see Hippolytus *Antichrist* 59; *Apostolic Constitutions* 2.547); Jesus will provide the bread that they truly require. The whole scene, in Drury's words ("Mark," 414), is "a classic little icon of the primitive Christian Church."

There is an obstacle, however, to the disciples' appropriation of the eucharistic bread, a bread that is linked with Jesus' teaching in the other Markan feeding story (see 6:34): the leaven of the Pharisees and of Herod, against which they are warned to be on their guard (8:15), and which the rest of the passage links with their incomprehension (cf. 8:17–21). Jesus' call to avoid leaven invokes the exodus/Passover typology, because Passover was the feast of unleavened bread, and before the feast began the Jewish household was diligently purged of leaven. In Passover contexts "leaven" is often synonymous with "leavened bread" (see the NOTE on "Beware of the leaven" in 8:15), and this equation would work well in the present context, where a contrast is being made between the bread that Jesus supplies and the leaven of the Pharisees and of Herod. If so, the situation is somewhat reminiscent of that in Proverbs 9, where people are called to eat the bread provided by Lady Wisdom but to shun that offered by the wanton woman who is her antithesis (Prov 9:5, 17).

But what more precisely is "the leaven of the Pharisees and the leaven of Herod," against which the disciples are warned to be on their guard? If we wish to penetrate what Mark means by this puzzling phrase, it is probably best to begin with the observation that "leaven" is a common Jewish metaphor for the Evil Inclination, the destructive and anarchic impulse within the hearts of human beings, which causes them to sin (see the NOTE on "Beware of the leaven" in 8:15). The applicability of this image to our passage is confirmed by the continuation, in which the "leaven" is associated with a hardened heart (8:17); because of its biblical rootage in Gen 6:5; 8:21, the Evil Inclination was intimately associated with defects of the heart, and in 1QS 5:4–5 it is synonymous with "stubbornness of heart" (cf. Marcus, "Evil Inclination in Paul," 20 n. 48).

Jesus, then, is warning his disciples against being infected by the same evil impulse that has hardened the hearts of his enemies, the Pharisees and Herodians (cf. 3:6; 12:13). It is probably not just a coincidence that the previous instance of Jesus' private instruction to the disciples also dealt with the Evil Inclination (see the COMMENT on 7:17–23). Indeed, the overall pattern of 8:10–21 matches that of 7:1–23:

Dispute with Pharisees	7:1–15; 8:10–12
Segregation with disciples	7:17; 8:13
Statement about Evil Inclination	7:21–23; 8:15

This pattern may be partly polemical, since the Pharisees of Mark's own time were probably much preoccupied with the Evil Inclination, as their successors the rabbis were, and they would have seen Law-free Christian communities such as Mark's as arenas in which this destructive, antinomian impulse ran rampant (see Marcus, "Scripture"). The disciples need special instruction about the Inclination, then, partly because Mark's community is being challenged about it. But it is also being challenged *by* it; the insidious influence of the Inclination is not only "out there," among the Pharisees, but also "in here," within the elect community itself. Mark's dual focus on the Twelve and the Evil Inclination reflects the increasing concentration of this section of the Gospel on the problems of discipleship; this concentration will become even more intense in the next major section, 8:21–10:52.

It is typical of these problems that the disciples completely miss the symbolic force of Jesus' reference to leaven, interpreting it literally as an allusion to their dearth of physical bread (8:16). As Lohmeyer (157) points out, this misunderstanding is comparable to the episodes in the Gospel of John in which the Samaritan woman misinterprets "living water" as a reference to physical water (John 4:10–15) and "the Jews" misinterpret "bread of God" as an allusion to material bread (John 6:31–34). The motif of misunderstanding makes it even more likely that "one loaf" in our passage should be interpreted in a symbolic, quasi-Johannine manner, for the function of the motif is to point to the deeper significance of what is being said and done.

8:17–21: *Jesus' rebuke of the disciples' misunderstanding.* Jesus discerns, perhaps supernaturally (see the NOTE on "when he knew it" in 8:17), the literalistic misinterpretation of the saying about the leaven that his disciples are retailing among themselves, and in response he unleashes a series of five critical questions that echo OT passages and themes (8:17–18). He then poses two additional questions that recall the two miraculous feedings (8:19–20) before returning to a final critical question (8:21).

The five critical questions all concern the disciples' lack of understanding. For readers of Mark, the most resonant of them is the penultimate one," Having eyes, do you not see, and having ears, do you not hear?" (8:18), which strongly echoes the terrible judgment pronounced on the "outsiders" in 4:12. That statement by Jesus was a citation of Isa 6:9–10, though our passage owes more to the related language in Jer 5:21 and Ezek 12:2, which speak of the blindness and deafness of the rebellious house of Israel "who have eyes, but do not see, who have ears, but do not hear."

This parallelism between the "outsiders" in 4:12 and the disciples in 8:17–18 is potentially very threatening to the Twelve, and it is an important weapon in the arsenal of those scholars who think that the Twelve ultimately belong among "those outside" and that Mark is pursuing a vendetta against them (see e.g. Kelber, *Mark's Story*, 41; Tolbert, 102–3, 199–200). But there are also significant differences between 8:17–21, on the one hand, and 4:12 and other passages about Jesus' enemies, on the other, and these differences tend to mitigate the threat. Gnilka, for example (1.311), notes that the disciples' hardness of heart is mentioned in a question, not in a statement as in 3:5 and 4:12, and that this question can be construed as a stimulus to further insight. This optimistic interpretation is supported by the placement of our story before the healing of a blind man, which implies that defective vision can be healed. Ambrozic (*Hidden Kingdom*, 69), similarly, points out that 8:17–21 lacks the "damning conclusion" of 4:12 ("lest they turn and be forgiven"). And Lemcio ("Evidence") has argued that our pericope and two other Markan passages (4:1–20; 7:14–23) exhibit a "dialogue form" with roots in the OT (e.g. Ezek 17:1–24; Zech 4:2–14): ambiguity, incomprehension, surprised or critical rejoinder, and explanation. In this form the hearer cannot really be expected to understand the initial statement, which is ambiguous, and the revealer's rebuke functions merely as a prelude to an explanation.

But if 8:19–20 is an explanation whose purpose is enlightenment, it is a strange example of this genre, since it is almost as enigmatic as the saying it is meant to explain (8:15). Indeed, even in a puzzling work such as Mark, our passage is singularly cryptic. Why has the disciples' misunderstanding elicited the severe rebuke of 8:17–18, when Jesus' initial remark about the leaven of the Pharisees and of Herod (8:15) was enigmatic enough to perplex interpreters from Matthew and Luke to the present (see the NOTE on "of the Pharisees and the leaven of Herod" in 8:15)? Are the disciples to be blamed for not comprehending it, especially when the subsequent interpretation seems at first to compound its obscurity? The initial response of readers of the passage, therefore, is likely to be a puzzlement as great as that of the disciples.

This readerly solidarity with the disciples in their confusion may, indeed, be part of the authorial purpose of the passage. Sternberg (*Poetics*, 47–48) has described, in terms easily transferable to Mark, the tendency of difficult Old Testament narratives to create solidarity between readers and certain characters in the story:

> With the narrative become an obstacle course, its reading turns into a drama of understanding ... The reader's drama is literally dramatized in and through an analogous ordeal of interpretation undergone by some character ... with variable success but under the same constraints of human vision. The resulting brotherhood in darkness and error thus cuts across the barrier separating participant from observer to highlight the barrier separating both from divine omniscience.

In Mark the "character" who dramatizes the Markan audience's frustration at trying to make sense of Jesus is the group of disciples, and this shared frustration serves both to tie the audience to the disciples and to point to the transcendence of Jesus (cf. Tannehill, "Disciples," 147–48).

Yet there is more to our enigmatic passage than a deliberate attempt to addle readers. The audience's "ordeal of interpretation," to use Sternberg's phrase, will eventually bear fruit, particularly if they remember the Passover/exodus typology that has prevailed since 6:6b and has been especially prominent since the beginning of chapter 8. This typology suggests an ultimately encouraging view of the disciples. As Myers (*Binding*, 225) points out, Jesus' queries in 8:17–18 echo not only the passages from Isaiah, Jeremiah, and Ezekiel referred to above but also Moses' words to Israel in Deut 29:2–4 LXX, which connect with the previous Markan passage as well:

> You have seen all that the Lord did before your eyes in the land of Egypt,
> . . . the great testings (*peirasmous*) which your eyes have seen, the signs
> (*sēmeia*) and those great wonders. But the Lord has not given you a heart to
> know (*kardian eidenai*), and eyes to see (*ophthalmous blepein*), and ears to
> hear (*ōta akouein*), to this day.

Here we see the themes of the insensitive heart, the blind eyes, and the deaf ears, all in the same order in which they appear in Mark 8:17–18, as well as the motifs of testing and signs, which appear in the previous Markan passage. A bit later in Deuteronomy, moreover, the Markan term "remember" (8:18 end) also comes to the fore (Deut 32:7). If Mark is making a deliberate allusion to these passages in Deuteronomy—and the prominence of the Pentateuchal Passover/exodus/wilderness traditions in this section of the Gospel makes such an allusion more likely—then the prospect for the disciples is more hopeful than exegetes such as Kelber and Tolbert allow: "to this day" they have not been granted perceptive hearts, eyes, and ears, but they will in the end receive them (cf. Deut 30:1–8). Jesus' concluding words to the disciples in our passage, "Do you not *yet* understand?," which repeat the question of 8:17, suggest a similarly hopeful message (cf. the NOTE on "not yet" in 8:21).

In the end, then, Jesus' questions in 8:19–20 are probably meant to be revelatory rather than obfuscatory, but it has to be admitted that they have often had the opposite effect. In particular, the emphasis on the numbers in these questions has occasioned a great deal of fascinated speculation (see the NOTE on "five . . . five thousand" in 8:19–20), but the truth is that there is no fixed OT or Jewish symbolism either for five thousand or for four thousand, and that five, seven, and twelve can signify many different things (cf. A. Collins, *Cosmology*, 55–138). Perhaps an initial step forward is to acknowledge Rau's point (*Markusevangelium*, 2123 n. 226) that the emphasis in our passage falls neither on the numbers in the respective crowds (five thousand and four thousand) nor on the number of loaves initially present (five and seven) but on the number of baskets of fragments left over, twelve and seven. It is these baskets of fragments that are the subject of Jesus' question, and the latter elicits the disciples' answers, "Twelve" and "Seven"—answers that Jesus' final question (8:21) suggests are self-explanatory.

In the biblical tradition twelve and seven and their multiples are used with a wide variety of nuances, but the one most relevant to the stories of miraculous feeding is their connotation of eschatological fullness, which derives from the root images of the twelve tribes of Israel and the seven days of creation. Some Jews, for example, expected that at the end the Ten Lost Tribes would return to restore Israel to its eschatological fullness of twelve tribes (see already Ezek 37:15–22 and cf. the later passages cited in Bergren, "People"). 11QTemple 18:16, similarly, expands the two loaves of Lev 23:17 to twelve, perhaps to emphasize the national and eschatological nature of the double Feast of the Counting of the Omer and of Weeks (cf. Swanson, *Temple Scroll*, 46). In Mark itself Jesus chooses twelve disciples as the nucleus of a new Israel (3:13–19). In Rev 4:1–6 there are twenty-four (= 2 × 12) elders sitting on twenty-four thrones around the throne of God, and in Rev 7:1–8 the angels seal twelve thousand servants of God from each of the twelve tribes as the nucleus of the elect. In Rev 21:9–21, moreover, the new Jerusalem has twelve foundations and twelve gates, and its measurements are all multiples of twelve. Seven is also an important number for Revelation and is associated there and elsewhere with eschatological judgment and grace; perhaps such apocalyptic associations of the number were partly responsible for the fact that the Jewish War, which forms the background to our Gospel, broke out at the beginning of the seventh decade after direct Roman rule over Judaea began (see the NOTE on "seven" in 8:8). Mark's use of seven, then, could be polemical: it is not the Jewish revolutionaries but Jesus who has brought in the age of eschatological fulfillment.

This impression that twelve and seven in our passage suggest eschatological completion is reinforced by the numbers' association with two different words having to do with fullness (*plēreis* and *plērōmata*, both translated "full of," though *plērōmata* literally means "fullnesses"; see the NOTE on "baskets full of bread fragments" in 6:43). Elsewhere in Mark, words with the *plēr-* root always have the connotation of eschatological realization (1:15; 2:21; 4:28; 6:43; 14:49). This eschatological interpretation of the passage also dovetails with Jesus' opening remark about avoiding the leaven of the Pharisees and of Herod. For that remark, as we have seen, recalls the removal of leaven, the symbol of evil, at Passover, and in some Jewish traditions and the New Testament the leaven becomes symbolic of the evil of the old age and of the Evil Inclination that is associated with it, while the leaven's removal and the eating of unleavened bread become symbolic of the final redemption (see the NOTE on "Beware of the leaven" in 8:15).

What the Pharisees and Herod do not realize, then, and what the disciples are in danger of forgetting, is that in Jesus God is bringing the new age into being. Blinded to this revolutionary divine change, the Pharisees ignore the clear signs of its advent (8:10–13) and object to Jesus' innovations with respect to fasting and the Sabbath (cf. 2:18–27); both Pharisees and Herodians, moreover, try to trap him into making subversive statements and surreptitiously plot his destruction (cf. 12:13; 3:6). Mark probably thinks that this Pharisaic and Herodian insensitivity to divine, eschatological realities is the reverse side of a hypersensitivity to this-worldly, human concerns; the "hypocritical" words of the Pharisees and Herodians in 12:14, in which they insincerely acknowledge that Jesus teaches the way of God and does not regard the opinion of human beings, are probably understood by Mark to boomerang on themselves and to reveal that they give too much attention to human evaluation (cf. John 5:44). This interpretation is supported by the way in which Mark has described Herod Antipas being manipulated into killing John the Baptist because of his excessive concern for his reputation among his dinner guests (6:26; cf. Acts 12:1–2, where Antipas' nephew Herod Agrippa I is portrayed as arresting Peter because "it pleased the Jews").

But our passage implies that the disciples themselves are in danger of falling into a similar sort of blindness about the fact and significance of God's eschatological action in Jesus, a similar fixation on the merely human, worldly concerns that are the quintessence of the dying evil age. The disciples, too, are in peril of ingesting and being infected by "the leaven of the Pharisees and the leaven of Herod"; indeed, Jesus will shortly excoriate Peter for his Satanically inspired preoccupation with "the things of human beings" rather than "the things of God." In the following section of the Gospel (8:22–10:52), Jesus will struggle to remove this leaven from the disciples' hearts, to eradicate their worldliness, to pull them out of the darkness and toward the light. This section, appropriately enough, will be inaugurated by a story of the healing of a blind man (8:22–26), and that narrative will underline both the distorted human vision and the sense of divine promise that are implicit in the concluding words of our passage, "Do you not yet understand?" (8:21).

APPENDICES

◆

THE SCRIBES AND
THE PHARISEES

◆

These two groups are closely linked in two Markan passages: 2:16, where "the scribes of the Pharisees" are outraged at Jesus' table fellowship with tax collectors and sinners, and 7:1, 5 (cf. 7:3), where "the Pharisees and some of the scribes" or "the Pharisees and the scribes" question why Jesus' disciples do not wash their hands before eating.

The groups, however, appear separately from each other in a number of passages, though often in alliance with other groups. The Pharisees, for example, are in alliance with the Herodians in 3:6 and 12:13 and are mentioned alongside of Herod in 8:15; they appear with the disciples of John in 2:18; they are unaccompanied in 2:24 and 8:11. The scribes are often in alliance with the chief priests (10:33; 11:18; 14:1; 15:31) or with the chief priests and the elders (8:31; 11:27; 14:43, 53; 15:1); they appear alone in 1:22; 2:6; 3:22; 9:11, 14; 12:28, 32, 35, 38.

The two groups also appear in different locations. Mark generally locates the Pharisees in Galilee. Only one of his ten references to them, 12:13, pictures them in Jerusalem. The other nine Markan references either picture the Pharisees in Galilee (2:16, 18, 24; 3:6; 7:1, 5; 8:11, 15; 10:2) or mention them in passages that take place in Galilee (7:3; 9:11). The scribes, on the other hand, are generally located in Jerusalem (8:31; 10:33; 11:18, 27; 12:28, 32, 35, 38; 14:1, 43, 53; 15:1, 31) or mentioned as coming from Jerusalem (3:22; 7:1; cf. 7:5); they are in Galilee or mentioned in it, however, in 1:22; 2:6, 16; 9:11, 14 (cf. Saldarini, *Pharisees*, 146–49). There is thus both overlap and differentiation in Mark's picture of the Pharisees and the scribes. But who were these two groups?

The Pharisees were one of the four major Jewish sects in the period before the revolt against the Romans of 66–73 C.E. Josephus describes them and the other major sects, the Sadducees, Essenes, and "Fourth Philosophy," in *J.W.*, 2.119–68 and *Ant.* 18.11–25. He pictures the Pharisees as the most accurate interpreters of the Jewish laws, as affectionate with each other and zealous for community harmony, and as influential among the common people (there are some differences between the portrayal of the Pharisees in the *History of the Jewish War* and the *Antiquities*, but the extent and nature of these differences are debated; see A. Baumgarten, "Rivkin and Neusner," 115–16). Partly no doubt because of this sort of reputation, the Pharisees' successors, the rabbis, became the leaders of the Jewish community in, and eventually outside of, Palestine after the war, which destroyed the other three sects. It is probable that the name "Pharisee," from the Hebrew *pārûš*, means "separated one" and was coined, like many designations for religious groups, by opponents, who would have used it pejoratively to speak of the sect's self-segregation from other Jews; as often happens, however, the members of the sect adopted the term and gave it a positive connotation, namely separation from impurity and sin (see Schürer, 2.396–98; cf. A. Baumgarten ["Name"], who thinks that the Pharisees would also have understood their name as meaning "specifiers" [of the exact interpretation of the Law]).

In Jesus' time the Pharisees' separation from impurity was graphically manifested by their participation in voluntary eating fellowships (*habûrôt*; for the near-synonymity of "Pharisee" with *hābēr* = "associate," compare *m. Hag.* 2:7 with *m. Dem.* 2:3). Ritually unclean outsiders were excluded from such table fellowships. Many Jewish scholars have argued that this policy should not be mistaken for misanthropy, as has often happened in Christian accounts. Its motivation, rather, was the magnification of God's holiness through the extension to laypeople of purity laws that in the OT had been applicable only to priests. As Neusner puts it (*Idea*, 3): "That the Pharisees required an act of purification before eating suggests that Pharisaism saw the act of eating as a cultic rite and further implies that Pharisaism compared the table to the altar, the home to the Temple, and the private person to the priest" (cf. *b. Hul.* 106a, where this reasoning is explicit, admittedly in a late tradition). The sect, moreover, maintained a welcoming attitude to all those, even Gentiles, who wished to repent of their sins and enter their holy fellowship through observance of the Law as Pharisaically interpreted (see the Matthean Jesus' reference to their missionary zeal in Matt 23:15).

Despite their hostility to the Pharisees, the Gospels are one of our earlier and best sources for knowledge about them. In Mark, for example, the Pharisees dispute with Jesus about fasting (2:18), Sabbath observance (2:24; 3:2), and divorce (10:2), and join with the scribes in disputing with him about eating with sinners (2:16) and handwashing (7:1; cf. Saldarini, *Pharisees*, 149). As Neusner points out, this corresponds in a general way with the earliest stratum of rabbinic law codified in the Mishnah and Tosefta, which is primarily concerned with ritual purity, tithing and other food laws, and Sabbath and festival observance (see Neusner, *Politics*, 80; Saldarini, *Pharisees*, 212–13). The two Pharisaic "houses" of Hillel and Shammai, moreover, disputed with each other about divorce (see Neusner, *Politics*, 113–15). Furthermore, both Mark and Josephus say that the Pharisees relied for their distinctive interpretation of the law on a "tradition of the elders" delivered to them from earlier times (Mark 7:3; *Ant.* 13.297, 408); in the post-70 era this idea developed into the full-blown theory of an oral law supplementary to the written law and handed down from Moses in an unbroken chain of transmission (see the theory's classic expression in *m. 'Abot* 1:1–12).

E. Sanders and other scholars, however, have expressed skepticism about key elements of Neusner's reconstruction. Most important, Sanders questions the claims that the Pharisees were primarily concerned with purity and table fellowship and that they wished to extend priestly purity rules to laypeople. Sanders notes, for example, that Josephus does not mention dietary matters in his description of the Pharisees, and he asserts that there is little evidence for Neusner's contention that the Pharisees ate ordinary food (food that was not holy, i.e. not second tithe [see GLOSSARY], sacrifices, or heave offering) in a state of ritual purity. Moreover, according to Sanders, when the Pharisees did express concern about purity, they were attentive only to the purity of members of their own eating clubs, not to that of people outside those clubs; overall, in fact, their influence on pre-70 Judaism was exceedingly limited (see E. Sanders, *Jesus*, 182–85; *Jewish Law*, 131–254; *Judaism*, 428–43). A further critique of Neusner's position is implicit in the assertion of D. Schwartz that, even if the Pharisees were concerned about purity, that does not prove that they wanted to live like priests: "One must differentiate uncompromisingly between priesthood and holiness" ("Kingdom," 63; cf. Poirier, "Why," 220–24).

It will take a while for the smoke (which has been thickened by the fierce polemics of both Neusner and Sanders) to clear completely on these issues, but in my view, while Sanders has pointed to some weaknesses in Neusner's arguments, the essential features of Neusner's reconstruction remain intact. On the crucial issue of ritual purity, for example, Dunn (*Jesus*, 61–88) plausibly suggests that Josephus' failure to mention a Pharisaic concern for dietary matters reflects his sensitivity to his Roman audience, who would have been suspicious of special dietary laws as an indication of strange cults. Sanders' dismissal of some of the NT evidence pointing to a Pharisaic concern for ritual purity, moreover, is troubling. As Dunn points out, for example, the issue between Jesus and the Pharisees in Mark 2:15–17 does seem to involve purity, because the Pharisees object to Jesus' *eating* with the tax collectors and sinners (see the NOTE on "Why does he eat with tax collectors and sinners?" in 2:16). This passage cannot be dismissed as late; it is at least pre-Markan, and that means that it almost certainly predates the transformation of the Pharisees from a sect to a ruling party, which took place in the decades after the Jewish War. Neither is Sanders convincing in his assertion that Mark simply does not know what he is talking about when he says that "the Pharisees, and all the Jews" wash their hands before every meal (Mark 7:3), presumably because they wish to eat all meals in a state of purity. Neusner and his advocates are more plausible in their assertion that Mark's evidence must be taken seriously, and that while "all the Jews" is probably an exaggeration, it reflects a degree of influence on other Jews that is corroborated by Josephus (*Ant.* 18.15; cf. the NOTE on "for the Pharisees, and all the Jews" in 7:3). This view has now been strengthened by the monograph of Deines (*Steingefässe*, 268–74), which argues on the basis of a review of literary and archaeological sources that the "stone water-jugs for the purification of the Jews" in John 2:6 are for handwashing, and that the abundance of such jugs found throughout Palestine in archaeological excavations of pre-70 sites testifies to the extent of the influence of Pharisaic purity concerns on large sectors of the Jewish population.

Just as critical as the evaluation of the NT evidence is the sifting of the rabbinic sources to determine which traditions can be reliably ascribed to the pre-70 Pharisees, and what they imply. Sanders, for example, lays great stress on the variant opinions in two passages in the Tosephta (*t. Ber.* 5:13, 27) which for him imply that some rabbis thought handwashing was not required at all meals (*Jewish Law*, 173). As he acknowledges elsewhere, however (ibid., 230), the first passage only records a dispute about whether or not the washing is to take place before or after the meal, not about whether it is to take place at all. As for the second passage, its wording, "Washing of hands for ordinary food is not," is grammatically incomplete, and Lieberman (*Tosefta*) suggests that "from the Torah" should be supplied, as in the parallel from the Babylonian Talmud (*b. Ber.* 52b); the passage, in other words, raises a question about the scriptural derivation of the requirement to wash the hands, not about its mandatoriness. On the other hand, Sanders dismisses as late, on insubstantial grounds, the anonymous traditions in *m. Yad.* 1–2 and *m. Ḥag.* 2:5, which call for handwashing before meals. Moreover, as Deines shows (*Steingefässe*, 269–70), Sanders really cannot explain away *m. Ber.* 8:2–4, in which the debates recorded between the Houses of Hillel and of Shammai about the order of handwashing (e.g. before or after mixing the wine?) presuppose that both of these pre-70 Houses practiced it. On other questionable aspects of Sanders' treatment of Pharisaic purity, see H. Harrington, "Did"; Poirier, "Why," 220–21.

While Sanders, D. Schwartz, and Poirier are right, moreover, to emphasize the distinction between purity and priestly purity, it still remains true that the OT limits handwashing before meals to priestly families, while the Pharisees seem to have extended the requirement to laypeople and to have challenged those who did not conform to it (Mark 7:1–5). Assuming, as seems incontestable, that the Pharisees knew the limitations of the biblical requirement, the most plausible explanation for their extension of the handwashing requirement to the laity would seem to be an aspiration that laypeople should live *in some ways* like priests (see Deines, *Steingefässe*, 268, 280). As de Lacey points out, Sanders twists Neusner's analysis into an assertion that the Pharisees meant to *replace* priestly purity with lay purity. This, however, is a misconstrual, since Neusner only claims that the Pharisees wanted to *extend* priestly rules to the laity ("Search," 362–63, 366). This does not mean that they thought that the distinction between priests and laity had thereby been totally eliminated; indeed, in view of the Bible's clear demarcation between the two groups, such an idea would be impossible. But within the constraints imposed by the Bible, which does after all treat priests and laity as distinct groups, the Pharisees nevertheless seem to have moved in the direction of the admittedly paradoxical notion of "lay priesthood." A certain parallel may be found in the internal tension within Episcopalianism, which on the one hand embraces the idea of the priesthood of all believers yet on the other hand maintains a distinct office for priests.

Although, as we have seen, the Markan portrayal of the Pharisees seems to be basically accurate, though biased, one aspect of it is puzzling: he locates them, as we have seen, primarily in Galilee rather than in Jerusalem. Josephus, on the other hand, most often describes them in Jerusalem contexts; the only Pharisees that he pictures in Galilee have been sent there from Jerusalem (*J.W.* 2.569; *Life* 189–98; see Saldarini, *Pharisees*, 147).

Dunn has attempted to diminish the clash between these testimonies by pointing out that Josephus was not writing a treatise on the social and religious life of Galilee but a military history, so his relative silence about Pharisees in Galilee is not decisive evidence against their presence there. Other sources, Dunn adds, suggest that during the early part of the first century the Pharisees were trying to extend their influence in Galilee (see e.g. the report in *y. Šabb.* 16:8 about Yohanan ben Zakkai's eighteen-year-long residence there; Dunn, *Jesus*, 77–79). It still remains puzzling, however, that the overwhelming predominance of Markan references to them occurs in Galilee, and that they effectively drop out of the story once it moves to Jerusalem, which according to Josephus was their major power center.

As for **the scribes**, literally a *grammateus* was a person who knew letters (Gk *grammata*), i.e. one who could write. The term is used in a variety of related senses in Greek, corresponding in some ways to the range in meaning of the English word "secretary," which can denote everything from a typist to a high government official. In Greek, analogously, a scribe may be a copyist, a government official in charge of records, an official with responsibility for enforcing the law, or a sage or teacher who interprets the law (see M-M, 131–32; D. Schwartz, "Scribes," 91–93; Saldarini, *Pharisees*, 241–76). The last is the word's sense in Mark. As Saldarini points out, the passage implies that the scribes are "the ordinary teachers with whom the people are familiar," since it is to them that the crowd reflexively compares Jesus (ibid., 152).

It has usually been assumed that the vast majority of Jewish scribes in New Testament times were Pharisees (see e.g. Jeremias, *Jerusalem*, 233–45). The evidence for this common conclusion, however, is surprisingly limited. Although the rabbis were the successors of the Pharisees, and they sometimes ascribed traditions they wished either to adopt or to oppose to ancient authorities they vaguely denoted "the scribes," evidence that first-century rabbis called themselves scribes is lacking. (They did, however, trace their traditions back to "Ezra the scribe"; see A. Cohen, *Everyman's Talmud*, xvi–xviii.) Indeed, rabbinic traditions are sometimes close to Mark 1:22 in their *derogation* of scribal authority, as, for example, in *m. Yad.* 3:2: "One may infer nothing about the words of the Law from the words of the scribes" (my trans.; cited by Saldarini, *Pharisees*, 270; see also *m. Para* 11:4–5, cited by E. Sanders, *Judaism*, 515 n. 8).

The real point of departure for the equation of scribes with Pharisees seems to be Matthew 23, where the phrase "scribes and Pharisees, hypocrites" runs as a refrain through the chapter, linking the two groups strongly. In contrast to Matthew, however, Mark maintains a nuanced distinction between scribes and Pharisees in 2:16 and 7:1, which seems to imply that only *some* scribes belonged to the Pharisaic party. He also locates the two groups in different locales: Pharisees, as we have seen, are usually in Galilee, whereas scribes are usually in or from Jerusalem (cf. Lührmann, "Pharisäer," 171–72).

Recently, D. Schwartz ("Scribes," 89–101) and E. Sanders (*Judaism*, 170–82), in apparent independence of each other, have challenged the prevailing equation of scribes with Pharisees and have made a strong case that most scribes were Levites (Schwartz) or priests and Levites (Sanders). (For a good short account of the Levites, a subordinate priestly group separate from priests proper, see J. Porter, "Levites.") Several late Old Testament passages (e.g. Neh 8:7–9; 2 Chr 17:7–9) assign to priests and Levites the task of interpreting the law, and the example of Ezra, who was both a priest and "a scribe skilled in the Law of Moses" (Ezra 7:6), was probably influential in postexilic times. There is no convincing evidence that the basic situation changed before the destruction of the Temple in A.D. 70 wiped out the priests' power base. Sirach sings the praises of Aaron, the ancestor of the priests, as a model interpreter of the Law (45:17), and Josephus assumes that priests are skilled in legal exegesis (*Life* 196–98) and twice mentions "the scribes of the Temple" (*Ant.* 11.128; 12.142), the latter time in conjunction with "the priests." Besides exegesis, the other major role of the New Testament scribe is judicial inquiry (see e.g. Mark 3:22; 14:53–55), and this role corresponds to that of the priests and Levites in John 1:19. The priests and Levites, moreover, were religious professionals who were forbidden to work the land and were on duty in the Temple only a few weeks a year; the pre-70 Pharisees, on the other hand, were laymen, most of whom probably worked six days a week at other jobs. The priests and Levites, therefore, would have had the leisure to expound and enforce the Law as a full-time occupation, whereas the Pharisees would not.

The combined arguments of Schwartz and Sanders add up to a compelling case for identifying most pre-70 scribes as members of the priestly orders— who might also be Pharisees (see e.g. Josephus *Life* 197; Josephus himself was a priest who claimed to be a Pharisee: *Life* 12; cf. D. Schwartz, "Scribes," 101 n. 65). After the destruction of the Temple, however, the situation changed drastically; the priests and Levites lost their power base and rapidly faded into obscurity, whereas the Pharisees emerged from the ruins of the war as the dominant Jewish party and took over legislation and enforcement of the law. Matthew's near-equation of scribes and Pharisees probably reflects this post-70 situation.

THE MESSIANIC SECRET MOTIF

◆

Throughout the Gospel of Mark, Jesus silences demons who shout out his identity (1:23–25, 34; 3:11–12), warns people whom he has healed and/or their friends or relatives not to make his healing miracles known (1:43–44; 5:43; 7:36; cf. 5:19; 8:26), and cautions his disciples not to let his messiahship or the secret of his Transfiguration become public (8:30; 9:9). He also tries to conceal his presence from the public (7:24; 9:30–31), deliberately hides the truth from outsiders (4:10–12, 33–34), and secludes himself with his disciples in order to impart secret teaching (4:13, 34; 7:17; 9:28, 30–31; 13:3). Even these intimates, moreover, frequently misunderstand or doubt him (4:13, 40; 6:52; 7:18; 8:14–21; 9:6; 14:41).

This theme of hiddenness is commonly referred to by scholars as "the messianic secret motif," though some have objected to this terminology because only one of the passages, 8:29–30, has to do specifically with Jesus' messiahship. The theme is more pronounced in Mark than in the other Gospels (Matthew and/or Luke, for example, expunge it from the parallels to 1:34; 3:11–12; 5:43; 7:17, 24, 36; 9:28–31; 13:3), and it demands explanation. Up until the beginning of the twentieth century, the usual explanations were historical or psychological: Jesus, for example, concealed his identity to ward off arrest, or because he did not want a false, military view of him to circulate, or simply because he was humble and modest.

These historical and psychological explanations were strongly challenged at the beginning of the twentieth century in William Wrede's classic monograph, *The Messianic Secret*. One by one, Wrede went through his contemporaries' explanations and highlighted their shortcomings, pointing out that some of the Markan stories are impossible to conceive historically. In 5:43, for example, Jesus' injunction against allowing anyone to hear about the girl's resuscitation is absurd in the face of the crowd's knowledge of her death and the certainty that she will now be seen alive. Wrede saw the messianic secret motif primarily as an expression of early Christian theology; by means of it the church (represented both by Mark and by the pre-Markan tradition) was trying to explain the tension between its belief in Jesus' messiahship and what Wrede presumed to be the fact that Jesus had not presented himself as the Messiah during his lifetime. The church's solution, Wrede thought, was to portray a Jesus who had indeed been the Messiah, and who had known that he was so, but who had kept this knowledge hidden from all but his closest followers.

This particular explanation of the messianic secret motif has not commanded overwhelming support, but most present-day exegetes would accept

Wrede's leading insight that the secrecy motif primarily reflects early Christian theology rather than the practice of the historical Jesus (see the surveys in
Blevins, *Messianic Secret*; Tuckett, *Messianic Secret*, 1–28; and Räisänen, 38–
75). Many, however, would distinguish among different aspects of the motif,
stressing plausibly that some messianic secret passages are pre-Markan and
others are Markan, and that Jesus' privacy has different motivations in different
places (see e.g. Luz, "Secrecy," and Räisänen). Theissen (140–52), for example, thinks that all the injunctions to secrecy in miracle stories are traditional
and have various magical motives, whereas all the silencings outside of miracle stories are editorial; while this generalization does not work in all instances
(5:43, for example, is probably redactional), it seems to be basically correct.
Most interest has centered on the secrecy motif in the editorial passages (1:34;
3:12; 5:43; 8:30; 9:9), and here the most influential and cogent view is that they
point toward the larger Markan story: Jesus' identity cannot truly be revealed
until his death (15:38–39) and resurrection (cf. 9:9); until that time, therefore,
any revelation of it must necessarily be veiled (see the discussion of the "his-
tory-of-revelation" view of E. Percy and G. Strecker in Tuckett, *Messianic
Secret*, 15, and Räisänen, 68–71).

The messianic secret motif also has a literary function, which may be
glimpsed by imagining what the Gospel would look like without it. In the traditions that have come down to Mark, Jesus is acknowledged to be the Messiah by one of his disciples (8:29), confessed to be the "holy one of God" and
the Son of God by demons (1:24; 5:7), and twice hailed as his Son by God
himself (1:11; 9:7). Mark has drawn these stories of human and superhuman
acknowledgment, which to a large degree reflect the early church's Christology, into the connected narrative of his Gospel and has associated them with
numerous other healing and exorcism stories that, in the work's overall context, confirm the acknowledgments of Jesus' messiahship and divine sonship.
But the creation of the Gospel has also joined the acknowledgment stories
with narratives in which Jesus jousts verbally with the Jewish leaders and with
the passion narrative in the Gospel's second half. By making this linkage,
however, Mark has created a literary problem for himself, to which the messianic secret motif is in part a solution. Without that motif, the stories of divine
and demonic acknowledgment would sit uneasily next to the motif of opposition that emerges in the controversy stories and comes to a climax in the passion narrative. The scribes' charge that Jesus casts out demons by the prince
of the demons (3:22), for example, would be nonsensical in view of the demons' public confession that Jesus had evicted them through the power of
God. Similarly, the Jewish leaders would be unable to accuse Jesus of blasphemy for claiming divine sonship (14:61–64), since that claim would have
been established publicly by irrefutable testimony from both the divine and
the demonic sides of the unseen world. Jesus, then, must hide his lamp under
a bushel (cf. 4:21–22)—in order that he may be opposed and, ultimately,
killed—in order that he may "give his life as a ransom for many" (10:45).

But the Markan Jesus is not always successful in suppressing reports that might lead to a perception of his identity. In 1:44–45 and 7:36 the healed person or his friends disobey Jesus' order not to say anything to anyone; indeed, the latter passage adds that "the more he commanded them, all the more greatly did they spread the news." These partial breaks in the secrecy motif, as Wrede already recognized, stem from the two-level nature of Mark's narrative (see Wrede, 113–14, 127–29). On the one hand, Mark is telling a story about what happened "way back when" in Jesus' earthly ministry, when the full truth about him could not yet be revealed because the epistemological revolution created by the crucifixion and resurrection had not yet occurred. Hence the messianic secret. On the other hand, because of the inherent power of a narrative about Jesus to grip and involve its Christian hearers, it is impossible for the separation between "then" and "now" to remain neatly in place. Rather, a narrative about Jesus' life inevitably shades off into a reflection on who Jesus *is* now, in the post-Easter period, for Mark and his community; hence the occasional breach of the secret. In the Markan narrative Jesus is such a powerful figure that the secret of his identity, which needs to be concealed during his lifetime at the end of the old evil age, cannot help punching occasional holes in the enveloping darkness (cf. the description of H. J. Ebeling's "epiphanic" interpretation in Tuckett, *Messianic Secret*, 13–15, and Räisänen, 60–62).

THE SON OF MAN

◆

The most frequent title for Jesus in Mark and the other Gospels is not "Christ" (eight Markan usages) or "Son of God" (five or six, depending on the text of 1:1) but "Son of Man" (fourteen). In the New Testament this title occurs almost exclusively in the Gospels (cf. Acts 7:56), where, with one exception, and that a Johannine one, it always appears on the lips of Jesus (cf. John 12:34). In the Synoptics the title is never explicated in any way; it is always assumed that Jesus' hearers will understand perfectly what he means when he speaks of "the Son of Man" (cf. Vermes, "Use," 310).

In this presumed knowledge, Jesus' audience is luckier than modern exegetes, who have been greatly perplexed by the title and have debated its significance heatedly (for a summary of the recent discussion, see Donahue, "Recent Studies," and Walker, "Son of Man"). All would agree, however, that the title has its roots in the Old Testament, where a "son of man" is a member of the human race, "man" being understood collectively. The term is often used in synonymous parallelism with terms for "human being," Ps 8:4 providing a well-known instance: "What is man, that thou art mindful of him, and the son of man, that thou dost care for him?" The most conspicuous example of this usage is in Ezekiel, where the prophet is addressed ninety-three times as "son of man" by God, thus emphasizing his human status in solidarity with those to whom he is sent and in contrast to the divine word with which he is commissioned (cf. Nickelsburg, "Son of Man," 137).

The book of Daniel, which is to be dated shortly after the beginning of the Maccabean Revolt (167 B.C.E.), takes up this OT usage and transforms it irrevocably, perhaps under the influence of ANE myths (see J. J. Collins, *Apocalyptic Imagination*, 78–80). As Nickelsburg sums up this transformation, "Paradoxically, a generic term meaning 'human being' develops a theological aura and, eventually, a set of highly technical meanings." The crucial passage is in Daniel 7. Here the term "one like a son of man," i.e. one like a human being, is applied to a figure who is enthroned beside God and granted worldwide dominion by him (Dan 7:13–14). Later in the chapter, however, the same prerogatives that are given to the "one like a son of man" in 7:13–14 (dominion, glory, kingship, etc.) are bestowed upon "the holy ones of the Most High" (7:18) or "the people of the holy ones of the most high" (7:21–22, 27). Some have concluded from this parallelism that the "one like a son of man" in Daniel is merely a collective symbol for Israel or the elect within Israel, analogous to Uncle Sam or John Bull (see e.g. Casey, *Son of Man*, 7–50).

Others, however, have argued that here, as elsewhere in the Bible, "the holy ones" are the angels (cf. Dan 4:10, 14, 20; 8:13) and the "one like a son of man" is Yahweh's chief angel, perhaps Michael, "the great prince who has charge of your people" (Dan 12:1; cf. 10:13, 21; see J. J. Collins, *Apocalyptic Imagination*, 81–85; Hurtado, *One God*, 76–77). Angels are often portrayed in the Bible as having a human form; later in Daniel, for example, the archangel Gabriel is described as "one having the appearance of a man" (Dan 8:15; 10:18). "One like a son of man," therefore, is a plausible designation for an angel.

The traditional view that the Danielic "Son of Man" figure is in fact the Messiah has not found much recent scholarly support. To be sure, this view is not totally without exegetical foundation; the beasts to whom the figure is contrasted all stand for kings (7:17), so it might be logical to see the "one like a son of man" as a king too. Dan 9:25, moreover, speaks of the coming of "an anointed one, a prince" at the the time of the end, and some exegetes link this reference with the traditional hope for an anointed king from the house of David, i.e. the Messiah. On the other hand, Dan 9:25 is the only Danielic mention of an "anointed one," and he is not literally linked with the Son of Man figure in Daniel 7. The visionary language "one like a son of man," moreover, suggests a figure who in some ways is like human beings (and thus in contrast to the *beasts* from the sea) but is also different from humans; there is no suggestion, however, that the figure in 9:25 is in any way transhuman. Nevertheless, later Jewish exegesis and the NT assume the identity of the Danielic figure with the Messiah (see below on *1 Enoch* and cf. 4 Ezra 7:28–29 with 4 Ezra 13; cf. also the rabbinic passages cited in Strack-Billerbeck, 1.486).

Some of the ambiguities about the Son of Man figure in Daniel are resolved in a later apocalyptic Jewish work, *The Similitudes of Enoch*. This is part of a pseudepigraphal corpus known as *1 Enoch*, most parts of which clearly predate the New Testament. Unfortunately, however, the dating of the *Similitudes* in particular is enveloped in controversy, because fragments of all of the sections of *Enoch* have turned up among the Qumran scrolls—*except* the *Similitudes*. This absence has caused some to date the *Similitudes* near the end of the first century C.E. or later (Qumran was destroyed in 68 C.E. by the Romans); Milik, for example, dates them to the third century (*Books of Enoch*, 89–98). Many others, however, think the *Similitudes* are pre-Christian and explain their absence from Qumran by their theological incompatibility with Qumran thought; J. J. Collins, for example, speculates that the Qumranians may have been put off by the equality of sun and moon presupposed in chapter 41 (*Apocalyptic Imagination*, 142).

The question of dating is important because the Son of Man in the *Similitudes* develops Daniel 7 in a way similar to the Gospels' elaboration of that biblical passage. In the *Similitudes* there is no more ambiguity about whether the Son of Man figure is an individual or a symbol for a collectivity. Although strongly linked with the elect people, he is clearly an individual, *the* Son of Man, a glorious, heavenly figure who has preexisted with God from the beginning (*1 Enoch*

48:2–3), reveals heavenly mysteries to the elect in the present (e.g. *1 Enoch* 46:2; 48:7), and will come at the end to usher in the new age and take the elect into eternal, blissful communion with him (e.g. *1 Enoch* 39:4–8; 45:3–6; 50:1; 62:13–16). His role as judge is especially emphasized (e.g. *1 Enoch* 45:3; 62:2–12; 69:27–29); this is a development from Daniel 7, where the holy ones associated with the "one like a son of man," not the "one like a son of man" himself, are given the prerogative of executing judgment (7:22). The Son of Man of the *Similitudes*, moreover, will be *seen* by his enemies at the eschaton (*1 Enoch* 62:3–5; cf. Mark 13:26), and he is explicitly identified with the Messiah (*1 Enoch* 48:10; 52:4). All of these points, which go beyond Daniel, can be paralleled in Gospel statements about the Son of Man.

Scholars are sharply divided as to which way the influence here runs. On the one hand, some (e.g. Lindars, Collins) think that Jesus and/or the early Christians knew the sort of ideas found in the *Similitudes*, if not the *Similitudes* themselves. Others, however (e.g. Milik), think the reverse, that the author of the *Similitudes* either was a Christian or knew about the early Christian usage of "Son of Man." Probably it is safe to say that the *Similitudes* were not written by a Christian, since it is difficult to imagine that a Christian would have spoken about the Son of Man without mentioning his death and resurrection, or that he would have listed him among a number of heavenly beings without giving him special prominence, as happens in *1 Enoch* 61:10. The *Similitudes* might, however, represent a Jewish response to Christian ideas, and the last two chapters of the *Similitudes* could be cited in support of this view. Here Enoch, the putative author of the book, is translated to heaven, spiritually transformed, and told that he himself is the Son of Man (*1 Enoch* 70–71); these chapters might be a Jewish attempt to disprove Christian claims for Jesus by showing that Enoch rather than Jesus is the Son of Man.

Many, however, have doubted whether these chapters originally belonged to the *Similitudes*, since they are so contradictory to the rest of the book (e.g. has Enoch been seeing visions of *himself* up to this point?). It seems more likely that chapters 70–71 were added to the *Similitudes* by a Jewish redactor as a counterblast to the Christian appropriation of the Son of Man figure. The most probable conclusion, therefore, would seem to be that, with the exception of chapters 70–71, the Son of Man figure in the *Similitudes* reflects pre-Christian ideas. This conclusion is supported by the way in which Jesus, in the Gospels, generally treats the Son of Man as a known quantity, never bothering to explain the term, and the way in which certain of this figure's characteristics, such as his identity with the Messiah or his prerogative of judging, are taken for granted. With apologies to Voltaire, we may say that if the Enochic Son of Man had not existed, it would have been necessary to invent him to explain the Son of Man sayings in the Gospels.

Those sayings, in their Synoptic form, are often divided into three groups: eschatological sayings, sayings about present earthly status, and sayings about suffering, death, and resurrection (see e.g. the influential short discussion in Bultmann, *Theology*, 1.30). Much of the scholarly debate has centered on trying to determine which, if any, of these sayings go back to the historical Jesus, and what they might have meant in his mouth. On the one hand, Bultmann argues that only the eschatological sayings are "authentic," but that in them Jesus distinguished himself from the coming Son of Man (see especially Mark 8:38). On the other hand, Vermes ("Use") thinks that only the sayings about the Son of Man's present earthly status and some of the sayings about suffering are authentic, but that "son of man" in these sayings is not a title drawn from Daniel but merely a circumlocution for "I." The circumlocution theory has been strongly questioned by, among others, Casey, who thinks that for Jesus "son of man" simply meant "man," as in the OT; Jesus used it for general statements that had a particular relevance to himself. On the really crucial point, however, Casey agrees with Vermes: Jesus' usage of the term was neither titular nor derived from Daniel 7 (*Son of Man*, 157–240; "General, Generic and Indefinite"; "Idiom").

The central issue, then, is whether the usage of "Son of Man" in the Gospels reflects the common OT idiom for "human being" or the apocalyptic transformation of that idiom which begins in Daniel 7. Certain of the sayings fall easily into place under the former supposition. In Mark 2:27–28, for example, Jesus says that the Sabbath was made for man, not man for the Sabbath, and that therefore "the son of man" is the lord of the Sabbath. The supposition that "son of man" here simply means "man" (i.e. humanity) yields an acceptable sense. On the other hand, a Danielic background would also yield good sense, since the "Son of Man" figure in Daniel 7 is strongly linked with the elect people, whether or not he is identical with them. It might seem more plausible at first that Jesus spoke of himself as a "son of man" in a non-apocalyptic sense, and that the church subsequently apocalypticized the sense in line with its developing view of Jesus' heavenly role. On the other hand, it is hard to imagine the church inventing apocalyptic sayings in which Jesus seems to distinguish himself from the Son of Man.

"Here is the end of the matter" (Dan 7:28): the meaning of "son of man" in the mouth of the historical Jesus may be an insoluble problem. Its meaning in Mark, however, is easier to track down. The Danielic echo is certainly there in at least three of the Markan sayings (8:38; 13:26; 14:62), so it is likely that Mark's readers, as they read and reread the Gospel, would learn to interpret even the "present status" and "suffering" sayings in a Danielic context. In this Danielic interpretation they would be helped by the fact that the "present status" sayings in Mark 2 share the theme of authority with Dan 7:13 LXX and that the Son of Man figure in Daniel 7 is linked with the elect people, who suffer. If *The Similitudes of Enoch* are pre-Christian, moreover, there was already within Judaism the beginning of a merger between the Son of Man figure and the Servant of Deutero-Isaiah, who suffers for his people's sin in Isaiah 52–53 (though the Son of Man in Enoch does *not* suffer; cf. Nickelsburg, "Son of Man," 138–39).

Both the Isaian Servant and the "one like a son of man" in Daniel 7 have a strong corporate dimension, and this corporate dimension continues to play an important role in later Jewish developments of the "Son of Man" figure, despite that figure's crystallization into an individual. In the *Similitudes*, for example, the Son of Man shares various epithets with the elect people (e.g. "righteous" and "elect"), and his hiddenness parallels their suffering. The people's ultimate hope, moreover, is that "with that Son of Man they shall eat and lie down and rise up for ever and ever" (62:14; cf. J. J. Collins, *Apocalyptic Imagination*, 147–49). Similar ideas seem to lie below the surface in Mark. In Mark 13:26–27, for example, the returning Son of Man vindicates not himself but the community of disciples. As Schaberg points out, moreover ("Daniel 7–12," 215–17), each of the three Markan predictions of the passion and resurrection of the Son of Man is followed by teaching on the subject of discipleship (8:31–38; 9:31–37; 10:32–45), as though the destiny of the Son of Man extended beyond himself to include those who followed him. Schaberg plausibly sees this extension as a reflection of the corporate dimension of the Son of Man figure in Daniel 7.

Our conclusion about the Danielic background of the Markan Son of Man raises a question about the claim of the "Perrin school" that in Mark the "Son of Man" title is meant to correct the theology of glory advocated by Mark's Christian opponents and associated by them with the Christological titles "Son of God" and "Christ" (see Perrin, "Christology"). For if "Son of Man" is itself a title implying glory, as it certainly is in Daniel 7, then it is difficult to see how it could function to correct the implication of glory that Perrin and his disciples find in the other two titles. (Perrin ["Christology," 103] simply dismisses the apocalyptic usages of "Son of Man" in Mark as remnants from pre-Markan tradition.)

Although Mark's "Son of Man" concept is probably not a polemic against Christian opponents, it may reflect another sort of polemic: one against the Jewish zealots whose revolutionary activity and theology form the probable background to the Gospel's composition. There is some evidence to suggest that these revolutionaries paid particular attention to Daniel 7–12 and that Mark's preoccupation with these chapters, especially in Mark 13, mirrors that of the revolutionaries (see Marcus, *Way*, 167–69). If this revolutionary usage of Daniel 7 and related traditions is granted, it becomes likely that the revolutionaries would have anticipated with eager longing the decisive intervention of the Son of Man to judge and destroy the evil Gentiles who were making war against Israel (cf. e.g. Dan 7:26–27; *1 Enoch* 46:4–8; 48:8–10; 4 Ezra 13:25–28). The unexpected and perhaps polemical twists in the Markan appropriation of this traditional pattern would be that, as Son of Man, Jesus forgives sinners rather than destroying them (2:10) and judges not the Gentiles but the leaders of Israel, who have condemned him (14:62).

GLOSSARY

♦

Apodosis	The "then" clause of a conditional sentence.
Asyndeton	In Greek rhetoric, the absence of the normal joining particles or conjunctions. In classical Greek, asyndeton is sometimes used for emphasis, but its frequency in the NT has often been taken as an indication of the primitive level of NT Greek.
Baraitha	An "extraneous" rabbinic tradition, i.e. one not found in the Mishnah, but supposed to be Tannaitic and quoted anonymously in the Talmud.
B.C.E.	"Before the common (or Christian) era"; corresponds to old-style B.C. ("before Christ").
Blank	An inadvertent disparity or failure to provide information within a narrative; contrast "gap."
C.E.	"Common (or Christian) era"; corresponds to old-style A.D. (*anno Domini* = "in the year of the Lord").
Chiasm, chiastic	Having a structure of ABA', ABCB'A', etc., so that a > pattern is formed. From the Greek letter chi, which is written X, since the pattern is one-half of an X.
Cola	Plural of "colon" = a single unit of poetry.
Diminutive	In Greek and other languages, a noun or adjective in a special form that indicates small size, familiarity, or affection.
Dissimilarity	A criterion for determining what goes back to the historical Jesus: features of the tradition that conflict with Judaism and the teaching or practice of the later church are likely to be authentic.

Divine passive	The use of a passive-voice verb (e.g. "it has been given") as a circumlocution for God's action (e.g. instead of saying "God has given").
Docetism	A Christian heresy according to which Jesus only seemed (Gk *dokein*) to be human but was really divine.
End-stress	A rhetorical principle according to which what comes at the end receives the greatest emphasis.
Eschaton	The end of the ages expected in Jewish and Christian theology; from the Greek word for "last."
Gap	An intentional discontinuity within a narrative such as the disparity between a parable and its explanation, unexplained motives, improbable or excessive actions, and discontinuities in plot (e.g. unnarrated endings); contrast "blank."
Gentile	Non-Jewish; a non-Jew.
Halakhic	Having to do with the observance of Jewish law.
Hapax legomenon	A word that occurs only once in a given corpus of literature, e.g. the OT or the NT.
Haplography	The inadvertent omission of letters, words, or lines in textual transmission.
Hendiadys	Lit. "one for two"; a rhetorical form in which a second term combines with a first one, which it may simply repeat or to which it may add something.
Homoeoarcton	In textual criticism, a situation in which two words have the same beginning; a cause of scribal omissions.
Homoeoteleuton	In textual criticism, a situation in which two words have the same ending; a frequent cause of scribal omissions.
Hypotaxis	An elaborate system of grammatical subordination, as opposed to parataxis.
Inclusion	The framing of a literary unit by the usage of the same or similar words at its beginning and end.

Intransitive   Not taking a direct object; an example would be the verb "procrastinate."

Kerygma   "Preaching" or "proclamation"; the content of the primitive Christian message about Jesus.

Koine   The "common" Greek of the Hellenistic period; the language in which most of the New Testament, including Mark, is written.

LXX   The Septuagint, the Greek translation of the Old Testament.

Mishnah   Authoritative compilation of Jewish law, promulgated under the authority of R. Judah the Prince at the beginning of the third century C.E.

MT   Masoretic Text, the traditional form of the original Hebrew and Aramaic text of the Old Testament.

Parataxis   Simple coordination of words, clauses, sentences, and paragraphs with "and." Mark's style is overwhelmingly paratactic, as are the narrative portions of the OT.

Parousia   The expected "Second Coming" of Jesus at the end of time; from the Greek word for "arrival" or "presence."

Pericope   A self-contained unit within the scripture; from the Greek for "cut around."

Pleonastic   Using more words than are necessary for mere sense; redundant.

Protasis   The "if" clause of a conditional sentence.

Q   Hypothetical source for the material shared by Matthew and Luke but not present in Mark.

Qumran   Site in the Judaean Desert, near the Dead Sea, where the Dead Sea Scrolls were found; home of a dualistic Jewish sect identical to or related to the Essenes.

Redaction   Editing; often used to describe an individual evangelist's adaptation of the traditions that have come down to him.

Sapiential   Having to do with wisdom.

Second tithe   According to Second Temple period Jewish law, a
                              tithe (tenth) of one's income was to be given to the
                              Levitical priests, but a second tithe was to be used for
                              sacrificial meals for oneself in Jerusalem.

Synoptic Gospels   Matthew, Mark, and Luke, the first three Gospels in
                              the New Testament; so called because they can be
                              laid out easily in parallel columns and read synopti-
                              cally ("with one eye").

Talmud   Lit. "learning"; commentary on the Mishnah that ap-
                              peared in two forms, the Palestinian (or Jerusalem)
                              Talmud (fifth century C.E.) and the Babylonian (ma-
                              jor redaction in the eighth century C.E.).

Tanna, Tannaitic   "Repeater" of traditions; a rabbinic teacher from the
                              time of Hillel and Shammai to R. Judah the Prince
                              and his contemporaries at the beginning of the third
                              century C.E. The opinions of the Tannaim (plural of
                              Tanna) are compiled in the Mishnah.

Tetragrammaton   The four-letter name of God, YHWH, from the He-
                              brew Bible.

Torah   The Hebrew word for "teaching" or "law"; often refers
                              to the first five books of the Old Testament, especially
                              the legal portions of those books.

Transitive   Taking a direct object; an example would be the verb
                              "hit." Opposite of "intransitive."

Two-Source Theory   The theory, accepted by the majority of scholars on
                              the Synoptic Gospels, that Mark was the earliest Gos-
                              pel and the major source for Matthew and Luke, who
                              also had available to them another source, Q.

INDEX OF COMMENTATORS
AND MODERN AUTHORS

◆

Titles of authors' works are given in an abbreviated form. Full titles may be found in the Bibliography.

INDEX OF SUBJECTS

◆

INDEX OF SCRIPTURAL AND OTHER ANCIENT REFERENCES

◆

560 MARK 1-8

Testament of Solomon
2:1 . . . 344
2:6 . . . 345
5:12–13 . . . 474

The Testaments of the Twelve Patriarchs

Testament of Asher
7:5 . . . 450

Testament of Benjamin
5:2 . . . 187

Testament of Dan
6:1–14 . . . 273

Testament of Gad
5:1 . . . 456

Testament of Joseph
19:1–7 . . . 267

Testament of Judah
23:5 . . . 150

Testament of Levi
14:4 . . . 450
18:6–12 . . . 159, 188, 193
18:9 . . . 217
18:10–12 . . . 275

Testament of Naphtali
6 . . . 337
8:3–4 . . . 170
8:4 . . . 168
8:6 . . . 274

Testament of Reuben
3:2–7 . . . 456

JOSEPHUS AND PHILO

Josephus . . . 151

Against Apion
1.70 . . . 471
1.281 . . . 208
2.133 . . . 464
2.282 . . . 248

Jewish Antiquities
1.193 . . . 270
3.47 . . . 266
3.91 . . . 248
3.217 . . . 464
3.219–22 . . . 266

3.261 . . . 357
3.400 . . . 204
5.169 . . . 445
6.77 . . . 183
6.336 . . . 20
7.365 . . . 168
8.354 . . . 181
8.408 . . . 487
11.128 . . . 524
11.133 . . . 267
11.346 . . . 440
12.142 . . . 524
13.297 . . . 441–42, 520
13.408 . . . 520
14.262 . . . 248
14.313–21 . . . 471
14.403 . . . 249
17.41 . . . 444
17.41–47 . . . 249
17.136 . . . 383
17.254 . . . 257
18.11–25 . . . 519
18.15 . . . 521
18.20 . . . 490
18.23 . . . 185
18.36–38 . . . 396
18.109–16 . . . 400
18.116–19 . . . 156, 399–400
18.117 . . . 155
18.136 . . . 396
18.289–304 . . . 402
18.356 . . . 423
19.331 . . . 249–50
20.97 . . . 184
20.97–99 . . . 421, 505
20.139 . . . 249–50
20.167 . . . 184
20.167–68 . . . 505
20.167–72 . . . 421
20.169 . . . 499
20.169–72 . . . 505
20.188 . . . 184, 421, 505
20.200 . . . 30, 32

Jewish War
1.123 . . . 507
1.319 . . . 249
1.571 . . . 249
1.657 . . . 384
2.43 . . . 257
2.119–68 . . . 519
2.125 . . . 383
2.147–49 . . . 455
2.258–59 . . . 505
2.261–62 . . . 499
2.261–63 . . . 505

2.433–34 . . . 34
2.444 . . . 34
2.456 . . . 247
2.463 . . . 36
2.478 . . . 471
2.517 . . . 247
2.569 . . . 523
2.652 . . . 34
4.151–57, 182–83, 201 . . . 35
4.335–44 . . . 34
4.388 . . . 35
4.582 . . . 197
5.5 . . . 35
6.95 . . . 35
6.250–87 . . . 38
6.284–86 . . . 505
6.300–9 . . . 38
6.313 . . . 34
7.1–4 . . . 38
7.29–31 . . . 34
7.31 . . . 360
7.45 . . . 464
7.323 . . . 140
7.437–42 . . . 421

Life
2.11 . . . 151
12 . . . 524
65 . . . 396
189–98 . . . 523
196–98 . . . 524
197 . . . 524
212–13 . . . 414
290 . . . 236
290–95 . . . 186

Philo

On Abraham
121 . . . 143
On the Change of Names
259–60 . . . 407
Cherubim
27 . . . 191
On the Contemplative Life
34 . . . 232
On the Creation
40–43, 80–81, 167 . . . 328
Decalogue
113–18 . . . 444
Every Good Man Is Free
75 . . . 490
Flaccus
121–24 . . . 186
Hypothetica
7:4–5 . . . 445